The Handbook of
Transformative Learning

The Handbook of Transformative Learning

Theory, Research, and Practice

Edward W. Taylor
Patricia Cranton
and Associates

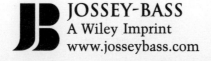
JOSSEY-BASS
A Wiley Imprint
www.josseybass.com

Published by Jossey-Bass
A Wiley Imprint
One Montgomery Street, Suite 1200,
San Francisco, CA 94104-4594   www.josseybass.com

Jossey-Bass books and products are available through most bookstores. To contact Jossey-Bass directly call our Customer Care Department within the U.S. at 800-956-7739, outside the U.S. at 317-572-3986, or fax 317-572-4002.

Wiley also publishes its books in a variety of electronic formats and by print-on-demand. Some material included with standard print versions of this book may not be included in e-books or in print-on-demand. If the version of this book that you purchased references media such as CD or DVD that was not included in your purchase, you may download this material at http://booksupport.wiley.com. For more information about Wiley products, visit www.wiley.com.

Library of Congress Cataloging-in-Publication Data

Taylor, Edward W. (Edward Woodbury), 1952 –
The handbook of transformative learning : theory, research, and practice / Edward W. Taylor, Patricia Cranton, and associates. – 1st ed.
p. cm. – (Jossey-Bass higher and adult education series)
Includes bibliographical references and index.
ISBN 978-0-470-59072-0 (hardback)
ISBN 978-1-118-21891-4 (ebk.)
ISBN 978-1-118-21892-1 (ebk.)
ISBN 978-1-118-21893-8 (ebk.)
1. Transformative learning.   2. Adult learning.   3. Adult education.
I. Cranton, Patricia.   II. Title.
LC1100.T38   2012
370.11′5–dc23
2012001578

Printed in the United States of America
FIRST EDITION

HB Printing   10 9 8 7 6 5 4 3 2 1

CONTENTS

About the Editors   ix

About the Contributors   xi

PART ONE: SETTING THE CONTEXT   1

1   Transformative Learning Theory: Seeking a More
    Unified Theory   3
    Patricia Cranton and Edward W. Taylor

2   Themes and Variations of Transformational Learning:
    Interdisciplinary Perspectives on Forms That Transform   21
    Elizabeth J. Tisdell

3   A Critical Review of Research on Transformative Learning
    Theory, 2006–2010   37
    Edward W. Taylor and Melissa J. Snyder

4   Studying Transformative Learning: What Methodology?   56
    Sharan B. Merriam and SeonJoo Kim

5   Learning to Think Like an Adult: Core Concepts of
    Transformation Theory   73
    Jack Mezirow

PART TWO: EXPLORING THE THEORY OF TRANSFORMATIVE LEARNING: DIVERSE PERSPECTIVES   97

6 Mezirow's Theory of Transformative Learning from 1975 to Present   99
Lisa M. Baumgartner

7 Nurturing Soul Work: A Jungian Approach to Transformative Learning   116
John M. Dirkx

8 Critical Theory and Transformative Learning   131
Stephen D. Brookfield

9 Transformative Learning: A Developmental Perspective   147
Kathleen Taylor and Dean Elias

10 Deep Transformation: Forging a Planetary Worldview   162
Edmund O'Sullivan

11 Transformative Learning and the Challenges of Complexity   178
Michel Alhadeff-Jones

12 Transforming Transformative Learning Through Sustainability and the New Science   195
Elizabeth A. Lange

13 An Existential Approach to Transformative Learning   212
Peter Willis

PART THREE: TRANSFORMATIVE LEARNING: CULTURE, POSITIONALITY, AND INTERNATIONAL PERSPECTIVES   229

14 Cultural-Spiritual Perspective of Transformative Learning   231
Nadira K. Charaniya

15 Women and Transformative Learning   245
Leona M. English and Catherine J. Irving

16 Positionality and Transformative Learning: A Tale of Inclusion and Exclusion   260
Juanita Johnson-Bailey

17 Transformative Learning Theory: A Perspective from Africa   274
Peggy Gabo Ntseane

18 Transformative Learning in Europe: An Overview of the Theoretical Perspectives 289
Alexis Kokkos

19 International and Community-Based Transformative Learning 304
Olutoyin Mejiuni

PART FOUR: TRANSFORMATIVE LEARNING: CENTRAL CONCEPTS AND SETTINGS 321

20 Critical Reflection and Transformative Learning 323
Carolin Kreber

21 The Role of Experience in Transformative Learning 342
Dorothy MacKeracher

22 Group Work and Dialogue: Spaces and Processes for Transformative Learning in Relationships 355
Steven A. Schapiro, Ilene L. Wasserman, and Placida V. Gallegos

23 Transformative Learning in the Workplace: Leading Learning for Self and Organizational Change 373
Karen E. Watkins, Victoria J. Marsick, and Pierre G. Faller

24 Fostering Transformative Learning in Higher Education Settings 388
Carol E. Kasworm and Tuere A. Bowles

25 Fostering Transformative Learning Online 408
Regina O. Smith

PART FIVE: FOSTERING TRANSFORMATIVE LEARNING: PRACTICES AND ETHICS 423

26 Transformation as Embodied Narrative 425
M. Carolyn Clark

27 Learner-Centered Teaching and Transformative Learning 439
Maryellen Weimer

28 Storytelling and Transformative Learning 455
Jo A. Tyler and Ann L. Swartz

29 Transformative Learning Through Artistic Expression: Getting Out of Our Heads 471
Randee Lipson Lawrence

30 Fiction and Film and Transformative Learning   486
    Christine Jarvis

31 Learning to Be What We Know: The Pivotal Role of Presentational
    Knowing in Transformative Learning   503
    Elizabeth Kasl and Lyle Yorks

32 Evaluating Transformative Learning   520
    Patricia Cranton and Chad Hoggan

33 Educator as Change Agent: Ethics of Transformative Learning   536
    Dorothy Ettling

PART SIX: REFLECTING ON THE FUTURE OF TRANSFORMATIVE LEARNING   553

34 Reflecting Back and Looking Forward   555
    Edward W. Taylor and Patricia Cranton

Name Index   575

Subject Index   588

ABOUT THE EDITORS

Edward W. Taylor is a professor of adult education at the Pennsylvania State University-Harrisburg. He received his Ed.D. in adult education from the University of Georgia. Research interests include adult cognition and learning (transformative learning), nonformal education, and medical education. His work has appeared in the *Adult Education Quarterly, International Journal of Lifelong Education, Studies in the Education of Adults,* and other scholarly journals. He has previously published two coedited books, *Transformative Learning in Practice* and *Adult Education in Cultural Institutions: Aquariums, Libraries, Museums, Parks, and Zoos.* He has been a coeditor of the *Adult Education Quarterly* and an active member of the planning committee for several international transformative learning conferences. Prior to joining the faculty at Penn State, he was a faculty member at Antioch University in Seattle.

Patricia Cranton is a retired professor of adult education, currently affiliated with the University of New Brunswick in Canada. She has been professor of adult education at St. Francis Xavier University, University of New Brunswick, and Brock University in Canada, and associate professor at McGill University. Patricia Cranton's previous books include *Planning Instruction for Adult Learners* (second edition, 2000, with a third edition currently in press), *Becoming an Authentic Teacher* (2001), *Finding Our Way: A Guide for Adult Educators*

(2003), and *Understanding and Promoting Transformative Learning* (second edition, 2006). Patricia has edited five volumes of New Directions in Adult and Continuing Education, most recently *Authenticity in Teaching* (2006) and *Reaching Out Across the Border: Canadian Perspectives in Adult Education* (with Leona English, 2009).

ABOUT THE CONTRIBUTORS

Michel Alhadeff-Jones is an adjunct assistant professor at Teachers College, Columbia University in New York City, New York, and an independent researcher associated with the Laboratoire EXPERICE at the University of Paris 8 in Paris, France.

Lisa M. Baumgartner is an associate professor of adult and higher education at Northern Illinois University in DeKalb, Illinois.

Tuere A. Bowles is an assistant professor in the Department of Leadership, Policy, Adult and Higher Education at North Carolina State University in Raleigh, North Carolina.

Stephen D. Brookfield is a distinguished professor at the University of St. Thomas in Minneapolis, Minnesota.

Nadira K. Charaniya is assistant dean and campus director at Springfield College School of Human Services in Los Angeles, California.

M. Carolyn Clark is an associate professor and program chair of adult education in the College of Education and Human Development at Texas A&M University in College Station, Texas.

John M. Dirkx is a professor of higher, adult, and lifelong education at Michigan State University in East Lansing, Michigan.

Dean Elias is a professor in the School of Education at St. Mary's College of California in Moraga, California.

Leona M. English is a professor of adult education at St. Francis Xavier University in Antigonish, Nova Scotia, Canada.

Dorothy Ettling is a professor in the Dreeben School of Education at the University of the Incarnate Word in San Antonio, Texas.

Pierre G. Faller is a doctoral candidate in adult learning and leadership at Teachers College, Columbia University. He currently oversees marketing activities for degree and nondegree programs at Columbia Business School in New York City, New York.

Placida V. Gallegos is a principal with ICW Consulting Group in Penn Valley, Pennsylvania.

Chad Hoggan is an instructor of organizational leadership in the Department of Leadership Studies in Education and Organizations at Wright State University in Dayton, Ohio.

Catherine J. Irving is a library specialist in the Coady Institute at St. Francis Xavier University in Antigonish, Nova Scotia, Canada.

Christine Jarvis is dean of education and professional development at the University of Huddersfield in Huddersfield, England, United Kingdom.

Juanita Johnson-Bailey holds the Josiah Meigs Distinguished Teaching Professorship, is the director of the Institute for Women's Studies, and is a professor in the Department of Lifelong Education, Administration, and Policy at the University of Georgia in Athens, Georgia.

Elizabeth Kasl is a retired professor of transformative learning and lives in California.

Carol E. Kasworm is the W. Dallas Herring Professor in the Department of Leadership, Policy, Adult and Higher Education at North Carolina State University in Raleigh, North Carolina.

SeonJoo Kim is a Ph.D. candidate and graduate assistant in adult education at the University of Georgia in Athens, Georgia.

Alexis Kokkos is a professor of adult education at the Hellenic Open University in Patras, Greece.

Carolin Kreber is a professor of higher education at the University of Edinburgh in Edinburgh, Scotland, United Kingdom.

Elizabeth Ann Lange is an assistant professor at St. Francis Xavier University in Antigonish, Nova Scotia, Canada.

Randee Lipson Lawrence is an associate professor at National-Louis University in Chicago, Illinois.

Dorothy MacKeracher is a professor emerita in education at the University of New Brunswick in New Brunswick, Canada.

Victoria J. Marsick is a professor of education/co-director of the J. M. Huber Institute at Teachers College, Columbia University in New York City, New York.

Olutoyin Mejiuni is a professor at Obafemi Awolowo University in Ile-Ife, Nigeria.

Sharan B. Merriam is a professor emeritus in the Department of Lifelong Education, Administration, and Policy at the University of Georgia in Athens, Georgia.

Jack Mezirow is a professor emeritus of adult and continuing education; former chairman, Department of Higher and Adult Education; and former director for adult education at Teachers College, Columbia University in New York City, New York.

Peggy Gabo Ntseane is the head of adult education at the University of Botswana in Gaborone, Botswana.

Edmund O'Sullivan is a retired professor of education, most recently from the Ontario Institute for Studies in Education at the University of Toronto in Toronto, Ontario, Canada.

Steven A. Schapiro is a professor in the School of Human and Organizational Development at Fielding Graduate University in Santa Barbara, California.

Regina O. Smith is an associate professor at University of Wisconsin in Milwaukee, Wisconsin.

Melissa J. Snyder is a D.Ed. candidate in adult education at the Pennsylvania State University, the Capital College in Middletown, Pennsylvania.

Ann L. Swartz is an instructor of nursing at the Pennsylvania State University, the Capital College in Middletown, Pennsylvania.

Kathleen Taylor is a professor in the School of Education at St. Mary's College of California in Moraga, California.

Elizabeth J. Tisdell is a professor of adult education at the Pennsylvania State University, the Capital College in Middletown, Pennsylvania.

Jo A. Tyler is an associate professor of training and development at the Pennsylvania State University, the Capital College in Middletown, Pennsylvania.

Ilene L. Wasserman is a managing principal of ICW Consulting Group in Penn Valley, Pennsylvania.

Karen E. Watkins is a professor of adult education and human resource and organizational development in the College of Education at the University of Georgia in Athens, Georgia.

Maryellen Weimer is a professor emerita in teaching and learning at the Pennsylvania State University, Berks Campus in Reading, Pennsylvania.

Peter Willis is a senior lecturer in the School of Education at the University of South Australia in Adelaide, South Australia, Australia.

Lyle Yorks is an associate professor of adult and continuing education and AEGIS program coordinator at Teachers College, Columbia University in New York City, New York.

The Handbook of
Transformative Learning

PART ONE

SETTING
THE CONTEXT

CHAPTER ONE

Transformative Learning Theory

Seeking a More
Unified Theory

Patricia Cranton and Edward W. Taylor

The purpose of this chapter is to explore the key issues in theory, practice, and research in transformative learning with a view of moving toward a more unified theory, one in which the current perspectives can be brought together under one theoretical umbrella. Currently, there is a diversity of theoretical perspectives, which brings a rich complexity to our understanding of transformation, but there is also a tendency to think in dualisms. For example, theorists and researchers write about rational *or* extrarational processes, a focus on individual change *or* a focus on social change, autonomous learning *or* relational learning. However, these perspectives, and many others that are presented in this volume, can coexist. It may be that for one person in one context, transformative learning is a rational endeavor; for that same person in another context, it could be emotional and intuitive; in some contexts, social change may need to precede individual change, and in another context, individual transformation drives social transformation, and so forth. The outcome is the same or similar—a deep shift in perspective, leading to more open, more permeable, and better-justified meaning perspectives (Mezirow, 1978)—but the ways of getting there can differ depending on the person or people and the context or situation. There are many examples in the chapters that follow—stories of individual change, organizational change, social change, and global change. A more unified theory allows us to continue to speak of transformative learning while maintaining the diversity of approaches that are so important to the complexity of the field of adult education.

In this chapter, first, we briefly set transformative learning in the general context of adult learning. We review the philosophical underpinnings of transformative learning theory and explore how these have led to the current dominant perspectives in the field. This takes us to the existing tensions and issues in the literature on transformative learning theory, research, and practice. We note how the diverse perspectives presented in this Handbook can point us toward a more unified theory.

THE CONTEXT: ADULT LEARNING

Over the decades since Lindemann's (1926) *The Meaning of Adult Education* was published, adult learning theory has evolved into a complex, multifaceted set of theoretical perspectives. Early adult educators (Moses Coady, Myles Horton, and Paulo Freire, for example) focused on emancipatory learning and achieving freedom from oppression, but when humanism became the prevailing philosophy underlying education in the 1960s, many theorists turned toward understanding individual learning processes.

Adult learning has been described consistently as a process that is different from children's learning since Malcolm Knowles (1975, 1980) made that distinction. In the 1970s and 1980s, adult learning was described as voluntary (individuals choose to become involved), self-directed, experiential, and collaborative. Adults "going back to school" were thought to be anxious and lacking in self-esteem based on their earlier childhood experiences in education. Brundage and MacKeracher (1980) provide a good example of the early efforts to define principles of adult learning. During that time, adult learning was seen to be a cognitive process that led to the acquisition of skills and knowledge. Early writings on transformative learning reflected this general trend (for example, see Mezirow, 1981). Instructional design and program planning models focused on setting objectives, finding appropriate learning strategies, and objective assessment of the learning. Knowles (1980) advocated that the learner be involved in making instructional design decisions, but aside from that, the process did not deviate much from instructional design in any other setting.

Things began to change after the publication of Brookfield's (1986) *Understanding and Facilitating Adult Learning.* He critiqued the automaton approach to meeting learner needs and discussed the political dimensions of self-directed learning (Brookfield, 1993). Attention returned to the social context of adult learning and to learning that goes beyond cognitive processes. As Merriam (2008) points out, adult learning theory began to draw on situated cognition theory, feminist theory, critical social theory, and postmodern theory. Adult learning is now described in relation to embodied learning, the emotions, spirituality, relational learning, arts-based learning, and storytelling.

Non-Western perspectives, which reject Western dichotomies such as mind-body and emotion-reason, are contributing to an interest in holistic approaches to understanding adult learning (Merriam & Sek Kim, 2008).

The evolution of transformative learning theory has paralleled and been strongly influenced by the development of adult learning theory in general. As Gunnlaugson (2008) suggests, we are now in the "second wave" of theory development in the field of transformative learning; that is, we are moving toward the integration of the various factions of the theory and into a more holistic perspective.

TRANSFORMATIVE LEARNING THEORY: PHILOSOPHICAL UNDERPINNINGS

The first comprehensive presentation of transformative learning theory was Mezirow's (1991) *Transformative Dimensions of Adult Learning*. This book was preceded by a companion volume of more practical strategies for fostering transformative learning, *Fostering Critical Reflection in Adulthood* (Mezirow & Associates, 1990). Both of these books drew on diverse disciplines—including developmental and cognitive psychology, psychotherapy, sociology, and philosophy—to come to an understanding of how adults learn, transform, and develop. Mezirow (1991, p. xiv) explained that transformative learning theory "does not derive from a systematic extension of an existing intellectual theory or tradition"; rather, it is an integration of his earlier research and concepts and theories from a wide array of disciplines. Transformative learning theory is based on constructivist assumptions, and the roots of the theory lie in humanism and critical social theory. In this section, we review the constructivist, humanist, and critical social theory assumptions underpinning transformative learning theory.

Constructivist Assumptions

Mezirow (1991) was explicit in saying that constructivist assumptions underlie his theory. He wrote about his "conviction that meaning exists within ourselves rather than in external forms such as books and that personal meanings that we attribute to our experience are acquired and validated through human interaction and experience" (p. xiv). Transformative learning theory is based on the notion that we interpret our experiences in our own way, and that how we see the world is a result of our perceptions of our experiences.

Transformative learning is a process of examining, questioning, and revising those perceptions. If we were to take the philosophical perspective that there are universal truths and constructs that are independent of our knowledge of them, then the goal of education would be to find those truths. Instead, argued Mezirow in 1991, we develop habitual expectations based on past experiences. We expect things to be as they were before. Or, put another way, we uncritically assimilate perspectives from our social world, community, and culture. Those perspectives include distortions, stereotypes, and prejudices. They guide our decision making and our actions until we encounter a situation that is not congruent with our expectation. At that point, we may reject the discrepant perspective or enter into a process that could lead to a transformed perspective.

Humanist Assumptions

Humanism is founded on notions of freedom and autonomy. Human beings are seen to be capable of making personal choices within the constraints imposed by heredity, personal history, and environment (Elias & Merriam, 2004). Humanist principles stress the importance of the individual and specific human needs. Among the major assumptions underlying humanism are the following:

- Human nature is inherently good.
- Individuals are free and autonomous, thus they are capable of making major personal choices.
- Human potential for growth and development is virtually unlimited.
- Self-concept plays an important role in growth and development.
- Individuals have an urge toward self-actualization.
- Reality is defined by each person.
- Individuals have responsibility to both themselves and to others (Elias & Merriam, 2004).

These humanist assumptions are inherent in transformative learning theory. If we could not make the assumptions that people can make choices, have the potential for growth and development, and define their own reality, transformative learning could not be described as it is described. What is problematic here is that the assumptions are rooted in a Western perspective; this may contribute to the challenges theorists encounter when transporting transformative learning theory into non-Western perspectives or attempting to integrate the two (Wang & King, 2008).

Humanist psychologists Maslow (1970) and Rogers (1969) had a strong influence on adult education in general and also specifically on Mezirow's conceptualization of transformative learning. Maslow's concept of self-actualization includes, among others, the characteristics of acceptance of self and others, and having peak experiences that lead to personal transformation. Rogers, known for his client-centered therapy, inspired Knowles's (1975) development of self-directed learning as a central concept in andragogy.

Critical Social Theory Assumptions

Critical social theory originated in the Frankfurt School of Critical Social Theory, especially from the work of Max Horkheimer. The goal of critical social theory is to critique and change society as a whole rather than explain or describe it. Brookfield (2005) gives three core assumptions of critical theory related to how the world is organized:

1. That apparently open, Western democracies are actually highly unequal societies in which economic inequity, racism, and class discrimination are empirical realities

2. That the way this state of affairs is reproduced and seems to be normal, natural, and inevitable (thereby heading off potential challenges to the system) is through the dissemination of dominant ideology

3. That critical theory attempts to understand this state of affairs as a necessary prelude to changing it (p. viii)

The dominant ideology in a society includes the beliefs, assumptions, and perspectives that people use to make sense of their experiences. If a part of the dominant ideology is, for example, capitalism, then it makes sense to center one's life on the acquisition of wealth and materials. In this way the dominant ideology perpetuates itself—it is seen to be the normal way to think and act, and it is seen to work in our best interests. Challenging and breaking through this cycle is the work of critical theorists.

At the center of transformative learning theory is the notion that we uncritically assimilate our values, beliefs, and assumptions from our family, community, and culture. In other words, we adopt the dominant ideology as the normal and natural way to think and act. When we are able to recognize that these beliefs are oppressive and not in our best interests, we can enter into a transformative learning process. Although early critiques of Mezirow's theory focused on his failure to address social change (Collard & Law, 1989) and his neglect of power issues (Hart, 1990), a careful reading of Mezirow's (1991) presentation of the theory reveals that he did pay attention to these issues, even though he was primarily interested in the perspective of the individual engaged in transformative learning.

Dominant Perspectives on Transformative Learning Theory

Transformative learning scholars have categorized the dominant perspectives on transformative learning in a variety of ways. Transformative learning is described as cognitive and rational, as imaginative and intuitive, as spiritual, as related to individuation, as relational, and as relating to social change, to name just a few of the most common perspectives. Each of these perspectives is described in this Handbook; the overlap between them and the fragile nature of the boundaries that have been artificially set up to distinguish between them becomes apparent.

Examining the philosophical assumptions underlying the dominant perspectives on transformative learning illuminates how these perspectives may simply be the result of scholars examining different facets of the same thing. It is our hope that this volume will help readers see the whole elephant.

Mezirow (1991) is explicit in describing transformative learning theory as being based on constructivist assumptions. Meaning is constructed through experience and our perceptions of those experiences, and future experiences are seen through the lens of the perspectives developed from past experiences. Learning occurs when an alternative perspective calls into question a previously held, perhaps uncritically assimilated perspective. Mezirow sees this as a rational process, but others suggest otherwise. This, however, does not negate the constructivist underpinnings of the theory. An imaginative and intuitive approach to learning or a spiritual approach to learning also relies on the construction of meaning from experience. The actual process involved in the construction of meaning may be different, but meaning is still constructed; it does not exist as an absolute truth outside of the self.

Dirkx (2001) and others who propose an extrarational (imaginative, intuitive, individuated, depth psychology) approach to transformative learning are easily associated with the philosophical assumptions of humanism—freedom, autonomy, choice, importance of the individual. If transformative learning is about differentiating the self from the collective through bringing the unconscious to consciousness as the depth psychologists propose, then it is about defining the self—a humanist goal.

The cognitive rational approach to transformative learning is also concerned with freedom, autonomy, and choice. People make a choice to engage with an alternative perspective; without this caveat, we move into the realm of manipulation rather than transformation.

Those theorists who focus on relational or connected transformative learning suggest that individuals learn through relationships with others. Autonomy therefore seems to take a back seat. However, if we look at this carefully, we see that relational learning is a process by which individuals suspend judgment and struggle to understand others' points of view from their perspective (Belenky & Stanton, 2000). The goal is to see holistically, not analytically. But we are still moving to the same place—individuals moving toward a better understanding of the self by engaging with others. It is interesting to note that one of the assumptions of humanism is that reality is defined by each person—a constructivist assumption.

When we come to critical social theory, at first glance there seems to be a serious disconnect with the previous philosophical perspectives (this was the basis of early critiques of Mezirow's work). It is helpful here to turn to

Brookfield's (2005) seven learning tasks associated with critical theory. The first of these learning tasks is *challenging ideologies*—the ideologies embedded in language, social habits, and cultural forms. Ideology is a "broadly accepted set of values, beliefs, myths, explanations, and justifications that appears self-evidently true, empirically accurate, personally relevant, and morally desirable to a majority of the populace" (p. 41). As such, ideologies are hard to detect (they appear to serve the interests of everyone), but they are what prevents us from realizing our true interests. The second learning task Brookfield extracted from critical theory is that of *contesting hegemony*. Hegemony occurs when people embrace (and see as normal) the conditions that serve those in power but work against the people's own best interests. For example, with the help of the media, we come to accept corporate takeovers and government bailouts as normal. The third learning task is *unmasking power* (Brookfield, 2005), based primarily on Foucault's ideas about individual interpersonal relationships (such as between teacher and learner or among learners) and in broader social structures. Unmasking power involves recognizing how power is exercised in our own lives in everyday actions. *Overcoming alienation* is the fourth learning task of critical theory. We are alienated when we are unable to be ourselves, unable to be authentic in the way in which we live and work. The learning task is to develop a sense of free agency and to realize how our lives are shaped by our social contexts. Brookfield lists *learning liberation* as the fifth adult learning task. Marcuse (1964), in *One-Dimensional Man*, argues that people can escape one-dimensional thought and ideological domination through imagination and the arts. *Reclaiming reason* is the sixth task in a critical theory approach to adult learning. Reclaiming reason involves applying reason to examining how our lives have been shaped by the lifeworld. The seventh and final learning task that Brookfield (2005) lists is *practicing democracy*. Brookfield claims that the word "democracy" is used in so many ways and with so many agendas that it has no real meaning. What we need to do is to practice democracy through rational discourse, paying attention to ideal speech conditions, increasing our awareness of the contradictions inherent in the ideal of democracy, and pay attention to power structures related to diversity (for example, race, class, gender, ethnicity, and sexual orientation).

There is a seeming disconnect between the critical social perspective and the constructivist and humanist perspectives: the former has a social "unit of analysis"; the latter, an individual "unit of analysis," to use Taylor's (2008) wording. A careful examination of the learning tasks of critical theory reveals that the focus is on critically questioning social structures that are the basis of inequities and oppression. It is the content of learning that is different—centered on the world outside of the self and the individual's position in that world rather than on the self, as it is in previously discussed perspectives. Mezirow (2000) refers to these processes as objective reframing (related to the external world) and subjective reframing (related to the self). Each of these learning tasks is about what individuals can and should do to increase their awareness of social conditions. Transformative learning theory need not be about individual transformation *or* social change; it is about both. Viewed in this way, this perspective is another leg of the elephant—an important leg, without which the elephant would fall down, but nevertheless, a part of the whole.

TENSIONS AND ISSUES IN THE FIELD

Scholars from a variety of perspectives within adult education and scholars from other disciplines other than adult education have been drawn to transformative learning theory. As a result, there are growing pains in the form of varied understandings of what transformative learning is and is not, seemingly conflicting perspectives on the learning processes involved, and unresolved issues related to theory development, which may in turn be creating stagnation in research and theory. Merriam, Caffarella, and Baumgartner (2007) list the following as unresolved issues: the role of context, rationality, and affect; the role of relationships in transformative learning; the place of social action; and the educator's role in fostering transformative learning. In this section, we highlight some of these tensions and issues in transformative learning theory.

Boundaries of the Field

Generally in the literature, there is an assumption that transformative learning is different from other kinds of learning (such as acquiring a new skill or elaborating on existing knowledge) (Mezirow, 2000). The *Journal of Transformative Education* maintains this distinction when the editors write that the journal is not another journal on education, but rather a "journal of another education" (Markos & McWhinney, 2003). But the boundaries remain unclear. Brookfield (2000) problematizes the idea of transformative learning, describing what he sees as the "misuse of the word *transformation* to refer to any instance in which reflection leads a deeper, more nuanced understanding of assumptions" (p. 139). He proposes that learning can be called transformative only if it involves a fundamental change at a very basic level, and he goes on to say that the indiscriminate use of the word "transformative" leads to the loss of its utility and validity. Similarly, and perhaps even more strongly, Newman (2011) presents examples of published works in which change of any kind (for example, becoming more open to other points of view, gaining self-confidence, "seeing things differently") are described as transformative. He challenges us to consider whether transformative learning exists as a distinct form of learning.

Teaching for transformation, he suggests, is simply good teaching. Scholars in the field need to continue to question the fundamental meaning of transformative learning and to refer back to original sources in doing so.

Fragmentation and Integration

As mentioned in the opening of this chapter, scholars and theorists tried to make meaning of the development of transformative learning theory by distinguishing one approach from another and categorizing accordingly. Early on, in response to Mezirow's (1991) work, individual and social change perspectives were defined, with the social change theorists critiquing the theory for overlooking social change. Within the focus on individual transformation, further splinters are immediately visible. Set up in contrast to Mezirow's cognitive approach is the extrarational approach or, as labeled by others, the depth psychology approach. Depth psychology theorists (Boyd & Myers, 1988; Dirkx, 2001) define transformation in relation to the Jungian concept of individuation, in which individuals bring the unconscious to consciousness as they differentiate Self from Other and simultaneously integrate Self with the collective. Also within the individual focus is a developmental perspective, wherein shifts are described in the way we make meaning—moving from a simplistic reliance on authority to more complex ways of knowing or higher orders of consciousness (for example, Kegan, 2000).

Within the focus on social change, some theorists see race and power structures as pivotal to ideology critique (Johnson-Bailey & Alfred, 2006). Tisdell and Tolliver (2003) add spirituality, symbolism, and narrative to what has been called the social-emancipatory approach. And there are those theorists who are interested in how groups and organizations transform.

In light of all of these fragments, what does transformative learning mean? When we use the phrase, what are we talking about? Clearly this is also related to the issue of boundaries discussed previously. However, some recent work is focusing on integration and holistic understandings in order to overcome a problematic plunge into a fragmented theory. At the 2005 International Conference on Transformative Learning, Dirkx and Mezirow engaged in a debate (Dirkx, Mezirow, & Cranton, 2006) that modeled an integrative process. They each presented their point of view, then looked for commonalities, overlap, and ways in which the two quite different perspectives could coexist without contradiction. Dirkx indicated that he was not denying the rational process of transformative learning; rather, he was simply more interested in the subjective world and the shadowy inner world. Mezirow acknowledged the significance of this dimension and added that there must also be a critical assessment of assumptions to ensure that they are not based on faith, prejudice, vision, or desire.

Gunnlaugson (2008) advocates working with a meta-analysis of what he calls the first-wave and second-wave contributions to the field of transformative learning in order to integrate perspectives. The first-wave contributions are those that build on, critique, or depart from Mezirow's account. Second-wave contributions are those that yield integrative, holistic, and integral theoretical perspectives. Gunnlaugson suggests that Taylor's (2006, 2008) integrative overview of the field is one example of how this supportive yet critical picture of the theory is beginning to emerge. Theorists and researchers need to identify what various perspectives on transformative learning theory have in common rather than continuing to try to distinguish between them. This is what we hope to encourage with our call for a more unified theory.

Social-Individual Tensions

The social-individual tensions go beyond the notion that some transformative learning is relevant to the individual and some is related to social change. Early on, Mezirow and Associates (1990) distinguished between the educational and political tasks of transformation. The educational task is to help people become aware of oppressive structures and develop the ability to change them (p. 210).

Taylor (2009) writes that "one framework...involves a collection of theoretical constructs that emphasize personal transformation and growth, where the unit of analysis is primarily the individual, with little attention given to the role of context and social change in the transformative experience" (p. 5). Social transformation, on the other hand, he describes as being about ideology critique whereby people "transform society and their own reality" (p. 5). The line between individual and social transformative learning is by no means clear. Rather than holding a dualistic viewpoint of "individual versus social" transformative learning, in a more unified theoretical stance we would think about how people engage in both ideology critique and individual transformation and how these processes complement each other.

Stagnation in Research and Theory

Considering the exponential growth of research on transformative learning theory over the last twenty years, it would be logical to conclude that the level of theoretical analysis is hard to contain and that many of the fundamental questions have been thoroughly explored. However, despite the intense interest in this theory, much of the research is redundant, with a strong deterministic emphasis of capturing transformative experiences and replicating transformative pedagogy in various settings, while overlooking the need for more in-depth theoretical analysis, including Mezirow's perspective as well new and emerging perspectives. Without an ongoing theoretical review, transformative learning becomes a theory that may begin lose its relevancy for the study of adult learning.

To address this concern, several approaches should be considered when in engaging in research on transformative learning theory. Most significantly, researchers should be thoroughly grounded in the primary sources and critiques of transformative learning (see, for example, Boyd & Myers, 1988; Clark & Wilson, 1991; Collard & Law, 1989; Freire, 1970; Hart, 1990; Merriam, 2004; Mezirow, 1991, 2000; Newman, 2011; O'Sullivan, 1999). Only through a thorough review of primary sources can scholars do research that both makes a significant contribution to the field and helps to continue an in-depth theoretical analysis of transformative learning.

Researchers should not rely solely on literature reviews to establish their study's contribution to the advancement of the field. Literature reviews are themselves not beyond critique. Often much can learned by returning to the original research and interpreting it anew—potentially from a different historical and theoretical perspective, as well as in relationship to the cumulative effect of ongoing research on transformative learning. Without this effort, literature reviews can foster an implicit assumption that the interpretation of research in a particular area is complete (when one has reviewed all the existing literature) and does not require further investigation. This may establish a baseline whereby everything begins with the review and not with the individual studies. An example of this is the criticism of Mezirow's overemphasis on rationality and lack of attention to affective ways of knowing (Boyd & Myers, 1988; Taylor, 1994). Often this critique is mentioned superficially in research studies with little awareness that the issue is far from resolved or of how it was conceptualized by Mezirow. The relationship between emotions and transformative learning is not yet well understood, and we know little about emotions and feelings in relation to other factors, such as how they foster and inhibit reflection; how they relate to the transformation of epistemic, sociolinguistic, and psychological perspectives; and how they manifest themselves in different cultures.

In response to this concern about giving too much weight to reviews, it would be helpful to use them more as a means to identify relevant research and provide direction for future research and less from an interpretive standpoint. Also, by identifying exemplar studies by literature reviews that provide models for research designs and theoretical analysis, we can minimize redundant studies and increase the opportunity for more forward-thinking research on transformative learning.

We further recommend that researchers give greater attention to theoretical analyses when developing a rationale and analyzing the findings of a study. Within the rationale of the study, attention should be paid to providing a critical review of related research and established theory and to considering how the research contributes to the advancement of transformative learning theory. Also, if multiple perspectives of transformative learning are engaged, researchers should discuss what these lenses offer. Furthermore, the findings of studies should be analyzed in relationship to the theoretical framework. Ideally the findings will be used to confirm or question theoretical assumptions, support prior critique or offer new critique in relationship to the literature, and raise new questions for further research about transformative learning theory.

Issues in Practice

Newman's comment (2011) that fostering transformative learning is just "good" teaching leads us to several challenges. What does it mean to foster transformative learning? What core assumptions provide the bases for fostering transformative learning, and what does it look like in practice? However, despite Newman's point and the related challenge, it is a worthy goal to identify what are effective educational practices for teaching adults. Of any area of research concerning transformative learning, exploring the practice of fostering transformative learning has been at the forefront among scholars particularly over the last ten years.

The research on fostering transformative learning confirms to a great extent what has been known about good teaching (for example, using direct and personally engaging experiences, involving prior experiences of learners, encouraging reflection, promoting dialogue), much of which falls under the mantle of transformative learning (Taylor, 2000, 2007; Mezirow & Taylor, 2009). In addition to these findings, there has been an emphasis on more holistic practices, such as attuning to the affective and relational aspects of learning, incorporating arts-based activities, and recognizing embodied learning. This can include a range of concepts, such as other ways of knowing, extrarational learning, whole person learning, and multidimensional learning. This identification of other essential practices of teaching has been both a problem and a blessing.

One aspect of the problem is the lack of clarity with the terminology. What is meant by all these terms? What practices do they include? How can they be applied in the teaching process? And how are they engaged in relationship to more instrumental forms of teaching (for example, lectures and presentations)? For example, what is the difference between whole person learning and other ways of knowing? Which practices are inclusive of these approaches, and what is not included? A recent analysis of different programs' and educators' descriptions of the importance of transformative learning reveals that the situation has become even more complicated. In addition to the importance of a more holistic approach, these identified other broad approaches to transformative learning, such as the importance of confronting power and engaging differences, promoting imagination, and leading learners to the edge of learning (Taylor & Jarecke, 2009).

Further compounding this problem is the fact that much of the terminology lacks a definitive theoretical grounding in transformative learning theory. If a theory is provided, it is most often based on Mezirow's perspective, with little recognition that some of the practices are incongruent or in conflict with this theoretical orientation. This is not to say there are not exemplars of how to theoretically frame the practice of fostering transformative learning. A good example can be found in the research by Yorks and Kasl (2006) in which they deconstruct expressing ways of knowing as a means of fostering transformative learning by drawing on the work of John Heron. However, despite the commendable efforts of a few, practices that are not theoretically framed lead to what could be referred to as "teaching arbitrary," where teaching methods are random, ill-defined, and disconnected strategies, with little acknowledgment of their underlying assumptions about learning in general and more specifically their association with transformative learning.

Without time spent making sense of these strategies and deconstructing them in relationship to current research, the context where they are applied, and a related theoretical framework, they continue to contribute to the ongoing difficulty of understanding the relationship between fostering transformative learning and "good" teaching. It may be that some teaching practices have more potential to foster transformative learning than others, or it may be that good teaching always has the potential to foster transformative learning and transformation is dependent on the readiness of the learners, the context in which the teaching takes place, or other factors outside of the teaching practice.

Further compounding the issue of the clarity of various practices is the lack of understanding about the impact of fostering transformative learning on learner outcomes. Literature has revealed that engaging in the practice of transformative learning can make a difference in the lives of learners (see, for example, Donaldson, 2009; Easton, Monkman, & Miles, 2009; Macleod & Egan, 2009); however, little is known about its impact on traditional measures of education (grades, test scores, performance). Definitive support is needed if educators are going to recognize transformative learning as a worthwhile goal of teaching adults.

Finally, the growing body of research and alternative perspectives reminds educators that fostering transformative learning is much more than implementing a series of instructional strategies with adult learners. It is first and foremost about educating from a particular educational philosophy, with its own assumptions about the purpose of education, the role of the educator, and the nature of knowledge.

Transformative Learning as the "New Andragogy"

A way to appreciate how transformative learning has impacted the field of adult education and adult learning more specifically is to think about it in relationship to andragogy (Taylor, 2008). It has accomplished what the study of andragogy had hoped to and much more. For example, andragogy is more a framework for teaching adults than a lens for explaining learning. Also, its related research is encumbered with host of challenges (for example, noncomparability of studies, the wide variation in definition and implementation, learner control and voluntarism) (Rachal, 2002). Transformative learning, on the other hand, although sharing some similar challenges, has persisted due to significant research and theoretical critique offering a framework for both understanding adult learning and guiding the teaching of adults (Taylor, 1998, 2007). As a result, it has overshadowed andragogy, moving from the margins to the center of the study of adult learning in both adult education and a variety of other disciplines (for example, archeology, medical education, distance education, religious studies). As previously discussed, a range of conceptions of transformative learning has emerged. In many ways transformative learning theory has brought a new and exciting identity to the field of adult education, one that builds on the previous work of andragogy.

However, despite the exponential growth of transformative learning theoretically, most research today continues to be based on Mezirow's work rather than the newer perspectives. This is unfortunate, not only for development of these perspectives but also for the general study of transformative learning theory. It is important to keep in mind that these theories emerged in response to the critiques of Mezirow's work. Through theoretical critique, other factors (relational, spiritual, context) were identified as relevant to transformation, along with an appreciation of multiple units of analysis (individual and social). It is our hope that this Handbook and its chapters on diverse conceptualizations of transformative learning will challenge scholars and researchers to engage these emerging perspectives, moving toward a more unified field of the study.

CONCLUDING THOUGHTS

Over thirty years have past since transformative learning was introduced to the field of adult education, and during that time no other theory of adult learning has experienced as much research, controversy, and promise. Transformative learning theory has far surpassed andragogy, providing a new identity for the field—a theoretical framework that guides both research and practice. As a consequence, many other disciplines have shown interest in engaging in transformative learning as way of making sense of progressive education. However, with all this growth there have also been struggles and shortfalls. Even though transformative learning epitomizes the core assumptions often associated with "good" practice of teaching adults, at the same time it reflects a tension between individual and societal change. Most significantly, its ubiquitous presence beyond the field of adult education has led to a construct that has come to mean many things to many educators. It is our hope that these tensions will move us toward a more unified theory of transformative learning. Both the potential and the challenges facing transformative learning theory are the motivation for this Handbook. It is our hope that through an academic engagement with host of recognized scholars, this Handbook will begin to address some of the concerns, but also offer even greater promise about the study of transformative learning as we move into the next decade.

References

Belenky, M., & Stanton, A. (2000). Inequality, development, and connected knowing. In J. Mezirow & Associates (Eds.), *Learning as transformation: Critical perspectives on a theory in progress* (pp. 71–102). San Francisco: Jossey-Bass.

Boyd, R. D., & Myers, J. B. (1988). Transformative education. *International Journal of Lifelong Education*, 7, 261–284.

Brookfield, S. D. (1986). *Understanding and facilitating adult learning.* San Francisco: Jossey-Bass.

Brookfield, S. D. (1993). Self-directed learning, political clarity, and the critical practice of adult education. *Adult Education Quarterly*, 43(4), 227–242.

Brookfield, S. D. (2000). Transformative learning as ideology critique. In J. Mezirow & Associates (Eds.), *Learning as transformation: Critical perspectives on a theory in progress* (pp. 125–150). San Francisco: Jossey-Bass.

Brookfield, S. D. (2005). *The power of critical theory.* San Francisco: Jossey-Bass.

Brundage, D., & MacKeracher, D. (1980). *Adult learning principles and their application to program planning.* Toronto: Ontario Institute for Studies in Education.

Clark, C. M., & Wilson, A. (1991). Context and rationality in Mezirow's theory of transformational learning. *Adult Education Quarterly*, 41, 75–91.

Collard, S., & Law, M. (1989). The limits of perspective transformation: A critique of Mezirow's theory. *Adult Education Quarterly*, 39, 99–107.

Dirkx, J. (2001). Images, transformative learning, and the work of soul. *Adult Learning*, 12(3), 15–16.

Dirkx, J., Mezirow, J., & Cranton, P. (2006). Musings and reflections on the meaning, context, and process of transformative learning. *Journal of Transformative Education*, 4(2), 123–139.

Donaldson, J. F. (2009). Fostering transformative learning in leadership development. In J. Mezirow, E. W. Taylor, & Associates (Eds.), *Transformative learning in practice* (pp. 67–77). San Francisco: Jossey-Bass.

Easton, P., Monkman, K., & Miles, R. (2009). Breaking out of the egg: Methods of transformative learning in rural West Africa. In J. Mezirow, E. W. Taylor, & Associates (Eds.), *Transformative learning in practice* (pp. 227–239). San Francisco: Jossey-Bass.

Elias, J. L., & Merriam, S. B. (2004). *Philosophical foundations of adult education* (3rd ed.). San Francisco: Jossey-Bass.

Freire, P. (1970). *Pedagogy of the oppressed*. New York: Herder & Herder.

Gunnlaugson, O. (2008). Metatheoretical prospects for the field of transformative learning. *Journal of Transformative Education, 6*(2), 124–135.

Hart, M. (1990). Critical theory and beyond: Further perspectives on emancipatory education. *Adult Education Quarterly, 40,* 125–138.

Johnson-Bailey, J., & Alfred, M. (2006). Transformation teaching and the practices of Black Women adult educators. In E. W. Taylor (Ed.), *Fostering transformative learning in the classroom: Challenges and innovations.* New Directions in Adult and Continuing Education, no. 109. San Francisco: Jossey-Bass.

Kegan, R. (2000). What "form" transforms? A constructive-developmental approach to transformative learning. In J. Mezirow & Associates (Eds.), *Learning as transformation: Critical perspectives on a theory in progress* (pp. 35–70). San Francisco: Jossey-Bass.

Knowles, M. (1975). *Self-directed learning: A guide for learners and teachers.* Chicago: Follet.

Knowles, M. (1980). *The modern practice of adult education: From pedagogy to andragogy.* New York: Cambridge.

Lindemann, E. (1926). *The meaning of adult education.* New York: New Republic.

Macleod, R., & Egan, T. (2009). Transformative palliative care. In J. Mezirow, E. W. Taylor, & Associates (Eds.), *Transformative learning in practice* (pp. 111–110). San Francisco: Jossey-Bass.

Marcuse, H. (1964). *One dimensional man.* Boston: Beacon Press.

Markos, L., & McWhinney, W. (2003). Editors' perspective: Auspice. *Journal of Transformative Education, 1*(1), 3–15.

Maslow, A. H. (1970). *Toward a psychology of being.* New York: Van Nostrand.

Merriam, S. B. (2004). The role of cognitive development in Mezirow's transformational learning theory. *Adult Education Quarterly, 55,* 60–68.

Merriam, S. B. (2008). Adult learning theory for the twenty-first century. In S. B. Merriam (Ed.), *Third update on adult learning theory* (pp. 93–98). New Directions for Adult and Continuing Education, no. 119. San Francisco: Jossey-Bass.

Merriam, S. B., Caffarella, R. S., & Baumgartner, L. (2007). *Learning in adulthood.* San Francisco: Jossey-Bass.

Merriam, S. B., & Sek Kim, Y. (2008). Non-Western perspectives on learning and knowing. In S. B. Merriam (ed.), *Third update on adult learning theory* (pp. 71–81). New Directions for Adult and Continuing Education, no. 119. San Francisco: Jossey-Bass.

Mezirow, J. (1978). Perspective transformation. *Adult Learning, 28,* 100–110.

Mezirow, J. (1981). A critical theory of adult learning and education. *Adult Education, 32,* 3–24.

Mezirow, J. (1991). *Transformative dimensions of adult learning.* San Francisco: Jossey-Bass.

Mezirow, J. (2000). Learning to think like an adult. In J. Mezirow & Associates (Eds.), *Learning as transformation: Critical perspectives on a theory in progress* (pp. 3–34). San Francisco: Jossey-Bass.

Mezirow, J., & Associates (Eds.). (1990). *Fostering critical reflection in adulthood.* San Francisco: Jossey-Bass.

Mezirow, J., Taylor, E. W., & Associates (Eds.). (2009). *Transformative learning in practice: Insights from community, workplace, and higher education.* San Francisco: Jossey-Bass.

Newman, M. (2011). Calling transformative learning into question: Some mutinous thought. *Adult Education Quarterly.* Retrieved August 15, 2011 as doi:10.1177/0741713610392768

O'Sullivan, E. (1999). *Transformative learning: educational vision for the 21st century.* New York: Palgrave Press.

Rachal, J. R. (2002). Andragogy's detectives: A critique of the present and a proposal for the future. *Adult Education Quarterly, 52*(3), 210–227.

Rogers, C. (1969). *Freedom to learn: A view of what education might become.* Columbus, OH: Merrill.

Taylor, E. W. (1994). A learning model for intercultural competency. *International Journal of Intercultural Relations, 18*(3), 398–408.

Taylor, E. W. (1998) Transformative learning: A critical review. ERIC Clearinghouse on Adult, Career, & Vocational Education (Information Series No. 374).

Taylor, E. W. (2000). Analyzing research on transformative learning theory. In J. Mezirow & Associates (Eds.), *Learning as transformation: Critical perspectives on a theory in progress* (pp. 285–328). San Francisco: Jossey-Bass.

Taylor, E. W. (2006). An update of transformative learning theory: A critical review of the empirical research (1999–2005). *International Journal of Lifelong Education, 26,* 173–191.

Taylor, E. W. (2007). An update on transformative learning theory: A critical review of the empirical research (1999–2005). *International Journal of Lifelong Education, 26*(2), 173–191.

Taylor, E. W. (2008). Transformative learning theory. In S. B. Merriam (Ed.), *Third update on adult learning theory* (pp. 5–16). New Directions for Adult and Continuing Education, no. 119. San Francisco: Jossey-Bass.

Taylor, E. W. (2009). Fostering transformative learning. In J. Mezirow, E. W. Taylor, & Associates (Eds.), *Transformative learning in practice* (pp. 3–17). San Francisco: Jossey-Bass.

Taylor, E. W., & Jarecke, J. (2009). Looking forward by looking back: Reflections on the practice of transformative learning. In J. Mezirow, E. W. Taylor, & Associates (Eds.), *Transformative learning in practice* (pp. 275–290). San Francisco: Jossey-Bass.

Tisdell, E., & Tolliver, E. (2003). Claiming a sacred face: The role of spirituality and cultural identity in transformative adult higher education. *Journal of Transformative Education, 1*(4), 368–392.

Wang, V.C.X., & King, K. P. (2008). Transformative learning and ancient Asian educational perspectives. *Journal of Transformative Education, 6*(2), 136–150.

Yorks, L., & Kasl, E. (2006). I know more than I can say. *Journal of Transformative Education, 4*(1), 43–64.

CHAPTER TWO

Themes and Variations of Transformational Learning

Interdisciplinary Perspectives on Forms That Transform

Elizabeth J. Tisdell

I sit quietly in my beloved community while the brass quintet plays Thomas Tallis's "If Ye Love Me."* I feel the vibration. My chest swells with awe as I'm filled with the majestic sound. Tears prickle behind my eyes as I'm enveloped in the music and the moment and the poignant present before me: The woman cradles her French horn, exhaling a breath of cosmic sound while her fingers dance and pause on each golden key. Her horn rests lightly on her swollen belly rising and falling with each breath, the ivory of her skin shimmering in her pregnant glow. To her left, her husband's tone echoes deep in the bass of his tuba, filling the space, lingering large and deep, the ebony of his skin and his soft dark eyes agleam and vibrant with sacred possibility. The trumpets sound, the trombone slides, at once drawing us inward, while also moving us outward. New being, old being, gathered and regathered, together and alone, we are. I come 'round again, seeming the same, but I'm transposed! Spiraling in, spiraling out, reflecting the themes and variations of transformational learning.

*This chapter is best read while listening to Tallis's piece, available online.

There are many themes and variations of transformational learning, just as there are in music. In many classical music pieces, the core melody serves as the theme, and then many variations are played on that theme as the piece moves along. The theme is announced, the variations provide depth, but the whole of the piece, and its effects on the listener, are always greater than the sum of its parts. Transformational learning experiences in our lives are like that.

There are different types of transformational experiences, and different "forms that transform" (Kegan, 2000, p. 35). Some alter our very being, our beliefs, and our core sense of self—the core *theme* by which we live and move and define our being. Mezirow (1991) refers to these as *transformative* learning experiences. Other types *transpose* our hearts and our moods and give us a glimpse of a larger learning about the Big Questions of life—what it means to be human, why we're here, what makes the universe go on, and the nature of human consciousness itself (Parks, 2000). These types often fill us with awe and wonder, yet they do not necessarily change our core identity or our core *theme*. Rather, they take our breath away in their profundity as we move to living more deeply (Schlitz, Vieten, & Amorek, 2007). We are *transposed*—as music is changed into a different key—to a *variation* on the theme of our core identity, and we live larger because of these types of experiences. The experience I had this morning, described at this chapter's opening (and to which I'll return later) is an example of this type of experience, which might function as a type of experience that transposes my consciousness in a given moment but not my core identity. Integrated together over time, however, such moments that transpose our consciousness can often—even on a daily basis, if we seek out such changes in consciousness through meditation or other active efforts at living more deeply—act as part of what Clark (1993) refers to as the integrating circumstance(s) of the transformative learning process.

Still a third type of transformational learning experience happens more in the context of working for social change in a community. People meet; their eyes and hearts and minds engage. They work together to make their communities better as they challenge systems of privilege and oppression, in what is often referred to as *emancipatory learning* efforts (Horton & Freire, 1990). Often communities are transformed in various ways, and so are the individuals within.

These three types of transformational experiences are neither mutually exclusive nor representative of all types of possible experiences. Further, the demarcations among them are not as clear as have been delineated here, as different authors use different terms to describe both similar and different types of experiences. But because there are many different types of transformational learning experiences (the collective term I will use for all types), they have been written about differently, both in adult education and in other disciplines. This has caused confusion, because often it is not clear what people mean when they refer to "transformative learning" or "transformational learning" as it is variously called; also, some people seem to use the term so loosely that it is almost a synonym for learning of any kind, rendering the term *transformative* nearly meaningless. Thus the purpose of this chapter is to explore the themes and variations in transformational learning from an interdisciplinary perspective, to glean further insights and provide greater clarity about what exactly is meant by *transformation* and *learning* or *experience* in these different discussions and different disciplines. Such an investigation will provide direction to researchers and practitioners hoping to glean new insights about the study or facilitation of this great capacity for human beings to grow, change, and to live more deeply through the various transformational learning experiences, in all their themes and variations, that inform their lives. First, I briefly consider some of the discussions specifically within the field of adult education, and the forms of transformative learning. Next, to give examples I offer an "interlude" largely based on my own experience. This sets the context and paves the way for exploration of how transformation has been discussed in other disciplines and what it might suggest for adult education.

ADULT EDUCATION AND TRANSFORMATIONAL AND EMANCIPATORY LEARNING

Most adult education readers are likely familiar with the most common discourses related to transformative learning and emancipatory education in the field; thus I only briefly summarize them here, to highlight their emphases. After doing so, I consider their more recent confluences within the field and influences beyond, and the particular "forms" of transformative learning.

Three Primary Discourses

Jack Mezirow (1991) is the initial architect of what has come to be known in U.S. adult education as transformative learning theory. His initial research—continued work that resulted in positing transformative learning theory as a ten-step process initiated by a disorienting dilemma that causes reflections on assumptions—has generated much discussion and critique over the years. One major critique had been that it is too driven by rationality, with not enough attention to other ways that individuals come to know and learn, such as through emotions, spirituality, or embodied forms of knowing. Thus other scholars (Cranton, 2006; Dirkx, 2001), seeking to develop a fuller model of transformative learning, have drawn on the literature in depth psychology and other disciplines that attend to these ways of knowing. Another major critique is that Mezirow's theory is too focused on the individual; it does not attend directly enough with power relations or social transformation (Taylor, 1997). All of these critiques have generated much debate, publication, and further adaptation of the theory and discussions for practice.

Another strand of transformative learning comes from the work of a Canadian adult educator, Edmund O'Sullivan (1999), who discusses a model of transformative education. His focus is more on articulating that vision and philosophy of transformative education rather than on the learning process itself. Drawing on the work of eco-theologian Thomas Berry (1999) and others, O'Sullivan articulates a transformative vision for planetary survival. He then highlights the importance of critique but cautions about the loss of the sense of the whole, at the same time that he critiques the individualist and marketplace-driven approaches to education that are dominant in Western culture. He also highlights the importance of creativity, ritual, symbol, and story in forging a creative vision. Whereas his 1999 work is quite philosophical, more recent edited collections drawing on his work have offered some specific transformative educational strategies relating to ecology, spirituality, sustainability, feminism, racism, and arts-based ways of knowing in specific situations (Gardner & Kelly, 2008; O'Connor, O'Sullivan, & Morrell, 2002).

The third discourse on transformation in the field is on emancipatory education; it focuses *specifically* on social transformation rather than individual transformation—on challenging power relations based on gender, race, class, sexual orientation, dis/ability, or religion. Scholars writing in these areas typically ground their work in theoretical frameworks that specifically attend to these issues, such as Paulo Freire's (1971) problem-posing education; the work of Myles Horton and the Highlander Folk School (Horton & Freire, 1990), which has influenced popular education movements (Walters & Manicom, 1996); and, from the emancipatory education literature, the work of those who foreground gender, race, class, or other structural systems of oppression to bring about social transformation. They tend not to refer to those scholars, such as Mezirow, who focus on individual transformation, but rather to focus on critical or feminist theory or critical race theory as their grounding point. Such discourses are generally seen as more relevant and specific, even though they often deal with transformative learning about social systems of oppression and privilege in the process of social transformation.

Overlaps and Integration in Adult Education and Beyond

More recent discussions of transformative learning and emancipatory education in adult education tend to draw on all three of these discourses, evidence of their mutual influence and integration. For example, several chapters of recent edited collections on transformative learning (Fisher-Yoshida, Geller, & Schapiro, 2009; Mezirow & Taylor, 2009) deal with challenging power relations based on difference and diversity, which has been the focus of the emancipatory discourses. Many authors also draw on other discussions of transformation from the wider field of education or other disciplines and bring insights back into the field from those disciplines, as Dirkx (2001) has done in relation to depth psychology, or Johnson-Bailey and Alfred (2006) have done in relation to race and gender discourses and transformative learning. This has also been my own strategy on considering the connections among spirituality and culture in transformative learning in my own research (Tisdell, 2003) and writing with my colleague (Tisdell & Tolliver, 2003). In any case, all of these examples serve as evidence of how those in the field are expanding the discussion of transformative learning in adult education and how it has been influenced by other disciplines.

But it is also important to point out that there are many discussions of transformative learning in the wider world of education that never refer to adult education discourses. For example, the critical multicultural education theorist James Banks (1996) refers to transformative teaching or transforma-tive pedagogy, though he never refers to Mezirow's work or others in adult education; rather, *transformative* in this sense refers to teaching to challenge power relations based on race or culture, so it is grounded in the more eman-cipatory literature. There are also discussions of transformation in other dis-ciplines that are useful in forging transformative learning theory and practice. Before considering these, it is helpful first to consider the "forms" of transfor-mative learning.

Considering "Forms" That Change and Transform

Robert Kegan (2000), in his discussion of epistemological shifts and cognitive restructuring in transformative learning, poses the excellent question: "What *form* transforms?" (p. 35). A corollary is "what form transforms *what*?" Some forms transform one's *being*, whereas others transform one's *thinking*, though obviously there are overlaps between the two. But trying to negotiate the reali-ties of falling in love and into a more mature relationship appears to be quite dif-ferent from having a breakthrough in understanding the chemical compounds of organic chemistry. The first appears to relate to a "form" involving more of the affective domain, whereas the latter is more in the cognitive domain. The "form" that transforms in both situations likely involves multiple dimensions of being, no matter what, but one domain is likely more primary than others, depending on what is being transformed.

Some transformative learning experiences transform our very core identity or worldview. Mezirow (2009) refers to these major shifts as "epochal," which he defines as "involving dramatic or major changes" (p. 23). He is writing about the kinds of experiences that alter one's core beliefs about oneself and the world, metaphorically one's *core theme.* He is not writing here about switching from regular lattes to soy lattes because one reads an article on the benefits of soy and learns to develop a taste for it! Although he acknowledges the fact that there are many types of transformative learning experiences, some of which are incremental, he appears to be primarily concerned with those that facilitate major identity or worldview shifts.

In their recent edited volume exploring "threshold concepts" in transfor-mative learning, editors Meyer, Land, and Baillie (2010) define threshold experiences as those that are like "passing through a portal" (p. ix), wherein a new view of some aspect of the world or one's life comes into view. They suggest such threshold experiences can be "transformative," as in a complete shift in consciousness about one's identity or a particular subject, or "integrative," as in "exposing a previously hidden inter-relatedness" (p. ix). In actuality, however, the chapter authors take on an examination of "threshold concepts" related to their academic disciplines, drawing on the cognitive sciences to understand the cognitive dimension of transformative learning and the interrelatedness of ideas. They consider components of integrational thinking that is transformative relating to new intellectual concepts rather than the type that transform one's identity. This is transforming one's *thinking* rather than transforming one's *being*—indeed, a different "form" that transforms. These kinds of transformative experiences may be integrative, but they are likely not what Mezirow would refer to as "epochal."

There are likely many times in one's life when one has transformational experiences that are integrative to transform one's *thinking*. But there are likely few instances of an epochal shift that transforms one's *being* and identity. In these instances the "form" that transforms involves multiple domains on a significant level—emotional, rational, physical, and perhaps spiritual as well. Moses's famous experience of the burning bush, described in Exodus 3 of the Hebrew Bible, serves as a classic example of an epochal or threshold experience. In it, Moses on Mount Horeb sees a burning bush that is not being consumed as it is burning. He approaches to look at the bush more closely, when reportedly the Lord calls to him. Moses responds with "Here I am!" Then the Lord tells him to come no nearer, but to take off his shoes and stand there, because where he is standing is "Holy Ground" (as cited in Steinmetz, 1993, p. 200). God then tells Moses of his mission to lead the people out of Egypt, and a rich dialogue unfolds between the two in regard to Moses and his abilities; Moses emerges with a transformed sense of identity. Steinmetz (1993) characterizes this as a transformation of epoch proportions and suggests that Moses was in a transformed state of consciousness and openness, an "ultraconsciousness" (p. 200) as a result of being in the desert and climbing the mountain where he encounters the burning bush. When he comes down from the mountain, he reportedly looks different, because he *is* different. He has stood on Holy Ground! He was able to understand his authentic self as he said anew "Here I am!"

It appears in this instance, at least in Steinmetz's (1993) interpretation, that the "form" that transformed involved the physical, emotional, and spiritual dimensions, the combination resulting in Moses's state of "ultraconsciousness." Obviously, it eventually included the cognitive dimensions in relation to his transformed identity, acted out in his leadership. Whether or not one believes the literal truth of the story, many of us have had moments of epochal transformation, in which we mark the moment or the place as Holy Ground for us (though we might not use that term), when we had a sense of our more authentic identity. Epochal experiences like this are likely rare over the course of one's life, and certainly most of us don't have a sense of mission like that of Moses. Nevertheless, such moments transform our hearts, our souls, and our very being, and the "form" that transforms involves multiple dimensions of who we are. Many see such moments as spiritual moments as well, though Mezirow never discusses epochal experiences as such. This is more in the purview of others who discuss transformational learning, many of whom are outside the field of adult education (see, for example, Abalos, 1998).

Some within adult education do touch on the notion of spirituality and other more holistic notions of transformative learning. My own work has been focused in this area, and Dirkx (2001) has highlighted attention to images in doing the work of the soul in transformative learning, as these are important forms that facilitate or encapsulate what transforms. O'Sullivan's transformative educational vision touches on the integration of cognition, spirituality, consciousness studies, critique, and creativity. Rereading his work since I've been working on this chapter helps explain partly why my mantra of late with my own students has been "Critique, but create!" Far too often in graduate programs we teach the importance of critique almost as if this is a form that transforms thinking, but we do not invite learners often enough to call upon the wonder of their own creativity, which is important in cultivating hope, possibility, and action. This is about engaging more aspects of oneself that can lead to the transformation of *being* as well as thinking.

Toward Expanding the Vision: Love, Death, and the Big Questions

So what is missing from the discourses of adult education and transformative learning? It is generally surprising that thus far in the field there's been limited attention to the Big Questions of life in transformative learning— what gives life meaning, why we're here, and the meaning of the universe—the very questions that have been the focus of organizations such as the Templeton Foundation or the Institute of Noetic Sciences. What form transforms in dealing with these questions? Perhaps more surprisingly, there are relatively few published studies in the transformative learning adult education literature dealing with two very fundamental aspects of human life that, to me, are intricately related to the most significant of transformative learning experiences: love and death. To some extent these concepts may be implied in research or discussion, but they have been given limited direct attention. I return to the importance of these concepts later, and their importance to much of what drives transformational learning experiences, particularly those that invite us to live more deeply.

INTERLUDE

It is now several days since I've begun writing this chapter. I reread what I've written. I listen again to a recording of Thomas Tallis's "If Ye Love Me" and think of that expectant young couple playing it in their quintet in the beloved community of my church. I am reminded of moments of transformational experiences, both in my life and in theirs, and I bet they are about to have one in the birth of their child!

I think about Moses and the burning bush, and about the only three epochal transformative learning experiences that I can identify in my own life—all having to do with love and death. The first was falling in love with a woman when I was thirty-one, when up until that time I had assumed my (hetero) sexual orientation was a stable given. It altered who I was and how I saw my identity, as I experienced the great awe and wonder of life and love with my beloved over the next ten years (including negotiating love's conflicts, and the ending of our partnership). Although I eventually fell in love again, with a man whom I have been with for twelve years, I came to understand my identity and my life in a different way from being in a committed long-term relationship with a woman. It altered a core theme about myself: the idea that sexual orientation is not a stable given—I fall in love with a person, not a gender. Indeed, there is nothing like the power of love to transform!

My experience listening to the music in church was a transformational experience, but not in the epochal sense; rather, it transposed me into a different key. I am reminded of Inayat Khan (1996), the Indian Sufi mystic who brought Universal Sufism to the West in 1910, who discusses the vibrational quality of music as sound that also changes the vibration of the brain waves of consciousness. Indeed, my consciousness was transposed in this instance. I found myself enveloped, not only in the embrace of such majestic music but also in the sacred scene of who was making the music in my beloved community. The sacred scene—the form that transformed—included the intertwined sound, sight, and vibrational feeling; all three together acted as the form that transformed. It pulled me open to life in a new way in those moments, as my skin tingled and I experienced what Sanders refers to as "the holy shimmer at the heart of things" (2006, p. 26). I also know the expectant young couple I described; I have worked with them in an emancipatory racial justice project. The scene, and the memory, the music, the project all were integrated into my new sense of consciousness in those moments. Such experiences help me celebrate the mystery of life itself—birth and death, music and creativity, the sensual and the communal—which affirms much of what it means to be human. It gives me courage to move forward, to embrace the more in them and the more in me, the more in our community. This is a kind of transformational learning; it transforms my consciousness and provides variation on what I've already come to know.

But amidst love and music I've also experienced two other epochal transformative learning experiences: that of walking the torrid but tender journey of death with each of my parents. I learned to believe in myself in a new way, that I could walk that really difficult journey; that I could stay till the very end, that amidst very labored breathing and my own fear, I could stay and hold my mother's hand as she crossed over. As she let go of her last breath, she squeezed my hand one last time as if she were passing her spirit right into me. I found a strength and source within that would give me courage in such times of difficulty and loss. There is power in this. I saw myself in a new way in terms of how to maintain presence and summon a deeper strength. I revisited this when my father died ten years later, when I saw a spark of the great mystery of life and creation, and the mystery of the interconnecting great web of life, in caring for his failing body at the same time his spirit shimmered with a different light. Amidst love and death comes transformation! Amidst transformation comes a new consciousness. I move forward . . . until I spiral back.

NEW VARIATIONS ON TRANSFORMATION LEARNING: INFLUENCES FROM OTHER DISCIPLINES

And so we come to a new moment in understanding transformational learning. Transformative and transformational learning and emancipatory education, as discussed in the field of adult education, have always been influenced by the disciplines of psychology and sociology, but there are new variations on these discussions. Although psychologists and social workers do not always discuss transformational *learning*, because their focus is generally on therapeutic healing, many are often engaged in facilitating its work; the therapeutic process often leads clients to a transformed sense of identity or shifts in worldview. Some actually do use the term "learning" in places. Loue (2008) for example, describes the transformative power of using and engaging metaphor in therapy. She talks about "roles and role transformation" and of engaging her clients in "learning new perspectives" (p. 63). Those who work in ministry, theology, or religious education circles sometimes refer to a "transforming moment" (Loder, 1989) and how to use such moments in one's own life or in working with others to facilitate transformation. Others use the language of liminality or conversion, in facilitating the ongoing work of transformation in pastoral ministry or religious education settings (Groome & Horell, 2003). Irwin (2002) also discusses this from a developmental psychology perspective, drawing especially on Robert Kegan's work relating to epistemological knowing and the structures of consciousness, as well as the cognitive restructuring and identity shifts that happen in light of "threshold" spiritual experiences, and in relation to meditation practices.

To an extent we see evidence of some of these influences in the transformational learning literature within adult education already, particularly in O'Sullivan's and his followers' work. Recent publications referring to transformative or transformational learning are being influenced by a variety of disciplines including theology, neuroscience, and consciousness studies. For example, Jackson, in his 2008 book on transformative learning for a worldview shift—which is based largely on his environmental work in India—discusses transformative learning from a global cultural perspective and argues for the need for a new world view. Nowhere does he refer to Mezirow, and he only refers to O'Sullivan's work briefly. Paul Hiebert (2008), in a somewhat similar vein, discusses anthropological perspectives on worldviews embedded in different cultures and what the process of transforming worldviews entails from a cognitive, cultural, and religious perspective, as conceptualized in anthropology. Thus we are beginning to see more expanded views on transformative learning, and what it means in this new century. Here I briefly summarize two of these interrelated perspectives—consciousness studies and neuroscience—that are starting to influence transformative learning.

Consciousness Studies and Transformational Learning

There are beginning to be a number of influences from consciousness studies in the more recent literature on transformative learning within the field of adult education. Tobin Hart (2001) has been involved in these discussions for a long time; his work on transformational learning from a transpersonal psychology and evolutionary consciousness perspective includes attention to the spiritual. He has tied his work specifically to adult education only in more recent years (Hart, 2008). Gunnlaugson (2007) also has recently brought discussions from consciousness studies into transformative learning and adult education, specifically in relation to understanding orders of consciousness. He draws on Kegan's (2000) work on different orders of consciousness and Ken Wilber's (2000) work on states of consciousness as developmental lines, and considers what this means for generative dialogue and how to help learners shift consciousness by drawing on multiple ways of knowing.

Various organizations and foundations devote their work to the realm of consciousness studies, which explore the connections among science, spirituality, and religion and what these interconnections suggests for transforming consciousness largely from a global perspective. The Templeton Foundation (www.templeton.org) and the Institute of Noetic Sciences (www.noetic.org) are two examples. Most relevant to our discussion here is a large mixed methods study on people's experiences of transformation from a consciousness studies perspective. The study was conducted through the Institute of Noetic Sciences and discussed in depth by Schlitz, Vieten, and Amorok (2007), outlining what the participants in this large study said about what it means to live deeply. They based their discussion on a study "of the transformative process—from analysis of hundreds of stories of transformation, teacher focus groups, fifty interviews with teachers and masters of transformative processes, and almost nine hundred surveys with people engaged in their own transformative journeys" (pp. 10–11). They further note that their discussion is informed by "leading theories of transformation" as well as "direct wisdom from a broad cross section of religious, spiritual, and transformative practices" and "scientific evidence from a diverse array of fields" (p. 11). They do not cite Mezirow, O'Sullivan, or Freire, but rather ground their work in transpersonal psychology and other consciousness studies scholars, from science, religion, and psychology. The foreword is written by famed Buddhist scholar and Columbia University professor Robert Thurman, who discusses the importance of consciousness and cultivating greater consciousness states for the fate of the earth. Throughout, they provide excerpts from their interview data on those who discuss the various portals of transformation in seeing with new eyes, and the way of cultivating transformation of consciousness through meditation and other means of living deeply, as well as some educational practices. Discussions of love and death come up often in these considerations of transformation.

In essence, the authors as well as the many interviewees caution against going in search of peak experiences; they advise instead engaging in daily practices that facilitate the development of higher states of consciousness that take one into the world. They foreground the interconnection of the "I" and the "we" and suggest that attention to both is necessary to facilitate individual and social transformation, and that one paradoxically leads to the other. They aver that we are currently a culture that is between worldviews in forging a new story:

> Both science and spirituality have a stake in the story that is being created. Each alone has only partial answers to the questions of who we are what we are capable of becoming. Indeed, as twenty-first century life unfolds, it is becoming increasingly clear that each of us has a voice in the answers to these questions. Through transformations in consciousness, each of us is empowered to help craft a new story—one that is more just, compassionate, and sustainable, now and for future generations. (pp. 210–211)

Indeed, it is through transforming our consciousness that we can contribute to crafting this new story. But what "form" transforms our consciousness? Epochal transformations seem to come with significant life experiences and how we deal with them, including those involving love and death that make us revisit the Big Questions of life. But transformations in consciousness seem to involve cultivation of daily attempts at living deeply. Recently in the field of adult education, Sussman and Kossak (2011), in drawing on consciousness studies, discuss teaching embodied meditation through music, chant, and movement or dance as one way to facilitate change in consciousness. They stress that long-term change involves regular practice, and they discuss recent efforts in neuroscience that show how the brain changes with sustained involvement with music and meditation. To be sure, there are many other types of meditation, and embodied or artistic practices that over time with sustained practice lead to changes in consciousness. There has been much media attention to some of the neuroscience research of late that indicates how meditation changes the brain (Hölzel et al., 2011), which is a part of changing one's consciousness that is part of transformative learning. This brings up the related area of neuroscience and complexity.

Neuroscience and Complexity

Consciousness studies tend to focus more on what changes consciousness, whereas the area of neuroscience examines the science of how it happens. Complexity science perspectives fundamentally examine how organisms (including single cells, entire human beings, and social units) "self-organize" in the face of threat and create new patterns of connection to ensure their survival (Capra, 1996). But these areas of complexity, consciousness studies, and neuroscience are interrelated. In essence, the emphasis in consciousness studies is on how to facilitate this reorganization of patterns of connection by focusing on the relationship of the disciplines of spirituality/religion and science, to facilitate a sense of greater global consciousness. Tobin Hart (2008) has recently discussed extensively how this plays out in contemplation states and its role in and relationship to transformative learning. Neuroscientists focus on the science of it all.

Daniel Siegel is one whose work in neuroscience is more accessible for those not schooled in the firing and mechanics of neurons. In his most recent book on the science of transformation, Siegel (2010) argues for the cultivation of consciousness that he calls "mindsight" and defines it as "a kind of focused attention that allows us to be aware of our mental processes rather than being swept away by them" (p. xi). His basic premise as that we can each developing the skill of mindsight, and that doing so physically and mentally changes the brain and hence the whole person. As one learns to cultivate mindsight and reorganizes to form new patterns of connection at the cellular intrapersonal, and interpersonal levels, one transforms and experiences a greater sense of well-being. Although he doesn't use the term "transformative learning" per se, he provides wonderful case studies and examples of how individuals have been transformed through cultivating mindsight and offers insights into how this is happening from a neuroscience perspective.

Siegel (2010) discusses the cultivation of "mindsight" more from a biological perspective than a spiritual perspective, though he acknowledges that religious and spiritual traditions offer help in finding ways to cultivate this greater consciousness. Other neuroscientists such as Newberg and Waldman (2009) from the University of Pennsylvania have more directly studied brain patterns through neuroimaging technology when subjects are engaged in meditation states. They then discuss the findings in relation to the varieties of spiritual experience. They offer specific suggestions for cultivating imagination and greater consciousness leading to "transforming your inner reality" (p. 149), and they offer both a biological and a spiritual explanation in naming the process.

New Directions for Transformative Learning and Research

These discourses related to transformation certainly have something to offer us in adult education. Most of the authors cited in this section do not necessarily put a learning lens to what they discuss, because they are not in education. Rather, they put the lens of their own discipline to their analysis of transformative processes. In essence, however, they are talking about the processes through which adults learn to change, and they examine those changes in their own terms for what form transforms. The world of consciousness studies, neuroscience, and complexity science variously examine different forms that transform people's lives and the evidence that can scientifically document some of it; nevertheless, science can never completely unlock the mysteries of all the forms that transform. That is part of the mystery of life itself; all that happens between birth and death, love and conflict, and our transformed sense of consciousness in the context of living in community and negotiating life in the complexity of a global world can never be captured completely through science. After all, the whole is still always greater than the sum of its parts. Nevertheless, it is up to those of us in adult education to put a learning lens to what the world of consciousness studies and neuroscience has unfolded, as we move toward a greater understanding of the multiple forms that transform. Thus adult education researchers can draw on this new literature on consciousness studies, spirituality, complexity, and neuroscience to find new ways to facilitate transformative learning, and to continue our own studies drawing on this new research and theory for what it means in various places of community.

CODA AND CONCLUSION

It is now several months since I've written this chapter's opening. I've revised the chapter in light of editors' and reviewers' comments. I listen again to Thomas Tallis's "If Ye Love Me," played so beautifully by the couple and their brass quintet described in the opening scene. The then-expectant young couple now have a new son, born just after his great-grandfather died. The circle of life continues. They have been transformed by his birth; they continue to make music that helps change my consciousness and theirs; the racial justice project they have initiated is transforming our beloved community in small and large ways through their emancipatory efforts. They experience and facilitate many themes and variations of transformative learning. People like them, people like you, in the various communities of which I am a part, inspire me to continue to try to change my own consciousness and live more deeply as I negotiate love and justice, birth and death, and all in between in the many places of community: church, university, city, country, world. All of these play a part in discovering ever new and ever multiple forms that transform.

In conclusion, it is clear that there are many themes and variations to transformational learning; some change our hearts forever as they transform our identity as a core theme. Others, in their many variations, bring us into a larger consciousness as we forge new patterns of connections that change the vibration of our cells and our souls, our brains and our beings. Still others happen when we summon the courage to stand up to power, on behalf of ourselves and others, to create a more just world. Ideally, all of them pull us open as we embrace the paradox of new life in the midst of death, creativity in the midst of critique, and love in the midst of apathy. May we continue to research and write about these new dimensions and directions of transformative learning and the forms that transform. More important, may we cultivate the consciousness that allows us to embrace them as we live and love ever more deeply.

References

Abalos, D. (1998). *La Communidad Latina in the United States*. Westport, CT: Praeger.

Banks, J. A. (Ed.). (1996). *Multicultural education, transformative knowledge, and action: Historical and contemporary perspectives*. New York: Teachers College Press.

Berry, T. (1999). *The great work: Our way to the future*. New York: Bell Tower.

Capra, F. (1996). *The web of life: A new scientific understanding of living systems*. New York: Random House.

Clark, M. C. (1993). Transformational learning. In S. B. Merriam (Ed.), *An update on adult learning* (pp. 47–56). New Directions in Adult and Continuing Education, no. 57. San Francisco: Jossey-Bass.

Cranton, P. (2006). *Understanding and promoting transformative learning: A guide for educators of adults*. San Francisco: Jossey-Bass.

Dirkx, J. (2001). Images, transformative learning, and the work of soul. *Adult Learning, 12*(3), 15–16.

Fisher-Yoshida, B., Geller, K., & Schapiro, S. (Eds.). (2009). *Innovations in transformative learning: Space, culture, and the arts*. New York: Peter Lang.

Freire, P. (1971). *Pedagogy of the oppressed*. New York: Herder & Herder.

Gardner, M., & Kelly, U. (Eds.) (2008). *Narrating transformative learning in education*. New York: Palgrave.

Groome, T., & Horell, H. (Eds.) (2003). *Horizons and hopes: The future of religious education*. Mahwah, NJ: Paulist Press.

Gunnlaugson, O. (2007). Shedding light on the underlying forms of transformative learning theory: Introducing three distinct categories of consciousness. *Journal of Transformative Education, 5*(2), 134–151.

Hart, T. (2001). *From information to transformation: Education for the evolution of consciousness*. New York: Peter Lang.

Hart, T. (2008). Interiority and education: Exploring the neurophenomenology of contemplation and its potential role in learning. *Journal of Transformative Education*, 6(4), 235–250.

Hiebert, P. (2008). *Transforming worldviews: An anthropological understanding of how people change*. Grand Rapids, MI: Baker Publishing Group.

Hölzel, B., Carmody, J., Vangel, M., Congleton, C., Yerramsetti, S., Gard, T., & Lazar, S. (2011). Mindfulness practice leads to increases in regional brain gray matter density. *Psychiatry Research: Neuroimaging, 191*(1), 36–43.

Horton, M., & Freire, P. (1990). *We make the road by walking: Conversations on education and social change*. Philadelphia: Temple University Press.

Irwin, R. (2002). *Human development and the spiritual life: How consciousness grows toward transformation*. New York: Klewer.

Jackson, M. G. (2008). *Transformative learning for a new worldview: Learning to think differently*. New York: Palgrave.

Johnson-Bailey, J., & Alfred, M. (2006). Transformative teaching and the practices of black women adult educators. In E. Taylor (Ed.), *Teaching for change: Fostering transformative learning in the classroom* (pp. 49–58). New Directions for Adult and Continuing Education, no. 109. San Francisco: Jossey-Bass.

Kegan, R. (2000). What "form" transforms? A constructive-developmental approach to transformative learning. In J. Mezirow & Associates (Eds.), *Learning as transformation: Critical perspectives on a theory in progress* (pp. 35–70). San Francisco: Jossey-Bass.

Khan, H. I. (1996). *The mysticism of sound and music: The Sufi teaching of Hazrat Inayat Khan*. Boston: Shambhala.

Loder, J. (1989). *The transforming moment*. New York: Helmers & Howard Publishers.

Loue, S. (2008). *The transformative power of metaphor in therapy*. New York: Springer.

Meyer, J., Land, R., & Baillie, C. (Eds.). (2010). *Threshold concepts and transformational learning*. Boston: Sense Publishers.

Mezirow, J. (1991). *Transformative dimensions of adult learning*. San Francisco: Jossey-Bass.

Mezirow, J. (2009). Transformative learning theory. In J. Mezirow, E. Taylor, & Associates (Eds.), *Transformative learning in practice* (pp. 18–32). San Francisco: Jossey-Bass.

Mezirow, J., Taylor, E. W., & Associates (Eds.). (2009). *Transformative learning in practice*. San Francisco: Jossey-Bass.

Newberg, A., & Waldman, M. (2009). *How God changes your brain: Breakthrough findings from a leading neuroscientist*. New York: Ballantine.

O'Connor, M., O'Sullivan, E., & Morrell, A. (Eds.). (2002). *Expanding the boundaries of transformative learning*. Palgrave Macmillan.

O'Sullivan, E. (1999). *Transformative learning: Educational vision of the 21st century*. Toronto, ON: Zed Books.

Parks, S. (2000). *Big questions, worthy dreams.* San Francisco: Jossey-Bass.

Sanders, R. (2006). *A private history of awe.* New York: North Point Press (Farrar, Straus & Giroux).

Schlitz, M., Vieten, C., & Amorok, T. (2007). *Living deeply: The art and science of transformation in everyday life.* Oakland, CA: New Harbinger Publications.

Siegel, D. (2010). *Mindsight: The new science of personal transformation.* New York: Random House.

Steinmetz, D. (1993). Moses' "revelation" on Mount Horeb as a near death experience. *Journal of Near Death Studies, 11*(4), 199–203.

Sussman, A., & Kossak, M. (2011). The wisdom of the inner life: Meeting oneself through meditation and music. In E. Tisdell & A. Swartz (Eds.), *Adult education and the pursuit of wisdom* (pp. 55–64). New Directions for Adult and Continuing Education, no. 131. San Francisco: Jossey-Bass.

Taylor, E. W. (1997). Building upon the theoretical debate: A critical review of the empirical studies of Mezirow's transformative learning theory. *Adult Education Quarterly, 48*(1), 32–57.

Tisdell, E. (2003). *Exploring spirituality and culture in adult and higher education.* San Francisco: Jossey-Bass.

Tisdell, E., & Tolliver, E. (2003). Claiming a sacred face: The role of spirituality and cultural identity in transformative adult higher education. *Journal of Transformative Education, 1*(4), 368–392.

Walters, S., & Manicom, L. (Eds.). (1996). *Gender in popular education.* London: Zed.

Wilber, K. (2000). *Integral psychology: Consciousness, spirit, psychology, therapy.* Boston: Shambhala.

CHAPTER THREE

A Critical Review of Research on Transformative Learning Theory, 2006–2010

Edward W. Taylor and Melissa J. Snyder

L iterature reviews help scholars distinguish research informative to a particular construct; they synthesize significant findings, help identify areas of concern and questions yet to be explored, and potentially provoke the status quo, challenging the field to question or rethink what is often unquestioned. They may also, although it is rarely discussed, stifle research when other researchers overly rely on and accept without question the conclusions from a literature review. This has been the case for the study of transformative learning theory (Mezirow, 1978, 1991), in which literature reviews of empirical research have played a role in stimulating research but are at times given too much authority in setting the research direction of the field.

Looking back at several past reviews, researchers find transformative learning constantly evolving. Early reviews found a more complex process of a perspective transformation, greater recognition of context in shaping transformative learning, a growing appreciation for other ways of knowing, and the varied nature of the catalyst process (Taylor, 1997). There was also a growing interest in research on fostering transformative learning. Findings revealed the importance of promoting group ownership, individual agency, shared experiential activities, interrelationship of critical reflection and affective learning, contextual influences, and value-laden course content, and the need for time when engaged in fostering transformative learning (Taylor, 2000). The most recent review (2007) found continued interest in fostering transformative learning, the emerging role of difference, the importance of the role of relationships, and a greater understanding of the meaning of a perspective transformation. There was also a call for researchers to look beyond Mezirow by involving other theoretical orientations of transformative learning (such as Boyd, 1991; Cranton, 2006; Freire, 1970; Kegan, 2000; O'Sullivan, 1999; Tisdell, 2003).

Essentially, these reviews over the last decade, as well as the related research, were predominantly wedded to what Gunnlaugson (2008) refers to as "first wave" questions of theory building (p. 129). They organized research "within a particular transformative learning theorist schemata" (p. 129), exploring how individuals experience transformative learning—in this case, predominantly from Mezirow's theoretical perspective. Although this has been helpful in accomplishing much of what is essential to a literature review—such as encouraging more research, providing insight into its intricacies, and fostering an interdisciplinary interest about transformative learning—there have also been some negative consequences. At times too much reliance has been placed on the reviews, to the point that the exemplar studies on which they are based are often not critiqued and discussed when establishing a rationale for further research. It is as if the review is the final interpretation and has captured all the published literature, and all the findings from each individual study have been reported.

To address some of these concerns, this chapter has four objectives. The first is to provide a general overview of trends in the present literature on transformative learning, similar to previous reviews made prior to 2006. The second is to offer an analysis of research of transformative learning theory that have used other theoretical conceptions of transformative learning. The third is to highlight, within the different sections of the review, exemplar studies of transformative learning that warrant greater discussion, encouraging their dissemination and providing models for further research. Finally, the review ends with a discussion of what has been learned about transformative learning since the last preceding review and suggestions for further research.

Identifying the literature for this review involved searching multiple databases—ERIC, Proquest, Medline, SAGE, and the Cumulative Index to Nursing and Allied Health Literature (CINAHL)—using several criteria for selecting studies. Each study reviewed here was published between 2006 and 2010; used transformative learning as its primary theoretical framework (for example, Freire, Mezirow, O'Sullivan, Tisdell, Cranton, Boyd); and included a methodology and findings section that informed the study of transformative learning theory. Forty-nine studies were identified and included in this review. The chapter is organized into a discussion of methodological and general trends, interdisciplinary approaches, the use of multiple theoretical frameworks, cross-cultural research, the growing significance of relationships, and research concerning the fostering of transformative learning.

METHODOLOGIES AND GENERAL TRENDS

Research trends concerning transformative learning from 2006 to early 2011 fall into several areas. Methodologically, the research designs use predominantly qualitative methods, although there is a growing specificity in the type of qualitative design, such as action/teacher research (Goulah, 2007b; Jaruszewicz, 2006; McBrien, 2008; Walton, 2010), narrative inquiry (Boyer, Maher, & Kirkman, 2006; Coleey, 2007; Cranton & Wright, 2008; Jokikokko, 2009; Nohl, 2009), autoethnography (Boyd, 2008), and case study (Choy, 2009; Goulah, 2007a; Hodge, 2010; Kerton & Sinclair, 2010; Marschke & Sinclair, 2008; Sandlin & Bey, 2006; Sands & Tennant, 2010; Sims & Sinclair, 2008). In addition, participant writing in journals, student writings, photography, and portfolios (Clare, 2006; Fetherston & Kelly, 2007; McBrien, 2008; Wittman, Velde, Carawan, Pokorny, & Knight, 2008) have continued to be viable data sources. Also, two teacher-research studies (Jaruszewicz, 2006; Goulah, 2007b) used video as documentation of student learning.

The designs have also expanded to include meta-analyses of several different but related transformative cases (King, 2008; Tisdell, 2008; Yorks & Kasl, 2006), mixed methods (Brown, 2006; Clare, 2006; Fetherston & Kelly, 2007; Forrester, Motteram, & Bangxiang, 2007; Glisczinski, 2007; Hanson, 2010; King, 2009a; Ntiri & Stewart, 2009), and exclusively surveys or questionnaires (Brock, 2010; Morris & Faulk, 2007; Stevens, Gerber, & Hendra, 2010). One survey in particular, the Learning Activities Survey Questionnaire (King, 2009a), has experienced a growth in its application (Brock, 2010; Glisczinski, 2007; Hodge, 2010), although it has never been thoroughly critiqued.

Further approaches that show promise are collaborative inquiry (Hanlin-Rowney et al., 2006) and group dialogue research (Wittman et al., 2008), in which participants research their transformative experience as a group. This method offers a means to exploring a collective transformation among participants and identifying the range of factors that influence the process.

In addition to the various methods just listed, there has also been a growing interdisciplinary interest in transformative learning, reflected in research from disciplines such as agriculture/sciences (Duveskog, Friis-Hansen, & Taylor, 2011; Kerton & Sinclair, 2010; Marschke & Sinclair, 2008; Sims & Sinclair, 2008; Tarnoczi, 2011), archeology (Sandlin & Bey, 2006), religious studies (Clare, 2006), health care (King, 2009b; Ntiri & Stewart 2010; Rush, 2008), critical media literacy (Tisdell, 2008), and spirituality (Chin, 2006). Exploration of transformative learning from new disciplines has helped address previously identified gaps found in participant selection and the application of TL in varied contexts (Taylor, 2007). In particular, there is growing application of research in settings outside the formal education classroom in other learning environments, including workshops and retreats (Clare, 2006; Sands &

Tennant, 2010; Wittman et al., 2008), the workplace (Choy, 2009; Isopahkala-Bouret, 2008; King, 2009b), online or technology supported learning environments (Boyer, Maher, & Kirkman, 2006; Goulah, 2007b; Hanlin-Rowney et al., 2006), hands-on or service learning experiences (Carrington & Selva, 2010; McBrien, 2008; Velde, Wittman, & Mott, 2007), nonformal groups or enclaves (Chin, 2006; Cooley, 2007; Wilhelmson, 2006a), and the high school classroom (Goulah, 2007a, 2007b). Despite this growing interest in nonformal settings, little attention is given to what is unique about these settings and their implications for fostering transformative learning.

A study that starts to identify how the setting can shape the transformative learning experience is found in Isopahkala-Bouret's (2008) research from Finland about the learning involved in transitioning to a managerial role. They found that a transition—a dilemmatic situation—was "self-transforming"; however, it did not result in a more inclusive worldview, but rather an adoption of the dominant perspective, in accordance with the new work setting and supportive of building human capital. They concluded that "instead of uncritically celebrating the self-discovery that newly appointed project managers and team leaders reflect upon, [the finding] calls for attention to sociocultural constraints that are discursively involved with reflections on 'self' and managerial roles" (p. 82). In addition, the study also highlights what possibly is unique about fostering transformative learning in organizational settings.

Research about fostering transformative learning is still most prevalent in formal classroom settings (Brock, 2010; Fetherston & Kelly, 2007; Glisczinski, 2007; Goulah, 2007a, 2007b; Hanson, 2010; King, 2008; Morris & Faulk, 2007; Jaruszewicz, 2006; Jokikokko, 2009; Rush, 2008; Walton, 2010). Also, these studies generally focused on a particular type of learner; for example, adult learners in English as a Second Language and Adult Basic Education programs (King, 2008), older African Americans in a diabetes education program (Ntiri & Stewart, 2009), nursing students (Morris & Faulk, 2007; Rush, 2008), teacher education students in large public universities and small private colleges (Glisczinski, 2007; Jokikokko, 2009; Walton, 2010), business students (Brock, 2010; Carson & Fisher, 2006), and students studying peace studies and conflict resolution (Fetherston & Kelly, 2007). However, as they focus on the various settings, few studies explore whether there was something unique about the participants' background, culture, and/or positionality and their experiences in relationship to transformative learning.

Concerning the research participants, the majority of studies reviewed focused on adults from early to middle adulthood. Little attention has been given to adults in later stages of adulthood, even though the overall population of older adults is growing more rapidly than any other age group. However, the theory has expanded to inform the learning of adolescents in a high school classroom (Goulah, 2007a, 2007b), and some efforts have been made to distinguish between age groups of adult learners (Nohl, 2009).

MULTIPLE THEORETICAL FRAMEWORKS

A theoretical framework, although often abstract, is profoundly helpful in bringing understanding of how the world is experienced. "It is the lens...framing and shaping what the researcher looks at and includes, how the researcher thinks about the study and its conduct, and in the end, how the researcher conducts the study" (Mertz & Anfara, 2006, p. 189). As previously discussed, there is a movement among researchers using additional theoretical lenses, beyond Mezirow's conception in the study of transformative learning theory. They include (1) the work of Belenky and Stanton, Boyd, Dirkx, Kegan, Tisdell, O'Sullivan, Freire, Dewey, Mead, and Vygotsky (Brock, 2010; Brown, 2006; Chin, 2006; Cranton & Wright, 2008; Clare, 2006; Goulah, 2007a, 2007b; Hanlin-Rowney et al., 2010; Hanson, 2010; Magro & Polyzoi, 2009; Nohl, 2009; Tisdell, 2008); (2) specific theoretical perspectives such as Africentrism (Duveskog, Friis-Hansen, & Taylor, 2011; Merriam & Ntseane, 2008; Mwebi & Brigham, 2009), critical theory (Sandlin & Bey, 2006; Heron, 1992; York & Kasl, 2006), critical social theory (Carrington & Selva, 2010), and new grief theory (Sands & Tennant, 2010); and (3) the introduction of a new lens of transformative learning, the Contextualized Model of Adult Learning (CMAL) (King, 2008).

Additional theoretical lenses were used primarily because the dominant conception (for example, Mezirow) did not adequately capture the assumptions on which the study was based. For example, Chin (2006), who explored the relationship between spirituality and transformative learning among women of the Bahá'i faith, used Tisdell (2003) and O'Sullivan (1999) to make sense of the construct of spirituality, as it is given little attention by Mezirow and Associates (2000). In another example, Sandlin and Bey (2006), who explored the transformation of archaeologists working in Yucatan, Mexico, used a critical lens, because of Mezirow's lack of attention to power relations. They viewed transformative learning from a more contextual perspective, located "at the intersection of personal biography with the societal structure" (Cunningham, 1998, p. 16).

However, there were studies that incorporated a variety of perspectives, with seemingly divergent underlying assumptions about the nature of transformative learning, without exploring the inherent tensions or how one theory possibly complemented the inadequacy of the other, as if, when taken together, they possibly represent an integral model of transformative learning (for example, Brown, 2006; Hanson, 2010; King, 2009a; Magro & Polyzoi, 2009). For example, Brown, in a study on preparing educational leaders' commitment to social justice and equity, states: "The andragogical process of critical reflection (Brookfield, 1985), rational discourse (Mezirow, 1991) and policy praxis (Freire, 1985), can lead to a transformation of one's personal agency and one's sense of social responsibility toward and with others" (p. 706). On the other hand, a good example of exploring differences among contrasting theoretical orientations of transformative learning can be found in Hanson's (2010) discussion of Freire and Mezirow and their varying emphasis on individual and social change.

When varied lenses are used there is often a significant lack of theoretical analysis of the findings affirming or questioning the underlying assumptions found in the theoretical framework. Instead, there is a tendency to be too deterministic where the data seems to fit easily, and to be unquestionably supportive of the theoretical framework, particularly Mezirow's orientation. Also, in studies that use multiple theoretical lenses, rarely if ever are the lesser-known conceptions of transformative learning (O'Sullivan; Freire; Boyd; Boyd & Myers; Dirkx) critiqued in relationship to the findings.

Despite these shortcomings, there were a few studies that offered some thoughtful theoretical insights into transformative learning (for example, Merriam & Ntseane, 2008; Nohl, 2009; Sands & Tennant, 2010). For example, Clare (2006), who looked at a case study of transformative learning theory (Mezirow) and Freireian pedagogy in context to religious education for social justice, offers greater clarity about the relationship between a hiatus (mediating factors between reflection and action), premise reflection, and action. She concluded that through a synthesis of each perspective of transformation, a more comprehensive understanding of transformative education emerges. In another study, which focused on transformative learning among war affected refugees in Canada and Greece, Magro and Polyzoi (2009) found that the early stages (disorienting dilemma, self-examination of feelings, critical reflection, and an awareness of a shared discontent) of transformation "appear to be more recursive and longer lasting" (p. 104). Also identified were multiple disorienting dilemmas (loss of culture, family, language) among the refugees.

Regardless of the efforts discussed here, researchers in the field have barely scratched the surface in engaging in-depth analysis of multiple theoretical perspectives of transformative learning, particularly involving comparative theoretical analysis. It is fundamental to theoretical growth for researchers to draw on multiple conceptions, inclusive of critique, that will potentially lead to a more integral view of transformative learning theory.

CROSS-CULTURAL RESEARCH

As previously discussed in the overview, there has been a significant increase in research involving transformative learning in other cultures and nationalities. More specifically, these studies explored transformative learning in cross-cultural experiences in language and teacher education (Hamza, 2010; Hutchison & Rey, 2011; Goulah, 2007b; Jokikokko, 2009; Mwebi & Brigham, 2009), refugees from war-torn countries (Magro & Polyzoi, 2009), women and leadership (Madsen, 2009), occupational therapy education (Velde, Wittman, & Mott, 2007), and e-learning (Forrester, Motteram, & Bangxiang, 2006), archeologist (Sandlin & Bey, 2006), agricultural development (Sims & Sinclair, 2008), and African indigenous knowledge systems (Merriam & Ntseane, 2008). The cultural sites included rural North Carolina and countries such as Botswana, Japan, Canada, China, Costa Rica, Finland, Gambia, Greece, Mexico, United Arab Emirates, United Kingdom, and Arab countries of the Gulf region. The predominant purpose for using transformative learning was theoretically to offer a lens that helped explain learning and professional development of individuals in the context of a cross-cultural experience. Despite this incredibly rich opportunity for exploring cultural differences and transformative learning theory—among, for example, Chinese and Finish educators or refugees from Greece, or within particular international settings such the United Arab Emirates or Africa—only a few studies made an effort in this direction (for example, Duveskvog, Friis-Hansen, & Taylor, 2011; Merriam & Ntseane, 2008; Sims & Sinclair, 2008).

For example, using a qualitative design framed from both psychocritical and Africentric transformative learning perspectives, Merriam and Ntseane's study analyzed adult Batswana's "experiences dealing with a life event that triggered a transformational learning process," focusing "on how the cultural context of Botswana shaped the way participants processed and interpreted the event" (p. 188). Like Mezirow's perspective, the Batswana shared similar disorienting dilemmas that triggered the learning process, such as the "death of loved ones, disrupted relationships, health crises" (p. 194) and the nature of change, had a psychological emphasis involving the questioning of assumptions that shaped the way they made meaning of their world. However, culturally unique to the transformative learning experience was an emphasis on the metaphysical (that is, the spiritual), community responsibility and relationships, and gender roles. "In this African context, the tools of culture (family, gender, spirits) shaped participants' interpretation of the experiences" (p. 195).

In another study, Sims and Sinclair (2008) explored "learning taking place through active citizen [farmers'] participation in the Watershed Management Agricultural Programme (WMAP) implemented by the Instituto Costarricense de Electricidad (ICE) in Costa Rica" (p. 152). Even though the authors did not foreground the Latin American culture, they found that "what happens through the WMAP is not such a cognizant process; it seems to be more organic that naturally led to a greater sense of agency" (p. 163) and "learning was rarely exclusively instrumental or communicative" (p. 164). These studies begin to shed light on the intercultural nature of transformative learning, identifying what in transformative process is culturally unique and what is universal.

GROWING SIGNIFICANCE OF RELATIONSHIPS

In every review of transformative learning, the role of relationships has been identified as being significant in the process of transformation. It happens "through trustful relationships that allow individuals to have questioning discussions, share information openly and achieve mutual and consensual understanding" (Taylor, 2007, p. 179). Insight into this phenomenon continues to grow. This review identified seven studies that deal with variety of issues associated with transformative learning and relationships, including: the inadequacy of personal relationships to a larger social vision (Sandlin & Bey, 2006), significant others in intercultural learning (Jokikokko, 2009), learning companions (Cranton & Wright, 2008), joint leadership (Wilhelmson, 2006b), repositioning of relationships (Sands & Tennant, 2010), social recognition (Nohl, 2009), social accountability (Chin, 2006), and a collective transformation (Wilhelmson, 2006a, 2006b).

A study of particular interest is Sands and Tennant's (2010) about suicide bereavement, drawing on "new wave of grief theory" (p. 101). They found that a transformation among the bereaved involved a repositioning of relationships "with the deceased, the self and others" (p. 116). This meant not only thinking of what kinds of relationships foster transformative learning but also "how our relationships changed, modified, reframed, or recast as a result of transformative learning" (p. 116). For the bereaved, transformative learning involved developing a healthy relationship with the deceased and that the repositioning of relationships is a natural outcome of a transformation, particularly "when significant others no longer share or even oppose your newly adopted world view" (p. 116).

Building on how relationships are changed by a transformation are the various roles they play in the process of transformation. For example, in Nohl's (2009) biographical exploration of transformative experiences, he found transformation from "spontaneous action" dependent to a great extent on "social recognition" (p. 294). "In light of the response of the others, an action that was originally incidental and spontaneous becomes significant" (p. 294). These studies further highlight the ideas that transformative learning does not happen in a vacuum solely through the free will of an autonomous learner; rather, it is contextually bounded and influenced by relationships with others.

Offering further insight into the nature of the "social" and transformative learning is the idea of "social accountability" (Chin, 2006, p. 41). Social accountability manifest as an "ethics of identity," whereby the outcome of transformative learning involves recognizing the reasons why, for what purpose, and for whom a new identity was constructed. This apparent moral underpinning as an outcome of transformative learning was also alluded to in Jokikokko's (2009) study of intercultural competence among Finnish teachers. She found that significant others played an important role in the development of an ethical orientation that included "values such as equality, justice, the appreciation of differences, a commitment to promote equity" (p. 158). These findings imply that as transformative learning occurs among trusting relationships with others, an essential component, by-product, or both is a sense of morality, well-being, and empathy toward others.

FOSTERING TRANSFORMATIVE LEARNING

Most of the research of transformative learning continues to focus on the practice of fostering transformative learning and provides support for major assumptions associated with Mezirow's perspective of practice—such as creating a safe and inclusive learning environment, focusing on the individual learner's needs, and building on life experiences, to mention a few. Unfortunately, the research does not expand the current understanding of these assumptions, nor does the research question their integrity. Despite this shortcoming, there are new insights about the practice of fostering transformative learning.

First, research reveals that fostering transformative learning is not a "one size fits all" approach, but rather it is necessary to consider the individual in a particular context. This finding emerges from the vast array of different contexts and strategies used by researchers from varying disciplines engaged in transformative learning. For instance, occupational therapy students practiced skills in a rural, primarily African American community (Velde, Wittman, & Mott, 2007). This hands-on experience enriched the student's learning, including skills, and also led to greater cultural competence and personal enrichment. "These changes were evidenced in their reflections on personal and professional growth and statements about changed beliefs and attitudes—key indicators that transformative learning is occurring" (p. 87). In a very different context—adult literacy—transformative learning was successfully fostered by educators who helped learners as learning companions to recognize their own expertise and experience (Cranton & Wright, 2008). The learning companion met each learner in his or her individual context; recognized the individual as central to the learning process; strove to create a safe, trusting relationship with the learners; engaged in a sense of discovery while helping the learner overcome fears and insecurities; and acknowledged the whole person in the fostering of transformative learning. Based on these findings, Cranton and Wright question Mezirow's emphasis on the cognitive aspects of learning and the lack of adequate attention to the whole being, and they suggest that other theorists offer an additional understanding of this teaching approach.

A second concern is the mix of related constructs that emphasize, for example, multidimensional ways of learning, whole person learning, or multiple ways of knowing when designing strategies to foster transformative learning. Most significantly, these terms lack clear and consistent definitions, are often used interchangeably as if they share similar assumptions about learning, and seem to apply to any combination of the following concepts (among others): cognitive or rational processes (Fetherstone & Kelly, 2007; Ntiri & Stewart, 2009), affect or emotions (Clare, 2006; Curry-Stevens, 2007; King, 2008; Wittman et al., 2008), creativity or expressive ways of knowing (Wittman et al., 2008; Yorks & Kasl, 2006), pleasure (Tisdell, 2008), kinesthetic learning (Velde, Wittman, & Mott, 2007), and individual and collaborative learning experiences (Boyer, Maher, & Kirkman, 2006; Choy, 2009; Cooley, 2007; Hanlin-Rowney et al., 2006; King, 2009a; Walton, 2010). Many of the studies focus on a combination of these ways of knowing and/or learning.

Despite lack of a clear definition, two studies begin to offer insight into the meaning of multidimensional or holistic learning. For example, Yorks and Kasl (2006) use empirical analyses of case studies of adult educators offering a taxonomy of expressive ways of knowing (that is, guided imagery, stories, music, art, poetry, art) framed in Heron's (1992) conception of presentational knowing to foster whole person learning and transformative change. "Expressive ways of knowing bring into awareness tacit and subconscious forms of knowing, making them accessible for critical reflection" (p. 61). This theoretical lens, in concert with transformative learning, offers much to future theory development and inquiry.

Similarly, Curry-Stevens (2007) studied community-based practitioners' transformations fostered through a pedagogy for the privileged (enabling learners to reconnect to all humanity, not just to those like themselves). The nature of the transformation was found to be multidimensional, including spiritual, ideological, psychological, emotional, behavioral, and cognitive changes. These changes emerged from a confidence-shaking process that created an awareness and understanding of the oppression of others, followed by a confidence-building process that led to agency. Through eliciting emotions and recognizing these various dimensions, new ways of bringing ideas into consciousness were revealed.

Additional dimensions relevant to fostering transformative learning, such as pleasure, were also identified. For example, in Tisdell's (2008) cross-case analysis in critical media literacy and implications for transformative learning, she found that the pleasure and humor of watching television or movies has the ability to facilitate transformative learning by drawing the learner into new experiences. This finding broadens the possibilities of catalysts for change, beyond the traditional conceptions of disorienting dilemmas associated with pain (emotional, physical) and suffering.

Also, this concept of pleasure was in contrast to the majority of studies that focus on conflict (Fetherston & Kelly, 2007; Walton, 2010) and a problem-based approach (Clare, 2006; King, 2008; King, 2009a; Ntiri & Stewart, 2009) as the means to fostering transformative learning. Learners faced varied types of problems or conflicts, including issues such as ethical dilemmas (Clare, 2006), workplace conflicts (King, 2008), diabetes control (Ntiri & Stewart, 2009), and confronting white privilege (Boyd, 2008). Despite the broad spectrum of issues, each of these learning experiences provoked critical reflection of previously held beliefs and prompted action through personal empowerment or group consensus.

DISCUSSION AND IMPLICATIONS

The research on transformative learning is ever growing, particularly as a means to frame pedagogy, with explicit practices for fostering critical reflection, self-efficacy, and an overall constructivist approach to teaching. In addition, there is an emerging interest from other disciplines outside education that are looking for a theoretical lens to help make sense of adult learning and a guide for practice. Along with these general trends, a number of points warrant further discussion. They include the emerging use of survey research designs, engagement of theoretical frameworks beyond the dominant perspective, the social nature of transformative learning, and implications for practice.

As noted, there is a growing sophistication in qualitative designs as well as data collection methods, beyond just relying on interviews. In addition, there is a significant increase of studies that use scales, surveys, and open-ended questionnaires. These initial efforts—asking participants to self-report on feelings and actions via a checklist of items that correspond to steps and components—although commendable as a first attempt, are far from adequate to accurately capture the process and outcome of a transformation from the perspective of the participant. More specifically, the most popular survey, King's (2009a), seems to lacks construct validity, which raises the question of whether inferences can be legitimately made between what has been operationalized in the survey and the theorized psychological constructs associated with transformative learning theory. Researchers need to engage in the development of an instrument that is not simply a reconstruction of the terminology found in the theory of transformative learning, but instead is a synthesis of both the theory and extensive qualitative data reflective of how people typically make meaning of transformative experiences. Even though King reports that the instrument was reviewed by experts, there is no statistical evidence demonstrating its validity and reliability. In addition, the survey lacks factorial validity, which involves having multiple questions that pertain to the same construct relevant to transformative learning. Additional questions allow the researcher to perform a factor analysis to determine the degree of relatedness between the questions and the construct. When there is a high correlation between the questions, then researchers can infer factorial validity. These concerns and others should remind scholars of the limitations of similar instruments until validity and reliability has been established.

A second area of discussion is the emerging application of additional theoretical frameworks, often with the intent to address assumptions, or concepts—or both—that the dominant perspective (Mezirow) does not adequately capture (for example, affective learning, spirituality, power). The various theoretical frameworks offer the opportunity to better understand the nature and practice of a transformation. For example, Kegan's (2000) perspective, which rests on the assumption that "genuinely transformational learning is always to some extent an epistemological change" (p. 48), offers a means to further distinguish transformative learning from other forms of learning, particularly when explored in relationship to increasingly complex epistemologies. A good example of a study that makes some headway in this direction is Lange's (2004) research on social and environmental responsibility.

Another example of how other theoretical lenses can offer new insight involves a race-centric perspective (for example, Johnson-Bailey & Alfred, 2006; Williams, 2003) of transformative learning. Essential to this view is engaging learners' polyrhythmic realities—"lived experiences within a sociocultural, political, and historical context" (Sheared, 1994, p. 36). Although there is little research on actual practice, the implications of this perspective for fostering transformative learning are significant, because it is seen as "a deliberate and conscious strategy to employing a political framework (for example, consciousness raising, activism)" in the classroom (Taylor, 2008, p. 9). To make the most of these different theoretical perspectives, researchers need to become steeped in the primary sources on which the theories are based.

A third discussion point is the emerging insight about the social nature of transformative learning revealed in the constructs of social recognition (Nohl, 2009), social accountability (Chin, 2006), and the significance of relationships. Starting with social recognition, Nohl (2009) introduces the reader to the idea that "a lack of social recognition" (p. 297) could be an explanation for a lack of transformation among some learners. This implies that social acceptance, acknowledgment, and possibly appreciation by peers are important to the transformative process, "because the reactions of [learners'] counterparts lend more relevance to their own ability and activity" (p. 294). This offers some insight into the role of students that educators should be aware of when fostering transformative learning. For example, when a student is on the threshold of transformation (Berger, 2004) and engaged in developing a more open and tolerant worldview, success or lack of success could rest on the degree of social recognition and acceptance from fellow students. Furthermore, in the transformative process relationships between the learner, peers, and educators are likely repositioned as the learner's transformation is recognized by others. Relationships become "not only a means to an end but an end in themselves" (Sands & Tennant, 2010, p. 116). These findings raise questions such as these: Is a transformation as much a product of individual change as of group acceptance of that change? How do individuals transform within settings that offer little social support or recognition?

The role of the "social" context in transformative learning is further foregrounded through the concept of social accountability, whereby the transformation includes the "how, from what, by whom, and for what" with which an individual's identity is constructed (Castells, cited in Chin, 2006, p. 41). A way to make sense of this concept is to reflect on Nohl's work described in the previous paragraph. Transformative learning is found at the intersection between the personal and the social, where a transformation is a reciprocal process (Scott, 2003)—a product both of others (social recognition, relationships) and of personal change—which potentially leads to a greater sense of individual responsibility for and about others (social accountability). This sense of social accountability seems to indicate a moral outcome associated with transformative learning, possibly reflective of greater empathy. Further research is needed about the role of others in "recognizing" an individual's transformation, as well as its implications for social responsibility as an individual transforms.

Continuing with the issue of constructs and transformative learning, we consider the clarity of terminology associated with theory. Though basic assumptions for fostering transformative learning have been accepted—for example, learner-centered teaching—there is a lack of a clear understanding of what it looks like in practice. This lack of clarity further complicates the task of assessing transformative learning. It becomes very difficult to assess both the outcome of transformative learning and which practices have contributed to those outcomes. This is particularly important not only when attempting to instruct future educators but also from a research perspective for educators trying to explore the effectiveness of this teaching approach.

Scholars engaged in research on fostering transformative learning need to take time not only to carefully define terms within the context of their research and framed from a particular theoretical perspective but also to consider how the terms have been defined historically, through a review of related literature. This practice allows for consistency of language within the field of transformative learning theory and will aid in the refinement of the theory.

With the growing application of transformative learning in other settings (beyond the formal), it will be important to better understand the role of context or setting and how it influences the process of transformative learning. Other areas of future research include the need to better understand the student's role in relationship to the educator when fostering transformative learning. Also, what are the peripheral consequences of fostering transformative learning in the classroom? For example, how does a student's transformation affect peers in the classroom, the teacher, the educational institution, and other individuals who play a significant role in the life of the student?

There is an ever-growing wave of research about the fostering of transformative learning that extends beyond the cognitive, taking into consideration multiple ways of knowing in areas such as creativity, spirituality, and emotion. These are intriguing new directions; however, it is important to understand the benefits and risks as educators engage with these very personal components of learning.

CONCLUSION

Looking back over this chapter, it is our hope that researchers will see this review as a beginning point, not an end point, when assessing the state of transformative learning. This means using this review and others to identify exemplar studies that will help inform their own research purposes and provide a basis to raise unexplored questions, going beyond the present understanding of transformative learning theory.

References

Berger, J. G. (2004). Dancing on the threshold of meaning. *Journal of Transformative Education*, 2, 366–351.

Boyd, R. D. (1991). *Personal transformations in small groups: A Jungian perspective*. London: Routledge.

Boyd, D. (2008). Autoethnography as a tool for transformative learning about white privilege. *Journal of Transformative Education*, 6, 212–225.

Boyd, R. D., & Myers, J. G. (1988). Transformative education. *International Journal of Lifelong Education*, 7, 261–284.

Boyer, N., Maher, P., & Kirkman, S. (2006). Transformative learning in online settings. *Journal of Transformative Education*, 4(4), 335–361.

Brock, S. (2010). Measuring the importance of precursor steps to transformative learning. *Adult Education Quarterly*, *60*(2), 122.

Brown, K. M. (2006). Leadership for social justice and equity: Evaluating a transformative framework and andragogy. *Educational Administration Quarterly*, *42*(5), 700–745.

Carrington, S., & Selva, G. (2010). Critical social theory and transformative learning: Evidence in pre-service teachers' service-learning reflection logs. *Higher Education Research and Development*, *29*(1), 45–57.

Carson, L., & Fisher, K. (2006). Raising the bar on criticality: Students' critical reflection in internship program. *Journal of Management Education*, *30*, 700–723.

Chin, S. S. (2006). I am a human and I belong in the world. *Journal of Transformative Education*, *4*(1), 27–42.

Choy, S. (2009). Transformative learning in the workplace. *Journal of Transformative Education*, *7*(1), 65–84.

Clare, R. (2006). Putting faith into action: A model for the North American middle-class. *Religious Education*, *101*(3), 368–388.

Cooley, L. (2007). Transformative learning and third wave feminism as potential outcomes of participation in women's enclaves. *Journal of Transformative Education*, *5*(4), 304–316.

Cranton, P. (2006). *Understanding and promoting transformative learning: A guide for educators of adults*. San Francisco: Jossey-Bass.

Cranton, P., & Wright, B. (2008). The transformative educator as learning companion. *Journal of Transformative Education*, *6*(1), 33–47.

Cunningham, P. M. (1998). The social dimension of transformative learning. *PAACE Journal of Lifelong Learning*, *7*, 15–28.

Curry-Stevens, A. (2007). New forms of transformative education pedagogy for the privileged. *Journal of Transformative Education*, *5*(1), 33–58.

Duveskog, D., Friis-Hansen, E., & Taylor, E. W. (2011). Farmer field school in rural Kenya: A transformative learning experience. *Journal of Development Studies*, 1–16.

Fetherston, B., & Kelly, R. (2007). Conflict resolution and transformative pedagogy. *Journal of Transformative Education*, *5*(3), 262–285.

Forrester, G., Motteram, G., & Bangxiang, L. (2006). Transforming Chinese teachers' thinking, learning, and understanding via e-learning. *Journal of Education for Teaching*, *32*(2), 197–212.

Freire, P. (1970). *Pedagogy of the oppressed*. New York: Seabury Press.

Freire, P. (1985). *The politics of education*. New York: Seabury Press.

Glisczinski, D. (2007). Transformative higher education: A meaningful degree of understanding. *Journal of Transformative Education*, *5*(4), 317–328.

Goulah, J. (2007a). Toward *pax terra-humana*: Cultural transformative learning and a planetary literacy in the foreign language classroom. *Journal of Transformative Education*, *5*(2), 163–176.

Goulah, J. (2007b). Village voices, global visions: Digital video as a transformative foreign language learning tool. *Foreign Language Annals, 40*(1), 62–78.

Gunnlaugson, O. (2008). Metatheoretical prospects for the field of transformative learning. *Journal of Transformative Education, 6*, 124–135.

Hamza, A. (2010). International experience. *Journal of Studies of International Education, 14*(1), 50–69.

Hanlin-Rowney, A., Kuntzelman, K., Lara, M., Roffman, K., Nichols, T., & Welsh, L. (2006). Collaborative inquiry as a framework for exploring transformative learning online. *Journal of Transformative Education, 4*(4), 320–334.

Hanson, L. (2010). Global citizenship, global health, and the internationalization of curriculum: A study of transformative potential. *Journal of Studies in International Education, 14*, 70–88.

Heron, J. (1992). *Feeling and personhood: Psychology in another key.* Thousand Oaks, CA: SAGE.

Hodge, S. (2010). Trainers and transformation: Facilitating the "dark side" of vocational learning. *International Journal of Training Research, 8*, 53–62.

Hutchison, A., & Rea, T. (2011). Transformative learning and identity formation on the smiling coast of West Africa. *Teaching and Teacher Education, 27*, 552–559.

Isopahkala-Bouret, U. (2008). Transformative learning in managerial role transitions. *Studies in Continuing Education, 30*(1), 69–84.

Jaruszewicz, C. (2006). Opening windows on teaching and learning: Transformative and emancipatory learning precipitated by experimenting with visual documentation of student learning. *Educational Action Research, 14*(3), 357–375.

Johnson-Bailey, J., & Alfred, M. V. (2006). Transformation teaching and the practices of black women. In E. W. Taylor (Ed.), *Teaching for change.* New Directions for Adult and Continuing Education, no. 109 (pp. 49–48). San Francisco: Jossey-Bass.

Jokikokko, K. (2009). The role of significant others in the intercultural learning of teachers. *Journal of Research in International Education, 8*(2), 142–163.

Kegan, R. (2000). What "forms" transforms? A constructive-developmental approach to learning. In J. Mezirow & Associates (Eds.), *Learning as transformation: Critical perspectives on a theory in progress* (pp. 35–70). San Francisco: Jossey-Bass.

Kerton, S., & Sinclair, A. J. (2010). Buying local organic food: A pathway to transformative learning. *Agriculture Human Values, 27*, 401–413.

King, K. (2008). Evolution of an educational research model: Transformative learning research intersecting with learner's lives across varied contexts. *International Forum of Teaching Studies, 4*(1), 13–20.

King, K. (2009a). *The handbook of the evolving research of transformative learning based on the learning activities survey.* United States: Information Age Publishing.

King, K. (2009b). Workplace performance—PLUS: Empowerment and voice through professional development and democratic processes in health care training. *Performance Improvement Quarterly, 21*(4), 55–74.

Lange, E. (2004). Transformative and restorative learning: A vital dialectic for sustainable societies. *Adult Education Quarterly, 54*(2), 121–139.

Madsen, S. (2009). Leadership development in the United Arab Emirates: The transformational learning experiences of women. *Journal of Leadership and Organizational Studies, 17*(1), 100–110.

Magro, K., & Polyzoi, E. (2009). Geographical and psychological terrains of adults from war-affected backgrounds. *Journal of Transformative Education, 7*(1), 85–106.

Marschke, M., & Sinclair, J. A. (2008). Learning for sustainability: Participatory resource management in Cambodian fishing villages. *Journal of Environmental Management, 90*, 206–216.

McBrien, J. (2008). The world at America's doorstep: Service learning in preparation to teach global students. *Journal of Transformative Education, 6*(4), 270–285.

Merriam, S. B., & Ntseane, G. (2008). Transformational learning in Botswana: How culture shapes the process. *Adult Education Quarterly, 58*(3), 183–197.

Mertz, N. T., & Anfara, Jr., V. A. (2006). Conclusion: Coming full circle. In V. A. Anfara, Jr., & N. T. Mertz (Eds.), *Theoretical frameworks in qualitative research* (pp. 189–196), Thousand Oaks, CA: SAGE.

Mezirow, J. (1978). *Education for perspective transformation: Women's re-entry programs in community colleges.* Teacher's College, Columbia University, New York.

Mezirow, J. (1991). *Transformative dimensions of adult learning.* San Francisco: Jossey-Bass.

Mezirow, J., & Associates (Eds.). (2000). *Learning as transformation: Critical perspectives on a theory in progress.* San Francisco: Jossey-Bass.

Morris, A., & Faulk, D. (2007). Perspective transformation: Enhancing the development of professionalism in RN-to-BSN students. *Journal of Nursing Education, 46*(10), 445–451.

Mwebi, B. M., & Brigham, S. M. (2009). Preparing North American preservice teachers for global perspectives: An international teaching practicum experience in Africa. *Alberta Journal of Educational Research, 55*(3), 414–427.

Nohl, A. M. (2009). Spontaneous action and transformative learning: Empirical investigations and pragmatist reflections. *Educational Philosophy and Theory, 41*(3), 287–306.

Ntiri, D., & Stewart, M. (2009). Transformative learning intervention: Effect on functional health literacy and diabetes knowledge in older African Americans. *Gerontology & Geriatric Education, 30*, 100–113.

O'Sullivan, E. (1999). *Transformative learning: Educational vision for the 21st century.* London: Zed Books.

Rush, B. (2008). Mental health service user involvement in nurse education: A catalyst for transformative learning. *Journal of Mental Health, 17*(5), 531–542.

Sandlin, J. A., & Bey, G. J. (2006). Trowels, trenches, and transformation: A case study of archaeologists learning a more critical practice of archaeology. *Journal of Social Archaeology, 6,* 225–276.

Sands, D., & Tennant, M. (2010). Transformative learning in the context of suicide bereavement. *Adult Education Quarterly, 60,* 90–121.

Scott, S. (2003). The social construction of transformation. *Journal of Transformative Education, 1*(3), 264–284.

Sheared, V. (1994). Giving voice: An inclusive model of instruction—a womanist perspective. In E. Hayes and S.A.J. Colin III (Eds.), *Confronting racism and sexism in adult education* (pp. 27–37). New Directions for Continuing Education, no. 61. San Francisco: Jossey-Bass.

Sims, L., & Sinclair, A. J. (2008). Learning through participatory resource management programs: Case studies from Costa Rica. *Adult Education Quarterly, 58,* 151–168.

Stevens, K., Gerber, D., & Hendra, R. (2010). Transformational learning through prior learning assessment. *Adult Education Quarterly, 60*(4), 377–404.

Tarnoczi, T. (2011). Transformative learning and adaptation to climate change in the Canadian Prairie agro-ecosystem. *Mitigation and Adaptation Strategies for Global Change, 16,* 387–406.

Taylor, E. W. (1997). Building upon the theoretical debate: A critical review of the empirical studies of Mezirow's transformative learning theory. *Adult Education Quarterly, 48,* 32–57.

Taylor, E. W. (2000). Fostering Mezirow's transformative learning theory in the adult education classroom: A critical review. *Canadian Journal of the Study of Adult Education, 14,* 1–28.

Taylor, E. W. (2007). An update of transformative learning theory: A critical review of the empirical research (1999–2005). *International Journal of Lifelong Education, 26,* 173–191.

Taylor, E. W. (2008). Transformative learning theory. In S. B. Merriam (Ed.), *Third update of adult learning* (pp. 5–15). New Directions for Adult and Continuing Education, no. 119. San Francisco: Jossey-Bass.

Tisdell, E. J. (2003). *Exploring spirituality and culture in adult and higher education.* San Francisco: Jossey-Bass.

Tisdell, E. J. (2008). Critical media literacy and transformative learning. *Journal of Transformative Education, 6*(1), 48–67.

Velde, B. P., Wittman, P. P., & Mott, V. W. (2007). Hands-on learning in Tillery. *Journal of Transformative Education, 5*(1), 79–92.

Walton, J. (2010). Examining a transformative approach to communication education: A teacher research study. *College Student Journal, 44*(1), 157–177.

Wilhelmson, L. (2006a). Dialogue meetings as nonformal adult education in a municipal context. *Journal of Transformative Education, 4*(3), 243–256.

Wilhelmson, L. (2006b). Transformative learning in joint leadership. *Journal of Workplace Learning, 18*(7/8), 495–507.

Williams, S. H. (2003). Black mama sauce: Integrating the theatre of the oppressed and Afrocentricity in transformative learning. In C. A. Wiessner, S. R. Meyer, N. L. Pfhal, & P. G. Neaman (Eds), *Proceedings of the fifth international conference on transformative learning* (pp. 463–468), Albuquerque, New Mexico.

Wittman, P., Velde, B. P., Carawan, L., Pokorny, M., & Knight, S. (2008). A writer's retreat as a facilitator for transformative learning. *Journal of Transformative Learning, 6*(3), 201–211.

Yorks, L., & Kasl, E. (2006). I know more than I can say. *Journal of Transformative Education, 4*(1), 43–64.

CHAPTER FOUR

Studying Transformative Learning

What Methodology?

Sharan B. Merriam and SeonJoo Kim

Although Jack Mezirow first presented his theory of adult learning in 1978, it wasn't until the 1990s that a substantial body of research on the theory began to appear in journals and conferences. Taylor's (1997, 2007) reviews updating readers on the research on transformative learning document the growth of this research base. His 1997 review was of thirty dissertations and only three journal articles; ten years later, his 2007 review was of forty-one peer-reviewed journal articles wherein this learning theory provided at least some portion of the theoretical framework of the study.

Whether dissertations or journal articles, most studies of transformative learning to date have employed a qualitative research methodology. And of course it is well known that the theory itself was derived from a grounded theory study of women returning to higher education (Mezirow, 1978a, 1978b). The qualitative nature of the majority of studies of transformative learning is not surprising, given that, as with any new area of investigation, the characteristics and nature of the phenomenon need to be uncovered and described before we can assess the distribution of the phenomenon or test causal relationships (Cresswell, 2009; Patton, 2002). The purpose of this chapter is to discuss factors involved in the selection of research methodologies that have been used or might be employed to advance our understanding of transformative learning theory.

To that end, this chapter first considers three factors that determine the selection of an appropriate research design or methodology to study transformative learning. The first factor is *one's philosophical perspective*; that is, what one believes about the world, about reality, and about the nature of knowledge—how it is created, whose knowledge counts, to what end knowledge is created, and so on. A second factor central to choice of methodology is *the question one is trying to answer*; different types of questions require different methodologies. A third factor is what we call *phenomenon maturity*. As we learn more about a phenomenon, we can ask different questions requiring different methodologies. Of course, these three factors overlap and interact in the course of selecting the methodologies for studying a phenomenon.

The second section of this chapter considers research methodologies beginning to be employed in the study of transformative learning at this point in the theory's development. Four such approaches that hold promise for extending our understanding of transformative learning are narrative analysis, arts-based inquiry, critical and emancipatory methods, and action research.

FACTORS IN THE SELECTION OF A RESEARCH METHODOLOGY

A number of factors play into the selection of research design, methodology, or method. First, however, we wish to clarify our use of the terms "design," "method," and "methodology." Although some might differentiate among these terms, we are using them interchangeably in this chapter to mean *how* we approach a phenomenon in order to learn more about it. Again, the three interrelated factors that we have identified as critical in the selection of a research methodology are one's philosophical perspective, the research question being posed, and the maturity of the phenomenon being studied.

Philosophical Perspective

The purpose of research is to contribute to the knowledge base in one's field; that is, anyone who conducts a research study is trying to find out more about the phenomenon of interest. The very questions that we ask and the design of a particular study reflect what we believe about the nature of reality (also called *ontology*) and the nature of knowledge, or our epistemological perspective. Is there a reality independent of our construction or interpretation of it? Is the goal of research to predict or to understand? To change or to question? Different researchers assume different epistemological perspectives. Drawing from several writers on the philosophical underpinnings of different types of research (Carr & Kemmis, 1995; Lather, 1992, 2006; Prasad, 2005), we now discuss the four common philosophical perspectives: positivist/postpostivist, interpretive/constructivist, critical, and postmodern.

A *positivist* perspective assumes that reality exists separate from the knower and that it is observable, stable, and measureable. Because reality is stable, we can measure its characteristics, "experiment" with conditions related to it, generalize to like phenomena, and predict future behavior. This type of research attempts to get at the "truth" about a phenomenon. As yet there are only a few studies of transformative learning that have attempted to measure a change in perspective. For example, using Mezirow's conception of transformative learning as a theoretical framework, Mallory (2003) adopted the Frommelt Attitude Toward Care of the Dying (FATCOD) scale in an attempt to assess nurses' attitudes toward dying patients and palliative care. Those nursing students who had participated in an end-of-life education course scored higher on the FATCOD than those in the control group. The educational program, which comprised experiences at hospice and the funeral home and role-playing, helped facilitate students' transformative learning.

In the context of mixed-method studies, King (2004) administered the Learning Activities Survey to examine participants' experiences with transformative learning in a graduate education program. Sixty-two percent were found to have experienced transformative learning. King (2009) also employed mixed methods in a study of a professional development program for a hospital workers' union (136 participants for survey, 28 individuals for interviews). The program embraced a learner-centered pedagogy designed to empower participants in terms of voice, attitude, communication, and problem solving. In a study that explored transformative learning experiences of Emirati female college students, Madsen and Cook (2010) adopted King's (1998) questionnaire and revised it with Likert scale–type responses. Madsen and Cook concluded that the female college students had experienced transformation in their opinions, expectations, and perspectives.

Similarly, Brown (2005) employed a mixed methods design using the Cultural and Educational Issues Survey (Version B), which is designed to measure preservice leaders' attitudes concerning cultural and educational issues. Seventy-six graduate students of educational administration participated in this study. Experiential activities such as diversity workshops, cross-cultural interviews, reflective journals, and activist assignments aided in participants' transforming their perspectives.

A second major philosophical orientation is *constructivist*, which assumes there is no single, objective reality. Reality for an individual is her or his interpretation of it; thus there are multiple possible constructions or interpretations of reality. Research is a meaning-making activity in that the researcher constructs an understanding of the phenomenon of interest from the perspectives of those who experience it. "Those meanings are varied and multiple, leading the researcher to look for the complexity of views" (Cresswell, 2007, p. 20); as mentioned earlier in this chapter, research on transformative learning has been mostly constructivist/interpretive or qualitative. Research from this perspective relies heavily on interviews in order to access participants' understanding of their experience of transformative learning. The discovery-oriented nature of this type of research led to Mezirow's original formation of the theory. In his study, interviews with eighty-three women who had returned to postsecondary education were conducted to identify factors that facilitated or impeded their progress in reentry programs (1978a, 1978b). Mezirow and his team discovered that participants had undergone a "personal transformation" that involved a ten-step process beginning with a "disorienting dilemma" and ending with a "reintegration" of the new perspective into their lives.

Subsequent qualitative studies of transformative learning focused first on confirming that "adults in different stages of their lives and in a variety of settings and conditions experience perspective transformations" (Taylor, 1997, p. 51). Early studies also explored the ten-step model, and how perspective transformation might be promoted. Later qualitative studies have been less about identifying the phenomenon's existence "and more about fostering transformative learning and the complex nature of critical reflection, relationships, the nature of a perspective transformation and the role of context" (Taylor, 2007, abstract, p. 173).

A third philosophical stance toward research is a *critical* one. This perspective goes beyond the constructivist goal of understanding a phenomenon and seeks to empower participants to be able to change their lives for the better. Critical research draws from critical theory, feminist theory, critical race theory, postcolonial theory, queer theory, and critical ethnography (Crotty, 1998; Kincheloe & McLaren, 2000; Patton, 2002). All of these orientations posit that reality is multiple and constructed as in a constructivist perspective, but it is also highly political, wherein power is unevenly distributed, leading to some being privileged and others being oppressed. The influence of Habermas, a critical theorist, and Freire, who spoke of a process of conscientization as well as empowerment and liberation, can be seen in Mezirow's theory, most prominently in his critical reflection and action components. However, the research that led to his theory was not critical in that he was not attempting to change and empower participants through the research. Nor did his research analyze the power dynamics involved in a transformative learning experience.

A few qualitative studies have been partially informed by a critical epistemological perspective and, in particular, how power in the social context shaped the transformative experience. McDonald, Cervero, and Courtenay (1999), for example, found that the transformative experience of ethical vegans was moderated by "the sustained power of normative ideology" in that they became "less outspoken" about their practice (p. 20). In another study, Carrington and Selva (2010) used critical social theory, which facilitates knowledge transformation through an emphasis on reflection, to study a group of preservice teachers who were engaged in service learning. This study focused on how critical reflection challenges the practices and assumptions in education that are interconnected with viewpoints held in society and in the world. The results showed that critical reflection promoted transformative learning, which in turn made them realize their responsibility to be change agents.

The fourth epistemological perspective is one of *postmodernism*, wherein there is no single reality—indeed, no single "truth," but rather multiple "truths." The world is diverse, with multiple realities, none of which is more privileged or more powerful than another. Postmodern research questions anything and everything; it "problematizes" assumptions and views; it "deconstructs" ideas, and it "interrupts" taken-for-granted narratives. Postmodern research is highly experimental and creative and is often combined with critical approaches. For example, Kilgore and Bloom (2002) studied women in crisis who, despite learning to speak of themselves in a more empowering way, did not experience a perspective transformation. Although the women in crisis used "the master discourses of transformation that they learn in their adult education classes" (p. 129), they did not change their perspectives. Rather, they held multiple but contradictory perspectives simultaneously, thus enabling them to navigate a fragmented, multiple, or nonunitary self.

In summary, one's philosophical perspective is intimately linked to the manner in which a research study is constructed and carried out. We have given illustrations of transformative learning studies drawing from a positivist, constructivist, critical, and postmodern perspective. Interrelated with the philosophical orientation is the nature of the question being asked and the maturity of the phenomenon being studied.

The Research Question and Maturity of the Phenomenon

One's view of reality is reflected in the construction of a research question—that overarching question specifying what one is trying to find out about a phenomenon. This question is often stated as the purpose of the research and addresses a perceived gap in our knowledge about the phenomenon. If, for example, one believes that reality is stable, knowable, and measureable, as in a positivist perspective, one could ask about the frequency of the phenomenon (for example, asking how many older adults have experienced a perspective transformation), variables that correlate with the phenomenon (asking whether age, level of education, marital status, gender or race is predictive of which older adults experience a perspective transformation), or conduct an experiment to see how an intervention program can bring about change (asking which is more effective in fostering perspective transformation in older adults: a psychological counseling or an educational intervention).

However, a researcher coming from a constructivist epistemology would ask questions about meaning and understanding from the participant's perspective. As Krauss (2005) points out: "Qualitative researchers believe that the best way to understand any phenomenon is to view it in its context. They see all quantification as limited in nature, looking only at one small portion of a reality that cannot be split or unitized without losing the importance of the whole phenomenon" (p. 759).

Further, human beings construct their "reality" of a phenomenon. They "impose order on the world perceived in an effort to construct meaning; meaning lies in cognition not in elements external to us" (Krauss, 2005, p. 760). Something as personal as transformative learning and subsequent perspective transformation lends itself to qualitative or constructivist research because we are interested in understanding the meaning of the experience for the participants involved. Using older adults as in the preceding examples, one might ask how life stage shapes transformative learning. In fact, Moon (2008) did ask a similar question in his study of how bereavement in late life precipitated transformative learning.

Yet other research questions are best approached from a critical or postmodern epistemological perspective. A critical stance shares with the constructivist perspective that there are multiple realities and that meaning and understanding are key. However, some realities are privileged over others and that for people to be empowered to free themselves from an oppressed state, the power dynamics of any situation must be uncovered and made visible. Using the hypothetical example of older adults, a researcher might ask about perspective transformations in those older adults who have become community activists, or how older adults have had transformative learning experiences that have enabled them to challenge aging stereotypes in our society. Finally, research questions drawing from a postmodern perspective might explore the concept of multiple selves versus the unitary self in a perspective transformation, or possibly deconstruct binaries—such as young/old, beautiful/ugly, competent/incompetent—that shape an older adult's transformative experience.

In most social science fields, the choice of a research methodology also reflects a third factor: the maturity of the phenomenon being studied. When a new concept, model, or theory is first proposed, research studies tend to be designed to advance an understanding of the phenomenon. Because understanding a phenomenon is best achieved through qualitative research, this design is often employed in the early stages of research. Cresswell (2009) points out:

> If a concept or phenomenon needs to be understood because little research has been done on it, then it merits a qualitative approach. Qualitative research is exploratory and is useful when the researcher does not know the important variables to examine. This type of approach may be needed because the topic is new, the topic has never been addressed with a certain sample or group of people, and existing theories do not apply. (p. 18)

This has certainly been true of transformative learning wherein the predominate mode of inquiry has been qualitative. Taylor noted that in his 1997 review of thirty-nine research studies on transformative learning, only two used a quantitative approach. Ten years later, however, Taylor reported that although the majority of studies were still qualitative, "The research processes have become more sophisticated through the use of longitudinal designs, action research, scales, surveys, content analysis of various documentation (e.g. emails, journals, portfolios) and the use of stimulated recall via video recordings and photo-elicitation interviews" (2007, p. 176).

A similar movement can be seen in the research on other adult learning theories. Self-directed learning, for example, was first conceptualized in the qualitative research of Houle (1961/1988) and Tough (1971). Houle interviewed twenty-two adults who were "conspicuously engaged in various forms of continuing learning" (p. 13), while his student Tough investigated the self-planned learning projects of sixty-six adults. This conceptualization of the phenomenon via qualitative research was followed by a number of survey studies verifying the widespread engagement of adults in self-directed learning (Merriam, Caffarella, & Baumgartner, 2007). Next came a period of research and model-building to further conceptualize this phenomenon. This same methodological movement can be seen with the most recent work in defining the nature of embodied learning, spirituality and learning, and narrative learning (see chapters in Merriam, 2008).

In summary, it is important to underscore the fact that these factors of epistemological perspective, research question, and phenomenon maturity are inextricably interrelated. The questions one asks about a phenomenon and the subsequent choice of methodology depend to some extent on what is known about the phenomenon. Further, one's perspective on reality and the nature of knowledge leads to raising certain questions and not others. In the case of research on transformative learning and perspective transformation, all three factors have come together to produce a vibrant body of research and theory-building. We turn now to discussing methodologies to further advance our knowledge of transformative learning—methodologies particularly appropriate at this point in the evolution of the knowledge base of transformative learning.

RESEARCH METHODOLOGIES FOR FUTURE RESEARCH ON TRANSFORMATIVE LEARNING

We suggest that the study of Mezirow's theory of transformative learning has matured to the point that researchers are experimenting with a variety of research approaches. However, we do not mean to imply that basic qualitative research designs are a thing of the past; in fact, much can still be learned about transformative learning and perspective transformation through studies employing a basic qualitative design and studies of its phenomenological, grounded theory and ethnographic variations (Merriam, 2009). This section of our chapter focuses on several approaches that are beginning to be used or might be employed to advance our understanding of this theory. In particular, we have chosen the following four approaches to review—narrative analysis, arts-based research, critical and participatory research, and action research.

Narrative Analysis

Narrative analysis is quite simply the analysis of people's stories. People use stories to make sense of their experiences; we "story" our lives and communicate with others through these stories. Stories are all around us in the form of news stories and stories about our families, our nation, and of course our lives. Stories are "the oldest and most natural form of sense making" (Jonassen & Hernandez-Serrano, 2002, p. 66). Stories are narratives, and when used in research, the first-person accounts of experience are told in story form with a beginning, middle, and end.

Narrative analysis is particularly well suited for the study of transformative learning because it allows people to convey their personal experience of this type of learning through stories. In an interesting discussion of storytelling and its intersection with Mezirow's conditions for critical discourse in the process of transformative learning, Tyler (2009) points out that stories of personal experience

> may be told from the heart rather than from the head. They may emerge as messy and as nonlinear as some of the events that they convey. They may be filled with sudden remembrances that prompt the teller to go back and fill the listeners in on an important detail. They may not start at the beginning, and they may not have the neat endings we have come to expect from performed stories, because the experiences of the tellers are not neat and are ongoing. (p. 138)

Yet another connection between narrative analysis and Mezirow's theory is in the developmental potential of both. Mezirow unequivocally states that the process of perspective transformation is "the central process of adult development" (1991, p. 155). Likewise, one's "story" can be restructured and reinterpreted to accommodate developmental change. Just as a perspective transformation leads to a "more inclusive, discriminating, permeable, and integrative perspective" (Mezirow, 1990, p. 14), one can re-story one's life in a way that is, as one author noted, "*big* enough, with a horizon *broad* enough, to account for as much as possible of my actual life and render it available to me as a coherent, re-membered whole" (Glover, cited in Randall, 1996, p. 240).

For instance, drawing on a theory of grief, Sands and Tennant (2010) explored meaning making as a form of "a repositioning of the relationships with the deceased, the self, and the others" (p. 116) among the suicide bereaved. The shift from the narrative of despair toward the narrative of hope established multiple perspectives on the ongoing construction of meaning, whereby grief experiences were constantly revisited and reinterpreted in a developmental way. In another narrative approach, Isopahkala-Bouret (2008) explored the experiences of transformative learning within an organizational setting. The in-depth narrative analysis of employees' stories of moving from specialist to managerial positions revealed how the participants adopt dominant organizational values as part of self-reflection.

From a methodological perspective, narrative analysis relies heavily on the "text" of the story, no matter how the story has been gathered—through interviews, journals, memoirs, letters, autobiography, or otherwise (Clandinin, 2007; Riessman, 2007). Narrative research makes use of a variety of approaches to analyzing these stories. including biographical, psychological, and linguistic approaches. Mishler (1995) reminds us that in doing this type of research, the researcher is also constructing a narrative and its meaning. "In this sense the story is always co-authored, either directly in the process of an interviewer eliciting an account or indirectly through our representing and thus transforming others' texts and discourses" (p. 117).

In summary, because people make meaning of their lives through stories, it would seem that narrative analysis is a particularly rich approach to understanding more about transformative learning. Various narrative approaches are also being used in learning contexts to foster transformative learning.

Arts-Based Research

Along with the traditional approaches to transformative learning, more creative research methods have emerged to gain a better understanding of transformative learning experiences. Drawing on people's unconscious, emotional, and intuitive ways of knowing, arts-based research forms an alternative approach to both fostering and studying transformative learning. Although Mezirow (2000) emphasizes the cognitive component of transformative learning, he does acknowledge alternative ways of understanding transformative learning: "Art, music, and dance are alternative languages. Intuition, imagination, and dreams are other ways of making meaning. Inspiration, empathy, and transcendence are central to self-knowledge and to drawing attention to the affective quality and poetry of human experience" (p. 6).

An arts-based approach is being used to foster transformative learning as well as a means of accessing participants' transformative experiences. It is particularly appropriate in understanding the affective, intuitive, relational, and often irrational ways of knowing beyond the limited cognitive perspective. Arts-informed research as an intuitive or nonrational means of transformation provides opportunities to empower people and help them create their own voices (Knowles & Cole, 2002). When the learners' imagination and intuition are engaged in diverse and expressive ways, learners have a better understanding of both their affective and conceptual meaning making, which leads to a holistic approach to transformative learning (Taylor, 2009).

An increasing amount of research has revealed unconventional ways of knowing through the arts, including photography, portraiture, painting, poetry, and theater, to mention just a few. Taylor (2003) used photography as an interview prompt in an attempt to understand the teaching belief change of entering graduate students. In another participatory photography project (Clover, 2006), marginalized groups such as homeless people and women in poverty and violence exhibited pictures of themselves and their families as a form for transformative narrative, thus becoming activist artists. By accessing symbolic and metaphoric levels of visual narratives in photography, these activist artists were nurtured, transformed, and ultimately empowered. Creating photos with their own cameras was a learning opportunity that allowed them to tell their stories and to locate their voices. The experiences of "turning the camera into a proactive, analytical, and empowering tool" (p. 285) facilitated a process of transformative learning. In the theater workshop developed by Butterwick and Lawrence (2009), the participants were given opportunities to learn new ways of responding to a situation that led to transformative learning. This activity of acting and witnessing their stories opened space to discuss and explore alternative realities. Clover and Butterwick and Lawrence's studies used an arts-based research method and in turn fostered transformative learning experiences.

In summary, the arts-based approach to fostering and researching transformative learning is a way of encompassing cognitive, affective, relational, and intuitive knowing through experiential learning. These experiential activities often allow learners to reveal inner worlds to an audience by creating materials that are witnessed by others. In this vein, tapping into multiple dimensions of knowing, an arts-based research method would promote transformative learning through giving voice to people, awakening the soul, and creating space for action, both privately and publicly.

Critical and Emancipatory Approaches

The third approach we have chosen to discuss is loosely labeled "critical" or "emancipatory" research. This perspective draws from the critical epistemological stance discussed in the first section of this chapter. This research is more than constructivist or interpretive; a critical stance has the goal of not only understanding a phenomenon but also analyzing the power dynamics of a situation. By critiquing the status quo, it is hoped that people can become empowered to transform their situation.

Any number of specific critical theoretical orientations can shape this research—critical race theory, feminist theory, critical ethnography, and so on. Participatory action research (PAR) also falls into this category, as the goal of PAR is the political empowerment of people through their involvement in the design and implementation of a research project. Understanding the power dynamics of a situation leads to fighting oppression and marginalization through collective action, and collective action as a result of the investigation is central.

With regard to Mezirow's theory, a critical perspective is beginning to have a presence. As mentioned in the first section of this chapter, the study by Kilgore and Bloom (2002) had a critical as well as a postmodern stance, in that the goal of the research was to understand how the perspectives of women at risk change. The learning experiences in adult basic education (ABE) and parenting classes did not support transformative learning among women in crisis, such as prisoners and drug abusers. The authors explain that because these women had to follow learning goals set by the institution, they experienced powerlessness, which hindered them from experiencing transformative learning. In another study of an educational program that tried to promote changes in teachers' worldviews, critical reflection played a pivotal role in changing their worldview and understanding their responsibility as change agents (Carrington & Selva, 2010). Combined with a more artistic way of transformative learning using autophotography, Armstrong (2005) explored the possibilities of social justice and democratic education. Critical reflection was enhanced as the participants interpreted the contents of photographs of "both people and places that [were] actual or metaphoric examples of his or her life world" (p. 34).

A number of discussions in the literature on transformative learning, especially research on how to foster this type of learning, are framed from this critical perspective. Taylor and Jarecke (2009), in their summary review of chapters in *Transformative Learning in Practice,* point out the critical dimensions of fostering transformative learning in an educational setting. They note that this view is framed in terms of "confronting power and engaging difference" (p. 278). Thus power relationships between instructor and students and among students are part of the analysis. Also, transformative educators who work "with learners who have been historically marginalized and oppressed by others" (p. 279) face enormous challenges. This kind of work, they point out, is "much more than personal empowerment; it is about developing political consciousness" (p. 279).

At the heart of Mezirow's theory is personal transformation. A personal perspective transformation can lead to social transformation, but it is a process. As Mezirow writes, "Personal transformation leads to alliances with others of like mind to work toward effecting necessary changes in relationships, organizations, and systems, each of which requires a different mode of praxis" (1992, p. 252).

Mezirow's perspective deviates somewhat from Freire's philosophy of transformative learning, in which personal and social transformation are inseparable processes (Freire, 2000). For Freire, the goal of education is to become aware, through critical reflection and action (praxis), of the various oppressive forces in the world in order to transform it. Freire's and other more recent conceptions of transformative learning—such as race-centric, cultural-spiritual, and planetary views (see Taylor, 2008 for a discussion of these orientations)—are philosophically congruent with critical and emancipatory research methodologies.

Action Research

Some recent research on transformative learning is focused on how to bring about this type of learning in an educational or organizational setting. What is the instructor or facilitator's role? What instructional activities are most effective? How should the emotional, affective, and spiritual aspects be handled in an ethical, respectful manner? These and other questions are beginning to be investigated using an action research methodology.

Action research is site-specific, designed to address a specific problem or issue within a specific setting, such as a classroom, a workplace, a program, or an organization. This kind of research often involves the participants in the research process, thus blurring the distinction between action and research. Taylor (2007) comments on the basic compatibility between transformative learning and action research:

> They share similar assumptions and outcomes about teaching for change, such as a participatory approach, the emphasis on dialogue, the essentiality of a reflective process in learning and the need for action. More research is needed that simultaneously engages action research and transformative learning to better understand their relationship, ultimately resulting in a more informed practice for fostering transformative learning and an effective method of classroom research. (p. 188)

In a study about fostering transformative learning in a teaching development program, Gravett (2004) used dialogical and reciprocal inquiry in an attempt to promote critical reflection that led to changes in the meaning structures of teachers in higher education. Jaruszewicz's (2006) action research project involved implementing visual documentation of student learning that led to transformative learning experiences for both students and the teacher. As both a teaching and learning process, this action research project allowed the teacher and students to engage in critical reflection that served to bring about transformations in meaning schemes on teaching, learning, communications, and identity.

We have reviewed four methodologies that are beginning to be used and hold promise for future research on transformative learning—narrative analysis, arts-based research, critical and emancipatory research, and action research. That is not to say that other designs shouldn't be used—and in fact we fully realize that most likely the majority of research on transformative learning will continue to be qualitative. We also recognize that attempts will continue to develop scales and other instruments to measure the phenomenon; however, it is difficult to see how the nature of the phenomenon at this time is particularly amenable to experimental or sophisticated statistical designs.

The affective and often intensely emotional component of transformative learning is more likely to lend itself to people telling their stories (narrative) and arts-based approaches.

CHALLENGES IN STUDYING TRANSFORMATIVE LEARNING

In this chapter, we found that the approaches to transformative learning theory bring one's philosophical perspective and the different types of questions that interconnect to the maturity of the phenomenon to the fore. As mentioned earlier, these factors of epistemological perspective, research question, and phenomenon maturity are inextricably interrelated. Whereas the positivist stance seeks to measure a change in transformative learning, the constructivist, critical, and postmodern perspectives have understood transformative learning and perspective transformation in more qualitative and natural ways, based on their epistemological stance and subsequent research questions. Given that qualitative methodology is a central way to understand phenomena, the four methods (narrative analysis, arts-based research, critical and emancipatory research, and action research) have expanded and deepened our sense of what transformative learning is.

There are, however, some challenges to doing research on transformative learning. First, Mezirow's theory basically lays out a cognitive process of change, yet we know from much of the research that transformative learning is much more than a rational process: it's complicated, personal, and often powerfully emotional. Given the increasing experimentation with arts-based inquiry to help capture these noncognitive dimensions, there is a need for clarification of research purpose, in that it's not always clear whether arts-based methods are being used to foster transformative learning or to study its occurrence. Narrative research would also seem to be able to capture the multidimensionality of transformative learning. People's stories are rich resources for accessing the depth of this type of learning. With imagination and creativity integrated by clear research purposes, researchers might strive to make something new out of the extant approaches to transformative learning and in turn enrich evolving TL theory without losing its essential nature and uniqueness.

Transformative learning is also about change and empowerment—and therein lies a second challenge. Mezirow emphasizes personal change and empowerment, but several theorists see a social dimension as equally important. The challenge, then, is how to design a research study that can assess the link between personal and social change and the power dynamics involved. A critical research approach would seem to be a suitable methodology, but, as with any study, there are issues that must be addressed in studying transformation and empowerment. For example, what are the ethical issues involved?

What might be the unanticipated consequences of engaging in this type of research? What types of interactions foster empowerment? To respond to these questions, the context must be attended to and, in particular, enough time allowed to closely examine contextual factors within which both personal and social changes are situated. Although difficult to carry out, assessment of the interaction between individual and social components over time is best accomplished through a longitudinal design.

Finally, although in our discussion of research methodologies we have focused on Mezirow's theory of transformative learning, there are a number of other conceptualizations. For example, Taylor (2008) has identified four alternative views: neurobiological, cultural-spiritual, race-centric, and planetary. Given that a neurobiological approach requires an understanding of neurobiological systems, what training would researchers need to examine neurobiological-based transformative learning? When we seek to understand "the interconnectedness among universe, planet, natural environment, human community, and personal world" (p. 9), how we can assess planetary consciousness changes? Determining how to study transformative learning from these perspectives may require even more creative and advanced methodological approaches.

In sum, research on transformative learning that integrates philosophical stance, research questions, and diverse methods has extended the knowledge base of transformative learning and will continue to do so. The evolution of transformative learning theory has been accompanied by methodological challenges. Currently, we see several challenges including the sensitivity or clarity of research purposes when employing creative methods, the importance of contextual factors in understanding both individual and social changes, and the question of investigating new conceptualizations of transformative learning in meaningful ways. These challenges offer additional opportunities to explore and expand transformative learning theory.

References

Armstrong, K. (2005). Autophotography in adult education: Building creative communities for social justice and democratic education. In R. L. Lawrence (Ed.), *Artistic ways of knowing: Expanded opportunities for teaching and learning* (pp. 33–44). San Francisco: Jossey-Bass.

Brown, K. M. (2005). Social justice education for preservice leaders: Evaluating transformative learning strategies. *Equity and Excellence in Education, 38*(2), 155–167.

Butterwick, S., & Lawrence, R. L. (2009). Creating alternative realities: Arts-based approaches to transformative learning. In J. Mezirow, E. W. Taylor, & Associates (Eds.), *Transformative learning in practice: Insights from community, workplace, and higher education* (pp. 35–45). San Francisco: Jossey-Bass.

Carr, W., & Kemmis, S. (1995). *Becoming critical: Education, knowledge and action research.* London: Hyperion Books.

Carrington, S., & Selva, G. (2010). Critical social theory and transformative learning: Evidence in pre-service teachers' service-learning reflection logs. *Higher Education Research and Development, 29*(1), 45–57.

Clandinin, D. J. (Ed.) (2007). *Handbook of narrative inquiry: Mapping a methodology.* Thousand Oaks, CA: SAGE.

Clover, D. (2006). Out of the dark room: Participatory photography as a critical, imaginative, and public aesthetic practice of transformative education. *Journal of Transformative Education, 4*(3), 275–290.

Cresswell, J. W. (2007). *Qualitative inquiry and research design* (2nd ed.). Thousand Oaks, CA: SAGE.

Cresswell, J. W. (2009). *Research design: Qualitative, quantitative, and mixed methods approaches.* Thousand Oaks, CA: SAGE.

Crotty, M. (1998). *The foundations of social research.* London: SAGE.

Freire, P. (2000). *Pedagogy of the oppressed* (20th anniversary ed.). New York: Continuum.

Gravett, S. (2004). Action learning and transformative learning in teaching development. *Educational Action Research, 12*(2), 259–272.

Houle, C. O. (1988). *The inquiring mind* (2nd ed.). Madison: University of Wisconsin Press and Norman: Oklahoma Research Center for Continuing Professional and Higher Education. (Original work published 1961).

Isopahkala-Bouret, U. (2008). Transformative learning in managerial role transitions. *Studies in Continuing Education, 30*(1), 69–84.

Jaruszewicz, C. (2006). Opening windows on teaching and learning: Transformative and emancipatory learning precipitated by experimenting with visual documentation of student learning. *Educational Action Research, 14*(3), 357–375.

Jonassen, D. H., & Hernandez-Serrano, J. (2002). Case-based reasoning and instructional design: Using stories to support problem solving. *Educational Technology Research and Development, 50*(2), 65–77.

Kilgore, D., & Bloom, L. R. (2002). "When I'm down, it takes me a while": Rethinking transformational education through narratives of women in crisis. *Adult Basic Education, 12*, 123–133.

Kincheloe, J. L., & McLaren, P. (2000). Rethinking critical theory and qualitative research. In N. K. Denzin & Y. S. Lincoln (Eds.), *Handbook of qualitative research* (2nd ed.) (pp. 279–314). Thousand Oaks, CA: SAGE.

King, A. P. (1998). *A guide to perspective transformation and learning activities: The learning activities survey.* Charlotte, NC: Information Age Publishing.

King, K. (2004). Both sides now: Examining transformative learning and professional development of educators. *Innovative Higher Education, 29*, 155–174.

King, K. (2009). Workplace performance—PLUS: Empowerment and voice through professional development and democratic processes in health care training. *Performance Improvement Quarterly, 21*(4), 55–74.

Knowles, J., & Cole, A. (2002). Transforming research: Possibilities for arts-informed scholarship? In E. O'Sullivan (Ed.), *Expanding the boundaries of transformative learning* (pp. 199–214). New York: Palgrave.

Krauss, S. E. (2005). Research paradigms and meaning making: A primer. *The Qualitative Report, 10*(4), 758–770.

Lather, P. (1992). Critical frames in educational research: Feminist and post-structural perspectives. *Theory into Practice, 31*(2), 87–99.

Lather, P. (2006). Paradigm proliferation as a good thing to think with: Teaching research in education as a wild profusion. *International Journal of Qualitative Studies in Education, 19*(1), 35–57.

Madsen, S. R., & Cook, B. J. (2010). Transformative learning: UAE, women, and higher education. *Journal of Global Responsibility, 1*(1), 127–148.

Mallory, J. L. (2003). The impact of a palliative care educational component on attitudes toward care of the dying in undergraduate nursing. *Journal of Professional Nursing, 19*(5), 305–312.

McDonald, B., Cervero, R. M., & Courtenay, B. C. (1999). An ecological perspective of power in transformational learning: A case study of ethical vegans. *Adult Education Quarterly, 50*(1), 5–23.

Merriam, S. B. (Ed.). (2008). *Third update on adult learning theory.* New Directions for Adult and Continuing Education, no. 119. San Francisco: Jossey-Bass.

Merriam, S. B. (2009). *Qualitative research: A guide to design and implementation.* San Francisco: Jossey-Bass.

Merriam, S. B., Caffarella, R. S., & Baumgartner, L. M. (2007). *Learning in adulthood* (3rd ed.). San Francisco: Jossey-Bass.

Mezirow, J. (1978a). *Education for perspective transformation: Women's re-entry programs in community colleges.* New York: Teacher's College, Columbia University.

Mezirow, J. (1978b). Perspective transformation. *Adult Education, 28*, 100–110.

Mezirow, J. (1990). How critical reflection triggers transformative learning. In J. Mezirow & Associates (Eds.), *Fostering critical reflection in adulthood: A guide to transformative and emancipator learning* (pp. 1–20). San Francisco: Jossey-Bass.

Mezirow, J. (1991). *Transformative dimensions of adult learning.* San Francisco: Jossey-Bass.

Mezirow, J. (1992). Transformation theory: Critique and confusion. *Adult Education Quarterly, 42*(4), 250–252.

Mezirow, J. (2000). Learning to think like an adult: Core concepts of transformation theory. In J. Mezirow & Associates (Eds.), *Learning as transformation: Critical perspectives on a theory in progress* (pp. 3–33). San Francisco: Jossey-Bass.

Mishler, E. G. (1995). Models of narrative analysis: A typology. *Journal of Narrative and Life History*, *5*(2), 87–123.

Moon, P. (2008). Bereaved elders: Transformative learning in late life. Unpublished doctoral dissertation, University of Georgia, Athens.

Patton, M. Q. (2002). *Qualitative research & evaluation methods* (3rd ed.). Thousand Oaks, CA: SAGE.

Prasad, P. (2005). *Crafting qualitative research: Working in the postpositivist traditions.* Armonk, NY: M.E. Sharpe.

Randall, W. L. (1996). Restorying a life: Adult education and transformative learning. In J. E. Birren, G. M. Kenyon, J. Ruth, J. Schroots, & T. Svensson (Eds.), *Aging and biography: Explorations in adult development* (pp. 224–247). New York: Springer.

Riessman, C. K. (2007). *Narrative methods for the human sciences.* Thousand Oaks, CA: SAGE.

Sands, D., & Tennant, M. (2010). Transformative learning in the context of suicide bereavement. *Adult Education Quarterly*, *60*(2), 99–121.

Taylor, E. W. (1997). Building upon the theoretical debate: A critical review of the empirical studies of Mezirow's transformative learning theory. *Adult Education Quarterly*, *48*(1), 34–59.

Taylor, E. W. (2003). Attending graduate school in adult education and the impact on teaching beliefs: A longitudinal study. *Journal of Transformative Education*, *1*(4), 349–367.

Taylor, E. W. (2007). An update of transformative learning theory: A critical review of the empirical research (1999–2005). *International Journal of Lifelong Education*, *26*(2), 173–191.

Taylor, E. W. (2008). Transformative learning theory. In S. B. Merriam (Ed.), *Third update on adult learning theory* (pp. 5–15). New Directions for Adult and Continuing Education, no. 119. San Francisco: Jossey-Bass.

Taylor, E. W. (2009). Fostering transformative learning. In J. Mezirow, E. W. Taylor, & Associates (Eds.), *Transformative learning in practice* (pp. 3–17). San Francisco: Jossey-Bass.

Taylor, E. W., & Jarecke, J. (2009). Looking forward by looking back: Reflections on the practice of transformative learning. In J. Mezirow, E. W. Taylor, & Associates (Eds.), *Transformative learning in practice* (pp. 275–290). San Francisco: Jossey-Bass.

Tough, A. (1971). *The adult's learning projects; A fresh approach to theory and practice in adult learning.* Toronto: Ontario Institute for Studies in Education.

Tyler, J. A. (2009). Charting the course: How storytelling can foster communicative learning in the workplace. In J. Mezirow, E. W. Taylor, & Associates (Eds.), *Transformative learning in practice* (pp. 136–147). San Francisco: Jossey-Bass.

CHAPTER FIVE

Learning to Think Like an Adult

Core Concepts of Transformation Theory

Jack Mezirow

A defining condition of being human is our urgent need to understand and order the meaning of our experience, to integrate it with what we know to avoid the threat of chaos. If we are unable to understand, we often turn to tradition, thoughtlessly seize explanations by authority figures, or resort to various psychological mechanisms, such as projection and rationalization, to create imaginary meanings.

MAKING MEANING AS A LEARNING PROCESS

As there are no fixed truths or totally definitive knowledge, and because circumstances change, the human condition may be best understood as a continuous effort to negotiate contested meanings. Milan Kundera, in *The Book of Laughter and Forgetting* (1981), wisely suggests that if there were too much incontestable meaning in the world we would succumb under its weight.

That is why it is so important that adult learning emphasize contextual understanding, critical reflection on assumptions, and validation of meaning by assessing reasons. The justification for much of what we know and believe, our values and our feelings, depends on the context—biographical, historical, cultural—in which they are embedded. We make meaning with different dimensions of awareness and understanding; in adulthood we may more clearly understand our experience when we know under what conditions an expressed idea is true or justified. In the absence of fixed truths and confronted with often rapid change in circumstances, we cannot fully trust what we know or believe. Interpretations and opinions that may have worked for us as children often do not as adults.

Our understandings and beliefs are more dependable when they produce interpretations and opinions that are more justifiable or true than would be those predicated on other understandings or beliefs. Formulating more dependable beliefs about our experience, assessing their contexts, seeking informed agreement on their meaning and justification, and making decisions based on the resulting insights are central to the adult learning process. Transformation Theory attempts to explain this process and to examine its implications for action-oriented adult educators.

Bruner (1996) identifies four modes of making meaning: (1) establishing, shaping, and maintaining intersubjectivity; (2) relating events, utterances, and behavior to the action taken; (3) construing particulars in a normative context—deals with meaning relative to obligations, standards, conformities, and deviations; (4) making propositions—applying rules of the symbolic, syntactic, and conceptual systems used to achieve decontexualized meanings, including rules of inference and logic and such distinctions as whole-part, object-attribute, and identity-otherness.

Bruner's list is incomplete. Transformation theory adds a fifth and crucial mode of making meaning: becoming critically aware of one's own tacit assumptions and expectations and those of others and assessing their relevance for making an interpretation.

Kitchener (1983, p. 230) has suggested that there are three levels of cognitive processing:

> At the first level, individuals compute, memorize, read and comprehend. At the second level [metacognition], they monitor their own progress and products as they are engaged in first-order cognitive tasks. . . . The third level . . . [the] epistemic cognition, must be introduced to explain how humans monitor their problem solving when engaged in ill-structured problems, i.e. those which do not have an absolutely correct solution. Epistemic cognition has to do with reflection on the limits of knowledge, the certainty of knowledge, and the criteria for knowing. . . . [E]pistemic cognition emerges in late adolescence, although its form may change in the adult years.

In this formulation, transformative learning pertains to epistemic cognition.

Learning is understood as the process of using a prior interpretation to construe a new or revised interpretation of the meaning of one's experience as a guide to future action. We appropriate symbolic models, composed of images and conditioned affective reactions acquired earlier through the culture or the idiosyncrasies of parents or caretakers—a highly individualistic "frame of reference"—and make analogies to interpret the meaning of our new sensory experience (Rosenfield, 1988). Learning may be intentional, the result of deliberate inquiry; incidental, a by-product of another activity involving intentional learning; or mindlessly assimilative. Aspects of both intentional and incidental learning take place outside learner awareness.

Construal in intentional or incidental learning involves the use of language to articulate our experience to ourselves or to others. A third type of construal Heron (1988) describes as presentational. In presentational construal we do not require words to make meaning, as when we experience presence, motion, color, texture, directionality, aesthetic or kinesthetic experience, empathy, feelings, appreciation, inspiration, or transcendence. We use language here only when we experience a problem in understanding or want to share the experience.

Beliefs do not need to be encoded in words. They may be encoded in repetitive interactions and generalized. Weiss reminds us that a person's beliefs about himself or herself and his or her world are intimately bound up with his or her affects. He writes:

> Indeed, research into the unconscious acquisition of knowledge demonstrates that the human being has an enormous capacity nonconsciously to make inferences from complex data, to solve difficult puzzles, and to make broad generalizations from particular experiences.... [T]he nonconscious capacity of people to acquire information is much more sophisticated and rapid than their conscious capacity to do this. Also human beings have no conscious access to the nonconscious process that they use to acquire information. People cannot describe them; they are conscious only of the *results* of their nonconscious mental activities. (1997, p. 428)

Art, music, and dance are alternative languages. Intuition, imagination, and dreams are other ways of making meaning. Inspiration, empathy, and transcendence are central to self-knowledge and to drawing attention to the affective quality and poetry of human experience. Dirkx (1997, p. 85) writes of "learning through soul" involving "a focus on the interface where the socioemotional and the intellectual world meet, where the inner and outer worlds converge." Psychotherapists use *transference* to facilitate the making of meaning by their patients. *Modeling* a way of learning by an educator, such as becoming critically reflective of one's assumptions, may also influence the way a learner makes meaning.

Cognition has strong affective and conative dimensions; all the sensitivity and responsiveness of the person participates in the invention, discovery, interpretation, and transformation of meaning. Transformative learning, especially when it involves subjective reframing, is often an intensely threatening emotional experience in which we have to become aware of both the assumptions undergirding our ideas and those supporting our emotional responses to the need to change.

As language and culturally specific social practices are implicated in learning, understanding will be enabled and constrained by the historical knowledge-power networks in which it is embedded. The assumptions of these historical networks and their supporting ideologies need to be brought into awareness and critical reflection by the learner to make possible a greater degree of autonomous learning. We need to focus on who is doing the learning and under what circumstances to understand the transformative learning process.

The who, what, when, where, why, and how of learning may be understood only as situated in a specific cultural context. However, the content of a comprehensive learning theory cannot be dictated exclusively by cultural interests. What we have in common are human connectedness, the desire to understand, and spiritual incompleteness. Cultures enable or inhibit the realization of common human interests, ways of communicating, and realizing learning capabilities.

Mindful learning is defined by Langer (1997, p. 4) as the continuous creation of new categories, openness to new information, and an implicit awareness of more than one perspective. Mindlessness involves relying on past forms of action or previously established distinctions and categories.

It should be understood that there are different degrees of comprehension and mindfulness regarding becoming aware of one's thoughts. In adulthood, knowing how you know involves awareness of the context—sources, nature, and consequences—of your interpretations and beliefs and those of others. In adulthood, informed decisions require not only awareness of the source and context of our knowledge, values, and feelings but also critical reflection on the validity of their assumptions or premises.

Transformative learning refers to the process by which we transform our taken-for-granted frames of reference (meaning perspectives, habits of mind, mind-sets) to make them more inclusive, discriminating, open, emotionally capable of change, and reflective so that they may generate beliefs and opinions that will prove more true or justified to guide action. Transformative learning involves participation in constructive discourse to use the experience of others to assess reasons justifying these assumptions, and making an action decision based on the resulting insight.

Transformation theory's focus is on how we learn to negotiate and act on our own purposes, values, feelings, and meanings rather than those we have uncritically assimilated from others—to gain greater control over our lives as socially responsible, clear-thinking decision makers. As such, it has particular relevance for learning in contemporary societies that share democratic values. Because this theory particularly addresses the interests of adult education, as this vocation has evolved in the West, it assumes the perfectibility of human beings when this refers to improving our understanding and the quality of our actions through meaningful learning.

Transformative learning has both individual and social dimensions and implications. It demands that we be aware of how we come to our knowledge and as aware as we can be about the values that lead us to our perspectives. Cultural canon, socioeconomic structures, ideologies and beliefs about ourselves, and the practices they support often conspire to foster conformity and impede development of a sense of responsible agency.

Domains of Learning

Habermas (1984) has helped us understand that there are two major domains of learning, with different purposes, logics of inquiry, criteria of rationality, and modes of validating beliefs. One is *instrumental learning*—learning to control and manipulate the environment or other people, as in task-oriented problem solving to improve performance. The other is *communicative learning*—learning what others mean when they communicate with you. This often involves feelings, intentions, values, and moral issues.

Understanding in communicative learning requires that we assess the meanings behind the words; the coherence, truth, and appropriateness of what is being communicated; the truthfulness and qualifications of the speaker; and the authenticity of expressions of feeling. That is, we must become critically reflective of the *assumptions* of the person communicating. We need to know whether the person who gives us a diagnosis about our health is a trained medical worker, that one who gives us direction at work is authorized to do so, or whether a stranger who talks to us on a bus is just passing the time or trying to sell us something, proselytize, or pick us up. The meaning of the words the stranger uses depends on his or her assumptions.

Assumptions include intent, sometimes implied as a subtext; what is taken for granted, like conventional wisdom; a particular religious worldview; whether one means what is said and in what sense it is meant—literally or metaphorically, as a joke or caricature; the frame of reference; the character—liar, zealot, crook—and qualifications of the person communicating; and the relevance and timing of the communication and the context—biographical, historical, and cultural—within which what is being communicated makes sense. Communicative learning often involves a critical assessment of assumptions supporting the justification of norms.

Most learning involves elements of both domains. Hart (1990) pointed out that challenging premises involved in instrumental learning itself involves communicative learning. In instrumental learning, problem solving and inquiry follow a hypothetical-deductive logic (test a hypothesis; analyze its consequences). In communicative learning, inquiry assumes a metaphorical-abductive logic (make an analogy; let each step in understanding dictate the next one). Learning may involve a transformation in frame of reference in either domain.

We establish the validity of our problematic beliefs in instrumental learning by empirically testing to determine the truth of an assertion. In communicative learning, we determine the justification of a problematic belief or understanding through *rational discourse* to arrive at a tentative best judgment. The only alternatives to discourse for justifying a belief are to appeal to tradition, authority, or force.

Here rationality refers to assessing reasons supporting one's options as objectively as possible and choosing the most effective means available to achieve one's objectives. In instrumental learning, rationality is judged by whether we are able to achieve technical success in meeting our objectives (for example, use methods that result in improved performance). In communicative learning, rationality is judged by our success in coming to an understanding concerning the issues at hand.

In coping with the external world, instrumental competence involves attainment of improved task-oriented performance. But communicative competence refers to the ability of the learner to negotiate his or her own purposes, values, feelings, and meanings rather than to simply act on those of others (what I later refer to as autonomous thinking). We test our interpretations and beliefs instrumentally by hypothesis testing and empirical measurement when we can and justify them communicatively through reflective discourse when we cannot.

Although Habermas suggests a third learning domain, *emancipation*, transformation theory redefines this as the transformation process that pertains in both instrumental and communicative learning domains. Habermas also suggests two additional learning domains: *normative learning*—learning oriented to common values and an expectation of certain behavior reflecting those values—and *impressionistic learning*—learning to enhance one's impression on others.

Reflective Discourse

Discourse, in the context of transformation theory, is that specialized use of dialogue devoted to searching for a common understanding and assessment of the justification of an interpretation or belief. This involves assessing reasons advanced by weighing the supporting evidence and arguments and by examining alternative perspectives. Reflective discourse involves a critical assessment of assumptions. It leads toward a clearer understanding by tapping collective experience to arrive at a tentative best judgment. Discourse is the forum in which "finding one's voice" becomes a prerequisite for free full participation. Kegan (1994) writes that the two greatest yearnings in human experience are to be included and to have a sense of agency. Of course, agency is intimately dependent on others and on one's inclusion in discourse. Discourse always reflects wider patterns of relationship and power.

Effective participation in discourse and in transformative learning requires emotional maturity—awareness, empathy, and control—what Goleman (1998) calls "emotional intelligence"—knowing and managing one's emotions, motivating oneself, recognizing emotions in others, and handling relationships—as well as clear thinking. Goleman elaborates emotional competencies for each of these dimensions of emotional intelligence. Major social competencies include empathy (understanding others and cultivating opportunity through diverse people and political awareness) and social skills (adeptness in getting desired responses from others). Self-regulation includes self-control and trustworthiness (maintaining standards of honesty and integrity). Based on his extensive qualitative research, Goleman claims that emotional intelligence accounts for 85 percent to 90 percent of success at work, more than I.Q. or expertise, a view that Warren Bennis (1998) shares.

Our culture conspires against collaborative thinking and the development of social competence by conditioning us to think adversarially, in terms of winning or losing, of proving ourselves smart, worthy, or wise. Deborah Tannen (1998) writes of ours as an "argument culture," a cultural paradigm that conditions us to approach anything we need to accomplish together as a fight between opposing sides, like a debate or like settling differences by litigation. Political discourse becomes reduced to negative advertising. In televised or radio talk shows, public discourse becomes a process of finding spokespersons for different points of view who are the most extreme and polarized. We tend to believe that there are two sides to every issue and only two. We set out to win an argument rather than to understand different ways of thinking and different frames of reference, and to search for common ground, to resolve differences, and to get things done.

In an argument culture, the quality of information that we get is compromised: however bizarre and unwarranted a viewpoint may be, such as denial of the Holocaust, it becomes "the other side," as though everything has another side. Tannen's analysis of our argument culture is a valuable sourcebook for those who would facilitate transformative learning and have a priority in helping adults learn how to move from self-serving debate to empathic listening and informed constructive discourse.

Consensus building is an ongoing process, and a best collective judgment is always subject to review by a broader group of participants. A best (or more dependable) judgment is always tentative until additional evidence, argument, or a different perspective is presented that may change it. This is why it is essential to seek out and encourage viewpoints that challenge prevailing norms of the dominant culture in matters of class, race, gender, technology, and environmental protection. Agreement based on the unchallenged norms of a culture will be obviously less informed and dependable than those based on a wider range of experience.

Ideally, a best judgment is based on the broadest consensus possible, but consensus is not always feasible. In striving for consensus, it is important not only to seek a wide range of views but to allow dissension. Discourse requires only that participants have the will and readiness to seek understanding and to reach some reasonable agreement. Feelings of trust, solidarity, security, and empathy are essential preconditions for free full participation in discourse. Discourse is not based on winning arguments; it centrally involves finding agreement, welcoming difference, "trying on" other points of view, identifying the common in the contradictory, tolerating the anxiety implicit in paradox, searching for synthesis, and reframing.

If one has a totally revolutionary way of expressing understanding, she may be unable to find support from others. It may take years to convince the world of the validity of a revolutionary idea, but for the concept to become validated, if it cannot be proven empirically, its justification must eventually be established through discourse.

Our option in the face of paradox is to bridge, through ongoing negotiations, the simultaneous existence of mutually exclusive internal, external, and relational realities. Bruner (1990, p. 30) defines open-mindedness as "a willingness to construe knowledge and values from multiple perspectives without loss of commitment to one's own values." Reflective discourse involves what the Greek Skeptics called *epoche*, a provisional suspension of judgment about the truth or falsity of, or the belief or disbelief in, ideas until a better determination can be made.

The generic role of discourse in human communication implies certain conditions for its full realization (and, by implication, a set of conditions for optimizing adult learning and education as well). To more freely and fully participate in discourse, participants must have the following:

- More accurate and complete information
- Freedom from coercion and distorting self-deception
- Openness to alternative points of view: empathy and concern about how others think and feel
- The ability to weigh evidence and assess arguments objectively
- Greater awareness of the context of ideas and, more critically, reflectiveness of assumptions, including their own
- An equal opportunity to participate in the various roles of discourse
- Willingness to seek understanding and agreement and to accept a resulting best judgment as a test of validity until new perspectives, evidence, or arguments are encountered and validated through discourse as yielding a better judgment

The claim is that if everyone could participate in discourse under these conditions there would be a consensus supporting them as norms. These ideal conditions constitute a principle; they are never fully realized in practice. They imply, in effect, what Bellah and others (1985) refer to as "democratic habits of the heart": respect for others, self-respect, willingness to accept responsibility for the common good, and willingness to welcome diversity and to approach others with openness.

There is also a close relationship between the ideal conditions of discourse and what Belenky and her colleagues (1986, pp. 143–146) refer to as "really talking," in which emphasis is placed on active listening, domination is absent, reciprocity and cooperation are prominent, and judgment is withheld until one empathically understands another's point of view: "Compared to other positions, there is a capacity at the position of constructed knowledge to attend to another person and to feel related to that person in spite of what may be enormous differences.... Empathy is a central feature in the development of connected procedures for knowing ... attentive caring is important in understanding not only people but also the written word, ideas, even impersonal objects."

Discourse is the process in which we have an active dialogue with others to better understand the meaning of an experience. It may include interaction within a group or between two persons, including a reader and an author or a viewer and an artist.

Fostering discourse, with a determined effort to free participation from distortions by power and influence, is a long-established priority of adult educators. The generally accepted model of adult education involves a transfer of authority from the educator to the learners; the successful educator works herself out of her job as educator and becomes a collaborative learner.

Although not necessarily a good example of connected knowing, the ideal of a graduate seminar may serve in some respects as a model of group discourse. In a model seminar, there are a set of commonly accepted norms that support the ideal conditions of discourse—there is no outside coercion (other than that internalized as a result of prior experience or of being expected to come to the seminar informed on the concepts and issues to be discussed), everyone has an equal opportunity to contribute, participants are informed on the topic to be discussed, and there are norms of courtesy, active listening, studying issues in advance, and taking turns to talk. Academic freedom permits anyone to be critically reflective of established cultural norms or viewpoints.

To assess and fully understand the way others interpret experience requires discourse, and to understand and assess the reasons for their beliefs and understandings requires the ability to become critically reflective of their assumptions and our own. Culture, history, and biography determine the manner and degree to which these human faculties for intersubjectivity, reflective discourse, and mindful learning become realized in time and place.

Values like freedom, equality, tolerance, social justice, and rationality provide essential norms for free full participation in discourse; that is, for fully understanding our experience. Cultures and societies differ in the degree to which critical reflection and discourse are encouraged. In a democracy, like all such norms that influence educational, political, and moral decisions, they are, at least in theory, dependent for their validity on an informed consensus by those affected. This is a consensus arrived at through discourse free from domination; ideally, under the conditions specified earlier.

Preconditions for realizing these values and finding one's voice for free, full participation in discourse include elements of maturity, education, safety, health, economic security, and emotional intelligence. Hungry, homeless, desperate, threatened, sick, or frightened adults are less likely to be able to participate effectively in discourse to help us better understand the meaning of our own experiences. This is one reason why adult educators are dedicated to social justice.

Full development of the human potential for transformative learning depends on values such as freedom, equality, tolerance, social justice, civic responsibility, and education. It assumes that these values are basic to our human need to constructively use the experience of others to understand, or make more dependable, the meaning of our experience. One might argue that their claim as human rights and their political significance are predicated on this foundation. To borrow a phrase from Camus, without these values "even a transformed world would not be worth living in, and man, even if 'new,' would not deserve to be respected" (quoted in Fulghum, 1997, p. 77).

MEANING STRUCTURES

A *frame of reference* is a "meaning perspective"—the structure of assumptions and expectations through which we filter sense impressions. It involves cognitive, affective, and conative dimensions. It selectively shapes and delimits perception, cognition, feelings, and disposition by predisposing our intentions, expectations, and purposes. It provides the context for making meaning, within which we choose what and how a sensory experience is to be construed and/or appropriated.

Frames of reference are the results of ways of interpreting experience. They may be either within or outside of our awareness. Many of our most guarded beliefs about ourselves and our world—that we are smart or dumb, good or bad, winners or losers—are inferred from repetitive affective experience outside of awareness. Because of such affectively encoded experience, each person can be said to live in a reality different from anyone else's.

Our frames of reference often represent cultural paradigms (collectively held frames of reference)—learning that is unintentionally assimilated from the culture—or personal perspectives derived from the idiosyncrasies of primary caregivers. We tend to embrace frames of reference that complement each other. Particularly comprehensive and dominant paradigms or systems of belief that unite the particular with the universal become "worldviews," like the concept of *logos* in ancient Greece, Christian belief in the Middle Ages and Reformation, and science and technology in the twentieth century. One's frame of reference may include intentionally or incidentally learned philosophical, economic, sociological, and psychological orientations or theories as well.

A frame of reference is composed of two dimensions: a habit of mind and resulting points of view. A *habit of mind* is a set of assumptions—broad, generalized, orienting predispositions that act as a filter for interpreting the meaning of experience. some varieties of habits of mind are the following:

- Sociolinguistic (cultural canon, ideologies, social norms, customs, "language games," secondary socialization)

- Moral-ethical (conscience, moral norms)

- Epistemic (learning styles, sensory preferences, focus on wholes or parts or on the concrete or abstract)

- Philosophical (religious doctrine, philosophy, transcendental world view)

- Psychological (self-concept, personality traits or types, repressed parental prohibitions that continue to dictate ways of feeling and acting in adulthood, emotional response patterns, images, fantasies, dreams; for a Freudian interpretation see Gould, 1978; for a Jungian interpretation, see Boyd, 1991)

- Aesthetic (values, tastes, attitudes, standards, and judgments about beauty and the insight and authenticity of aesthetic expressions, such as the sublime, the ugly, the tragic, the humorous, the drab, and others)

Habits of mind include conservative or liberal orientation; tendency to move toward or away from people; approaching the unknown fearful or confident; preference to work alone or with others; ethnocentricity (seeing people different from your group negatively or as inferior); tendency to respect or challenge authority; thinking like a scientist, soldier, lawyer, or adult educator; interpreting behavior as a Freudian or a Jungian; approaching a problem analytically or intuitively; focusing on a problem from whole to parts or vice versa; introversion or extroversion; patterns of acting as a perfectionist, victim, or incompetent; fear of change; thinking conventionally about one's roles; occupational, disciplinary, religious, educational, capitalist, Marxist, or postmodernist; and many other orientations and worldviews.

A habit of mind becomes expressed as a *point of view*. A point of view comprises clusters of meaning schemes—sets of immediate specific expectations, beliefs, feelings, attitudes, and judgments—that tacitly direct and shape a specific interpretation and determine how we judge, typify objects, and attribute causality. Meaning schemes commonly operate outside of awareness. They arbitrarily determine what we see and how we see it—cause-effect relationships, scenarios of sequences of events, what others will be like, and our idealized self-image. They suggest a line of action that we tend to follow automatically unless brought into critical reflection.

Our values and sense of self are anchored in our frames of reference. They provide us with a sense of stability, coherence, community, and identity. Consequently they are often emotionally charged and strongly defended. Other points of view are judged against the standards set by our points of view. Viewpoints that call our frames of reference into question may be dismissed as distorting, deceptive, ill intentioned, or crazy.

Who we are and what we value are closely associated. So questions raised regarding one's values are apt to be viewed as a personal attack. Learning tends to become narrowly defined as efforts to add compatible ideas to elaborate our fixed frames of reference. However, this disposition may be changed through transformative learning.

A frame of reference that is more dependable, as we have seen, produces interpretations and opinions that are more likely to be justified (through discursive assessment) or true (through empirical assessment) than those predicated on a less dependable frame of reference. A more dependable frame of reference is one that is more inclusive, differentiating, permeable (open to other viewpoints), critically reflective of assumptions, emotionally capable of change, and integrative of experience. Insofar as experience and circumstance permit, we move toward more dependable frames of reference to better understand our experience.

TRANSFORMATIONS

Learning occurs in one of four ways: by elaborating existing frames of reference, by learning new frames of reference, by transforming points of view, or by transforming habits of mind.

Transformation refers to a movement through time of reformulating reified structures of meaning by reconstructing dominant narratives. The process may itself become a frame of reference, a dispositional orientation. As mentioned earlier, we transform frames of reference—our own and those of others—by becoming critically reflective of their assumptions and aware of their context—the source, nature, and consequences of taken-for-granted beliefs. Assumptions on which habits of mind and related points of view are predicated may be epistemological, logical, ethical, psychological, ideological, social, cultural, economic, political, ecological, scientific, or spiritual, or may pertain to other aspects of experience.

Brookfield (1995) emphasizes the importance of three common assumptions for critical reflection: paradigmatic assumptions that structure the world into fundamental categories (the most difficult to identify in oneself), prescriptive assumptions about what we think ought to be happening in a specific situation, and causal assumptions about how the world works and how it may be changed (the easiest to identify).

Transformative learning refers to transforming a problematic frame of reference to make it more dependable in our adult life by generating opinions and interpretations that are more justified. We become critically reflective of those beliefs that become problematic. Beliefs are often inferential, based on repetitive emotional interactions and established outside of our awareness. Frames of reference may be highly individualistic or shared as paradigms. Transformative learning is a way of problem solving by defining a problem or by redefining or reframing the problem. We often become critically reflective of our assumptions or those of others and arrive at a transformative insight, but we need to justify our new perspective through discourse.

Imagination is central to understanding the unknown; it is the way we examine alternative interpretations of our experience by "trying on" another's point of view. The more reflective and open we are to the perspectives of others, the richer our imagination of alternative contexts for understanding will be.

In instrumental learning we can transform our points of view by becoming critically reflective of assumptions supporting the *content* and/or *process* of problem solving. For example, in deciding how to assign grades to learners in a class, we may become critically reflective of the content of the problem: How might one select and assign value to different indicators—standardized tests, written work, teacher-made tests, participation, group work, and others? We may also become critically reflective of the process of solving the problem: Do we have a sufficiently representative sample of student performance in the selected indicators to make a fair judgment? Critical analysis of content or process in instrumental learning can lead to significantly improved performance by the educator.

We may transform our habit of mind by becoming critically reflective of our *premises* in defining the problem, such as by questioning the validity of our assumptions supporting the concept of competitive grading in the first place rather than focusing assessment on individual learner gains, and perhaps we take action on our reflective insight by turning to another form of evaluation, such as portfolio assessment.

Becoming critically reflective of assumptions underlying content, process, or premise is common in both instrumental and communicative learning. Reflectivity involves reasoning and/ or intuition. Both are significantly influenced by conditioned emotional responses. Many beliefs are generalized from repetitive interactions outside of consciousness. Transformations may be focused and mindful, involving critical reflection, the result of repetitive affective interaction or of mindless assimilation—as in moving to a different culture and uncritically assimilating its canon, norms, and ways of thinking.

Transformations in habit of mind may be *epochal*—a sudden, dramatic, reorienting insight—or *incremental*, involving a progressive series of transformations in related points of view that culminate in a transformation in habit of mind. For example, a traditionally oriented woman takes a late-afternoon adult education class. She may come to wonder why the other women in the class stick around to discuss interesting issues when she has to rush home to make dinner for her husband. She may engage in transformative learning by becoming critically reflective of her point of view on this topic. If she experiences a related progression of such critically reflective questions about her assumptions in several different situations, this can lead to a transformation in her habit of mind regarding her role as a woman.

Cohen (1997) describes how an educator can help adult students with negative experiences in school to feel more secure as learners in doing classwork. Over time, a series of these transformations in point of view about oneself as a learner ("I *can* understand these ideas") may cumulatively lead to a transformation in self-concept ("I am a smart, competent person")—a habit of mind.

We change our point of view by trying on another's point of view. We are unable to do this with a habit of mind. The most personally significant and emotionally exacting transformations involve a critique of previously unexamined premises regarding oneself ("A woman's place is in the home, so I must deny myself a career that I would love").

Transformations often follow some variation of the following phases of meaning becoming clarified (see Chapter 11):

1. A disorienting dilemma
2. Self-examination with feelings of fear, anger, guilt, or shame
3. A critical assessment of assumptions
4. Recognition that one's discontent and the process of transformation are shared
5. Exploration of options for new roles, relationships, and actions
6. Planning a course of action
7. Acquiring knowledge and skills for implementing one's plans
8. Provisional trying of new roles
9. Building competence and self-confidence in new roles and relationships
10. A reintegration into one's life on the basis of conditions dictated by one's new perspective

Clark (1993) found that an earlier stage of exploration may be followed by encountering a "missing piece" that provides the integration necessary for a transformative experience.

Frosty (1998, p. 72) observes, "From women's and black consciousness movements come insights that psychic transformations involve a revisioning of self in the eyes and responses of similar others and/or a beneficial cycle of desire, identification and re-apportion of a stronger subjectivity through relations with those who themselves successfully transcend oppression."

Boyd (1991, p. 198) has identified two fundamental steps toward a personal transformation: "making public, primarily for ourselves, the historical dimensions of our dilemma" and "confronting it as a difficulty to be worked through."

Transformative learning may occur through objective or subjective reframing. *Objective reframing* involves critical reflection on the assumptions of others encountered in a narrative or in task-oriented problem solving, as in "action learning" (Revans, 1982). *Subjective reframing* involves critical self-reflection of one's own assumptions about the following:

- A narrative—applying a reflective insight from someone else's narrative to one's own experience
- A system—economic, cultural, political, educational, communal, or other—as in Freire's (1970) *conscientization,* consciousness raising in the women's movement and the civil rights movement
- An organization or workplace—as in Argyris's (1982) "double loop learning"
- Feelings and interpersonal relations—as in psychological counseling or psychotherapy
- The ways one learns, including one's own frames of reference, per se, in some adult education programs—as in Isaacs's (1993) "triple loop learning"

Critical reflection in the context of psychotherapy focuses on assumptions regarding feelings pertaining to interpersonal relationships; in adult education its focus is on an infinitely wider range of concepts and their accompanying cognitive, affective, and conative dimensions. This distinction is important in differentiating between these two professional fields. Subjective reframing commonly involves an intensive and difficult emotional struggle as old perspectives become challenged and transformed.

A mindful transformative learning experience requires that the learner make an informed and reflective decision to act on his or her reflective insight. This decision may result in immediate action, delayed action, or reasoned reaffirmation of an existing pattern of action. Taking action on reflective insights often involves overcoming situational, emotional, and informational constraints that may require new learning experiences in order to move forward. As challenging one's cherished beliefs (a leap into the unknown) often invokes a threatening emotional experience, the qualities that constitute emotional intelligence are essential conditions of transformative learning. Freedom involves not just the will and insight to change but also the power to act to attain one's purpose. As Novak claims: "Perspective transformation represents not only a total change in life perspective, but an actualization of that perspective. In other words life is not *seen* from a new perspective, it is *lived* from that perspective" (quoted in Paprock, 1992, p. 197).

Tennant (1998, p. 374) sees as a test of transformative learning "the extent to which it exposes the social and cultural embeddedness and taken-for-granted assumptions in which the self is located; explore[s] the interests served by the continuation of the self thus positioned; incite[s] a refusal to be positioned in this way when the interests served are those of domination and oppression; and encourage[s] alternative readings of the text of experience."

Critical reflection, discourse, and reflective action always exist in the real world in complex institutional, interpersonal, and historical settings, and these inevitably significantly influence the possibilities for transformative learning and shape its nature. The possibility for transformative learning must be understood in the context of cultural orientations embodied in our frames of reference, including institutions, customs, occupations, ideologies, and interests, which shape our preferences and limit our focus. We need to become critically reflective of their assumptions and consequences.

ADULTHOOD

An adult is commonly defined as a person old enough to be held responsible for his or her acts. The assumption in democratic societies is that an adult is able to understand the issues; will make rational choices as a socially responsible, autonomous agent; and, at least sometimes, is free to act on them. Even partial autonomy requires communicative competence and transformative learning.

A sense of agency implies that one can understand perceptively. Such understanding requires the ability and disposition to become critically reflective of one's own assumptions as well as those of others, engage fully and freely in discourse to validate one's beliefs, and effectively take reflective action to implement them.

But learning theory must recognize the crucial role of supportive relationships and a supportive environment in making possible a more confident, assured sense of personal efficacy, of having a self—or selves—more capable of becoming critically reflective of one's habitual and sometimes cherished assumptions, and of having the self-confidence to take action on reflective insights. The power to control and determine our actions in the context of our desires and intentions is a definition of will. Transformative learning includes this conative dimension. The development of these dispositions is intimately dependent on others and, by extension, on wider patterns of relationship and power. Maxine Greene observes: "It is actually through the process of effecting transformations that the human self is created and re-created" (1988, p. 21).

Although it is clear that our interests and priorities change in the different seasons of our lives, development in adulthood may be understood as a learning process—a phased and often transformative process of meaning becoming clarified through expanded awareness, critical reflection, validating discourse, and reflective action as one moves toward a fuller realization of agency. For Robert Kegan, "transforming our epistemologies, liberating ourselves from that in which we are embedded, making what was a subject into object so that we can 'have it' rather than to 'be had' by it—this is the most powerful way I know to conceptualize the growth of the mind" (1994, p. 34).

Döbert, Habermas, and Nunner-Winkler (1987, p. 296) comment: "Finally adolescents form the notions of *heteronomy* and *autonomy*; they recognize the difference between existing conventions and justifiable norms. The orientation guiding action becomes increasingly abstract, focusing first on concrete need, then duty and finally autonomous will."

Although adolescents may learn to become critically reflective of the assumptions of others, becoming critically reflective of one's own assumptions appears to be much more likely to occur in adults (see Chapter 2). King and Kitchener (1994) have found that it is well into adulthood that we develop reflective judgment—the process of participation in critical discourse to assess reasons and make tentative judgments regarding contested beliefs.

TOWARD A PHILOSOPHY OF ADULT EDUCATION

Adult education may be understood as an organized effort to assist learners who are old enough to be held responsible for their acts to acquire or enhance their understandings, skills, and dispositions. Central to this process is helping learners to critically reflect on, appropriately validate, and effectively act on their (and others') beliefs, interpretations, values, feelings, and ways of thinking. Our human need to understand our experience, the necessity that we do so through critical discourse, and the optimal conditions enabling us to do so freely and fully provide a foundation for a philosophy of adult education. Kegan (1994, p. 232) notes that learning that reflects on itself can only be accomplished through transformational education—"a 'leading out' from an established habit of mind," an order of mental complexity that enables self-direction, a qualitative change in *how* one knows.

Siegal (1990, p. 58) describes a liberated person as one "free from unwarranted and undesirable control of unjustified beliefs, unsupportable attitudes and paucity of ability which can prevent one from taking charge of her own life." Fostering these liberating conditions for making more autonomous and informed choices and developing a sense of self-empowerment is the cardinal goal of adult education.

Acquiring the ability to make more autonomous choices is a process never fully realized. An autonomous choice is one in which the individual is "free to act and judge independently of external constraints on the basis of her own reasoned appraisal" (p. 54).

This process has to do with assessing reasons supporting beliefs. To do so effectively, this involves becoming critically reflective of their assumptions, validating assertions through empirical test or discourse, and making a decision to act on one's critical insight. For Siegal and Transformation Theory, critical thinking is coextensive with rationality.

The process of self-empowerment—acquiring greater control of one's life as a liberated learner—is, of course, always limited by social, historical, and cultural conditions. Sociologists, feminists, and ecologists have helped us become aware that human beings are essentially relational. Our identity is formed in webs of affiliation within a shared life world. Human reality is intersubjective; our life histories and language are bound up with those of others. It is within the context of these relationships, governed by existing and changing cultural paradigms, that we become the persons we are. Transformative learning involves liberating ourselves from reified forms of thought that are no longer dependable.

Jansen and Wildemeersch (1998) point out that social conditions for acquiring a sense of autonomy in our society often imply *qualifications*—that only through a particular kind and quantity of education may one acquire the abilities to participate fully in social and economic life. This assumes social integration; marginalized groups are often excluded. The implication is that social identity and full-fledged social and economic participation require the proper qualifications and that we all have equal access to the necessary education and training to become qualified. Of course, this is a shibboleth. A further assumption is that there are always rewarding career opportunities out there for those who are qualified. Adult educators are committed to efforts to create a more equal set of enabling conditions in our society, to the ideal of social justice.

The postmodern emphasis that a person is constructed from sources outside oneself is a valuable insight. Rubenson (1998, p. 257) observes: "Lifelong learning for all is conditional on a working life organized in a way that promotes the use of literacy and a society where people are encouraged to think, act, and be engaged."

There are obvious inequities in the social structure reflecting asymmetrical power relationships and perpetuating inequalities that profoundly influence the way one understands experience. Learners need to become critically reflective of how these factors have shaped the ways they think and their beliefs so they may take collective action to ameliorate them.

There is a reciprocity between democratic theory and transformation theory. Warren (1992, p. 8) contends that democracies inherently create opportunities for self-transformation: "[W]ere individuals more broadly empowered, especially in the institutions that have most impact on their everyday lives (workplaces, schools, local governments, etc.), their experiences would have transformative effects: they would become more public spirited, more tolerant, more knowledgeable, more attentive to the interests of others, and more probing of their own interests."

Transformation theory suggests that transformative learning inherently creates understandings for participatory democracy by developing capacities of critical reflection on taken-for-granted assumptions that support contested points of view and participation in discourse that reduces fractional threats to rights and pluralism, conflict, and the use of power, and foster autonomy, self-development, and self-governance—the values that rights and freedoms presumably are designed to protect.

Autonomous thinking may be understood as a competence acquired through transformative learning. Learning to become a more autonomous thinker clearly involves the interaction of personal and situational variables. We must ask: Who is granted the opportunity to achieve autonomous thinking? Who is excluded, cast as the Other to be excluded and, by implication, dominated? Tennant (1998, p. 370) challenges the postmodernist notion that autonomy implies an internalization of externally imposed disciplines of regulation, a way to produce cultural conformity.

Fostering greater autonomy in thinking is both a goal and a method for adult educators. (For a different view see Candy, 1991, p. 8.) As used here, achieving greater autonomy in thinking is a product of transformative learning—acquiring more of the understandings, skills, and dispositions required to become more aware of the context of interpretations and beliefs, critically reflective of assumptions, able to participate freely and fully in rational discourse to find common meaning and validate beliefs, and effective in acting on the result of this reflective learning process.

Autonomy here does not represent a fixed goal to be achieved or an arbitrary norm, but movement in the process of transformative learning toward greater understanding of the assumptions supporting one's concepts, beliefs, and feelings and those of others. Emancipation in this context is no search for certainty and control through totalizing explanations and the elimination of difference. Nevertheless, concepts such as autonomy, emancipation, rationality, education, and democracy are all contested meanings that require continuing critical reflection on their assumptions and practices, and validation through continuing discourse.

Learners may be helped to explore all aspects of a frame of reference: its genealogy, power allocation, internal logic, uses, affective and intuitive dimensions, advantages, and disadvantages. The frame may be understood as a coherent, meaningful way to organize events and feelings with costs and benefits that may be assessed. An intellectual and emotional grasp of a particular frame of reference opens space for the operation of others. The learner can look at the same experience from a variety of points of view and see that concepts and feelings depend on the perspective through which they occur. Kegan writes: "This kind of learning cannot be accomplished through *in*formational training, the acquisition of skills, but only through *trans*formational education, a 'leading out' from an established habit of mind" (1994, p. 232).

The broader purpose, the goal, of adult education is to help adults realize their potential for becoming more liberated, socially responsible, and autonomous learners—that is, to make more informed choices by becoming more critically reflective as "dialogic thinkers" (Basseches, 1984) in their engagement in a given social context. Adult educators actively strive to extend and equalize the opportunities for them to do so.

It is important to differentiate this goal of adult education from its objective—to help adult learners assess and achieve what it is they want to learn. Learning objectives may be personal, such as getting a better job or helping a child do homework, or may focus on social change (in the context of a social movement, some community development and literacy programs, or labor union education) or on organizational change. We need to recognize the difference between our goals as educators and the objectives of our learners that we want to help them achieve.

Transformative learners, with social or organizational change as objectives, seek out others who share their insights to form cells of resistance to unexamined cultural norms in organizations, communities, families, and political life; they become active agents of cultural change.

Adult educators are never neutral. They are cultural activists committed to support and extend those canon, social practices, institutions, and systems that foster fuller, freer participation in reflective discourse, transformative learning, reflective action, and a greater realization of agency for all learners. Justification for the norms derived from these commitments is continually open to challenge through critical discourse.

Adult educators do not indoctrinate (for an alternative view, see Hart, 1990, p. 136); in our culture they create opportunities and foster norms supporting freer, fuller participation in discourse and in democratic social and political life.

They make every effort to transfer their authority over the learning group to the group itself as soon as this is feasible, and they become collaborative learners. They model and share their commitment and act on their convictions by encouraging and assisting learners to critically assess the validity of norms from alternative perspectives, arrive at best tentative judgments through discourse, and effectively act on them. In social action contexts, such as social movements, labor and popular education, or community development programs, adult educators may choose to work with learners with whom they have a feeling of solidarity.

In fostering transformative learning efforts, what counts is what the individual learner wants to learn. This constitutes a starting point for a discourse leading to a critical examination of normative assumptions underpinning the learner's (and often the educator's) value judgments or normative expectations. (For methods of fostering critical reflection, see Mezirow & Associates, 1990, and Brookfield, 1995.)

Adult educators create protected learning environments in which the conditions of social democracy necessary for transformative learning are fostered. This involves blocking out power relationships engendered in the structure of communication, including those traditionally existing between teachers and learners. Central to the goal of adult education in democratic societies is the process of helping learners become more aware of the context of their problematic understandings and beliefs, more critically reflective on their assumptions and those of others, more fully and freely engaged in discourse, and more effective in taking action on their reflective judgments. Curricula, instructional methods, materials, assessment, and faculty and staff development should address both learner objectives and this goal of adult education.

References

Argyris, C. (1982). *Reasoning, learning, and action.* San Francisco: Jossey-Bass.

Basseches, M. (1984). *Dialectical thinking and adult development.* Norwood, NJ: Ablex.

Belenky, M., Clinchy, B., Goldberger, N., & Trule, J. (1986). *Women's ways of knowing.* New York: Basic Books.

Bellah, R., & Associates. (1985). *Habits of the heart: Individualism and commitment in American life.* Berkeley: University of California Press.

Bennis, W. (1998, Oct. 25). It ain't what you know. *New York Times Book Review*, p. 50.

Boyd, R. (1991). *Personal transformations in small groups.* London: Routledge.

Brookfield, S. (1995). *Becoming a critically reflective teacher.* San Francisco: Jossey-Bass,

Bruner, J. (1990). *Acts of meaning.* Cambridge, MA: Harvard University Press.

Bruner, J. (1996). Frames for thinking: Ways of making meaning. In D. Olson & N. Torrance (Eds.), *Modes of thought.* New York: Cambridge University Press, pp. 93–105.

Candy, P. (1991). *Self-direction for lifelong learning.* San Francisco: Jossey-Bass.

Clark, C. (1993). Changing course: Initiating the transformational learning process. In *Proceedings* of the 34th Annual Adult Education Research Conference (pp. 354–361). State College: Pennsylvania State University.

Cohen, L. (1997). I ain't so smart, and you ain't so dumb: Personal reassessment in transformative learning. In P. Cranton (Ed.), *Transformative learning in action: Insights from practice.* New Directions for Adult and Continuing Education, no. 74. San Francisco: Jossey-Bass.

Dirkx, J. (1997). Nurturing soul in adult learning. *Adult Education Quarterly, 74,* 79–87.

Döbert, R., Habermas, J., & Nunner-Winkler, G. (1987). The development of the self. In J. Broughton (Ed.), *Critical theories of psychological development* (pp. 275–301). New York: Plenum.

Freire, P. (1970). *Pedagogy of the oppressed.* (M. Ramos, Trans.). New York: Herter and Herter.

Frosty, S. (1998). *Psychoanalysis and psychology: Minding the gap.* London: Macmillan.

Fulghum, R. (1997). *Words I wish I wrote.* New York: HarperCollins.

Goleman, D. (1998). *Working with emotional intelligence.* New York: Bantam Books.

Gould, R. (1978). *Transformations: Growth and change in adult life.* New York: Simon & Schuster.

Greene, M. (1988). *The dialectic of freedom.* New York: Teachers College Press.

Habermas, J. (1984). *The theory of communicative action: Vol. 1. Reason and the rationalization of society.* (T. McCarthy, Trans.). Boston: Beacon Press.

Hart, M. (1990, Spring). Critical theory and beyond: Further perspectives on emancipatory education. *Adult Education Quarterly, 40,* 125–138.

Heron, J. (1988). Validity in cooperative inquiry. In Peter Reason (Ed.), *Human inquiry in action* (pp. 40–59). London: SAGE.

Isaacs, W. (1993). *Taking flight: Dialogue, collective thinking and organizational learning.* Cambridge: Organizational Learning Center, Massachusetts Institute of Technology.

Jansen, T., & Wildemeersch, D. (1998). Beyond the myth of self-actualization: Reinventing the community perspective of adult education. *Adult Education Quarterly, 48,* 216–226.

Kegan, R. (1994). *In over our heads: The mental demands of modern life.* Cambridge, MA: Harvard University Press.

King, P., & Kitchener, K. (1994). *Developing reflective judgment.* San Francisco: Jossey-Bass.

Kitchener, K. (1983). Cognition, metacognition, and epistemic cognition. *Human Development, 26,* 222–232.

Kundera, M. (1981). *The book of laughter and forgetting.* New York: Viking Penguin.

Langer, E. (1997). *The power of mindful learning.* Reading, MA: Addison-Wesley, p. 4.

Mezirow, J., & Associates (Eds.). (1990). *Fostering critical reflection in adulthood.* San Francisco: Jossey-Bass.

Paprock, K. (1992). Book review. *Adult Education Quarterly, 42,* 195–197.

Revans, R. (1982). *Origins and growth of action learning.* Bickly, Kent, UK: Chartwell-Bratt.

Rosenfield, I. (1988). *The invention of memory.* New York: Basic Books.

Rubenson, K. (1998). Adults' readiness to learn: Questioning lifelong learning for all. *Proceedings,* 39th Annual Adult Education Research Conference. San Antonio, TX: University of the Incarnate Word, pp. 257–262.

Siegal, H. (1990). *Educating reason.* New York: Routledge.

Tannen, D. (1998). *The argument culture.* New York: Random House.

Tennant, M. (1998). Adult education and technology of the self. *International Journal of Lifelong Learning, 16,* 364–376.

Warren, M. (1992). Democratic theory and self-transformation. *American Political Science Review, 86,* 8–23.

Weiss, J. (1997, Summer). The role of pathogenic beliefs in psychic reality. *Psychoanalytic Psychology, 14*(3), 427–434.

PART TWO

EXPLORING THE THEORY OF TRANSFORMATIVE LEARNING: DIVERSE PERSPECTIVES

Mezirow's Theory of Transformative Learning from 1975 to Present

Lisa M. Baumgartner

Individuals create theories that develop over time. Although scholars often cite the most recent version of a theory, there is immense value in exploring a theory's evolution. Only then can the theory be truly understood. When we observe its development, we can ponder the influence of historical time and other social forces on the theory, see the theorist's decision-making processes, and predict future developments.

The purpose of this chapter is to explore the progression of Mezirow's theory from its inception in the 1970s to the present. Next, I explore the theory's development in the 1980s, including Habermas's influence, the two paths to transformative learning, and Mezirow's differentiation between meaning schemes and perspectives. Key developments in the 1990s and 2000s include the expansion of critical reflection, the acknowledgment of relationships in the transformative learning process, and changes in terms. Critiques are noted throughout. I discuss the effect of the prominent educational philosophies in the field of adult education during the theory's development. Last, I reflect on the theory's development and future directions.

PUBLICATIONS PRIOR TO TRANSFORMATIVE LEARNING: INKLINGS OF FUTURE THEORY DEVELOPMENT

Scholars' writing agendas evolve over time, and Mezirow's is no exception. Mezirow's early writings regarding community development (1954), international program evaluation (Mezirow & Santopolo, 1960), and international adult education (Mezirow & Epley, 1965) demonstrate his interest in adult education initiatives abroad. By 1969, Mezirow lamented that theorists in adult education concerned themselves with "questions of social philosophy" (abstract) and Mezirow advocated "developing a research based body of theory, indigenous to adult education and of practical utility to practitioners" (1969, abstract). He explored ideas that appear in his early writings on transformative learning theory. For example, Blumer's (1969) concept of symbolic interactionism appeared in Mezirow's early work on transformative theory. Second, Mezirow's promotion of grounded theory (an inductive approach to data analysis) for the creation of theory (Glaser & Strauss, 1967) foreshadowed its use in his study on programs for reentry women.

Mezirow called for a theory indigenous to adult education when there was a nascent interest in theory building in adult education in the United States. Knowles (1968) had written about andragogy, and Tough (1968) had started investigating self-directed learning in adults. In short, the field of adult education appeared to be ready for theory development.

Mezirow's interest in deriving theory using a grounded theory methodology was perhaps unusual given the rise in data-based research using quantitative methodologies in the field of adult education at that time (Dickinson & Rusnell, 1971; Long & Agyekum, 1974). The use of sophisticated qualitative research methodologies was not as prevalent in adult education research during the mid-1970s as it is today. A rise in qualitative research-based articles appearing in *Adult Education Quarterly* would not occur until the 1990s (Taylor, 2001).

In addition to the adult education field being ready for a theory, larger sociohistorical events—namely the women's movement in the United States and its intersection with adult education—contributed to the development of Mezirow's transformative learning theory. By the mid-1970s, the work of liberal feminists and the women's liberation movement had been in the media for some time (Davis, 1999). Women's reentry programs had sprung up across the nation (Mezirow, 1978a). Discussions in these reentry programs prompted "a critical appraisal of sex stereotypes" (Mezirow, 1978a, p. 8), which led women to "new vistas of self-realization" (p. 8). This process would later be called transformational learning (Mezirow, 1978a).

TRANSFORMATIVE LEARNING THEORY: THE BEGINNING

Mezirow's transformative learning theory emerged from a study designed to "identify factors that characteristically impede or facilitate the progress of [women's] re-entry programs [at community colleges]" (1978a, p. 1). These programs helped women resume their education or return to the workforce after "an extended hiatus" (p. 1). The initial fieldwork involved twelve programs that were geographically, ethnically, and socioeconomically diverse. Data was collected on eighty-three women from four two-year colleges. In a follow-up study, an additional twenty-four campuses were included. Also, a survey was sent to 1,172 two-year colleges affiliated with the American Association of Community and Junior colleges, of which 314 had reentry programs. After the initial field data was analyzed, twenty women who attended consciousness raising groups and over fifty alumnae were interviewed "to secure evidence on the development of participants after the re-entry experience" (p. 57).

From this data, Mezirow and his research team unearthed a nonsequential, nine-phase process that resulted in a change in "meaning perspective," which he defined as "psychological structures with dimensions of thought, feeling and will" (Mezirow, 1978a, p. 108) and "a personal paradigm for understanding ourselves and our relationships" (p. 101). Mezirow continued, "By recognizing the social, economic, political, psychological and religious assumptions that shape these structures . . . we can reconstruct our personal frame of reference on self-concept, goals and criteria for evaluating change" (p. 7).

The phases were:

> (1) a disorienting dilemma; (2) self-examination; (3) a critical assessment of sex role assumptions and a sense of alienation from taken-for-granted social roles and expectations; (4) relating one's discontent to a current public issues; (5) exploring options for new ways of living; (6) building competence and self-confidence in new roles; (7) planning a course of action and acquiring knowledge and skills for implementing one's plans; (9) [sic] provisional efforts to try new roles; (10) [sic] a reintegration into society on the basis of conditions dictated by the new perspective. (Mezirow, 1978a, p. 12)

Elements integral to the transformative learning process included: "Taking the perspective of others" (Mezirow, 1978b, p. 104), making a "critical appraisal of assumptions underlying our roles, priorities, and beliefs" (p. 105), and deciding whether to take action on the new perspective. The decision to take action was more important than taking action. Stalling at certain points was common (Mezirow, 1978a).

Mezirow noted components essential to transformative learning and commented on the process. He believed it impossible for individuals to revert to the old perspective. He observed that culture enhanced and inhibited individuals' ability to engage in perspective taking and argued that societies that emphasized individuality and valued "contractual" relationships might encourage perspective transformation, in contrast to group societies that valued "organic" relationships steeped in family traditions, and "caste and class" (Mezirow, 1978b, p. 106).

Mezirow's theoretical underpinnings included references to Freire, Kuhn, and Fingarette (see Kitchenham, 2008 for more information). Mezirow saw similarities between Freire's concept of "conscientização" or conscientization and perspective transformation (Freire, 1970, p. 90). Freire's process included educators soliciting problems from villagers and facilitating critical reflection on these issues through dialogue (Freire, 1970). Mezirow stated that Freire "identif[ied] the development of critical consciousness as prerequisite for liberating personal and social action" (1978b, p. 103), recognized that the process began with a disorienting dilemma, and understood the importance of dialogue. Kuhn's paradigms or "universally recognized scientific achievements that for a time provide model problems and solutions" (Kuhn, 1962, p. vii) "became [Mezirow's] frame of reference" (Kitchenham, 2008, p. 106).

In addition to taking concepts from philosophers, historical time and educational philosophies shaped Mezirow's theory. Humanism was popular in the field of adult education, and Mezirow's theory appeared to fit somewhat with this philosophy. He focused on the ability of the individual to change and to achieve a more integrated perspective, and he recognized the role of others' support in the process (Mezirow, 1978a). Humanists believe that people are good, each person is unique and valuable, and everyone has the ability to self-actualize (Elias & Merriam, 2005). Humanistic teachers are student centered and believe that growth occurs in a supportive environment (Elias & Merriam, 2005). Some of the adult education literature at the time also showed a humanistic bent. For example, Knowles's attention to the self-concept of learners, their uniqueness, and the fact that learning needs to be personally relevant demonstrated his commitment to the humanistic philosophy (Elias & Merriam, 2005).

THE 1980s: EXPANSION AND REFINEMENT

In the 1980s, Mezirow refined definitions, expanded concepts, and absorbed some of Jürgen Habermas's ideas into his theory. Mezirow borrowed the concept of meaning schemes and perspectives from Kuhn's (Kitchenham, 2008) and Fingarette's (1963) work. Mezirow contended that perspective transformation was "the emancipatory process *of becoming critically aware of how and why the structure of psycho-cultural assumptions has come to constrain the way we see ourselves and our relationships, reconstituting this structure to permit a more inclusive and discriminating integration of experience and acting upon these understandings*" (italics in original) (Mezirow, 1981, p. 6). A perspective transformation involved a change in "meaning perspective," which Mezirow defined as "a personal paradigm involving cognitive, conative, and affective dimensions" (Mezirow, 1985, p. 22). A meaning perspective comprised meaning schemes—"sets of related expectations governing cause-effect relationships ... roles ... social action ... values ... and making connections between feelings and action [that] guide the way in which we experience, feel, understand, judge and act upon our situation" (p. 22).

Mezirow adopted Jürgen Habermas's three learning domains or "cognitive interests" (Mezirow, 1981, p. 4). Technical learning (or Mezirow's "instrumental" learning [p. 18]) concerned learning through deductive reasoning and hypothesis testing. Practical knowledge or "dialogic learning" (Mezirow, 1985, p. 19) happened through discussion with others, and meaning was validated though consensus. Emancipatory learning (or self-reflective learning) (p. 21) and knowledge occurred through "critical self-awareness" (Mezirow, 1981, p. 5). Critical reflection on one's belief systems or ideologies led to "emancipatory action" or "perspective transformation" (p. 6).

Mezirow asserted that the three learning processes could occur within meaning schemes, a new meaning scheme could also be created, and a meaning scheme or perspective could be transformed. Regarding the change within meaning schemes, the meaning scheme did not change but the "specificity of response" did (Mezirow, 1985, p. 23). For example, from a dialogical perspective, a person could learn that lying meant making up falsehoods *and* omitting facts. Regarding learning new meaning schemes, an individual might learn that leading a more balanced life is better than constantly giving to others. The meaning scheme's context does not change, and the perspective of helping others is strengthened and refined. When a transformation of a meaning scheme or perspective occurs, a false assumption is changed. For example, through discussions with others (dialogic learning), women recognized the sex-role stereotypes they believed to be oppressive (Mezirow, 1985).

Another concept that Mezirow borrowed from Habermas was the ideal conditions under which discourse could occur. Discourse was integral to transformative learning. Under ideal conditions, people could assess the validity of assumptions. Some of these conditions included having sufficient self-knowledge to avoid self-deception and enjoying an exchange of ideas sans constraints and coercion (Habermas, 1971, as cited in Mezirow, 1985).

Mezirow articulated the importance of various types of "reflectivity"—a concept that would be refined in later publications (1981, p. 11). Reflectivity occurs when we become "aware of a specific perception, meaning, or behavior of our own or of habits we have of seeing, thinking or acting" (p. 12). Types of reflectivity include affective, critical, conceptual, and theoretical. Theoretical reflectivity is central to perspective transformation and involves examining "taken-for-granted cultural or psychological assumptions" (p. 13).

In addition to claiming concepts from Habermas and championing reflectivity, Mezirow expanded his theory from nine to ten "elements" (Mezirow, 1981, p. 7) and declared that perspective transformation could occur through "sudden insight" (p. 7) or multiple transitions of assumptions. Phase three changed from critically assessing "sex role assumptions" to "internalized role assumptions" (p. 7). In phase four, Mezirow added that people recognized that their problem was shared with others. Phase five evolved from "exploring options for new ways of living" (1978a, p. 12) to "exploring options for new ways of acting" (Mezirow, 1981, p. 7). Step seven split into steps seven and eight and became (7) Planning a course of action and (8) acquiring knowledge and skills. Step nine changed from "provisional efforts to try new roles" (Mezirow, 1978a, p. 12) to "provisional efforts to try new roles *and to assess feedback*" (italics added) (Mezirow, 1981, p. 7).

In sum, during the 1980s Mezirow refined and added depth to his theory. People learned in a variety of ways, individuals engaged in types of "reflectivity," and dialogue became an important component in the transformative learning process (Mezirow, 1981, p. 11). Yet critics noted the theory lacked a focus on social change (Collard & Law, 1989).

A Critique of Mezirow's Theory: Collard and Law's Perceptions

As the decade closed, a critique of Mezirow's theory surfaced. Collard and Law (1989) charged that Mezirow's theory was not "a comprehensive theory of social change" (p. 102) and that it emphasized the psychological and individual. Mezirow's theory was not a critical theory because he failed to "address adequately questions of context, ideology, and the radical" (p. 106). Mezirow (1989) countered that social action was only one goal of education. He argued that individual transformation could lead to social action. However, action might not be taken because of barriers including a "lack of information" and an "absence of required skills" (p. 172). Mezirow asserted that Collard and Law saw sociocultural distortions solved only through "collective social action" and ignored "epistemic or psychic" distortions (p. 172). Although Mezirow defended his theory, Collard and Law's observations would shape future theory development.

THE 1990s: OF MEANING PERSPECTIVES, REFLECTION, AND PHASE REVISION

During the 1990s, Mezirow discussed different types of meaning perspectives and their distortions. He elaborated on the importance of relationships and types of reflection in the transformative learning process. He also received many critiques (Mezirow, 1991a).

Mezirow (1991a) discussed the three types of meaning perspectives including the epistemic (what knowledge is and how we use it), sociolinguistic (how language and society influence each other), and psychological. Each type was prone to distortions and remedied by a perspective transformation. Kitchener and King's (1990) reflective judgment scale exemplified changes in epistemic distortions. Stage one individuals believe knowledge is absolute, whereas people at stage seven understand that knowledge is constructed through "reasonable inquiry" (p. 124) (as cited in Mezirow, 1991a).

Sociolinguistic distortions included social norms and roles assimilated by people as children and reinforced by language (Mezirow, 1991a). For example, infant girls are described as "sweet" and "delicate" whereas infant boys are described as "strapping" and "active."

Psychological premise distortions are rules learned in childhood that prevent people from being fully functioning human beings. These beliefs might stem from childhood traumas. An example is Susan's belief that she cannot confront people because of a frightening experience from childhood (Mezirow, 1991a).

Perhaps the most notable addition to the theory was Mezirow's continued refinement of reflection. He defined reflection as "the process of critically assessing the content, process, and premise of our efforts to interpret and give meaning to an experience" (1991a, p. 104). If someone is investigating graduate programs, reflecting on the content of the problem might mean asking questions such as "What criteria should I use to determine the best graduate school to attend?" Process reflection might mean asking oneself, "Have I gathered enough material to determine which graduate school is the best?" If a person assumed she would attend graduate school and then asks, "*Why* am I attending graduate school?" this is a premise reflection. Mezirow contended that content and process reflections were made daily and precipitated changes in meaning schemes. Only premise reflection led to perspective transformation.

Mezirow (1998a) clarified the importance of critical reflection and proposed two kinds: critical reflection of assumptions (CRA) and critical reflection on self-assumptions (CRSA). CSA occurred when individuals engaged in content or process reflection. CRSA was synonymous with premise reflection. He noted that the term "critical reflection" was limiting and that perhaps "reframing" was more accurate, because it encompassed changes on the spiritual, psychological, and cognitive levels (p. 192).

Mezirow also proposed a taxonomy of CRA and CRSA. Objective reframing included narrative CRAs, which involved "critically examining the validity of the concepts, beliefs, feelings or actions being communicated" (Mezirow, 1998a, p. 192). Action CRAs meant stepping back to examine one's assumptions about a problem in order to solve it (Mezirow, 1998a, p. 192).

Subjective reframing included several types of CRSAs. Narrative CRSAs are "the application of Narrative CRA to oneself" (Mezirow, 1998a, p. 193). For example, a supervisor tells a student teacher that creating grading rubrics are a waste of time. The student teacher uses the grading rubrics and receives fewer challenges to his grading. He decides to continue using the rubrics. The systemic CRSA "involves critical reflection on one's own assumptions pertaining to . . . taken-for-granted cultural systems" (Mezirow, 1998a, p. 193). Organizational CRSAs include those "embedded in the workplace" (p. 193). The moral-ethical CRSA "involves a critique of the norms governing one's ethical decision-making" (p. 194). The therapeutic CRSA meant assessing "assumptions governing one's problematic feelings and related dispositions and their action consequences" (p. 194). A person might be afraid to engage in a group-based art project because of previous experiences in art class. Last, the epistemic CRSA looks at the "causes . . . nature . . . and consequences of . . . frames of reference" to understand why a person learns in a particular way (p. 195).

Mezirow also delineated the importance of rational discourse in the transformative learning process (Mezirow, 1991a). Conditions for this discourse expanded to include openness to alternative perspectives and the ability to weigh arguments "objectively" (p. 77) and to accept "an informed, objective, and rational consensus as a legitimate test of validity" (p. 78).

Mezirow refined and reordered his transformative learning phases. In phase two, he added that self-examination occurred "with feelings of guilt or shame" (1991a, p. 168). Phase three changed from "a critical assessment of personally internalized role assumptions and a sense of alienation from traditional social expectations" (Mezirow, 1981, p. 7) to "a critical assessment of epistemic, sociocultural, or psychic assumptions" (Mezirow, 1991a, p. 168). In phase five, Mezirow noted that there was an "exploration of new roles and relationships" (p. 168). The former phase six (building competence and confidence in new roles and relationships) changed to phase nine and the role of relationships was added. The former phase seven (planning a course of action) became phase six and the former phase eight, "acquisition of knowledge and skills for implementing one's plans," became phase seven (p. 169). The emphasis on critical self-reflection was evident in Mezirow's discussion of meaning existing inside oneself rather than in external items (Mezirow, 1991a). In 1994, Mezirow penned an eleven-phase process, adding "Renegotiating relationships and negotiating new relationships" between the 1991 phases eight and nine (Mezirow, 1994b, p. 224).

Critiques of Mezirow's Work in the 1990s

During the 1990s, the adult education field embraced critical and postmodern philosophies. Critiques on Mezirow's theory reflected this philosophical shift from humanism. Critical theorists examined how "society's ideas, structures, and actions are dominated by a single class" (Elias & Merriam, 2005, p. 173) and how positionalities (such as race, class, gender, and sexual orientation) privilege and oppress individuals in the educational context. Postmodernists resist "the unified, coherent subject as a human being" (p. 226). Humans are not "free, conscious, and self-determining," and truth is relative (p. 226).

Clark and Wilson (1991) analyzed Mezirow's theory through critical and postmodern lenses and asserted that context "play[ed] a subordinate role to individual agency" (p. 78) and ignored the influence of gender, class, and historical time. Second, Mezirow assumed a unified self, whereas individuals are multifaceted. Third, the theory reflected white, Western values of independence, self-direction, and human agency, which Mezirow presented as a universal experience. Further, Mezirow decontextualized rationality by introducing ideal conditions for discourse. Clark and Wilson acknowledged that "Mezirow has increasingly acknowledged [that] rationality is a highly contingent process with its meaning infused by its historical location in specific communities, its judgmental nature and its value-driven orientation" (p. 90). They recommended that Mezirow abandon his Habermasian ideal conditions for discourse in favor of "Bernstein's, Hawkensworth's, and Kuhn's understanding of rationality" (p. 90) because the importance of context was delineated in these theories. Mezirow (1991b) responded that he accounted for the cultural context, and that learning through rational discourse was embodied in a culture. An emphasis on individualism did not mean he advocated for individualism over collectivism. Further, his theory examined how adult learning is influenced by the cultural context. The theory showed how changing our cultural frames of reference can lead to transformative learning. Mezirow stated that he found Kuhn, Bernstein, and Hawkensworth's work "elaborative and supportive of transformative learning" (p. 192).

Michael Newman (1994) lauded Mezirow for "*recontextualiz[ing] the act of reflection*" (p. 239) but challenged Mezirow's decontextualization of action. People simply readjusted to society after their transformation, which could be seen as a "mainstream kind of action" (p. 240). Mezirow (1994a) countered that he "decontextualized both reflection and action in an effort to construct an abstract theoretical model of adult learning" (p. 243). Mezirow reminded Newman that reintegration was based on the new meaning perspective, which was not "a 'readjustment' to the status quo" (p. 244).

In another postmodern critique, Pietrykowski (1996) stated that Mezirow's theory was mired in modernism. Mezirow's education for emancipation "implicitly accepts a unitary conception of power and . . . leaves unquestioned the disciplinary matrix within which education takes place" (p. 90). Mezirow (1998b) agreed that learning took place in a social context and said he never proposed the ideal conditions of discourse as a goal; rather, he saw them as a set of standards "for . . . facilitating significant adult learning" (p. 239).

Cunningham (1992) charged that Mezirow believed that personal transformation was sufficient, regardless of social transformation. Mezirow (1992) countered that he addressed the influence of power by mentioning "hegemonic ideology, false consciousness, and other sociolinguistic premise distortions" (p. 251). He said that power relationships shaped epistemic and psychological factors but "the relationship between these factors and economic and cultural power relationships is seldom direct or easy to establish" (p. 251).

Mark Tennant (1993) criticized the intersection of perspective transformation and adult development. Tennant argued that Mezirow saw "'normative' psychological development as instances of perspective transformation" (p. 34). Tennant asserted, "[Mezirow] underestimates the power of social forces to shape, not only the lives of individuals, but theoretical accounts of those lives" (p. 37). Mezirow (1994b) replied that he saw no reason to differentiate between adult development and transformative learning; after all, "Perspective transformation is the engine of adult development" (p. 228).

Taylor's (1997) review of thirty-nine empirical studies that used Mezirow's model confirmed many of the aforementioned critiques. Researchers found the importance of "affective learning, nonconscious learning, relationships and the collective unconscious" was downplayed or not mentioned (Taylor, 1997, pp. 51–52). Second, studies showed the importance of context in the transformative learning process. Last, researchers found no empirical support for the ideal conditions for fostering transformative learning, ignored context in the fostering of transformative learning, and disregarded the practical consequences of fostering transformative learning.

Mezirow's responses to his critics included the refutation of a criticism, further explanation of a concept believing that he had not adequately explained his position, and a general welcoming of further debate. He retained his theoretical bases. For example, he maintained his belief in modernist concepts such as the unified self rather than adopting the postmodern concept of multiple selves (Mezirow, 1991b).

Nevertheless, Mezirow's critics pushed him to expand his theory. He responded to the charges that he did not adequately address the role of power in his theory but instead focused on the individual transformation over societal transformation, and that he gave short shrift to social action as "the essential objective of all transformative learning" (Mezirow, 1991a, p. 206). In his text *Transformative Dimensions of Adult Learning* he expounded on the role of power in discourse and the role of transformative learning as regards "social goals versus personal development" (p. 208), and he discussed the adult educator's place in social action.

THE 2000s: A THEORY-IN-PROGRESS

When Mezirow published his edited text (for example, Mezirow & Associates, 2000), he refined terminology, acknowledged the role of feelings in the transformative learning process, added a fourth way of learning, and recognized that a wider array of emotions could occur during the self-examination period.

In his terminology revision, "frame of reference" became synonymous with "meaning perspective" and was defined as "the structure of assumptions and expectations through which we filter sense impressions" (Mezirow & Associates, 2000, p. 17). Frames of reference are composed of a "habit of mind," expressed as a "point of view" (p. 17). A habit of mind is "a set of assumptions—broad, generalized, orienting predispositions that act as a filter for interpreting the meaning of experience" (p. 17). These habits of mind include sociolinguistic (such as "social norms," p. 17), moral-ethical, epistemic (such as "learning styles," p. 17), philosophical (such as "worldview," p. 17), psychological (such as personality types), and aesthetic (such as "judgments about beauty," p. 17). Mezirow stated, "A point of view comprises clusters of meaning schemes—sets of immediate specific expectations, beliefs, feelings, attitudes and judgments—that tacitly direct and shape a specific interpretation and determine how we judge, typify objects, and attribute causality" (p. 18). They are generally not conscious but determine how people see things. Rational discourse became "reflective discourse" (p. 10). Perhaps Mezirow changed this term to portray more accurately the role of reflection and to distance himself from the critiques of transformational learning being too cognitive and rational.

In a nod to his critics, Mezirow acknowledged the role of emotions and other components in the transformative learning process. Mezirow added fear and anger to his second phase and gave examples of transformative learning through emotion (Wiessner & Mezirow, 2000). Mezirow noted Clark's (1991) discovering of an integrating circumstance that might be necessary in the transformative learning process and recognized the importance of intuition.

In addition to updating terms and recognizing the importance of context, emotions, and integrating circumstances in his theory, Mezirow added an additional way to learn. He had stated in earlier work (1985, 1991a) that learning could occur through learning new meaning perspectives (or frames of reference), by elaborating new meaning perspectives, and by transforming habits of mind. He added that people could learn through transforming points of view by "trying on another's point of view" (Mezirow, 1985, p. 21).

By the mid-2000s, Mezirow's theory had been fodder for critique for thirty years. Merriam (2004) suggested that perspective transformation might require higher levels of cognition and suggested that Mezirow "substantively expand the theory . . . to include more 'connected,' affective, and intuitive dimensions" (p. 67). In 2006, Mezirow clearly summarized issues that had been raised over the years. He admitted that the role of emotion, intuition, and imagination had been underrepresented (Mezirow, 2006). He noted that intuition was necessary in transformations outside of one's consciousness and addressed the charge that his theory promoted decontextualized learning. He contended that critical self-reflection on assumptions involved "influences like power, ideology, race, class, and gender differences" (p. 29) but these factors could be "rationally assessed and social action taken appropriately" (p. 29). In answer to the criticism that social action was underemphasized, Mezirow responded that transformative learning theory is a foundation for learning how to take social action. In response to Brookfield's challenge that transformative learning theory was narrowly conceptualized and ignored issues of power and the questioning of hegemonic assumptions, Mezirow responded that Brookfield's focus concerned "critical reflection as ideological critique" which concerned individuals' recognition of how capitalism shaped their belief systems (Brookfield, 1991, as cited in Mezirow, 2006, p. 34). Also, "Brookfield is not suggesting a critique of all relevant ideologies" (p. 31). Transformation theory, Mezirow maintained, involved a critical reflection on "one's assumptions" and "it is not primarily to think politically" (p. 34).

REFLECTIONS ON THE PAST AND PREDICTIONS FOR THE FUTURE

Since 1975, Mezirow's theory has evolved from a rational process grounded in a particular context, with reference to concepts from psychology and critical pedagogy, to an increasingly holistic theory infused with ideas from Jürgen Habermas's (1971) conception of critical theory and open to the importance of emotion, context, intuition, and relationships in the transformative learning process. The nature of change to the theory tends toward seeing transformative learning as more a holistic, emotional, and intuitive process and perhaps a little closer in sentiment to the psychodevelopmental and psychoanalytic approaches of Robert Boyd and Laurent Daloz (Taylor, 2005).

Recent research seems to confirm this move toward more emphasis on spirituality (Merriam & Ntseane, 2008; Roberts, 2008) and the influence of childhood experiences (Maney, 2008), mindfulness (Matthieson & Tosey, 2008), and emotion (Snyder, 2010) on the transformative learning process. Researchers also noted that reflective discourse and critical reflection were not as important in the process (Bradshaw, 2008; Merriam & Ntseane, 2008).

An explicit discussion of the holistic process of socialization and its role in the transformative learning process would also make the theory seem more integrated. Because socialization is woven throughout the transformative learning process and includes talking and listening to others (for example, reflective discourse) as well as such social learning principles such as learning through observation and being reinforced by peers for appropriate behavior (Bandura, 1986), perhaps the explicit inclusion of social learning theory might be a path of future theoretical development for those who carry Mezirow's theory forward.

It is difficult to say what further theoretical developments will occur. Will neo-Mezirowians remain true to Mezirow's Habermasian-inspired theory but deemphasize Habermas's ideal conditions for reflective discourse and instead infuse the theory with concepts that expressly emphasize the role of context from Bernstein, Hawkensworth, and Kuhn, as suggested by Clark and Wilson (1991)? Will they adopt more ideas from depth psychology to make the theory closer to Boyd's (1989) conception of transformative learning? Will the theory change from a model presented in a linear fashion to an interactive model?

Regarding changes in the theory's ten phases, perhaps more thought will be given to listing the seven main emotions (fear, sadness, anger, joy, surprise, disgust, and contempt) in the second phase instead of restricting emotional reactions to self-examination as "fear, anger, guilt, or shame" (Mezirow & Associates, 2000, p. 22). Second, a discussion of how emotions are implicitly embedded in other phases of the transformative learning process might be in order.

How will this theory-in-progress evolve? As Taylor (2007) pointed out, studies have shown that context influences perspective transformation outcomes. Continued exploration of the effects of various contexts on the transformative learning process is warranted including the sociocultural (race, class, gender, and culture), interpersonal (such as the effect of support and stigma), temporal (for example, developmental stages in a person's life or social time, historical time, chronological time, and the passage of time), and situational (contexts specific to that person's experience, such as pregnancy) (Ickovics, Thayaparan, & Ethier, 2001; Neugarten & Datan, 1973).

In addition, one remaining question about the influence of context on the transformative learning process is how to effectively recognize its influence (Taylor, 2007). This can be challenging, because individuals occupy multiple contexts simultaneously. However, one could begin by critically reviewing studies from a particular context, looking for similarities in the transformative learning process. Second, a research focus on a particular context as it applies to transformative learning would be helpful. For example, how does the interpersonal context (such as support and stigma) affect the transformative learning process of those living with HIV/AIDS?

The effect of power in the transformative learning process remains a topic for further investigation. How does power affect the transformative learning process in different contexts? How is power evidenced in cultural expectations, and how does that affect the transformative learning process?

Another potential area for future development is a deeper investigation into the role of relationships in the transformative learning process. Scholars are beginning to discuss the nature of a transformative relationship, but more work needs to be done. It has been asserted that there was a "need for greater understanding of . . . aspects of relationships such as intimacy, trust, and empathy and their relationship to transformative learning" (Taylor, 2007, p. 188).

The role of emotions and their intersection with critical reflection in transformative learning will be an area of interest. "Little is known about how to effectively engage emotions in practice, particularly in relationship to its counterpart critical reflection, and the role of particular feelings . . . in relationship to transformative learning" (Taylor, 2007, p. 188). How does a transformative learning process triggered by happiness differ, if at all, from one in which the initial emotional reaction is fear? It has been argued that a certain level of cognitive development is necessary for transformative learning to occur (Merriam, 2004). Do individuals also need to achieve a particular level of emotional maturity to engage in transformative learning? Mezirow notes that transformative learning also requires a certain level of emotional intelligence (Mezirow & Associates, 2000). Perhaps new developments in brain research will also inform this area of interest.

Only time will tell how Mezirow's transformative learning theory will evolve. What is certain is that over the past thirty-five years, Mezirow's transformative learning theory has become more inclusive and integrative. Colleagues' critiques have caused Mezirow to expand the theory. Future critiques will only strengthen this theory-in-progress.

References

Bandura, A. (1986). *Social foundations of thought and action: A social cognitive theory.* Prentice-Hall series in social learning theory. Englewood Cliffs, NJ: Prentice Hall.

Bradshaw, E. I. (2008). When does transformation end? A phenomenological study of sustaining an intended change in behavior through perspective transformation in overweight management. Retrieved from ProQuest Digital Dissertations. (AAT 3297155)

Blumer, H. (1969). *Symbolic interactionism: Perspective and method.* Englewood Cliffs, NJ: Prentice Hall.

Boyd, R. D., & Meyers, J. G. (1989). Transformative education. *International Journal of Lifelong Education, 7*(4), 261–284.

Clark, M. C. (1991). The restructuring of meaning: An analysis of the impact of context on transformational learning. Retrieved from ProQuest Digital Dissertations. (AAT 9133460)

Clark, M. C., & Wilson, A. L. (1991). Context and rationality in Mezirow's theory of transformational learning. *Adult Education Quarterly, 41*(2), 75–91.

Collard, S., & Law, M. (1989). The limits of perspective transformation: A critique of Mezirow's theory, *39*(2), 99–107.

Cunningham, P. M. (1992). From Freire to feminism: The North American experience with critical pedagogy. *Adult Education Quarterly, 42*(3), 180–191.

Davis, F. (1999). *Moving the mountain: The women's movement in America since 1960.* Chicago: University of Illinois Press.

Dickinson, G., & Rusnell, D. (1971). A content analysis of adult education. *Adult Education Quarterly, 21*(3), 177–185.

Elias, J. L., & Merriam, S. B. (2005). *Philosophical foundations of adult education.* (3rd ed). Malabar, FL: Krieger Publishing.

Fingarette, H. (1963). *The self in transformation: Psychoanalysis, philosophy and the life of the spirit.* New York: Harper & Row.

Freire, P. (1970). *Pedagogy of the oppressed.* New York: Herder and Herder.

Glaser, B. G., & Strauss, A. L. (1967). *The discovery of grounded theory: Strategies for qualitative research.* Chicago: Aldine Publishing.

Habermas, J. (1971). *Knowledge and human interests.* (J. J. Shapiro, Trans.). Boston: Beacon Press.

Ickovics, J. R., Thayaparan, B., & Ethier, K. A. (2001). Women and AIDS: A contextual analysis. In A. Baum, T. A. Revenson, & J. E. Singer (Eds.), *Handbook of health psychology* (pp. 817–839). Mahwah, NJ: Erlbaum.

Kitchenham, A. (2008). The evolution of John [sic] Mezirow's transformative learning theory. *Journal of Transformative Learning, 6*(2), 104–123.

Knowles, M. S. (1968). Andragogy, not pedagogy. *Adult Leadership, 16*(10), 350–352, 386.

Kuhn, T. S. (1962). *The structure of scientific revolutions.* Chicago: University of Chicago Press.

Long, H. B., & Agyekum, S. K. (1974). Adult education 1964–1973: Reflections of a changing discipline. *Adult Education Quarterly, 24*(2), 99–120.

Maney, J. S. (2008). The child is the father of the man: Understanding transformative experiences of white college presidents around racial understanding. Retrieved from ProQuest Digital Dissertations. (AAT 3306517)

Matthieson, J., & Tosey, P. (2008). Riding into transformational learning. *Journal of Consciousness Studies, 15*(2), 67–88.

Merriam, S. B. (2004). The role of cognitive development in Mezirow's transformational learning theory. *Adult Education Quarterly, 55*(1), 60–68.

Merriam, S. B., & Ntseane, G. (2008). Transformative learning in Botswana: How culture shapes the process. *Adult Education Quarterly, 58*(3), 183–197.

Mezirow, J. (1954). The coordinating council in community development: An evaluation. *Adult Education Quarterly, 8*, 231–240.

Mezirow, J. (1969). Toward a theory of practice in education with particular reference to the education of adults. Paper presented at the Adult Education Research Conference, Minneapolis, MN. February 27–28, 1970. (ERIC No. ED 036 755)

Mezirow, J. (1978a). *Education for perspective transformation: Women's re-entry programs in community colleges.* New York: Teachers College, Columbia University.

Mezirow, J. (1978b). Perspective transformation. *Adult Education Quarterly, 28*(2), 100–110.

Mezirow, J. (1981). A critical theory of adult learning and education. *Adult Education Quarterly, 32*(1), 3–24.

Mezirow, J. (1985). A critical theory of self-directed learning. In S. Brookfield (Ed.), *Self-directed learning: From theory to practice* (pp. 17–30). New Directions for Continuing Education, no. 25. San Francisco: Jossey-Bass.

Mezirow, J. (1989). Transformation theory and social action: A response to Collard and Law. *Adult Education Quarterly, 39*(3), 169–175.

Mezirow, J. (1991a). *Transformative dimensions of adult learning.* San Francisco: Jossey-Bass.

Mezirow, J. (1991b). Transformation theory and cultural context: A reply to Clark and Wilson. *Adult Education Quarterly, 41*(3), 188–192.

Mezirow, J. (1992). Transformation theory: Critique and confusion. *Adult Education Quarterly, 42*(4), 250–252.

Mezirow, J. (1994a). Response to Mark Tennant and Michael Newman. *Adult Education Quarterly, 44*(4), 243–244.

Mezirow, J. (1994b). Understanding transformation theory. *Adult Education Quarterly, 44*(4), 222–232.

Mezirow, J. (1998a). On critical reflection. *Adult Education Quarterly, 48*(3), 185–198.

Mezirow, J. (1998b). Postmodern critique of transformation theory: A response to Pietrykowski. *Adult Education Quarterly, 49*(1), 65–76.

Mezirow, J. (2006). An overview of transformative learning. In P. Sutherland and J. Crowther, *Lifelong learning: Concepts and contexts* (pp. 24–38). New York: Routledge.

Mezirow, J., & Associates (Eds.). (2000). *Learning as transformation: Critical perspectives on a theory in progress.* San Francisco: Jossey-Bass.

Mezirow, J., & Epley, D. (1965). Adult education in developing countries: A bibliography. Pittsburg, PA: Pittsburg University. (ERIC Document Reproduction No. ED022086)

Mezirow, J., & Santopolo, F. A. (1960). Community development in Pakistan: The first five years. *International Social Science Journal, 12*(3), 433–439.

Newman, M. (1994). Response to *Understanding transformation theory. Adult Education Quarterly, 44*(4), 236–242.

Neugarten, B. L., & Datan, N. (1973). Sociological perspectives on the life cycle. In P. B. Baltes & K. W. Schaie (Eds.), *Life-span developmental psychology: Personality and socialization* (pp. 53–69). New York: Academic Press.

Pietrykowski, B. (1996). Knowledge and power in adult education: Beyond Freire and Habermas. *Adult Education Quarterly, 46*(2), 82–97.

Roberts, N. A. (2008). The role of spirituality in transformative learning. Retrieved from ProQuest Digital Dissertations. (AAT 3377924)

Snyder, C. (2010). "We see things not as they are. We see things as we are." Capturing the transformation of career changing women from STEP fields. Retrieved from ProQuest Digital Dissertations. (AAT 3391424)

Taylor, E. W. (1997). Building upon the theoretical debate: A critical review of the empirical studies of Mezirow's transformative learning theory. *Adult Education Quarterly, 48*(1), 34–59.

Taylor, E. W. (2001). *Adult Education Quarterly* from 1989 to 1999: A content analysis of all submissions. *Adult Education Quarterly, 51*(4), 322–340.

Taylor, E. W. (2005). Making meaning of varied and contested perspectives of transformative learning theory. In D. Vlosak, G. Kielbaso, & J. Radford (Eds.), *Proceedings of the 6th International Conference on Transformative Learning* (pp. 459–464). East Lansing, MI: Michigan State University.

Taylor, E. W. (2007). An update on transformative learning theory: A critical review of the empirical research (1999–2005). *International Journal of Lifelong Education, 26*(2), 173–191.

Tennant, M. C. (1993). Perspective transformation and adult development. *Adult Education Quarterly, 44*(1), 34–42.

Tough, A. (1968). Why adults learn: A study for the major reasons for beginning and continuing a learning project. Paper presented at the National Seminar on Adult Education Research (Toronto, February 9–11, 1969). (ED 025688)

Wiessner, C. A., & Mezirow, J. (2000). Theory building and the search for common ground. In J. Mezirow & Associates (Eds.), *Learning as transformation: Critical perspectives on a theory in progress* (pp. 329–358). San Francisco: Jossey-Bass.

CHAPTER SEVEN

Nurturing Soul Work

A Jungian Approach to Transformative Learning

John M. Dirkx

Transformative learning suggests not only change in *what* we know or are able to do but also a dramatic shift in *how* we come to know and how we understand ourselves in relation to the broader world. Most scholars of transformative learning would agree that this form of learning involves the making or remaking of meaning (Boyd, 1991a, 1991b; Cranton, 2006; Merriam & Clark, 1991; Mezirow, 1991; O'Sullivan, Morrell, & O'Connor, 2002). Although often perceived as a rational process, from a depth psychology perspective, meaning-making stresses more unconscious, imaginative, and extrarational processes. Scholars working from a Jungian or post-Jungian perspective (Davis, 2003; Stein, 1998; Whitmont, 1969; Young-Eisendrath & Dawson, 1997) focus on understanding the meaning of emotion-laden images that spontaneously and autonomously populate our consciousness within a given learning experience (Hillman, 1975; Watkins, 1984, 2000a, 2000b) and the stories or personal myths around which we seem to unconsciously construct our lives (Bond, 1993; McAdams, 1993; Stevens, 1995). Jung referred to this dimension of the human person as "soul." By this he was referring to the hidden, inner self (Stein, 1998). From this perspective, transformative learning involves making sense of these outward expressions of our inner selves.

In this chapter, I build on the application of depth psychology to adult learning initiated by Boyd and his colleagues (Boyd, 1991a, 1991b; Boyd & Myers, 1988; Boyd & others, 1991). In contrast to Mezirow's (1991) approach to transformative learning, which is characterized by a central reliance on fostering rational processes of critical reflection in adult learning, the theoretical perspective reflected here arose out of Boyd's long-standing efforts to understand more deeply and fully the unconscious forces that characterize dynamics of small, adult learning groups (Boyd, 1991a, 1991b). Boyd argued that Mezirow's theory focuses on the adaptive task of instrumentally responding to reality demands, whereas the depth perspective emphasizes relational, emotional, and largely unconscious issues associated with development of the individual, interpersonal interactions, and social development (Boyd & Myers, 1988). Although Boyd's approach may be seen as augmenting aspects of Meizow's theory, such as his characterization of the human psyche, it is important to recognize that this perspective stems from a research tradition initiated independent of Mezirow's work.

Relying on several Jungian and post-Jungian scholars, I have extended Boyd's work to the deeply emotional and image-laden contexts of transformative learning. I refer to this approach as nurturing soul or soul work (Dirkx, 1997, 2000, 2008a, 2008b).

A MAP OF THE SOUL

Jungian psychology provides a complex and unique understanding of human nature. Although many accounts of this approach are available, I rely primarily on the lucid and succinct descriptions of Stein (1998) and other Jungian and post-Jungian scholars (Davis, 2003; Young-Eisendrath & Dawson, 1997; Whitmont, 1969). They provide a kind of map that helps us better understand what it means to nurture soul in higher and adult education.

Central to our understanding of a Jungian approach to transformative learning is the concept of individuation. According to Stein (1998), "Jung used the term individuation to talk about psychological development, which he defines as becoming a unified but also unique personality, an undivided and integrated person" (p. 175). Psychological wholeness involves conscious and unconscious aspects of one's psyche. This idea "speaks directly to the interplay of conscious and unconscious, of outer and inner worlds" (Sonik, 2008, p. 97). The concept depicts people as naturally moving toward wholeness through recognition of and relationships with the unconscious and consciousness. By working on these relationships, individuals differentiate aspects of themselves and foster integrated connections among the various parts of their psyches.

Compensation reflects the process through which the unconscious expresses itself in a life largely dominated by the ego (Stein, 1998). As the ego gains strength and dominance in our adult lives, the unconscious compensates by manifesting itself in dream images and in other states in which the ego's control is reduced, such as emotional arousal. Perceived over time, these compensatory images demonstrate patterns or themes, which reflect important aspects of the unconscious. For example, recurrent dreams of being in an airplane that struggles to become airborne may mirror vague unease that one feels consciously about the direction of one's career. The ego is viewed not as captain of one's psychic ship but rather as one of several important structures in relationship with the greater whole of the psyche.

The Idea of Ego Consciousness

Educators working from a depth psychology perspective are concerned with the totality of the human psyche (Jones, Clarkson, Congram, & Stratton, 2008; Mayes, 2005, 2007; Neville, 1989). Understanding what this means and its implications for teaching and learning requires consideration of two sets of ideas that constitute an important foundation for understanding a Jungian approach to transformative learning: consciousness and the unconscious, and the personal and the transpersonal. As the term "depth psychology" implies, scholars working in this theoretical tradition stress the importance of understanding our "inner" worlds, of which we may be unaware. Conscious expressions of learning are interpreted as also possibly reflecting unconscious meanings.

For example, in a professional development workshop I attended, I found myself becoming increasingly agitated about how the leader was facilitating the experience. I initially attributed this agitation to sharp disagreements with the leader's approach to and depictions of the topic. From a depth psychology perspective, however, such an explanation fails to really account for the powerful emotional reactions I experienced. Something below the surface of this otherwise ordinary-looking experience seemed to be contributing in a powerful way to how I was making sense of this particular context of learning.

This concern for the inner, unconscious world arises from an abiding interest among Jungian-oriented scholars and practitioners in helping foster consciousness among individuals and collectives. Jung refers to this kind of awareness as "ego consciousness." According to Stein (1998), Jung defines "ego" as a term that "refers to one's experiencing of oneself as a center of willing, desiring, reflecting, and acting" (p. 15). It is the ego that comes to represent or mirror conscious content of the psyche. For us to become conscious or aware of unconscious content in our lives, it must be represented in some manner in the ego. Insights or epiphanies are examples of the ego making conscious connections with psychic content that was previously unconscious. Such experiences are usually associated with a surge of psychic energy or emotion, such as surprise, enthusiasm, excitement, or, in the case of the workshop example, anger.

Consciousness always stands in relation to the unconscious. Whereas consciousness refers to what we know, the unconscious constitutes what we do not consciously know. Psychic content that is conscious can be reflected on, examined, and worked with by the ego, but content that is unconscious cannot be readily accessed by ego consciousness. As with most matters that characterize the human person, consciousness develops; that is, we become more aware of our outer and inner worlds. For most people, the content that makes up consciousness constitutes relatively stable objects, such as thoughts, memories, and images. As we mature and develop, this content becomes expanded and more elaborate and our relationship with the unconscious more fluid.

The presence of the ego or a sense of "I-ness" emerges very early in our lives, expressing itself in the form of intentionality or willfulness. As we develop, many changes occur with our egos, related to "cognition, self-knowledge, psychosocial identity, competence, etc." (Stein, 1998, p. 21). These changes reflect a complex interaction of physiological processes, the press of and collision with factors in the outer world, and psychic energy. As we physically mature, we develop a growing awareness of our bodies, which contributes to a somatic basis for ego consciousness. The will, desire, and intentionality that gradually come to constitute ego consciousness sometimes clash with the outer environment, which also serves to shape this evolving sense of I-ness. Then, too, we gradually become aware of a sense of inner voice that, although sometimes reflecting or responding to demands from an outer reality, at other times seems to express a sense of autonomy that can surprise us and catch us off-guard, such as an emerging sense of calling or vocation that takes us in a different direction.

An ego develops that can either provide the person with a solid foundation for further growth and expansion of consciousness or limit development of consciousness. In the former case, ego development provides for an I-ness that, although sometimes frightened and uncertain, continues to seek challenges that serve to enlarge ego-consciousness (McRae & Short, 2010; Stapley, 2006). If a solid foundation for ego consciousness does not develop, a sense of I-ness may emerge that responds to new challenges or conflicts with heightened anxiety and seeks to draw back or retreat from growth and development. For example, learners with a less well-developed ego consciousness may find interpersonal conflict very threatening.

Amidst the emerging ego consciousness and the change associated with this development, however, we retain a sense of continuity reflecting the essence of our ego. As a middle-aged adult, I recognize aspects of myself that seem the same as when I was five or fifteen. Sometimes when I feel abused in my relationships with authority figures, my consciousness is animated by the image of myself in seventh-grade gym class, being grabbed around the back of my neck by an angry teacher. Our here-and-now experiences are constantly visited by images from our past, providing us with both a sense of continuity and a sense of change. There remains amidst this evolving sense of consciousness a sense of I that suggests an enduring presence of the self—an important element in a Jungian approach to transformative learning.

The Structures and Dynamics of the Unconscious

Enlargement of ego-consciousness, through our interactions and relationships with both our inner and outer worlds, represents an important aim of transformative learning. The primary focus of soul work is the establishment and elaboration of a conscious relationship with one's unconscious. Helping adult learners represent in consciousness psychic content that was previously unconscious characterizes a significant dimension of this particular approach (Boyd, 1991a; Boyd & Myers, 1988; Dirkx, 2000; Dobson, 2008) and represents the heart of what nurturing soul means.

As we mature, the need for adaptation arises from forces within ourselves. Reflecting a process of compensation (Stein, 1998), these forces manifest themselves as disruptions of consciousness, such as powerful feelings, emotions, or images that seem out of proportion to any demands originating from the outer environment, what I have referred to as "messengers of the soul" (Dirkx, 1997). Palmer (1998) talks about a "loss of heart" among experienced, deeply committed teachers. A redistribution of psychic energy occurs and there seems to be no external event or change that can readily be identified as responsible for such a shift. Loss of heart and midlife issues (Hollis, 1993, 2005) often represent explicit or empirical expressions of soul—manifestations of the unconscious compensating for the one-sidedness of the ego in one's life.

Psychic energy associated with these unconscious elements will manifest itself in various ways in our lives and provide us with invitations for further growth of consciousness. These "disturbances" of consciousness constitute the growing importance of our inner worlds or what Stein refers to as the "interior" of our lives. Take, for example, Mary, a middle-aged woman (Boyd, 1991a). She had enrolled in a course on group dynamics and found, after a few meetings, that her involvement in the group reminded her of her relationship with her mother and some of the difficulties that she had experienced in that relationship. Mary eventually came to see how the group had come to be for her an image of a powerful containing mother, evoking in her emotions related to her relationship with her own mother. She realized how she had been projecting these difficult inner forces onto the group and her relationship with it. Although the explicit focus of this experience was on developing a deeper understanding of the dynamics of instructional groups, it stimulated in Mary semi-autonomous forces that shaped her awareness and consciousness of the experience and how she made sense of her being in the group. Working through these experiences was, for her, a powerful example of transformative learning.

Another important term in a Jungian approach to transformative learning is the notion of "constellation." Jung refers to a person who is "constellated" as taking "up a position from which he can be expected to react in a quite definite way" (Jung, CW, vol 8, cited in Stein, 1998, p. 43). For example, certain teacher behaviors or situations will evoke among some learners fairly predictable responses, such as heightened anxiety over what might be perceived to be a lack of structure or direction, or smoldering anger arising from a teacher who is perceived as overly directive. Reacting in this manner manifests the constellation of a complex, reflecting a continuum ranging from a modest emotional arousal to being completely overwhelmed and losing touch with the reality of a given situation. We fear this loss of control over our emotions, our behavior, or even our bodies because we recognize that we become subject to a force that is greater than the will arising from ego consciousness.

The process of constellating complexes or, more colloquially, having our buttons pushed, suggests that these psychic entities possess their own energy, and it is this energy that sometimes threatens to break through or even overwhelm ego-consciousness, occasionally obliterating our sense of I-ness. If this occurs, the ego is no longer "in charge" of one's relationships and interactions with one's outer reality. When we act under the influence of powerful emotions, without the mediation of a conscious ego, we often do or say things we later tend to regret, or even deny.

Fortunately, most individuals with a well-developed sense of ego-consciousness are able to modulate the influence of complexes in most contexts. In a given situation that may constellate some aspect of a complex, we are usually able to control the ways in which this emotion becomes manifest; sometimes we even manage to completely avoid its expression in the social context in which we find ourselves. We readily experience a variety of emotions in such contexts (Dirkx, 2008a), and sometimes, as teachers or learners, these emotions influence and even direct our classroom behaviors. Rarely, however, do these emotional forces overwhelm our consciousness to the point where we completely lose control or are not able to behave in ways that are appropriate to the context. The ability to recognize and address these powerful emotional reactions represents a major focus for soul work and transformative learning for the educator (Dirkx, 2008b).

The downside of this ability to modulate or control emotions associated with constellated complexes is that we may do it so often and get so good at it that we loose touch with these powerful inner voices. Then the psychic energy associated with these complexes fails to gain conscious expression or voice and may, when we least expect it, erupt into consciousness in powerful and very disruptive ways. We often see this when people "overreact" to a particular event or stimulus in their environment—as we often say in the American Midwest, making a mountain of a molehill. Before we explore what this work looks like in teaching and learning, we need to consider one more important facet of Jung's theory. As it turns out, the unconscious is more complex than we might imagine, but it is this very complexity that represents the heart of the transformative process in Jungian psychology—the realization of wholeness of the self (Harding, 1956).

The Role of the Transpersonal in Transformative Learning

Although this role is less well known in the scholarship on transformative learning, several authors have argued for the importance of the transpersonal in understanding and facilitating this phenomenon in teaching and learning (Ferrer, 2002). In addition to the personal dimension, our unconscious lives reflect collective dynamics as well, such as may be evident in families, peer groups, professional affiliations, and even the broader society. This phenomenon is referred to as a cultural complex (Gozawa, 2009; Singer & Kimbles, 2004). People who grow up in the same family, community, or culture share a common unconscious structure (Stein, 1998). This collective phenomenon is readily apparent within education in the dynamics that often come to characterize learning groups (Boyd & Dirkx, 1991; Dirkx, 1991; Stapley, 2006). These groups tend to develop their own personalities, complete with their own hot buttons.

Similar to the individual, groups or broader collectives develop ways to limit the disruption of unconscious forces in the broader context of reality, usually in the form of some kind of defense mechanism, such as denial, scapegoating or, more commonly in academic circles, rationalization or intellectualization. Defense mechanisms are ways that the ego seeks to prevent certain unconscious contents that it may not be ready to address. Yet the psychic energy associated with these dynamics will continue to seek expression in some form in the social context. Unless these powerful emotional dynamics are recognized and integrated with the broader consciousness of the collective, they may at some point overwhelm the collective's ability to develop and sustain effective adaptations to the demands of the broader reality. This development is often evident in learning groups that seem to lose steam or energy, in cohort groups that develop cliques or subgroups that engage in ongoing but fruitless conflict, or in the development of scapegoats within broader society, such as the desire to define a common enemy after some kind of attack, as occurred after the September 11, 2001, terrorist attacks in the United States.

NURTURING SOUL IN ADULT LEARNING

The process of soul work reflects an appreciation for that which is not at the surface in specific contexts, of the ways in which the inner worlds of the individual come to be a voice for the inner worlds of the collective (Sardello, 2004), and how the inner worlds of the collective shape the meanings we construct at an individual level. Being in relationship is a dominant theme in the research and theory in transformative learning. From a Jungian perspective, the dynamics and processes of relationship are approached mythopoetically (Dirkx, 2008b); that is, the meaning we construe through and in relationships about our selves and our being in the world arises from our innate ability to generate or frame our lives in the context of stories (Bond, 1993; McAdams, 1993; Stevens, 1995). These stories reflect both the personal trajectories of our individual lives and the ways in which these personal lives participate in and reflect their presence in a broader, collective story. Nurturing soul depends on imaginative engagement and elaboration of the inner stories, the private myths (Stevens, 1995) that seem to implicitly guide and inform our lives. Deepening our understanding of our relationship with the unconscious requires our ability to name, describe, elaborate, and give life to the stories that reflect the voice of the soul.

Attending to Expressions of Soul in Teaching and Learning

The first step in nurturing soul is to simply awaken and attend to its manifestation in the learning setting. Soul becomes expressed or awakened through several avenues in teaching and learning. The subject matter and the assigned texts or readings are often evocative of underlying unconscious issues in groups and individuals. For example, in one class students were engaged in discussing assigned readings for the week. Discussion over the first couple readings seemed forced and somewhat lifeless, without much spirit or heart. As the group began to discuss a third reading, however, participation in the discussion rose suddenly and dramatically, as did the actual volume in the room. Almost all members of the group were actively engaged, animatedly arguing and disputing one another's claims and introducing counterarguments.

A literal and manifest interpretation of this experience would perhaps suggest that the discussion got participants to think and reflect at a fairly high level, and that through the discussion a deeper understanding of the content was being fostered. Soul, however, appears here not in the manifest content of the interactions but in the symbolic meaning revealed through the group's dynamics in response to the assigned reading. Why was so much energy invested in discussing this particular article but not in the first two? Was there something about the topic that connected with more of the students in some way? If so, what was it? From a symbolic perspective, what was this high level of energy and excitement saying about what was emotionally meaningful to this group? By raising such questions with the learning group during a debriefing of the class discussion, a facilitator is attending to matters of soul. The questions themselves suggest seeing or understanding the discussion in a way that invites the learners to consider what is less visible in the room but still quite powerful.

A couple of years ago I observed a math class for dislocated workers who were pursuing retraining. For many of these former factory workers, the idea of math itself provoked high levels of fear and anxiety. A literal interpretation of these emotions might attribute their appearance to the students' self-perceptions of their math abilities. In talking with many of these students later, it became clear to me that these emotions expressed much more about the learners' relationships with themselves and with the teacher, informed by earlier, emotionally negative experiences of schooling (Dirkx & Dang, 2009).

In addition to the content of learning, the relationships and interactions that comprise the contexts of learning groups can also be an invitation to the expression of soul. For example, the case of Mary, discussed earlier, demonstrates how the relationships she established with the group as a whole provided for a more symbolic understanding of unconscious issues that were shaping her understanding and meaning-making within the group. Online courses that make extensive use of collaboration and interaction also can awaken soul (Dirkx & Smith, 2003). Entering into and working within relationships online requires not only that students have skills to work collaboratively but that they also are able to work given the emotional uncertainty and ambiguity that such learning arrangements often evoke.

Working with Emotions and Emotion-Laden Images in Adult Learning

Attending to emotions and emotion-laden images in teaching and learning is a little like waking up and realizing you have been dreaming and that in the dreams were very some disquieting images. The question now is, what will you as a teacher do with this awareness that there is another reality evident in the learning experience—one beyond the literal and manifest, one that suggests an imaginal knowing (Leonard & Willis, 2008)?

The general approach used to nurture soul work is referred to as the imaginal method (Corbin, 2000; Durand, 2000; Watkins, 2000a, 2000b), consisting of several components. Specific emotion-laden images or issues represent the focus for this method. These issues or images are attended to through careful observation and description, including the context, feelings associated with the experience, actors involved, and relationships and interactions.

Another component of the imaginal method is the process of association. In this part of the method, the student describes how this particular image or issue reflects similar experiences from the past. For example, a learner finds that she is irritated by the teacher's unwillingness to provide more structure and direction for her group. In reflecting on this issue, she notes that there have been several other instances in which she experienced similar emotions relative to other teachers' actions. She describes these situations and realizes that, in each instance, similar emotions were evoked and the circumstances of the situation were similar. She observes that some of these experiences occurred as early as high school and that such experiences have been occurring with some regularity in similar contexts throughout college and graduate school.

A third component of the imaginal method is amplification. In this process, the student makes use of popular culture, literature, and mythology to enlarge and expand the meaning of the original image. This step broadens the work beyond the individual to the collective. For example, in reflecting on her irritation with her teacher, Jane notices similar experiences in certain popular movies, in which students' interactions with teachers reflect similar content and emotions. She notices how related stories are depicted in well-known novels and even in mythology. This work demonstrates to Jane that her experiences of irritation and impatience with the teacher are shared experiences, not only with others in her time but also in other historical periods and cultures. These experiences suggest that she is participating in something that transcends her own individual experiences. Although she may continue to experience similar emotions in the future, she is less likely to act out these emotions in ways that are not helpful to her or to her peers in the learning group.

The fourth aspect of an imaginal method is animating the original image. In this process, students are encouraged to engage the image and to enter into an imaginal dialogue with the image (Waktins, 2000a). This process is usually undertaken in written form but can also make use of the empty chair technique. In written form, the learner begins a written dialogue with the image of interest and invites the image to respond. The learner is encouraged not to think about the entries but to simply record what enters consciousness. The imaginal dialogue is usually limited to a set period of time, such as twenty minutes.

The empty chair technique is simply a role-playing variation of the written method. In this technique, an empty chair can be placed opposite where the learner is seated. The student personifies the emotion-laden image and then initiates a dialogue with this image. As the dialogue unfolds, the student moves to the empty chair and assumes the role of the personified image, speaking back to the chair of the student. Again, this process continues for a set period of time. Following this process, the student is encouraged to reflect on the dialogue and the affect associated with the process. Often, the student will experience new and deeper insights into the original experience, identifying and connecting with aspects of the self of which he or she was previously unaware.

The imaginal method helps students identify emotion-laden issues that often represent various manifestations of unconscious issues evoked in the context of teaching and learning. Through the process of observing and reflecting, they befriend powerful aspects of their inner lives and establish a relationship with unconscious psychic content.

IMPLICATIONS FOR A TRANSFORMATIVE EDUCATION

In this chapter I present a particular view of transformative learning that is theoretically grounded in a depth understanding of the human psyche.

Others have provided similar efforts, using different theoretical lenses (Cranton, 2006; Freire, 1976; Kegan & Lahey, 2001; Mezirow, 1991; O'Sullivan, Morrell, & O'Connor, 2002). Still others argue for developing a more integral approach to transformative learning and transformative education (Ferrer, Romero, & Albareda, 2010; Kriesberg, 2010). This scholarship suggests that the theory and practice of transformative learning reflects ways of knowing and helping adults learn that extends well beyond the initial ideas framed by the notion of andragogy. The kinds of learning and change reflected in these different theoretical perspectives underscores the complexity of the human condition and how our sense of self and ways of coming to know are intimately bound up with our deep relationships with ourselves, as well as one another, our social contexts, and the broader world. Bringing about deep change involves far more than just developing and implementing new policy or providing workshops for faculty on new techniques and strategies for fostering transformative learning. The kinds of change represented in this chapter, as well as in the work of others who seek to understand more deeply the theoretical foundations of transformative learning, require a deeper sense of self-knowing. This change process involves and occurs in relationships that range from the relationship of the learner with unknown aspects of herself or himself to relationships with other learners, teachers, groups, the organization, and broader society. To bring about the deep and lasting change that is the aim of transformative learning is to bring about deep and lasting change in these relationships.

Jungians and post-Jungians are not known for their contributions to critical theory. At the core of such theory, however, is the task of addressing the potentially distorting effects of coercive forces on human consciousness from both within and without. Our present political environment in the United States represents a good example of how forces from without can quite effectively mold and shape the consciousness of individuals and groups in a society.

The struggle for ego consciousness and, later, for a constructive role of the unconscious in our lives can create experiences of unease and anxiety. It takes courage to embrace such messages, which populate our everyday experiences and seek to give voice to the powerful inner forces being evoked by the particular sociocultural contexts in which we live. How we come to understand and make sense of their manifestations in our lives depends on our individual and collective willingness to engage in the inner work—the soul work—that is necessary to avoid being possessed by these forces (Zweig & Wolf, 1997).

Our learning contexts in adult and higher education represent microcosms in which these broader psychological, social, and cultural dynamics play out. These contexts often mirror in various ways many of the processes and structures that characterize larger sociocultural contexts in which they are embedded. As such, they have the potential to evoke powerful emotions and emotion-laden images at the personal and group levels. Jungian and post-Jungian theory, through its emphasis on the symbolic and the imaginal, is well-suited to help educators and learners understand more deeply the symbolic meanings associated with many of the actions, processes, and structures that evolve in our learning settings. The imaginal is not intended to take the place of more analytic, reflective, and rational processes that have been associated with transformative learning. Rather, it is intended to provide a more holistic and integrated way of framing the meaning-making that occurs in contemporary contexts for adult learning.

As practitioners who work with adults in various educational contexts, we play a critical role, whether we choose to consciously acknowledge it or not, in the individuation processes of our learners. Hardly a day goes by in my own work with students in which I don't witness the gentle and sometimes not so gentle knocking of the soul on the doors of consciousness. Sometimes this seems to occur primarily with individuals, but other times it feels like a group phenomenon. Even in my online teaching, I am challenged on a regular basis by dramatic and potentially disruptive emotional dynamics that occur within and among the learning teams. If I am honest and step back away from my academic program, I can sometimes even sense invitations from the soul in the broader collective of our faculty group or our relationships as a group with our students.

The kind of transformative education being advocated here, however, requires a true paradigm shift in one's ways of thinking about teaching and learning. I am referring to a fundamentally different way of making sense of our lives as teachers and learners. This paradigm shift involves decentering the ego and ego consciousness in the learning process and allowing our inner selves greater expression and voice, allowing for a deeper and more meaningful presence of the imagination and the spontaneous and semi-autonomous forces of the unconscious to which it is giving voice. This paradigm shift requires a reconnection, an ongoing dialogue of the ego with these deeper, unconscious, and extrarational aspects of the human psyche, both individually and collectively. It is a way of thinking about our work that recognizes the experience of meaning as always coming from both within and without. It is about attending to and nurturing soul.

References

Bond, D. S. (1993). *Living myth: Personal meaning as a way of life*. Boston: Shambala.

Boyd, R. D. (1991a). Mary: A case study of personal transformation in a small group. In R. D. Boyd & others (Eds.), *Personal transformation in small groups: A Jungian perspective* (pp. 179–202). London: Routledge.

Boyd, R. D. (1991b). The matrix model: A conceptual framework for small group analysis. In R. D. Boyd & others (Eds.), *Personal transformation in small groups: A Jungian perspective* (pp. 14–40). London: Routledge.

Boyd, R. D., & Dirkx, J. M. (1991). Methodology for the study of the development of consciousness in the small group. In R. D. Boyd & others (Eds.), *Personal transformation in small groups: A Jungian perspective* (pp. 41–64). London: Routledge.

Boyd, R. D., & Myers, J. G. (1988). Transformative education. *International Journal of Lifelong Education*, 7(4), 261–284.

Boyd, R. D., & others (Eds.). (1991). *Personal transformation in small groups: A Jungian perspective.* London: Routledge.

Corbin, H. (2000). Mundus Imaginalis, or the imaginary and the imaginal. In B. Sells (Ed.), *Working images: The theoretical base of archetypal psychology* (pp. 70–89). Woodstock, CN: Spring.

Cranton, P. (2006). *Understanding and promoting transformative learning: A guide for educators of adults* (2nd ed.). San Francisco: Jossey-Bass.

Davis, R. H. (2003). *Jung, Freud, and Hillman: Three depth psychologies in context.* Westport, CN: Praeger.

Dirkx, J. M. (1991). Understanding group transformation through the focal person concept. In R. D. Boyd & others (Eds.), *Personal transformation in small groups: A Jungian perspective* (pp. 65–96). London: Routledge.

Dirkx, J. M. (1997). Nurturing soul in adult learning. In P. Cranton (Ed.), *Transformative learning in action: Insights from practice* (pp. 79–88). San Francisco: Jossey-Bass.

Dirkx J. M. (2000). Transformative learning and the journey of individuation. ERIC Digest, No 223, ED ED448305.

Dirkx, J. M. (Ed.). (2008a). *Adult learning and the emotional self.* New Directions for Adult and Continuing Education, no. 120. San Francisco: Jossey-Bass.

Dirkx, J. M. (2008b). Care of the self: Mythopoetic dimensions of professional preparation and development. In T. Leonard & P. Willis (Eds.), *Pedagogies of the imagination: Mythopoetic curriculum in educational practice* (pp. 65–82). Dordrecht, Netherlands: Springer.

Dirkx, J. M., & Dang, N.L.T. (2009, April 16). "Betwixt and between": The role of liminality in fostering a learner identity among dislocated workers in developmental education. Presented at the annual meeting of the American Educational Research Association, San Diego, CA.

Dirkx, J. M., & Smith, R. O. (2003). Thinking out of a bowl of spaghetti: Learning to learn in online collaborative groups. In T. S. Roberts (Ed.), *Online collaborative learning: Theory and practice.* Hershey, PA: Idea Group Publishing.

Dobson, D. (2008). The symbol as teacher: Reflective practices and methodology in transformative education. In R. A. Jones, A. Clarkson, S. Congram, & N. Stratton (Eds.), *Education and imagination: Post-Jungian perspectives* (pp. 142–159). London: Routledge.

Durand, G. (2000). Exploration of the imaginal. In B. Sells (Ed.), *Working images: The theoretical base of archetypal psychology* (pp. 52–69). Woodstock, CN: Spring.

Ferrer, J. (2002). *Revisioning transpersonal theory: A participatory vision of human spirituality*. SUNY Press.

Ferrer, J., Romero, M., & Albareda, R. (2010). Integral transformative education: A participatory proposal. In S. Esbjörn-Hargens, J. Reams, & O. Gunnlaugson (Eds.), *Integral education: New directions for higher learning* (pp. 79–103). Albany, NY: SUNY.

Freire, P. (1976). A few notes on conscientization. In R. Dale (Ed.), *Schooling and capitalism*. London: Routledge.

Gozawa, J. (2009). The cultural complex and transformative learning environments. *Journal of Transformative Education, 7*(2), 114–133.

Harding, M. E. (1956). *Journey into self*. Boston: Sigo Press.

Hillman, J. (1975). *Re-visioning psychology*. New York: Harper Colophon.

Hollis, J. (1993). *The middle passage: From misery to meaning in midlife*. Toronto: Inner City Books.

Hollis, J. (2005). *Finding meaning in the second half of life*. New York: Gotham.

Jones, R. A., Clarkson, A., Congram, S., & Stratton, N. (Eds.). (2008). *Education and imagination: Post-Jungian perspectives*. London: Routledge.

Kegan, R., & Lahey, L. L. (2001). *How the way we talk can change the way we work: Seven languages for transformation*. San Francisco: Jossey-Bass.

Kriesberg, J. (2010). Integral education, integral transformation, and the teaching of mind-body medicine. In S. Esbjörn-Hargerns, J. Reams, & O. Gunnlaugson (Eds.), *Integral education: New directions for higher learning* (pp. 229–244). Albany, NY: SUNY.

Leonard, T., & Willis, P. (Eds.). (2008). *Pedagogies of the imagination: Mythopoetic curriculum in educational practice*. Dordrecht, Netherlands: Springer.

Mayes, C. (2005). *Jung and education: Elements of an archetypal psychology*. Latham, MD: Rowman and Littlefield Education.

Mayes, C. (2007). *Inside education: Depth psychology in teaching and learning*. Madison, WI: Atwood.

McAdams, D. P. (1993). *Stories we live by: Personal myths and the making of the self*. New York: William Morrow.

McRae, M. B., & Short, E. L. (2010). *Racial and cultural dynamics in group and organizational life: Crossing boundaries*. Thousand Oaks, CA: SAGE.

Merriam, S. B., & Clark, M. C. (1991). *Lifelines: Patterns of work, love, and learning in adulthood*. San Francisco: Jossey-Bass.

Mezirow, J. (1991). *Transformative dimensions of adult learning*. San Francisco: Jossey-Bass.

Neville, B. (1989). *Educating psyche: Emotion, imagination, and the unconscious in learning*. Melbourne, AU: Collins Dove.

O'Sullivan, E. V., Morrell, A., & O'Connor, M. A. (2002). *Expanding the boundaries of transformative learning: Essays on theory and praxis*. New York: Palgrave.

Palmer, P. J. (1998). *The courage to teach: Exploring the inner landscapes of a teacher's life.* San Francisco: Jossey-Bass.

Sardello, R. (2004). *Facing the world with soul: The reimagination of modern life.*

Singer, T., & Kimbles, S. L. (Eds.). (2004). *The cultural complex: Contemporary Jungian perspectives on psyche and society.* London: Routledge.

Sonik, M. (2008). Literary individuation: A Jungian approach to creative writing. In R. A. Jones, A. Clarkson, S. Congram, & N. Stratton (Eds.), *Education and imagination: Post-Jungian perspectives* (pp. 96–117). London: Routledge.

Stapley, L. F. (2006). *Individuals, groups, and organizations beneath the surface: An introduction.* London: Karnac.

Stein, M. (1998). *Jung's map of the soul: An introduction.* Chicago: Open Court.

Stevens, A. (1995). *Private myths: Dreams and dreaming.* Cambridge, MA: Harvard University Press.

Watkins, M. (1984). *Waking dreams* (3rd ed.). Woodstock, CN: Spring.

Watkins, M. (2000a). *Invisible guests: The development of imaginal dialogues.* Woodstock, CN: Spring.

Watkins, M. (2000b). Six approaches to the image in art therapy. In B. Sells (Ed.), *Working images: The theoretical base of archetypal psychology* (pp. 186–207). Woodstock, CN: Spring.

Whitmont, E. C. (1969). *The symbolic quest: Basic concepts of analytical psychology.* Princeton, NJ: Princeton University Press.

Young-Eisendrath, P., & Dawson, T. (Eds.). (1997). *The Cambridge companion to Jung.* Cambridge: Cambridge University Press.

Zweig, C., & Wolf, S. (1997). *Romancing the shadow: A guide to soul work for a vital, authentic life.* New York: Ballantine Books.

CHAPTER EIGHT

Critical Theory and Transformative Learning

Stephen D. Brookfield

Transformation is one of the most powerful words in the English language. When something is transformed, its component elements undergo a profound metamorphosis so that what emerges is fundamentally different from what went before. As a body of work, critical theory has a transformative, metamorphosing impulse, so its connection to transformative learning seems natural and obvious. In critical theory's case, the metamorphosis sought is the change from the competitive, individualist ethics and systems of capitalism to the collective, interdependent, and cooperative ethics and systems of democratic socialism. In its own terms, critical theory studies how to usher in social and economic arrangements fundamentally different from postindustrial capitalism. Its project is to explain how social control works so that current systems of capitalist control can then be dismantled and society transformed into a democratic socialist model. The kind of transformative learning that is endemic to critical theory is learning how to create the cooperative and collective structures, systems, and processes necessary for democratic socialism (Gramsci, 1971; Horkheimer, 1995; Brookfield and Holst, 2010). In this chapter I outline the central tenets of critical theory and my understanding of learning. I explore the learning that critical theory mandates and the degree to which this learning can be considered transformative. Throughout, I argue that critical theory's focus on how adults learn to challenge dominant ideology, uncover power, and contest hegemony is crucial for scholars of transformative learning to consider if transformative learning is to avoid sliding into an unproblematized focus on the self. Understanding the self to be socially and politically created, and understanding commonsense choices and actions as therefore ideologically manipulated, are central elements of critical theory. When applied to the research and practice of transformative learning, critical theory therefore ensures that the transformation of social and political systems is seen as necessary for any transformation of the self. If the self is understood as politically sculpted, then learning to transform the self is a political project requiring political transformation. Hence any research on transformative learning must, in critical theory's terms, attend to the ways dominant ideology fosters or constrains what people consider to be transformative.

This emphasis on political transformation is one distinctive to critical theory. In his crucial contributions to building a critical theory of adult learning, Welton (1991, 1993, 1995) argues that "the consequences of forgetting Marx for the construction of a critical theory of adult learning are enormous, inevitably binding us to an individualistic model of learning" (1995, p. 19). Marx's political economy (Marx, 1973)—his understanding of all human phenomena (including learning) as framed and explained by the material relations existing in society—means that a critical theory interpretation of what transformation comprises will always center it in economic transformation. In Marx's analysis, this means we can talk about transformation in a meaningful sense only when capitalism has been transformed into socialism and human nature has been transformed from a focus on individual competition into a focus on collective identity and responsibility. In his influential collection *In Defense of the Lifeworld* (Welton, 1995), Welton includes a dialogue with Mezirow in which the differences between the critical theory perspective of Welton and of Collins (1991, 1998), among others, and Mezirow's own understanding are clarified. Over the years, Mezirow himself has responded to criticisms that his perspective is overly individualistic (Mezirow, 1989, 1994, 1997), arguing that his critics do not acknowledge the comprehensive nature of his theory, which includes but is not limited to an analysis of politically inclined reflection on social systems.

Two interwoven strands of analysis in critical theory have direct relevance for understanding the process of transformative learning. The first concerns critical theory's focus on understanding the power dynamics that are just as present in the smallest micro-actions in families, classrooms, and personal relationships as they are in the wider political sphere. Critical theory can help us understand how teacher power is used, or abused, in classrooms that claim to be zones of transformative empowerment for students. For example, Foucault (1980) alerts us to the fact that what educators fondly believe are activities that foster agency in learners can just as easily be understood as processes of manipulation when seen from the learner's perspective. Even something as seemingly innocent as moving classroom chairs into a circle to signify to learners that now they are in a democratic environment can be interpreted instead as an act of surveillance. From Foucault's viewpoint learners now experience themselves as being in full view not only of the teacher but also of peers. So as educators are congratulating themselves on rearranging the furniture in ways that make learners feel welcomed and respected, and that consequently create conditions under which transformative learning can occur, those same learners feel themselves to be under the gaze of teachers and peers and focused chiefly on not making a humiliating mistake that will be noticed by both groups.

The second analytical component of critical theory that goes straight to the heart of transformative learning concerns critical theory's focus on understanding how adults learn the component elements of dominant ideology and how they fail to understand how that same ideology constrains their life choices—and hence prevents the possibility of transformation. If transformation entails a fundamental reordering of the most deep-rooted and paradigmatic assumptions we hold, and if it can happen only when the full range of transformative possibilities is open to us, then we need to be able to recognize how dominant ideology limits both those processes. From a critical theory standpoint transformative learning is equivalent to recognizing and challenging such dominant ideological tenets as: a majority vote represents the most democratic outcome, capitalism fosters the spirit of individual entrepreneurship that is vital to liberty, free speech exists in the United States, whites are natural leaders, or, same-sex relationships should never attain the legal status of marriage.

Let's take a potentially dramatic example of transformative learning—learning to create a political party intended to foster revolutionary change. Learning to create such a party would challenge an unchallenged element of dominant ideology: that because all politicians are the same (cynical, opportunistic crooks who will say anything to get elected and then will break all their promises), and because political office holders are beholden to lobbyists and special interests, involvement in political organizing is meaningless. If we assume that politicians are all the same, and that it doesn't matter who holds office, this constitutes a source of powerful ideological resistance to political action. If you believe these things, then learning to create revolutionary new political parties is pointless. So a critical theory analysis holds that ideology has effectively limited transformative possibilities, and prevented the learning necessary for such transformation, without our being consciously aware of that act.

In their analysis of ideological control, Herman and Chomsky (1980) point out how in the United States the idea that socialist forms of economics comprise a legitimate alternative to capitalism has been expunged from popular consciousness. So when people are considering answers to the most fundamental question of social life—how should we arrange things to make sure that freedom and democracy are ensured?—a whole area of thought, replete with alternative possibilities, is closed to them. If transformative learning entails expanding our meaning perspectives to include ever wider experiences and possibilities, it is hard to see how political learning can ever be transformative if there is a massive "no-go" area called socialism. Essentially, an alternative way of organizing the production and distribution of goods and services that is considered as normal and unremarkable by millions outside the United States is considered to be off limits. Learning to create cooperative, grassroots economic forms would be an example of transformative learning for anyone who has grown up with the idea that private enterprise is the only way to guarantee freedom and liberty. Yet, as critical theory points out, dominant ideology has rendered such a transformative learning project all but impossible for many.

WHAT IS CRITICAL THEORY?

Critical theory has as its starting point the illumination and resolution of a difficult conundrum. How is it that the majority of people who are limited and constrained by a grossly iniquitous society come to accept this state of affairs as not only normal, but actually desirable? Its central hypothesis is that dominant ideology is organized to convince people that this is an acceptable state of affairs and that people learn this ideology throughout their lives. As a body of work, then, critical theory is grounded in three core assumptions regarding the way the world is organized: (1) that apparently open, western democracies are actually highly unequal societies in which economic inequity, racism, and class discrimination are empirical realities; (2) that the way this state of affairs is represented as seeming to be normal, natural, and inevitable (thereby heading off potential challenges to the system) is through the dissemination of dominant ideology; and (3) that critical theory attempts to understand this state of affairs as a prelude to changing it.

Dominant ideology comprises the set of broadly accepted beliefs and practices that frame how people make sense of their experiences and live their lives. When it works effectively it ensures that an unequal, racist, and sexist society is able to reproduce itself with minimal opposition. Its chief function is to convince people that the world is organized the way it is for the best of all reasons and that society works in the best interests of all. Critical theory regards dominant ideology as inherently manipulative and duplicitous. From the perspective of critical theory, a critical adult is one who can discern how the ethic of capitalism and the logic of bureaucratic rationality push people into ways of living that perpetuate economic, racial, and gender oppression. Additionally, and crucially, critical theory views a critical adult as one who takes action to create more democratic, collectivist, economic, and social forms. Some in the tradition (for example, Cornel West) link social change to democratic social-ism; others (for example, Erich Fromm) link it to socialist humanism. Clearly, then, the way critical theory defines being critical is far more politicized than the way humanistic psychology—until recently the dominant discourse in adult education—regards this idea.

Critical theory is usually not written in terms immediately recognizable to those of us primarily interested in adult learning. Yet an analysis of adult learning is usually implicit in its propositions, particularly in that strand of theorizing (initiated by Mezirow, 1981) that draws its inspiration from Jürgen Habermas (1984, 1987). Subsumed within the general desire of critical theory to understand and then challenge the continuous reproduction of social, political, and economic domination are a number of related concerns. One of these is to investigate how dominant ideologies educate people to believe certain ways of organizing society are in their own best interests when the opposite is true. Another is to illuminate how the spirit of capitalism and of technical and bureaucratic rationality enters into and distorts everyday relationships (what Habermas calls the colonization of the lifeworld by the system). A third concern (and this is particularly important to a theory of adult learning) is to understand how people learn to identify and then oppose the ideological forces and social processes that oppress them.

A theory of adult learning originating in these general concerns of critical theory would attempt to answer a series of more specific questions focused on the way people learn to awaken and then act on their human agency. These questions would ask how people learn to challenge beliefs and structures that serve the interests of the few against the well-being of the many, and how they then learn to build structures, systems, and processes that are cooperative and collective, rather than individual and competitive; in other words, how they learn to build democratic socialism.

Understood this way, a critical theory of adult learning is clearly a theory of social and political learning. It studies the systems and forces that shape adults' lives and oppose adults' attempts to challenge ideology, recognize hegemony, unmask power, defend the lifeworld, and develop agency. Such a theory must recognize its explicitly political character. It must focus consistently on political matters such as the way formal learning is structured and limited by the un-equal exercise of power. It must not shy away from connecting adult learning efforts to the creation of political forms, particularly the extension of economic democracy across barriers of race, class, and gender. It must understand adult education as a political process in which certain interests and agendas are always pursued at the expense of others, in which curriculum inevitably pro-motes some content as "better" than other content, and in which evaluation is an exercise of the power of some to judge the efforts of others. Critical theory springs from the desire to extend democratic socialist values and processes, to create a world in which a commitment to the common good is the foundation of individual well-being and development. A critical theory of adult learning will always come back to the ways in which adults learn to do this.

WHAT IS LEARNING?

I use "learning" as both a noun and a verb. As a noun it refers to an identifiable change that has occurred in the learner; as a verb, to the process that contributes to that change. Let's take the noun first. From my perspective, transformative adult learning is an observable shift in knowledge and skill regarding the creation and maintenance of democratic socialism. A single instance of such learning can cross the three learning domains famously identified by Habermas (1979) that have been so influential in adult education generally and in transformative learning in particular—technical, communicative, and emancipatory. For example, learning how to stand up to racist speech and racist acts—including one's own—involves technical aspects (becoming alert to how certain metaphors are used uncritically and instinctively in everyday speech), communicative dimensions (learning how to bring racism to another's consciousness so that it is considered seriously and not rejected dismissively), emancipatory processes (integrating an alertness to racism into one's daily reasoning and practice), and also emotional intelligence (learning to acknowledge yet not be derailed by the frustration, self-doubt, self-disgust, and embarrassment that antiracist work involves, especially for whites).

But these intrapersonal and interpersonal learning activities are only the beginning. The critical theory tradition requires such individual acts to be tied to political action—to creating structures, systems, parties, and institutions that equalize access to common resources to democratize access to education and health, and to organize around common interests. Learning to recognize and oppose racism—to take the example already mentioned, for example—involves people organizing to enact legislation, create educational programs, establish alternate media networks, set up housing and other cooperatives, and launch neighborhood businesses. This project is pursued on different terrains and using different strategies and tactics. One person might be concerned to develop an Africentrically grounded adult school in which teaching and learning are in harmony with African centered values, practices, and conceptual referents. Another might be concerned to set up a media watch to monitor the presence of racist stereotypes in local news reporting. Still another might organize rallies to lobby for the civil rights of undocumented immigrants, for the establishment of neighborhood health centers staffed by native speakers of the language predominantly spoken by community members, or for stronger legal sanctions for clearly racist behavior. Such learning is not just concerned with changing individuals' perceptions and promoting individual changes of attitude. It is just as focused on political projects, all of which entail adult educational dimensions—people teaching people skills, knowledge, and understanding in collective settings—and all of which are tied together by an interest in extending participatory democracy.

So a critical theory understanding of adult learning is not that it is any effort by people over twenty-one to increase knowledge, enhance understanding, or develop insight or skill. Rather, critical theory inextricably ties adult learning to creating and extending political and economic democracy—to equalizing control of, and access to, wealth, education, health care, and creative work, and to promoting collective and cooperative forms of decision making and labor. This is sometimes seen most clearly in community movements. Every act of adult learning in such a movement will entail alternating and intersecting dimensions. None of these activities is wholly technical, communicative, emancipatory, or emotional in terms of the learning that ensues; rather, each involves a complex web of actions, choices, and reasoning, with different forms and processes highlighted more strongly than others at different times (Ceballos, 2006).

To transform capitalism into economic democracy, adults also need to learn about a range of alternative social and economic arrangements: socialist economics, participatory budgeting, worker cooperatives, collective decision making, negotiation strategies, conflict management, and so on. They also need to learn a structural world view; that is, one that sees supposedly individual crises and dilemmas as produced by the intersection of larger structural and systemic forces—particularly the intersection of monopoly capitalism and white supremacy—and one that analyzes the global dimensions that inform the seemingly most mundane daily decisions and practices.

Let me take an example of learning currently in fashion within the scholarly discourse of adult education—workplace learning—and show how this is understood from a critical theory perspective. Workplace learning is currently one of the most frequently touted projects within adult education; the workplace is, after all, an important setting in which we exercise creativity and from which we draw aspects of our identity. The stigmatization of unemployment and the shame and self-laceration it produces in those laid off pays eloquent testimony to how meaningful the concept of productive work is for people. But workplace learning does not happen just in waged situations. The unwaged doing motherwork and providing health care for family members, or those doing grassroots organizing or eking out existence while being artistically creative, are also engaged in workplace learning. The workplace, however it is defined, is where many of us develop networks, meet spouses and partners, locate friends, and realize our contribution to society.

From a critical theory perspective, workplace learning is tied not to enhancing U.S. competitiveness within the global marketplace but to the creation of more meaningful work—work in which learners feel they are exercising creativity and control, which feels as fulfilling as possible, and which is undertaken for ends that are seen as inherently important and socially necessary. Establishing the conditions for this kind of meaningful work necessitates a major learning project; that is, learning to recognize and then combat the alienation induced by capitalism. This understanding of adult workplace learning takes us directly to critical social theory's illumination of how the workplace impedes adult learning for creative fulfillment, while enhancing learning that supports becoming efficient consumers of the goods we produce.

WHAT IS THE ADULT LEARNING PROJECT EMBEDDED IN CRITICAL THEORY?

As I have argued, the overarching task of critical theory is to understand how capitalism manages to perpetuate itself, despite events such as the financial crash of 2008. Critical theory is therefore initially concerned with learning, particularly with how people learn consent. It begins with questions such as: How do the majority of disenfranchised and dispossessed people learn to accept a system that is clearly set up against their interests? How do they learn to collude in, even celebrate, their own oppression? Critical theory then moves to understanding how people learn to identify and challenge the mechanisms of social control that have secured their consent; in other words, how they become aware of power and hegemony's influence over them. Finally, critical theory concerns itself with the kinds of learning that people then need to undertake to build a qualitatively new form of society that is organized around collective, cooperative, and interdependent values; in other words, how they learn to dismantle capitalism and replace it with democratic socialism.

In the popular consciousness, capitalism is seen as the guarantor of freedom and liberty and as the quintessentially democratic economic system guaranteeing that all have the opportunity to taste the fruits of life. Learning liberation from this ideology and these structures involves an imaginative leap to envision a form of humanistic socialism in which the valuing of human dignity and creativity is viewed as inseparable from the common stewardship of social resources. It also entails the sorts of technical and interpersonal learning required when families, neighborhoods, workplaces, communities, and societies learn to conduct themselves to serve the interests of all their members rather than the narrow, sectional interests of a privileged minority. This kind of learning requires a qualitative—a truly transformative—change in the way people think, not just a change in external political and economic arrangements. It involves learning to define one's interests as the interests of the group as a whole rather than as the pursuit of individual advantage, learning to view identity as collectively created and maintained rather than individually crafted, and learning to view the personal alienation one feels in one's life, work, relationships, and recreational pursuits as inextricably linked to the way one's labor is defined and controlled by the interests of capital via large corporations. Finally, it requires a kind of ethical learning of the maxim that we cannot seek any individual advantage unless that same benefit is sought for all.

One form of this learning involves adults learning to recognize how dominant ideology is inscribed within them and the way they come to understand how this ideology shapes, or perhaps more accurately circumscribes, their individual choices, decisions, and actions. A major element in this learning is coming to realize the collective formation of personal identity—the way that personal identity is not developed in a series of purely self-contained, individual choices, but is shaped by collectively generated and maintained roles, assumptions, images, and expectations associated with one's race, class, or gender. Even something as seemingly individualistic as what one buys is, of course, a culturally and economically framed choice reflecting aspirations and needs that are felt as individual but in reality are socially induced. Getting adults to realize this is the focus of the kind of critical adult consumer education proposed by Sandlin (2005) and others (Ozanne, Adkins, & Sandlin, 2005). Learning to counter dominant ideology also involves realizing that what people see as purely individual changes (for example, getting a better—or any—employment, a better—or any—access to health care or decent education, stopping spousal abuse, or escaping slum housing) are made possible only when structures and systems change, and that such change happens only as a result of collective pressure. To paraphrase Frederick Douglass, power never gives up its position of preeminence unless it is forced to, and this usually happens only as a reaction to the power of numbers.

Individual acts, quixotic solo gestures, and going down in a martyr's blaze of glory are challenges to power that are much more easily deflected than an organized and determined mass movement. Ideologically, if the power of numbers is depicted in popular imagination as potentially dangerous and uncontrollable (that is, large numbers of people are really mobs waiting for a spark of unrest to ignite them into spontaneous and destructive violence) or as overly controlling (large numbers of people will soon ossify into structures that restrict individual liberty and freedom), then the impulse to organize collective action is successfully stopped in its tracks. Anyone seeking to organize a grassroots organization, union, or social movement quickly becomes ideologically defined as either a loose cannon primed to lead people into violent confrontation or a Stalinist waiting to impose his views on everyone and brooking no deviation. This kind of ideological manipulation is part of the reason why socialist ideals have become less influential in recent years.

A particularly subtle form of learning studied by critical theory is how people learn to recognize when they are victims of what Herbert Marcuse (1965) called repressive tolerance. Repressive tolerance is what happens when individuals, or a whole system, realize a threat is emerging against the entrenched power of that system and head it off by appearing to concede the demands being made while in reality making no real changes. This is sometimes described as being coopted by the system. By allowing a limited amount of protest that is carefully managed, a societal pressure valve is created to release into thin air the stream of energy that would otherwise cause the system to make real change. Diversity days, Black History Month, having people of color take positions as newscasters on local TV stations, colleges and universities featuring a majority of photos of black, brown, or Asian students on their publicity materials (when such students form only a small minority of actual students), profiling what are touted as quintessentially U.S. success stories of wealthy black entertainers or athletes—all these can be seen as examples of repressive tolerance. How do people learn that such measures are Band-Aids covering much deeper cultural, political, and economic wounds? How do they learn a measure of vigilance so they are alert when repressive tolerance springs into action? How do they learn to communicate its presence to skeptical friends and colleagues who believe that racial problems have been solved, fundamental inequalities abolished? And how do they learn to carry on fighting against such tolerance when they are the only ones who notice what's happening? What learning do they need to undertake to avoid radical pessimism?

Another form of learning that captures the interest of critical theory is learning within—and learning how to build—communities and movements that challenge existing relations of power and advantage (Holst, 2004). How do people learn to build grassroots coalitions? How, for example did local organizers of a march protesting the 2003 American invasion of Iraq get ten thousand people to the center of Minneapolis to express their opposition to the Bush administration? The march's organizers had to learn how to publicize its existence, how to coordinate a mass protest with law enforcement agencies, how to alert media to this march without the march's logic being distorted, and how to direct the march as it occurred. Participants in the march had to learn how to make their voices heard, how to explain their participation to those who were uninformed about the war (such as very young children) and to those who were active supporters of the war. Clearly, such a day of protest involves a massive amount of adult learning.

On a different scale, what skills and knowledge does one need to acquire to establish a local food cooperative or to organize a local chapter of a union in a nonunionized workplace? And what learning must be accomplished for workers to set up their own independent local chapter when they feel their national union has betrayed them? When worker-employees take over a business, what do they have to know and how do they ensure they locate and then assimilate all necessary information? When tenants organize a rent strike, or citizens take on city hall to demand action on environmental pollution or to advocate for better housing, education, or health facilities, what must people who never completed high school learn to do? What learning was involved when workers set up factory councils in Turin or took control of the Scottish Clydeside shipbuilding plants? When mothers who had family members kidnapped by Argentinian security forces during the military dictatorship of the 1970s formed the *Mothers of the Plaza de Mayo*, how did they learn to face their fear, establish networks of communication, publicize their cause, and bring international attention to the government's "dirty war," as it came to be known, waged by the dictatorship against dissidents amongst its own citizenry? How did members of the previously all-powerful South African security forces learn to acknowledge they had detained and tortured black South Africans, and how did the citizenry learn to face their torturers at the Truth and Reconciliation Commission hearings?

These kinds of learning are subsets of a much larger democratic project—learning to organize the economy, political system, civil society, and cultural production for the benefit of all. This kind of learning is truly transformative, requiring that many existing structures be transformed in the public interest so that they work for the benefit of the mass of so-called "ordinary" working people, rather than to increase profits enjoyed by a small minority. This is why some emphasize the inseparability of democracy and socialism. In the United States, dominant ideology (in particular, the discourse of democracy) has very effectively and brutally severed this link so that socialism is seen as a form of state tyranny, with a small band of grey demagogues ensuring that everybody thinks and acts alike and a determination to rid the world of individual liberty and creativity. It is an interesting exercise to ask students—even those in critical theory courses—who they think wrote that the organizing principle of society should be "securing for every member of society . . . an existence not only fully sufficient materially, and becoming day by day fuller, but an existence guaranteeing to all the free development and exercise of their physical and mental faculties." Liberty and justice (not to mention creative fulfillment) for all, indeed. Washington? Lincoln? Jefferson? The answer, of course, is none of these. It was Friedrich Engels in his essay on *Socialism* (Engels, 1950). Socialism is the freedom for people to realize their own creativity without being forced to devote their lives to working for institutions that have the maximization of profit as their overarching purpose. When socialism is defined as creating systems whereby those who are most affected by social and economic decisions have the chief responsibility for making those decisions, its democratic core is apparent. What is democracy other than trusting people enough to give them control over the decisions that affect their lives? If socialism is regarded as a project to develop structures in which labor is an enjoyable source of personal fulfillment, its connection to individual creativity is clear. But as long as rampant Marxophobia (McLaren, 1997) causes socialism to be equated with totalitarian thought control and the denial of creativity, democratic adult educators face a massive challenge in transformative adult learning.

HOW IS THIS LEARNING TRANSFORMATIVE?

In no less an august authority than the *International Encyclopedia of Adult Education,* transformative learning is defined as "a process by which previously uncritically assimilated assumptions, beliefs, values, and perspectives are questioned and thereby become more open, permeable, and better validated" (Cranton, 2005, p. 630). In the recent decennial *Handbook of Adult and Continuing Education,* transformative learning is also identified as a dominant theoretical paradigm in the field (Brookfield, 2010). Central to this paradigm is Mezirow's argument that the developmental imperative of adulthood is to transform one's meaning schemes (sets of assumptions governing particular situations) and meaning perspectives (broader worldviews) so that they explain the disorienting dilemmas (situations that take us by surprise and cause us to question assumptions) we inevitably encounter as we journey through adulthood. In the process we alter how we see ourselves, our purpose in the world, and the way that purpose can be realized.

For Mezirow and Associates, then, "development in adulthood may be understood as a learning process—a phased and often transformative process of meaning becoming clarified through expanded awareness, critical reflection, validating discourse, and reflective action as one moves towards a fuller realization of agency" (2000, p. 25). Mezirow sees this kind of transformation as happening both as a result of intentional critical reflection and as something we are catapulted into by events. Mezirow describes the arc of transformative learning as a ten-stage process in which a disorienting dilemma causes one to question assumptions, seek others also going through this experience, contemplate new roles, develop new skills and knowledge to match these, and then integrate these into a reordered life.

For critical theorists, transformative learning is a rich hermeneutic. The kinds of learning described in the previous section as the adult learning project of critical theory are undoubtedly transformative. This is because all of them—whether they be technical, communicative, or emancipatory kinds of learning—are undertaken in the context of fundamentally transforming society into a democratic socialist form. Moving toward more cooperative, collective, democratic, and socialist ways of thinking and living requires a transformation in the ways we think, the ways we act toward each other, the ways we organize society and politics, the ways we distribute the resources available to us, and the ways we understand the purpose of life. On a broad social stage it usually takes a societal disorienting dilemma—the collapse of the stock market, a declaration of war, a military coup, a major economic depression—to trigger a critical mass of transformations in individual circumstances that coalesce into a massive act of transformational change. My position—similar to that of situated cognition theorists (Lave & Wenger, 1991)—is that cognition is fundamentally a function of social organization and location. This is also Mezirow's view. For him, "identity is formed in webs of affiliation within a shared life world" and "it is within the context of these relationships, governed by existing and changing cultural paradigms, that we become the persons we are" (Mezirow, 2000, p. 27). How and what one thinks is shaped by one's class, race, and gender (one's social location or positionality), by the cultural streams in which one swims (and which, like a fish in water, one is unaware one is swimming in), and by dominant ideology (the set of beliefs and practices, reflected in the structures and systems of a society, that are accepted as natural, commonsense, and working for the good of all).

If cognition is situated in these phenomena—as theorists of situated cognition (Lave, 2003) hold—then, by implication, changing cognition depends on changing culture and ideology. In Mezirow's terms, "transformative learning involves liberating ourselves from reified forms of thought that are no longer dependable" (2000, p. 27). "Reified forms of thought" is as good a shorthand definition of ideology as one could have—implying, as it does, that dominant ideas and practices have an existence somehow independent of the environment that produced them. In reality, reified forms of thought and their associated practices (decisions, actions, and behaviors) are produced, buttressed, and nourished by sociopolitical and economic structures and systems. By implication, then, reified forms of thought and practice can be changed only if the structures producing and sustaining those phenomena are changed. And if capitalist structures produce and sustain individualized, competitive practices, with people acting on the basis of self-advancement and assuming that others' poverty or oppression is the result of "natural" forces working to favor the most capable (the survival of the fittest), then only a move to cooperative, democratic, socialist structures will serve to instigate a truly transformative change of consciousness.

From a critical theory perspective, then, transformative adult learning theory is a useful way to explain how adults learn to recognize the way in which the exchange dynamic of capitalism (*I give you this labor and you give me that wage in return*) has permeated their life worlds, to use Habermas's (1987) term. It also constitutes a theoretical starting point for understanding how people learn a whole new way of being—a way of thinking, acting, feeling, and creating—that moves from acquisition to creative fulfillment in association with others. This is what Erich Fromm described as the movement from having to being (Fromm, 1968). The logic of both situated cognition and transformative learning is that such a developmental project can happen only through people creating new collective forms of social, political, cultural, and economic association. Such forms would embed ways of ordering common affairs that have as their chief rationale the attainment of liberty and justice for all. In other words, learning new forms of being can happen only when a socialist ethic informs how we live together, regulate our common affairs, and decide how necessary tasks are to be fairly distributed and how the products of our collective labors are fairly enjoyed. It is hard to imagine a more profound example of transformative learning. This is why studying the processes and conditions under which people learn the transformation to socialism is one of the most important transformative learning research agendas.

References

Brookfield, S. D. (2010). Theoretical frameworks for understanding the field. In A. C. Kasworm, A. Rose, & J. Ross-Gordon (Eds.), *Handbook of adult and continuing education, 2010* (pp. 71–82). Thousand Oaks, CA: SAGE.

Brookfield, S. D., & Holst, J. D. (2010). *Radicalizing learning: Adult education for a just world.* San Francisco: Jossey-Bass.

Ceballos, R. M. (2006). Adult education for community empowerment: Toward the possibility of another world. In S. B. Merriam, B. C. Courtenay, & R. M. Cervero (Eds.), *Global issues and adult education* (pp. 319–331). San Francisco: Jossey-Bass.

Collins, M. (1991). *Adult education as vocation: A critical role for the adult educator.* New York: Routledge.

Collins, M. (1998). *Critical crosscurrents in education.* Malabar, FL: Krieger.

Cranton, P. (2005). Transformative Learning. In L. M. English (Ed.), *International encyclopedia of adult education* (pp. 630–637). New York: Palgrave Macmillan.

Engels, F. (1950). Socialism: Utopian and scientific. In K. Marx & F. Engels (Eds.), *Selected works* (vol. 2). London: Lawrence & Wishart.

Foucault, M. (1980). *Power/Knowledge: Selected interviews and other writings, 1972–1977.* New York: Pantheon.

Fromm, E. (1968). *The revolution of hope: Toward a humanized technology.* New York: Harper and Row.

Gramsci, A. (1971). *Selections from the prison notebooks* (Q. Hoare & G. N. Smith, Trans.). London: Lawrence & Wishart.

Habermas, J. (1979). *Communication and the evolution of society.* Boston: Beacon Press.

Habermas, J. (1984). *The theory of communicative action: Volume One. Reason and the rationalization of society.* Boston: Beacon Press.

Habermas, J. (1987). *The theory of communicative action: Volume Two. Lifeworld and system—a critique of functionalist reason.* Boston: Beacon Press.

Herman, E., & Chomsky, N. (1980). *Manufacturing consent.* New York: Pantheon.

Holst, J. D. (2004). Globalization and education within two revolutionary organizations in the United States of America: A Gramscian analysis. *Adult Education Quarterly, 55*(1), 23–40.

Horkheimer, M. (1995). *Critical theory: Selected essays.* New York: Continuum.

Lave, J. (2003). *Cognition in practice.* New York: Cambridge University Press.

Lave, J., & Wenger, E. (1991). *Situated learning: Legitimate peripheral participation.* Cambridge: Cambridge University Press.

Marcuse, H. (1965). Repressive tolerance. In R. P. Wolff, B. Moore, & H. Marcuse (Eds.), *A critique of pure tolerance* (pp. 81–123). Boston: Beacon Press.

Marx, K. (1973). *Capital: A critical analysis of capitalist production: Vol. 1.* (S. Moore & E. Aveling, Trans.). New York: International Publishers.

McLaren, P. (1997). *Life in schools: An introduction to critical pedagogy in the foundations of education* (3rd ed.). White Plains, NY: Longman.

Mezirow, J. (1981). A critical theory of adult learning and education. *Adult Education Quarterly, 32*(1), 3–27.

Mezirow, J. (1989). Transformation theory and social action: A response to Collard and Law. *Adult Education Quarterly, 39*(3), 169–175.

Mezirow, J. (1994). Response to Mark Tennant and Michael Newman. *Adult Education Quarterly, 44*(4), 243–244.

Mezirow, J. (1997). Transformation theory out of context. *Adult Education Quarterly, 48*(1), 60–62.

Mezirow, J. (2000). Learning to think like an adult: Core concepts of transformation theory. In J. Mezirow & Associates (Eds.). *Learning as transformation: Critical perspectives on a theory in progress* (pp. 3–33). San Francisco: Jossey-Bass.

Ozanne, J. L., Adkins, N. R., & Sandlin, J. A. (2005). Shopping (for) power: How adult literacy learners negotiate the marketplace. *Adult Education Quarterly, 55*(4), 251–268.

Sandlin, J. A. (2005). Culture, consumption, and adult education: Refashioning consumer education for adults as a political site using a cultural studies framework. *Adult Education Quarterly, 55*(3), 165–181.

Welton, M. R. (1991). Shaking the foundations: The critical turn in adult education theory. *Canadian Journal for the Study of Adult Education*, 5, 21–41.

Welton, M. R. (1993). The contribution of critical theory to our understanding of adult education. In S. B. Merriam (Ed.), *An update on adult learning theory*. (pp. 81–90). New Directions for Adult and Continuing Education, no. 57. San Francisco: Jossey-Bass.

Welton, M. R. (Ed.). (1995). *In defense of the lifeworld: Critical perspectives on adult learning*. Albany, NY: State University of New York Press.

CHAPTER NINE

Transformative Learning

A Developmental Perspective

Kathleen Taylor and Dean Elias

We live in a time of great promise and great peril. In the richest countries, effects of wealth suggest no upper limit to longevity (Besci, 2001); yet in the poorest countries child mortality exceeds 12 percent (World Health Organization, 2005). A manned trip to Mars is being planned, yet our current energy usage threatens the biosphere. Nations once ruled by dictators now have freely elected governments, yet factional leaders incite violence and genocide between neighbors.

Given Einstein's insight that "You cannot solve a problem from the same consciousness that created it," what can we adult educators make of these juxtapositions? Apparently, despite success with teaching that supports technological, economic, and political progress, we are less effective at facilitating the kind of learning, thinking, or imagining that would lead to understanding of how today's "solutions" can turn out to be tomorrow's even more intractable problems. Lindeman's description of what should be the underlying purpose of adult education seems newly relevant: "a quest of the mind which digs down to the roots of the preconceptions which formulate our conduct" (1925, p. 3).

The major theoretical framework of this chapter is Kegan's (1994) model of *transformations of consciousness*, which describes lifespan development in terms of increasing epistemological complexity. We have found that using this theory to inform practice can help adult educators to foster in learners capacities to perceive, feel, understand, act, relate, and *know* in ways more responsive to the crises our species must address with new imagination, if we are to preserve our planet and ourselves. We also interweave reference to Jack Mezirow's (1991, 2000) *transformative learning theory*, which introduced the language of transformative learning to the world of adult education.

This chapter comprises four parts: *Illustration* describes two stories of transformation related to learning and knowing; *Analysis* uses these stories to illuminate the theoretical constructs; *Application* examines factors that affect such development in awareness and capacity, with implications for practice; and *Invocation* calls adult educators to exploration of the "growing edge."

ILLUSTRATION

Development means successively asking broader
and deeper questions of the relationship between
oneself and the world.
—Daloz (1986)

The students introduced in this section chose an adult-serving program within a liberal arts Catholic college because of its reputation and rigorous, student-centered curriculum, and also because their deep ties to a faith tradition necessitated an environment that welcomed and honored such perspectives. But it is significant that the learning experiences they describe did not occur in courses connected to religious themes or viewpoints.

A New Relationship to God

Jim's end-of-course self-assessment began: "Are truths absolute? Are values situational? Should one ever question the church . . . is it a sin to question God?" In his early forties when he returned to college, Jim had been a gang-member as an adolescent and had had several run-ins with the law. Eventually, through the intercession of a caring priest, he left that life, got married, had children, and became a counselor to other youthful gang members.

Jim's first papers detailed his concerns about course activities focused on questioning assumptions: "I had heard that upper-level education could threaten my belief system," he wrote in his required weekly journal, "and cause me to doubt my established truths. This was a major concern to me as my entire being revolves around my Creator."

However, in the weeks that followed, during which class activities and his instructor welcomed Jim's ongoing inquiry, something shifted for him. He later wrote:

> When I first came to the church, I had no true sense of direction. My views of
> right and wrong were warped and had led me down a destructive path. . . . I
> needed clear-cut direction. I needed to be told what my next step should

be... God provided this through the Bible, the church, and the pastor who helped me to change.... In essence, my moral compass was given to me by my new environment.

He found himself discovering—not without anxiety—a need to define and assert his own moral compass. "I don't want to believe in God because someone else told me that I should. I want to believe in God because *I* believe in Him.... The point is that I am searching for myself, not my created self that is based on others' perceptions."

At course end he reassessed his earlier fears: "I believe that these [new] thoughts will enlighten me and strengthen my beliefs.... This is exciting and still somewhat threatening, but I am okay with that. My belief in God is strong. On the other hand, the way that I react to that belief is changing."

A God of Love

Shirley, an African American woman in her forties, described her world being turned upside down. Raised in a strict Baptist "bible-teaching and -adhering family," where "my faith and belief were my foundation... my faith was who I was!" she was dumbfounded when her dearest friend admitted he was gay and dying of AIDS.

Sermons about homosexuality—that "AIDS was God's way of punishing [gay] people"—were frequent in her church. "But this time it was not other people, it was a beloved friend who did not deserve to die." She finally came to the wrenching decision that her church was wrong; that "It was up to me to decide what my beliefs were or not... I am responsible for establishing my own value system. At the time, I could not label it, but I knew I had tasted wisdom."

Distancing herself from her church, she saw parallels between her experiences as an African American in a racist society and her gay friend in a homophobic society. Though changes in her relationship to her church antedated her return to college, subsequent classroom discussions and reflective papers led her to a deeper awareness. She found her new way of thinking "an exhilarating and liberating experience... [and one that more closely reflected] the essence of Jesus and his teachings. I find it rather ironic that something I struggled with so desperately because of my love for God, would ultimately draw me closer to Him."

ANALYSIS

In the transformation of meaning lies
the meaning of transformation.
—Daloz (1999)

Something momentous occurred as these adults expanded their sense of possibility and wonder. They began to understand themselves and their world in new ways and discovered a more autonomous sense of self characterized by "agency, choice, reflection, and rationality" (Tennant, 2005, p. 105). Rather than strangely different, this "new" self was "the self I know plus something bigger"—a new *capacity* for exploring and even embracing a broader array of ideas, feelings, and beliefs. Developing this more expansive conception of faith, God, and belief had effects beyond their religious practice (explored further later in this chapter in "Beyond Socialization").

How did these students come to question what had seemed self-evident; how did they dare to challenge what had heretofore been the ultimate authority? When Jim reflected uneasily that his educational experiences might lead him to question the church, his instructor—by happenstance a former Jesuit seminarian—noted reassuringly in the margin, "Don't worry—God can handle it." In so doing, his instructor contributed to what Kegan (1982) calls a *holding environment* (described later in "Application")—an essential support for development because it provides the safety, and security, and encouragement that makes the often-painful transformation possible.

The irreconcilable contradiction between Shirley's deep emotional connection to her friend and the belief that gay people are sinful, deserving of death, and destined for hell, is an instance of a "disorienting dilemma" (Mezirow, 2000, p. 21). Such experiences illuminate and challenge heretofore invisible and unquestioned assumptions that determine how we know ourselves and the world around us. Here again the process of transformation is greatly enhanced when we are encouraged to engage the dilemma in a manner that inspires new ways of perceiving it. In Shirley's case, subsequent course activities, including faculty and peer support, enabled her to reframe losing her church community as gaining a new and even more meaningful relationship with God.

As is evident, the social surround often acts powerfully to maintain distorted perspectives. When one's community holds steadfast against challenges to its ideas—not just questions of faith, but the more pervasive and pernicious distinctions between who "we" are and who "they" are, and what our relationship "should" be—the individual, already burdened by self-questioning, faces the added anxiety of potential loss of the group (family, "tribe") that is a primary source of identity and belonging. If adults instead find themselves in a discourse community that welcomes various viewpoints, "the social process of perspective transformation... [including testing] new perspective on friends, peers, and mentors... can be vitally important in making transformation possible" (Mezirow, 1991, p. 185). Thus a process begins to unfold that can lead to new perspectives, self-concept, commitments, behaviors, and actions—and the awareness that one's assumptions *are* assumptions.

This emphatically does not mean all assumptions are rejected. Jim does not reject his relationship to his Creator; rather he constructs a new relationship no longer limited by fear of questioning the church, which he comes to *embrace in a more complex* way. Shirley, by contrast, cannot reconcile her new definition of God as love with the teaching of her church, and she relinquishes her connection to that *institution*, though not to her newly reconstructed *faith*. Furthermore, in conversations with her white, gay friend she sees prejudice itself—how it creates "otherness"—from a *qualitatively different perspective*. This is the essence, Mezirow tells us, of thinking like an adult in democratic societies: to "be able to understand the issues . . . make rational choices as a socially responsible, autonomous agent and, at least sometimes, [be] free to act on them" (2000, p. 25).

It is also, in terms of Kegan's constructive-developmental theory, aspects of a transformed *epistemology*—a new way of knowing or "making meaning." Throughout the lifespan, Kegan claims, "It is not that a person makes meaning as much as that the activity of being a person is the activity of meaning-making" (1982, p. 11).

At every moment, we seek to make sense of what goes on around and within us; however, the process of that sense-making changes as it becomes more complex. We do not merely *gain knowledge* and experience as we mature (the *informational* explanation for change and growth); we also *know in a different way* (the *transformational* explanation).

The "subject-object" relationship is the core of such transformation. Think of nested matryoshka dolls, most of which are contained in a larger doll and contain a doll smaller than itself. We are subject to that which is "larger"—has greater capacity, is more complex. That which is object to us is "smaller"—has less capacity, is less complex. As Kegan (2000) describes it: "That which is 'object' we can look at, take responsibility for, reflect upon, exercise control over, integrate with some other way of knowing. That which is 'subject' we are run by, identified with, fused with, at the effect of. . . . We 'have' object; we 'are' subject" (p. 53).

It is the distinction between what we *know we know* (our recognition makes it object to us) and what we *don't know we don't know* (its invisibility makes us subject to it). We also hold as object that which *we know we don't know* because our awareness of our shortcoming means we can try to remedy it. The Oracle at Delphi declared Socrates the wisest of men. Not believing that pronouncement, Socrates asked his fellow Athenians various questions for which he did not have answers. Though many responded who thought themselves wise, Socrates' questioning proved their replies inadequate. He concluded that being able to recognize the limits of one's wisdom was indeed a greater wisdom.

Conversely, and similar to the unwise Athenians, we are subject to that which *we don't know we "know"*—meaning we do *not* realize that what appears to be self-evidently "so," "reality," and "the way things are" (or "I am") is actually our *belief* or *assumption*. Because we "know" it, we cannot subject it to questioning. We therefore have no choice—it is in charge. We don't have it, *it has us*.

Two subject-object shifts. Kegan's model specifies five such transformations in ways of knowing, or "orders of consciousness." We focus here on third order (epistemological/psychological adulthood) and fourth order (beyond socialization; self-authorization); the latter occurs many years later, *if at all*, when the earlier way of knowing is once again transformed. (The even less prevalent fifth order of consciousness, self-transformation, is briefly introduced in "Invocation.")

To understand the accomplishments and limitations of third order, we first sketch the outlines of second order, which is common to adolescents.

Shortly after leaving for summer vacation, a grandchild learned that his beloved grandfather, whom he visited often, had unexpectedly needed surgery. "Oh," responded the just-turned eleven-year-old, "it's good that happened while we're gone, because we wouldn't have had much fun visiting you." As a child progresses through the teen years, most adults find such typically egocentric attitudes irritating. Second-order knowers perceive situations in terms of their personal needs and preferences. Second-order knowers also lack empathy; they cannot "feel with" or imagine another's perspective and therefore don't see what the fuss is about. Hence they have no guilt about their actions, though they may alter their behavior to avoid undesirable consequences to themselves. It is important to emphasize that *they don't know* they are subject to (and driven by) their own perspectives and desires.

Though this epistemology is the hallmark of psychological adolescence, it is not always coterminous with the teen years (Kegan, 1986). Development of third order consciousness occurs when one can make object—and therefore be aware and in charge of—the personal wants and needs to which one was formerly subject. However, as is always the case, the new, more complex way of knowing is subject to a fresh set of invisible assumptions—in this instance, the imperative to abide by the newly internalized "rules" of adulthood.

Epistemological adulthood. With this move to "socialized" consciousness, we adults are subject to the "shoulds" that every community inculcates in its members—but *we don't know* that we are now run by these new dictates. (We use *socializing* and *socialized* more or less interchangeably; as we do with *self-authorizing/self-authorized* and sometimes also with *self-authoring/self-authored*.) What we experience as the rightness or wrongness of various feelings, actions, and perspectives is determined by what we "know" as reality and truth. To deviate is literally unthinkable, as that requires holding these prescriptions and proscriptions as object.

Among the hidden assumptions of the socialized way of knowing (in Mezirow's terms, *frame of reference*) is the delineation between "us" and "them." Whether the boundary is broad (for example, national, racial, religious identity) or narrow (for example, sports team or workplace), we know we are in important ways "righter" than those who are "not like us." Our basis for defining difference also extends to less obvious identifications—for example, "personality type"—that we nevertheless unconsciously use as a basis for distinction and judgment (Kegan, 1994). At best, we simply ignore (perhaps "tolerate") those whom we perceive as "other." Sometimes, however, we interpret the distinction as an invitation (even obligation) to "help" them gain our (superior) perspective. We can also be manipulated by those who confirm our group's fundamental beliefs and assumptions. For example, we can be provoked to act with self-righteous aggression toward those whom we have been led to believe are intolerable. This way of knowing is clearly inadequate to meet the modern demands of increasingly diverse schools, neighborhoods, and workplaces—let alone to establish mutual respect and understanding among nation-states and the ethnic or religious subgroups within them (Kegan, 1994).

Beyond socialization: self-authorizing. Not until we make object our group-formed identities and become aware of and challenge the associated assumptions and dictates can we cross the threshold to fourth order, "self-authorizing" consciousness. As we construct more complex identities and values, differences formerly experienced as uncomfortable or threatening can become instead a welcome source of new possibilities and perspectives. Rather than avoiding conflict for fear of damaging relationships, we find that "difficult dialogues" improve mutual understanding. Intrapersonally, challenging the hidden imperatives that have, since the end of adolescence, directed our lives may trigger a "mid-life crisis." However, as we become increasingly autonomous and better able to explore the roots of our beliefs, we move toward consciously constructing knowledge, making our own choices, and accepting responsibility for the outcomes (Taylor, 2006). This description of self-authorizing consciousness accords with Mezirow's (2000) suggestion that adult education must "help adults realize their potential for becoming more liberated, socially responsible, and autonomous learners" (p. 30) who can think critically and dialogically about their participation in their social context.

Yet a majority—even among professional, well-educated, and relatively affluent adults—have not fully reached the fourth order threshold (Kegan, 1994, p. 197). Thus the primary focus of our task as adult educators may be to foster this epistemological transformation.

All adults in contemporary America share citizenship with people whose skin color, gender, age, social position, sexual orientation, and physical capacity differ from their own . . . present[ing] us with a vast variety of expectations, prescriptions, claims, and demands. . . . [This requires a change in] *how* we know, [in] the complexity of our consciousness. (Kegan, 1994, p. 5)

The metaphor Kegan uses to represent third order certainty and unques-tioned assumptions is "family religion"—not to be conflated with *religious faith.* "The religion to which I refer is *not [a] denominational affiliation* ... [but rather] *the family's deepest idiosyncratic beliefs* of what life is *really about,*" based on the "rules, values, ideals, prejudices, passions, promises, betrayals, terrors, demons, and angels" that determine how one is required to think, feel, and behave both within the family and in relation to the wider community (our emphasis, 1994, p. 267). Thus embarking on the sometimes harrowing journey from socialized to self-authoring consciousness does *not* require one "to leave the family or the religion" (p. 270). Rather, as Jim and Shirley discovered, one can create new ways of being in relation to, rather than being at the behest of, these connections. One can *have* (hold as object) those relationships, values, goals, and beliefs rather than *be had by* (be subject to) them.

Jim's final self-assessment gives voice to that realization. It traces his de-velopment not only from one form of socialization to another (from the family religion of street gangs to the socially acceptable religion of Catholicism) but also toward a new awareness of what lies *beyond* that way of knowing:

> Once upon a time the streets owned me. I thought I owned the streets but I was a captive of my own perception ... I possessed values and morals, only they were not what society would deem as such. ... I valued my family [the gang], and ... would do anything for them (even if society thought it was wrong). ... Once upon a time the church owned me. ... I became a productive member of society ... I identified with those around me ... but I didn't really know who I was. ... One day I went back to college. I began to question ... I began to take ownership of my values. ... The greatest thing I learned was that I was an individual and there was value in my individuality. ... Some may feel threatened by my new perspectives, but I am at peace with my Creator ... I am comfortable with the knowledge I have because I realize that on any given day I may have to question it.

Thus Jim poignantly describes the experience of those embarked on the "trembling bridge" (Kegan, 1994, p. 270) toward self-authorized ways of knowing.

APPLICATION

Constructivist, active, and experiential forms of teaching and learning, marked by high levels of uncertainty, ambiguity, contradiction, and paradox, invite expressions of soul.
—Dirkx (1997)

As described earlier, development requires a *holding environment.* Though the particulars vary according to the "culture of embeddedness" with which the developing individual is always in tension (Kegan, 1982), it must accomplish three things: support or *confirmation*—validation and acceptance as one now is; challenge or *contradiction*—encouragement to stretch beyond one's current limitations and comfort zone; and *continuity,* as one negotiates the developmental path.

An optimal holding environment requires both *high* challenge and *high* support (Daloz, 1986, p. 214). Unfortunately, although most educators readily communicate to adult learners what they did not do sufficiently well and have yet to accomplish, we are far less specific about what they have achieved, where growth has occurred, and what they can be rightly proud of. *"Emphasize positive movement,"* Daloz (1986) insists; "underline it, restate it, praise it" (p. 127). From a developmental perspective, the most effective educators balance critical feedback with telling learners *what they did right.*

Support and Challenge

The adult educator's ongoing task is to determine which supports and challenges are most meaningful, given where learners are in their process. For example, learners closer to third order feel supported when the relational context includes their instructor's explicit validation and at least tacit acceptance of their ideas by their peers; they feel challenged when asked to engage unfamiliar perspectives and assumptions. They may also interpret critical feedback as directed toward them, personally, rather than at their accomplishment of a task. Adults closer to fourth order, however, revel in their increasing sense of self-authorship and enjoy engaging in discourse about competing ideas and differing values. They also appreciate guidance toward improvement, as they no longer conflate critique with disapproval.

This is not to suggest that adult educators should try to identify each learner's point along a line of development and individualize curriculum accordingly; rather, that we should focus on designing learning environments that provide an array of supports and challenges. The overarching challenge for the adult educator may be first to develop in the learning environment a sense of nurturant community, trust, and security, then to introduce disorienting dilemmas and provide opportunities for discourse and reflection that can lead to consideration of new perspectives.

Schapiro's (2009) description of *facilitating environments* elaborates on Kegan's holding environment by including a fourth element, creation, derived from Lewin's model of personal or organizational change: "confirmation... → feeling safe and affirmed; contradiction... → anxiety and disequilibrium; creation... → changed behavior, attitudes and consciousness; continuity... → reintegration, equilibrium." Shapiro also reframes what he sees as the "sequential and close-ended" nature of Kegan's model: "the change process is probably more cyclical and open-ended; all four kinds of facilitating environments exist to some extent at the same time, and change occurs all of the time" (p. 96).

What might this look like in practice? The following vignettes briefly describe classroom activities designed to "hold" aspects of the transformational process, such as forging a new mutuality that at the same time values and welcomes difference, shifting focus from authorities to one's own authority, and cultivating a more complex kind of empathy.

Forging Mutuality and Welcoming Difference

A particularly effective timing for this approach is in a course that introduces a program or sequence of courses. To focus on forging bonds, initial activities would include small groups sharing stories, such as rich or meaningful learning experiences they have had in some earlier class, group, or team. The small groups are invited to seek common themes to share with the large group; active listening is encouraged, especially paraphrasing one another—thus requiring careful attention and an open perspective.

The facilitated conversation that ensues builds on these themes to develop agreements and expectations for the emerging collective in terms of what a meaningful, productive, appropriate learning environment entails. All themes are accounted for—if not immediately as part of the newly drafted guidelines, then as prompts for later examination. Such an approach confirms learners' needs for affiliation, common values, and bonds of mutuality before asking them to engage in sustained dialogue about possibly contentious topics; it also confirms the more complex construction that appreciates and welcomes exploration of multiple perspectives.

In a similar vein, one might introduce an instrument such as Kolb's Learning Style Inventory (1985) or the Myers-Briggs Type Indicator (Myers & Myers, 1987). Participants, grouped first with their "own kind," identify their distinctive characteristics; then in mixed groups they explore how differences can be complementary.

Shifting Authority

Because socialized knowers vest authority in teachers, texts, and other external, capital-A "Authorities" (Perry, 1998), we encourage movement from validation provided by formal authority to that of peers—and eventually to self-validation. When carefully focused through faculty feedback, learners' written self-assessments may encourage such movement toward greater autonomy and self-direction in learning (Taylor, 1995, 2006).

The following multipart "scaffolded" approach (Applebee & Langer, 1983) also promotes such shifts, though the individual parts may be used independently. Initially, when providing feedback on papers or classroom activities, the educator authentically and explicitly validates the learner's many strengths: for example, "I appreciate risks you took when you ___" or "I like the connection you make between ___ and ___" (such as described in Cranton, 1994, p. 144). This can lead adults to (unconsciously) think to themselves: "Aha! So *that's* what I'm supposed to do. Welllll, if I did it there, I can do it elsewhere." By offering learners the possibility of "self-modeling," the faculty's role as ultimate arbiter is attenuated.

Another incremental shift follows when feedback comes from peers. Using an established rubric as a common referent, participants examine one another's work. As they identify others' shortcomings similar to their own, they develop greater confidence in their capacity to self-assess. Next, learners use the rubric to evaluate their own work, citing evidence to support their judgment. The final step—facilitated by the faculty member—involves the class developing its own grading rubric, which is then used throughout the course.

Cultivating Empathy

Initially, Kegan (1986) used *lack of empathy* to describe the inability of most adolescents to hold simultaneously their own perspective and a conflicting one—the "absence of a shared reality" that the socialized way of knowing transcends (p. 54). He later connected empathy with a self-authorizing capacity to be warm, inclusive, and emotionally available, yet not subject to others' perspectives (1994, p. 227). It is this fourth order empathy that we wish to cultivate.

Beyond imagining ourselves in another's mindset (Geller, 2009, p. 184), such empathy involves the capacity to hold conflicting viewpoints with appreciation and respect. This is difficult to achieve when one feels that directly communicating such viewpoints could threaten one's relationships. There is an anxiety-reducing tactic that has learners begin the dialogue by paraphrasing the other's perspective. This requires that each listen attentively and be somewhat permeable to the other's thoughts and feelings, thus enhancing the likelihood of continued engagement toward greater understanding.

The essence of all these activities is to provide both support and challenge (for additional examples, see Taylor, 2006). Because we agree with Mezirow (1991) that "transformation can lead developmentally toward a more inclusive, differentiated, permeable, and integrated perspective" (p. 155), we believe it is incumbent upon adult educators to teach with such *developmental intentions* (Taylor, Marienau, & Fiddler, 2000) focused primarily on the epistemological movement most prevalent in adult learners. We nevertheless accept that some learners may feel it impossible to accept that invitation (Daloz, 1988).

INVOCATION

*In the history of the collective as in the history
of the individual, everything depends on the
development of consciousness.*
—Carl Jung

The increasing polarization of the political process and the gradual extinction of thoughtful discourse—as in the media "echo chambers" in which a given set of beliefs and assumptions are reinforced and grow more strident—appear to evince what Mezirow (1991) identified as "rigid or highly defended thought patterns" (p. 156) and Kegan (1994) described as limitations of third order consciousness.

Currently, technological advances and economic interrelationships create an ever more interdependent global village, yet the communities in that village are widely divergent in terms of belief in human rights, access to human necessities, availability of education, and economic and political stability. Resolving these tragic challenges calls for a new consciousness—one that is at once empathic and creative, that is attuned with the whole that embraces a vision in which the needs of all are satisfied, and that inspires the courage to realize that vision. Using Kegan's (1994) terminology, we suggest this implies that as adult educators we must also focus our efforts *beyond* self-authorizing, toward the fifth order—the *self-transforming* way of knowing. This is emphatically *not* movement toward a new way of centering on the self; if anything, it is toward the *non-self* described in the wisdom literature of the East.

Where self-authorizing knowers are successful at negotiating across multiple boundaries, self-transforming knowers recognize that these boundaries are self-constructed. As such, they can be reconsidered and reframed, transcending both third order's limited identification with *particular* communities and fourth order's more expansive ability to invite engagement with *disparate* communities. Fifth order has the capacity to see *beyond* such apparently clear delineations. Though many appropriate distinctions certainly exist, each time we draw a line of demarcation we must also question what part of ourselves we have failed to recognize in what we have deemed "other" and what part of that "other" we have failed to recognize in ourselves.

We interpret the following story as a concrete example of seeing beyond the successful coordination of multiple "institutions" that is the hallmark of self-authorizing consciousness (Kegan, 1982). After his release from prison for his insistent anti-apartheid activities, Nelson Mandela led negotiations that constructed a fully democratic political system, and he was elected president of South Africa in 1994. He was faced with governing two highly antagonistic populations: white Afrikaners, who reacted with fear and suspicion at their loss of primacy, and black Africans, who felt entitled, after years of brutal repression, to replace Afrikaners in major public roles and to replace traditional Afrikaner symbols with symbols reflecting black culture and tradition.

Mandela, however, made a point of retaining Afrikaners in many major roles because he felt it was essential that the government reflect the makeup of the nation. Furthermore, he saw how deeply the South Africa rugby team, the Springboks—although rejected by most black Africans—was a unifying symbol for Afrikaners. Therefore, as depicted factually in the film *Invictus* in a leap of imagination beyond pragmatic "inclusion," he actively embraced the Springboks, wore their symbols, and persuaded his party, the African National Congress, to support the team as a fraternal act (Rollings, 2011). When the Springboks heroically won the rugby world cup a year later, the entire stadium of spectators sang two anthems with gusto—the traditional Afrikaner anthem, and the ANC anthem. In that moment, differences were transcended.

We see such an integrative perspective in the practices of other political figures such as Eleanor Roosevelt and Aung San Suu Kyi, and the exhortations of martyred leaders such as Gandhi, Robert Kennedy, and Martin Luther King, to view issues of race, religion, ethnicity, and power through the lens of a transcendent human community. As Martin Luther King eloquently said in an address to Oakwood College in 1962:

> Every individual and every nation must see . . . that all life is interrelated, and all [people] are caught in an inescapable network of mutuality tied in a single garment of destiny, and whatever affects one directly affects all indirectly . . . [U]ntil we come to see this . . . we will end up with a cosmic elegy. (Warren, 2001, p. 174)

Caveat and Challenge

We—Kathleen and Dean—are operating at our own "growing edge" in attempting to imagine the self-transforming way of knowing. Most adult educators, ourselves included, are likely to be traveling a developmental trajectory similar to that of our adult learners—toward achieving and crystallizing our capacities for fourth order. We can therefore offer little guidance about how attention to fifth order might differ from our current practice; plus, it might seem contradictory to suggest that one might facilitate another's *self*-transformation. But ultimately, we concur with what Larry Daloz wrote to us in August 2010: "*[N]obody does it alone.* [An educator's] assignment is to help arrange a world in which the transformation of the self may be accomplished."

At a minimum, teaching adult learners about theories of transformative learning and development of consciousness may be part of that arrangement, as they provide both visions of potential destinations and guidance when the journey seems arduous. We also do well to acknowledge—to ourselves and our adult learners—that we are as much fellow travelers as guides.

If our planet is to survive and its people to prosper, it seems to us that third order consciousness has become a way station, fourth order a gateway, and working actively toward fifth order an urgent need, so that we may develop the capacity to perceive and imagine how to effectively engage the world's constantly emerging and changing crises. To that end, we hope to challenge our colleagues and ourselves to discover and share adult educational practices that will ultimately enable us to realize a quality of consciousness that knows, beyond all question, that as King put it, "all life is interrelated, and all [people] are caught in an inescapable network of mutuality tied in a single garment of destiny" (Warren, 2001, p. 174).

References

Applebee, A. N., & Langer, J. A. (1983). Instructional scaffolding: Reading and writing as natural language activities. *Language Arts, 60,* 168–175.

Becsi, Z. (2001). *Longevity and the life cycle.* Working paper, Department of Economics, Louisiana State University. Retrieved August 11, 2010, from http://www.bus.lsu.edu/economics/papers/pap01_12.pdf

Cranton, P. (1994). *Understanding and promoting transformative learning.* San Francisco: Jossey-Bass.

Daloz, L. (1986). *Effective teaching and mentoring.* San Francisco: Jossey-Bass.

Daloz, L. (1988). The story of Gladys who refused to grow. *Lifelong Learning, 11*(4), 4–7.

Daloz, L. (1999). *Mentor: Guiding the journey of adult learners.* San Francisco: Jossey-Bass.

Dirkx, J. M. (1997). Nurturing soul in adult learning. In P. Cranton (Ed.), *Transformative learning in action* (pp. 79–88). New Directions for Adult and Continuing Education, no. 74. San Francisco: Jossey-Bass.

Geller, K. D. (2009). Transformative learning dynamics for developing relational leaders. In B. Fisher-Yoshida, K. D. Geller, & S. A. Schapiro (Eds.), *Innovations in transformative learning* (pp. 177–200). New York: Peter Lang.

Kegan, R. (1982). *The evolving self.* Cambridge: Harvard University Press.

Kegan, R. (1986). The child behind the mask: Sociopathology as developmental delay. In W. D. Reid, J. W. Bonner III, D. Dorr, & J. I. Walker (Eds.), *Unmasking the psychopath* (pp. 45–77). New York: Norton.

Kegan, R. (1994). *In over our heads.* Cambridge: Harvard University.

Kegan, R. (2000). What form transforms? A constructive-developmental approach to transformative learning. In J. Mezirow & Associates (Eds.), *Learning as transformation: Critical perspectives on a theory in progress.* (pp. 35–69). San Francisco: Jossey-Bass.

Kolb, D. A. (1985). *Learning style inventory.* Boston: McBer.

Lindeman, E. C. (1925). What is adult education? Unpublished manuscript. Columbia University Rare Books and Manuscripts Library, Eduard C. Lindeman Papers (Box 4, Folder 1925), New York.

Mezirow, J. (1991). *Transformative dimensions of adult learning.* San Francisco: Jossey-Bass.

Mezirow, J. (2000). Learning to think like an adult. In J. Mezirow & Associates (Eds.), *Learning as transformation: Critical perspectives on a theory in progress* (pp. 3–33). San Francisco: Jossey-Bass.

Myers, P. B., & Myers, K. D. (1987). *Myers-Briggs Type Indicator.* Palo Alto, CA: Consulting Psychological Press.

Perry, W. G. (1998). *Forms of intellectual and moral development in the college years.* San Francisco: Jossey-Bass.

Rollings, G. (2011, June 15). When Mandela wore Springbok jersey, it changed my nation. *The Sun.* Retrieved from http://www.thesun.co.uk/sol/homepage/features

Schapiro, S. A. (2009). A crucible for transformation: The alchemy of student-centered educations for adults at mid-life. In B. Fisher-Yoshida, K. D. Geller, & S. A. Schapiro (Eds.), *Innovations in transformative learning* (pp. 87–111). New York: Peter Lang.

Taylor, K. (1995). Sitting beside herself. In K. Taylor & C. Marienau (Eds.), *Learning environments for women's adult development: Bridges toward change* (pp. 21–28). New Directions for Adult and Continuing Education, no. 65. San Francisco: Jossey-Bass.

Taylor, K. (2006). Autonomy and self-directed learning. In C. Hoare (Ed.), *Handbook of adult development and learning* (pp. 196–218). New York: Oxford University Press.

Taylor, K., Marienau, C., & Fiddler, M. (2000). *Developing adult learners.* San Francisco: Jossey-Bass.

Tennant, M. (2005). *Psychology and adult learning.* London: Routledge.

Warren, M. A. (2001). *King came preaching.* Downers Grove, IL: InterVarsity Press.

World Health Organization. (2005). Annex table 2b: Under-five mortality rates (per 1000) directly obtained from surveys and vital registration, by age and latest available period or year. In *World health report 2005: Make every mother and child count.* Retrieved from http://www.who.int/whr/2005/annex/annexe2b_en.pdf

CHAPTER TEN

Deep Transformation

Forging a Planetary Worldview

Edmund O'Sullivan

A few years into a new century, we live in a paradoxical moment. Ours is a time of great possibilities and also of grave dangers, both arising from the capability of our species to pursue its goals effectively and single-mindedly. New achievements in science, technology, industry, commerce, and culture have brought benefits to millions of people and ushered the human community into a new age. However, a lack of comprehension has accompanied our frequently arrogant sense of accomplishment. We have been blind to the devastation that has led us to an impasse in our relations with the natural world. In the broadest historical and global context, our commercial industrial obsessions have disturbed the biosystems of this planet to a degree never before known in the historical course of human affairs.

The eminent historian Paul Kennedy anticipated this situation in his book, *Preparing for the Twenty-First Century*, written as the last century came to a close:

> Many earlier attempts to peer into the future concluded either in a tone of
> unrestrained optimism, or gloomy forebodings, or (as in Toynbee's case) in
> appeals for spiritual renewal. Perhaps this work should finish on such a note.
> Yet the fact remains that simply because we do not know the future, it is
> impossible to say with certainty whether global trends will lead to terrible
> disasters or be diverted by astonishing advances in human adaptation. What is

clear is that as the cold war fades away, we face not a "new world order" but a troubled fractured planet; whose problems deserve the serious attention of politicians and publics alike. (Kennedy, 1993, p. 349)

In line with Kennedy's assessment, we see that three hundred years of technological advance and extension of our basic physical abilities have resulted in the possibility for us to reach most parts of the globe within twenty-four hours, communicate instantly through cyberspace, visually apprehend within minutes events as they occur around the world, launch disaster relief in one part of the world from any other within a day, walk on the moon and maneuver in space, provide every child on the earth with vaccines and other medicine that eliminate most life-threatening and debilitating childhood diseases, and produce food on a scale to eliminate starvation. And the list goes on (O'Sullivan & Taylor, 2004).

At the same time, we are able to lay waste vast portions of the earth and entire populations with nuclear arms delivered with laser precision from unmanned crafts on earth and from space. On a daily basis, more garbage is being created than can be disposed of safely. Manufacturing and refining processes around the globe are generating toxic wastes that pollute the earth, water, and air, threatening all species of life on earth, including our own. Destructive environmental changes—precipitated by industry, hydrocarbon-based transportation systems, and the military—are becoming ever more apparent.

Yet our decisions and priorities do not reflect an intention toward life. We are not using our knowledge and technical ability to reverse the dangerous course we seem to be on. The pattern of choices with respect to how and for whose benefit we use our technical expertise is creating deep resentment and rage that sometimes manifests as continuing war and terrorism. Instead of improving the general human condition, the capability to produce wealth and material goods is creating rapidly widening gaps between the rich minority and the poverty-stricken majority. Clearly, traditional science and its applications have brought mixed results to the health and well-being of the earth. As the species at the forefront of the creation of our present perplexities, we are an enigma to ourselves and—as they would no doubt tell us, if they could speak—to all other species. In the midst of our creative capacities, we seem to be gripped by powerful forces of ignorance. In Alan Clements's *Instinct for Freedom* (2002), he suggests that our brains are hardwired toward impulsiveness, irrationality, rage, and violence. He suggests that our future depends on developing the capability to deprogram our minds from these primordial forces and instead reconfigure them toward wisdom and goodness. Although these ideals are ancient in origin, the need to cultivate them in our present world is an ambition no longer confined to spiritual or philosophical circles. The profound dangers that accompany the human venture in this moment of history reveal our immense vulnerabilities. Clements ponders:

> The harsh realities of the modern world have shown us how just a few people with hostile fantasies can rain hell down on the multitude. The need to identify the forces giving rise to ethnocentricity, xenophobia, and any other form of human degradation has never been greater. Equally, we must provide concrete and innovative solutions to deal with these denigrating forces, at international, national, and individual levels. . . . The transformation of human consciousness is a political and social imperative. The promotion of global human rights, exploration of the human mind, and the indivisibility of freedom should be standard subjects taught in every school serious about the preservation of life. (pp. 58–59)

Dealing with the complexities that Clements has engaged, I think it appropriate to give to the reader a provisional definition of what dimensions are included in my formulation of transformative learning. The reader should understand in advance that I am using transformative learning to mean a profound change in worldview. Schlitz and Miller (2010) articulate clearly and succinctly my sense of worldview, as follows:

> A worldview combines beliefs, assumptions, attitudes, values, and ideas to form a comprehensive model of reality. Worldviews also encompass formulations and interpretations of past, present, and future. In our worldviews, we construct complex conceptual frameworks to organize our beliefs about who we are and the world we live in. (p. 5)

My specific formulation of transformative learning is as follows:

> Transformative learning involves experiencing a deep, structural shift in the basic premises of thought, feelings, and actions. It is a shift of consciousness that dramatically alters our way of being in the world. Such a shift involves our understanding of ourselves and our self-locations; our relationships with other humans and with the natural world; our understanding of relations of power in interlocking structures of class, race, and gender; our body awarenesses, our visions of alternative approaches to living; and our sense of possibilities for social justice and peace and personal joy. (O'Sullivan, Morrell, & O'Connor, 2002, p. 11)

The definition of transformative learning just suggested deserves a much more thorough elaboration than is possible within the confines of this volume. As the reader can conclude, this definition holds very complex and differentiated social processes and practices. I refer the reader to the collection of articles that make up *Expanding the Boundaries of Transformative Learning*

(O'Sullivan, Morrell, & O'Connor, 2002), commissioned by the Transformative Learning Centre, where this definition is unpacked in greater detail.

THE GREAT TURNING AND THE GREAT WORK: A TIMELINE FOR DEEP TRANSFORMATION

The deep transformations just suggested are only just starting. This century must be one of deep transformation if there is to be a next century in a human earth context. We need to do our immediate work while at the same time operating in a longer visionary time perspective. The energy needed for this longer time frame is the energy that comes from a place of hope. The cultural historian Thomas Berry (1999) identifies this hopeful context in what he calls the "great work" (p. 1). He notes that human history in different time periods has been governed by overarching movements that give shape and meaning to life by relating the human venture to the larger destinies of the universe. He notes that creating such a movement is the great work of a people. Berry holds that the great work of our time is to carry out the transition from a period of human devastation of the earth to a period in which humans will be present to the planet in a mutually beneficial manner. Joanna Macy and Molly Brown (1998) refer to this larger perspective as the "Great Turning," a way of naming the vast revolution that is going on because our way of life cannot be sustained (see also Korten, 2006). This Great Turning involves three main dimensions. The first dimension is holding actions in defense of life on earth. Holding actions are important because they buy time. They are like a first line of defense; they can save a few species, a few ecosystems, and some of the gene pool for future generations. But holding actions are not enough to create a sustainable society. It is essential to have new social and economic structures, new ways of doing things. The second dimension involves an analysis of structural causes and creation of alternative institutions. It is an understanding of the structural dynamics that fuel the industrial growth society. Macy and Brown (1998) make the point that in this dimension we are not only studying structural causes of the global crisis but also seeking to create alternatives. Finally, the third dimension involves a shift in perception of reality, both cognitively and spiritually. The creation of alternative institutions will not take place unless they are rooted in deeply held values—in our sense of who we are, who we want to be, and how we relate to each other and the living body of earth. This is the third dimension of the Great Turning. It has at its foundation a spiritual revolution, awakening perceptions and values that are both very new and very ancient, linking back to rivers of ancestral wisdom (Macy & Brown, 1998).

INTEGRAL MODES OF TRANSFORMATIVE LEARNING: THE TRIPARTITE DISTINCTION OF SURVIVE, CRITIQUE, AND CREATE

In a very similar vein relating to Macy and Brown's (1998) characterization of the Great Turning, I introduce the tripartite distinction of survive, critique, and create in my formulation of transformative learning (O'Sullivan, 1999; O'Sullivan, Morrell, & O'Connor, 2002; O'Sullivan & Taylor, 2004). Learning takes place in three modes that are distinct but interdependent. There is a holding matrix in my conception of transformative learning that encompasses an education for survival, an education for critical understanding, and an education for integral creativity. In this definition of transformative learning, there is an imperative to survive, critique, and create.

Survival Education (Survive)

Survival means creating conditions for the continuance of living. The terminal aspects of our historical moment, which I have already described, involve educational concerns at the personal, communal, and planetary levels. The sense of all of the locations of survival can be crystallized in the awareness that something is very amiss with the practices of an economic system that has led to both human suffering and environmental disaster. Patterns of devastating destruction, which are neither random nor accidental, have arisen from a consciousness that fragments existence. This dynamism, which is now embedded in the onslaught of the global market, is withering away our vital sustenance at the personal, communal, and planetary levels of existence. We see its effect in environmental devastation, human rights violations, the hierarchies of race, the prevalence of violence, the idea of technological progress, and the problem of failing economies. To understand these complex issues as an intricate piece of our awareness of ecological crisis is the survival task of transformative learning. In terms of facing these profound issues of survival, there are three learning aspects that one does not ordinarily identify with learning.

Here I am thinking about the dynamics of denial, despair, and grief. Denial is a defense mechanism that prevents us from being overwhelmed by the deeply problematic nature of our times. But in order to solve problems it is necessary to come out of denial. Once the depth of our problems is allowed into awareness, we must contend with despair. Despair will be one of the major difficulties in facing survival issues. Without the development of a critical understanding and creative vision, despair potentially has the capacity to overwhelm. Finally, grieving is a necessary ingredient in the survival mode. The sense of loss at the personal, communal, and planetary level that is part and parcel of the survival mode demands a grieving process at deeply profound levels. Therefore, transformative learning in the survival mode is a learning process that requires the ability to deal with denial, despair, and grief (see also Metzger, 2006).

Critical Resistance Education (Critique)

A deep cultural pathology calls for a deep cultural therapy. Part of this cultural therapy involves a transformative mode of cultural criticism. We need to examine the factors and conditions that have brought us to this devastating historical moment. We are in need of a resistance education that moves in the direction of cultural criticism. We are basically dealing with a transformative learning that includes moments of resistance and critical pedagogy. A critical pedagogical moment will cover several areas that are in need of deep critical reflection.

The first dimension of critical resistance education to be examined is the matrix of thought that provides the frame of reference and worldview for the forces of the modern world. Here we need to be attentive to the deep ontological basis of western European thinking. In relation to the natural world, the dynamics of the modern scientific-industrial worldview has moved an agenda that has had profound effects on how the modern western European human views the natural world. The sense of the world that views nature as a mechanism that is enmeshed in mechanical forces has led to a profound disenchantment with the natural world. There is within these forces of modernism a loss of the sense of a wider cosmology in which human actions are embedded.

The philosopher Stephen Toulmin, in his book *The Return to Cosmology* (1985), gives us a convenient entry point for our discussion of the term "cosmology." He observes that there appears to be a natural attitude toward a cosmological sense taken by humans at all times and in all places when reflecting on the natural world. Within this cosmological sense there appears to be a comprehensive ambition to understand and speak about the universe as a whole. Toulmin notes that, in practical terms, this desire for a view of the whole reflects a need to recognize where we stand in the world in which we have been born, to grasp our place in the scheme of things, and to feel at home within it.

A second dimension of critical resistance education is dealing with the saturation of commodity consciousness. Marshall McLuhan once quipped, "I don't know who discovered water, but it certainly wasn't the fish." This image succinctly conveys the problem of a submerged consciousness that critical resistance education must encounter. Given the incredible saturation of information that our modern consciousness demands we attend to, we are, according to John Ralston Saul (2005), an *unconscious civilization*. We are caught up in a situation in which our knowledge does not make us conscious. Reflecting back to the earlier discussion of a fractured cosmology, we see a loss of coherence because we no longer have a coherent conception of ourselves, our universe, and our relation to one another and our world. Within the context of a broader cosmological background, information diversity is as critical to our long-term survival as biodiversity.

The third dimension of of critical resistance education is the critical examination of hierarchical power. Our modern western historical inheritance is deeply embedded in a hierarchal conception of power that comes to us in the structures of patriarchy and imperialism (Korten, 2006). In its simplest interpretation, patriarchy is a system of power in which men dominate. Our culture exists within the matrix of patriarchal power. In reflecting on our western heritage, we see male dominance in the four establishments that have been in control of western history over the centuries: the classical empires, the ecclesiastical establishment, the nation state, and the modern corporation. Historically, women have had a minimal role, if any, in the direction of these establishments. Simultaneously, with the deconstruction of patriarchy, the deep structure of hierarchal power and violence will need to be critically examined in such areas as race, class, gender, and sexual orientation. The structures of imperialism, which have characterized the expansiveness of western culture in the modern era, are now being brought into the light of profound criticism.

Visionary Transformative Education (Create)

I develop the idea of a creative transformative learning by highlighting the themes of education for planetary consciousness, education for integral development, education for quality of life, and education and the sacred. Let us first consider education for a planetary consciousness. In spite of its powerful dynamics in our world today, the idea of the global market is a small idea. Brian Swimme (1996) points out that we can be fooled into thinking that our lives are passed in political entities, such as the state or a nation, or the bottom-line concerns in life having to do with economic realities. He invites us to understand that we live in the midst of immensities. I realize that, in presenting a larger cosmological context for our lives, it is not enough to defend a new cosmology in opposition to the cosmology that has underpinned modernity. In a visionary context for transformative learning, we must articulate a planetary context for learning, expressed in such a way that it can effectively challenge the hegemonic culture of the market vision and can orient people in practice, in their daily lives, to create and sustain an environmentally viable world, starting now. The philosopher Alan Gare (1995) maintains that we need a new grand narrative that helps us to find our way in our present situation in a narrative story larger than the market. We need stories of sufficient power and complexity to orient people for effective action to overcome environmental problems, to address the multiple problems caused by environmental destruction, to reveal what possibilities are available for *transforming* these problems, and to guide people in the roles they must play in this project. The scope and magnitude of transformative stories brings many cultural pieces together in creative dynamic tension.

In my own work on transformative learning, I suggest that we need to expand our horizon of consciousness to the universe itself. The cultural historian and ecologist Thomas Berry (1989) reveals the scope of a vision where the universe is the matrix:

> The universe in its full extension in space and its sequence of transformations in time is best understood as story; a story in the twentieth century for the first time with scientific precision through empirical observation. The difficulty is that scientists have until recently given us the story only in its physical aspects not in the full depth of its reality or in the full richness of its meaning. The greatest single need for the survival of the earth or of the human community in this late twentieth century is for an integral telling of the Great Story of the Universe. This story must provide in our times what the great mythic stories of earlier times provided as the guiding and energizing sources of the human venture. (p. 1)

I am using Berry's ideas as entry point into a broader cosmological context. I have found that this point of entry has opened up a system of larger meaning that can help create an organic planetary context for educational endeavors that transcends the myopic vision of the global marketplace.

Planetary Context

I believe that educational vision in the twenty-first century must be accomplished within a planetary context. We live on a planet, not on a globe. When we look at the universe story that we have just depicted, we encounter an organic totality, not a cartea logical map. We are one species living on a planet called Earth, and all living and vital energies come out of this organic cosmological context. The globe is a construct of human artifice. For Europeans, Columbus transformed the mapping systems for commerce from a flat surface to a globe. The globe was made for commerce today, and the language of globalization today is first and foremost for commercial purposes. For all of the major issues that we have discussed under "Critique," the language of globalization is the background context. All over the world, at this moment, nation state governments are delivering their inhabitants to transnational business. Therefore we cannot dispense with global language, and it is absolutely necessary that it be the subject of deep order cultural criticism at a world level.

The second visionary theme is education for integral development. The words "integral" and "development" have been carefully chosen. In spite of the very critical analysis of the concept of development that can be ventured against market-driven development, there is still a very core need to retain a conception of development in a treatment of transformative education. It is one thing to severely criticize our western conceptions of development; it is quite another to try to conceive of education in the absence of an overarching conception of development. Creative visionary education must include a conception of development that will transcend the limitations of our western ideas about development and its attendant conception of underdevelopment. Therefore, integral development links the creative evolutionary processes of the universe, the planet, the earth community, the human community, and the personal world. It is a development that must be understood as a dynamic wholeness, where wholeness encompasses the entire universe and vital consciousness resides both within us and at the same time all around us in the world. The endpoint of all this moves toward a deep personal planetary consciousness that one can identify, at a personal level, as ecological selfhood.

THE DYNAMISM OF TRANSFORMATION AT THE PERSONAL LEVEL

In this personal ecological context, it is important for the reader to be apprised of the integral nature of what we are suggesting. As people, we seem to have a deep primordial need for reciprocal acknowledgment, and in the absence of this aspect of deep sociability there appears to be a breakdown in the development of the person at these early vulnerable stages that can be devastating. It would seem that humans are possessed of a compulsion to share their conscious understanding and emotions as intimately as possible. Intimacy here means a presence to one another at our deepest levels of subjectivity. It is clear that each species carries a deep coding of its responsibilities for the enhancement of its own life processes. We are also very much aware of an interspecies awareness that from our very beginnings is opening us up to a wider world. This wider sense of connection with all of the powers of the world is a primary matrix for all of our subsequent development.

The framework for personal transformation just articulated must be formulated in an evolutionary understanding of personal development. Here I will briefly draw on general systems theory to give us a specific entry point into the world of the individual learner. In the systems theory viewpoint, during the process of learning, the mind organizes itself by virtue of feedback—that is, by monitoring its interactions with its environment. The key term in systems theory is "monitoring." The basic assumption is that open systems, like the mind, self-monitor. In the context of learning, monitoring assumes that the mind watches what it is doing and adjusts. The mind initially operates through preconceptions; these preconceptions not only shape our interpretations of the world but also impinge on the world itself.

To comprehend how the world and the mind shape each other, it is necessary to examine the two main ways that feedback works. The first is homeostatic or negative feedback, a process that brings the world around us in line with our assumption and goals. The second is adaptive or positive feedback, which leads to change in internal codes or presuppositions. Thus negative feedback indicates that one is on track, with no need for adjustment, whereas positive feedback signals deviation from the objective and a need to correct or alter course.

In this particular context, living systems adapt by transforming themselves, and learning occurs. Thus, from the perspective of transformative learning, real learning is not something added to a system in adaptation. Transformation means, in essence, the reorganization of the whole system. In this process, the viewed world is different and so is the viewpoint of the viewer. Transformative learning processes are counted as the creative function of cognitive crisis. Creativity occurs in a cognitive system when old habitual modes of interpretation become dysfunctional, demanding a shifting of ground or viewpoint. The breakdown, or crisis, motivates the system to self-organize in more inclusive and comprehensive ways of knowing, embracing, and integrating data of which it had been previously unconscious.

At the Transformative Learning Centre, we are interested in the generation of energy for radical vision, action, and new ways of being. If we are to survive on this planet we need new connections to each other and to the natural world. Changing of political and economic relationships is part of the larger project of reconstituting and revitalizing all of our relationships. Thus our purpose in transformative learning is not to delineate abstract principles about how adults learn; we are not interested in theoretical "generalizibility"—at least not in the terms in which this concept is ordinarily used (O'Sullivan, Morrell, & O'Connor, 2002, p. 11).

In such a context, where might we seek direction regarding change? Where are the voices of vision in this century? What must our points of emphasis be as we learn new types of consciousness? I am not looking for vision from nation-state governments or even from universities for that matter. Too often both are embedded and implicated in current problems to the extent that nothing changes. We need a different conception of how knowledge is going to be garnered in this century.

TRANSFORMATIVE LEARNING AT THE LEVEL OF EMERGENT PRACTICES

In *Expanding the Boundaries of Transformative Learning*, we asked contributors to reflect upon and question the purposes of transformative learning

(O'Sullivan, Morrell, & O'Connor, 2002). At the same time, these questions require us to understand the content of learning in ways that other approaches have shied away from. This edited volume offers a much more open space for the marginal, the liminal, the unconscious, and the embodied. Contributors to this volume include those who use embodied praxis of artful inquiry and arts-informed research, contributors who apply meta-analyses of the media and of global capital, and contributors who draw from various types of indigenous knowledge to shape their pedagogical strategies. Our particular vision or visions of transformative learning also differs from other visions in this current volume with respect to the centrality and potential of dialogue or rational discourse. There is no question that challenging discussion can stimulate change, particularly when there is safety, trust, and respect. In my view, however, there are also other routes to transformative learning, which are illustrated in this volume. We also understand that crucial learning often takes place nonverbally, in the inarticulate dimensions of our bodies.

In 2004, Marilyn Taylor and I put out an edited volume entitled *Learning Toward an Ecological Consciousness: Selected Transformative Practices* (O'Sullivan & Taylor, 2004). This collected volume of thirteen authors brought together types of practices in a variety of fields addressing ecological consciousness. The wide-ranging selection of transformative practices documented therein offered avenues toward an emerging ecological consciousness that reshapes us, our actions, and our understanding. These practices, as a collection, are an expression of the principle of equifinality; that is, the principle that there are many paths to a destination. A corollary is that we begin where we are and in a way in which we are moved and able to begin. The contributors and those whose experience and reflections are represented (where identified) in the chapters begin in multiple cultures, at least three indigenous, on at least four continents, in at least eight countries. They are men and women who speak through a gendered experience implicitly if not explicitly. Signifying transformation through connection in multiple ways, these practices cross layers and domains of the social and cultural processes of the social and natural world. These practices are holding together interpersonal and primary groups, cultural and other communities, the workplace, educational institutions, and the wider society.

One chapter in that volume exemplifies the transdisciplinary, embodied, participatory, and more-than-rational arising from our definition of transformative learning. In "Holding Flames: Women Illuminating Knowledge of s/Self Transformation," Eimear O'Neill draws on embodied and critical artful heuristic research, within a participatory transformative learning framework, to literally and figuratively display women's understandings and process in the breakdown of previous worldviews toward more integral ecological consciousness. Together the community installation of thirty-six lanterns from a diversity of women indicated that women were transforming from limiting traumatic experiences, and that their journeys of transformation were multilocal (changing communities, cultures, and institutions, not just individual selves), participatory (cocreated) and indigenous (drawing on the histories of their own peoples and on the natural world as teacher and spiritual resource [O'Neill, 2004, 2005]). In her more recent writing, O'Neill (2011) demonstrates how these research findings changed educational praxis in developing the circle processes of the three extraordinary Spirit Matters Gatherings in 2004, 2007, and 2010. At these Gatherings, wisdom leaders from multiple traditions met with participants and each other in deep conversation, artful celebration, and commitment to action toward social, political, and environmental change.

The work of the Fielding Institute and Associates deserves mention as also expanding the boundaries of transformative learning. The edited volume entitled *Innovations in Transformative Learning* demonstrates how transformative learning can be introduced to a variety of settings and cultures and synergistically integrated with theories of communication and participatory action research. The editors organize this volume around themes of creating space for learning through the lenses of culture, diversity, and difference as well as animating awareness through the experience and performance of the arts (Fisher-Yoshida, Geller, & Schapiro, 2009).

Gardner and Kelly (2008) have put together an edited volume on transformative learning entitled *Narrating Transformative Learning in Education.* The opening chapter for this volume draws on the inspiration of the work that I am doing at the Transformative Learning Centre. Finally, Jason Goulah (2007a, 2007b), in a study carried out in Japan, used my take on transformative learning as a theoretical underpinning for a research study entitled "Cultural Transformative Learning and Planetary Literacy in the Foreign Classroom."

INTEGRAL TRANSFORMATIVE LEARNING

In conclusion, I elucidate dimensions of transformative learning that characterize the integral nature of my work in this field. I end by highlighting five central components or points of emphasis of such a shift of consciousness.

Holism

Complexity theory reminds us that our mechanistic belief structures are ill conceived. We cannot control everything, and we must now engage in more emergent, integrative thinking to envision change. Complexity theory encourages a "learning while moving" kind of education that teaches a response to contingency. Creativity is the basis of such education, and it must be restored in contemporary education. We need to reengage whole areas of creativity to honor holism and to honor ourselves as whole persons in relation to a cosmos and a biosphere. We must learn to attend to our surroundings as whole persons in the web of life. We must also begin to think and to talk in terms of webs and circles rather than hierarchies. We must build a participatory consciousness and set up our institutions to encourage this kind of consciousness, so that we actually participate with one another and cross boundaries to negotiate and to develop a consensus that helps people feel like parts of a learning process that enhances the quality of their lives. So it is a web—the web of life—making connections not only to the human world but also to the natural world. We must begin to look at, appreciate, and learn from cultures that have honored the natural processes as a matter of course.

Wisdom of Women

The institutions of patriarchy place men in a hierarchical relationship with women in terms of what is important and not important. But the world needs what women provide. If we look at other periods of history, there have been different constellations in which women were much more prominent. I believe that the idea of the feminine, even in men, will be important to break through the processes that are forcing so much destructive violence on the world and its people.

Wisdom of Indigenous Peoples

Indigenous, aboriginal peoples are in the process of reconstituting their heritage. The reenchantment of the natural world will not be accomplished by a return to older ways of thinking and acting in the world. We will not be able to romanticize or imitate indigenous peoples' participatory mystique with the world. We cannot copy worldview systems that we do not occupy or live in. We nevertheless must appropriate certain aspects of wisdoms from the past. We must have a sober accounting of the wisdom and sagacity of cultures that have preceded us. Although magic, religion, and mystical traditions were prey to errors and follies of the spirit, they nevertheless carried within them a wisdom of the awareness of humanity's organic embeddedness in a complex and natural system. This type of appreciation does not abolish modernity, but it may help us transcend it. The major problem is for us to discover how to recapture older wisdoms in a mature form. Modern scientists are beginning to understand that traditional indigenous wisdom is extremely sophisticated and of considerable practical value.

Native science preceding our own western systems has developed systems for identifying, naming, and classifying soils, plants, insects, and other elements of local environments and deriving medical and economic benefit from them. Because of the deep understanding of the earth processes and a frame of reference that is planetary in vision, it will be both prudent and wise for educators to pay careful attention to indigenous wisdom because of its rich and varied planetary emphasis. Our cultural history with the indigenous first peoples of the Americas has been marked by arrogance and disrespect for a worldview that for the most part we neither understood nor appreciated. We are now coming to see, with the help of postmodern deconstruction, that we have ignored worldviews that were rich in cosmological significance. The worldviews of indigenous peoples can now give us a new appreciation of the historical and contemporary significance of native cosmologies.

Spirituality

It is possible that if you spoke to someone at the beginning of the past century, he or she might have said that religion would no longer be around by the mid-twentieth century and that with increased secularization, there would no longer be a need for God, religion, or spirituality. But that did not happen. Atheism no longer has the same kind of currency, even in universities. Different manifestations of religion are on the rise across the world. This rise in religious participation seems to be a two-edged sword. Although there are many positive features of renewed interest in religion, one must recognize a downside. As the world is becoming more religious, is it also becoming a lot more dangerous as a result of religious intolerance? On another level, secular modernity masks the fact that we are material spirits, spirits of matter. Our spirituality is a mystery. The type of spirituality that will become important is marked by what Brian Swimme and Thomas Berry (1992) outline as differentiation, subjectivity, and communion. There are diverse expressions of what it means to be a human spirit, and we should be interested in and appreciative of these, while still being ourselves. Our spirituality should open us to differences and to the "inscape," the inner mysteries of life. As Swimme and Berry remind us, "The universe is a communion of subjects, not a collection of objects" (1992, p. 243). The Universe Story and a deep sense of interiority and an appreciation of difference invite us to a wider, more inclusive community (Swimme & Berry, 1992).

These voices, these points of emphasis I have just named, lead us toward and enliven a transformative education. As I have indicated elsewhere, along with other cowriters, transformative education involves experiencing a deep structural shift in the basic premises of our thoughts, feelings, and actions. It is a shift of consciousness that dramatically and permanently alters our way of being in the world. Such a shift involves an understanding of ourselves and our self locations, our relations with other humans and with the natural world; an understanding of the relations of power in the interlocking structures of class, race, and gender; our body awareness; our visions of alternative approaches to living; and our sense of possibilities for social justice and peace and personal joy

(O'Sullivan, Morrell, & O'Connor, 2002, p. 11). Such a transformative education involves emancipation from servitude, yes, but also from the blinders that servitude places on us in relation to the rest of the world. It is felt at the personal, community, institutional, global, and planetary levels.

In this sense, it is an integral education, or what some might call a holistic education. It is that web that holds together the many elements that constitute a transformative learning and teaching process. Transformation is a process of learning that has a sense of adventure. It is learning embraced as a journey, less concerned with trying to find fixed facts and more concerned with identifying what we need to learn to live well—ecologically, peacefully, and justly. Finally, a transformative education requires modes of survival and sustainability, resistance and critique, and creativity and vision. It is deeply ecological and integrative.

As we stand at the beginning of this new century, our time to change is here. The transition period is upon us, and there is an urgency to these changes that compels us. Transformative education holds the hope of a different kind of education. It is our work to do, our promise to fulfill, our legacy to leave.

References

Berry, T. (1989, July). Twelve principles for understanding the universe and the role of the human in the universe. *Teilhard Perspective, 22,* 1–3.

Berry, T. (1999). *The great work: Our way into the future.* New York: Bell Tower Books.

Clements, A. (2002). *Instinct for freedom.* Novato, CA: New World Library.

Fisher-Yoshida, B., Geller, K., & Schapiro, S. (Eds.). (2009). *Innovations in transformative learning: Space, culture, and the arts.* New York: Peter Lang.

Gardner, M., & Kelly, U. (Eds.). (2008). *Narrating transformative learning in education.* New York: Palgrave Press.

Gare, A. (1995). *Postmodernism and the environmental crisis.* New York: Routledge Press.

Goulah, J. (2007a). Cultural transformative learning and planetary literacy in the foreign language classroom. *Journal of Transformative Education, 5*(2), 163–176.

Goulah, J. (2007b, Spring). Village voices, global visions: Digital video as a transformative foreign language tool. *Foreign Language Annals, 40,* 62.

Kennedy, P. (1993). *Preparing for the twenty-first century.* New York: Harper.

Korten, D. C. (2006). *The great turning: From empire to earth community.* Bloomfield, CT: Kumarian Press.

Macy, J., & Brown, M. Y. (1998). *Coming back to life: Practices to reconnect our lives, our world.* Gabriola Island, BC: New Society Publishers.

Metzger, D. (2006). *From grief into vision.* Topango, CA: Hand to Hand Publishers.

O'Neill, E. (2004). Holding flames: Women illuminating knowledge of s/Self transformation. In E. O'Sullivan & M. Taylor (Eds.), *Learning toward an ecological consciousness: Selected transformative practices* (pp. 183–200). New York: Palgrave Macmillan.

O'Neill, E. (2005). *Holding flames: Women illuminating knowledge of s/Self transformation.* Unpublished dissertation, OISE/UT. Available at www.eimearoneill.com.

O'Neill, E. (2011). The place of creation: Transformation, trauma and creative praxis. In L. Williams, R. Roberts, & A. McIntosh (Eds.), *Radical human ecology: Intercultural and indigenous approaches.* London: Ashgate Publishing Group.

O'Sullivan, E. (1999). *Transformative learning: Educational vision for the 21st century.* New York: Zed Books.

O'Sullivan, E., Morrell, A., & O'Connor, M. (Eds.). (2002). *Expanding the boundaries of transformative learning: Essays on theory and praxis.* New York: Palgrave Press.

O'Sullivan, E., & Taylor, M. (Eds.). (2004). *Learning toward an ecological consciousness: Selected transformative practices.* New York: Palgrave Press.

Saul, J. R. (2005). *The unconscious civilization.* Toronto: Anansi Press.

Schlitz, M., & Miller, E. (2010). Worldview transformation and the development of social consciousness. *Institute of Noetic Sciences, 2*(5), 5.

Swimme, B. (1996). *The hidden heart of the cosmos.* New York: Orbis Books.

Swimme, B., & Berry, T. (1992). *The universe story.* San Francisco: HarperOne.

Toulmin, S. (1985). *The return to cosmology.* Berkeley, CA: University of California Press.

CHAPTER ELEVEN

Transformative Learning and the Challenges of Complexity

Michel Alhadeff-Jones

T ransformative learning is "an approach to teaching based on promoting change, where educators challenge learners to critically question and assess the integrity of their deeply held assumptions about how they relate to the world around them" (Mezirow & Taylor, 2010, p. xi). The study of transformative learning itself is grounded in systems of thoughts (for example, behaviorism, cognitivism, constructivism, feminism, Marxism, positivism, poststructuralism, psychoanalysis, structuralism, systems theories, and so on) characterized by "deeply held" epistemic assumptions. Each of these paradigms defines and legitimates how knowledge should be produced in order to establish some kind of "truth" about individual and collective learning and transformation. Each of them also defines what kind of "error" should be avoided in the scientific process. As practitioners, the way we conceive our educational practice is strongly influenced by the epistemic assumptions that frame such systems of thought. As researchers, our inquiry is determined by methodologies that are rooted in one or another of these paradigms. For transformative educators, challenging assumptions is at the core of what we promote among learners—despite the fact that we seldom consider questioning the legitimacy of the paradigms that frame our own educational practice and research.

In this chapter, I discuss some implications inherent to theories of complexity, because I believe, as many other educational theorists currently do (for example, Ardoino, 2000; Banathy & Jenlink, 1996; Clénet & Poisson, 2005; Complicity: An International Journal of Complexity and Education; *La Pensée*

Complexe en Recherches et en Pratique, 2008; Morin, 1999; Osberg & Biesta, 2010; Paul & Pineau, 2005; Sinnott, 2003) that they provide us with a set of assumptions and principles that are needed in order to challenge some significant limitations associated with dominant systems of thought. Located at the intersection of philosophy, physics, biology, and human sciences, the paradigm of complexity formulated by Morin (1977/1992; 1977–2004/2008; 1990/2008, 2007) criticizes contemporary sciences and philosophies that compartmentalize and reduce the way we understand ourselves and the world around us without critically reflecting on the limitations they introduce.

Interpreting the way knowledge is produced as a "complex" phenomenon means that it embraces or comprehends heterogeneous elements plaited together, interwoven in a way that is hardly apprehended by the mind and not easily analyzed or disentangled (Ardoino, 2000; Alhadeff-Jones, 2008a). In the contemporary context, most of us have access to a sum of knowledge (scientific or not) so abundant that we face a major challenge: to learn not only to identify what is relevant to know but also how to organize heterogeneous explanations and interpretations so that they remain meaningful. As a learner, practitioner, or researcher, when dealing with complexity one must systematically challenge the way everyday situations and scientific problems are reduced. Indeed, a complex way of thinking "represents a shift away from the simplifying, reductionist approach that has traditionally shaped scientific enquiry" (Morin, 1996, p. 10).

To illustrate what is at stake in the definition and in the development of a complex epistemology of transformative learning, this chapter introduces the paradigm of complexity and explores six challenges that appear particularly illustrative with regards to the advance of research and practices related to transformative learning.

INTRODUCING THE PARADIGM OF COMPLEXITY

Throughout the history of modern sciences, there have been several ways to conceive the complexity of problems tackled by scientists (Weaver, 1948). From the seventeenth to the nineteenth century, it was conceived following the models offered by classical physics: valorizing objectivity, causal explanation, quantitative data, and certainty.

According to this "paradigm of simplification" (Morin, 1990/2008)—which still grounds dominant scientific paradigms and organizes scientific disciplines—complex problems must be tackled by reducing them to more simple issues, explaining or solving them independently and successively. Since the second half of the nineteenth century, several discoveries made in physics have contributed to the emergence of another paradigm, which considers disorder as a fundamental part of natural phenomena (for instance, physical matter appearing to be made of disordered particles and the universe being born from initial chaos). The forms of order observed in the physical and biological world are born from disorder and in some ways dominate it. However, the emergence of systems (from a swirl of water to life itself) organizing order and disorder does not follow a simple causality. Complex phenomena are both predictable and unpredictable. For instance, it is easy to predict that water heated up is going to boil, however it is impossible to predict where in the pot the boiling will start. They combine antagonistic, complementary, and contradictory principles such as fluctuation and stability, linearity and nonlinearity, randomness and nonrandomness. In addition, discoveries made in the early twentieth century forced scientists to acknowledge that the study of complex phenomena cannot be done without taking into consideration the role of the observer in the way complexity is described (Morin, 1977/1992). The recognition of complexity therefore appears at the roots of a new kind of scientific explanation, which perceives simplicity as a specific provisional phenomenon. Complication refers to the idea of an intricate situation waiting to be disentangled; complexity supposes the fundamental nonsimplicity of studied phenomenon (Ardoino, 2000) requiring the acknowledgment of researchers' own uncertainty about the way they conceive it. As formulated by Bachelard (1934/2003, p. 152, my translation): "There is no simple idea, because a simple idea [. . .] is always inserted, to be understood, in a complex system of thoughts and experiences." From the 1940s until today, several theories have emerged, providing scientists with resources that help them question and understand the relationship between order and disorder among complex phenomena (for a more exhaustive overview, including full bibliographical references, see Alhadeff-Jones, 2008a).

Considering research on transformative learning through these contributions requires one to navigate between at least three intertwined levels. The first level is conceptual and theoretical. It involves reconsidering one's understanding of transformative learning based on a renewed vocabulary (including chaos, disorder, emergence, nonlinearity, self-organization, and systems). The second level is epistemological. It requires one to revisit the way one conceives scientific activity and the processes through which knowledge is produced through the inclusion of a set of assumptions legitimizing innovative logics and methodologies (for example, complex causalities, dialogical principle) (Morin, 1977–2004/2008; 1990/2008). The third level requires researchers and practitioners to reflect more systematically on the personal and institutional dynamics shaping the way research is conducted and knowledge created (Alhadeff-Jones, 2010; Montuori, 2005, 2010; Paul & Pineau, 2005).

REVISITING TRANSFORMATIVE LEARNING THROUGH THE PARADIGM OF COMPLEXITY

To revisit the way knowledge about transformative learning is produced according to a complexivist perspective, the following section explores six challenges that represent some of the core issues associated with the paradigm of complexity.

Negotiating the Tensions Between Generality and Singularity

Assuming that transformative learning is a complex process invites one to consider it as both predictable, according to determined general principles (such as the crucial role of disorienting dilemma, dialogue, and so on), and unpredictable (such as the randomness of the experience of epiphany). Educational practices and theoretical contributions informing our understanding of transformative learning are therefore caught into a double bind, shaped by both the need to generalize and abstract the way transformative learning is interpreted and promoted, as well as the necessity to acknowledge its contingency. On one hand, transformative learning is growing as a dominant teaching paradigm that is becoming a standard of practice in a variety of disciplines and educational settings, as well as the focus of a growing amount of scientific research suggesting some kind of universality. On the other hand, individual experience and an awareness of the context of learning remain two essential components that frame a transformative approach to teaching (Mezirow & Taylor, 2010). A respect for this tension is at the core of a complex understanding of transformative learning. From an epistemological perspective, during the past twenty years the influence of postmodern and poststructuralist critiques have challenged the claim of universality legitimizing many educational contributions, including initial writings on transformative learning theory (for example, Mezirow, 1999; Usher, Bryant, & Johnston, 1997; Pietrykowski, 1996). Nevertheless, traditional (for example, Mezirow, 1991) and radical "postmodern" interpretations (Bagnall, 1999) both tend to reduce the complexity that can be found in transformative learning. The former focuses on the search for the underlying order shaping transformative learning experiences and the identification of a totalizing discourse, which tends to reduce the diversity of variables determining real-life experience in order to highlight universal characteristics. Conversely, the latter privileges the reintroduction of disorder into educational practice and theory, mainly by focusing on what has been neglected, forgotten, repressed, rejected, disqualified, excluded, or silenced by traditional methodologies (Rosenau, 1992). A complex conception of learning and research encourages one to embrace such an antagonism rather than minimizing it. This requires researchers and practitioners to continuously nurture the tensions between what makes the universality and the singularity of transformative learning. For instance, in spite of the relevance of life history and biographical approaches (for example, West, Alheit, Andersen, & Merrill, 2007) regarding the promotion of perspective transformation in adult and higher education, the transformative dimension inherent in such methods remains often uncertain and always contingent on the constitution and the dynamics of the group as well as the institutional environment surrounding it (such as status and prior knowledge of participants, mutual trust, power dynamics) (Dominicé, 2000). Considering a process of transformation according to the "catastrophic" (literally "overturning") and "chaotic" nature of "nonlinear phenomena" (exemplified through the well-known "butterfly effect") requires learners, researchers, and practitioners to privilege interpretations starting from the local and the singular (Morin, 1977–2004/2008; 1990/2008). To be generalized, the meaning of a transformative approach to education also requires the inclusion of the micro and macro historical contexts of the training (for example, individuals, group, institution, and country's history) in order to grasp the extent of its transformative effects (Lani-Bayle & Mallet, 2010). Considering the increasing expectations formulated by practitioners and institutions favoring "ready-made tools," "standardized" tests and methods framing their research and training, such a position is a challenging one. It questions what kinds of resources are required for practitioners and researchers to learn to claim the value of a paradoxical perspective on transformative learning, looking for generality while simultaneously embracing the singularity of every learning event.

Reconsidering the Linearity and Nonlinearity of Transformative Learning

Individual perspective transformation is most often explained as being triggered by a significant personal event. However, there is still little understanding of why some disorienting dilemmas lead to a transformation and others do not (Taylor, 2000). This fact encourages one to revisit common assumptions about the type of causality involved in transformative learning (Sinnott, 2003). The principle of "complex causality" (including mutual causalities, feedback loops) informs the understanding of self-regulating systems (Morin, 1977–2004/2008). It breaks with the principle of linear causality, stressing the fact that cause acts on its effect, as effect acts on its cause through positive and negative feedbacks (exemplified by the thermostat's mechanism of temperature regulation). Transformative learning is often described through the linear succession of different phases (for example, disorienting dilemma, self-examination, critical assessment of assumptions, recognition that one's discontent and transformation are shared, exploration of new science options, planning action, acquisition of knowledge and skills, trying new roles, building self-confidence, reintegration of the new perspective) (Mezirow & Associates, 2000). Each of these phases is made of multiple changes affecting the learner and the learner's environment.

Each step involves a variety of outcomes (emotions, beliefs, behaviors) that affect the other phases of the transformative process. The principle of complex causality invites one to pay attention to theses mutual relationships, not only through a linear but also through circular dynamics. It stresses the role of the positive and negative reinforcements (such as radicalization and inhibition) that regulate the emotions, beliefs, and behaviors at each stage of the process and in between. Beyond the idea of regulation, complexity theories also introduced the notion of "recursive loop" in order to understand and describe processes of "self-organization" and "self-production" (Morin, 1977/1992). It refers to a generating loop through which products and effects are themselves producers of what produces them. Such a principle can be observed, for instance, in social life: society produces who we are at the same time that we contribute to what society becomes. At an individual level, recursive loops characterize the "vicious and virtuous circles" often described by learners or practitioners when they interpret their personal or professional experiences and their self-development. Transformative learning emerges from what each stage of its own development produces—dilemma, reflection, awareness, community, alternatives, new knowledge, feelings, identity, and so on. A critical incident, such as a traumatic event, may retrospectively appear at the source of a transformation, but transformative learning can also be triggered by the repetition of the same unsatisfactory experience through multiple cycles, building up to a critical mass, leading one day to a bifurcation in one's own way of being. For instance, such cycles may characterize the evolution described when someone is finally able to quit smoking after several unsuccessful attempts. Recursive loops stress the relationships among circularity, repetitions, and innovation involved in the process of transformation. Paying attention to these processes provides resources to interpret the generative dynamics associated with transformative learning according to linear and nonlinear developmental perspectives (Sinnott, 2003). It is congruent with studies establishing the evolving and spiraling nature of transformative learning (Taylor, 2000). Such a perspective is challenging because it claims that single causes explaining the presence or the absence of transformative learning are the exception, not the rule. Transformative learning is produced and/or inhibited by the multiple changes that constitute the learner's own evolution. According to this assumption, the evaluation and description of transformative learning therefore becomes much more difficult to anticipate, describe, and evaluate.

Conceiving the Emerging Nature of Transformation Through Its Levels of Organization

Several streams of research have approached the complexity of transformative learning through holistic and interdisciplinary perspectives favoring open spaces for the marginal, the liminal, the unconscious, the embodied, and the affective, stressing the importance of promoting an ecological vision, and highlighting the interconnectedness between individuals and their social and natural environment (for example, Davis-Manigaulte, Yorks, & Kasl, 2006; O'Sullivan, 1999; O'Sullivan, Morrell, & O'Connor, 2002). Despite such contributions, the mutual influences among context, culture, and transformative learning remain only marginally examined (Taylor, 2000), and regrettably there is still no sound connection between individual perspective transformation and social change (Finger & Asùn, 2001). Embracing a holistic perspective and the complexity of the relationships between individual and collective transformations requires one to establish strong connections between psychological, social, anthropological, economical, and political theories. It also requires one to systematically bind knowledge of parts to knowledge of the whole(s). Adopting a systemic and organizational perspective encourages one to conceive transformative learning through the new properties that emerge from a whole, influencing its environment and recursively determining its own components (Morin, 1977–2004/2008). This privileges research design that articulates multiple levels of analysis (individual, organizational, institutional, societal) in order to question what characterizes their mutual relationships and how they are intertwined with each other. For instance, in their research on power dynamics in a corporate multinational company, Pagès, Bonetti, de Gaulejac, and Descendre (1979) articulated three theoretical frameworks (Marxism, psychoanalysis, and psychosociology) in order to interpret the correspondences between social organization and the unconscious structures of the individuals' personalities. They demonstrated that for individuals and an organization to be transformed requires understanding of both the unconscious ties that attach individuals to the collectivity and the organizational policy implemented in order to reinforce such ties. Adopting a systemic and organizational perspective also invites one to consider the different temporalities shaping transformative learning and how they intertwine (Alhadeff-Jones, Lesourd, Roquet, & Le Grand, 2011). For instance, the international survey coordinated by Lani-Bayle and Mallet (2010) questions and differentiates the relationships between personal transformation and the different temporal frames shaping individual and collective experience (that is, biological age, generational belonging, local and national history). It is challenging to consider transformative learning as an emergence involving several levels of organization simultaneously because this requires researchers and practitioners to consider relationships, interactions, and mutual interdependences among phenomena that are usually fragmented, compartmentalized, and simplified by scientific theories and disciplines.

Beyond Diversity of Perspectives: Recognizing Heterogeneity and Multireferentiality

The literature on transformative learning includes a growing number of contributions originating from heterogeneous academic disciplines (from sociology to psychology and neurosciences). From an epistemological perspective, such a process of inclusion is often grounded in misrepresentations of adjacent disciplines in an attempt to simplify their contributions and preserve the coherence of one's own field of study (Pagès, 2002). For instance, according to Finger and Asùn (2001), Marxists' criticism of Mezirow's theory claiming that it has no theory of social action and social change (Collard & Law, 1989; Welton, 1995) should be conceived not as a political question but rather as an epistemological one: "Mezirow has not really integrated Freire's and Habermas's political analysis; this has led him to focus ... on the way adult learners adapt to rather than criticize society. As a result, Mezirow simply assumes, like the [humanist tradition in adult education] that perspective transformation and adult learning will automatically lead to social action and social change" (Finger & Asùn, 2001, p. 59). Acknowledging how much a complex way of doing research is embedded in the articulation between academic disciplines, Ardoino's contribution to the concept of "multireferentiality" stresses the need to identify what is constitutive of their heterogeneity: "A multireferential approach promotes the adoption of a plural way of reading its objects (practices or theories), adopting various angles and involving as many specific views [regards] and languages, appropriate to the required descriptions, based on distinct systems of references, acknowledged as explicitly irreducible to each other, in other words as heterogeneous" (Ardoino, 1993, p. 15, my translation). Multireferentiality requires that researchers systematically identify the cores and boundaries as well as the rules, logic, and assumptions specific to the different disciplines, theories, and concepts used to interpret transformative learning. It has been initiated, for example, around the concepts of "self" (Dirkx, 2007), "critique" (Alhadeff-Jones, 2007a, 2007b, 2010; Brookfield, 2000) and "complexity" itself (Alhadeff-Jones, 2008a) in order to nuance their use. The acknowledgment of multireferentiality is required in order to avoid the pitfalls of eclecticism associated with the incompatible mix of philosophies and epistemologies sometimes denounced in the literature on transformative learning (Finger & Asùn, 2001). Indeed, a complex method does not aim to merge, aggregate, or integrate theories in order to build unifying syntheses; rather, it privileges the conception of their mutual relationships based on the recognition of their boundaries (Pagès, 2002). From a practical point of view, for instance, such a perspective invites practitioners and researchers to distinguish what is constitutive of heterogeneous realities (for example, biological, psychic, or social ones) in order to interpret their relationships. Pagès (2002) mentioned, for example, his collaboration with a sociologist in order to collectively interpret the life histories of patients that he was following in psychotherapy. The understanding of transformative learning appears complexified by the articulation of two roles acknowledged as distinct: while the sociologist was raising questions related to the way the participants were interacting with objective social realities (including places, people, family names, money); according to his psychoanalytical background, Pagès was asking participants to be in touch with unconscious memories. Exploring complexity not only challenges disciplinary boundaries but also requires researchers and practitioners to acknowledge and understand the epistemological assumptions shaping how knowledge is created and organized among heterogeneous disciplines (Montuori, 2010).

Reconsidering the Relationship Between Autonomy and Dependence

In spite of the value attributed to them as processes located at the core of transformative learning theory, traditional conceptions of critical reflection, critical thinking, and engagement in dialogue are regularly contested because of their paradoxical effects. On one hand, they may ground an individual process of empowerment, which can be experienced as emancipatory. On the other hand, the narrative and the group dynamics that shape critical practices raise resistances and may also be interpreted as constraining and potentially alienating (Alhadeff-Jones, 2007a, 2010; Ellsworth, 1992; Schugurensky, 2002; Usher, Bryant & Johnston, 1997). For instance, research referring to the use of personal narrative in higher education shows how the process of writing one's own life history can trigger critical insights that help to increase some participants' autonomy. At the same time, other participants may experience this exercise and the process of sharing their narratives in group as overwhelming or threatening (Dominicé, 2000). In addition, transformative learning may be promoted in formal institutions where the established knowledge, power base and institutional dynamics require learners to conform to conventions and procedures contrary to the learners' own preferences. The critical aim of the training may therefore be challenged by institutional and program policy and procedures (for example, admission requirements, lack of flexibility in the program approval policies, lack of faculty resources, kinds of research sanctioned, work requirements overload, lack of flexibility in the curriculum) (Bitterman, 2000). To understand how an opportunity for transformative learning can become disempowering, one must revisit the assumptions framing common conceptions of control and autonomy. Among others, the autonomy-dependence principle formulated by Morin (1990/2008) focuses on the property characterized by the fact that what makes a system (a person, a group, a theory) self-sufficient and autonomous is also what makes it dependent. Indeed, the case, common in the United States, of students going deeply into debt to cover the cost of an academic degree—a degree that may or may not be transformative—illustrates well the ambivalent nature of education as a source of both autonomy and dependence. The autonomy-dependence principle encourages one to systematically consider transformative learning as a manifestation of the complex interplay among complementary, contradictory, and antagonistic forms of self and mutual control (embedded in individuals, groups, and institutions). Acknowledging and going beyond a critique of the alienating dimension of educational institutions (Illich, 1971), this principle brings researchers and educators to systematically question their contribution to both, the learners' autonomy and dependence, in order to critically assess and negotiate such a tension without reducing it. Doing so is challenging because it nuances the benefits (in terms of autonomy) usually associated with transformative education, and also because it stresses ethical dilemmas that cannot be easily solved.

Reintroducing the Knower in Any Knowledge

Recognizing transformative learning as an individual or collective, brief or long-lasting emergence is a matter of convention. Any complex system requires a subject (such as the researcher) who isolates it, cuts it up, qualifies it, and hierarchizes it, based on selective interests and the cultural and social context of scientific knowledge (Montuori, 1993; Morin, 1977–2004/2008). In educational sciences, "systems" always involve human factors referring to meanings, values, behaviors, and histories, which are never indifferent to the researchers who study them, be it consciously or not (Devereux, 1967). Researchers and practitioners are therefore required to position their own contributions based on the expression of the filiations framing their own beliefs, assumptions, and practices. They must constantly clarify the epistemological, ethical, and existential issues, as they appear influenced by unconscious, emotional, cognitive, social, historical, or political determinants. In France, Lourau (1997) defined as "implication" every aspect that intellectuals refuse, consciously or not, to analyze in their practice. Ardoino (1993) establishes a distinction between "libidinal implications" (inherent to unconscious psychic life) and "institutional implications" (inherent to the social, economical, and political status, ideology, and so on).

In North America, close to the concept of "institutional implications," the notion of "positionality" describes how the researcher's or practitioner's own class, ethnicity, and gender influence their own research and educational practice (for example, Johnson-Bailey, 2004; Taylor, Tisdell, & Hanley, 2000). Considering researchers' and practitioners' implications corresponds to the heuristic intuition that it can be as much a source of knowledge than a factor of distortion (Ardoino, 2000). For instance, from an educational perspective, paying attention to psychological implications, such as transference and countertransference (Devereux, 1967) allows us to understand how a subject (learner, trainer, researcher, and so on) actualizes and projects onto another person unconscious desires (seduction, aggressiveness, fear, and so on) replicating relationships from her/his own past life (such as with parents or siblings) and influencing her/his own learning. For educators, interpreting their own countertransference—that is, reactions that echo their learners' transference—is a valuable strategy for understanding the role played by attraction, repulsion, suspicion, or competition as behaviors originating in the past, whose actualization during the training stimulates or prevents transformative learning among learners. From a research perspective, Devereux (1967) demonstrated how traditional scientific methods, including tests, tend to reduce the understanding of the role played by the researcher's psychological implications, by facilitating the denial of emotional overload—for example, anxiety or fear—involved in the study of phenomena that they may perceive as traumatic or taboo, such as sexual or violent behaviors. Questioning implications and positionality requires one to challenge the normative dimension of research and education. It appears therefore as a delicate ethical and political operation with numerous pitfalls. On one hand, it can be distorted by objectivist paradigms of research, through its integration as additional pseudo-transparency aiming to identify specific bias. On the other hand, it can become inoperative, as when it is used to legitimize a hypersubjectivist conception incompatible with scientific pretentions (Lourau, 1997). It is difficult to systematically consider practitioners and researchers' implications, not only because this challenges the assumption of neutrality deeply rooted in positivist epistemology but also because it requires the development of research and pedagogical methods that valorize the practitioner's self-inquiry.

THE CHALLENGES OF COMPLEXITY AS SOURCES OF TRANSFORMATIVE LEARNING

Several traditions of research conceive transformative learning through the adoption of nondualistic, dialectical, or postformal ways of thinking, reframing the way conflicting issues are understood (for example, Basseches, 1984; Belenky, Clinchy, Goldberger, & Tarule, 1986/1997; Mezirow, 1991; Sinnott, 2003). These approaches invite one to bring together two notions, concepts, options, or assumptions that seemingly exclude each other, but which appear as an integral part of the same reality. By rationally assuming the association of contradictory or even paradoxical views, we can expect a deeper transformation of the learner's assumptions. Such theoretical contributions are crucial in order to understand the adoption of more complex and inclusive worldviews (Alhadeff-Jones, 2007b). As we discussed earlier, the six challenges described in this chapter introduce various forms of antagonisms, contradictions, and complementarities (dealing with singularity and generality, predictability and unpredictability, linear and circular causalities, considering the relationships between levels of an organization, transgressing and respecting disciplinary borders, giving autonomy and creating dependence, referring to subjectivity and looking for objectivity). They introduce tensions, which make up—among other dimensions—a complex conception of transformative learning. It appears therefore that the recognition of some of the challenges raised by the idea of complexity carries by itself a potential for transformation. In other words, conceiving the complexity of transformative learning may require or trigger transformative learning. Such circularity characterizes the recursive dimension of a complex way of thinking.

Stressing the importance of discursive principle privileging the association of complementary, concurrent, and antagonistic notions with each other, the paradigm of complexity encourages us to go one step further. Honoring complexity not only values nondualistic ways of thinking but also requires that we give a central position in the research process to the deep ambivalences, contradictions, and paradoxes experienced not only by the learners but also by the practitioners and researchers (Morin, 1977–2004/2008). Rather than reducing contradictions, the adoption of a dialogical principle requires the researcher to question what can be learned from the study of paradoxes and double binds framing both transformative dynamics and the scientific processes aiming to study them (Alhadeff-Jones, 2007b; Bitterman, 2000; Montuori, 2005, 2010). It therefore suggests that a complex way of thinking about education and research systematically involves some levels of transformation inherent in the act of challenging the assumptions framing traditional educational and research practices.

TRANSFORMATIVE LEARNING: OBJECT OF STUDY, DIMENSION OF RESEARCH

As Morin (1990/2008) formulates it, complexity can neither be defined in a simple way nor serve as a replacement for simplicity. Complexity is a word problem, not a word solution. It does not provide us with any kind of standardized tools or methods. It requires ingenuity and creativity (Montuori, 2005, 2010).

> Thinking in terms of complexity is clearly not a mode of thought that replaces certainty with uncertainty, separation with inseparability, and logic with all kinds of special exceptions. On the contrary, it involves a constant toing and froing between certainty and uncertainty, between the elementary and the global, between the separable and the inseparable. The aim is not to abandon the principles of classical science—order, separability and logic—but to absorb them into a broader and richer scheme of things. . . . Linkage must be made between the principles of order and disorder, separation and connection, autonomy and dependence, which are at one and the same time complementary, concurrent and antagonistic. (Morin, 1996, p. 14)

Challenging our conceptions of transformative learning, both theoretically and practically, according to a complexivist perspective requires one to explore the ways this field is interpreted and defined, according to a reflexive epistemology. Indeed, it suggests the development of a systematic skepticism that continuously questions the legitimacy of one's own teaching and research assumptions. This is an ambitious project that requires navigating through heterogeneous theories, involving a process of translation between foreign disciplines and unknown natural and conceptual languages. Dealing with their complementarities, contradictions, and antagonisms requires the adoption of ways of knowing that cannot be taken for granted. Embracing a complex epistemology is not only a challenging process intellectually but also involves every dimension of one's own being (Alhadeff-Jones, 2007a, 2007b; *La Pensée Complexe en Recherches et en Pratique*, 2008; Heshusius & Ballard, 1996; Montuori, 2005, 2010). For researchers and practitioners alike, a complex way of thinking suggests the conception of the scientific process as continuous learning, a source of potential transformations, grounded in the experience of doing research itself. From an educational perspective, a complex way of thinking may be understood as a method of learning involving human error and uncertainty (Morin, 1977/1992). It involves taking into consideration both the individual and collective experiences grounding any activity of research and—more deeply—the transformative learning processes associated with them (Alhadeff-Jones, 2007a, 2007b, 2008b; Montuori, 2005, 2010).

The good news for researchers working on transformative learning is that the growing interest in academia and in education for transdisciplinary approaches informed by the idea of complexity (Montuori, 2010; Paul & Pineau, 2005) constitutes a new field of exploration allowing us to study how we learn—or not—to question the assumptions framing our worldviews. There is no doubt that transformative learning theory can play a significant role in the understanding of current academic and scientific transformations triggered by the need to develop an intelligence of complexity (Morin, 1990/2008). But there is no certainty about how this field of study will contribute to the advance of science and education during the coming decades. Therefore the best way to find out may be to sustain a systematic effort aimed at confronting our own transformation as we try to conceptualize the transformations we are studying.

References

Alhadeff-Jones, M. (2007a). *Education, critique et complexité: Modèle et expérience de conception d'une approche multiréférentielle de la critique en Sciences de l'éducation*. Université de Paris 8 & Université de Lille: Atelier National de Reproduction des Thèses.

Alhadeff-Jones, M. (2007b). Beyond the heterogeneity of critique in education: Researchers' experiences of antagonisms and limits as transformative learning opportunities. In P. Cranton & E. W. Taylor (Eds.), *Proceedings of the 7th International Transformative Learning Conference* (pp. 1–6). Albuquerque, NM: University of New Mexico College of Education, Central New Mexico Community College.

Alhadeff-Jones, M. (2008a). Three generations of complexity theories: Nuances and ambiguities. *Educational Philosophy and Theory*, *40*, 1, 66–82.

Alhadeff-Jones, M. (2008b). Promoting scientific dialogue as a lifelong learning process. In F. Darbellay, M. Cockell, J. Billotte, & F. Waldvogel (Eds.), *A vision of transdisciplinarity: Laying foundations for a world knowledge dialogue* (pp. 104–112). Lausanne, Switzerland: Swiss Federal Institute of Technology Press.

Alhadeff-Jones, M. (2010). Challenging the limits of critique in education through Morin's paradigm of complexity. *Studies in Philosophy and Education*, *29*, 5, 477–490.

Alhadeff-Jones, M., Lesourd, F., Roquet, P., & Le Grand, J.-L. (2011). Questioning the temporalities of transformative learning in a time of crisis. In M. Alhadeff-Jones & A. Kokkos (Eds.), *Transformative learning in time of crisis: Individual and collective challenges*. Proceedings of the 9th International Transformative Learning Conference (pp. 394–407). New York and Athens, Greece: Teachers College, Columbia University and the Hellenic Open University.

Ardoino, J. (1993). L'Approche multiréférentielle (plurielle) des situations éducatives et formatives. *Pratiques de Formation/Analyses*, *25–26*, 15–34.

Ardoino, J. (2000). *Les avatars de l'éducation*. Paris: Presses Universitaires de France.

Bachelard, G. (1934/2003). *Le nouvel esprit scientifique*. Paris: Presses Universitaires de France.

Bagnall, R. G. (1999). *Discovering radical contingency. Building a postmodern agenda in adult education*. New York: Peter Lang.

Banathy, B. H., & Jenlink, P. M. (1996). Systems inquiry and its application in education. In D. H. Jonassen (Ed.), *Handbook of research for educational communications and technology* (pp. 37–57). New York: Simon & Schuster Macmillan.

Basseches, M. (1984). *Dialectical thinking and adult development*. Norwood, NJ: Ablex.

Belenky, M. F., Clinchy, B.M.V., Goldberger, N. R., & Tarule, J. M. (Eds.). (1986/1997). *Women's ways of knowing*. New York: Basic Books.

Bitterman, J. E. (2000). Antilogical aspects of graduate study in adult education: Reflections on motivational conflicts in the AEGIS program experience. In K. Illeris (Ed.), *Adult education in the perspective of the learners: 5th report from the Adult Education Research Project* (pp. 81–115). Frederiksberg, Denmark: Roskilde University Press.

Brookfield, S. (2000). The concept of critically reflective practice. In A. L Wilson & E. R. Hayes (Eds.), *Handbook of adult and continuing education* (pp. 33–49). San Francisco: Jossey-Bass.

Clénet, J., & Poisson, D. (2005). *Complexité de la formation et formation à la complexité*. Paris: L'Harmattan.

Collard, S., & Law, M. (1989). The limits of perspective transformation: A critique of Mezirow's theory. *Adult Education Quarterly, 39*, 2, 99–107.

Complicity: An International Journal of Complexity and Education. Available at: http://ejournals.library.ualberta.ca/index.php/complicity

Davis-Manigaulte, J., Yorks, L., & Kasl, E. (2006). In E. W. Taylor (Ed.), *Expressive ways of knowing and transformative learning* (pp. 27–35). New Directions for Adult and Continuing Education, no. 109. San Francisco: Jossey-Bass.

Devereux, G. (1967). *From anxiety to method in the behavioral sciences*. The Hague: Mouton.

Dirkx, J. M. (2007). Making sense of multiplicity: Metaphors of self and self-change in transformation theory. In P. Cranton & E. W. Taylor (Eds.), *Proceedings of the 7th international transformative learning conference* (pp. 110–115). Albuquerque, NM: University of New Mexico College of Education, Central New Mexico Community College.

Dominicé, P. (2000). *Learning from our lives: Using educational biographies with adults*. San Francisco: Jossey-Bass.

Ellsworth, E. (1992). Why doesn't this feel empowering? Working through the repressive myths of critical pedagogy. In C. Luke & J. Gore (Eds.), *Feminisms and critical pedagogy* (pp. 90–119). New York: Routledge.

Finger, M., & Asùn, J. M. (2001). *Adult education at the crossroads. Learning our way out*. New York: Zed Books.

Heshusius, L., & Ballard, K. (Eds.). (1996). *From positivism to interpretivism and beyond: Tales of transformation in educational and social research (the mind-body connection)*. New York: Teachers College Press.

Illich, I. (1971). *Deschooling society*. New York: Harper & Row.

Johnson-Bailey, J. (2004). Enjoining positionality and power in narrative work: Balancing contentious and modulating forces. In K. DeMarais & S. D. Lapan (Eds.), *Foundations for research, methods of inquiry in education and the social sciences* (pp. 123–138). Mahwah, NJ: Erlbaum.

Lani-Bayle, M., & Mallet, M. A. (Eds.). (2010). *Evénements et formation de la personne*. Editions L'Harmattan.

La Pensée complexe en recherches et en pratique. (2008). *Chemins de Formation, 12–13*. Paris: Téraèdre.

Lourau, R. (1997). *Implication, transduction*. Paris: Anthropos.

Mezirow, J. (1991). *Transformative dimensions of adult learning*. San Francisco: Jossey-Bass.

Mezirow, J. (1999). Transformation theory, postmodern issues. Paper presented at the Adult Education Research Conference, Northern Illinois University, De Kalb, Illinois.

Mezirow, J., & Associates (Eds.). (2000). *Learning as transformation. Critical perspectives on a theory in progress.* San Francisco: Jossey-Bass.

Mezirow, J., Taylor, E. W., & Associates (Eds.). (2010). *Transformative learning in practice: Insights from community, workplace, and higher education.* San Francisco: Jossey-Bass.

Montuori, A. (1993). Knowledge, learning, and change: Exploring the systems/cybernetic perspective. In L. Bradburn & J. Petranker (Eds.), *Mastery of mind* (pp. 252–297). Berkeley, CA: Dharma Press.

Montuori, A. (2005). Literature review as creative inquiry: Reframing scholarship as a creative process. *Journal of Transformative Education, 3,* 4, 374–393.

Montuori, A. (2010). Transdisciplinarity and creative inquiry in transformative education: Researching the research degree. In M. Maldonato (Ed.), *Research on scientific research: A transdisciplinary study* (pp. 110–135). Portland, OR: Sussex Academic Press.

Morin, E. (1977–2004/2008). *La Méthode* (new edition including the six volumes published between 1977 and 2004). Paris: Seuil.

Morin, E. (1977/1992). Method. *Towards a study of humankind* (Vol. 1: The nature of nature). New York: Peter Lang.

Morin, E. (1990/2008). *On complexity.* Cresskill, NJ: Hampton Press.

Morin, E. (1996, February). A new way of thinking. *UNESCO Courier, 49*(2), 10–14.

Morin, E. (1999). *Seven complex lessons in education for the future.* Paris: UNESCO.

Morin, E. (2007). Restricted complexity, general complexity. In C. Gershenson, D. Aerts, & B. Edmonds (Eds.), *Worldviews, science and us: philosophy and complexity* (pp. 5–29). London: World Scientific.

Osberg, D., & Biesta, G. (Eds.). (2010). *Complexity theory and the politics of education.* Rotterdam: Sense Publishers.

O'Sullivan, E. (1999). *Transformative learning: Educational vision for the 21st century.* New York: Zed Books.

O'Sullivan, E., Morrell, A., & O'Connor, M. A. (Eds.). (2002). *Expanding the boundaries of transformative learning: Essays on theory and praxis.* New York: Palgrave Press.

Pagès, M. (2002). Complexité. In J. Barus-Michel, E. Enriquez, & A. Lévy (Eds.), *Vocabulaire de psychosociologie* (pp. 83–93). Ramonville, France: Eres.

Pagès, M., Bonetti, M., de Gaulejac, V., & Descendre, D. (1979). *L'Emprise de l'organisation.* Paris: Desclée de Brouwer.

Paul, P., & Pineau, G. (Eds.) (2005). *Transdisciplinarité et formation.* Paris, L'Harmattan.

Pietrykowski, B. (1996). Knowledge and power in adult education: Beyond Freire and Habermas. *Adult Education Quarterly, 46*(2), 82–97.

Rosenau, P. M. (1992). Into the fray: Crisis, continuity, and diversity. In *Post-modernism and the social sciences: Insights, inroads, and intrusions* (pp. 3–24). Princeton, NJ: Princeton University Press.

Schugurensky, D. (2002). Transformative learning and transformative politics. In E. O'Sullivan, A. Morrell, & M. A. O'Connor (Eds.), *Expanding the boundaries of transformative learning* (pp. 59–76). New York: Palgrave Press.

Sinnott, J. D. (2003). Learning as a humanistic dialogue with reality. New theories that help us teach the whole person. In T. Hagström (Ed.), *Adult development in post-industrial society and working life* (pp. 78–152). Stockholm: Stockholm University.

Taylor, E. W. (2000). Analyzing research on transformative learning theory. In J. Mezirow & Associates (Eds.), *Learning as transformation: Critical perspectives on a theory in progress* (pp. 285–328). San Francisco: Jossey-Bass.

Taylor, E. W., Tisdell, E. J., & Hanley, M. S. (2000). The role of positionality in teaching for critical consciousness: Implications for adult education. Paper presented at the Adult Education Research Conference, University of British Colombia, Vancouver, B.C., Canada.

Usher, R., Bryant, I., & Johnston, R. (1997). *Adult education and the postmodern challenge: Learning beyond the limits.* London: Routledge.

Weaver, W. (1948). Science and complexity [electronic version]. *American Scientist, 36,* 536. Retrieved August 20, 2004, from http://www.ceptualinstitute.com

Welton, M. (1995). *In defense of the lifeworld: Critical perspectives on adult learning.* Albany, NY: State University of New York Press.

West, L., Alheit, P., Andersen, A. S., & Merrill, B. (Eds.). (2007). *Using biographical and life history approaches in the study of adult and lifelong learning: European perspectives.* Frankfurt am Main: Peter Lang.

CHAPTER TWELVE

Transforming Transformative Learning Through Sustainability and the New Science

Elizabeth A. Lange

E ducators have a historic opportunity to put transformative learning theory and practice into the service of what historian Paul Kennedy calls "nothing less than the reeducation of humanity" (quoted in Orr, 1994, p. 126). To take on such a role, the current theory and practice of transformative learning will need to shed its modernist clothing. This chapter offers a pastiche of emerging, contested ideas that share commonalities but derive from diverse theoretical roots and disciplinary histories. In particular, the principles of "strong sustainability" and the emerging scientific thinking that informs it will be brought into play with the orthodox assumptions of transformative learning, yielding new insights and pointing to new pathways for theory and practice.

I steer off the gravel road onto the matted grass parking lot, nestling between several cars. Striding quickly past picnic tables and interpretive signs, I step onto the boardwalk suspended several feet above the marsh. I hold my breath, hopeful. I have been frequenting this bird sanctuary a few kilometres outside the city for fifteen years—alone, with my family, and with my classes—learning lessons from this ecosystem, particularly the importance and dynamics of wetlands. I am disappointed. There is no water in sight. To my right, the cattails that used to border the boardwalk are now crowded out by an expanding ring of willows and birch and aspen saplings around what was once a lake, now a mudflat. To my left, we used to watch Canada geese nesting on distant grassy hummocks, protected by the surrounding marsh, now dry. Underneath the boardwalk, muskrats would weave around bent rushes and sedge clumps, heading for their well-worn mud trenches, where they could glide to safety in the water. As we rounded the bend, pungent wild mint would caress our senses. Farther along, my young children used to lie and hang their heads over the boardwalk while my husband pointed out water striders, dragonfly nymphs, diving beetles, whirligigs, and mayflies, twirling among the algae-encased reeds. Meanwhile, I would study the shallow wetland lake, teeming with mallard and ruddy ducks, scaups, teals, shovelers, buffleheads, and pin-tails. Over the surrounding prairie forest, red-tailed hawks and merlins would circle, swoop, and cry. The myriad of trails around this protected area have been a place I go to celebrate good news, casting flowers and other symbolic gifts into the water, or to cleanse the bad, getting lost in the deep grasses hidden up in the trees.

Today, however, the marsh is completely quiet. I zip my jacket up against the chill wind, the only sound filling my ears. So where did they all go? I fight the despair pushing its way into my consciousness, as I survey the exposed mud bottom, dotted by a few coins of water and some webbed footprints. My eighty-something father, well attuned to natural cycles, sparingly offers, "The water will return." Realizing his intention of hope, I do not counter with the science of climate change and the receding likelihood that many Alberta lakes like this will ever fill again. This lake has been drying for over ten years, now filling only briefly in spring. In some areas, farmers have already brought this land under the plough or the city has built over them. How do I explain to him—a living bridge spanning the horse-and-buggy, space travel, and globalization eras—that a profoundly different frame of understanding is needed. Such an understanding would in part resurrect some of the nature knowledge Dad carries, but build on cutting-edge science as well. Should I suggest that the largely human-caused transformation of global land and ocean is calling for an equally significant human transformation—one that can take us into a new era shaped by the values of social and environmental sustainability and a rediscovery of relations and ways of knowing that have been suppressed since the Enlightenment?

Andres Edwards (2005) claims we are already in the midst of a sustainability revolution, which will be more sweeping than the eighteenth-century Enlight-enment. What is not widely known is that the sustainability movement is now considered the largest social movement in history—a profoundly moving, un-precedented good-news phenomenon that rarely surfaces in the mainline media (Hawken, 2007). Many authors call for a personal and social transformation that will "lift ourselves to a new level of species maturity and potential ... birthing a new era of Earth Community" (Korten, 2006, p. 21). The generations alive today are considered to be *the* transitional generation—the first with a global consciousness as well as the capacity to reimagine our communities to be truly life-giving.

The need for transformative learning theory to inform sustainability education and to help build sustainable communities is critical. This was recognized at the 8th International Transformative Learning Conference, through its theme *Reframing Social Sustainability in a Multicultural World*. The website captured the challenge: "Social sustainability calls for rethinking and reframing basic ideas about LIFE itself." However, sustainability theorizing, and the New Science informing it, pose a number of fundamental challenges to transformative learning theory.

The New Science refers to a new paradigm of scientific thinking predicated on relativity theory, quantum mechanics, process physics, complexity and chaos theory, enactivism, Gaia theory, and deep ecology. This new knowledge from the physical and biological sciences as well as mind and consciousness studies has coalesced into an emerging vision of science (Laszlo, 1996; Capra, 1996). This emerging vision brings into question the modernist epistemological, cosmological, and ontological roots that currently inform transformative learning theory and practice.

CONTESTED VISIONS OF SUSTAINABILITY

Edwards (2005) suggests that sustainability is more than a social movement. He claims it is a social revolution given the new consciousness, social ethos, and widely shared objectives of a large and diverse number of global groups. Edwards has documented five understandings and objectives that are shared among these groups:

a. environmental protection;

b. economic and social equity;

c. acknowledgement of human dependence on natural systems for our health and survival;

d. acknowledgement of the limits of Earth's ecosystems and regenerative powers; and

e. advocacy for long term, intergenerational perspectives. (p. 7)

Despite the commonalities among these groups, David Orr (1992) argues that within sustainability thinking, there are two poles in a rather wide and diverse ideological spectrum. He identifies these poles as *sustainable development* and *sustainability*, with key differences in assumptions and outcomes. The differences between sustainable development and sustainability are now called the debate between weak and strong sustainability. Table 12.1 summarizes key assumptions of each approach.

Table 12.1 Sustainable Development and Sustainability

Assumptions	Sustainable Development or "Technological Sustainability" — Weak sustainability	Sustainability or "Ecological Sustainability" — Strong sustainability
Assumptions about growth	Argues that more rapid growth is required to ensure that developing countries can address poverty; developed nations should "green" their growth.	Argues that unlimited growth in a finite natural system is impossible; there are limits to the human capacity to comprehend and coordinate at the global scale. Rather than growth, what's needed is a rethinking of agriculture, shelter, energy use, urban design, transportation, economics, resource use, forestry, and wilderness, as well as localization and selective globalization.
Assumptions about technology	Argues that humans will develop the needed technology fixes and market solutions before the limits of nonrenewable resources are reached; humans can control and manage the environment; global-scale social engineering is possible.	Argues that we cannot determine carrying capacity (the level at which the total population times the resource-use level exceeds the ecosystem capacity to renew itself and thus begins to break down) or fully understand other vital ecological limits; the principle of precaution counsels alternatives that move beyond industrialism and economic measures; coevolution and coherence between social and ecological systems within bioregions is needed; biomimicry—using the living world as the matrix—should be the model for all technological design; elegant design is valued over quantity or bigness.
Assumptions about public participation and education	Argues that decisions ought to be a centralized responsibility; the answer will be found among policymakers, scientists, corporate executives, banks, and international agencies through a rational and managerial process. Education needs to be used to inform citizens about the thinking of experts and the decisions they have made.	Argues that decisions ought to be a decentralized responsibility; change best occurs at the regional level among grassroots groups where self-organizing can predominate; communities need to shed political systems that bred passivity and reactivate participation; education is key to social change, developing an ecologically competent citizenry; rediscovering and honoring traditional place-based knowledge systems is necessary.
Assumptions about humans, knowledge, and values	Dominated by the model of the "economic human" who maximizes gain and minimizes loss (utilitarianism) and is fundamentally self-interested; uses Cartesian rational logic and reductionism.	Advocates a stewardship model; ecocentrist ethics recognize responsibility to the whole living world; living systems thinking is based on holistic science; humans need humility, realizing they are part of, not above, ecosystems; seeks union among knowledge, livelihood, living, and place.

In sum, technological or weak sustainability stays rooted in the modernist paradigm, following core enlightenment assumptions. Strong sustainability, however, is predicated on what Charlene Spretnak (1999) calls a "reconstructive or ecological postmodernism," building on the more positive advances of the modern tradition, but rooted in an earth-based epistemology, cosmology, and ontology. In the end, David Orr concedes that these two polar views can be complementary, if sustainable development is the stopgap strategy to stabilize current crises and sustainability is the long-term solution, leading toward a new way of thinking and living predicated on respect for and symbiosis with the living world. The following section counterpoints the modernist assumptions embedded in transformative learning and some of the insights from New Science for reconceptualizing transformative learning.

SHEDDING THE MODERNIST CLOTHING

The modernist paradigm presumes that the scientific epistemology of empiricism and logical rationalism offers superior knowledge-creating processes and ways of knowing, "untainted by emotions, sensate knowledge, social constructions, and noncognitive awareness" (Spretnak, 1999, p. 220). In contrast, ecological postmodernism recognizes the need for groundedness rather than abstractionism, recognizing that our well-being is predicated on our physical connections with the earth (Spretnak, 1999). Spretnak elaborates that humans are not fixed, thoroughly contained entities bounded by skin, but are fluid and connected in multiple ways, particularly at the energy level, within a vast creative living network. Emerging from the New Science, space and time are now considered connected by a vast sea of energy. All human experience and knowledge is embedded in this subtle energy force field across space and time (Laszlo, 1996).

Modernism has also been founded on a mechanistic cosmology of a linear cause-effect universe. If all nonhuman matter is machine-like, then it is dead. It follows, then, that humans can subjugate it through industrialism and technological prowess to achieve "progress." In contrast, Einstein, Bohr, Heisenberg, and others found that the existentials of form, matter, time, and space are not fixed, linear, or only three-dimensional, but are dynamic, curved, and flowing on a multidimensional space-time continuum, humbling scientific aspirations of certainty (Capra, 1996). At the subatomic level, matter and energy are interchangeable, as either particles or waves, affecting each other synergistically and emergent with the act of human observation (Maturana & Varela, 1980). Thus matter and mind co-emerge as an intimately interlinked system within a larger biosphere. Consciousness is not just individual but also transpersonal. Potentially, we have access to this transpersonal consciousness based on our holistic or expansive self, which connects with the world through the collective unconscious and is usually available to us through dreams, deep meditation, prayer, and conscious breathing (Scott, 1997). As Laszlo (1996) suggests, "Our constant, though not necessarily conscious, dance with other minds and the world around us should give us a new sense of responsibility . . . it reinforces our sense of oneness with nature and the universe" (pp. 220, 224).

The Enlightenment spawned the reified belief in change and transformation, understood as the reconstructibility of the natural world, societies, the body, and the mind. Typically, modern social change is linear, highly interventionist, and the result of power struggles, favoring the interests of the dominant culture. In contrast, living systems at all levels are self-organizing, called *autopoiesis*. Systems self-regulate by constantly receiving input from negative feedback loops and adjusting to maintain fluctuations within stable parameters, called dynamic balance (Macy & Young Brown, 1998, p. 41). When significant stress occurs and it reaches a bifurcation point, these systems either fall apart and die, or adapt by spontaneously reorganizing themselves into more complex, coherent patterns—a process called emergence. Chaos theory also suggests that there is an underlying connectedness in apparently random events (Briggs & Peat, 1999) and that chaos generates a multitude of creative possibilities that keep living systems vibrant. Further, the butterfly effect describes how small changes can become unpredictably magnified to a point of crisis, through a nonlinear chain of events (Gleick, 1987). In sum, according to the New Science and living systems theories, reality is highly sensitive, nonlinear, relational, and self-renewing—more lifelike than machinelike (Karpiak, 2005), predisposed to generating and maintaining the conditions for life (Laszlo, 1996).

The Enlightenment paradigm accepts an anthropocentric morality wherein humans are separate from and above the natural world. Moral decisions privilege human society, an attitude now considered a form of human chauvinism wherein humans are the measure of all things and the source of all value. Associated with this are andocentrism and enthnocentrism, breeding the contemporary domination ethos in which structural violence toward other groups is accepted as the fabric of society. In contrast, living systems theory moves from the premise that humans are radically interrelated to, and part of, living systems, which are networks within networks, or nested systems. All organisms are interdependent, functioning best through cooperation, partnership, synergy, and symbiosis.

Another Enlightenment assumption is the ontology of autonomous individualism, wherein the individual is the locus of morality guided by individual conscience and private judgment, seeking no greater purpose than individual fulfillment. In contrast, many scientists, including Einstein, realized that separation and autonomy are a delusion. A new cosmology is emerging, telling the story of an unfolding universe, starting from the primordial flaring forth or big bang, ever expanding outward (Swimme & Berry, 1992), in which we are all embedded and participating. This cosmology provides for a meaningful and connected place for humans, rather than a random place maintained by brutish survival. Historian Tarnas (1991) notes that the modern determination to forge an autonomous rational human self led to the repression of imagination, emotion, instinct, intuition, the body, women, the "exotic Other," and other species, all of which now require restoration to a rightful place.

Finally, within Enlightenment thought, humans are viewed as *homo economicus*: economics is the driving force in human affairs, economic acquisition is the logical end to disciplined work, each individual pursuing monetary self-interest constitutes the common good, and mass consumption is the utilitarian "most good for the highest number." In this view, urbanization and mobility for economic reasons are valued over ties to place of birth, family, religion, or community. The continued spread of industrialism, bureaucratism, and an impersonal, abstract market society has been intensified by neoliberal corporate globalization. As Max Weber (1930/1992) asserted, modern technicians and cost-benefit instrumentalism reduces people, beings, and things to resources or instruments, avoiding key ethical questions and precluding higher principles. In sum, the contrast between modernism and the New Science can allow us to think afresh about transformative learning, and begin to reconceptualize the theory and practice of transformative learning.

TRANSFORMING TRANSFORMATIVE LEARNING

"The conventional wisdom holds that all education is good, and the more of it one has, the better" (Orr, 1994, p. 5). However, Orr then goes on to challenge the idea that more people should be equipped with diplomas and degrees representing theories without values and responsibility, short- rather than long-term thinking, abstraction rather than consciousness, mastery of content rather than of self, answers instead of questions, ideology and economics without ecological literacy, and efficiency and management over conscience. Orr (2005) encourages educators to attend to the art of rehabitation—reeducating people in the art of living well and justly where they are. In short, we are challenged to rethink the purpose and processes of adult education, particularly transformative learning, in this challenging historical moment. As educators providing conditions for transformative learning, what kind of reality are we bringing into being through our efforts?

Rethinking the Etymology of Transformation

Transformative change—considered the most radical, complete form of change—has been central to modern thinking. What sets the idea of transformation apart from other forms of change is that is it "a change of" not just "a change in" (Sztompka, 1994, p. 27). *Trans* means "to go across" indicating that there is a dynamism or force in this type of change. *Formation* comes from the root *formus* or *morpheus*, which means "morphing" or "to take a new shape." In other words, *trans-form* means to move across forms, to change the very form of the organism (person or society). The fundamental deep structure of the organism is changed, not just the surface appearance and not just a developmental evolution of certain elements.

However, additional understandings of transformation emerge from the New Science. The etymology of *in-formation* is any type of pattern that influences the formation or transformation of other patterns. If mind and matter co-emerge, and information is transmitted across space and time through the energy sea, then transformation involves an entanglement of mind and body with this information-rich energy field. In this view, the locus of transformation is not the individual or society, as currently debated, but the relations, system interactions, and perturbations that reverberate throughout a system or nested systems (Fenwick, 2003). This questions fundamental conceptions of knowledge, reframing it as emergent, participatory, and inclusive of the conscious and unconscious, rather than given, static, and developmental. It also questions fundamental distinctions between the human and nonhuman—as interconnected and related, not discrete.

Rethinking the Process of Transformation

The typical perception of a transformative learning process is linear and mechanistic, in the search for cause and effect. Yet living systems are fluid and responsive, continuously oscillating between habitual and novel patterns. Living systems require stability, and thus patterns of repetition are maintained within a state of dynamic balance, through negative feedback loops that buffer any changes with an opposite reaction. However, living systems also require change to maintain vibrance; thus living systems regularly encounter "splittings," in which a choice point occurs between habitual or novel patterns. Typically these are small choices; yet with an unpredictable complex of influences, these choices can become amplified through positive feedback loops that augment the change with similar types of changes. When there is an accumulation of these splittings and amplifications, a living system can reach an unexpected breaking point, called a *bifurcation point*, at which the stasis is broken. The state of bifurcation is characterized by wide, unstable fluctuations or unusual, perhaps temporarily contradictory patterns (Gleick, 1987).

One key insight here is that the transformation process is not linear but rather a looped process with many feedback cycles that can either amplify or buffer the changes, explaining the diversity with which learners respond to a transformative pedagogy. Further, the potential for transformation likely always exists; in fact, continual adaptation and innovation is the normal order of things. The potential for transformation may always be occurring through small daily choices. When the choices consistently do not adhere to established patterns and a certain accumulation occurs, a breaking or bifurcation point has been reached, and the transformative process becomes visible. This explains the manifestation of transformation as both epochal and incremental. One of the most important insights of chaos theory, for an analysis of transformative learning, is that linear and reductionist analyses are unlikely to reveal the complexity of transformative learning, given the influence of numerous cofactors and the invisibility and contingency of the choice points. Chaos is as much about what we cannot know and about accepting limits as it is about celebrating the mystery and complexity of a fascinating phenomenon like transformative learning (Gleick, 1987).

It is also intriguing that at the point of greatest instability lies the greatest potential. This confirms the importance of Mezirow's disorienting dilemma as a pedagogical opportunity for transformative learning. Briggs and Peat (1999) suggest that the goal is to embrace chaos and confusion as the pregnant space of creativity and learning. Negative feedback loops are limiting loops that keep people rooted in familiar patterns. To become creative participators in the potential of chaos is to become attuned to subtle nuances, irregular orders, insignificant things, and ambiguity. As Vaclav Havel, the playwright and past Czech president, demonstrated, attention to the accumulation of small and creative actions can topple seemingly impenetrable power systems (in Briggs & Peat, 1999). By encouraging people to name their automatic or habitual patterns that collude to create consensual power structures, we can reveal perceived constraints, open up hidden degrees of freedom, and catalyze unexpressed creativity, to generate new patterns that reverberate through nested social systems.

These insights raise a new question about transformative learning: How do chaos and order coexist in the process of transformative learning? What may be important about transformation is not the initial disorientation, stages of change, or the discarded old form, but how the entanglements of structures, processes, and energy co-emerge into new patterns. In my own research on sustainability education, I call the phenomena of order and stability "restorative learning," which works in dialectical relation with transformative learning. Before engaging participants in a social or environmental analysis that unleashes powerful emotions and unsettling societal critique, the educator invites individuals to undertake personal reflection activities to identify their core ethics and values. This later provides a touchstone to guide them through their examination of lived contradictions. This preliminary reflective process involves not only a conscious values clarification but also a "restoration" of knowledge back up into conscious thought. For instance, many adults have had special experiences in the natural world as children. In recalling this, they reflect on its healing attributes, their strong sense of belonging to a larger world, their freedom of movement (not afforded children today), and their learning about natural processes. Finally, they identify their deepest yearnings, as a precursor for thinking about what a sustainable society could mean. Remembering these powerful embodied learnings, reconnecting with their internal value framework, and recovering their deepest yearnings provided a sense of order required to survive the disorder of transformative change, as they went on to probe every facet of their working and living. It also generates personal and collective energy to drive the process of change. Thus restorative learning is needed as a stable platform from which learners may transform toward sustainability thinking, which often co-emerges with transformed patterns of living and working (Lange, 2009, 2004). Scientist Laszlo (1996) concurs: "Our separation from each other and from nature is at the root of many of our problems; overcoming them calls for a recovery of our neglected, but never entirely forgotten, bonds and connections" (p. 230).

Rethinking the Pedagogy of Transformative Learning

The often unspoken assumption of educators is the felt need to provide activities and content to induce desired modifications in an individual or society—toward either certain characteristics or an ideal state. Deeply rooted in this assumption are modernist ideas of causality, calculability, reconstructibility or manageability, and dualism.

Yet Davis and Sumara (2007), drawing from complexity theory, acknowledge that "humans are highly inconsistent and conflicted beings, subject to a diversity of influences... [with] the capacity to maintain incompatible beliefs" (p. 55). Not only are learners not unitary selves, but it is impossible for any educator to know enough about the past histories, knowledge base, and influential relationships in which each individual is embedded, or the range of cultural and ideological beliefs present, for any educational planning to be effective (Clark & Dirkx, 2000). For the most part, each individual, as a self-organizing system, will learn in a way that may stretch that person toward horizons of new possibilities and new choice points. However, the person may still maintain a dynamic balance within livable parameters—parameters unknown to the educator.

Although a transformative learning practitioner may engage learners in some deliberative ways, the impact will be unpredictable, nonlinear, and often nonsequential—perhaps related to the teaching but certainly not determined by it. It is difficult to know when a bifurcation point may be reached for a learner, when enough confusion and disorientation occurs to prompt the emergence of new patterns in ways of knowing, being, or doing. In honest humility, we educators must acknowledge that learning is what occurs beneath any pedagogical plans, with facilitation simply "a conscientious participation in expanding the space of the possible by creating the conditions for the emergence of the not-yet-imaginable" (Davis & Sumara, 2007, p. 64). Transformative facilitators can act as the "consciousness of the collective" or a mirror against which assumptions are evaluated. Although educators may begin with mechanistic planning for their own comfort, the real task is watching for, listening for, and intuiting emergent changes while pointing to possibilities for freedom. Conscious teaching can help to surface the potential for transformation, but it does not create it, decentering the managerial role of the educator.

Feminism, consciousness studies, and psychoanalytic thought have challenged the concept of the unitary self, individuals as the locus of change, and autonomy as the ultimate stage of human development (Gilligan, 1982; Belenky, Clinchy, Golberger, & Tarule, 1986; Clark, 1999). Now the materialist notion of a private mind is also being challenged, through an intriguing and controversial area known as the *field studies*, particularly the field dynamics of mind (McTaggart, 2008; Laszlo, 1996). In transpersonal teaching, the teaching occurs at two levels—the content exchange and what Bache (2008) calls the Mind-Field—where the "transindividual fabric of life" can be triggered, activating the latent collective intelligence that is part of the larger field of consciousness (p. 31). When attentive to this, Bache witnessed deep transformational processes being triggered. Moreover, individuals often do not know their potential until a specific community brings it forth—explaining in part how a Gandhi or Rosa Parks emerges. Thus transformation is highly participative, spontaneously emerging in connection with others. Taylor (1991) concurs that individual meaning has significance only against a horizon of community meaning, a framework from which we derive, measure, and enact individual meaning. The World Café process is one that Bache uses extensively to generate the power of deep listening and whole system dialogue as a vehicle for social transformation and collective intelligence.

Rethinking the Outcomes of Transformative Learning

Although you can never direct meaningful change, you can disturb a system by introducing a meaning-rich idea, question, or practice that responds to a shared need. When groups gather around a shared self-interest, Wheatley (1996) suggests they become living systems where energy is created and new practices flow out rapidly to other parts of the networks. Suddenly it reaches a tipping point, and a marginal practice becomes the accepted standard. The insight here is that transformation is an elastic, moving, living process that is not time-specific or bound to individuals, but is carried within and among networks. Like flowing energy, it circulates outward through intentions, dialogue, and actions.

For instance, in a sustainability education process, individuals carried various sustainability concepts into their families, workplaces, and peer networks. They excitedly articulated the ideas of carrying capacity, biomimcry, ecological footprints, or voluntary simplicity; they reimagined what their work and living could look like according to sustainability principles and then tested the reactions. Receiving strong feedback either reinforced conformist responses or energized the desire for change, somewhat dependent on the strength of the relationship and the openness to explore reframed meanings, but this was wholly unpredictable. Many participants experienced powerful dreams or images through visualization that tapped other ways of knowing and transpersonal knowledge. Thus the transformative learning process was continually responsive to a perturbation as it rippled through webs of connections.

Similarly, social movements are self-organizing systems that converge into moments of counter-hegemonic critique and social action but also disperse, before taking on another form, much like the Occupy movement. The resistance strategy of modernist movements is important, but opposition can also inadvertently energize the dominant system. Rather than railing at a wall of power indiscriminately, using up valuable resources and energy, social movements can practice active stillness, like the heron silently watching and waiting in the water: vigilant, aware, and waiting for opportunities to seize the fish. So, too, social change is as much preparation, positioning, and timing as well as finding appropriate opportunities for decisive action (Ming-Dao, 1992, p. 14). To use another analogy, like flying a kite, one harnesses the forces that are naturally occurring in a system, borrowing and redirecting that energy to create alternative systems (Ming-Dao, 1992, p. 35).

Rethinking the Ethics of Transformative Learning

The literature has already moved beyond a solely rationalist epistemology—which states that transformation is transforming people's minds or their cognitive and ideological understandings—toward exploring extrarational ways of knowing, such as intuitive, emotional, somatic, embodied, and imaginal knowing. Yet transformative learning most often does not account for embeddedness in bodies, in a species, and in natural ecosystems. Assisting this shift from anthropocentrism, Abrams (1996) asserts that there is an essential reciprocity between our sensing body and the sensuous earth, reflected in our knowledge systems. Our task is to honor the direct experience of the body, emotions, and spirit in relation to the earth as legitimate knowledge sources. Lakoff (1980) suggests that we reach embodied understanding by co-constituting meaning through creative conceptual organizations—such as myth, metaphors, and symbols—as carriers for human meaning and knowledge. Learning is *learning to live symbiotically* in a participatory universe, often best accessed through meditation, ritual, and contemplation, and often best expressed in music, poetry, art, and story. Teaching these practices in educational spaces repatterns habitual ways of knowing and being.

Indigenous educator Gregory Cajete (2004) considers education to be "breathing in life" or to "be with life" (p. 103). Aboriginal epistemologies issue from a story of origin that provides guidance for two key relationships—how we get along with others and how we approach our relationship to the earth. Cajete (2004) identifies the key tasks of a "true and rightful education" as finding one's face or true identity, finding one's heart or motivating desires, and finding one's foundation or the work that enables you to express your face and heart. Then, one must explore "all their relations" by understanding their relationships to self, family, clan, natural world, and cosmos, learning to move in a harmonious relationship within one's inner and outer worlds (p. 110). This approach helps to reorient the ethics of transformative learning—rethinking human practices toward that which is life-giving, and learning to honor all these relations.

Historically, indigenous knowledge systems have developed in specific places among specific groups or people. Wade Davis (2009) asserts, "[T]he myriad of cultures make up an intellectual and spiritual web of life that envelops the planet and is every bit as important to the well being of the planet as is the biological web of life" (p. 2)—yet it is being lost at an astonishing rate. Respect and space for such epistemologies and cosmological stories can disrupt the modernist epistemology and the dominator ethic.

Consistent with this, Edmund O'Sullivan (1999), in his groundbreaking book *Transformative Learning: Educational Vision for the 21st Century,* proposed an *ecozoic* understanding of transformative learning. His core thesis is that the "fundamental educational task of our times is to make the choice for a sustainable planetary habitat of interdependent life forms over and against the dysfunctional calling of the global competitive marketplace" (p. 2). He builds on the new science-based cosmological story, called *The Universe Story* (1992), which Brian Swimme, a mathematical cosmologist, and Thomas Berry, a theologian and historian, developed by integrating their fields. This story, which can be used as a spiral meditative walk activity, has tremendous transformative potential by shifting the perceptual framing of the role of humans in the cosmos and teaching about deep time, or geological and cosmological passages of time since the Big Bang.

Learners also move beyond anthropocentric ethics and their estrangement from natural places when they are brought back into engagement with the natural world. Experiential activities in wild, unmanicured areas can cultivate a re-attunement to senses, breathing, body movements, and biorhythms, re-developing an organic relatedness to nature, body, and the cosmos (Lange, 2004). Reverential, slow learning, in which they explore the minutia of the natural world for clues to ecosystem health, fosters a relational mode of knowing. Orr (1992) and Sobel (2005) believe that this kind of place-based education is most effective for activating emotional attachments to places and nonhuman species and for offering living spaces for teaching ecological literacy. The Landscape and Human Health Lab at the University of Illinois now links adult aggression and poor cognitive, social, and emotional functioning to the lack of green spaces, and Richard Louv (2005/2008) identified "nature-deficit disorder" among children lacking natural place-based experiences. These are entry points for a transformative pedagogy based on a living systems approach.

Rethinking the Scope of Transformative Learning

Reimagining life-centered forms of development beyond Western "maldevelopment" and neoliberal globalization (Clover, 2004) is vital to counteract the creation of a global capitalist monoculture that is dismembering many Southern hemisphere communities. Esteva and Prakash (1998) report that in Latin America, Africa, and Asia, "so-called illiterate 'masses' are pioneering radical postmodern paths out of the morass of modern life...regenerating their own traditions, their cultures, their unique indigenous and other non-modern arts of living and dying" (pp. 3, 5)—important exemplars to examine. In the North, Jennifer Sumner (2005) asserts, rural communities have a special role in sustainability, being at the interface of corporate power, the environment, and the civil commons. The goal, she says, is to avoid further deruralization by rebuilding their civic cooperative basis and resisting further corporate enclosure of land and people for the purposes of profit-making. This degrades local ecosystems and undermines the possibility of community self-reliance and long-term sustainability. Shiva (2005) illustrates that corporate dynamics, common to both the North and the South, require collective efforts to protect public access to seeds, food sources, water, life forms, and medicines. Further, the voluntary simplicity movement stresses that increased consumption far beyond basic comfort has not made the global middle and upper class any happier and has actually decreased the quality of life. Fromm (1976) advocates for the need to move from the mode of having—the craving and possessing mode—to the mode of being fully present to life, with a focus on relational and spiritual wealth. These global issues are additional pedagogical entry points for transformative sustainability learning.

CONCLUSION

Although it may not bring the water back into the marsh I love, transformative learning has a key role to play in the reeducation of humanity. Strong sustainability offers realistic principles for thoughtful consideration and global exemplars that inspire as well as unmask limiting feedback loops that perpetuate social inaction and a sense of futility. Rehonoring "all our relations" can reorient the purpose of transformative learning and reactivate a relational mode of knowing. Engaging adults in deep learning—learning that is both transformative and restorative, that deals with the contradictions of this historical moment that we enact daily—can crack open degrees of freedom and break through a dispirited time to rejuvenate the human art of sustainable habitation.

Moreover, the assumptions of New Science assist in transforming modernist ideas about reality and transformative learning—enlarged by attention to chaos and complexity, energy fields of circulating knowledge, relations rather than beings, bifurcation points and butterfly effects, the self-organizing of living systems, cosmic connectedness, and deep time. In particular, relations are the locus of transformation, and the global social and economic realities can inform the deliberative scope of transformative learning. Nonlinear looping cycles, daily choice points, complexity of cofactors, self-organizing, a nonunitary self, and the creativity of chaos all shape the nature of transformative change. Intuiting possibilities for emergent change, introducing meaning-rich perturbations, activating transpersonal processes and an expansive sense of self, flowing with and energizing emergent change processes at any system level from individual to the social, and offering opportunities for embodied learning, contemplative and cosmological practices, earth engagement, civic participation, and ecocentric participatory ethics—all of these characterize the transformative educator role. As Laszlo proposes, "The concept of a subtly interconnected world, of a whispering pond in and through which we are intimately linked to each other and to the universe, assimilated by our intellect and embraced by our heart, is part of humanity's response to the challenges that we now face in common" (1996, p. 230).

References

Abrams, D. (1996). *The spell of the sensuous.* New York: Vintage Books.

Bache, C. (2008). *The living classroom.* Albany, NY: SUNY.

Belenky, F. M., Clinch, B. M., Golberger, N. R., & Tarule, J. M. (1986). *Women's ways of knowing.* New York: Basic Books.

Briggs, J., & Peat, D. (1999). *Seven life lessons of chaos.* New York: HarperCollins.

Cajete, G. (2004). A Pueblo story for transformation. In E. O'Sullivan & M. Taylor (Eds.), *Learning toward an ecological consciousness* (pp. 103–114). New York: Palgrave Macmillan.

Capra, F. (1996). *The web of life.* New York: Anchor Books.

Clark, M. C. (1999). Challenging the unitary self: Adult education, feminist theory, and nonunitary subjectivity. *Canadian Journal for the Study of Adult Education, 13*(2), 39–48.

Clark, C., & Dirkx, J. (2000). Moving beyond a unitary self: A reflective dialogue. In A. Wilson & E. Hayes (Eds.), *Handbook of adult and continuing education* (pp. 101–116). San Francisco: Jossey-Bass.

Clover, D. (Ed.). (2004). *Global perspectives in environmental adult education.* New York: Peter Lang.

Davis, B., & Sumara, D. (2007). Complexity science and education: Reconceptualizing the teacher's role in learning. *Interchange, 38*(1), 53–67.

Davis, W. (2009). *The wayfinders.* Toronto, ON: House of Anansi Press.

Edwards, A. (2005). *The sustainability revolution.* Gabriola Island, BC: New Society Publishers.

Esteva, G., & Prakash, M. (1998). *Grassroots postmodernism.* London: Zed Books.

Fenwick, T. (2003). Reclaiming and re-embodying experiential learning through complexity science. *Studies in the Education of Adults, 35*(2), 123–141.

Fromm, E. (1976). *To have or to be?* New York: Continuum.

Gilligan, C. (1982). *In a different voice.* Cambridge, MA: Harvard University Press.

Gleick, J. (1987). *Chaos.* New York: Penguin Books.

Hawken, P. (2007). *Blessed unrest.* New York: Penguin Group.

Karpiak, I. (2005). Chaos theory. In L. English (Ed.), *International encyclopedia of adult education* (pp. 96–100). Basingstoke, UK: Palgrave Macmillan.

Korten, D. (2006). *The great turning.* San Francisco: Berrett-Koehler.

Lakoff, G. (1980). *Metaphors we live by.* Chicago: University of Chicago Press.

Lange, E. (2004). Transformative and restorative learning: A vital dialectic for sustainable societies. *Adult Education Quarterly, 54*(2), 121–139.

Lange, E. (2009). Fostering a learning sanctuary for transformation in sustainability education. In J. Mezirow, E. W. Taylor, & Associates (Eds.), *Transformative learning in practice* (pp. 193–204). San Francisco: Jossey-Bass.

Laszlo, E. (1996). *The whispering pond.* Boston: Element.

Louv, R. (2005/2008). *Last child in the woods.* Chapel Hill, NC: Algonquin Books.

Macy, J., & Young Brown, M. (1998). *Coming back to life.* Gabriola Island, BC: New Society Publishers.

Maturana, H., & Varela, F. (1980). *Autopoiesis and cognition.* Dordrecht, Netherlands: D. Reidel.

McTaggart, L. (2008). *The field.* New York: Harper.

Ming-Dao, D. (1992). *365 Tao.* New York: HarperCollins.

Orr, D. (1992). *Ecological Literacy.* Albany, NY: SUNY.

Orr, D. (1994). *Earth in mind.* Washington, DC: Island Press.

Orr, D. (2005). Place and pedagogy. In M. Stone & Z. Barlow (Eds.), *Ecological literacy* (pp. 85–95). San Francisco: Sierra Club Books.

O'Sullivan, E. (1999). *Transformative learning: Educational vision for the 21st century.* Toronto, ON and London, UK: University of Toronto Press and Zed Books.

Scott, S. (1997). The grieving soul in the transformation process. In P. Cranton (Ed.), *Transformative learning in action: Insights from practice* (pp. 41–50). New Directions for Adult and Continuing Education, no. 74. San Francisco: Jossey-Bass.

Shiva, V. (2005). *Globalization's new wars: Seed, water and life forms.* New Delhi: Women Unlimited.

Sobel, D. (2005). *Place-based education.* Great Barrington, MA: Orion Society.

Spretnak, C. (1999). *The resurgence of the real.* New York: Routledge.

Sumner, J. (2005). *Sustainability and the civil commons.* Toronto, ON: University of Toronto Press.

Swimme, B., & Berry, T. (1992). *The universe story.* New York: HarperOne.

Sztompka, P. (1994). *The sociology of social change.* Oxford: Blackwell.

Tarnas, R. (1991). *The passion of the western mind.* New York: Ballantine Books.

Taylor, C. (1991). *The malaise of modernity.* Concord, ON: House of Anansi Press.

Weber, M. (1930/1992). *The protestant ethic and the spirit of capitalism.* New York: Routledge.

Wheatley, M. (1996, Spring). The unplanned organization. *Noetic Sciences Review, 37.*

CHAPTER THIRTEEN

An Existential Approach to Transformative Learning

Peter Willis

In this chapter I explore some existential dimensions of learners in transformation. The existential dimensions pay attention to what the experience of transformative learning might mean to the learner in her or his actual experience of these processes. Using a narrative phenomenological approach, I explore the ways in which learning events, which the learners name as being in some way transformative, are like as lived experiences. This inquiry seeks to add another frame to intersecting approaches to transformative learning, and to add educational approaches to its fostering.

In recent years the idea of transformative learning has opened out and become more nuanced. In the second edition of her foundational work on transformative learning, Cranton (2006) tracks the significant development of transformative theory's two major approaches, first as an outcome of critical thinking (Freire 1972a, 1972b; Mezirow 1978, 1991) and then enriched by nonrational thinking (Boyd & Myers, 1988; Dirkx, 2000, 2001; Cranton, 2006). The approach of my inquiry would see these as essentialist structural approaches that could be enriched by a perspective that looked not so much at changes to rational and nonrational cognitive structures as to actual processes of human existence—to the processes of human being and becoming.

This is more a matter of emphasis, as existing writers have hinted at this dimension. Mezirow's reference to a "disorientating dilemma" that precipitates the transformative process carries a narrow meaning focused on the cognitive frameworks through which the learner was reflecting on her situation. It seems that this can also have a wider meaning, referring to the person's life stance, her way of being in the world—which becomes unstable.

From this perspective the experience of learning is viewed not so much in its structure (a change in perspective) but more in its overall experience (a change in "being," becoming different). This response to learning is not restricted to a change in intellectual perspective, which it often is, but to a deep sense of enrichment, of becoming somehow better and brighter, more potent and alive. Dirkx (2006, p. 32) confirms this overlap when he writes, "These [transformative learning] experiences foster radical shifts in one's consciousness, in one's ways of being."

In a research study of the learning experiences of retired women in rural Australia enrolled in higher degrees (Lear, 2010), one informant spoke of her sense of enrichment, satisfaction, and excitement as she received her next package of notes and books from the university. It was evident to Lear that this woman saw herself as significantly transformed, but not specifically in her thinking. Her progressive thinking was confirmed and enriched rather than radically modified. It was as though her black-and-white world had become suffused with color. It seemed that this form of transformative learning needed further exploration— not so much from an essentialist perspective, looking for structural change in her thinking, but existentially in her enthusiasm and appreciative life stance; not so much what she had come to *know* and *understand* but what she had come to *be*. Elizabeth Lange (2004) speaks of *restorative transformation*, specifically in citizenship education. Here it seems to be more a kind of illumination.

These two kinds of learning have also been referred to as the "inspirational" and the "scientific." As early as 1989, Oliver and Gershman suggested two kinds of knowledge could be gained by two kinds of learning: technical and ontological. They write:

> Technical knowledge refers to adaptive, publicly transferable information and skills: ontological knowing refers to a more diffuse apprehension of reality, in the nature of liturgical or artistic engagement. In this latter sense, we come to know with our whole body, as it participates in the creation of significant new occasions—occasions which move from imagination and intention to critical self definition, to satisfaction and finally to perishing and new being. (p. 63)

Ideas of learning that have built on Oliver and Gershman's ontological notion have a strong link to the existential approach.

THE EXISTENTIAL PERSPECTIVE

Existentialist approaches to learning draw on a European tradition most famously linked to the writings (1956) of Sartre (1905–1980) but developed in a pedagogic and less individualistic way by Maxine Greene (1967a, 1967b, 1988, 1995), who drew as well on the pragmatism of John Dewey (1938). Many of the primary resource texts and their commentators belong to the early and middle twentieth century, but I think there is relevance in this approach when considering the dimensions of transformative learning, which are linked to a strong desire for resolution to an experienced dilemma in which learners are confronted by contradictory perspectives and related life choices. The existential approach seeks to underpin and encourage the personal energy of people facing this dilemma. Morris (1966) summed up the existential project:

> It summons us onward . . . to a new level of awareness: of self, of freedom, of choice, of responsibility, of authenticity. It summons us to take charge of our own symptoms, to assume personal control of our anxiety and make it the occasion for achieving a new kind of life. (p. 32)

An existential approach to learning and pedagogy contrasts with the more essentialist, objective, or so-called "scientific" approach. Under the essentialist approach, learning is considered to occur when information and skills are taken into the learner's repertoire. The existential approach, in contrast, points out that learning, and particularly transformative learning, is a personal dynamic process. It is made up of a series of chosen acts of self-orientation in response to some life challenge. These personal acts of learning are pursued by people with specific personalities and desires in particular social contexts (Rasheed, 2006).

In his writings on the existential outlook, the historian of ideas Jack Cross (2005) points to three recurring dialectic tensions requiring ongoing resolution that characterize the existential outlook: "existence and transcendence," "choice and boundary situations," and "self and other." From an existential perspective, transformative learning refers to radical learning choices by which a person orients her- or himself wisely and authentically within the forces of these dialectics.

Existence and Transcendence

This dialectic highlights the human tension between *existing* in specific circumstances and simultaneously seeking to *transcend* these circumstances. The existentialist seeks to develop a capacity, while in the confines of the real circumstances of life, to contemplate these as if from a distance; to imagine alternative circumstances and to make choices that lead toward desirable changes.

Cross (2005) writes of this:

> My capacity for transcendent thought tells me that everything I do or say takes its relevance and point from my own existence, in ever widening circles—how I

live with (1) myself, (2) others, (3) society, and (4) the universe. Yet I know with great certainty that comparatively soon I will cease to exist—at least in the present form that is me. (p. 3)

Out of this sense of finitude can come a tragic sense of life, on the one hand—the famous existential angst—and, on the other, the creativity, courage, and nobility of those who seize the moment for acts of love, honor, and courage. The tension between existence and transcendence becomes exacerbated in difficult circumstances, which are referred to as *boundary situations*.

Choice and Boundary Situations

The existential psychiatrist Karl Jaspers (1932/1969–1971) pointed out that at different times in life, people are called upon to confront difficult and precarious states such as illness, loss of employment, natural disasters, and the like. In these boundary situations, one needs to develop authenticity: to take responsibility for choices and actions and stand behind them in order to perform honorably and to avoid colluding in a downward spiral of dishonesty to oneself. Strenger (2009) wrote that, for Jaspers, it is significant that for many people caught up the challenges of life-changing learning, which presents itself as somehow transformational, the learning challenge itself is often linked to a boundary situation and accompanied by prolonged and accumulated stress. Strenger (2009) claims that for Jaspers,

> The encounter with boundary situation was essential to human life...human beings could find their freedom through this encounter. In being thrown back to the failure intrinsic to human existence, as in finitude, illness, and death, human beings can also experience the freedom to choose how to deal with these problems. We can choose between love and hate, between facing reality and avoiding it, between dignity and cowardly avoidance of pain. (p. 52)

Self and Other

The third dialectic in the existential tradition, with its quest for meaning in the choices of life and the need to establish and safeguard personal identity, is the tension between self and other. Cross (2005) observes that the close personal relations that people need can also be a source of distress. This dialectic can generate empathy and compassion but sometimes forms of hatred as well. He writes:

> Because we all share common existential experiences with others, we all share a common humanity or humanness—the humanism of existentialism.... We need significant others to help relieve existential loneliness...having others helps up map out our own identity which in turn influences the way we behave. (p. 6)

There is thus a significant tension between social relationships and individual independence. For instance, Gloria Dall'Alba (2009) speaks of how Heidegger's existential phenomenology was strongly aware of the self/other dialectic:

> For Heidegger (1962/1927), being-in-the-world more generally, necessarily incorporates being with others . . . that through being with others, we learn to think and act as the generalised "they" do. In learning to think and act as "they" do, we also take a stand on those thoughts and actions, as well as on who we are becoming. (p. 42)

The significant point in this context is that transformation takes place in an environment in which these tensions exist and where, at least from time to time and to a greater or lesser extent, human learning can easily be a boundary situation with all the accompanying stress. When this is applied to education, the curriculum stresses the development of the person as well as her or his competencies. For example, Sinha (2008), writing of Maxine Greene's existential approach, says that education can serve to help students "to experience different perspectives as their own, to help students experience the radical modification in their own consciousness so they may be enabled to truly see that to which they would not ordinarily be open, and to experience the limitlessness of the range of human possibility" (p. 274).

TRANSFORMATIVE LEARNING AS AN EXISTENTIAL PROCESS

As explored in this chapter, transformative learning can be understood as an *existential act* (compare with Estrela, 2008; Greene, 1974; Rasheed, 2006), which engages the whole person of the learner. From this perspective, such learning involves significant personal change and is identified by learners themselves as transformative. Apart from its cognitive structure, which has been carefully discussed by Mezirow and his interpreters and critics mentioned earlier, there is the question of what the existential quality of such a transformative learning event might be.

Phenomenologist John Heron (1992) suggests that the experience of human knowing and learning involves four interconnected modalities. The first modality encompasses forms of embodied sensation and feeling. This leads to the second modality, experienced as metaphoric, intuitive, and heartfelt image creation. The third modality involves conceptual analysis and critique, which leads finally to praxis or reflective action. Kasl and Yorks (2002) explored Heron's approach in relation to transformative learning. They summarized Heron's four modalities in this way: "Heron presents the four ways of knowing as a cycle: the learner experiences a felt encounter which is grasped and presented intuitively, expressed propositionally and extended into practical action. Action creates a new experience of 'felt encounter' and the cycle begins anew" (p. 2).

In this chapter, I consider how these four modalities are verified existentially in self-identified transformative learning events.

The first mode of knowing and learning, *embodied sensation and feeling*, is generated in the initial awareness of a new sensation or feeling. Because transformation by definition involves some form of radical change, in what ways does this impact the human knower as a new sensation or feeling? In some transformative narratives the learner feels physical resonances of a basic and deep change. Indeed, existentially it is hard to imagine a person reporting a moment of transformative learning without bodily responses being involved.

In Heron's second mode of knowing and learning, the *imaginal*, the learner sees and dwells on the sensations or feelings of the first mode in a metaphoric and narrative way. This mode is linked to the significant personal change that the learner may identify as transformative; she or he produces a metaphoric or imaginal presentation of the power and reach of the learning experience. Imaginal knowing (Hillman, 1981; Corbin, 1969) is not the same as the workings of the imagination, which are much broader and full of real and unreal possibilities. Imaginal processes are not concerned with fantasy; they are linked to images through which people consciously or unconsciously represent and value things and experiences, seemingly instinctively and often without full awareness. These, according to Hillman (1981), are supported by "generative" images that hold the imagination and move the heart, the influence of which is somehow present deep in the person's psyche. This imaginal approach suggests further that these personal generative images and ideals are influenced by powerful, more or less hidden images, which Jung called *archetypes*, located in the unconscious mind. Following a general Jungian line, Hillman suggests that, with varying degrees of self-awareness, people build and develop their own images and stories of self through which they create their own style, values, and personal myths.

Thus this imaginal representation of an experience of transformative knowing and learning is linked to human mythopoesis (Macdonald, 1981; Holland & Garman, 2008), which is the creation of significant life-interpreting and life-guiding stories. This metaphoric and imaginal representational process is usually carried in colorful immediate stories, with their revelatory and imaginal character. Heron highlighted this second mode as an intervening step between raw embodied awareness and critical analysis.

The third mode of knowing, *conceptual analysis and critique*, is the foundation of logical rational approaches to transformative knowing and learning. This is the radical moment of intellectual insight when chaotic and disturbing questions are in some way brought to resolution. Here I focus on the experiential dimensions of these analytical and critical elements. What does this transformative process feel like for the learner? Archimedes running from his bath into the streets of Athens crying "Eureka!" is a strong example of transformative knowing and learning as cognitive discovery.

Finally, this existential inquiry into self-defined transformative learning explores the lived experience of the fourth mode of knowing and learning, *reflective action.* Sometimes called *praxis*, this final mode refers to the feedback from chosen action. There is an implicit suggestion that transformative thinking, feeling, and imagining leads to new knowledge and ways of being in the world and takes on yet another dimension when put into action in the context of embodied life with others. Whereas cognitive forms of transformative knowing and learning can be represented in logical and careful reports, the existential dimensions often find natural representation in stories.

NARRATIVE DIMENSIONS OF EXISTENTIAL TRANSFORMATION

This section considers how stories are able to represent the existential dimensions of transformative learning, within the dialectics of existence and transcendence, choice and boundary situations, and self and other. An actual story of such transformation follows. Before this is a brief sketch showing how this existential approach can be discerned in the four modalities of knowing and learning when describing a learner's transformative experience. Resonances from the existential approach can be discerned in the four modalities.

A carefully wrought story can integrate Heron's four modes of knowing in representing the texture and appeal of a transformative learning episode. The storyteller, who may or may not be the learner, often begins by mentioning a raw and troubling event or events that the learner has encountered. Its existential dimension can be represented by describing the learner's responsive awareness and bodily responses. The storyteller can then move to more expressive representation by using metaphors from her or his repertoire to represent the raw impact of the event. These metaphors tend to be drawn from archetypal images in the storyteller's culture. The story picks up intensity in this imaginal mode; it displays with color and urgency the texture and impact of the challenging event on the learner.

The storyteller then shows how the learner appraises the event, seeking analytical categories to which it might belong, its causes, and finally what action is required in response. The existential dimension of this third, more logical and rational mode of knowing and learning tends to be represented as a cool and rational process. It tells of the analytical reflection and considered choice for action characterizing transformation rather than a more impulsive response, which would be less likely to be named as transformative. The story then moves to praxis, the fourth modality of learning, wherein the transformation is validated in action.

In this praxis mode of learning, the storyteller can report on the learning that took place when the chosen responses to the unsettling new situation were put into practice. In the challenge of personal and social change, this final mode of reflective action is a specific kind of learning. Its existential dimension is linked to what it was actually like when the chosen change was implemented. What actually happened? How did it feel? How did others react? Were there unexpected consequences? What did it achieve? Was it actually the right thing to do?

It is this overall narrative agenda, with its links to the four modalities of learning, that has influenced the approach to education and learning explored here. John Howard Griffin's story of transformation, which follows, highlights the existential dimensions of transformative learning in action.

JOHN HOWARD GRIFFIN'S EXISTENTIAL NARRATIVE OF TRANSFORMATION

This existential story of transformative learning draws on events that took place in America after the Second World War. It concerns John Howard Griffin's radical change from a mystical, aesthetic, and sociable musician, journalist, and scholar to a tireless antiracist activist. Griffin is best known for his popular book *Black Like Me* (1961). The book tells the story of how, in 1959, Griffin dyed his skin black and spent nearly a month as an itinerant black man looking for work in white-controlled and racist America. During this time he experienced and wrote about the deep transformative learning challenge he encountered. Quotations from his unpublished journal and other information have been drawn from Bonazzi's (1997) book on Griffin and his brief life history by his wife Elizabeth Griffin-Bonazzi (1999).

Griffin was born in 1920 to a musical rural family in Fort Worth, Texas. In 1946, as a consequence of shrapnel wounds suffered during military service in World War Two, he lost his sight. In 1956, apparently due to the effects of medication he was prescribed for another illness, his sight returned. During his time of blindness in his home in Texas, his natural kindly, aesthetic, and spiritual disposition, enhanced by his study with religious academic mentors, was affronted by the contrast he heard between the warmth and courtesy with which American whites spoke to each other and the demeaning and hostile way they spoke to their black fellow citizens. He realized that although such unjust and cruel differences had always been present, he had become aware of them only because of his changed circumstances—blind, religious, and hypersensitive to injustice. His daily journal writing helped him to confront and critique events and experiences that troubled him, and it acted as a kind of reflective existential pedagogy.

Griffin defined himself as a writer seeking to experience intensely and to portray every element of his life. He attempted to discover and create beauty in every part of his world: music, religion, friendship, and social justice. His journaling seemed to act as a catalyst to authenticity, to aesthetic rapture and disgust, to careful logical analysis and to prophetic protest against the ugliness of human cruelty and prejudice. There is little of the social activist in the early days of Griffin's adulthood when he first returned, blind, to his parents' home, but by the time he regained his sight he was looking for ways to reform America's unchallenged racism.

BLACK LIKE ME

After 1956, with his sight restored, Griffin entered his period of greatest productivity. His book *Black Like Me* came out in 1961. The month-long "white man dyed black" experiment had taken place at the end of 1959. Once his experiment started, he couldn't believe his exclusion from familiar citizen activities. He would walk for miles in search of work; he was refused a seat in cafes, unable to get service at bus stops, and excluded from public toilets unless there were ones specially designated for blacks. He was ignored and sometimes abused by white people in public places. He started to keep a low profile to avoid being the target of white violence, knowing that the law would not protect him. He noted the strength of his distaste, fear, and distress. He also pointed out more analytically that the racist behavior of individual whites was condoned, if not encouraged, by mainstream American culture. He saw himself and many other so-called good white Americans as unwittingly compliant.

Griffin's book became a best seller. He was feted and threatened at the same time. The book acted as a catalyst for the "white awareness" movement, and contributed to a more inclusive U.S. culture in which black voices no longer required a white interpreter and amplifier. From the transformative learning perspective, it was Griffin's experience before and during his "black" period that led to his transformation into a special kind of nonviolent activist. To read this book now is to hear an aesthetic and cultivated person confronted with an inhuman social regime operating in the Southern region of the United States almost under his nose. He began to realize that the form of egalitarian and respectful whiteness practiced by him and his family was often not the one in common use. He felt wretched: images of black degradation and neglect stayed with him, and his analytical mind was spinning as he tried to understand how a nominally Christian country could condone or even promote such rejection and subjugation. He concluded that much of this neglect was not known and certainly the experience of such disdainful exclusion was not understood. He decided to tell white America his stories of what it is like to be black: what he saw and felt, how his mind spun in confusion and his heart in disarray.

In the light of earlier descriptions of existential transformative learning, Griffin's story of becoming and changing carries significant elements of Heron's four modes of learning. His heightened bodily awareness of a kind of disorientation—his hearing, when blind, of the sound of patronizing white voices and fearful black voices, and his bodily experiences of life as a black man—form much of the power of his book.

Griffin's vivid story of his life as a black itinerant worker conveys not only his initial bodily reactions and feelings but metaphorically his initial "unreflected upon" imaginal awareness of being black in America. He feels images of himself as dirty, feral, dangerous under the white gaze, and images of himself as welcome and acceptable under the inclusive black gaze.

Dwelling on the shocking images that he had seen and registered, he struggled to find analytical categories to understand the racist regime with which he had to admit that, as an unaware and nonresistant white, he was at least to some extent complicit. With these disturbing images fresh in his mind, he then reflected on the weakness in America's unequal and demeaning version of Western democracy. He also revealed and challenged the racial blindness of his own powerful Christian religion, which, for reasons he struggled to understand, had not condemned racism and promoted equality and inclusivity. His analytical reflection also identified possibilities for reform in American democracy. He pointed to its constitution and its acceptance of the power of individual citizens exercising their right to free speech to reveal injustice and to mobilize public opinion against it. His transformative experience, with its images and analytical critique, led to his choice of active engagement in civil rights campaigning, which he pursued until his death.

Griffin's deep change from mystical musician and writer to social activist can be seen as an existential event realized in the four modes of knowing and learning described earlier. The comprehensive power of Griffin's story seems to me to be revealed by examining the ways in which his writings covered and evoked these four modes. His powerfully evocative narrative of awakening and transformation carried an implicit invitation for others to engage in similar learning and to allow room in their hearts for a similar experience. This story of an event as experienced (which can be referred to as an "existential narrative") seems often to carry an implicit "evocative pedagogy" when someone's story of transformation moves the heart of the listener. This is common in religious witnesses of being saved and narratives of satisfaction from contented purchasers of a particular product.

The last part of this chapter looks briefly at the nature of such existential pedagogy and the ways in which it may be understood and pursued.

EXISTENTIAL PEDAGOGY AND TRANSFORMATIVE LEARNING

Existential pedagogy seeks to be attuned to and evocative of human learning as a major life-shaping project and quest: its energies and vulnerabilities. The processes of facilitation as an existential invitation to learning have been examined in the work of Maxine Greene, who has joined ideas of Sartre with those of Dewey. Sinha (2008) writes that for Maxine Greene, existential pedagogy can help students to "experience different perspectives as their own, to experience the radical modification in their own consciousness so they may be enabled to truly see that to which they would not ordinarily be open, and to experience the limitlessness of the range of human possibility" (p. 274).

This evocative approach is a form of invitation to learn, a form of existential pedagogy.

Awareness of the existential dimensions of education would also acknowledge the importance of supporting a *transcending process*. One of the ways this can be done is by seeking meta-narratives relating to learning activities. The learner is invited to ask her or himself the existential meta-question: *What are you doing?* It is not the specific activity that needs to be named but the more general interpretive frame in the light of the person's life project that is being pursued. When the stonemason is asked "What are you doing?" the reply can be "I am shaping this stone," "I am working to feed my family," or "I am building a cathedral." Thoughtful answers to the meta-question can precipitate a useful transcending response and possibly a refreshed and focused return to learning.

An appropriate pedagogy, aware of transformative learning as an existential border situation, can be enriched by supportive elements. Learners in life-challenging situations can develop an ecology to protect their body through exercise, sleep, good nutrition, healthy social connections, and the like, and mentors and educators can enrich such an ecology. Mentors' stories of their own learning struggles can helpfully encourage resistance to vulnerability, and of course the educator can refer the learner to supportive resources and people where necessary.

Finally, a pedagogy attuned to the "self and other" dialectic encourages relational action: social links, networking, conferencing, and study, reading, and support groups all have been key processes in meeting this existential dialectic.

In earlier work (Willis, 2002), I explored the notion of "invitation" as a useful way to represent the existential challenge of promoting learning in a democratic and nonintrusive way. In this context, "invitation" refers to an approach that seeks to engage the learner in friendly, interpersonal exchanges that respect the learner while encouraging her or him to take up specific learning agendas, because in this way the learner can be enriched. This invitational stance tends to place the learner "on the line." It is essentially an engaged rather than detached approach: warm rather than cool, holistic rather than purely logical or rational.

In the following poem (Willis, 2002, p. 18), I attempted to portray the contradictory and risky nature of invitation to a shared meal.

Invitation
I risk inviting;
I want you here.
And when you come
I'll feel enriched, believe
you feel the same.
If you refuse,
that says
I have no worth to you,
And if, when you agree to come,
you don't appear,
your absence makes a wound
and I fall below
the place I was
when first I asked you.
No-one invites for fun;
If you say "drop in if you like,"
that's not a real inviting;
there's no risk, a dollar each way
against rejection.
Inviting is for keeps
a friend, a lover in pursuit:
no half measures.
It's black or white,
not blurred or lukewarm.
And guests know the rules
to dress up, cradle
the eggshell of friendship
at your place;
And trust that
while you stand
unarmed and welcoming
your guests will not turn;
refuse to dance the party's tune;
humiliate and bring you down
and turn your grapes of bounty
into ash.

The poem sees to portray the tension that hosts can feel when they invite people to an event. There are two sources of tension. The first is if the invitation is not accepted, for no convincing reason. The second is if invited guests at the event abuse the welcoming host in some way. This element of risk seems to me to belong to the existential pedagogy of learning invitation to transformative processes. Newman (2006) referred to a catalytic stance inclining democratic educators to their reflective and intuitive work as an example of "proactive consciousness" which is "the aliveness we feel when we are assertively engaging with reality, when we are taking action, when we are continually making choices. . . . It is the consciousness which combines reflection and action" (p. 66).

It is thus the agenda of an existential inclusive pedagogy to evoke proactive, holistic consciousness in learners. This is done in two steps, which emerged in the *Black Like Me* story: establishing credibility and setting out the invitational path.

The first step is to somehow achieve pedagogic credibility. Not only does the educator have to embody the learning being promoted, but she or he must be seen as one who achieved this form of transformative learning by risking being damaged and discredited in the process. The ancient ideal of the existentially credible educator comes from Homer's *Iliad*, in which Mentor—a member of Homer's household and a seasoned, compassionate, righteous warrior and veteran of many journeys and battles—is entrusted as the adviser and educator of Homer's son Telemachus. Mentor uses his hard-won credibility to engage Telemachus in the existential, transformative learning of coming to manhood by embarking on the perilous journey to find his father. (I am indebted to Dr. Anne Morrison for her insight into the importance of existential credibility in educators who seek to invite people to engage in the experience of transformative learning.)

The second step is the invitation to the learning process, using the invitations of immersion, myth making, and critical and practical appraisal, finally calling (but not forcing) learners to choose to engage passionately in the work of their transformation.

CONCLUSION

This chapter has explored (1) an existential approach to transformative learning and (2) narrative pedagogy as one of its natural precipitators, drawing on the experiences and writings of John Howard Griffin, author of *Black Like Me*. I have explored an invitational pedagogy in each of the four ways of knowing proposed by John Heron: to feel, to dream, to appraise, and to engage in tactful praxis. The existential tone has a utopian and holistic character and seeks to complement more essentialist approaches. It seeks ways for educators promoting forms of transformational learning to consider the value of adopting a nuanced existential invitation to be explored on Heron's four levels of learning. An existentially credible educator who has had a chance to feel, dream, appraise, and practice tactfully in her or his educational craft may be well equipped to invite learners to explore a similar range of learning opportunities. After all, the narrative and oblique teaching of Griffin's book and related presentations were one of the notable catalysts of the antiracism movement in the United States and throughout the world.

References

Bonazzi, R. (1997). *Man in the mirror: John Howard Griffin and the story of* Black Like Me. Maryknoll, NY: Orbis Books.

Boyd, R. D., & Myers, J. G. (1988). Transformative education. *International Journal of Lifelong Education, 7*, 261–284.

Corbin, H. (1969). *Creative imagination in the Sufism of Ibn Arabi.* Princeton, NJ: Princeton University Press.

Cranton, P. (2006). *Understanding and promoting transformative learning: A guide for educators of adults* (2nd ed.). San Francisco: Jossey Bass.

Cross, J. (2005). The existential outlook. Unpublished lecture notes, University of South Australia).

Dall'Alba, G. (2009). Learning professional ways of being: Ambiguities of becoming. *Educational Philosophy and Theory, 41*(1), 34–45.

Dewey, J. (1938). *Experience and education.* New York: Collier Books.

Dirkx, J. M. (2000). Transformative learning and the journey of individuation. ERIC Digest 223.

Dirkx, J. M. (2001). Images, transformative learning, and the work of soul. *Adult Learning, 12*(3), 15–16.

Dirkx, J. M. (2006). Authenticity and imagination. In P. Cranton (Ed.), *Authenticity in teaching* (pp. 27–39). New Directions for Adult and Continuing Education, no. 111. San Francisco: Jossey-Bass.

Estrela, A. (2008). Delfim Santos. An innovator and precursor in the field of education. *Sísifo: Educational Sciences Journal, 6*, 101–104. Retrieved from http://sisifo.fpce.ul.pt

Freire, P. (1972a). *Cultural action for freedom.* Harmondsworth, UK: Penguin.

Freire, P. (1972b). *Pedagogy of the oppressed.* Harmondsworth, UK: Penguin.

Greene, M. (1967a). *Existential encounters for teachers.* New York: Random House.

Greene, M. (1967b). *Releasing the imagination: Essays on education, arts and social change.* San Francisco: Jossey-Bass.

Greene, M. (1974). Literature, existentialism, and education. In D. E. Denton (Ed.), *Existentialism and phenomenology in education: Collected essays* (pp. 63–86). New York: Teachers College Press.

Greene, M. (1988). *The dialectic of freedom.* New York: Teachers College Press.

Greene, M. (1995). *Releasing the imagination: Essays on education, the arts, and social change.* San Francisco: Jossey Bass.

Griffin, J. H. (1961). *Black like me.* New York: Houghton Mifflin.

Griffin-Bonazzi, E. (1999). Griffin, John Howard, in *Handbook of Texas Online.* Texas: The Texas State Historical Association.

Heron, J. (1992). *Feeling and personhood: Psychology in another key.* Thousand Oaks, CA: SAGE.

Hillman, J. (1981). *The thought of the heart.* Dallas, TX: Spring Publications.

Holland, P., & Garman, N. (2008). Watching with two eyes: The place of the mythopoetic in curriculum inquiry. In T. Leonard & P. Willis (Eds.), *Pedagogies of the imagination: Mythopoetic curriculum in educational practice.* Dordrecht, Netherlands: Springer.

Jaspers, K. (1932/1969–1971). *Philosophie.* Berlin: Springer. Translated as *Philosophy* (E. B. Ashton, Trans.). Chicago: Chicago University Press.

Kasl, E., & Yorks, L. (2002). An extended epistemology for transformative learning theory and its application through collaborative inquiry. TCRecord Online, http://www.tcrecord.org/Content.asp?ContentID=10878

Lange, E. (2004). Transformative and restorative learning: A vital dialectic for sustainable societies. *Adult Education Quarterly, 54,* 121–140.

Lear, G. (2010). *There's got to be more: Rural women of action in their third age.* Unpublished draft Ph.D. manuscript, School of Education, University of South Australia.

Macdonald, J. (1981). Theory, practice, and the hermeneutic circle. *Journal of Curriculum Theorising, 3,* 130–138.

Mezirow, J. (1978). *Education for perspective transformation: Women's re-entry programs in community colleges.* New York: Center for Adult Education, Teachers College, Columbia University.

Mezirow, J. (1991). *Transformative dimensions of adult learning.* San Francisco: Jossey-Bass.

Morris, V. C. (1966). *Existentialism in education: What it means.* New York: Harper & Row.

Newman, M. (2006). *Teaching defiance: Stories and strategies for activist educators.* San Francisco: Jossey-Bass.

Oliver, D., & Gershman, K. (1989) *Education, modernity and fractured meaning: Toward a process theory of teaching and learning.* Albany, NY: SUNY Press.

Rasheed, S. (2006). *An existential curriculum of action.* Washington, DC: University Press of America.

Sartre, J. (1956). *Being and nothingness* (H. E. Barnes, Trans.). New York: Philosophical Library.

Sinha, S. (2008). Review of Rasheed: An existentialist curriculum of action; creating a language of freedom and possibility. *Educational Studies, 43,* 273–277.

Strenger, C. (2009, Winter). Sosein: Active self acceptance in midlife. *Journal of Humanistic Psychology, 49,* 46–65.

Willis, P. (2002). *Inviting learning: An exhibition of risk and enrichment in adult education practice.* Leicester, England: NIACE.

PART THREE

TRANSFORMATIVE LEARNING: CULTURE, POSITIONALITY, AND INTERNATIONAL PERSPECTIVES

Cultural-Spiritual Perspective of Transformative Learning

Nadira K. Charaniya

The relevance of spirituality in adult education and to transformative learning is not a new idea. Much has been written on the idea of soul and its importance to the transformative learning process (Dirkx, 1997; Davis, 2003); on the role and impact of spirituality and culture in adult education practice (Tisdell, 2001, 2002, 2003; Tolliver & Tisdell, 2006; English & Tisdell, 2010), on the spiritual dimension of learning (English & Gillen, 2000; English, 2001; Miller, 2002); and on the potential of learning to facilitate spiritual development (English, 2001).

The premise of this chapter is that the journey of transformation, when considered in the context of spirituality or culture, often follows a repeating three-part sequence that begins with a strong sense of identity that is confronted by anomalies and challenges. This identity is then expanded through engagement with experiences that are intellectual, relational, and reflective. Finally, the culmination is a clearer or more pronounced understanding of self and of one's role in the world, a goal that is very much reflective of the transformative learning process. Although the outcome of this process has definite implications for social justice work, it must begin from an individual and personal perspective. It is from this premise that this chapter proceeds.

The beginning point of this journey is an identity that is deeply rooted in the socialization processes of religion and culture but somehow incomplete. The learning process through which this incomplete identity seeks completion is not a single, static occurrence but rather an ongoing series of events and experiences through which one's understanding of the world and of one's place in it are formed and reformed through contact with the unexpected, the unfamiliar, and the challenging. It is also a process through which the sojourner finds strength in both personal reflection and a "mentoring community" (Daloz, 2000).

More specifically, this journey of transformation usually begins with a questioning of one's deeply held beliefs and attitudes and a "challenging of certain culturally based assumptions" and results in "the construction of [a] new perspective" (Merriam & Ntseane, 2008). It is "an experience leading toward wholeness" (Tisdell, 2008, p. 28) and is often "the culmination of an earlier stage of exploration and searching" (Clark, 1993, p. 81). It is a "change or shift [that is] long in coming and its possibility [is] prepared for in myriad ways" (Daloz, 2000, p. 106). Seen from a cultural-spiritual perspective, "Transformation is an *extrarational* process that involves the integration of various aspects of the Self" (Baumgartner, 2001, p. 18). It is a change that ultimately redefines the individual's place in the world.

BEGINNING THE JOURNEY

Before going further in this discussion of the spiritual-cultural dimensions of transformative learning, we must clarify what is meant by "spiritual," how that is the same as or different from "religious," and how it relates to the cultural dimension referred to in this chapter. Tolliver and Tisdell (2006) identify several assumptions in trying to define spirituality. The most important of these assumptions, for our purposes, is that spirituality is an honoring of a "life-force" that permeates all living things and that this life-force is always present, albeit usually unacknowledged, in the learning environment. There are contemporary differentiations between spirituality and religion—identifying religion as "an organized community of faith" and spirituality as "an *individual's* personal experience of making meaning of the sacred" (English & Tisdell, 2010, p. 287). Although these authors differentiate between spirituality and religion, they also acknowledge that for many who have been socialized in a particular faith tradition, it is often difficult to separate spirituality from religion; particularly as their spiritual experiences may be intimately linked with, and have occurred within, their community of faith.

For the purposes of this chapter, spirituality is not separated from religion or religiosity, yet it is also not necessarily assumed to be inherently linked to formal religion. The reference to spirituality in this chapter is based on an understanding of it as "an awareness of something greater than ourselves ... [that] moves one outward to others as an expression of one's spiritual experiences" (English & Gillen, 2000, p. 1) and that may or may not be influenced by a formal religious tradition or organized community of faith. Organized communities of faith "offer guidance on how to live a spiritual life and have personal experiences of the sacred. They also come with rituals, music, symbols, prayers, and sacred stories that connect with or honor many of life's transitions that serve as gateways to the sacred" (Tisdell, 2008, pp. 28–29).

In so doing, these organized communities of faith provide us with inroads to our own spirituality and opportunities for spiritual experiences. These opportunities then live on in our psyche even if we choose to consciously distance ourselves from the ritualized communal practice of faith. Thus it is often difficult to separate the potential impact of religion from one's personal spirituality.

This understanding of spirituality is further nuanced for the purposes of this chapter with an assumption that one's spirituality is intimately connected with culture. Hill et al. (2000) define spirituality as "the feelings, thoughts, experiences, and behaviors that arise from a search for the sacred" (p. 66) and tell us that "cultural and social forces are at work in defining the sacred. . . . What is sacred, therefore, is a socially influenced perception of either some sense of ultimate reality or truth or some divine being/object" (p. 67).

Thus the search that one engages in as a spiritual being is influenced by one's culture. The process is a holistic one that involves the integration of all dimensions of the learner.

As an Afro-Indian, British, Canadian, American Muslim woman, I have a lot to say about the intersections between culture and spirituality. Each of my multifaceted identities—religious, ethnic, geographical, gender—informs who I am as a cultural being. As a person who was raised in four different countries on three different continents, my understanding and experience of culture is very different from that of someone who was born and raised in a single geographical context. Similarly, my socialization as a Muslim woman raised in a Western context is different from a Muslim woman socialized in Saudi Arabia. My life experiences have been heavily influenced by this socialization and my resulting worldview. I am, however, not unique in this. Mezirow tells us, "Human reality is intersubjective; our life histories and language are bound up with those of others. It is within the context of these relationships, governed by existing and changing cultural paradigms, that we become the persons we are" (2000, p. 27).

At a time when the world is rife with conflict, dogmatic interpretations, and misunderstanding, it is important that adults engage in a sharing and exploration of perspectives so that they move toward "meaning perspectives that are more inclusive, discrimination, permeable, and integrative of experience" (Mezirow, 1991, p. 225).

We live at a time that the Aga Khan (2008) has referred to as a "clash of ignorance" in which it is our responsibility "to listen to one another and learn from one another" (p. 128). This is an exciting opportunity for us, particularly in the field of adult education. The opportunity provides an opening for us to find ways to help adults explore their taken-for-granted assumptions and replace them for more informed, more nuanced, and more discriminating knowledge. Because much of the ignorance is based on socialization that is inherently influenced by our cultural and spiritual perspectives of life, these perspectives are just as important in the solution to take us forward. The spiritual and cultural foundations with which the adult learner enters into the educational encounter are inherent to the learner's identity and are the stepping-off point for transformation.

There are several possibilities for how adult learners can begin this journey of transforming the ignorance that leads to conflict. One way, when they are aware of and enthusiastically confront the ignorance, is by seeking more knowledge. A second way is when they are confronted by the ignorance or the inadequacy of their own understanding by circumstance and thus are forced to seek more information. Finally, they can simply build more informed insight through engaging in experiences that expose them to greater knowledge and more diverse perspectives. In a study on adult learning in the context of interreligious dialogue (Charaniya & West Walsh, 2001), these three entryways were defined as diving in, being pushed in, and testing the waters.

Divers—those who dive in—are individuals who have been preparing for transformation throughout their lives and take advantage of an integrating cir-cumstance that drew them in "to greater depths of understanding and personal growth" (Clark, 1993, p. 83). Bill, for example, remembered being taunted and physically attacked as a child because he was a Jew. All of his life he won-dered about this, not really understanding how a person who purports to be a Christian could do such a thing to a Jew, as Jesus himself was a Jew. Hav-ing the opportunity years later, as an adult, to engage in Christian and Jewish dialogue gave him the context in which he could work out the answer to this old and very personal question. In the process, he was able to transform his understanding of the experiences of his childhood in a new adult learning con-text and to then move toward a more activist stance in dealing with issues of religious intolerance (Charaniya & West Walsh, 2001). Divers actively seek out the experience in a variety of ways, as they find the integrating circumstance a form of opportunity to learn and move on in their lives.

Those who are pushed in are those who encounter disorienting dilemmas that cause them to question their frame of reference. Their reaction to the disorienting dilemma pushes them toward dialogue rather than running away from it. An example of this is the story of Reshma, a Muslim participant in the interreligious dialogue study, who shared how having been confronted by an older Jewish women who did not "want [her] making bombs in her backyard" made her realize that contrary to her previous assumptions, understanding the "other" is more important than simply minding one's own business (Charaniya & West Walsh, 2001, p. 168). This pattern of transformation is echoed by participants in an informal study on the influence of culture and spirituality on adult learning in progress. One participant, who identifies herself as Amij, says, "Being in an abusive marriage caused me to question the 'til death do us part doctrine of the church and the belief that a woman should subjugate herself to the man, as well as traditional roles for women." For Amij, the disorienting dilemma was incremental and a result of her negative experiences in her marriage. More important, it led her to confront her culturally based beliefs and create positive change in her life.

Those who enter the journey to test the waters are not confronted with a dilemma, nor does the invitation present itself as "an opportunity for exploration and development" (Clark, 1993, p. 82), as is the case with an integrating circumstance. Rather, they are intrigued, interested, or simply curious about the possibilities. These individuals are those who have a strong foundation but who are open to, and ready for, the possibilities of transformation. Although several of the participants in the Charaniya and West Walsh study (2001) started out by testing the waters, at the time the research data was collected they were fully engaged and participating in the cycles of emerging and reimmersion that leads to transformation. These participants are representative of those whom Dirkx (2000) suggests "are caught up with the images and symbols which swirl around the learning environment" (p. 247).

Each of these aspects of the adult learners' lives—their culture, their spirituality, and the experiences they encounter—serve as a base from which the transformative journey can potentially be launched. Not all learners necessarily set out on that journey, but those that do are helped through certain pedagogic and situational tools and opportunities. The next section explores these tools and opportunities in more detail.

CONDITIONS FOR TRANSFORMATION

Mezirow (1991) asserts that learning is all about making meaning; that one learns through a process of making explicit, connecting with, interpreting, remembering, validating, and acting on "some aspect of our engagement with the environment, other persons, or ourselves" (p. 11). When cultural and spiritual perspectives are invited into the mix, this process of making meaning, or learning, involves a range of experiences in which knowledge is socially and collaboratively constructed. It is a process of listening, hearing, questioning, relating, symbolizing, feeling, and sharing of stories. It is a site for sharing understandings as a process of "finding coherence in and giving meaning to the multiple forces and relations that make up our lives" (Fowler, 1981, p. 4). It is a context in which spiritual development, and the learning that accompanies that process, can take place.

When seen from a cultural-spiritual perspective, transformative learning is not limited to intellectual and logical dimensions alone, nor is it necessarily a linear progression. Rather, it is a spiraling, creative, collaborative, and intertwining journey of discovery. As Miller (2002) tells us, "From a spiritual perspective, learning does not just involve the intellect; instead, it includes every aspect of our being including the physical, emotional, aesthetic, and spiritual" (p. 97).

Taylor, in his update on transformative learning theory (2008), tells us that the goal of a cultural-spiritual view of transformative learning "is to foster a narrative transformation—engaging storytelling on a personal and social level through group inquiry" (p. 9). Similarly, Tisdell (2003) tells us "spirituality and culture in adult and higher education are always about stories and people's experiences" (p. 21). In the study on the experiences of adults engaged in interreligious dialogue (Charaniya & West Walsh, 2001), participants painted a picture of experiences in which knowledge was socially and collaboratively constructed.

Although each of these elements can be part of a transformative experience without necessarily being spiritual in nature, when the resulting learning moves the learner to that metaphysical plane where the impulse to connect with others is strengthened by a holistic awareness of the interconnectedness of life, that is when the spiritual-cultural perspectives are most prominent. Participants in the study mentioned earlier described their experiences as more than a rational exercise in "constructive discourse to use the experience of others to assess reasons justifying [one's] assumptions, and making an action decision based on the resulting insight" (Mezirow, 2000, p. 8). For example, one participant described it in this way:

> I really think that the heart of any conversation . . . is just people being linked
> together and people being willing to put on the table in the conversation some
> part of themselves, and it doesn't have to be the deepest part of yourself. It can
> be something entirely different. But that once you do that, the two outside
> circles have some sense of concentricity to them—they link—there's a center,
> and that center changes the outside circles because you've shared something.
> (Charaniya & West Walsh, 2001, p. 225)

When the cultural and spiritual aspects of the learner's identity are included in the learning process, the result is a sharing, re-visioning, and enlargement of learner narratives about their identities, life, and the world, and a profound sense of interdependence. It is grounds for a transformation that goes beyond the individual's place in the world to a more active engagement with the world.

The transformative learning process thus involves interacting with co-learners from a holistic perspective. It is what Dirkx (1997) refers to as "learning through soul," which occurs when "the socioemotional and the intellectual world meet" (p. 85). It is collaborative knowledge construction. According to Lee (1998, 2000), core values of collaborative learning include cultivating critical openness, engaging the whole person, stimulating critical thinking through dialogue, appreciating diverse perspectives, dwelling with questions, touching the affective, strengthening the cognitive, and enhancing the social. All of these are conditions for transformation when the cultural and spiritual are partners in the learning environment. It should be noted, however, that having the cultural and spiritual dimensions as partners in the learning environment does not necessarily lead to the kind of transformation suggested here. In fact, when the cultural and spiritual dimensions are buried in ignorance, resistance, or simply fear of the unknown, the resulting barriers are often impossible to break down.

In order for the learning environment to reach out and invite transformative learning that is positively influenced by the cultural and spiritual aspects of the learner, the learner must be able to bring certain prerequisite tools to the table. For example, the personal characteristics of intellectual curiosity and being comfortable with ambiguity are crucial in any encounter in which one's cultural and spiritual assumptions are to be challenged. Intellectual curiosity allows the learner to be open to asking questions; tolerance of ambiguity gives the learner a certain comfort level with the unknown and with having his or her own beliefs challenge without being devastated. As one participant in the Charaniya and West Walsh study put it, "Knowing what I don't know gives me a chance to learn more . . . you learn that what you've been taught all your life, maybe it's not true, but it doesn't matter" (p. 190).

Another learner attitude that is important for transformative learning and that is closely related to intellectual curiosity and comfort with ambiguity is intellectual and social humility. Intellectual humility allows the learner to be open to more divergent points of view. Social humility enables the learner to be willing to listen to those divergent points of view with minimal resistance. Both of these stances are integral to a cultural-spiritual perspective, and both invite the possibility for transformation. These attitudes, when combined with opportunities in the learning environment, enable the learner to be touched and transformed intellectually, affectively, and socially. One of the interreligious dialogue study participants captured this idea when he described what happens in the process:

> The person you see is moved. I mean they are really, usually when these people talk about their experiences religiously, or about this particular episode—they are talking about it because it has moved them somehow. And you see that and you can't help but share, if you are really listening—if you are really listening, you can't help but be moved by whatever it is that moved them. So you have to say, "Wow, that's a pretty powerful force that has made this person's . . . ," you know it resonates with you. (Charaniya & West Walsh, 2001, p. 191)

Peters and Armstrong (1998) tells us that "collaboration means that people labor together in order to construct something that did not exist before the collaboration, something that does not and cannot fully exist in the lives of individual collaborators" (p. 75). This is what happens when adult learners are open to and inviting of the *extrarational* process (Baumgartner, 2001) that is an inherent aspect of attending to cultural and spiritual dimensions in the transformative learning process. It is something that cannot happen when the exploration is limited to intellectual discourse. It is a sharing of more than just ideas.

The examples just presented are based on the experiences of individuals whose very focus was on the spiritual and cultural dimension of life because they were engaged in interreligious dialogue. The experiences they describe and the tools and environments they portray, however, are not unique to their context. Brown-Haywood (Tisdell, Brown-Haywood, Charaniya, & West Walsh, in press) describes the impact of a workshop entitled "Singing My Way Through in Sacred Face: The Healing Properties of Black Sacred Music" on participants. The workshop uses slave spirituals as a way to give voice to the human condition and, through that voice, to move toward healing and hope that is transformational. The power of this approach is evident in the response of one participant in a workshop for women residing in shelters: "no one has ever told me I can release my feelings by sounds and a song; it's still hard but this way makes it easier." This woman is an example of how the transformative process can be profound when it is stimulated through stories and creative expression—both of which are evident in the workshop's approach.

What is most significant about the spiritual-cultural dimensions of transformative learning—and what makes this dimension so different from Mezirow's original conception—is that the experiences involved are not simply a linear progression of a ten-step process. Rather, they are an ongoing, cyclical smorgasbord of opportunities to dialogue, share stories, explore symbols, and learn from each other. In the case of the interreligious dialogue study, it is "a dance between partners from two different religious traditions within which the content knowledge they brought into the experience was bolstered by how they interacted with the 'other,' their reflections upon their own inner selves, and by the manner in which this knowledge was shared and communicated" (Charaniya & West Walsh, 2001, p. 197).

WHAT TRANS-FORMS

A feature of a cultural-spiritual perspective of transformative learning is that what transforms is usually multidimensional. When one's spirituality and one's culture are invited guests at the table, they become an inherent part of the transformation. Participants at the table are transformed in terms of how they see the world, how they see their own identities, and how they see their role in the world.

Kegan (2000) suggests that for learning to be trans-*form*-ative (p. 49) it must put the "form" itself at risk of change. He suggests that the difference between what he terms "in-*form*-ative" learning (p. 49) and trans-*form*-ative learning is that although the former is limited to an increase in one's knowledge, the latter occurs only when one's very frame of reference is changed. Using the language of constructive-developmental theory, he argues that "when a way of knowing moves from a place where we are 'had by it' (captive of it) to a place where we 'have it,' and can be in relationship to it, the form of our knowing has become more complex, more expansive" (pp. 53–54).

He identifies two processes in the epistemological process: meaning forming and reforming our meaning forming. He says, "We do not only form meaning and we do not only change our meanings; we change the very form by which we are making our meanings. We change our epistemologies" (pp. 52–53). This same idea of transformative learning as epistemological change is echoed by Daloz (2000): "What shifts in the transformative process is our very epistemology—the way in which we know and make meaning" (p. 104). The epistemological change described by Kegan and echoed by Daloz describes a circular process by which the learner revisits previous meanings and changes both the meanings formed and the way in which the new meanings are formed.

Tisdell (2008) suggests a similar process when she tells us how educators in her study on spirituality "reclaimed aspects of the sacred in their own cultural or gender story, or found new power in reframing some of the cultural symbols, mythic stories, music, or metaphors that were part of their earlier life experience" (pp. 31–32). Referring to the ideas of Bateson (1995), she describes a process of spiral learning in which adults remap earlier understandings when they revisit them in new contexts. She goes a step further than Kegan or Daloz, however, when she tells us that "just as events and experiences of the past can be infused and remapped with new meaning, so too can symbols, mythic story, metaphor, and music" (p. 32).

The process of transformation is not always easy, especially when spirituality and culture are key partners. As Tolliver and Tisdell (2006) tell us, "Spirituality can involve not only positive and constructive understandings, but also struggle and confrontation of the more shadowy aspects of human existence" (p. 45). Ultimately, however, the learning can lead to "reflectively transforming the beliefs, attitudes, opinions, and emotional reactions that constitute our meaning schemes" (Mezirow, 1991, p. 223).

IMPLICATIONS FOR THE ADULT EDUCATOR

Depending on the particular site for adult education activity, the conditions for learning just detailed may or may not be appropriate. There are certainly some instances (such as technical education, for example) in which the interdependent, interrelational, and affective conditions just described may be out of place. In appropriate contexts, however, there are many ways in which the preceding discussion has implications for the field. Two key areas are the role of the adult educator and the role of pedagogy and environment. In the remainder of the chapter, I briefly explore these two areas.

If the spiritual and cultural dimensions of the adult learner are to be allowed to filter into the learning that occurs within a given context in the manner described in the preceding section of this chapter, then the adult educator is a vital link in the process. First, the educator must be open to the prospect of having these dimensions of the learner be part of the dynamic of the classroom experience. The educator has the power to set the tone for the learning experience, and someone who is not open to the cultural and spiritual possibilities is less likely to create the kind of enabling environment in which the cultural-spiritual strength of the learners is given space to allow transformative learning to occur.

Educators who foster these qualities of intellectual curiosity, tolerance for ambiguity, and intellectual and social humility invite those same characteristics from the learners. Tolliver and Tisdell (2006) tell us, "When our practice is informed by our authenticity and fullness of being that includes the spiritual . . . we invite learners to participate in the learning process in their own level of desire and comfort" (p. 45). Our modeling behavior as facilitators of adult learning can enable rich, collaborative openness to new ideas and unsettling cognitive challenges, or it can limit exploration to rigid formulaic ideas.

In addition to the four attitudes just identified, the adult educator needs to be comfortable with being vulnerable, because he or she is no longer the expert who will amaze the students with expertise and knowledge. In this spiral dance in which the spiritual and cultural dimension of the learners are invited and encouraged to partner with exposure to new knowledge and new perspectives, the role of the educator is that of facilitator rather than expert. He or she invites the dancers onto the floor and engages with them as they allow the rhythm and the beat to guide them through their experience. In so doing, the educator teaches from the heart, which Apps (1996) tells us means "teaching from the depths of who we are with the hope that we will touch the hearts of those with whom we work. To begin discovering the core of who we are requires that we work to become aware of our beliefs and values" (p. 63).

Although Apps was not explicitly referring to transformative learning when he said this, the sentiment he expresses is certainly an important one for understanding the educator's role in that process. Mezirow (2003) tells us that transformative learning involves "learning to decide more insightfully for oneself what is right, good and beautiful is centrally concerned with bringing into awareness and negotiating one's own purposes, values, beliefs, feelings, dispositions and judgments rather than acting on those of others" (p. 326). What this implies is that if adult educators are to invite learners to participate in, and grown from, the transformative learning process, they should be willing to engage in the process for themselves.

The purposeful use of pedagogy and environment is another crucial area in which adult educators can create conditions for transformation influenced by the spiritual and cultural dimensions of the learner. Daloz (2000) identifies four conditions for transformation: the presence of the other, reflective discourse, a mentoring community, and opportunities for committed action. Although he was not explicitly referring to spiritual-cultural dimensions of transformation, the conditions he identifies are certainly important in order for these dimensions to be nurtured. To his list, I would add a fifth: opportunity for holistic engagement. This fifth item on our list is crucial because it is the ingredient that allows learners to explore, build on, and re-vision their cultural and spiritual understanding and attitude so that transformation is possible.

There are many ways in which these conditions can be made possible in a learning environment, even when that environment is not explicitly religious in nature. One example comes from my experiences as an instructor for a four-term required undergraduate group community research class. This series of classes brings together relative strangers from different cultural, religious, and ethnic groups to common ground from which they can identify and effect needed community change. They must first create a community of their own from which to draw the skills, knowledge, and expertise to accomplish their task.

Daloz's four conditions are all present in this learning opportunity. The students themselves are representative of both the community and the pluralism within it. The reflective discourse is a natural part of the course design— discourse within the classroom and in the wider community. The mentoring community includes me as the instructor, content experts, and key stakeholders from the community who serve as community partners. Also, previous cohorts who have gone through the process are invited in to serve as informal mentors. The opportunity for committed action is the goal of the sixteen-month journey. All that is missing is the opportunity for holistic engagement.

This is brought in through a mask-making activity that is implemented very early on in the process. The activity requires them to work in intimate contact with each other as they mold and shape each other's masks. For many students, this requires a level of trust they are not used to in a classroom environment. For those students who begin the activity insisting that they are not creative, it also requires getting comfortable with the process and believing they are capable. As they laugh, struggle with the task and the discomfort of being in a new situation, learn how to manipulate the materials, and wonder what the activity has to do with community research, they slowly become more comfortable with each other and begin to share stories about their lives and hopes of being able to share the experience with their grandchildren. By the end of that particular class session, this diverse group of thirty-, forty-, and fifty-year-olds has made a perceptible transition from being strangers assigned to work together to being collaborators.

A second aspect of this particular activity is for the students to take the mask home and decorate it in such a way that it represents who they are, what they believe they bring to the group, and why they have chosen the project they have. This process is very much an intrapersonal activity, but it too takes on collaborative dimensions when they bring the completed mask and share it with their peers. The completed masks almost always use symbols from and references to the students' cultural and spiritual lives. Moreover, as the project advances, there is evidence of how this inclusion of the students' cultural and spiritual backgrounds has helped transform the students' understanding of their place in the world. One poignant example is that of a thirty-five-year-old African American woman who had been struggling with reconciling culturally accepted understandings of domestic violence with her own experiences. She used her insights from the activity to reclaim her culture and to become an advocate for culturally responsive support. The project that her group ultimately completed was the creation of a culturally based, culturally relevant support group for victims of domestic violence.

CONCLUSION

This chapter provided one view of the spiritual and cultural perspective of the educational journey and suggests how the journey itself can lead to transformative learning. In doing so, it explored spirituality and its relationship to religion and to culture and their relationship to transformative learning in general. It also discussed the implications of this spiraling journey for adult education practice. It does not assume that the spiritual or cultural perspective is uniquely different from others presented in this Handbook. However, it does highlight what is inherent in a spiritual cultural perspective and advocates for the purposeful consideration of spirituality and culture as influencing factors in the transformative learning process.

References

Aga Khan, K. (2008). *Where hope takes root: Democracy and pluralism in an interdependent world*. Vancouver, BC: Douglas & McIntyre Ltd.

Apps, J. W. (1996). *Teaching from the heart*. Malabar, FL: Krieger.

Bateson, M. C. (1995). *Peripheral visions*. San Francisco: Harper Perennial.

Baumgartner, L. M. (2001). *An update on transformational learning* (pp. 15–24). New Directions for Adult and Continuing Education, no. 89. San Francisco: Jossey-Bass.

Charaniya, N. K., & West Walsh, J. (2001). *Adult learning in the context of interreligious dialogue: A collaborative research study involving Christians, Jews, and Muslims.* (Doctoral dissertation). Retrieved from http://digitalcommons.nl.edu/diss/15

Clark, C. M. (1993). *Changing course: Initiating the transformational learning process.* Paper presented at the Adult Education Research Conference, Penn State University.

Daloz, L. A. (2000). Transformation for the common good. In J. Mezirow & Associates (Eds.), *Learning as transformation: Critical perspectives on a theory in progress* (pp. 103–124). San Francisco: Jossey-Bass.

Davis, D. (2003). *Dialogue of the soul: Transformative dimensions of the experience of spirit* (pp. 137–142). Paper presented at the Fifth International Transformative Learning Conference: Transformative Learning in Action—Building Bridges Across Contexts and Disciplines, Teachers' College, Columbia University.

Dirkx, J. (1997). Nurturing soul in adult learning. In P. Cranton (Ed.), *Transformative learning in action: Insights from practice* (pp. 79–88). New Directions for Adult and Continuing Education, no. 74. San Francisco: Jossey-Bass.

Dirkx, J. M. (2000). *After the burning bush: Transformative learning as imaginative engagement with everyday experience.* Third International Transformative Learning Conference, New York.

English, L. M. (2001). Reclaiming our roots: Spirituality as an integral part of adult learning. *Adult Learning, 12*(3), 2+. Retrieved November 9, 2010, from Questia database: http://www.questia.com/PM.qst?a=o&d=5001963626

English, L. M., & Gillen, M. A. (Eds.). (2000). *Addressing the spiritual dimensions of adult learning: What educators can do.* New Directions for Adult and Continuing Education, no. 85. San Francisco: Jossey-Bass.

English, L. M., & Tisdell, E. J. (2010). Spirituality and adult education. In C. E. Kasworm, A. D. Rose, & J. M. Ross-Gordon (Eds.), *Handbook of adult and continuing education* (pp. 285–293). Thousand Oaks, CA: SAGE.

Fowler, J. W. (1981). *Stages of faith: the psychology of human development and the quest for meaning.* San Francisco: Harper & Row.

Hill, P. C., Pargament, K. I., Hood, R. W., McCullough, M. E., Swyers, J. P., Larson, D. B., & Zinnbauer, B. J. (2000). Conceptualizing religion and spirituality: Points of commonality, points of departure. *Journal for the Theory of Social Behaviour, 30*(1), 51–77.

Kegan, R. (2000). What "form" transforms: A constructive-developmental approach to transformational learning. In J. Mezirow & Associates (Eds.), *Learning as transformation: Critical perspectives on a theory in progress* (pp. 35–70). San Francisco: Jossey-Bass.

Lee, G.C.M. (1998). *Collaborative learning in three British adult education schemes.* Unpublished doctoral dissertation, University of Nottingham, Nottingham, U.K.

Lee, M. (2000). *Collaborative learning in three British adult education schemes.* Paper presented at the Adult Education Research Conference, Vancouver, BC.

Merriam, S. B., & Ntseane, G. (2008). Transformational learning in Botswana: How culture shapes the process. *Adult Education Quarterly, 58*(3), 183–197.

Mezirow, J. (1991). *Transformative dimensions of adult learning.* San Francisco: Jossey-Bass.

Mezirow, J. (2003). Epistemology of transformative learning. Proceedings from the Fifth International Conference on Transformative Learning: *Transformative Learning in Action: Building Bridges Across Contexts and Disciplines.* Teachers College, Columbia University.

Mezirow, J., & Associates (Eds.). (2000). *Learning as transformation: Critical perspectives on a theory in progress.* San Francisco: Jossey-Bass.

Miller, J. (2002). Learning from a spiritual perspective. In E. O'Sullivan, A. Morrell, & M. O'Conner (Eds.), *Expanding the boundaries of transformative learning: Essays on theory and praxis* (pp. 95–102). New York: Palgrave.

Peters, J. M., & Armstrong, J. L. (1998). Collaborative learning: People laboring together to construct knowledge. In I. Saltiel, A. Sgroi, & R. Brockett (Eds.), *The power and potential of a collaborative learning partnerships* (pp. 75–86). San Francisco: Jossey-Bass.

Taylor, E. W. (2008). *Transformative learning theory* (pp. 5–15). New Directions for Adult and Continuing Education, no. 119. San Francisco: Jossey-Bass.

Tisdell, E. J. (2001). Spirituality in adult and higher education. Columbus, OH: ERIC Clearinghouse on Adult Career and Vocational Education.

Tisdell, E. J. (2002). Spiritual development and cultural context in the lives of women adult educators for social change. *Journal of Adult Development, 9*(2), 127–140.

Tisdell, E. J. (2003). *Exploring spirituality and culture in adult and higher education.* San Francisco: Jossey-Bass.

Tisdell, E. J. (2008). *Spirituality and adult learning* (pp. 27–36). New Directions for Adult and Continuing Education, no. 119. San Francisco: Jossey-Bass. doi:10.1002/ace.303

Tisdell, E. J., Brown-Haywood, F., Charaniya, N., & West Walsh, J. (in press). The intersecting roles of religion, culture, and spirituality in feminist popular education in a post 9–11 US context. In S. Walters & L. Manicom (Eds.), *Feminist popular education.* Houndmills, Basingstoke, Hampshire, UK: Palgrave Macmillian.

Tolliver, D. E., & Tisdell, E. J. (2006). *Engaging spirituality in the transformative higher education classroom* (pp. 37–47). New Directions for Adult and Continuing Education, no. 109. San Francisco: Jossey-Bass.

CHAPTER FIFTEEN

Women and Transformative Learning

Leona M. English and Catherine J. Irving

Transformative learning is a helpful lens through which to view the experience of women and adult learning. Transformative learning has the potential to help us understand the ways in which women encounter learning in the community, in higher education, and in the workplace. Yet the links are not always clear, and insufficient attention has been paid to the gendered dimensions of transformative learning. This chapter addresses this gap by reviewing and analyzing the extant literature and making suggestions for research practice.

BACKGROUND AND RATIONALE

Beyond the fact that Mezirow's (1978) empirical work started with women returning to college after a hiatus, neither his deliberation on that study nor his more recent work have focused specifically on women. The same might be said of theorists such as Clark and Dirkx (2008), Taylor (2008), and Cranton (2006), though the reason is not exactly clear, in much of the literature there are implications that women have a particular experience of transformative learning that differs from men's. When Taylor, for instance, develops his taxonomy

Note: The authors would like to acknowledge the Social Sciences and Humanities Council of Canada for financially supporting this study.

of transformative learning perspectives, he does not name gender as a central category. Not naming women (and gender) in a discussion of transformative learning is problematic for a number of reasons. A recent comprehensive review of gender and learning showed that the category of gender had virtually disappeared from the adult education literature as a named and separate unit of analysis, though women's issues floated beneath the surface, and women continue to make up the majority of the student body and professoriate in adult education (English & Irving, 2007).

We speculate that in the attempt to unite with other causes in the struggle for equality and to tone down feminist rhetoric, adult education scholars have forgone special attention to women; this depoliticization means that women's needs and causes are increasingly hidden. Aspects such as race, disability, and class are increasingly highlighted (for example, English & Irving, 2007); yet the reality is that women are disproportionately affected by the issues they raise. Naming women's transformative learning as a central concern puts the spotlight on these interlocking issues and on women specifically. Those who come into our field from the worlds of health, nursing, and business, for instance, often have not had exposure to social science insights on women, feminism, or gender, and they need this knowledge.

Turning to the adult education literature on women and learning, we propose that much of that literature has presupposed transformation, dealing as it does with personal and institutional challenges that affect women's entry into educational programs and their active participation in them (Belenky, Clinchy, Goldberger, & Tarule, 1986; Hayes, Flannery, & others, 2000). The reality (and subsequent study) of women's challenging location in the workplace, the community, higher education, and the development sphere has lent itself to extended discussions of transformation, albeit in a variety of discourses. Arguably, women's historically disadvantaged position has necessitated a unique framing and body of work that has seen little need for the discourse of transformative learning. A second possibility is that while much of the literature on feminism, in particular, is based on a community, civil society, and collective experience, there may be an erroneous perception that transformative learning is always individualistic. It may at last be the right time for theorists focusing on women to learn and benefit from the transformative learning literature.

In preparing this chapter, we reviewed the main journals and textbooks in transformative learning including works by Cranton (2006), Mezirow (2000), and Mezirow, Taylor, and Associates (2009). We chose women and learning as the specific term in the title, because it is a broad term that can include gender, the ways in which women and men are socialized into roles and behaviors, and feminism, the political intent to change society and conditions for women (English & Irving, 2007). Our intent was to span the spectrum from more individualistic and humanistic expressions of transformative learning to more collective, radical, and civil society–oriented expressions. Use of the term "women and learning" allows this latitude.

OBSERVATIONS ON THE LITERATURE

Our search revealed that direct linkages between the theory and women's learning were few and far between, which was surprising give the overall commitment of adult educators to women and learning and to feminism more specifically (for example, Belenky et al., 1986; Hayes et al., 2000). In fact, the primary publication for articles on transformative learning, the *Journal of Transformative Education*, has published few related articles (Clover, 2006; Cooley, 2007; Elvy, 2004; Kluge, 2007; Mayuzumi, 2006; Nash, 2007; Williams, 2006). The proceedings of the biennial Transformative Learning Conference contain a similarly low number of papers directly focused on women's transformation (Armacost, 2005; Balan, 2005; Buck, 2009; Cooley, 2005; Forest, 2009; Hamp, 2007; Hansman & Wright, 2005; Jeanetta, 2005; Jeris & Gajanayake, 2005; Lee & Na, 2009; Mejiuni, 2009; Muhammad & Dixson, 2005). Significantly, only one of these publications uses the word "feminist" in the title (Brookfield, 2003).

Searches of other adult education journals through the SAGE and Proquest databases yield similar results when the specific terms "transformative learning" and "women/gender/feminism" are used (see, for example, Cooley, 2007; Elvy, 2004). Yet there is a considerable literature in cognate areas. It appears that the term "transformative learning," like the term "women and learning," has several synonyms or near synonyms, such as "conscientization," "radical social change," and "transition" (for example, Arnot, 2006; Stromquist, 2006). We include both the explicitly named concept and its cognates, with the intent of encouraging mutual exchange and broadening the scope of the field.

From our reading of the literature, a number of issues and themes arose. We comment on each of these here and then move on to implications for teaching and learning.

ENGAGEMENT OF WOMEN'S LEARNING WITH THE THEORY

Some of the literature makes a concerted effort to build on the literature in women's transformative learning. We concentrate here on Belenky, Clinchy, Goldberger, and Tarule (1986), one of the most significant publications in women's learning because it seems that most of the work on women's transformation pays homage to it, directly or indirectly (for example, Cranton & Wright, 2008; Ettling & Guilian, 2004; Forest, 2009). Belenky and Stanton (2000) bring the lens and theory of transformative learning to the understandings of the original *Women's Ways of Knowing* (Belenky et al., 1986), which include concepts such as voice, subjectivity, and silence. In traversing the *Women's Ways of Knowing* theory of women as connected knowers, they point also to the preferred styles of knowing of women. They are also gently critical of Mezirow's linear and rational version of transformative learning, noting that "critical discourse, the doubting game, can only be played well on a level playing field" (Belenky & Stanton, p. 89), suggesting that the field is rarely level for women.

Belenky and Stanton (2000) observe that Mezirow's attention to "reflective discourse, critical thinking, and evaluating one's basic assumptions" (p. 91) seems to celebrate separate knowing as opposed to connected knowing. They offer practical strategies for integrating their theory in teaching and learning situations, stressing the metaphors of voice (also see Buck, 2009; Hamp, 2007; Jeanetta, 2005) and midwifing (also used by Buck, 2009; Cranton & Wright, 2008; Ettling & Guilian, 2004), and of focusing education on what adults need and want to know. Similarly, Forest (2009) points to the value of enabling women to examine the underlying meaning in their life experience and focusing on their interests and needs.

Interestingly, Belenky and Stanton (2000) do not refute Mezirow's separate knowing but rather suggest that it not occupy the central place that Mezirow would give it, especially for collective action. They note that critical-thinking skills are important, in particular for oppressed groups whose voices have not been heard. For Belenky and Stanton and researchers such as Hamp (2007), Jeanetta (2005), Meyer (2009), and Nash (2007), it is important to first build these capacities so women's transformation is possible. Cranton and Wright (2008), in their study of eight female literacy teachers, stress these teachers' capacities to be nurturing learning companions and supports for the literacy learner. Ultimately, their emphasis is less on the end goal of learning and more on the collaborative way in which this goal is achieved.

CONNECTION TO RACE, CLASS, AND OPPRESSION

Much of the writing on transformative learning and women is derived from studies of women in oppressive conditions, which has helped to contextualize an originally middle class and white experience. For instance, Meyer (2009) studied lower class women in East Harlem, Nash (2007) examined the impact of intimate partner violence and social dynamics on African American women, and Jeris and Gajanayake (2005) worked with Mezirow's theory to examine perspective transformation among women in Sri Lanka. Implicit in these articles is that tragedy, violence, or other social factors can be instigators of a disorienting dilemma; yet this is not developed well, and its links to transformative learning theory are not specifically named.

Also focusing on oppressed women, Hamp (2007) writes about the transformative dimensions of the lives of women who make the transition from welfare to work. Using Mezirow's theory as a starting point, she documents how women experience the theory slightly differently. She emphasizes how their experience of poverty and domestic violence affects their ability to manage emotions and to experience transformative learning. Kilgore and Bloom (2002) similarly draw from their work with women in crisis to point out the challenges of facilitating transformative learning with people who are struggling. They suggest that educators work to really hear the voices and experiences of these women and to reinterpret the transformative learning theory in light of their insights. Theirs is a challenge to the rational and linear expectations of Mezirow's theory.

Johnson-Bailey and Alfred (2006) bring in the experience of black women educators, noting the relevance of their own experiences of race and transformative learning. They stress that educators need to understand their own process of transformation as precursor to their own teaching. Similarly, Brooks (2000a) underscores the importance of recognizing that transformative learning theories (for example, Mezirow, Kegan, Buddhist, feminist) each have their own cultural story that ought to be named and understood. Speaking from the perspective of feminist poststructuralism, Brooks highlights the importance of valuing the cultural stories of the learners as well, and of allowing multiple narratives to emerge in the teaching and learning encounter.

SILENCE ON TRANSFORMATIVE LEARNING THEORY

One of the most troubling findings in our review is the lack of direct attention to the theoretical frameworks that support transformative learning. Many of the articles used the language of transformative learning in a very superficial way and did not attempt to refute or contribute to the development of theory, actions that are necessary for its ongoing conceptualization. For instance, in one of the articles in the *Journal of Transformative Education*, Brookfield (2003) describes bell hooks and Angela Davis as exemplars of the social action and transformative struggle, yet he does not directly engage the transformative learning theory to any great degree. Like many other writers, he sees many of the social action–oriented educators as proponents of critical transformative learning, though they themselves are not working explicitly in that theoretical framework. Others who seem to evade direct discussion of the theory include Mayuzumi (2006), who highlights the role of the Japanese tea ceremony in the healing and presumably the transformation of women. Williams (2006) describes students' perceptions of women in leadership as an instance of transformative learning, and Kluge (2007) looks at women's personal growth through an adventure model. Kluge's is a pedagogical paper on using an out-door model of teaching to help women transform. Elvy (2004) narrates the lives of forty women working in the Cuban Literacy Campaign in the 1960s and uses photographs and poetry to illustrate their lives. She briefly discusses the devel-opment of consciousness through the women's experiences as literacy tutors. Yet there is little in this study or indeed in any of these studies that directly engages the transformative literature, making us wonder how writers might be enabled to directly engage with it to make it more robust.

Similarly, Grant (2008) writes about Jewish women's learning and how it highlights tensions between institutions and personal growth. According to Grant, their transformative learning is affected by their conflicted allegiances to Jewish teaching and religion and their own feminist development. This is an ongoing tension that raises questions about the context and sociocultural factors that affect development. Although Grant's stated goal in her study addresses "whether this transformative learning educational process will win out over historical context and potentially indoctrinating influences" (p. 100), she does not work with transformative learning concepts and ideas.

FACILITATING WOMEN'S TRANSFORMATION

From our review of this transformative learning literature and our own back-ground in researching gender and learning, we point to some particular areas that can be developed to make the transformative learning theory on women more robust and the practice in the field stronger (see also English & Peters, in press). In naming these elements we recognize the importance of the core elements of transformative learning theory—such as individual experience, critical reflection, dialogue, holistic orientation, context, and authentic rela-tionships (Taylor, 2009)—but we argue that the elements we describe in this section are especially important for women's transformation. We do this heed-ing Cranton's (2006) caution that gender divisions are dangerous.

The Importance of Relationships

The studies that we have cited and explored elucidate the importance of rela-tionships in women's transformative experiences (see Brookfield, 2003; Buck, 2009; Carter, 2002; Ettling & Guilian, 2004; Grant, 2008; Hamp, 2007; Wittman, Velde, Carawan, Pokorny, & Knight, 2008). This connects to Brooks's (2000b) notion that the opportunity for women to share their life narratives is at the heart of their transformative experience. Cooley (2007) explores the significance of an enclave or gathering for women, which can facilitate friendship, trust, and transformative learning. Similarly, Mejiuni (2009) speaks to the value of col-laboration and support, using the term "transformative mentoring" (p. 277) to describe transformative learning among women in academe in Nigeria. Meyer (2009) stresses journaling and coaching to support women's transformation, and Forest, the role of the "coach" in assisting women who live in poverty; Carter points to a "love relationship" (p. 76).

Although relationships and mentors arguably are an integral part of transformative learning for both sexes, as identified by Taylor (2009) and Cranton (2006), these studies suggest that they are especially important for women and even more for women in crisis. The collective aspect of women's experience in groups seems to be very important as well. For instance, in Hamp (2007), relationships were the catalyst for transformation of women who were making the transition to work. Telling is Cranton and Wright's (2008) observation that the relationship is the impetus for the transformation, more so than a major event or disorienting dilemma. Given that few of the studies even discuss disorienting dilemmas (for example, Muhammad & Dixson, 2005; Kucukaydin & Flannery, 2007; Lee & Na, 2009) and many identify supportive relationships, we find support for Cranton and Wright's observation; we go further to suggest that it is especially true for women. We encourage adult educators to continue to build relationships and supportive conditions in which women's transformation might occur. Yet we also encourage them to ensure that they establish appropriate boundaries around relationships, especially those arising in professional settings.

The Importance of the Body

A decidedly female version of transformative learning is developed by Armacost (2005), who writes on menopause and its transformative dimensions; Buck (2009), who looks at the use of photography to understand women's midlife spirituality; and Mayuzumi (2006), who examines the physical ritual of the tea ceremony for healing and transformation of women. The body is the impetus and the site of learning, creating change and enacting new possibilities. Likewise, in the Kluge (2007) publication, women are encouraged to undertake physical activity as a means of challenging stereotypes of aging. Through the body they learn potential and are transformed in self-perception, moving from stereotypes and negative self-image to "increased connection with and confidence in their bodies" (p. 187).

A number of writers in adult education have showcased the role of the body in women's learning. Clark (2001), for instance, has written of embodied knowing, as has Michelson (1998), who has focused specifically on experiential learning. Similarly, Barnacle (2009) examines the role of the body in learning and challenges the ascendancy of rational ways of knowing and concomitant dismissal of mind-body relations. Like Clark, Michelson and Barnacle are interested in the noncognitive modes of knowing and engagement. These theorists' insights about the body can be used to inform transformative learning theory and to move it beyond the metaphors of midwifing that have stalled development of the theory. They also lend support to the teaching domain by encouraging us to give pride of place to the body in learning and to refuse to give rational, cognitive learning all the space in the teaching and learning encounter.

The Importance of Emotion

Much of the transformative learning literature on women focuses on oppressive conditions, which affect women's learning. These conditions directly and indirectly affect women's transformation either by stymieing it or by serving as a catalyst. It seems that women who become stirred up by their circumstances, who work together with other women, have the ability to be transformed. Hamp (2007) identifies the "drama and extreme emotional distress" (p. 176) that is part of women's learning. Muhammad and Dixson (2005) name resistance and anger, latent pain, and discomfort among white and black women as they discuss race. Mayuzumi (2006) examines the transformation to a state of peace and tranquility following a Japanese tea ceremony, and Mejiuni (2009) looks at the role of emotion in female academics' transformative learning. This suggests that emotion plays a particular role in transformation for women, yet in most of the other studies it remains beneath the surface and is not named directly. For instance, Jeanetta (2005), Forest (2009), and Nash (2007) speak to the critical awareness fostered in women about their desperate life circumstances but never directly name anger, resentment, or even peace and love among the women. Curiously, emotion is virtually absent from these narratives. Yet we know from bell hooks (2001) and Freire (1970) that emotion plays a role in transforming one's life circumstances. Clark and Dirkx (2008) have discussed emotion in transformative learning but have not focused attention directly on women's experience. We encourage practitioners to pursue this very obvious link in their everyday communities. Naming and working with emotion can be key to facilitating the learning of women.

The Importance of Race and Class

Social, cultural, and economic factors affect transformative learning and women. Race, class, gender, and ability are dealt with a little in the literature, yet collectively we see that they are major factors to be considered in understanding the intersection of women and transformative learning. Johnson-Bailey's (2006) work, for instance, highlights the role of race and suggests that struggle is part of the transformative learning process, yet few other writers take on these issues directly. Her race-centric perspective has much in common with certain strands of feminism and is reminiscent of Hill Collins's (1998) work, which suggests definite links for those interested in pursuing the transformative dimensions of women's learning. Although there may be an uneasy alliance between some aspects of feminism and some of the theory of transformative learning, given occasional competing claims between transformative learning and social change adherents, the benefits of a critical lens would be useful. From our Canadian perspective we realize that attention to the First Nations communities is especially needed. There are no studies that we are aware of in this area, and our practice is correspondingly weak.

A number of adult educators have pursued the links among women, class, and learning. These links have been developed primarily in the United Kingdom, by researchers such as Sue Jackson (2003) at Birbeck College and Jane Thompson (2007) of NIACE, among others. This literature focuses on the interlocking nature of the multiple systems of oppression—race, class, gender, and sexual orientation—and on how these have affected or facilitated learning. It would be a logical leap to conjoin these insights with transformative learning and to make deliberate attempts in practice to be aware of how race, class, gender, and power affect learning for women. We cannot avoid discussing these interdependent social factors with our participants, even if the dialogue is charged and challenging.

The Importance of Creativity and the Arts

A theme in the literature is the role of creativity and the arts in supporting transformation for women. Armacost (2005), Elvy (2004), Clover (2006), and Wittman et al. (2008) all employ photographic research methods to examine women's transformative learning. Clover emphasizes that the arts are very important for women and transformative learning. She found that having homeless participants use cameras helped to engage them in a participatory process and to become active agents in their own learning and empowerment. Others, such as Brooks (2000b), have examined the role of the narrative arts of storytelling as important to women's learning. In a similar vein, Wiessner (2009) examines women's use of music-based activities to foster transformation. And Wittman et al. examine collective writing as a transformative tool for women. Hansman and Wright (2005) develop the role of popular education techniques such as role-plays and storytelling as a means of facilitating women's transformation. Although all these means are part of any strong pedagogy—Taylor calls them "instructional aids" (2009, p. 8)—they seem to be very important for women and their transformative learning. Adult education practitioners would do well to incorporate these insights into their pedagogical encounters.

DIRECTIONS FOR FUTURE RESEARCH AND PRACTICE

In addition to the areas just named for teaching and learning practice, there are other areas in which researchers need to help the literature become more robust. Few researchers have made an attempt to situate their work in a particular body of transformative learning theory, yet there clearly were separate preferences with a number of writers following the Freirean-based global, social change direction (for example, Clover, 2006; Hansman & Wright, 2005; Jeanetta, 2005; McCaffery, 2005) and others more interested in the more individual orientation of Mezirow (for example, Armacost, 2005; Balan, 2005; Buck, 2009; Carter, 2002; Cooley, 2007; Forest, 2009). Notable too were those writers who made a concerted effort to tie their findings or conclusions to either theory (for example, Belenky & Stanton, 2000; Cranton & Wright, 2008). It would seem to be a minimum requirement that scholars working in transformative learning be asked to name their theoretical framework and identify the ways their work contributes to the theory. We challenge each researcher to ask: Which theory is operative here and how am I building or refuting this theory?

We encourage theorists interested in women and learning to work further on healing the divisions between the two basic directions of the theory: individually oriented and social justice oriented transformative learning (Johnson-Bailey, 2006). It seems that the writing in transformative learning and women has been predominantly influenced by Mezirow (1978) and Belenky et al. (1986; Belenky & Stanton, 2000; Brooks, 2000b). The latter group might learn from the more global and social justice strain of transformative learning pursued at the Institute for Development Studies at Sussex in the United Kingdom and at the OISE/University of Toronto. These perspectives are decidedly revolutionary, change oriented, and rooted in the conscientization process envisaged by Freire (1970), Stromquist (2006), and Walters and Manicom (1996). The same recommendation to diversify might be made of the Freire group and their seeming division from personally oriented transformation. The inability to see change on a continuum from personal to global has halted our understanding of transformative learning for women. It must also enable transformative learning theory to become more robust and to further strengthen its claims to both social and personal transformation. We encourage researchers to ask: Are we building bridges between varying perspectives, or are we further bifurcating the field?

As well, we encourage theorists in women's transformative learning to look not only to a variety of contexts in which the theory might be examined, but to build alliances with other disciplines and their theories. For instance, Blunt (2007) serves as an exemplar of how theoretical perspectives on social work might inform and strengthen transformative learning. Other likely areas for investigation are nursing and health promotion theory, where little work has been done. We challenge researchers in these health-related areas to ask: Where might transformative learning theory inform our work? How do we foster or suppress transformative learning in our teaching and scholarly enterprises?

We recognize here that many of the historic contributions from studies of feminist theory and pedagogy have become mainstream in adult education. For instance, Brookfield (2010) observes that we have now come to consensus that "learning is holistic" (p. 76), an attribute that was once applied only to women's learning. Therefore we encourage researchers in transformative learning to examine whether some of the gendered dimensions of learning that we have identified for women, such as emotion and the body, might be applied to all of transformative learning. In part, we see this focus on women's transformative as a possible incubator of ideas and practices for adult education generally. We suggest, therefore, that researchers ask questions like these: Is the body is as important to men's learning as it is to women's? Does emotion play a key role in men's transformation?

CONCLUDING REMARKS

Transformative learning theorists need to directly focus on women's learning in order to address a serious gap in the existing literature. Because women's learning is central to adult education, given the gendered nature of our field, there are many reasons why we need to pursue this line of inquiry. Our chapter has shown that there is little research that connects gender and transformative learning and that makes a deliberate attempt to contribute in a systematic way to building the theory. Transformative learning offers a strong theoretical framework from which to understand learning and the particular challenges that women face in gaining access; consequently, we encourage research in this area. Yet we want to be careful not to further essentialize women and their experiences or contribute to their further marginalization in society. We need to be mindful of this tension in this important area of inquiry.

References

Armacost, L. K. (2005). Menogogy: The art and science of becoming a crone: A new perspective on transformative learning. *Proceedings of the Sixth International Transformative Learning Conference, Michigan State University, Oct. 6–9.* Available at http://transformativelearning.org/

Arnot, M. (2006). Gender equality, pedagogy and citizenship: Affirmative and transformative approaches in the UK. *Theory and Research in Education, 4*(2), 131–150.

Balan, B. N. (2005). Perceptions of transformative learning during workplace transition. *Proceedings of the Sixth International Transformative Learning Conference, Michigan State University, Oct. 6–9.* Available at http://transformativelearning.org/

Barnacle, R. (2009). Gut instinct: The body and learning. *Educational Philosophy and Theory, 41*(1), 22–33.

Belenky, M. F., Clinchy, B. M., Goldberger, N. R., & Tarule, J. M. (1986). *Women's ways of knowing: The development of self, voice, and mind.* New York: Basic Books.

Belenky, M. F., & Stanton, A. V. (2000). Inequality, development and connected knowing. In J. Mezirow & Associates (Eds.), *Learning as transformation: Critical perspectives on a theory in progress* (pp. 71–102). San Francisco: Jossey-Bass.

Blunt, K. (2007). Social work education: Achieving transformative learning through a cultural competence model for transformative education. *Journal of Teaching in Social Work, 27*(3/4), 93–114.

Brookfield, S. D. (2003). The praxis of transformative education: African American feminist conceptualizations. *Journal of Transformative Education, 1*(3), 212–226.

Brookfield, S. D. (2010). Theoretical frameworks for understanding the field. In C. E. Kasworm, A. D. Rose, & J. M. Ross-Gordon (Eds.), *Handbook of adult and continuing education* (pp. 71–81). Thousand Oaks, CA: SAGE.

Brooks, A. K. (2000a). Cultures of transformation. In A. L. Wilson & E. R. Hayes (Eds.), *Handbook of adult and continuing education* (pp. 161–170). San Francisco: Jossey-Bass.

Brooks, A. K. (2000b). Transformation. In E. Hayes, D. D. Flannery, & others (Eds.), *Women as learners: The significance of gender in adult learning* (pp. 139–153). San Francisco: Jossey-Bass.

Buck, M. A. (2009). Discovering the transformative learning potential in the spirituality of midlife women. *Proceedings of the Eighth International Transformative Learning Conference, College of Bermuda.* Available at http://transformativelearning.org/

Carter, T. J. (2002). The importance of talk to mid career women's development: A collaborative inquiry. *Journal of Business Communication, 39*(1), 55–69.

Clark, C. (2001). Off the beaten path: Some creative approaches to adult learning. In S. B Merriam (Ed.), *The new update on adult learning theory* (pp. 83–91). New Directions for Adult and Continuing Education, no. 89. San Francisco: Jossey-Bass.

Clark, C., & Dirkx, J. (2008). The emotional self in adult learning. In J. M. Dirkx (Ed.), *Adult learning and the emotional self* (pp. 89–95). New Directions for Adult and Continuing Education, no. 120. San Francisco: Jossey-Bass.

Clover, D. (2006). Out of the dark room: Participatory photography as a critical, imaginative, and public aesthetic practice of transformative education. *Journal of Transformative Education, 4*(3), 275–290.

Cooley, L. (2005). Transformational learning and third wave feminism as potential outcomes of participation in women's enclaves. *Proceedings of the Sixth International Transformative Learning Conference, Michigan State University, Oct. 6–9, 2005.* Available at http://transformativelearning.org/

Cooley, L. A. (2007). Transformational learning and third-wave feminism as potential outcomes of participation in women's enclaves. *Journal of Transformative Education, 5*(4), 304–316.

Cranton, P. (2006). *Understanding and promoting transformative learning* (2nd ed.). San Francisco: Jossey-Bass.

Cranton, P., & Wright, B. (2008). The transformative educator as learning companion. *Journal of Transformative Education, 6*(1), 33–47.

Elvy, J. C. (2004). Notes from a Cuban diary: Forty women on forty years. *Journal of Transformative Education, 2*(3), 173–186.

English, L. M., & Irving, C. (2007). A review of the Canadian literature on gender and learning. *Canadian Journal for the Study of Adult Education, 20*(1), 16–31.

English, L. M., & Peters, N. (in press). Transformative learning in feminist organizations: A feminist interpretive inquiry. *Adult Education Quarterly.* First published on December 15, 2010, as doi:10.1177/0741713610392771

Ettling, D., & Guilian, L. (2004). Midwifing transformative change In E. O'Sullivan & M. Taylor (Eds.), *Learning toward and ecological consciousness: Selected transformative practices* (pp. 115–131). New York: Palgrave.

Forest, C. (2009). Transformative development in U.S. women living in poverty. *Proceedings of the Eighth International Transformative Learning Conference, College of Bermuda.* Available at http://transformativelearning.org/

Freire, P. (1970). *Pedagogy of the oppressed.* New York: Continuum.

Grant, L. D. (2008). Authenticity, autonomy, and authority: Feminist Jewish learning among post-Soviet women. *Journal of Jewish Education, 74*(1), 83–102.

Hamp, J. (2007). Voice and transformative learning. *Proceedings of the Seventh International Transformative Learning Conference, Michigan State University, Oct. 24–26, 2007.* Available at http://transformativelearning.org/

Hansman, C. A., & Wright, K. J. (2005). Popular education in Bolivia: Transformational learning experiences. *Proceeding of the Sixth International Transformative Learning Conference, Michigan State University, Oct. 6–9, 2005.* Available at http://transformativelearning.org/

Hayes, E., Flannery, D., & others. (2000). *Women as learners: The significance of gender in adult learning.* San Francisco: Jossey-Bass.

Hill Collins, P. (1998). *Fighting words: Black women and the search for justice.* Minneapolis: University of Minnesota Press.

hooks, b. (2001). *All about love: New visions.* New York: Perennial.

Jackson, S. (2003). Lifelong earning: Lifelong learning and working-class women. *Gender and Education, 15*(4), 365–376.

Jeanetta, S. (2005). Finding voice in a community-based learning process. *Proceedings of the Sixth International Transformative Learning Conference, Michigan State University, Oct. 6–9, 2005.* Available at http://transformativelearning.org/

Jeris, L., & Gajanayake, J. (2005, October 6–9). Transformation on the ground in Sri Lanka: Just who is transformed? Tales from the inside/out and the outside/in. *Proceedings of the Sixth International Transformative Learning Conference,* Michigan State University. Available at http://transformativelearning.org/

Johnson-Bailey, J. (2006). Transformative learning: A community empowerment conduit for African American women. In S. B. Merriam, B. C. Courtenay, & R. M. Cervero (Eds.), *Global issues and adult education: Perspectives from Latin America, Southern Africa and the United States* (pp. 307–318). San Francisco: Jossey-Bass.

Johnson-Bailey, J., & Alfred, M. V. (2006). Transformational teaching and the practices of black women adult educators. In E. W. Taylor (Ed.), *Teaching for change: Fostering transformative learning in the classroom* (pp. 49–58). New Directions for Adult and Continuing Education, no. 109. San Francisco: Jossey-Bass.

Kilgore, D., & Bloom, L. R. (2002). "When I'm down, it takes me a while": Rethinking transformational education through narratives of women in crisis. *Adult Basic Education, 12*(3), 123–133.

Kluge, M. A. (2007). Re-creating through recreating: Using the personal growth through adventure model to transform women's lives. *Journal of Transformative Education, 5*(2), 177–191.

Kucukaydin, I., & Flannery, D. (2007). Transformative learning of a Kurdish woman in Turkey. *Proceedings of the Seventh International Transformative Learning Conference, Michigan State University, Oct. 24–26, 2007.* Available at http://transformativelearning.org/

Lee, E., & Na, S. (2009). A phenomenological study on transformative learning of married female immigrant farmers. *Proceedings of the Eighth International Transformative Learning Conference. College of Bermuda, Bermuda.* Available at http://transformativelearning.org/

Mayuzumi, K. (2006). The tea ceremony as a decolonizing epistemology: Healing and Japanese women. *Journal of Transformative Education, 4*(1), 8–26.

McCaffery, J. (2005). Using transformative models of adult literacy in conflict resolution and peacebuilding processes at community level: Examples from Guinea, Sierra Leone and Sudan. *Compare, 35*(4), 443–462.

Mejiuni, O. (2009). Potential for transformative mentoring relationships among women in academia in Nigeria. *Proceedings of the Eighth International Transformative Learning Conference*, College of Bermuda. Available at http://transformativelearning.org/

Meyer, S. (2009). Promoting personal empowerment with women in East Harlem through journaling and coaching. In J. Mezirow, E. W. Taylor, & Associates (Eds.), *Transformative learning in practice: Insights from community, workplace, and higher education* (pp. 216–226). San Francisco: Jossey-Bass.

Mezirow, J. (1978). *Education for perspective transformation; Women's re-entry programs in community colleges.* New York: Teacher's College, Columbia University.

Mezirow, J. (2000). Learning to think like an adult: Core concepts of transformation theory. In J. Mezirow & Associates (Eds.), *Learning as transformation: Critical perspectives on a theory in progress* (pp. 3–33). San Francisco: Jossey-Bass.

Mezirow, J., Taylor, E. W., & Associates (Eds.). (2009). *Transformative learning in practice: Insights from community, workplace, and higher education.* San Francisco: Jossey-Bass.

Michelson, E. (1998). Re-membering: The return of the body to experiential learning. *Studies in Continuing Education, 20*(2), 217–233.

Muhammad, C. G., & Dixson, A. (2005). Examining the baggage: First steps towards transforming habits of mind around race in higher education. *Proceedings of the Sixth International Transformative Learning Conference, Michigan State University, Oct. 6–9, 2005.* Available at http://transformativelearning.org/

Nash, S. T. (2007). Teaching African American women's experiences with intimate male partner violence: Using narratives as text in gender violence pedagogy. *Journal of Transformative Education, 5*(1), 93–110.

Stromquist, N. P. (2006). Gender, education and the possibility of transformative knowledge. *Compare, 36*(2), 145–161.

Taylor, E. T. (2008). Transformative learning theory. In S. B. Merriam (Ed.), *Third update on adult learning theory* (pp. 5–15). New Directions for Adult and Continuing Education, no. 119. San Francisco: Jossey-Bass.

Taylor, E. T. (2009). Fostering transformative learning. In J. Mezirow, E. W. Taylor, & Associates (Eds.), *Transformative learning in practice: Insights from community, workplace, and higher education* (pp. 3–17). San Francisco: Jossey-Bass.

Thompson, J. (2007). *More words in edgeways: Rediscovering adult education.* Leicester, UK: NIACE.

Walters, S., & Manicom, L. (Eds.). (1996). *Gender in popular education: Methods for empowerment* (pp. 1–22). London: ZED.

Wiessner, C. (2009). Noting the potential for transformation: Creative expression through music. In C. Hoggan, S. Simpson, & H. Stuckey (Eds.), *Creative expression in transformative learning: Tools and techniques for educators of adults* (pp. 103–127). Malabar, FL: Krieger.

Williams, I. D. (2006). Southern community women teach a new generation lessons of leadership for social change. *Journal of Transformative Education, 4*(3), 257–274.

Wittman, P., Velde, B. P., Carawan, L., Pokorny, M., & Knight, S. (2008). A writer's retreat as a facilitator for transformative learning. *Journal of Transformative Education, 6*(3), 201–211.

CHAPTER SIXTEEN

Positionality and Transformative Learning

A Tale of Inclusion and Exclusion

Juanita Johnson-Bailey

We all occupy positions in society that continually affect our lives—in ways that are obvious and routine and in ways that are unseen and perhaps unimaginable. Positionality, or social location, is a way of classifying other people, *the unknown*, by placing them into groups, connecting them with what we know as a way of figuring out who people are and, more important, who people are in relation to us, *the known*. The major classifications in our society seem obvious and innocuous: gender, race, and age. Other ways of categorizing that we also use to ascertain who's who are determined through interactions or closer observations, religion, class, sexual orientation, and ability or disability.

Consideration of the learners' and the educators' social positions or postionalities has gained prominence in the academy in the last two decades (Alfred, 2002; Colin & Preciphs, 1991; Johnson-Bailey & Cervero, 2000; Tisdell, 1995). As we have transitioned into this new millennium, teachers and learners have experienced a major shift in how the academy views education and learning (Guy, 1999; Ross-Gordon, Martin, & Briscoe, 1990; Tisdell, 1995). There is a growing emphasis on using a globally informed perspective to research, teach, and learn. To that end, we have seen a new significance placed on multicultural and social justice education. The education of this new era moves beyond the canonical and insists on a critique that asks essential questions of the traditional canon: What perspective informs the scholarship and what perspective is omitted? And what happens when the new teaching and learning that seeks to transform meets the old way of understanding, informing, and ordering our world?

Indeed, the intersection of positionality and transformative learning is complex, unpredictable, and possibly volatile because the place where the two meet can be dynamic and tense. As educators and learners, we are faced with several questions; the primary queries involve weighing risk and balancing experiential knowledge claims. First, there is a definite vulnerability for teachers and students when the intent is to disrupt status quo thinking by creating the disorienting dilemma critical to transformation. Therefore it is prudent to ask what matters most: the possible growth through transformation or the potential harm or painful cognitive dissonance that may be experienced? A second important issue is the political quagmire of positionality—the complex and shifting mix of who we think we are and the social locations that others assign us to or place us in. As societal beings, we all reason and negotiate from our cultural base, our history, and our experiences. Because there are existing norms ordering our culture, norms grounded in the majority standard, how do positional claims fit with transformative learning?

To illustrate how personal and historical perspective, which are directed by positionality, can affect a transformational learning experience, think about the following example:

In an attempt to globalize their missions and curricula, many universities have added study abroad programs as a staple component of undergraduate education and as a growing part of graduate education, especially in light of the growing number of first-generation college students who are now entering graduate education. At the Tower of London, an adult educator noticed that two of her students, a white female and a black female, were moved to tears while they stood transfixed in front of a display of the British Crown Jewels.

In the afternoon debriefing, the teacher facilitated the discussion and asked the two students to share what they each had found so moving about touring the castle. Surprisingly, the teacher discovered that the same experience had created a chasm between the two students that would affect the rest of the study abroad, with each woman using the new perspective as a way of understanding the trip. The teacher had taken for granted that there would be some commonality in the women's experiences. But the white student related how she was struck by the rich and ancient heritage of the British Empire and how proud she was to be a descendent of British grandparents. And in stark contrast, the black student said that she was saddened and shocked that the African continent had been plundered and nearly destroyed so that the natural resources of her mother continent—gold and diamonds—could be used in such a frivolous and conspicuous manner: putting two thousand diamonds in a tiara for a child monarch and fashioning a thirty-five-pound scepter. The goal of the study abroad, which was to introduce students to a culture other than their own and to help them view the world from a different perspective, had been achieved. However, the students had been impacted by their disparate historical and cultural locations.

THE COMPLEXITY OF POSITIONALITY

Although diversity is a treasured gift that makes our world—indeed, each inhabitant in our world—unique, the social locations that we attach to the positions that people occupy in the world are not so harmless. This ordering of the world along set queues occurs because, as a person is categorized as belonging to a race, that person is also accorded all the rights, privileges, and baggage that accompany the classification (McIntosh, 1995). Take into account what it means to be classified as a *raced being* in our world: the person of color, the some categorized as the other. For example, the experience of having Asian ancestry in the United States is completely different from that of having Hispanic ancestry. According to Takaki (1993), Asian Americans are much more likely to be asked how long they have been in the United States, with the assumption being that at one point their family legally immigrated to the United States from another county. Whereas to be of Hispanic ancestry is accompanied by the often unexpressed concern, held by others, that Hispanic persons or their ancestors might have illegally immigrated to the United States. However, persons of white European ancestry are unlikely to be questioned about their origins or legal residency status, with the assumption being that they are regular American citizens. Race is an ongoing troubling classification system that plagued the social justice goals and concerns of the twentieth century (DuBois, 1903/1953), and doggedly continues to be a major divide into the twenty-first century. The President's Commission on Race (*One America*, 1998, p. 46) defined the value connected to being designated a "real American"—a white American—as a type of currency that has the "institutional advantages based on historic factors that have given an advantage to white Americans . . . we as a nation need to understand that whites tend to benefit, either unknowingly or consciously, from this country's history of white privilege."

Additionally, gender, another major social construction system, uses the sex-based categories of male and female to classify, assign, and order society. The gender-bound culture of Western civilization has shaped our educational and learning experiences in profound ways. Although women make up over half of the world's population and over half of the learners in higher education, males are still advantaged in wealth, earning, education, and social positions. Gender affects the distribution of power and privilege in society. Although gender and race are both social constructs, they intersect with other positions—such as class, age, and sexual orientation—to affect and order our everyday lives, invariably permeating our educational institutions. Classes, practices, programs, and research reflect what students and teachers have experienced and believe about ourselves and others. "We all speak from a particular place, out of a particular experience, a particular culture, without being contained by that position" (Hall, 1992, p. 258)—all the while making assumptions and overgeneralizing.

As humans, whether adult or adolescent, we come to know and learn through our cultural filters. Maher and Tetreault (1994) argue that learning is a function of positionality and situatedness, in that learners are significantly affected by their backgrounds and the context in which the learning occurs. Specifically, Maher and Tetreault are suggesting that the learning of a migrant Mexicana student who lives in a large metropolitan area and attends a community college will be affected by both her Mexican culture and her urban and schooling environments. Part of the hidden curriculum that might influence her learning will be her traditions and customs as well as the educational setting. Yet it is likely that another Mexican American woman who is a second-generation American citizen living in a similar urban environment and attending a research-intensive private university would be affected differently even if exposed to the same curriculum.

More often than not, the mechanisms that help us to sort and categorize our world are shaped by our social positions or societal locations: race, gender, class, sexual orientation, age, physical and mental abilities. Such factors not only affect how we view the world but also influence how the world sees us. So an integral and often unexplored part of this positional existence is the consciousness of one's position. As educators and students, do we have a conscious and evidence-based understanding of our place in society?

Moreover, positionality and the understanding of one's place in the society is fluid, subject to time and experiences, and complicated by intersection and overlap of the positions and of understandings of the subject and the person attempting to know the subject. Over the years, the higher education classroom has provided me with numerous examples of students, of all races, who maintain that they belong to only the human race and that no other racial affiliation matters. In addition, there have been students who have stressed that their only positionality or the only one that they allow for is their Christian identity. Consequently, I have witnessed such students reject course readings or argue fervently about the illegitimacy of difference and any collective conditions said to result from societal disparities. Such classroom discussions are complicated equally by students who are locked into one standpoint, usually race or gender or class, or by students who are held captive by interlocking postionalities and thus cannot move beyond the complexity of the intersection. For example, in a course entitled Gender, Media, and Mis-Education, in which mass media was examined as our society's most powerful educational force, black women students seemed particularly disoriented when the discussion turned to voting your positionality in the 2008 primaries. The black women students struggled with their interlocking postionalities of race and gender and could not separate these two identities, which they believed to be fused. Were they influenced most by their race or their gender, in judging the women candidates, Hillary Clinton and Sarah Palin, or by their race, in assessing the black male candidate, Barack Obama?

The learning outcome for me was that even though an awareness of positionality can be introduced in the learning/teaching exchange, a transformational awareness about what or how a learner's position affects learning cannot be forced. Furthermore, although teaching can be situated so as to encourage transformational learning, transformational learning can not be guaranteed (Cranton, 2002). And furthermore, who can predict whether awareness of social position precipitates transformative learning or if transformative learning fosters consciousness of one's positionality?

This question, about the ability of educators and learners to move beyond or in spite of their positions in order to participate in transformative learning, poses a most difficult predicament, as most teachers and learners are in different positions of understanding and enfranchisement. And it is challenging for students and teachers alike to see their assumptions and to critically examine what they regard as their universal truths (Takacs, 2002), because as humans we are inevitably mired in seeking out data to support what we already know. It can become an exercise in relativism and futility (Moser, 2008), with positional stances being simultaneously significant and insignificant, bearing in mind the situation, the discourse, or both.

TWO PERSPECTIVES OF TRANSFORMATIVE LEARNING AND SOCIAL LOCATIONS

Transformational learning is one of adult education's most thriving and vigorous areas of scholarship (Baumgartner, 2001; Boyd & Myers, 1988; Clark & Wilson, 1991; Cranton, 1994, 2002; Dirkx, 1998, 2006; Kitchenham, 2008; Kroth & Boverie, 2009; Merriam & Caffarella, 1999). Two main bodies of literature relating to transformative learning have developed around (1) the scholarship of Mezirow and his transformative learning theory and (2) the writings relating to Freire's concept of conscientization (Baumgartner, 2001; Cranton, 1994, 2002; Dirkx, 1998, 2006). Introduced in the 1970s, the concept of transformative learning, as described by Mezirow, speaks to how adults use learning to make meaning of life events (Mezirow, 1978). Mezirow based his theory on how a group of reentry women incorporated new learning that they gleaned from life-changing events. Ultimately, it is a theory about change—about how lives are forever altered by circumstances and the meaning that we make from the surrounding state of affairs. Although Mezirow eventually described ten phases, he set forth three as principal: critical reflection on the assumptions held at the time of the life event, a language or discourse to speak about or make sense of the event, and a new schema that is incorporated into one's life as a result of the recently developed understanding.

Mezirow's theory, which is individualistic, essentially posits that a *disorienting dilemma* triggers the process that forces learners to begin self-examination and to scrutinize their set of assumptions or beliefs. Eventually learners will realize the universality of their experience and will use their new perspective to look for new solutions. Such a perspective relies heavily on rationality, encourages an artificial separation of the rational and the intuitive (Clark & Wilson, 1991; Collard & Law, 1989; Dirkx, 2006; Johnson-Bailey & Alfred, 2006; McDonald, Cervero, & Courtenay, 1999), and embraces the notion that all things are possible through discourse. However, the concept of rationality that Mezirow offers is a Western concept that does not account for emotions or alternative forms of knowing.

From this viewpoint the sociocultural aspects of life—how a learner's social location can affect all learning and meaning making—is ignored (Baumgartner, 2001; King & Biro, 2006; McDonald, Cervero, & Courtenay, 1999; Taylor, 1994). For example, disenfranchised groups experience life differently from enfranchised groups and consequently may construct meaning differently. From the standpoint of a person whose social location is not white, middle class, and male, Mezirow's transformative learning theory would be more acceptable if it addressed the relationship of the disenfranchised other to society. For if transformative learning is truly applicable beyond the individual level, then how does the individual initiate change at the societal level? Finally, because Mezirow's perspective calls for adult educators to engage in transformative teaching and learning, there is an implicit understanding that contains a hierarchically based argument that puts power and righteousness in the hands of the all-knowing and best-knowing adult educator. Mezirow (1997) asserts it is the "educator's responsibility to help learners reach their objectives in such a way that they will function as more autonomous, socially responsible thinkers" (p. 8).

This indictment discounts the positional and social relations of the students and the teacher and idealistically assumes that we live in a just, fair, and power-neutral society, placing an extremely heavy burden on the educator to create a perfect classroom environment for the supposedly willing and fully participating adult learner. The teacher in Mezirow's world acts with the highest degree of honor and is caring, empathic, and sincere, while creating a safe, trusting, and learner-centered environment (Baumgartner, 2001; Boyd & Myers, 1988; Brookfield, 1995; Cranton, 1994; Daloz, 1986; Dirkx, 1998).

Separate from Mezirow's transformative learning theory is the body of knowledge that has developed around Freire's scholarship. Although not readily noted as either an architect or a founding theoretician of transformative learning, Freire certainly contributed significantly to embedding the idea of learning's transformational powers into the practice and literature of adult education, and Mezirow acknowledges Freire's influence in his book *Transformative Dimensions of Adult Learning* (Mezirow, 1991). In addition, comprehensive reviews of Mezirow's theory reference Freire's influence (Baumgartner, 2001; Dirkx, 1998; Kitchenham, 2008; Taylor, 1998). Indeed, Freire's work has found more resonance beyond the field than has that of any other adult educator. His groundbreaking *Pedagogy of the Oppressed* (1970) presented a thorough discussion of how new learning can be used to change and empower learners. Eventually criticized for being too context specific, Freire, a white Brazilian, wrote about literacy issues for the socioeconomically disadvantaged masses in Brazil. Whereas Mezirow's theory was about change at the individual level, Freire spoke about making social change from the community level and thus fostering societal changes.

The type of learning that Freire encourages is a new form of learning designed to transform learners by showing them a new way of seeing and being in their world. Freire views traditional education as value-laden, disempowering, and designed to reproduce the status quo. For Freire, the teaching and learning transaction is a politically charged site of struggle. According to Freire, if the masses were informed and or adequately educated they would rise up and save themselves. He believed that that traditional education was about *banking* or filling the minds of learners with facts. He encouraged educators to ask questions of learners about building a better world for themselves. It is Freire's hypothesis that education is designed to reproduce the underclasses (Freire, 1970, 1973; Freire & Faundez, 1989).

In this idealized Freirean world, the teacher-student liaison is devoid of power imbalances; rather, it is reciprocal in nature. Dialogue is to Freire as discourse is to Mezirow. Although Freire does reflect on how the context of the learning affects the student, he nevertheless brings an idealized notion of the educator and learner to the conceptual table, believing that by freeing the minds of learners an educator can jump-start the process of transformation. This "conscientization" forgoes important variables—the weight, trauma, and dailiness of oppression—placing the onus of liberation squarely on the backs of the oppressed. Freire emphasizes the importance of dialogue to the process of change and empowerment, but he does not persuasively trouble the notion that the language and therefore dialogue does not easily reside with the powerless or in his case the low literate. Although Freire does not mention positionality, race, or ethnicity, it is known that the socioeconomically disadvantaged learners who populated his Brazilian practice were people of color. Therefore one is left to wonder why Freire did not directly address culture, ethnicity, or the race of his learners.

THE COEXISTENCE OF TRANSFORMATIONAL
LEARNING AND POSITIONALITY

Given the critique of Mezirow's transformational learning theory as individualistic, rational, and lacking cultural consideration, and the critique of Freire's transformative learning as emancipatory both at the individual and social levels (Baumgartner, 2001; Dirkx, 1998), but with the obvious dimension of race excluded, it would seem that transformational learning theory as presented by Mezirow and Freire has no regard for matters of positionality and that transformational learning and positionality are mutually exclusive. However, it is more probable that transformational learning as set forth by Freire can implicitly encompass ethnicity and race, because when Freire addresses the challenges of talking back to power, the learner's position or social location is certainly a factor. Indeed, Freire clarified this position in a conversation with Macedo (Freire & Macedo, 1995) in a published dialogue in which they discussed how culture and race were embedded in Freire's work. And although Mezirow's transformative learning theory in its purest form does not address culture or social constructs, his foundational study was bounded by the culture of reentry women's gender and has inevitably had positionality fitted into its frame and has sufficiently accommodated the inclusion (Johnson-Bailey, 2006; King & Biro, 2006; McDonald, Cervero, & Courtenay, 1999; Pope, 1996).

Making an allowance for the ways in which students' perspectives might affect learning further complicates the issue of transformational learning. As Merriam (2004) first asked, are most students prepared cognitively and emotionally to engage in transformational learning? Extrapolating from this stance and factoring in positionality, I would ask: are most educators and learners aware of their social positions and accompanying connected privileges or lack thereof? And are they then able to enter into the negotiations and understanding necessary for transformative learning to occur?

The answer to these questions is a nebulous and resounding: it depends. A person's awareness of her or his own racial and cultural identity is dependent on several variables, the most important two being whether the person grew up in heterogeneous or homogenous surroundings, and whether the person was in a position as a minority or a majority (Cross, 1991; Helms, 1984, 1990). Research suggests that existing in settings in which one is in the minority will influence an early awareness of difference and diversity.

Examine the case presented by King and Biro (2006) in their article "A Transformative Learning Perspective of Continuing Sexual Identity Development in the Workplace," in which they argue that transformational learning offers useful tools for LGBT sexual identity development, allowing "a basis for adults to reflect on their experiences using adult learning and a heuristic, self-understanding framework" (p. 19). And using a similar line of reasoning, Johnson-Bailey (2006), in her book chapter "Transformative Learning: A Community Empowerment Conduit for African American Women," views transformational learning as ideally suited for a learning community of American black women because these women have shared cultural experiences of resistance and collective transformational markers. She goes on to explain that for African American women there does not need to be a single and isolating triggering event; thus she embraces Mezirow's later assertion that transformational learning does not have to be sudden and severe, but can be cumulative. In taking this position, Johnson-Bailey is in accordance with Pope (1996), who sets forth, in her work on the impact of education on a group of ethnically diverse learners, that the process of change was long term, evolutionary, and driven to a large extent by their positionalities. Johnson-Bailey's stance is that a consciousness of the group's positionality preceded and fostered transformative learning. Such an idea was indeed declared previously by hooks and Freire, who assert that transformation is born out of talking back and acting out (Freire, 1970; hooks, 1989).

King and Biro (2006) found that there were components of transformational learning well suited for the lesbian women who were coming out, attempting to claim their gay identity. For example, this group used critical questioning and critical reflection to construct a new way of understanding the world and as a way of finding new meaning, using a new language and new identity. Likewise, Johnson-Bailey's community of black women scholars found that their transformative shared understanding was rooted in an understanding of power based on Foucault's (1980) concept that power operates through our discourses and our practices. In addition, their brand of transformative learning incorporates the work of theorists who explore issues of power and culture (Bourdieu, 2000; Collins, 1990; Giroux, 1997; Foucault, 1980; hooks, 1989). Employing their positional lens to filter interpretations, they also used many of the methods encouraged by Mezirow: life histories, case histories, role-play, and reframing questions (Mezirow, 1997). However, Johnson-Bailey contends that these activities are rooted in a rich African tradition that precedes Mezirow's transformational learning and Freire's contributions of community grassroots activism. For example, reframing questions becomes calling for the question, which is a culture-bound form of talking back and is similar to the call and response of the black church. In such a give and take dialogue, it is typical for unseasoned and young complainants who are decrying the conditions of indifference and isolation to be asked about the threat of death or physical harm. This is one method of putting the risk into perspective, comparing the current legal and often societal discomfort to the Civil Rights movement struggles of the 1960s and 1970s that involved the ever-real threat of physical pain and possible death. And if, upon inquiry, they learn that life and limb are not threatened, then they are questioned as to the inherent risk or lack thereof. This procedure of calling the question is a way of reminding younger group members of the price paid by their ancestors who were killed and physically assaulted as they struggled through their transformation in an effort to teach and transform a nation (Guy-Sheftall, 1995; hooks, 1990; Johnson-Bailey, 1998, 2006).

It is further opined that the theory of transformative learning is parsimonious, as all good theories are, and that the theory of transformative learning can be reflexive on the micro, mezzo, and macro levels. Using the experiences of these two groups of marginalized learners—King and Biro's lesbian workers, who were coming into their conscious gay identities in the workplace, and Johnson-Bailey's African American women in white academe—it is posited that transformational learning is adaptive and is not confined by positionality. The theory's notion of rationality is easily extended beyond what many perceive as Mezirow's and Freire's stated intentions to construct a discourse or dialogue that easily moves between the rational and the intuitive to perhaps create a synergy of knowing that is based on and values both logic and instinctive ability as ways of understanding and affecting change.

An overarching recommendation would be that this theory should be regarded as a living, breathing entity, introduced by Mezirow, to which significant contributions were made by Freire. Furthermore, the theory is not meant to be interpreted and used only by like-minded scholars. If transformative learning is to have an afterlife that extends beyond the definitions and reinterpretations breathed into it by Mezirow and Freire, then we must take up the process of sculpting transformative learning to our needs, by testing it and adjusting it, as has been the work contributed by Daloz (1986), in his text *Effective Teaching and Mentoring: Realizing the Transformational Power of Adult Learning Experiences*; by Cranton, in *Understanding and Promoting Transformative Learning: A Guide for Educators of Adults* (1994) and *Professional Development as Transformative Learning* (1996); by Wangoola and Youngman (1996), in *Towards a Transformative Political Economy of Adult Education: Theoretical and Practical Challenges*; and by Boyd (1991) in *Personal Transformation in Small Groups: A Jungian Perspective*.

The limitations that the literature finds in transformative learning are merely points of departure for maximizing the existing frame. Therefore, it is recommended that transformative learning theory be adapted for use in varied settings, inside and outside of the academy with learners, regardless of and perhaps because of their disenfranchised positions. It is used with groups like those in the cases discussed by King and Biro (2006) and Johnson-Bailey (1996) as possible tools for group understanding and empowerment. It is first necessary that there be positional consensus, bounded by common experiences and common goals. In addition, two other elements seem essential: trust and open dialogue. Because critical reflection drives the process of transformative learning, learners must be able to honestly discuss and appraise the position. The practices recommended for the classroom—such as role-playing, reframing the question, and studying case histories—are appropriate in any group setting for carrying particular risk when teachers and learners are working across boundaries—that is, in the murky waters of heterogeneity. To find success or to move forward, the learners must be able to develop a discourse that transcends regular discussions and is informed by research while valuing positional experiences and intuition-based knowledges. Such discourse must be culturally sensitive. In such responsiveness and sensitivity, transformative learning theory can find the ability to stretch past its comfortable location in a traditional Western teaching and learning environment. Addressing such issues provides a means of broadening transformative learning theory from the individual micro level to the mezzo community level and beyond.

References

Alfred, M. V. (2002). The promise of sociocultural theory in democratizing adult education. In M. V. Alfred (Ed.), *Learning and sociocultural context: Implications for adults, community, and workplace education* (pp. 3–13). New Directions for Adult and Continuing Education, no. 96. San Francisco: Jossey Bass.

Baumgartner, L. M. (2001). An update on transformational learning. In S. B. Merriam (Ed.), *The update on adult learning theory* (pp. 15–24). New Directions for Adult and Continuing Education, no. 109. San Francisco: Jossey-Bass.

Bourdieu, P. (2000). Social space and symbolic space. In C. Calhoun, J. Gerteis, J. Moody, S. Pfaff, & I. Virk (Eds.), *Contemporary sociological theory* (pp. 259–267). Oxford: Blackwell Publishers Ltd.

Boyd, R. D. (1991). *Personal transformation in small groups: A Jungian perspective.* London: Routledge.

Boyd, R. D., & Myers, G. J. (1988). Transformative education. *International Journal of Lifelong Education, 7*(4), 261–284.

Brookfield, S. D. (1995). Becoming a critically reflective teacher. San Francisco: Jossey-Bass.

Clark, M. C., & Wilson, A. (1991). Context and rationality in Mezirow's theory of transformational learning. *Adult Education Quarterly, 41*(2), 75–91.

Collard, S., & Law, M. (1989). The limits of perspective transformation: A critique of Mezirow's theory. *Adult Education Quarterly, 39*(2), 99–107.

Colin, S.A.J., III, and Preciphs, T. K. (1991). Perceptual patterns and the learning environment: Confronting White racism. In R. Hiemstra (Ed.), *Creating environments for effective adult learning*. New Directions for Adult and Continuing Education, no. 50. San Francisco: Jossey-Bass.

Collins, P. (1990). *Black feminist thought: Knowledge, consciousness, and the politics of empowerment*. New York: Routledge.

Cranton, P. (1994). *Understanding and promoting transformative learning: A guide for educators of adults*. San Francisco: Jossey-Bass.

Cranton, P. (1996). *Professional development as transformative learning*. San Francisco: Jossey-Bass.

Cranton, P. (2002). Teaching for transformation. In J. M. Ross-Gordon (Ed.), *Contemporary viewpoints on teaching adults effectively* (pp. 63–71). New Directions for Adult and Continuing Education, no. 93. San Francisco: Jossey-Bass.

Cross, W. E. (1991). *Shades of Black: Diversity in African American identity*. Philadelphia, PA: Temple University Press.

Daloz, L. (1986). *Effective teaching and mentoring: Realizing the transformational power of adult learning experiences*. San Francisco: Jossey-Bass.

Dirkx, J. M. (1998). Transformative learning theory in the practice of adult education: An overview. *PAACE Journal of Lifelong Learning, 7*, 1–14.

Dirkx, J. M. (2006). Engaging emotions in adult learning: A Jungian perspective on emotion and transformative learning. In E. W. Taylor (Ed.), *Fostering transformative learning in the classroom: Challenges and innovations* (pp. 15–26). New Directions for Adult and Continuing Education, no. 109. San Francisco: Jossey-Bass.

DuBois, W.E.B. (1903/1953). *The souls of black folk*. Greenwich: Fawcett Publications.

Foucault, M. (1980). *Power/knowledge*. New York: Pantheon.

Freire, P. (1970). *Pedagogy of the oppressed*. New York: Herter and Herter.

Freire, P. (1973). *Education for critical consciousness*. New York: Continuum.

Freire, P., & Faundez, A. (1989). *Learning to question*. New York: Continuum.

Freire, P., & Macedo, D. P. (1995). A dialogue: Culture, language, and race. *Harvard Educational Review, 65*(3), 377–402.

Giroux, H. (1997). Rewriting the discourse of racial identity: Towards a pedagogy and politics of whiteness. *Harvard Educational Review, 67*, 285–320.

Guy, T. C. (1999). (Ed.). *Providing culturally relevant adult education: A challenge for the twenty-first century*. New Directions for Adult and Continuing Education, no. 82. San Francisco: Jossey-Bass.

Guy-Sheftall, B. (1995). *Words of fire: An anthology of African-American feminist thought*. New York: The New Press.

Hall, S. (1992). New ethnicities. In D. J. Donald & A. Rattansi (Eds.), *Race, culture, and difference* (pp. 252–259). Thousand Oaks, CA: SAGE.

Helms, J. E. (1984). Toward a theoretical explanation of the effects of race on counseling: A black and white model. *Counseling Psychologist, 17*, 227–252.

Helms, J. E. (1990). Toward a model of white racial identity development. In J. E. Helms (Ed.), *Black and white racial identity: Theory, research, and practice* (pp. 67–80). Westport, CT: Greenwood Press.

hooks, b. (1989). *Talking back: Thinking feminist, thinking black.* Boston: South End.

hooks, b. (1990). *Yearning: Race, gender, and cultural politics.* Boston: South End Press.

Johnson-Bailey, J. (1998). Sonia Sanchez: Telling what we must hear. In P. Bell-Scott & J. Johnson-Bailey (Eds.), *Flatfooted truths: Telling black women's lives* (pp. 209–222). New York: Henry Holt.

Johnson-Bailey, J. (2006). Transformative learning: A community empowerment conduit for African American women. In S. B. Merriam, B. Courtenay, & R. M. Cervero (Eds.), *Global issues in adult education: Perspectives from Latin America, Southern Africa, and the United States* (pp. 307–318). San Francisco: Jossey-Bass.

Johnson-Bailey, J., & Alfred, M. (2006). Transformative teaching and the practices of black women adult educators. In E. W. Taylor (Ed.), *Fostering transformative learning in the classroom: Challenges and innovations* (pp. 49–58). New Directions for Adult and Continuing Education, no. 109. San Francisco: Jossey-Bass.

Johnson-Bailey, J., & Cervero, R. M. (2000). The invisible politics of race in adult education. In A. L. Wilson & E. R. Hayes (Eds.), *Handbook of adult and continuing education: New edition* (pp. 147–160). San Francisco: Jossey-Bass.

King, K. P., & Biro, S. C. (2006). A transformative learning perspective of continuing sexual identity development in the workplace. In R. Hill (Ed.), *Challenging homophobia and heterosexism: Lesbian, gay, bisexual, transgender and queer issues in organizational settings* (pp. 17–27). New Directions for Adult and Continuing Education, no. 112. San Francisco: Jossey-Bass.

Kitchenham, A. (2008). The evolution of John Mezirow's transformative learning theory. *Journal of Transformative Education, 6*(2), 104–123.

Kroth, M., & Boverie, P. (2009). Using the discovering model to facilitate transformational learning and career development. *Journal of Adult Education, 38*(1), 43–47.

Maher, F., & Tetreault, M. (1994). *Feminist classrooms.* New York: Basic Books.

McDonald, B., Cervero, R. M., & Courtenay, B. C. (1999). An ecological perspective of power in transformational learning: A case study of ethical vegans. *Adult Education Quarterly, 50*(2), 5–23.

McIntosh, P. (1995). White privilege and male privilege: A personal account of coming to see correspondences through work in women's studies. In M. Anderson & P. Hill Collins (Eds), *Race, class and gender: An anthology* (pp. 70–81). Belmont, CA: Wadsworth.

Merriam, S. B. (2004). The role of cognitive development in Mezirow's transformational learning theory. *Adult Education Quarterly, 55,* 60–68.

Merriam, S. B., & Caffarella, R. S. (1999). *Learning in adulthood: A comprehensive guide.* San Francisco: Jossey-Bass.

Mezirow, J. (1978). *Education for perspective transformation: Women's re-entry programs in community colleges*. New York: Teacher's College Press.

Mezirow, J. (1991). *Transformative dimensions of adult learning*. San Francisco: Jossey-Bass.

Mezirow, J. (1997). Transformative learning: Theory to practice. In P. Cranton (Ed.), *Transformative learning in action: Insights from practice* (pp. 5–12). New Directions for Adult and Continuing Education, no. 74. San Francisco: Jossey-Bass.

Moser, S. (2008). Personality: A new positionality. *AREA*, *40*(3), 383–392.

One America in the 21st century: Forging a new future. (1998). *The President's Initiative on Race: The Advisory Board's Report to the President*. Washington, DC: One America.

Pope, S. J. (1996). *Wanting to be something more: Transformation in ethnically diverse working class women through the process of education* (Unpublished doctoral dissertation, Fielding Institute).

Ross-Gordon, J. M., Martin, L. G., & Briscoe, D. B. (Eds.). (1990). *Serving culturally diverse populations*. New Directions for Adult and Continuing Education, no. 48. San Francisco: Jossey-Bass.

Takacs, D. (2002). Positionality, epistemology, and *Social Justice* in the classroom. *Social Justice*, *29*(4), 168–181.

Takaki, R. (1993). *A different mirror: A history of multicultural America*. Boston: Back Bay Books.

Taylor, E. W. (1994). Intercultural competency: A transformative learning process. *Adult Education Quarterly*, *44*(3), 154–174.

Taylor, E. W. (1998) Transformative learning: A critical review. Columbus, OH: ERIC Clearinghouse on Adult, Career, and Vocational Education Selected Journal Articles (Information Series no. 374).

Tisdell, E. J. (1995). Creating inclusive learning environments for adults: Insights from multicultural education and feminist pedagogy. Columbus, OH: ERIC Clearinghouse on Adult, Career, and Vocational Education Selected Journal Articles (Information Series no. 361).

Wangoola, P., & Youngman, F. (Eds.). (1996). *Towards a transformative political economy of adult education: Theoretical and practical challenges*. DeKalb, IL: LEPS Press.

CHAPTER SEVENTEEN

Transformative Learning Theory

A Perspective from Africa

Peggy Gabo Ntseane

As an African woman, historically colonized and marginalized, I am a product of academic learning traditions and methodologies founded on the culture, history, and philosophies of Euro-Western thought. My own African learning traditions have been marginalized and pushed further to the periphery of science and knowledge construction. Chilisa (2011) observes that these excluded knowledge systems are often presented as "other" and "fall under broad categories of non-Western, Third World, developing, underdeveloped, first nations, indigenous people, and so on" (p. 1). The main thrust of this chapter is that current learning theories, especially transformative learning theory, should not exclude from the knowledge production other knowledge systems of formerly colonized, marginalized cultures, because lived experiences enhance the quality of useful knowledge. Through reflection, which is embraced by transformative learning theory, an identification of oppressed learning experiences can help individuals and groups to turn an oppressive feature into a source of critical insight appropriate for epistemological developments. According to feminist theorists (Harding, 2004; Hundleby, 1997), knowledge is socially situated because different situations result in different knowledge. This chapter demonstrates that a learning theory implies a methodological approach with a philosophical base that informs assumptions about perceptions of reality, about what counts as knowledge—ways of knowing—as well as values.

The chapter starts with an overview of Mezirow's version of transformative learning. Then it presents an African view that informs learning and argues that in addition to what Mezirow says about this adult learning theory, transformative learning experiences in the southern African context can enrich this theory in several ways. For instance, adult learning in the African context is a webbed connection and collective process that cannot be realized without a theory that is culturally sensitive. Using examples from empirical research in Botswana, the chapter demonstrates how the African historical experience of culturally based learning values (such as respect, common good, spirituality, and a collective approach to learning) have been used to critically analyze disorienting life experiences, thus setting in motion transformative learning or realization of what one learner affectionately calls the "second heart." Finally, the chapter compares this African context for transformative learning conditions to the Western value system and concludes that although there are similarities, the collective approach to human existence and development in the African context is significant for opening dialogue critical for defining new worldviews.

If one is to understand transformative learning as referring to fundamental changes in what we know about ourselves, others, and the world in which we live (Kegan, 2000; Mezirow, 2000), then the continued development of a transformative learning theory must benefit from many transformative learning experiences in different cultural settings. As a researcher and an adult educator who belongs to the Bantu people of Africa, living a communal life based on connectedness that stretches from birth to death and continues beyond death and extends to the living and nonliving, I have always been disturbed by the way the Euro-Western research processes and teaching and learning methods disconnect me from the multiple relations and connections that define my reality. I am happy to have been invited to write this chapter as it adds to the growing evidence that social science research and adult learning theory in particular "needs emancipation from hearing only the voices of Western Europe, emancipation from generations of silence, and emancipation from seeing the world in one color" (Guba & Lincoln, 2005, p. 212). I believe that adult learning theories need to respect communal forms of living that are non-Western and create inquiries based on relational realities as well as forms of knowing that are predominant among non-Western "others" like my African context.

Another important form of knowing is the Afrocentric view of the role of the elderly. In an oral tradition society such as those found in Africa, the role of elders is also important for transformative learning because of the knowledge embedded in their wisdom and experiential learning. In fact, Fennell and Armot (2009, p. 13) state that "the role of the elders is central not just to the maintenance of the corpus of knowledge but their collective presence directs the transmission of knowledge and draws together the supernatural, the temporal and the spatial aspects of life." The next section presents African worldviews that in my view are relevant for the development of a theory of transformative learning.

AFRICAN WORLDVIEWS THAT INFORM TRANSFORMATIVE LEARNING

This section presents African worldviews that, although context specific, are perceived as having the potential to contribute to the continuing development of transformative learning theory. In particular, African traditional education, *übuntu*, and the Afrocentric paradigms are discussed.

Traditional Education

Prior to Africa's colonial experience, traditional education was indigenous to the local inhabitants of different geographic regions of the continent. For example, in Botswana, different tribes had varieties of traditional education depending on the domination of tribal subcultures. The instruction process was embedded in the whole system of raising children and nation building. The system embraced elements of child rearing, entrepreneurship, trading, economic demand and supply concepts, societal hierarchies and power structures, safety and homeland security, and welfare skills. People born at the same time belonged to certain *mephato* (cohorts or regiments), which would be called to receive training or mobilize each other to construct useful knowledge together as a collective. These *mephato* would also be called for various social services, such as fighting during wars and times of conflict (Makgoba, 1999). This reminds me of the time when I told my great-grandfather (now deceased) that I was going to the United States of America for further studies. He said, "My child, come back after acquiring useful knowledge from the white man; my people will only respect you, our family name, and the new knowledge that you will bring from there if you come back to the village to live happily with your family, your people, and the spirits of your ancestors." Although I did not find my great-grandfather when I brought back the American Certificate, it does not bother me because I am connected to his spirit, his people, and his geographic space. This is what the southern African indigenous principle of knowledge emphasizes by the concept *übuntu* (collective humanism of human beings), because to learn is to live usefully and happily with other people, the earth, and its inhabitants as well as spirits of those who have died. According to Adeyinka (2003), traditional educational systems had three interrelated goals: to preserve and conserve the cultural heritage of the family, clan, tribe, and community; to adapt children to their physical, social, and spiritual environment so that they could exploit and benefit from it; and to instill in them the value placed on a rational autonomous individual whose actions reflect the values of communities and societies.

Another distinguishing feature of African indigenous education is informality (Ocitti, 1988; Ntseane, 2007). The instruction process, though structured, was not formalized in the manner of most educational systems we know today. Bureaucrats and leaders were born artisans, warriors, teachers, lawyers, traders, shepherds, farmers, and other occupations; they learned their skills from role models and mentors who used participatory learning methods such as song, drama, stories, proverbs, poetry, observation, demonstration, dialogues, and problem-solving techniques. Training methods included the oral mode of instruction and acquisition as well as knowledge revealed through the processes of dreams and visions. Although marginalized in the current African education systems, this informality survived colonialism and thus can be researched and reconstructed to inform transformative learning.

Colonization and Imperialism

Colonization—the imposed rule over one country by another—was a brutal and humiliating process whereby two thirds of the world experienced invasion, which resulted in loss of territory; destruction of political, social, and economic systems; and loss of control and ownership of the knowledge systems. Chilisa (2011) argues that one of the worst outcomes of colonialism is "scientific colonialism," which she describes as the "imposition of the colonizers' ways of knowing—and the control of all knowledge produced in colonies" (p. 9). In Africa, colonial occupation occurred in 1884 when the European powers (Britain, Belgium, France, Germany, Italy, Portugal, and Spain) met at the Berlin Conference and divided Africa amongst themselves. In addition, African states were given names related to the colonial power, settlers, explorers, or missionaries. For example, Zimbabwe was named Rhodesia after the explorer Cecil Rhodes. European explorers, travelers, and hunters were notorious for claiming discovery of African lands, rivers, lakes, and waterfalls. One can't help but concur with (Chilisa & Preece, 2005), who argue that this was a violent way of dismissing the indigenous people's knowledge as irrelevant and a way of disconnecting them from what they knew and how they knew it.

This colonial experience is important for transformative learning in this context because scientific colonization has implications for a decolonization process. According to Smith (1999), decolonization is a process of centering the concerns and worldviews of the colonized or "other" so that they understand themselves through their own assumptions and perspectives. Decolonization has also been associated with the restoration and development of cultural practices, thinking patterns, beliefs, and values that were suppressed but are still relevant and necessary to the survival and birth of new ideas. According to Laenui (2000), five phases of the decolonization process are (1) rediscover and discovery; (2) mourning; (3) dreaming; (4) commitment; and (5) action. Both transformative learning and *the decolonization process* highlight the fact that worldviews and concerns of the colonized are important because human beings have to understand themselves through their own assumptions and perspectives. In fact, a number of scholar who have written about decolonization (Smith, 1999) argue that thinking patterns, beliefs, and values that were suppressed but are still relevant are necessary for the survival and birth of new ideas, thinking, and techniques.

The persistent determination of Third World scholars—myself and many others—speaks to our marginalization in knowledge construction circles and is indicative of the resistance against scientific colonization. The relevance of this framework to this chapter is that current dominant and Western-based learning theories should be decolonized to legitimate and enable the inclusion of knowledge production processes that accommodate the shared knowledge and wisdom of those suffering from the oppressive colonial teaching and learning paradigms. As an example, one of the African belief systems that could inform transformative learning theorizing and processes in the Southern African context, is *übuntu*.

Übuntu

The worldview described by *übuntu* or *botho* (Tswana version) is African humanism, which involves sharing, compassion, respect, commitment and sensitivity to the needs of others, patience, and kindness. By being *botho* or behaving with dignity (that is, with honesty, integrity, and trustworthiness) among the collective, the individual becomes part of an empowered group of people who are honest and accommodating, sharing a commitment to a safe life at all costs and respecting the youth and the old. In the African context, the opposite of *botho* or humanism is selfishness, greediness, and self-centeredness. Humanism or *botho* is crucial for promoting cooperation among individuals, cultures, and nations. Most African communities—with particular reference to Bantu people of Southern Africa—view human existence in relation to the existence of others; hence the popular concept *Motho ke motho ka batho ba bangwe*. According to Goduka (2000, p. 7), an English translation that comes close to this principle is "I am we; I am because we are; we are because of I am." All of these underscore the fact that communality, collectivity, human unity, and pluralism define this African principle. This is in direct contrast to the Eurocentric view of humanity of "I think, therefore I am," expressed by Descartes (cited in Chilisa, 2011), which emphasizes autonomy in transformative learning.

Spirituality is also important in helping Africans understand humanity or reality. Our connectedness to the earth (*lefatshe*) and all its inhabitants—including animals, birds, plants, and spirits, especially those of our departed ancestors (*badimo*)—help us to view human existence in relation to the existence of others. This connectedness is embraced and celebrated through taboos and totems. For instance, my totem is a springbok; this animal is sacred to me, my family, and my ethnic group. This means that we have a responsibility to respect and conserve this animal, as evidenced by not killing or eating its meat.

As a collective, when people see their totem (usually an animal) we see one another, including the ancestral spirits; we recognize ourselves and God, in whose image all people are made. According to Tournas (1996), because Botswana people see the human and physical world as one, and self and world as one, separating them from God can deprive them of their source of knowledge as a people.

Education systems have neglected this African philosophy of life because of the emphasis on materialistic and instrumental value systems (Cunningham & Curry, 1997). I would add that the major shortcoming of adult education in Africa has been that it elevates rationality over other forms of knowledge, human thought, and discourses that are probably critical for reflection and transformative learning.

The Afrocentric Paradigm

The Afrocentric paradigm, as explained by Asante (1995, 1987), deals with the question of African identity from the perspective of African people who have been marginalized and dislocated by colonialism. He explains Afrocentricity as follows:

> To say that we are decentered... we have lost our own cultural footing and become other than our cultural and political origins, dislocated and disoriented. We are essentially insane, that is living an absurdity from which we will never be able to free our minds until we return to the source. Afrocentricity as a theory of change intends to re-locate the African person as a subject.... As a pan-African idea, Afrocentricity becomes the key to the proper education of children and the essence of an African cultural revival and, indeed, survival. (Asante, 1995, p. 1)

In agreement, Mazama (2001) asserts that "in the process Afrocentrism also means viewing the European voice as just one among the many and not necessarily the wisest one" (p. 388). Insistence on a clear definition of space is the central distinguishing characteristic of the Afrocentric inquiry. Space here refers not only to physical space but also to the idea of giving voice to the marginalized.

Because the ultimate aim of Afrocentricity is people's liberation, the Afrocentric methodology is supposed to generate knowledge that will free and empower people. Mazama (2001) argues for the production of "knowledge that opens the heart" (p. 399). This was affirmed by one of the respondents in my 2007 study on Botswana women, who described her transformative learning experience as her "realization of her second heart." Based on shared experiences from my research, I see the relevance of the Afrocentric idea to adult learning as identifying African cultural values that can be incorporated in transformative learning theory to make it more culturally sensitive. Furthermore, transformative learning provides a unique opportunity for Africans to define themselves and their agenda according to their realities as well as taking into account the realities of others. Validating this view, Prah (1999) noted: "We cannot in all seriousness study ourselves through the eyes of other people's assumptions. I am not saying we must not know what others know or think of us. I am saying we must think for ourselves like others do for themselves" (p. 37).

Afrocentrism is a paradigm reflecting an African–centered worldview that establishes a conceptual framework for how the world is seen and understood. In fact, Asante is credited with identifying two indigenous concepts. *Maat* means interrogating the manner in which knowledge and information process is in harmony with culture of the people and pursuing issues of truth and justice. *Nomma,* from the Nile Valley civilization, describes the creation of knowledge as a vehicle for improvement in human life and human relations. Although these African worldviews survived colonialism and Western imperialism, unfortunately they have not survived marginalization by the dominant Western culture in relation to the process of knowledge production, validation, and acquisition.

This section has discussed African value systems that inform human existence in this cultural context and argued that these can enrich the transformative learning theory if it is culturally sensitive to the diverse context of adult learners. Key African learning values, such as "communal/collective/participatory" and "interconnectedness/independence" for social change and empowerment, are unique ways in which African philosophies and theoretical perspectives inform ways of seeing, knowing, and reconstructing reality.

TRANSFORMATIVE LEARNING IN BOTSWANA: EVIDENCE FROM THE FIELD

Although most adults in different African contexts and cultural settings may not be familiar with the term "perspective transformation," their life is nevertheless characterized by encounters that changed their perspectives. For example, in addition to traumatic experiences referred to in the literature on transformative learning (Mezirow, 2000; Merriam & Ntseane, 2008), African people have a history of transformative learning as a result of social change periods driven by colonialism, imperialism, and most recently global capitalism (Konate, 2007). Observations about the relationship between traditional African value systems and learning have concluded that such values embrace a collective rather than an individual concept of responsibility; interdependence instead of independence; a unity of spirit, mind, body, and emotions in learning rather than a focus on the cognitive; as well as the valuing of life experience and wisdom over formal knowledge.

Three scenarios from research data in a study on transformative learning in Botswana (Ntseane, 2007) are presented. Case 1 demonstrates the role of spirituality in the transformative learning process.

Case 1: Visionary Transformative Learning: Interview with a Sixty-Year-Old Divorcee

INTERVIEWER: How did you get out of this marriage then?

RESPONDENT: God knows how to do his things. One night when I was sleeping I had a dream. In this dream I heard a voice saying, "This man will kill you. This man will kill you." That was the turning point.

INTERVIEWER: Which incident really made you to decide once and for all that you were getting out of this marriage?

RESPONDENT: Many things, but the dream was like the last straw. You know the dream made me realize that this man has said that he was going to kill me several times in the past every time we had a misunderstanding or when he was kicking me and beating me, but I never thought he could do that. I kept telling myself that I was the mother of his three children and a wedded wife. But the dream was *beyond me*. It was like a whole tray of my past sad life was brought in front of me, I mean on my face with the dream being in front. I knew I had to leave with or without money this time. It was that powerful. I left everything but my children and I felt it in my heart, blood, and bone that this man should not find me in the house when he comes for lunch that day. So yes! Yes! It was the dream more than the beatings.

INTERVIEWER: *Wao*! I see that. If you were to advise young women on marriage, what would you say?

RESPONDENT: My daughter's marriage lasted three years and she was out of it. I told her, "My babe an abusive man is an abuser! Period! You don't need more than three years to decide to leave." That is what I will tell every woman. I stayed too long and the damage was also great. Here I am on wheelchair; I don't want anybody to go through that, even my worst enemy. So I will say marriage is a gift from God and if it is not your gift, don't waste time. Move on and you will find peace and happiness with something else.

Case 1 illustrates the role of vision in cultural transformative learning. Because of a cultural belief in connection with the earth, the dead, and the living as well as dreams and visionary experiences, the solution to this woman's marriage problems was not only an individual or close family issue but also a collective responsibility. Case 1 also links the idea of critical thinking and transformative learning within a broader context of problem-based learning (Thomas, 2009). The critical reflection of the women's cultural belief system against her marriage life experiences helped her to go through a paradigmatic shift that cannot be reversed. Not only has she seen the larger picture, but she is ready to educate others about the new perspective, which to her will be more effective. This demonstrates that there has been a transformative shift or what Quinn (1996, p. 22) calls "deep change."

Case 2: The Role of Community Support

INTERVIEWER: Really? You are one of the people who came out nationally about your HIV status?

RESPONDENT: Yes! Yes! I am happy I did. I have made presentation at schools and national conferences about my experience with the disease. I have traveled to two countries with the national HIV/ AIDS health team to share my experience with other people living with the virus from the world. This is what has made my life worth living even in the face of AIDS.

INTERVIEWER: Why changes from being afraid of the HIV stigma to actually publicizing your status like that?

RESPONDENT: I think it is the support I got from people. I never thought anybody would sympathize with an HIV positive or AIDS person. This support helped me to realize things that I had always taken for granted. For example, I now see the value of being a member of a group of people called the family or ethic group. The support I got helped me to want to give back to my people something in return to what they are doing now. They really took my sickness as their illness. For example, people fund raised for the ARV's for me in 2004 when I almost died. Some lobbied government to introduce free ARV's. People from faraway places like America and Europe talked at the top of their voices for the need to help people living with HIV and AIDS. The support group of people living with AIDS in this country is given money by people who don't even know us. With this support you would be "dead alive" not to want to give back to the society that perceives you as one of them no matter what.

INTERVIEWER: That is powerful. So what are you giving back as a result of this experience, apart from making presentations?

RESPONDENT: You know in my culture there is a saying that *go swa motho go sala motho* or "one dies, another remains." This proverb has really empowered me because it is relevant to my experience. I am dying as you can see that I am just bones. But I now believe that my death must be for a good reason. Maybe I had to be the one infected with HIV so that others (those remaining, as the proverb says) would learn from me that they have to contribute to the good of their society. I have taught the young people that they need to prevent HIV infection, otherwise they will be sick like me, but I have also shown them that every individual owes their society a legacy. So I am ready to die even today because I am at peace with myself and my people.

INTERVIEWER: Very good. Have you talked about death with anybody and why?

RESPONDENT: Ohoo Yes! My church members in particular have done nothing else but to give me hope in an effort to prepare for life after death.

INTERVIEWER: Lastly, if you were to summarize the lessons from this experience, what would you say?

RESPONDENT: I will say, everyone is here on earth for a purpose. I had to be infected with HIV and die from AIDS for me to accomplish my mission here on earth. I have been given support by my family, church, community, and the world at large to succeed. I have also given something worthwhile to my people, thanks to HIV and AIDS. I am now ready to join the spirits of my ancestors to continue the good work. Search for your calling and do likewise.

Case 2 illustrates the point that the development of transformative learning theory can benefit from local meanings attached to experiences. For example, this data shows that the respondent used an appropriate proverb (common understanding), which is part of the oral local literature review and a source of problem identification and meaning-making to legitimize the new worldview. This case also demonstrates the interconnectedness of humans to the living and the dead.

Informed by the concept *übuntu*, most African worldviews emphasize belongingness, connectedness, community participation, and people-centeredness. Botswana, like many African societies, has a long history of diverse ways of processing and producing knowledge collectively in centers such as the Kgotla (Chief's Palace), shrines, and religious centers. This case supports the literature on the process of transformation from a more spiritually oriented approach (Tolliver & Tisdell, 2006). Furthermore, this case is used here to argue that in some contexts the spiritually oriented approach is facilitated through sociocultural content and experiences. The next case illustrates how this is done.

Case 3: Dingaka (Diviners) Practices: Communal Practices to Transformative Learning

The process starts with a sick individual who shows signs of confusion.

The family members see the strange behavior and conclude that maybe it is a sign that ancestral spirits are not happy (for example, it could be they have not been fed in a long time).There is a cultural belief that this bad response could easily be manifested in the most vulnerable, namely a child. In agreement, the family consults the extended family and a date is set for a cultural event to appease the ancestors' spirits.

A short time after the festive event, the child is sick again and shows similar signs. This time the family decides to engage a *ngaka* or diviner who uses bones. The bones, as many as sixty, symbolize divine power, evil power, foreign spirits (good or bad), elderly men and women, young and old, homesteads, family life or death, and ethnic groups that include *makgoa* (white people) to construct a story about the consulting client's life. The sixty pieces of bone represent experiences and networks as well as relationships of people and the environment. In constructing a story, the diviner consults the patterns of the divine set as the client throws them to the ground. This is done in the presence of the extended family of the child.

The diviner asks the client to confirm the interpretation of the set as a true story about the troubled aspect of his or her life. The family members present are also expected to comment on the consultation reading results. In the process, both are contributing to an interpretation, a construction of reality. The client and family members are invited to talk freely about the life of the client and to reject the constructed story if it does not tally with his or her life experiences.

I see the collective process of constructing knowledge as expanding on aspects discussed in the Western conception of transformative learning; namely, spirituality, context, and dialogue (Taylor, 2007). In the context of the diviner, there is no absolute knowledge because the three—the diviner, the set, and the client (patient and family)—construct knowledge.

Context is complex and expansive as well as infinite, because there is no claim to a description of any context. Instead, symbolic representations of the surroundings are brought to the diviner and the clients. The story, in whatever form, is read and agreed upon, and no interpretation occurs in the absence of any one of the three. Dialogue with others, belief systems, and other realities assist the learner in expanding worldviews.

The worldview represented by divining in Case 3 challenges the positivist view of health knowledge as absolute, the medical doctor as the sole objective constructor of knowledge, and the patient as a passive object. This worldview appeals to community construction of knowledge as opposed to the individual's rational and cognitive construction. Furthermore, as Chilisa (2005) observed, the diviner's knowledge construction method "challenges Western research's control of knowledge" (p. 680).

Case 3 illustrates transformative journeys that African adult educators must investigate through reflection on their identities as creative individuals and collectives. Palmer (2004) affirms this experience by relating identity to integrity and argues that this struggle catalyzes transformational change. If a reflective process that uses this African worldview (such as Afrocentism) has resulted with transformation that has expanded our understanding of the self as well as our understanding of the world, then experiences shared in case 3 on divining are relevant to culturally sensitive processes of transformative theory. Examples like this one offer alternative ways in which adult educators may work with communities to theorize and build transformative learning systems that not only are owned by people but that also restore their dignity and integrity in the process of generating useful knowledge. Useful knowledge is context specific; thus it does not have to be appropriate or ethical for Western adult educators not practicing in the relevant context to emulate.

CONCLUSION

In the African context, the historical space of indigenous knowledge systems and the legacy of colonialism and *übuntu* show that communality and inter-dependence, rather than autonomous learning, are valued as a community-building activity in the African context. Other African learning values highlighted in the case studies are (1) a unity of spirit, mind, and body as well as emotions instead of a focus on cognitive qualities and (2) a valuing of experience and wisdom over formal knowledge. If transformative learning theory is to be culturally sensitive to the African context, the deconstruction of earlier proverbs and myths should be sources of problem solving and meaning-making. As Chilisa (2005) observed, "proverbs represent cultural theories or models of experience, evaluation assertions from a moral perspective, gener-alized knowledge that can be applied to the interpretation of particular events and a point of view or certain ways of looking at problems" (p. 2). This African communal approach to learning is an important source of making meanings, which has the potential to enable a multidirectional borrowing and lending of knowledge across nations and within nations. According to Hoppers (2000), education and training of various types should begin by building on what people have and knowledge they have acquired through indigenous methods. Because the world is becoming a global village, it is therefore crucial that citizens of the world learn through and about each other so that they can coexist in peace and harmony.

References

Adeyinka, A. A. (2003). Philosophical foundations of educational policy and practice in Africa with special reference to Botswana. Paper presented to the Fulbright-Hays group. Gaborone, Botswana, July 2, 2003.

Asante, M. K. (1995). *Afrocentricity: The theory of social change.* Retrieved on September 15, 2004, from http://64.233.187.104/search?q=cache:Vrrntf9t3DsJ :www.africawithin.com/asante/social_change.htm+Afrocentricity:+The+theory +of+social+change&hl=en&ie=UTF-8

Asante, M. K. (1987). *The Afrocentric idea.* Philadelphia: Temple University Press.

Chilisa, B. (2005). Educational research within postcolonial Africa: A critique of HIV/AIDS research in Botswana. *International Journal of Qualitative Studies in Education, 18*(6), 659–684.

Chilisa, B. (2011). *Indigenous research methodologies.* Thousand Oaks, CA: SAGE.

Chilisa, B., & Preece, J. (2005). *Research methods for adult educators in Africa.* Cape Town: Pearson and UNESCO.

Cunningham, P., & Curry, R. (1997). Learning within a social movement: The Chicago African American experience. In R. E. Nolan & H. Chelesvig (eds.), *38th Annual Adult Education Conference Proceedings* (pp. 73–78). Knoxville, TN: University of Tennessee.

Fennell, S., & Armot, M. (2009). Decentring hegemonic gender theory: Implications for educational research. *RECUP Working Paper No. 21: Research Consortium on Educational Outcomes and Poverty.*

Guba, E. G., & Lincoln, E. Y. (2005). Paradigmatic controversies, contradictions and emerging confluences (pp. 191–215). In N. K. Denzin & Y. S. Lincoln (Eds.), *The SAGE handbook of qualitative research* (3rd ed.). Thousand Oaks, CA: SAGE.

Goduka, I. N. (2000). Africa/Indigenous philosophies: Legitimizing spirituality centered wisdoms within the academy. In P. Higgs, N.C.G. Vakalisa, T. V. Mda, & N. T. Assie-Lumumba (Eds.), *African voices in education.* Lansdowne, South Africa: Juta Academic.

Harding, S. (2004). *Introduction: Standpoint theory as a site of political philosophical and scientific debate.* New York: Routledge.

Hoppers, C.A.O. (2000). Africa voices in education: Retrieving the past, engaging the present, and shaping the future. In P. Higgs, N.C.G. Vakalisa, T. V. Mda, & N. T. Assie-Lumumba (Eds.), *African voices in education* (pp. 1–12). Lansdowne, South Africa: Juta Academic.

Hundleby, C. (1997). Where standpoint theory stands now. *Women and Politics*, *18*(3), 25–43.

Kegan, R. (2000). What form transforms? A constructive-development approach to transformative learning. In J. Mezirow & Associates (Eds.), *Learning as transformation: Critical perspectives on a theory in progress* (pp. 35–70). San Francisco: Jossey-Bass.

Konate, M. (2007). Experiences of post-colonial women in grassroots organizations in Mali. In L. Servage & T. Fenwick (Eds.), *Learning in community* (Vol. 1). Proceedings of the Joint International Conference of Adult Education Research Conference (AERC) 48th National Conference. Halifax, Nova Scotia.

Laenui, P. (2000). Processes of decolonization. In M. Battiste (Ed.), *Reclaiming indigenous voice and vision.* Vancouver: University of British Columbia Press.

Makgoba, M. W. (1999). *African renaissance.* Cape Town: Mfube and Tafelberg Publishers.

Mazama, A. (2001). The Afrocentric paradigm: Contours and definitions. *Journal of Black Studies*, *31*(4), 387–405.

Merriam, S. B., & Ntseane, P. G. (2008). Transformational learning in Botswana: How culture shapes the process. *Adult Education Quarterly*, *58*(3), 187–193.

Mezirow, J. (1991). *Transformative dimensions of adult learning.* San Francisco: Jossey-Bass.

Mezirow, J. (2000). Learning to think like an adult: Core concepts of transformation theory. In J. Mezirow & Associates (Eds.), *Learning as transformation: Critical perspectives on a theory in progress* (pp. 3–33). San Francisco: Jossey-Bass.

Ntseane, P. G. (2007). African indigenous education: the case of Botswana. In S. B. Merriam & Associates (Eds.), *Non-western perspectives on learning and knowing* (pp. 113–136). Malabar, FL: Krieger Publishing.

Ocitti, J. P. (1988). Indigenous education today: The necessity of the useless. *Adult Education and Development*, *30*, 53–73.

Palmer, P. J. (2004). A hidden wholeness. San Francisco: Jossey-Bass

Prah, K. K. (1999). African Renaissance or Warlords? In M. W. Makgoba (ed.), *African Renaissance.* Capetown: Mafube.

Quinn, R. E. (1996). *Deep Change: Discovering the manager within.* San Francisco: Jossey-Bass.

Smith, L. (1999). *Decolonizing methodologies: Research and indigenous peoples.* London: Zed Books.

Taylor, E. W. (2007). An update of transformative learning theory: A critical review of the empirical research (1999–2005). *International Journal of Lifelong Education*, *26*, 173–191.

Thomas, I. (2009). Critical thinking, transformative learning, sustainable education, and problem-based learning in universities. *Journal of Transformative Education* *7*(3), 245–264.

Tolliver, D. E., & Tisdell, E. J. (2006). Engaging spirituality in the transformative higher education classroom. In E. W. Taylor (Ed.), *Teaching for change: Fostering transformative learning in the classroom* (pp. 37–48). New Directions for Adult and Continuing Education, no. 19. San Francisco: Jossey Bass.

Tournas, S. A. (1996). From sacred initiation to bureaucratic apostasy: Junior secondary school-leavers and the secularization of education in Southern Africa. *Comparative Education, 32*(1), 10–17.

CHAPTER EIGHTEEN

Transformative Learning in Europe

An Overview of the Theoretical Perspectives

Alexis Kokkos

The theory and practice of transformative learning was developed mainly in the United States. The scholars leading the development of transformative learning theory live and work in North America, and all of the eight International Conferences on Transformative Learning have been organized in North American countries. However, adult educators in other countries, and especially in Europe, have also formed communities within which they explore and develop the theory and practice of transformative learning (for example, in the United Kingdom, Greece, and Sweden). Europe comprises the following forty-nine countries: Albania, Andorra, Armenia, Austria, Azerbaijan, Belarus, Belgium, Bosnia Herzegovina, Bulgaria, Czech Republic, Croatia, Cyprus, Denmark, Estonia, Finland, France, F.Y.R.O.M., Georgia, Germany, Great Britain, Greece, Holy See, Hungary, Iceland, Ireland, Italy, Latvia, Liechtenstein, Lithuania, Luxembourg, Malta, Moldova, Monaco, Montenegro, Netherlands, Norway, Poland, Portugal, Romania, Russia, San Marino, Serbia, Slovakia, Slovenia, Spain, Sweden, Switzerland, Turkey, Ukraine.

Note: Author Alexis Kokkos would like to thank colleagues Agnieszka Bron, Christine Delory-Momberger, Jerôme Eneau, Ted Fleming, Laura Formenti, Tom Hagström, Pierre Hebrard, Marianne Horsdal, Ewa Kurantowicz, Paris Lintzeris, and José Gonzalez Monteagudo, who offered some basic information concerning the impact of transformative learning theory in their countries, as well as his colleague George Koulaouzides, with whom he discussed the criteria for the selection of the examined papers, and Dimitra Andritsakou, Marilena Fragedaki, and Louloudi Chalatsi, who helped with the collection of the necessary data.

A few interesting questions emerge from this reality, particularly if we wish to have a better understanding of the impact of transformative learning theory in the field of adult education in Europe:

1. What is the attitude of European adult educators toward the theoretical framework of transformative learning?

2. To what extent and depth do they incorporate this framework in the development of their own ideas?

Additionally, European adult educators are active in a social, political, and cultural environment that has its own historic background, from which paradigms concerning the phenomenon of learning emerge. Such traditions include community education, critical pedagogy for emancipation, and adult education for social change (Jarvis, 1995). Consequently, one more question arises: In what way do European colleagues combine their own traditions with their perception of transformative learning?

The aim of this chapter is to explore opinions developing in Europe via a literature review. For this reason we consider as "European adult educators" those who were not only born and educated in Europe but also developed the vast majority of their work and research in Europe. Undoubtedly, in the current transnational world we may be hard-pressed to imagine that a writer's ideas are situated in a single country or even a continent. Nevertheless, we argue that the historical, ideological, and sociocultural context in which a writer is active, as well as the policies implemented by decision-making centers, such as the European Union and the government of each country, considerably influence the formation of the writers' ideas. Therefore, to take one example, although we acknowledge the significance of Stephen Brookfield's work, we do not include him in the category of adult educators active in Europe, because he has been mainly working in the United States in recent decades. On the other hand, we have included scholars like Julia Preece, who has worked for a long time in the United Kingdom and moved only very recently to the University of Lesotho.

In the first section of the chapter we try to define the theoretical framework of transformative learning, in an attempt to set the boundaries of the approaches in which European adult educators express their opinions. In the second section we introduce the methodology of our literature review: the criteria for choosing the papers, the sources used, the barriers faced during our research, and the way in which the chosen material was analyzed. In the third section we critically comment on the data. In the last section we use Greece as an object of a case study, attempting to interpret the findings of the literature review that are related to this country in the light of the social and educational context from which they emerged.

DEFINING THE THEORETICAL FRAMEWORK OF TRANSFORMATIVE LEARNING

The theory of transformative learning is described by Jack Mezirow in his article "A Critical Theory of Adult Learning and Education" (1983), as well as in his later work (for example, 1991; Mezirow & Associates, 1990, 2000). However, he cautions that this theory is not binding but mainly concerns a central body of ideas open to enrichment and new approaches. This approach is made evident in the subtitle of his book *Learning as Transformation: Critical Perspectives on a Theory in Progress*, in the preface of which he refers to the "Transformative Learning movement" (2000, p. xi), which "has produced several books, well over fifty doctoral dissertations, dozens of conference presentations and articles" (2000, p. xi). Indeed, during the last twenty-five years many scholars have adopted the principles and the basic concepts of Mezirow's theory and have developed their own ideas within this framework, providing new elements and research data as well as suggestions for critical reevaluation of its various aspects.

But which of the different theoretical approaches suggested can be considered to be part of the transformative learning movement, corresponding to its original theoretical framework? The criteria to answer this question are far from concrete and hard to definitively set. Mezirow himself has avoided singling out the scholars who have significantly contributed to the progress of his theory. That said, however, he has in fact acknowledged that a number of colleagues have broadly contributed to that process. In all three books he has edited (1990, 2000, and 2009 along with Edward Taylor), the words "and Associates" appear next to his name on the book cover. It is obvious that this American scholar as well as those whose papers were embodied in the three books have been collaborating in the development of the transformative learning theory. With this in mind, we argue that the authors included in the three books, especially those who have worked extensively on transformative learning in their own published works, are those who work toward a common theoretical framework: transformative learning. The best-known of these scholars are Belenky, Brookfield, Cranton, Daloz, Dirkx, Dominicé, Duveskog, Elias, Friis-Hansen, Gould, Green, Kasl, Kegan, King, Kitchener, Lipson Lawrence, Marsick, Taylor (Edward), Taylor (Kathleen), Tisdell, and Yorks. The approaches developed by these scholars will be referred to in the remainder of the chapter as *theoretical conceptions related to transformative learning*.

On the other hand, in the existing literature there is a convergence of opinions (Cranton, 2006; Dirkx, 1998; Merriam, Caffarella, & Baumgartner, 2007; Taylor, 2007, 2008) that important scholars like Freire and Boyd and Myers share the same emancipating educational goals as those supporting the theory of transformative learning, even though the cited researchers depart from an alternative understanding of perspective transformation and use a different conceptual framework. Given that, we decided not to overlook the views of European adult educators in relation to those scholars' work.

LITERATURE REVIEW METHODOLOGY

The papers concerning the issue at hand could be drawn from a number of sources: books, journals, conference papers, databases, and websites. Due to the obvious difficulty of collecting all this data, we thought it would be best to apply a set of criteria for collecting the data necessary for the research. We rejected sources that are difficult to cite because of their wide range, such as books, databases, and web pages. We limited the survey to theoretical and empirical approaches published in international scientific journals or presented at peer-reviewed international conferences. Nevertheless, we had to set limitations in some of these cases as well. In regard to scientific journals, we chose to limit our research to English-language publications because most adult education publications in Europe are in English, which is also the language of the major international conferences. Among the different publishing houses, we chose to draw data from those who have shown significant publishing activity in the field of adult education, namely:

- SAGE (including journals such as *Adult Education Quarterly, Journal of Transformative Education, Action Research, Human Resource Development Review, and Management Learning*)
- Taylor and Francis—Routledge (*International Journal of Lifelong Education, Research in Post-Compulsory Education, Studies in Continuing Education*, etc.)
- Wiley (New Directions for Adult and Continuing Education)
- NIACE (*Studies in the Education of Adults, Convergence and Adults Learning Journal*)
- Emerald (*Journal of Workplace Learning, Education and Training*)

As for conference papers, we drew data from the Transformative Learning Conferences (5th through 8th) and the conferences of SCUTREA, the European conference institution of university departments engaged in adult education.

In the framework set by the aforementioned resources, we looked for papers written by European adult educators which met three criteria: (1) the title, subtitle, or abstract of the paper contains words or phrases that relate to the concept of transformative learning theory ("transformative learning," "transformative education," "transformative goals," and so on); (2) the paper makes direct references to one or more of: Mezirow's work, the theoretical conceptions related to transformative learning, and the alternative views of perspective transformation; and (3) in the case of papers written by more than one author, at least one author is active in Europe.

FINDINGS

We tracked twenty-three papers written by European adult educators (Alhadeff, 2003; Dominicé, 2003; Duveskog & Friis-Hansen, 2007, 2009; Duveskog, Friis-Hansen, & Taylor, 2009; Fenson & Chesser-Smyth, 2009; Fetherston & Kelly, 2007; Fleming, 2000; Gray, 2006; Harvey & Langdom, 2009; Hunt, 2009; Illeris, 2003, 2004; Karalis, 2010; Kokkos, 2009; Nieuwenhuis & Van Woerkom, 2007; Preece, 2003; Taylor & Pettit, 2007; Taylor, Pettit, & Stackpoole-Moore, 2005; Tosey, Mathison, & Michelli, 2005; Wilhelmson, 2005, 2006; Wilner & Dubouloz, 2010). These papers are a small part of the relevant international literature. For example, among the 126 papers published from 2003 to 2009 in the *Journal of Transformative Education,* only 6 were written by European authors. Also, from the 339 papers available on the Internet from the International Conferences on Transformative Learning, only 11 were written by Europeans. This initial information shows that reflection on the theory of transformative learning has not, so far, been an issue of central scientific concern in Europe.

As far as the *country of origin of* the authors and coauthors of the examined papers is concerned, the review revealed that most of them (thirteen) were located in Great Britain, followed by three from Switzerland. Two authors were from Denmark, two from Greece, two from Ireland, two from the Netherlands, and two from Sweden.

To find more information about the transformative learning activities in European countries, we sent out a questionnaire to the European colleagues participating in the Scientific Committee of the 9th International Transformative Learning Conference, which was held in 2011 (names are mentioned in the Acknowledgments). It was revealed that there are several relevant activities in Great Britain, such as postgraduate courses, research, and published books or chapters in collective works. In Denmark, France, Italy, Poland, Spain, and Sweden, transformative learning theory is not so popular in the field of adult education. In all these countries there is a limited number of authors (two to four) whose work on transformative learning has been published in books or journals; in France, Italy, and Poland, a small number of theses have been written. In contrast, Greece seems to be one country where there is a vivid engagement of the adult educators' community in transformative learning. Therefore Greece is presented in detail in the last section of this chapter in the form of a case study.

Another finding is that interaction among European writers from different countries is modest, and they do not seem to have formed a network. The only exceptions are the collaborative papers of Duveskog (Sweden) and Friis-Hansen (Denmark); Gray's (2006) reference to the paper of Tosey, Mathison, & Michelli (2005); and Wilhelmson's (2006) reference to Preece's paper (2003). Regarding the *year of publication*, all the texts have been published relatively recently (since 2000).

Concerning the *context of adult education*, five papers refer to community development (Duveskog & Friis-Hansen, 2007, 2009; Duveskog, Friis-Hansen, & Taylor, 2009; Harvey & Langdom, 2009; Wilhelmson, 2005). Among those, the first four deal with cases in Africa. There are also five papers on professional development (Dominicé, 2003; Fenson & Chesser-Smyth, 2009; Gray, 2006; Wilhelmson, 2006; Nieuwenhuis & Van Woerkom, 2007). Only a few works are situated in the context of higher education (three papers: Fetherston & Kelly, 2007; Hunt, 2009; Taylor & Pettit, 2007), and one refers to a cultural context (Fleming, 2000). Nevertheless, the larger category consists of the remaining nine papers, which cannot be placed in a particular context because they constitute pure theoretical approaches.

We should mention here that Taylor's review (2007) on forty papers—mainly written by American authors published between 1999 and 2005—had quite different outcomes. Most papers were concerned with higher education and professional development. The comparison of those data to our findings shows that European writers do focus more on activities of community development that take place in other continents, but mainly on theoretical research. These findings could be connected to the fact that, up to now, no significant nucleus of adult educators working on the implementation of transformative learning has been formed in Europe.

As far as the *issues* with which the papers are concerned, these are also different from those in Taylor's review. He has found that there was an emphasis on references to the analysis of the nature and components of transformative learning, as well as to the processes of its application and the methods that reinforce the process of perspective transformation. In our survey, we found that European writers focus only to a certain extent on the research of the very nature of transformative learning (there is one relevant reference: Alhadeff, 2003) and also that there is just one paper that describes the applications of transformation in a certain context (Fenson & Chesser-Smyth, 2009), while three others refer to the methods that reinforce transformative learning processes (Tosey, Mathison, & Michelli, 2005; Hunt, 2009; Kokkos, 2009). On the other hand, four papers elaborate on the issue of the relationship between transformative learning and social action (Duveskog & Friis-Hansen, 2007, 2009; Duveskog, Friis-Hansen, & Taylor, 2009; Harvey & Langdom, 2009). Still, the main finding is that most papers (fourteen) use several transformative learning theory concepts (such as "perspective transformation," "disorienting dilemma," "frame of reference") as well as its components (such as critical reflection, symbolic dimensions of learning, and the role of emotions) in relation to the exploration of various subjects, such as learning processes (Fertheston & Kelly, 2007; Fleming, 2000; Gray, 2006; Illeris, 2003, 2004; Karalis, 2010; Wilhelmson, 2005), research methods (Dominicé, 2003; Taylor & Pettit, 2007), social change (Preece, 2003; Taylor, Pettit, & Stackpool-Moore, 2005; Wilner & Dubouloz, 2010), and workplace processes (Nieuwenhuis & Van Woernom, 2007; Wilhelmson, 2006).

These findings indicate that the dominant trend for European writers is to not set the very nature and the applications of transformative learning theory as the main focus of their approaches. It appears that they tend to adopt its elements in order to assign further depth and argumentation in the elaboration of issues on which they intensively work. For instance, Fleming cites transformative learning theory only in the last part of his paper (2000), which focuses mainly on learning in the third age. He links the conclusions with the discussion of the role of critical reflection in transformative learning and argues that the emphasis on rational process was not easily identified in his study of educational work.

To further explore the *attitude of the European writers toward the framework of transformative learning*, we take a two-sided approach. The first was quantitative; it concerns the frequency in which references to (1) Mezirow's work, (2) the theoretical conceptions related to transformative learning, and (3) alternative views of perspective transformation (Freire, Boyd, Myers) appear in the papers. The second approach was qualitative; it aimed to investigate the way in which European writers integrate their works into the theoretical framework of transformative learning, as well as the ways in which they combine it with their own intellectual traditions on adult education.

Among the twenty-three papers that we examined, twenty-one contain references to Mezirow's work. The conclusion derived is that his conception is the basic resource in the European writers' work on transformative learning. However, most of them do not seem to have a comprehensive and up-to-date view of his entire work. It is characteristic that only two papers refer to his texts published after the year 2000. Furthermore, only ten papers refer to his articles or chapters in collective books and only five papers contain more than two references to his works.

There are very few references to the work of scholars who express conceptions related to transformative learning. Particularly, seven papers have references to Brookfield's work, seven to E. Taylor's, six to Cranton's, four to Kegan's, three to Greene's, two to Dirkx's and Marsick's, one paper to Belenky's, Elias's, and Kasl's, and another one to King and Kitchener's common work. These findings show that European writers are not highly involved in the ongoing discussion on transformative learning.

As far as references to the work of scholars who expressed alternative theoretical views of perspective transformation are concerned, Freire's work on critical pedagogy seems to maintain a crucial position in European adult educators' thoughts. Nine papers contain references to him and one more to his colleague Ira Shor. In contrast, only two papers have references to Boyd and Myer's work. This indicates that most of the European writers are not particularly concerned with the learning processes that take place outside awareness.

Concerning the results of our qualitative approach, first, it was confirmed that a few papers are framed in transformative learning theory (for example, Wilhelmson, 2005; Tosey, Mathison, & Michelli, 2005; Duveskog, Friis-Hansen, & Taylor, 2009; Kokkos, 2009). Also, four more attempt to combine the transformative learning framework with other approaches (Fetherston & Kelly, 2007; Gray, 2006; Preece, 2003; Karalis, 2010). Nevertheless, the rest of the papers (fifteen), which are the majority, do not use transformative learning theory as their primary theoretical framework. Their reflections derive from other theoretical origins, and their reference to the transformative learning framework aims at proving that they have globally covered the literature relevant to their subject matter. Characteristically, Taylor and Pettit (2007) write:

> Learning happens in action, however, and the complexity of working with processes of social change and associated power relationships leads to complexities of learning. There are useful theories of learning emerging, such as transformative learning theory (Mezirow & Associates, 2000), but there is not much evidence that application of this theory actually leads to transformation in the context of social change. (p. 239)

As far as European writers' conception of the theoretical framework of transformative learning is concerned, they focus on Mezirow's conception, and in most cases they are critical of his work. The dominant view is that his approach has strong cognitive emphasis and neglects other ways of knowing, such as the intuitive and emotional dimensions of learning (Fleming, 2000; Tosey, Mathison, & Michelli, 2005), the emotional and social aspects (Illeris, 2003, 2004), the collective dimension (Harvey & Langdom, 2009; Wilhelmson, 2006), the relational processes (Duveskog, Friis-Hansen, & Taylor, 2009), the relationship between learning and social change (Taylor & Pettit, 2007), and the impact of spirituality (Preece, 2003). Finally, two papers claim that Mezirow does not recognize the unconscious modalities for revising meaning structures (Hunt, 2009; Fetherston & Kelly, 2007).

On the other hand, the vast majority of the twenty-three papers contain many references to other theoretical approaches; the writers use these as background to their argumentation or combine them with components of the transformative learning framework. The scholars of the different theoretical approaches emphasized are mainly Europeans whose works contain a great number of elements of critical thinking and social dimensions of learning: Bourdieu, Foucault, Illeris, Giroux, Morin, Adorno, Horkheimer, Held, Outhwaite, Engeström, Gagné, hooks, Apps, Heron, Thompson, Jarvis, Kanpol, Bakhtin, Mayo, McLaren, and others. At this point we should mention that Stephen Brookfield's approach (2005) is very similar to this. Although he has been working in the United States for many years now, like his European colleagues he engages the work of European theorists, such as Marx, Gramsci, Althusser, Foucault, Habermas, and Fromm.

The basic *conclusion* that emerges from the survey is that the theory of transformative learning does not have concrete roots in the conceptual formation of the European adult educators. Most of the texts examined mainly build on European theoretical paradigms, and the authors do not see the need to place their work within the relatively new theory of transformative learning. On the other hand, it appears that adult educators in Europe believe that the theory of transformative learning shares elements with their own theoretical background and also that it needs to be enriched with various approaches.

This very fact leads us to the proposal for a process of more intense convergence between the European and the North American perspective. European scholars could gain much if they were more actively engaged with the discourse of a theory that is supposed to be "the most researched and discussed in the field of adult education for over 25 years" (Taylor, 2007, p. 73). And, mutually, incorporating elements of the European thought in the theory and practice of transformative learning—especially in what concerns the components of critical thinking, social context, societal change, and collective ways of knowing—would broaden its base and expand its potential.

A CASE STUDY: GREECE

Apart from the two papers to which we have already referred (Karalis, Kokkos), ten more works that concern transformative learning have been published by Greek authors: two books (Lintzeris, 2007; Chasidou, 2009), three chapters in collective books (Kalogridi, 2010; Lintzeris, 2010; Kokkos, 2010), and five papers (Lazaridou, Bokou, & Tsabouri, 2008; Kagiavi, 2009; Koulaouzides, 2008; Sifakis, 2007; Zarifis, 2004). All these texts have commonalities with those of the European writers. They all consider Mezirow's conception as dominant in the theoretical framework of transformative learning. Most of them (seven) include references to Freire's work and, additionally, contain many references to European scholars. On the other hand, most Greek papers, when compared to the European ones, deal more comprehensively with Mezirow's work and the theoretical resources that he drew on (mainly the Frankfurt School), as well as with the work of other transformative learning scholars (eight refer to Brookfield, seven to Cranton, five to Dirkx, five to E. Taylor, and so on).

Thus a question emerges: Why do we find such an intense interest on transformative learning in a country like Greece, with no strong tradition in adult education? We will attempt to approach this issue by connecting the findings from our review to the social and educational contexts in Greece.

Up to 1980, adult education activities in Greece were inconsequential (Karalis & Vergidis, 2006). However, 1981 saw the election to power of a social-democratic government, which placed as one of its priorities the consolidation of the institution of popular education, whose main objectives were citizens' personality development and their conscious participation in the social realm. Learner participation increased rapidly: from 60,000 in 1980 to 180,000 in 1985 (Karalis & Vergidis, 2006, p. 51). Simultaneously, the general secretariat of popular education (G.S.P.E.) was founded, assigning advisers of popular education in all fifty-one prefectures of the country. Their duties were to study educational needs, to coordinate educational activities, and to train the educators. Also, 1982 saw the founding of a nongovernmental institution, the Center for Studies and Self-Directed Learning, which, financed by the G.S.P.E., undertook the responsibility to supply the institution of popular education with ideas, theoretical support, texts, and materials. In addition, it undertook the training of the executive staff of G.S.P.E. and of the advisers of popular education. Those actions helped spread ideas and methods concerned with the growth of critical reflection in the field of adult education (Kokkos, 2008).

The members of the Center were inspired by the ideas of the School of Frankfurt but mainly by Freire's ideas, which were the ones suited to the radical sociopolitical climate prevailing in Greece at the time. Nevertheless, there was significant resistance against the efforts of the Center deriving mainly from the traditionally conservative Ministry of Education, to which G.S.P.E. and the advisers referred, but also from a considerable number of advisers and trainers, who were nurtured in the teacher-centered educational mentality. In any case, the period of 1982–1986 may be considered as the first in which discussions concerning the principles and the methods with which adult education can incorporate critical reflection activities took place. In the "Stone Age" that followed until the end of the twentieth century, a core of people safeguarded these ideals, brought them into their work settings, and paved the way for the new creative activities that started on a larger scale in the beginning of the twenty-first century (Kokkos, 2008).

Since 1987 and until the end of the twentieth century, within the frame of an ongoing conservatism in Greek social life, a by-product of the entanglement of the country in the processes of globalization and the concurrent predominance of the principles of extreme competition, consumerism, and individualism, the field of adult education faced a barren period. The financing of the institution of popular education shrank, and in the second half of the 1990s participants did not exceed fifteen to twenty thousand per year (Karalis & Vergidis, 2006, pp. 51–55). The financing of the Center of Studies and Self-Directed Learning stopped, which led to the end of its activities. Professional training provided mainly by speculative institutions prevailed in the field, while the quality of services and the production of scientific work remained at a very low level (UNESCO, 1997; Karalis & Vergidis, 2004).

However, new institutions were gradually developed. In 1998, Oone publishing house started a series entitled *Adult Education*, which as of this writing has published fifteen books, one of which is a translation of Mezirow and Associates' work (2000). The postgraduate program "Adult Education" of the Hellenic Open University started operating in 2003, followed by similar postgraduate programs at the Universities of Macedonia, Patras, and Athens. Two national programs for adult educators' training were organized from 2003 to 2008. These activities were facilitated by the Hellenic Adult Education Association, which was founded in 2004. The Association, which has nine hundred members, publishes the peer-reviewed Greek journal *Adult Education* (twenty-four volumes so far) and has also published five books. Simultaneously, the Association has organized international conferences, as well as experiential workshops on the training of trainers. In effect, the appropriate conditions were created that allowed the beginning of a new circle of essential discussion on the aims and methods of adult education. This discussion was developed mainly around transformative learning theory, which became the point of reference for adult educators who adopt emancipatory learning views (see Lintzeris, 2010; see also volumes 9, 11, 12, 17 of the journal *Adult Education*, including special tributes to transformative learning, as well as volumes 19, 23, and 24, with tributes to the 8th and 9th International Transformative Learning Conferences).

We identify two main reasons for this trend. First, the only theoretical tradition of adult education that ever existed in Greece arose in the 1980s, derived from Freire's idea of conscientization and the critical theory of the School of Frankfurt. Then, when after almost fifteen years the appropriate conditions were created for the development of theoretical reflection, Mezirow's ideas, which had been partially inspired by those theoretical resources (see Mezirow & Associates, 2000, p. xiii), were welcomed with enthusiasm by Greek adult educators, particularly those who had earlier participated in the movement of popular education and were now able to influence the new institutions. Second, because discussion on critical reflection in the Greek field of adult education takes place nowadays mainly in the private sector, in universities and in the Hellenic Adult Education Association, it is meeting less resistance. In particular, the Association's activities, which are organized and financed by its members and have voluntary attendance, ensure participation by those who are genuinely interested.

In these circumstances, the Greek movement for transformative learning has been evolving rapidly. A peak moment of these efforts was Mezirow's visit to Athens in 2007 and the undertaking by the Association of the responsibility to host the 9th International Conference on Transformative Learning in 2011. We hope that this conference contributed to the strengthening of the collaboration among European colleagues and to the reinforcement of the worldwide network of those who care for an adult education that strives for human emancipation.

References

Alhadeff, M. (2003, October 23–25). Rethinking transformative learning and the concept of "critical reflection" through the paradigm of complexity. In *Proceedings of the Fifth International Transformative Learning Conference*, New York, available at http://transformativelearning.org/

Brookfield, S. (2005). *The power of critical theory.* San Francisco: Jossey-Bass.

Chasidou, M. (2009). *Critical reflection and transformation in adult education through the art of theatre.* Athens: Hellenic Adult Education Association.

Cranton, P. (2006). *Understanding and promoting transformative learning.* San Francisco: Jossey-Bass.

Dirkx, J. (1998). Transformative learning theory in the practice of adult education: An overview. *PAACE Journal of Lifelong Learning, 7,* 1–14.

Dominicé, P. (2003, October 23–25). Transforming biography through the process of transformative learning. In *Proceedings of the Fifth International Transformative Learning Conference*, New York, available at http://transformativelearning.org/

Duveskog, D., & Friis-Hansen, E. (2007, October 24–26). Transformative learning in Farmer Field Schools: An entry point for change among resource-poor farmer in Africa. In *Proceedings of the Seventh International Transformative Learning Conference*, Albuquerque, New Mexico, available at: http://transformativelearning.org/

Duveskog, D., & Friis-Hansen, E. (2009, November 18–20). Farmer Field Schools and the agro/human eco-system analysis exercise. In *Proceedings of the Eighth International Transformative Learning Conference*, Bermuda, available at: http://transformativelearning.org/

Duveskog, D., Friis-Hansen, E., & Taylor, E. (2009, November 18–20). Perspective transformation in Kenyan Farmer Field Schools as a catalyst for relational change within the household and wider community. In *Proceedings of the Eighth International Transformative Learning Conference*, Bermuda, available at: http://transformativelearning.org/

Fenson, S., & Chesser-Smyth, P. (2009, November 18–20). Is critical practice prepared for nurses who journey through a transformative learning curriculum? In *Proceedings of the Eighth International Transformative Learning Conference*, Bermuda, available at http://transformativelearning.org/

Fetherston, B., & Kelly, R. (2007). Conflict resolution and transformative pedagogy: A grounded theory research on learning in higher education. *Journal of Transformative Education, 5*, 262–285.

Fleming, T. (2000, 3–5 July). Adding life to your years: Transformative learning for older people at the Irish Museum of Modern Art. In *Proceedings of SCUTREA's 30th Annual Conference*, Nottingham, available at: http://www.leeds.ac.uk/educol/documents/00001443.htm

Gray, D. (2006). Executive coaching: Towards a dynamic alliance of psychotherapy and transformative learning process. *Management Learning, 37*, 475–797.

Harvey, B., & Langdom, J. (2009, November 18–20). "Transformative learning in the defence and equitable use of natural resources: Experiences from Senegal and Ghana," in *Proceedings of the Eighth International Transformative Learning Conference*, Bermuda, available at: http://transformativelearning.org/

Hunt, C. (2009, November 18–20). Creative writing as a tool for transformative learning. In *Proceedings of the Eighth International Transformative Learning Conference*, Bermuda, available at: http://transformativelearning.org/

Illeris, K. (2003, October 23–25). Defence and resistance towards transformative learning. In *Proceedings of the Fifth International Transformative Learning Conference*, New York, available at: http://transformativelearning.org/

Illeris, K. (2004). Transformative learning in the perspective of a comprehensive learning theory. *Journal of Transformative Education, 2*, 79–89.

Jarvis, P. (1995). *Adult and continuing education: Theory and practice.* London: Routledge.

Kalogridi, S. (2010). The contribution of self-directed learning to adult education. In D. Vergidis & A. Kokkos (Eds.), *Adult education: International approaches and Greek trajectories* (pp. 127–163). Athens: Metaixmio.

Karalis, T. (2010). Situated and transformative learning: Exploring the potential of critical reflection to enhance organizational knowledge. *Development and Learning in Organizations, 24*, 17–20.

Karalis, T., & Vergidis, D. (2004). Lifelong education in Greece: Recent developments and current trends. *International Journal of Lifelong Education, 23*, 179–189.

Karalis, T., & Vergidis, D. (2006). *Evaluation de l'impact de la politique des fonds structurels européens sur l'institution de l'éducation polulaire en Grèce. Carrefours de l' Education, 21*, 45–58.

Kagiavi, M. (2009). The social dimension of AIDS: A seminar based on Mezirow's, Freire's, and Perkins's theories and techniques. *Adult Education, 17*, 3–10.

Kokkos, A. (2008). Adult education in Greece. *Convergence*, pp. 2–3, 59–73.

Kokkos, A. (2009, November 18–20). Transformative learning through aesthetic experience: Towards a comprehensive methodology. In *Proceedings of the Eighth International Transformative Learning Conference*, Bermuda, available at: http://transformativelearning.org/

Kokkos, A. (2010). Critical reflection: A critical issue. In D. Vergidis & A. Kokkos (Eds.), *Adult education: International approaches and Greek trajectories* (pp. 65–93). Athens: Metaixmio.

Koulaouzides, G. (2008). Transformative learning: A learning theory for adult education. *Pedagogical Review*, *46*, 21–32.

Lazaridou, T., Bokou, P., & Tsabouri, U. (2008). Simulating a teaching session: Kolb's learning circle and transformative learning in educational practice. *Adult Education*, *15*, 10–18.

Lintzeris, P. (2007). *The significance of critical reflection and discourse in Jack Mezirow's theory of transformative learning.* Athens: Hellenic Adult Education Association.

Lintzeris, P. (2010). Theory of transformative learning: Possibility for a critical and emancipatory turn of adult education. In D. Vergidis & A. Kokkos (Eds.), *Adult education: International approaches and Greek trajectories* (pp. 94–123). Athens: Metaixmio.

Merriam, S., Caffarella, R., & Baumgartner, L. (2007). *Learning in adulthood: A comprehensive guide.* San Francisco: Jossey-Bass.

Mezirow, J. (1983). A critical theory of adult learning and education. In M. Tight (Ed.), *Adult learning and education* (pp. 124–139). Maidenhead, Berkshire, UK: Open University Press.

Mezirow, J. (1991). *Transformative dimensions of adult learning.* San Francisco: Jossey-Bass.

Mezirow, J., & Associates (Eds.). (1990) *Fostering critical reflection in adulthood.* San Francisco: Jossey-Bass.

Mezirow, J., & Associates (Eds.). (2000). *Learning as transformation: Critical perspectives on a theory in progress.* San Francisco: Jossey–Bass.

Mezirow, J., Taylor, E. W., & Associates (Eds.). (2009). *Transformative learning in practice.* San Francisco: Jossey–Bass.

Nieuwenhuis, L., & Van Woerkom, M. (2007). Goal rationalities as a framework for evaluating the learning potential of the workplace. *Human Resource Development Review*, *6*, 64–83.

Preece, J. (2003). Education for transformative leadership in Southern Africa. *Journal of Transformative Education*, *1*, 245–263.

Sifakis, N. (2007). The education of teachers of English as a lingua franca: A transformative perspective. *International Journal of Applied Linguistics*, *17*, 355–375.

Taylor, E. (2007). An update of transformative learning theory: A critical review of the empirical research (1999–2005). *International Journal of Lifelong Education*, *26*, 173–191.

Taylor, E. (2008). Transformative learning theory. In S. Merriam (Ed.), *Third update on adult learning theory* (pp. 5–15). New Directions for Adult and Continuing Education, no. 119. San Francisco: Jossey-Bass.

Taylor. P., & Pettit, J. (2007). Learning and teaching participation through action research: Experiences from an innovative masters programme. *Action Research*, *5*, 231–247.

Taylor, P., Pettit, J., & Stackpool-Moore, L. (2005, July 5–7). Learning and teaching for transformation: insights from a collaborative learning initiative. In *Proceedings of SCUTREA's 35th Annual Conference*, Sussex, available at: http://www.leeds.ac.uk/educol/documents/142030.doc

Tosey, P., Mathison, J., & Michelli, D. (2005). Mapping transformative learning: The potential of neuro-linguistic programming. *Journal of Transformative Education*, *3*, 140–167.

UNESCO. (1997). *Adult education since the fourth international conference on adult education, Paris (1985)*. UNESCO, ED-97/WS/5.

Wilhelmson, L. (2005, October 6–9). Dialogue meetings as non-formal adult education in a municipal context, In *Proceedings of the Sixth International Transformative Learning Conference*, Michigan, available at: http://transformativelearning.org/

Wilhelmson, L. (2006). Transformative learning in joint leadership. *Journal of Workplace Learning*, *18*, 495–507.

Wilner, A., & Dubouloz, C.-J. (2010). Homegrown terrorism and transformative learning: An interdisciplinary approach to understanding radicalization. *Global Change, Peace, and Security*, *22*, 33–51.

Zarifis, G. (2004). Motivation, reflection, and transformative learning in Balkan languages learning programmes. In *Proceedings of ESREA's 4th European Research Conference*. Wroclaw: ESREA.

CHAPTER NINETEEN

International and Community-Based Transformative Learning

Olutoyin Mejiuni

Community-based transformative learning is collective transformative learning (Mezirow, 1991) of and among groups of people who share common interests and or identities and occupy a particular territory at a particular point in time. This chapter explores informal pedagogical activities and nonformal educational interactions that resulted in examining, questioning, validating and revising problematic frames of reference (sets of fixed assumptions and expectations—habits of mind, meaning perspectives, and mind sets) (Cranton, 1994; Mezirow, 2003) of members of some communities in some parts of the world outside North America. Although there is abundant literature on how transformative learning theory explains transformative learning at the individual level, not much has been written about how transformative learning theory explains, and enhances our understanding of, the process of perspective transformation at the collective or social level, especially as a result of nonformal education and pedagogical activities in community settings.

SOME COMMUNITY-BASED TRANSFORMATIVE LEARNING PROJECTS AND ACTIVITIES

In this section, summaries of five potentially transformative educational activities are provided, focusing on the purpose or objective of the activities, the participants in and the context of the educational endeavors, the frameworks that informed the contents and the methods of educational activities, and the fundamental shifts in perspectives observed. The five educational activities discussed in this section were chosen because they had been identified by either authors who documented them or this author as potential transformative learning activities; they had discernible pedagogical structures; they focused on a wide range of interest groups in different, yet similar contexts; and they took place in continents outside North America.

Kenya and Uganda (East Africa)

Duveskog and Friis-Hansen (2009) explored the transformative aspects of Farmer Field Schools (FFS) in Kenya and Uganda, in East Africa, and reflected on "how the learning tools applied facilitated critical thinking and transformation of mind-sets among rural poor" (p. 240). The authors were involved in the FFS program as advisors, consultants, and researchers. The FFS approach, developed in Indonesia, was introduced to East Africa in 1996 as "a means of facilitating critical decision-making skills among learners to deal with complex farming problems" (p. 242) in the East African context, where the poor derive their livelihood from agriculture and farmer education and extension are important tools for improving people's lives. The authors, however, observed that in traditional farmer education and extension service, "farmers are pushed into preconceived behaviours and actions, often with a form of uptake of externally designed technologies" (p. 241).

The approach of the FFS is guided by adult education, experiential, and action learning principles; the FFS is an institutional platform whereby farmers meet regularly in groups to study a particular topic in the areas of crop or livestock management and special topics that address broader livelihood issues. Participants hold regular weekly or biweekly meetings over a period scheduled and defined by group members. The process of learning involves regular field observations, relating such observations to the ecosystem, and "blending previous experience with new information to make improved crop or livestock management decision" (p. 241). Participants learn through hands-on practical learning situations, information sharing among peers, reflection on experiences, discussion and testing of ideas, and defining of strategies for action. Participants generate their own learning materials (drawings and posters), based on their observations in the field and consistent with local conditions. The skilled facilitators who guide the learning process are usually extension workers, agricultural technicians, or local farmers, trained for FFS facilitation. Facilitators are taught to take the backseat role, offer help and guidance in group learning processes, and stimulate dialogue and reflection, so that farmers can challenge habitual ways of thinking and acting.

Duveskog and Friis-Hansen (2009) reported that participants diversified farming systems, tried technological solutions to a greater extent than nonparticipant farmers, gained confidence to experiment with selling produce to higher levels of value chain, and changed from the mind set of risk minimization to opportunity search. Participants also demonstrated an increase in self-confidence in terms of how they perceive their roles versus the role of experts. A female farmer enthused: "Before I joined the FFS, if somebody asked me what I do, I used to say 'nothing.' Now I proudly answer: 'I am a farmer'" (p. 240). These changes are congruent with the definition of collective transformative learning provided at the beginning of this chapter. Farmers challenged authorities and participated more in community decision-making processes—community meetings, voting in local elections, and holding leadership positions. Farmer networks and associations also emerged as a follow-up effect of FFS. They work to break manipulative relationships with trade middlemen and so gain access to more lucrative markets to sell their products.

South Africa (Southern Africa)

In her autobiography, Govender (2007) described how, as media officer for the Garment Workers' Industrial Union (GWIU) in Durban, Natal Province, South Africa, and the national educator for the Garment and Allied Workers' Union (GAWU) of South Africa in 1987, she initiated the first campaign against the practice of strip-searching in Durban's largest clothing factories, and organized and facilitated at workshops that sought to develop and empower women (leaders) within GAWU. In 1987, South Africa was under white minority and apartheid rule, the majority of clothing workers were women, and they endured strip-searching and sexual harassment on top of poor wages. The women also seldom elected women into leadership positions at all levels, because they had internalized society's beliefs about women's roles and capabilities.

After Govender was employed as media officer (a role in which she was also expected to work on everything from education to organizing) for GWIU, two women were strip-searched at one of Durban's largest clothing factories. She convened a lunchtime meeting with shop stewards in the factory. Women, old and young, wept as they shared their experience of strip-searching of the most private parts of their bodies and beings, which had become routine practice in the industry. They reflected on their experiences, mapped a course of action, investigated more cases, and made a list of demands. Govender described the meeting as a catalyst for resistance. At a meeting with the personnel manager, who consistently ignored the women workers, the manager told their media officer that the women were being strip-searched because of theft in the factories and that the search was done decently.

On the Friday after the meeting, workers joined hands as they marched out of the factory, singing the anthem of the African National Congress (ANC) loudly, even though it was banned at that time. The ANC was one of the leading anti-apartheid organizations in South Africa. Govender reported that in the face of this solidarity no guard dared strip and search any of them. Although management responded to this action with hostility, many more creative strategies were employed in factories to stop strip-searching. In one case, women refused to vacate the factory floor after work. They instead invited the manager over and started exposing different parts of their bodies to the manager, taunting him to search them. The manager fled as the women howled with laughter. Govender said strip-searching stopped even before any written agreement was negotiated.

During the workshops for women leaders within GAWU, Govender got women to share their ideas and images of women. She said they shared "a depressing litany of all the stereotypes we are told we are" (p. 96). She challenged them to think about the logic of their beliefs about women (about themselves) and placed this in the context of their work conditions and the fact that women constituted the majority of garment workers. Intense discussions followed; women recounted painful experiences from girlhood that had weakened their sense of self and embroiled them in power play (driven by men) with other women, instead of exercising collective power with women. Two years after these workshops, the leadership of GAWU at all levels had become overwhelmingly female. This is a result of collective transformation of beliefs and mind-sets about who women are—and can be.

Nigeria (West Africa)

In their review of the transformational learning potential of the intervention efforts of a nongovernmental organization—Women Against Rape, Sexual Harassment, and Sexual Exploitation (WARSHE) that operates in Southwest Nigeria, Mejiuni and Obilade (2004) indicated that WARSHE intervention efforts, which include education, counseling, and support, are not just consciousness-raising projects; they are also "grounds for mobilizing young women (and men) for collective action for improving women's social status" (p. 242). WARSHE was established in 1998 to help children, girls, and women prevent sexual violence and abuse (SVA) and cope with these abuses when they happen.

The authors, who are WARSHE volunteers and facilitators at WARSHE education program, observed that in Nigeria, different modes of power—gender, seniority, and class—interact to result in varying degrees of oppression of women, and so sexual violence and abuse of children, girls, and women is commonplace. They analyzed WARSHE awareness raising talks (ARTs), which are education program for mothers who attend child welfare clinics; symposia and intensive training workshops (ITW) that target female students and a few male students, as well as academic and nonacademic staff of tertiary institutions; and her counseling and support efforts. The ARTs, symposia, and ITWs run for fifteen to twenty minutes, three to three-and-a-half hours, and a whole day, respectively. The language of instruction for the ARTs is Yoruba (the language of the people of Southwest Nigeria) and pidgin English, whereas English is used for the symposia and ITWs. The education programs address the different dimensions of the problem of sexual violence and abuse, and volunteers focus on and deconstruct power that shapes the Nigerian sociocultural context in their intervention efforts. WARSHE adopts the Freirean approach and feminist framework in her intervention work.

The techniques adopted by WARSHE include provision of information through short talks and presentation of lead papers, questioning and contesting positions, witnessing to sexual violence and abuse and other forms of oppression of women, sharing experiences, and group work. Participants also put forward suggestions for action, point out priority actions, and, in the case of ITWs, select the steering committee of WARSHE in the concerned institution that will work with the secretariat of WARSHE to implement priority actions. Facilitators are WARSHE volunteers and specialists who share the vision of WARSHE. Mejiuni and Obilade said that as a result of a symposium, a university lecturer changed her belief about why young women are harassed and raped, and that as a result of WARSHE counseling and support, two rape victims and a relation gained confidence and challenged their assailants, even though the assailants had brought economic, state, and generational power to bear on the cases. This is an illustration of transformative learning in action. In addition, student volunteers actively "supported rape victims as they sought medical attention, and during court appearances" (p. 242). Mejiuni and Obilade also wrote about one rape victim who appeared disoriented after an ART, and another woman who taught that making men happy was the best way to proceed after an ITW.

Malta (Europe)

Mayo (2003, 2007) described the transformations that occurred as a result of a parental empowerment project in a state primary school in a working-class locality in the South of Malta. At the time of the project in 1995, the school in question was one of the most densely populated in Malta, and formal educational achievement in the locality was low. Mayo indicated that a middle-class parent who was a member of the school council approached him and a colleague with the council's wish to begin a parental empowerment project.

Fifty parents, all women, attended the first meeting that addressed the issue of homework. The parent coordinator and staff had identified homework as a topic on the minds of mothers and female guardians. The first session, coordinated by one of the two resource persons, was a mixture of teaching and dialogue. Subsequent agendas were introduced by parents after discussions with project coordinators and identification of priority areas. Other themes identified included creative expression and teaching of English. Mayo described the process of teaching and dialogue as a process of co-investigation, so that sessions do not degenerate into laissez-faire pedagogy, and the authority enjoyed by the guest speaker does not harden into authoritarianism. The Freirean approach shaped the project.

The author said that only thirty of the fifty women consistently attended each meeting. When asked why this was so, the women said their husbands work in the evenings, and there was the patriarchal notion that a child's schooling is the mother's business. One mother opined that others did not attend the meetings because they thought it was "being held the way it used to be held in the past . . . that he (the speaker) is the only one who speaks" (Mayo, 2007, p. 257). Mayo (2007) recorded participants as saying that in the meetings they held before, they just listened to the experts. They were, according to one woman, "like fools" (p. 257). But in this project, they found that someone was prepared to listen to them, they discussed among themselves, and even when they did not agree on everything, they said what they felt was good for their children's education, and the organization of learning transaction was also different.

According to Mayo (2003, 2007), participants noted that their demands were immediately taken up. The school arranged a visit to a museum and similar places the week after cultural outings were mentioned at a meeting. Parents said pupils were beginning to speak English at home and during English lessons in school. They were satisfied that things were happening, even if not quickly. Author surmised that parents clamored for a role that was at odds with that ascribed to them by educational administrators and teachers, and through this project they moved from the role of "adjunct" to that of "subjects." Mayo said the "victories" have inspired confidence, such that parents placed pressure on the school to publish its own newsletter and run a family literacy program. Illustrating a collective transformative experience, the female participants have also organized into a women's group called MaraMediterra, which is based in the locality, and deals with issues larger than parental involvement in the child's primary schooling.

Bolivia (South America)

Hansman and Wright (2009) reported that in Cochabamba, Bolivia, South America, the education department of a community-based popular education organization, the Oficina Juridica Para la Mujer (Women's Legal Office: OJM) runs a legal promoters' course. The OJM was conceived in 1984 as "an option for poor women who needed training in the defense of their rights, and protection from family and societal violence" (p. 208). Participants in the OJM's legal promoters' course are trained to provide legal assistance to women, particularly those with limited resources, and to refer them to the OJM for further free legal assistance. The course covers training in the knowledge of the law and how to facilitate learning. The authors' reflections on the OJM program is based on data that one of them collected as a participant-observer in the legal promoters' course.

The framework that informed the work of the OJM was critical theory and popular education, and the contents of the workshops for the legal promoters are "constantly revised and enriched according to the perceptions of the facilitators, the needs of the participants, and social conditions" (p. 210). The content is planned strategically to fall within the most effective time frames—to prepare for elections and to address violence against women at a time during the course when the mostly female participants would be comfortable speaking to those issues.

The course is organized into workshops in the classroom, institutional visits, workshops for evaluation and reinforcement, and special events (seminars and field trips) as they arise; the program runs from February to October each year. There is also an action component of the curriculum. The authors described the methodology of the OJM program as participatory and living, as it uses role-play, small group work, storytelling, field visits, research homework, and multimedia tools. The technique for connecting learners to the subject of interest was reflection and discussion; the language of facilitation was Spanish for urban area courses and indigenous languages (Quechua and Aymara) in rural areas.

There were shifts in attitudes and self-images. One woman said she used to be shy and fearful but the OJM program has given her courage and taught her to honor herself; once she started valuing herself, her husband began to value her. A facilitator expressed the view that some of those who take part in the program as leaders become more powerful when they return to their organizations and communities; they move higher up in the leadership and motivate others to critically reflect on the situation of women in Cochobamba and around the world. They also reported the action part of a particular course. Thirty course participants attended the sentencing of a public official who had raped and impregnated his employee. The rapist reportedly received six years in prison. Though not the ideal punishment for the offense, it went beyond the realistic expectations of the OJM defense attorneys, given prevailing power relations.

COMMON THEMES

In this section I tease out those factors and issues that are enablers of transformative learning in the community-based educational endeavors discussed in the preceding section.

Experience and Frame of Reference

Participants in the educational interactions that led to transformative learning have had a deep personal experience of a situation or relationship, and this included the experience of a pedagogical practice. Some have held beliefs and attitudes that constricted their lives. Hansman and Wright (2009) reported that in Bolivia, the women OJM works with have often faced domestic violence in their personal lives and historical marginalization in the traditional male sphere of social action. In Malta, parents said that in the meetings they held prior to the parental empowerment project they only listened to experts; the experts did not listen to them, so they felt like fools. In Kenya, a female farmer's experience of farming before joining the Farmer Field School was such that she denied being a farmer. In South Africa, female factory workers had experienced humiliating strip searches conducted in clothing factories, and they had also believed that "women are gossips," they "can't unite over anything," and so on (Govender, 2007, p. 96). In Nigeria, a female lecturer had believed the dominant discourse that young women cause rape and sexual harassment by the way they dress, even though a teenager and a young woman had experienced rape and continuous harassment and humiliation by their assailants. Participants in the educational interactions reviewed brought negative experiences, feelings, and beliefs to the educational setting.

Triggers for Transformative Learning

The content of educational interactions, the methods adopted, the frameworks that informed them, and the dialogue that took place among learners and between learners and facilitators were the triggers for transformative learning in the cases cited in this review. Mayo (2003) told us that the Freirean approach was adopted in the parental empowerment program in Malta, and the project was "socially committed action research" (p. 51). Through consultation and dialogue, themes were selected for "co-investigation," and the process ensured that the object of investigation connected with parents' thematic universe. Mayo (2003) said they also listened to parents, as Freire advocated in *Pedagogy of Freedom.* For their part, Duveskog and Friis-Hansen (2009) said the approach adopted by the FFS is guided by adult education, experiential, and action learning principles. Their description of the FFS project fits Boud's (2005) description of experiential learning and Marsick and Kuhn's (2005) description of action learning. The other education projects identified their frameworks and approaches. WARSHE in Nigeria used consciousness raising (Hart, 1990), the Freirean approach, and the feminist framework. The OJM in Bolivia adopted popular education and critical theory. Although Govender (2007) self-identified a feminist influence on her work, it is clear that she also employed consciousness raising, which was influenced by critical theory (Merriam & Cafarrella, 1999).

From the foregoing, one can say that the content and methods that these approaches and frameworks inspired were counter-discourses (Hernendez, 1997; Mayo, 2003) to the dominant discourses that participants had known, had been made to believe, had believed, or had lived with.

The Role of Facilitators

The role of facilitators in the educational interactions reviewed here can be placed along a continuum ranging from those that took the back seat (facilitators in the FFS project) to those that were "directive," interspersing dialogue with brief expositions (the parental empowerment project), to those that were interventionist, in which facilitators and participants share experiences that they all critically reflect on; facilitators take participants through a process of meaning-making, such that they feel challenged to act, and facilitators guide the process of action. The projects in South Africa, Nigeria, and Bolivia fall into the last two categories identified on the continuum. Whereas participants and facilitators, regardless of their position on the continuum, were cocreators of knowledge, it seems that the facilitators who were interventionist on the continuum overtly pushed for social change.

It is significant that almost all the authors of the education projects under review were participants in the projects, as facilitators, consultants, and so on. The reflections of the authors on the educational projects they had participated in hold a lot of possibilities and pose some challenges. Some of those challenges are highlighted later in this chapter.

From the Particular to the General, from the Personal to the Social

Almost all the education projects reviewed focused first on participants' personal experience and the beliefs held by individuals and groups. These were then placed in a wider socioeconomic, political, and cultural context. Through reflection on these experiences and beliefs, the programs exposed and interrogated what Merriam and Caffarella (1999) referred to as "the structured nature of power relations and interlocking systems of oppression based on gender, race, and class" (p. 359). The meetings and workshops for female garment workers in South Africa began with the exploration of the problem of strip-searching in factories and the gross underrepresentation of women in the leadership of the garment workers' union, then moved to the interrogation of women's social status in the context of racism and apartheid rule. The WARSHE education interaction in Nigeria focuses on sexual violence and abuse and moves to questioning women's inferior social status in Nigeria. In Bolivia, the OJM program that demystifies the law and teaches women their legal rights and how to teach others their legal rights helps women to "develop critical consciousness about themselves, their context, and their society" (p. 214); the FFS project in East Africa addresses technical issues, group dynamics, and special topics relating to broader livelihood issues.

Bonding and Unity Forged During Educational Interactions

Hansman and Wright (2009) said "a sense of community in an educational setting emerged as essential to transforming . . . lives" (p. 214) in the OJM program. Participants in the FFS projects in East Africa attributed achievements to "the social bonding that take place within the FFS context" (Duveskog and Friis-Hansen, 2009, p. 244). Govender (2007) reported unity and bonding among African and Indian women garment workers in the actions they took to stop strip-searching and also reported that unity was built through the workshops organized for shop stewards. Unity and bonding were implied in the reflections on the Nigeria and Malta projects. Mejiuni and Obilade (2004) said that student volunteers actively supported rape victims as they sought medical attention and during court appearances, and Mayo (2007) reported that women participants in the parental empowerment project have organized into a women's group dealing with issues larger than their involvement in their children's education. Essentially, bonding and unity forged during educational interactions contributed to transformative learning and also served as the basis for social action.

The common themes just identified enable transformative learning and so enhance our understanding of why transformative learning occurred in the cases cited. The question now is: What remaining issues are relevant to transformative learning yet unresolved or not properly addressed in the educational interactions cited in this chapter?

ISSUES THAT ARE YET UNRESOLVED

From the reflections on the educational interactions cited in this chapter, one came away with the impression that all participants in three of the five projects (the Bolivia, Malta, and South Africa projects) experienced transformative learning and perhaps also sustained it such that social change resulted. The authors of the OJM project implied that it resulted in personal and large-scale structural and political change. However, Duveskog and Friis-Hansen (2009) said there were instances when farmers felt powerless and unable to make significant changes in their lives after they had participated in FFS. Mejiuni and Obilade (2004) reported that one woman was deeply pained and confused after a WARSHE program; another had not made any movement toward transformative learning.

There is no evidence to show that the changes in feelings, beliefs, and behavior that resulted from the five educational interactions reviewed are sustainable. Perhaps the authors did not set out to attend to such concerns. The example of powerlessness felt by farmers in Kenya after participation in FFS ought to compel us to focus on the sustainability of transformative learning (whether the observed fundamental changes in attitudes, beliefs, feelings, and behavior remain with the individual or community for a long time) because of the peculiar nature of the contexts and periods in which educational interactions take place and in which transformative learning occurs. We should therefore be alert to possibilities of backsliding (Mezirow, 1991) and reverting back to a previous perspective after a transformative learning experience.

This review also highlights the challenges of fostering transformative learning, reflecting on it, and writing about one's practice. The authors of the five projects cited in this chapter are practitioners and researchers. As researchers, they were participant observers in the projects they described, so they probably faced the dilemma that Marshall (1998) said participant-observers are forever trapped in: how to balance adequate subjectivity with adequate objectivity. To resolve this dilemma, participant-observers may understate or overstate the impact of the processes they had been a part of. Although it is difficult to measure the overall impact of community-based transformative learning on the social change that occurs in a community, a useful approach would be to explicitly state the specific social changes that have occurred as a result, as Duveskog and Friis-Hansen did, and or situate collective transformative learning that occurred within other social change processes, as Govender did. The reflections of Mejiuni and Obilade and Hansman and Wright were not keyed into local, national, and international social change processes. Although Mejiuni and Obilade did not say that all women who took part in WARSHE programs experienced transformative learning, they could have assessed transformative learning resulting from WARSHE educational interactions in the context of the clamor for democracy and respect for human rights and women's rights in Nigeria, beginning from the early 1990s. After all, it is usually a series of micro educational interventions that target different interest groups within communities that result in macro community transformative learning in particular circumstances. It is perhaps this lack of connection of the impact of collective transformative learning involving small groups to other social change processes that makes Hansman and Wright's (2009) position about the impact of the OJM program seem like an overstatement. They said, "We believe that the legal Promoter's Course, with this combination of personal and large-scale structural and political change, can serve as a guide for popular education programs that seek to empower women and create long-term social change" (p. 215).

Another outstanding issue is how to manage the (potential) consequences of fostering transformative learning. Duveskog and Friis-Hansen (2009) and Mejiuni and Obilade (2004) did not speak to how participants who had experienced powerlessness and pain were supported. The experiences of the participants in FFS and WARSHE projects can lead to frustration and despair—and grave consequences, if support is not forthcoming. There is also the issue of compulsion in educational interactions. Adults ought to access and participate in education programs voluntarily. Therefore, if there have indeed been or are to be fundamental shifts in attitudes, beliefs, feelings, and new insights on issues, adults should voluntarily participate in actions meant to effect social change. One is therefore uncomfortable that Hansman and Wright said the OJM facilitators "found that compelling course participants to action, followed by reflective activities, enhanced learning and transformation among participants" (p. 213). Or is this compulsion by force of argument?

Finally, there is a need for finer details on how facilitators assisted learners in the educational interactions cited in this chapter to center and or decenter culture and cultural identities, given the influence of culture on transformative learning (Merriam & Ntseane, 2008)—especially on collective transformative learning. An examination of how culture may impact dialogue and discourse—an important element in the transformative learning process—is relevant here. In line with the theme of this chapter, the culture that I focus on is one defined by the degree of cohesion among group members, identified as collectivist and individualistic cultures. In collectivist cultures, individuals see themselves first as members of one or more groups, and they are motivated by the values, norms, duties, and obligations imposed by the group. They are loyal to the group (Liu, 2010), or they completely identify with the group. Mezirow (1991) described this as having an organic relationship with the group. Liu (2010) posited that in contrast to collectivist cultures, persons in individualist cultures have less respect for and loyalty to their groups. Whether in individualist or collectivist cultures, dialogue with others to validate an alternative perspective may not be required in individual perspective transformation, because the individual can dialogue with herself, her forebears, and with the Almighty. However, dialogue with fellow humans in the social world is a requirement for collective perspective transformation. Unfortunately, in collectivist cultures, dialogue and discourse, which involves the examination of existing frames of reference and validation of alternative perspectives, is problematic because participants are expected to question both the self that is loyal to the group and the values and norms that the group holds true and dear and that shape their social context. This is not to say that collectivist groups and communities do not gain emancipatory knowledge—the third domain of knowledge identified by Habermas, whose work had an influence on

Mezirow's (1991) transformative learning theory. They do gain it—and that is why we need more information about how facilitators assist adults to negotiate and balance group loyalty in questioning constricting perspectives and examining alternative perspectives.

DIALOGUE, REFLECTIVE DISCOURSE, AND THE CASE FOR COUNTER-DISCOURSE

Discourse is one of the essential components of transformative learning theory and process. In the literature, rational reflective discourse and dialogue are used interchangeably to mean the process of learning through validity testing and consensus building in speech acts (Mezirow, 1991; Cranton, 1994). Taylor (2009), delicately sorts dialogue from discourse, when he says, "Dialogue becomes the medium for critical reflection to be put into action, where experience is reflected on, assumptions and beliefs are questioned, and habits of mind are ultimately transformed" (p. 9). Mezirow (1991) distinguishes theoretical, practical, and therapeutic discourse by what they challenge; respectively, the claim to truth about the knowledge we hold about the world; the rightness of norms, ideal, values, and moral decisions, especially when used as standards; and the authenticity of feelings or intents.

I wish to step back from Mezirow's conception of discourse as challenge, or ability to reason, and apprehend discourse as speech, writing, and other communicative acts, "seen from the point of view of the beliefs, values and categories which it embodies; these beliefs, etc. constitute a way of looking at the world, an organization or representation of experience" (Roger Fowler, cited in Mills, 2004, p. 5). Mezirow also came to this position, in his paper titled "Transformative Learning as Discourse" (2003). The point here is that statements and writings about the knowledge we hold true about the world, the norms that we use as standards, or our feelings and intents, "are enacted within a social context . . . determined by that social context . . . and contribute to the way that social context continues its existence" (Mills, 2004, p. 10). This is an integration of power relations into the understanding of the term "discourse." Before Mills, Gee (1990) had posited that discourse, the "little d," refers to language-in-use, whereas the combination of language with other social practices within a specific group is Discourse the "big D." Gee believes that language is always used from a perspective and always occurs within a context.

Mezirow himself admitted that the conditions that he prescribed as necessary for his widely known conception of reflective discourse (or should we just say dialogue?) assume "perfectability of human beings" (2000, p. 8). Surely, given that productive and also hegemonic and oppressive "power and influence are endemic in our lives" (Mezirow, 2003, p. 53), the conditions that are necessary for reflective discourse do not exist in many communities and institutions in most parts of the world. This is especially so in communities where social and collective identities are strong, which is the case in almost all the countries where the educational interactions described in the chapter took place. Too often, persons, groups, and institutions that possess power resources shape the discourse around problematic frames of reference that individuals and groups in a community and adult educators may want to change. But because dialogue is a requirement for community transformation, counter-discourses are required. At any rate, counter- and alternative discourses are often present in groups and communities even if they exist on the edge. Transformative learning occurred in the educational interactions cited in this chapter because the discourses offered and imagined in those spaces, which participants reflected on and juxtaposed with their prior experiences and beliefs, were alternative discourses or counter-discourses to the ones offered and generally agreed on in the groups and communities to which participants belong. Cranton (1994) said as much when she indicated that "learning occurs when an individual enters a process of reconciling newly communicated ideas with the presuppositions of prior learning" (p. 27). In reality, discourses do not occur in isolation but in dialogue, and in relation to or in contrast and opposition to other discourses (Mills, 2004). It is when there are discourses and counter-discourses that a broad consensus, which Mezirow advocates, can be reached. Otherwise, groups mobilize power resources (numerical strength, economic, and political and cultural power, including power of knowledge production and dissemination and at times, regrettably, violence) around a discourse (a counter-discourse), to displace the discourse that has become dominant or hegemonic.

So when we talk about the core elements of transformative learning theory and process, should we not be talking about "discourse(s) and counterdiscourse(s)" instead of "discourse"? In practice, adult educators who wish to foster transformative learning deliberately provide, or help learners imagine, alternative discourse(s).

IMPLICATIONS FOR PRACTICE AND FUTURE RESEARCH

From this review, one can conclude that adult educators, who wish to foster collective transformation in informal and community settings, can draw from a rich reservoir of approaches (Freirean, experiential learning, action learning, and consciousness raising) and frameworks (popular education, feminist framework, and critical theory, among others).

From the concerns raised about the need to situate collective transformative learning within other social change processes, it appears there is a need to focus more on narratives as an approach for documenting practitioners' reflections on their practice of fostering transformative learning. Narratives such as biography, autobiography, history or herstory, and also fiction, afford authors the space to place observed changes in context.

There is a need for longitudinal studies in the area of sustainability of collective transformation, and also to track backsliding during and after a (potentially) transformative learning process. Finally, we ought to incorporate counter-discourse along with discourse as an important component of transformative learning theory and process.

References

Boud, D. (2005). Experiential learning. In L. M. English (Ed.), *International encyclopedia of adult education* (pp. 243–245). New York: Palgrave Macmillan.

Cranton, P. (1994). *Understanding and promoting transformative learning: A guide to educators of adults.* San Francisco: Jossey-Bass.

Duveskog, D., & Friis-Hansen, E. (2009). Farmer Field Schools: A platform for transformative learning in rural Africa. In J. Mezirow, E. W. Taylor, & Associates (Eds.), *Transformative learning in practice: Insights from community, workplace, and higher education* (pp. 240–250). San Francisco: Jossey-Bass.

Gee, J. P. (1990). *Social linguistics and literacies: Ideology in discourses. Critical perspectives on literacy and education.* London: Falmer Press.

Govender, P. (2007). *Love and courage: A story of insubordination.* Aukland Park, SA: JacanaMedia (Pty) Ltd.

Hansman, C. A., & Wright, J. K. (2009). Popular education, women's work, and transforming lives in Bolivia. In J. Mezirow, E. W. Taylor, & Associates (Eds.), *Transformative learning in practice: Insights from community, workplace, and higher education* (pp. 205–215). San Francisco: Jossey-Bass.

Hart, M. U. (1990). Liberation through consciousness raising. In J. Mezirow & Associates (Eds.), *Fostering critical reflection in adulthood: A guide to transformative and emancipatory learning* (pp. 47–73). San Francisco: Jossey-Bass.

Hernendez, A. (1997). *Pedagogy, democracy, and feminism: Rethinking the public sphere.* Albany, NY: State University of New York Press.

Liu, J. (2010). Culture and knowledge transfer: Theoretical considerations. *Journal of Service Science and Management, 3*(1), 159–164. Retrieved from http://www.doaj .org/doaj?func=openurl&genre=journal&issn=19409893&volume=03&issue= 01&date=2010&uiLanguage=en

Marshall, G. (1998). *Oxford dictionary of sociology.* Oxford: Oxford University Press.

Marsick, V. J., & Kuhn, J. S. (2005). Action learning. In L. M. English (Ed.), *International encyclopedia of adult education* (pp. 15–19). New York: Palgrave Macmillan.

Mayo, P. (2003). A rationale for a transformative approach to education. *Journal of Transformative Education*, *1*(1), 39–57.

Mayo, P. (2007). Learning communities: Schools, parents, and challenges for wider community involvement in schools. *International Journal About Parents in Education*, *1*(0), 256–264.

Mejiuni, O., & Obilade, O. O. (2004). No pains, no gains: Exploring the dimensions of power in poverty reduction, through transformational learning. In J. Preece (Ed.), *Adult education and poverty reduction: A global priority* (pp. 240–245). Gaborone: Department of Adult Education, University of Botswana. Retrieved from http://www.gla.ac.uk/centres/cradall/docs/Botswana-papers/mejiunifinal_53.pdf

Merriam, S. B., & Caffarella, R. S. (1999). *Learning in adulthood: A comprehensive guide.* San Francisco: Jossey-Bass.

Merriam, S. B., & Ntseane, G. (2008). Transformational learning in Botswana: How culture shapes the process. *Adult Education Quarterly*, *58*(3), 183–197.

Mezirow, J. (1991). *Transformative dimensions of adult learning.* San Francisco: Jossey-Bass.

Mezirow, J. (2000). Learning to think like an adult: Core concepts of transformation theory. In J. Mezirow & Associates (Eds.), *Learning as transformation: Critical perspectives on a theory in progress* (pp. 3–33). San Francisco: Jossey-Bass.

Mezirow, J. (2003). Transformative learning as discourse. *Journal of Transformative Education*, *1*(1), 58–63.

Mills, S. (2004). *Discourse.* New York: Routledge. Retrieved from Questia Media America, Inc., www.questia.com

Taylor, E. W. (2009). Fostering transformative learning. In J. Mezirow, E. W. Taylor, & Associates (Eds.), *Transformative learning in practice: Insights from community, workplace, and higher education* (pp. 3–17). San Francisco: Jossey-Bass.

PART FOUR

TRANSFORMATIVE LEARNING: CENTRAL CONCEPTS AND SETTINGS

Critical Reflection and Transformative Learning

Carolin Kreber

T he ability to reflect critically on the assumptions underlying what is communicated to us, and those informing our own perceptions, thoughts, feelings, and actions, is of fundamental importance in order to address the challenges, responsibilities, and complexities associated with adult life. It is seen as imperative for sustaining positive personal relationships (Brookfield, 1987), productivity and well-being in the workplace (Fook & Askeland, 2007; Rigg & Trehan, 2008; Yorks & Marsick, 2000; Schön, 1983), and a healthy democracy (Brookfield, 2001; Dewey, 1916; Giroux, 1983, 2010; Habermas, 1983; Nussbaum, 2010). Critical reflection is considered essential for reaching decisions on complex issues affecting individuals and society and, therefore, is widely espoused as a principal goal of adult and higher education (Barnett, 1997; Brookfield, 1987; Freire, 1970; Giroux & Giroux, 2004; Lindeman, 1926; Mezirow & Associates, 1990; Nussbaum, 1997, 2010). There is a general sense that engagement in critical reflection makes adult learning more profound (for example, Mezirow, 1991), and some go so far as to contend that without it not only our learning and professional practice but also our life opportunities would be constrained and diminished (Brookfield, 1995, 2000; Nussbaum, 2000). However, critical reflection is also a contested concept. The theorists just referenced would presumably agree on a good number of features they associate with this notion but argue over others. How then might we understand "critical reflection"?

In this chapter I explore the meaning of critical reflection in the context of Mezirow's (1991) Transformation Theory. I first discuss its concern with ideology critique to differentiate it from more traditional notions of critical thinking. I then briefly review several theoretical influences on Mezirow's conception of critical reflection before focusing my discussion on Habermas and Dewey. I show that Mezirow's later distinction between objective and subjective reframing (1998, 2000) can be traced back to these two traditions. Later in the chapter I turn to strategies that might foster critical reflection, offer a brief analysis of the role of emotions in relation to critical reflection, and raise some issues relevant to researching critical reflection.

WHAT IS "CRITICAL" ABOUT CRITICAL REFLECTION?

Critical reflection is certainly closely related to reflective thinking (for example, Dewey, 1910/1991), critical thinking (Siegel, 1988), and reflective practice (for example, Schön, 1983); however, an important feature that distinguishes critical reflection from these other constructs is its strong foundation in critical theory (for example, Freire, 1970; Habermas, 1971, 1983; Gramsci, 1971) and variations of it enriched by postmodern ideas (Brookfield, 1995, 2000; Giroux, 1983, 2010; Tierney, 1993; Tierney & Rhoads, 1993). It is this critical theory tradition that connects reflection explicitly with social and political purposes and ideology critique, and hence makes it *critical.* According to this perspective, the focus of critical reflection is on revealing "submerged power dynamics and relationships" and on surfacing assumptions "that we accept as being in our own best interest without realizing that these same assumptions actually work against us in the long term by serving the interests of those opposed to us" (Brookfield, 2000, pp. 137–138)—the latter, in keeping with Gramsci (1971), often referred to as "hegemonic assumptions."

There are obviously similarities but also differences between a conception of critical reflection inspired by critical theory and that underlying the traditional critical-thinking literature. The latter conceives of a critically thinking person as someone who is "appropriately moved by reasons" (Siegel, 1988, p. 32) and has acquired the reasoning skills, abilities, and dispositions—including various judgmental, reflective, and creative/intuitive ones—needed to define and solve a problem in a logical way (for example, Ennis, 1991; Paul, 1992; Siegel, 1988). Critical thinking thus construed is principled and based on *criteria.* Taken by itself, it is also "politically neutral." Of course this does not mean that some dispositions, skills, and abilities do not matter when examining power relations or hegemonic assumptions; to the contrary, they would seem essential for that. Nussbaum (1997, 2010), for example, argues that developing the ability to think critically about one's beliefs is a necessity for promoting greater intercultural understanding and challenging traditions.

An important distinction between the traditional conception of critical thinking and that informed by critical theory is the latter's direct link to social action. For Freire (1970) in particular, critical reflection and social change were inextricably connected, a relationship he expressed in the term "praxis." Unlike those who produced the traditional critical-thinking literature, which tends to separate the cognitive (albeit not purely rational) process from that of acting, critical theorists seek not only to understand and solve complex problems but also to transform consciousness and practice (although, as intimated in the earlier quote by Harvey Siegel, the philosophical question is whether one can be a critical thinker without then also acting on one's insights). Jürgen Habermas, a descendant of the Frankfurt School of critical theory, emphasizes this emancipatory potential. His later work (1983) takes a different analytical approach to the relationship between critique and social action, and I will explore shortly how this newer conception informs Mezirow's theory of transformative learning. First, however, it is useful to briefly review some of the other influences on Mezirow's conception of critical reflection.

OTHER THEORETICAL INFLUENCES

Whereas critical theory brought to the surface sociocultural or linguistic distortions that limit experience and understanding, Gould's (1978) psychoanalytic theory of adult growth pointed to psychological distortions. Research on lifespan development (for example, Loevinger, 1976), dialectical thinking (Basseches, 1984), and the development of reflective judgment (Kitchener, 1983) had suggested that adults were capable of complex reasoning processes; however, it was also apparent that adult meaning-making often revealed epistemic distortions; for example, naive assumptions regarding the certainty, limits, and criteria for knowing. Mezirow (1991) argued that distorted assumptions of any kind lead people "to view reality in a way that arbitrarily limits what is included, impedes differentiation, lacks permeability or openness to other ways of seeing, or does not facilitate an integration of experience" (p. 118). Although in earlier formulations of a theory of perspective transformation (for example, Mezirow, 1981) distortions in presuppositions were seen to relate to psychological, sociolinguistic, and epistemic meaning perspectives, Mezirow (2000) more recently proposed that distortions may pertain also to one's moral-ethical, philosophical, and aesthetic meaning perspectives, the latter now called "habits of mind."

The notion that meaning perspectives, or habits of mind, become more inclusive and differentiated as a result of assumptions being confirmed or disconfirmed through critical reflection is informed by the philosophical position of constructive alternativism (Kelly, 1955). This position holds that people make meaning based on their own experiences, which in turn influences how they perceive and act. Kelly's corresponding idea of a personal construct system that may become progressively differentiated through negation, as expectations are disconfirmed by new experiences, clearly resonates with Mezirow's concept of perspective transformation. Likewise, Kuhn's (1970) notion of a paradigm shift, describing a major revolution in science in response to anomalies that the previous paradigm was unable to assimilate, reverberates through Mezirow's theory.

Argyris and Schön's (1974) distinction between single- and double-loop learning emphasized the significance of problem reframing through premise reflection, a process central to the transformation of meaning perspectives. Schön's (1983) later work highlighted the distinction between knowing-in-action and reflection-in/on-action, which Mezirow (1991) expressed as the difference between "thoughtful action" (p. 106) and content, process, and premise reflection. More generally, Schön's argument that matters of practice (or human relations) cannot be understood through reliance on a technical rationality but call for an alternative epistemology (a point also central to Habermas) is reflected in Mezirow's (1981, 1991) view that adult learning cannot be reduced to behavioral changes.

Earlier in this chapter I noted critical theory's concern with ideology critique. Although we tend to understand ideologies as broad cultural canons or worldviews, they can also be construed more liberally as something that has been socially learned and now works within us or affects our personalities and, as such, "frames our moral reasoning, our interpersonal relationships, and our ways of knowing, experiencing, and judging what is real and true" (Brookfield, 2000, p. 130). Once this broader definition of ideology—as the taken-for-granted assumptions we hold about what is right or true, which then give rise to certain practices—is adopted, one might further argue that the various distortions described in the theories offered by Gould, Kelly, Kitchener, and Schön, given that these also have been acquired in social contexts defined by certain relations of power, constitute ideologies. Reflection on these distortions could then, by extension, be viewed as a form of ideology critique.

Clearly, this is not to say that the theorists just cited consider their own work to be concerned with ideology critique. The distortions their theories point to can be construed as ideologies only to the extent that it is recognized that the social contexts in which they were acquired are undergirded by power relations that legitimize certain ways of thinking and acting over others.

Of the critical theory tradition noted earlier, it was the work of Habermas (1971, 1983) in particular that inspired the prominent role attributed to critical reflection in Mezirow's learning theory, and it is Habermas's notion of communicative action that we will turn to next.

THE THEORY OF COMMUNICATIVE ACTION AND CRITICAL REFLECTION

Rather than conceiving of critique as a third interest aimed at emancipation, separate from the technical and practical that generate their own forms of knowledge (Habermas, 1971), the Theory of Communicative Action (Habermas, 1983) envisages critical reflection to become an inherent part of people's lifeworld where important decisions about how to live together as a society are reached. This fusion of critique and practice, through which individuals exercise their responsibility and autonomy, is seen to encourage emancipation and progress. Hannah Arendt's (1958) influence on Habermas is perhaps apparent in the trust he places in the power of the public sphere. In her major philosophical work the *Human Condition*, Arendt (1958) describes action as the public engagement whereby people practice their freedom and engage with the opportunity of renewing and creating a common world. Her statement: "the fact that man [sic] is capable of action means that the unexpected can be expected from him" (p. 178) points to both the unpredictability of human action and the possibility of change. This view resonates with Habermas's (1983) main thesis that through communicative action, a practice infused by critical discourse, it is possible to arrive at knowledge that is uncontaminated by ideology, where the only power at work, allegedly, is that of the better argument.

Recognizing that human consciousness is largely shaped by language, and that ideology therefore is systematically distorted communication, Habermas (1983) proposes that we need universal standards by which any speech act could be held accountable in terms of the validity claims it makes. A true consensus would be maintainable in an environment of ideal speech conditions. In case conditions are not ideal—and they rarely are—doubt could be cast on what has been accepted as the "consensus" and it could be revealed as a form of ideology. Critical reflection, then, describes the practice of critical questioning of validity claims.

Two levels of Critical Reflection

Since the purpose of Habermas's (1983) critical theory is to diminish the power of prejudgmental attitudes, norms, and traditions, his theory of communicative action has interesting implications for the expert discourses associated with the instrumental and communicative learning or knowledge domains and reveals two different levels of validity testing involved in critical reflection.

Habermas suggests that there are different discourses; for example, the theoretical, practical, and aesthetic, concerned respectively with claims to truth, rightness, and truthfulness or authenticity. On the one hand adherence to these established discourses, with their disciplined methods of inquiry, is immensely useful, as they assist us in continuously testing (or contesting) the validity claims underlying assertions (see also Dewey, 1910/1991); on the other hand, however, these same discourses may be conceived of as cultural traditions themselves and hence, at least in principle, are open to contestation and critique with respect to their adequacy for informing decisions in particular contexts.

In some instances, we are able to redeem validity claims by referring to accepted ways of constructing knowledge (for example, the sciences and their claims to the "truth"). In other instances the premises underlying how a problem is defined are heavily contested, and reaching consensus is not a straightforward matter. Most complex problems affecting individuals and society—for example, the AIDS pandemic, poverty, land use, the oil disaster in the Gulf of Mexico, global warming, and even promoting student success in education—are not solvable through "science" alone but require the consideration of moral implications. This is why in most serious discussions all validity claims (truth, rightness, and truthfulness or authenticity) would seem important and need to be considered.

Habermas's and Dewey's Influence on Mezirow's Concept of Critical Reflection

Mezirow (1991) incorporated some of Habermas's (1983) insights into his own evolving theory of adult learning, arguing, first, that most acts of learning involve instrumental and communicative processes; second, that "emancipatory reflective learning can be involved in both instrumental and communicative learning" (Mezirow, 1991, p. 98); and third, that ideal speech conditions are also ideal conditions of adult learning.

Mezirow (1991) extends Dewey's (1910/1991) work, arguing, first, that problem-solving is also part of communicative learning, although it takes on a different form; and second, that validity testing of assumptions and premises, in the domains of instrumental and communicative learning, occurs through the established methods of inquiry in these fields. However, the more important extension of Dewey's (1910/1991) analysis of reflective thinking is Mezirow's focus on another dimension of reflection; namely, that which is directed at identifying "how habits of expectations (meaning perspectives) affect reflective thought—as in problem posing—or how reflective thought might affect them—as in consciousness raising or psychotherapy" (Mezirow, 1991, pp. 101–102).

Mezirow (1991) defines reflection as "the process of critically assessing the content, process and premise(s) of our efforts to interpret and give meaning to an experience" (p. 104). All three forms of reflection are considered to involve critique, but premise reflection is the form of reflection central to empower-ment and emancipation. Now, as became obvious in the earlier discussion of disciplinary discourses, premises are not necessarily personal presupposi-tions, and hence one might note that there are two different kinds of premise reflection. This point was left underexplored in Mezirow's (1991) core text, but he later draws attention to it when he explicitly distinguishes between objective and subjective reframing, the first referring to critical reflection on assumptions (CRA) and the second to critical self-reflection on assumptions (CSRA) (Mezirow, 1998, 2000). Objective reframing includes reflection on con-tent, process, and premises in the area of interpreting what is communicated to us ("narrative" CRA) or in task-oriented problem solving ("action" CRA). In contrast, "subjective reframing" refers to self-reflection or critical reflection on one's own psychological and cultural assumptions or premises that limit one's experiences.

Although Mezirow refers to both objective and subjective reframing as eman-cipatory dimensions of learning, I would argue that it is in CSRA that we can see a stronger link to ideology critique. CRA shares greater similarity with Dewey's notion of reflective thinking, whereby we draw on established or sanctioned expert discourses to verify solutions or, in this case, interpretations. We do not question why we consult these rather than other discourses, but we use them to test validity claims. In CRSA we consider how our own presuppositions have arisen and how they influence consciousness.

FOSTERING CRITICAL REFLECTION

Engagement in critical reflection is never a direct function of employing a set of techniques that seemed to be conducive to such an experience in some con-texts with some people. It seems important to appreciate as well that there are numerous psychological and sociocultural factors that can make engagement in critical reflection difficult. Cranton (1996, 2000) points to personality differ-ences, and Brookfield (1995) to prevailing cultures in work settings (specifically the cultures of silence, individualism, and secrecy), which can inhibit critical reflection. Although it is beyond the scope of this chapter to delve into the ethical implications associated with fostering critical reflection (see Mezirow, 1991; Baumgartner, 2001), it would seem imperative that educators attempt to be as open and clear as possible with learners about the "the qualities, risks and likely consequences of the experience they are about to undergo" (Brookfield, 1994, p. 215).

With these brief caveats in mind, educators who hold the view that adult learning, to be most meaningful, ought to involve engagement in critical reflection may find some inspiration in the literature on feminist, critical, and radical pedagogy (for example, Bracher, 2006; hooks, 1994; Maher & Tetreault, 1994; McLaren & Hammer, 1989) and also in the concrete strategies discussed by several authors (for example, Brookfield, 1987, 1995; Cranton, 1996; Fook & Askeland, 2007; Loads, 2009; Mezirow & Associates, 1990; Moon, 1999; Osmond & Darlington, 2005). Although the use of critical dialogue or conversations is frequently mentioned in the literature, the assumptions underlying such practice may differ.

Rather than agreeing with the notion that it is possible to arrive at ideology-free knowledge based on universal validity claims, many educators, leaning on Foucault (1980), argue that knowledge and power cannot be separated and that "power is already there...one is never 'outside' it" (p. 141). Brookfield (2000) suggests that "by turning logic on its head, reversing images, looking at situations sideways, and making imaginative leaps, we realize that things are the way they are for a reason" (p. 130).

Further suggestions made in the literature on how to foster critical reflection include, for example, the skilful employment of critical incidents, autobiographies, role play, repertory grids, concept maps, working collaboratively (for example, collaborative inquiry groups), critical questioning, free writing and journaling, metaphor analysis, and creative/expressive activities such as collages, drawings, or sculpture. Some of these approaches rely principally on confronting participants with the unexpected, unfamiliar, surprising, and perhaps even disturbing, thereby calling into question the presuppositions they hold and possibly revealing them as "distorted." Brookfield (2000) also stresses the importance of critical friends in stimulating reflection.

Commenting specifically on the nature of dialogue that should govern learning in higher education settings, Barnett (1992) noted that "true conversation means taking seriously the critical viewpoints of others, perhaps even entering a different world held open by those others" (p. 27). Rowland (2006) emphasizes the importance of dialogue across disciplinary boundaries, as this would develop the capacity to challenge the ideological positions and assumptions that underlie different disciplinary perspectives.

Common to all approaches is the intent to offer contexts in which participants are encouraged to identify the assumptions underlying their meaning perspectives or habits of minds that give rise to how they interpret particular situations, subject these to critical scrutiny, and explore alternatives. As for exploring alternatives, Maxine Greene's (1995) discussion of how engagement in art may release the imagination seems particularly relevant. Critical reflection then is not only a rational activity but also calls for creative and emotive capabilities (Brookfield, 1987, 1994; Boud, Keogh, & Walker, 1985; Garrison,

1991; Paul, 1992; Schön, 1983). I further explore the role of emotions in critical reflection in the next section.

CRITICAL REFLECTION AND EMOTIONS

When entrenched views and convictions are revealed to be "distorted," finding the mental space to be creative, and mustering the courage to develop alternatives, can be enormously challenging (Mezirow, 2000). It is also emotionally draining and possibly demoralizing when we become aware of the pervasiveness of power structures and how limited we are in our capacity to challenge the orthodox views and practices around us (Brookfield, 2000). Mackenzie (2002) offers an account of critical reflection that emphasizes the importance of emotional flexibility and investment involved in envisaging alternatives. Although not focusing on critical reflection *per se* but instead arguing that transformative learning involves both discernment through soul work and critical reflection, Dirkx (1997) and Scott (1997) highlight the deeply personal and emotional dimension of experiencing challenges to one's ways of understanding the world. Recently van Woerkom (2010) argued against critical reflection as a rationalist ideal, highlighting the importance of implicit learning and the emotions. The implication for educators is to offer environments that demonstrate respect and support for the emotive aspects of transformative learning. The various studies on fostering critical reflection reviewed by Taylor (2000) also confirm this.

Emotions are also relevant to critical reflection in another way. As Brookfield (1987) and Boud, Keogh, and Walker (1985) argued, very positive emotions can be a strong trigger for critical reflection, as when we unexpectedly encounter a situation in which we feel we have "come home," leading us to reflect critically on the assumptions we had taken for granted up to this point. The student who is the first of her family to attend university, who has self-doubts and yet excels on a difficult term paper and, as a result, questions her assumptions and considers whether she might go on with postgraduate studies, is an example of such an experience. The implication for educators is that critical reflection, in this case on psychocultural assumptions, might be promoted by giving learners opportunity to succeed in areas they may not have thought of themselves as very capable of mastering.

A third way in which emotions are relevant in critical reflection is associated with the notion of authenticity (for example, Cranton & Carusetta, 2004; Kreber, Klampfleitner, McCune, Bayne, & Knottenbelt, 2007; Kreber, 2010). Earlier we saw that there is a distinction between objective and subjective reframing, the latter focusing on one's own meaning perspectives (Mezirow's CSRA). We might also say that when engaged in critical reflection, whereby we then gain greater insight into our real rather than perceived needs and choices, we move beyond rational autonomous decision making and toward greater authenticity, the latter being much more challenging and emotionally charged. Bonnett (1976) suggested that we act authentically, rather than just autonomously, when our choices are bound up with our own inner motives. Daloz (1986) points to this link between critical self-reflection and authenticity, arguing that "the struggle to be something more than the person others have made, is one of the most compelling struggles of our adult lives" (p. 154). However, as Adorno (2003) noted, there is a risk of viewing the process of moving toward greater authenticity as only inwardly directed self-reflection.

There is yet another way in which critical reflection is linked to the emotions. Nussbaum (2004) showed that emotions are complex judgments we make. When in relation to a particular disadvantaged individual or marginalized social group we make a judgment that their "misfortunes...are serious...that they have not brought this misfortune on to themselves, and...that they are themselves important parts of one's own scheme of ends and goals" (Nussbaum, 2004, p. 335), the emotion we experience as we make these judgments is one of compassion. When we encounter suffering in others—for example, the adult student who never speaks in class discussions—we might also recognize our related vulnerability, which implies that we see others as important to our own flourishing (Nussbaum, 2004). Nixon (2008) argues that "through courage I assert my own claims, or those of my clan, to recognition; through compassion I assert the rights of others to recognition" (p. 89). We might also say that through showing compassion we allow for the authentic engagement of others who without our compassion would remain unrecognized. Encouraging authenticity in others is linked to my own authenticity. Although experiencing compassion is, of course, not necessarily a transformative experience for people, it may involve critical reflection and judgment in relation to one's sociolinguistic meaning perspective or ethical deliberation. We might then also observe that the emotion of compassion can be learned, at least to a certain extent, by becoming more critically reflective. The latter could have profound implications for social justice education.

RESEARCHING CRITICAL REFLECTION

There is no shortage of studies on critical reflection, although not all studies that use the term "critical refection" in the title or abstract are necessarily embedded in a discourse of power. Some of the issues that continue to require deeper understanding include: why some people engage in critical reflection more easily than others; why the same person might demonstrate considerable critical reflectivity in one domain but little in another; why the same person might easily engage in CRA but not in CSRA; how different people experience engagement in certain phases of critical reflection; the relative weight of rational, emotive, imaginary, and creative experiences in this process, and whether intuition and imagination possibly replace the rational aspects of critical reflection in some contexts (Dirkx, 1997); the role of significant others in triggering and sustaining critical reflection; the extent to which important policy decisions are indeed made on the basis of critical reflection; the kinds of distortions that may occur during important decision-making processes, and which ones are most difficult to overcome; and the conditions under which insight or critical awareness of distortions are sustained and lead to changes in meaning structures—to mention but a few.

Extensive case studies carried out in natural settings based on observation and interviews with people engaged in an activity likely to involve critical reflection (for example, exploring the space for critical reflection in organizational development, Rigg & Trehan, 2008; Jacobs, 2008) could yield significant insights into the conditions under which some individuals experience critical reflection. It would also be interesting to carry out more detailed analyses of what happens in discussions that presumably foster critical reflection (for example, Servage, 2007) and whether individual group members experience the process differently (Cranton, 2000). Phenomenological studies similar to Mezirow's (1975) original research on women returning to higher education after a long hiatus could explore how participation in a program of study affects CRA and CSRA (one might think of how the higher education experience influences different students' identities).

Studies that explore more thoroughly whether and how critical reflection informs decision making on important policy matters would be particularly enlightening. Such a study was carried out by Lauber, Knuth, and Deshler (2002), and because such work is still rare, it will be featured here in greater detail. Lauber et al. interviewed different stakeholder groups about what they thought should be done to address a particular social problem they were campaigning for; they then were asked to provide reasons for their decisions. The authors were able to identify several distortions, among them "prescription distortions, inadequate problem definition, unsupported contentions, inadequate word choice, stereotyping, and dismissal of alternative perspectives" (p. 593) that constrained decisions and made communication across stakeholders difficult. More studies of this kind would reveal whether the same distortions also impede good decision making in other contexts.

Studies relying on interviews that explore people's recollections of past critical reflection episodes are perhaps the easiest to do, but these are obviously limited by the extent to which participants are willing to accurately represent their experience or can correctly remember it, given the time that has lapsed. Asking participants to keep a journal (or portfolio; see, for example, Lyle & Hendley, 2007) over a certain period of time during which critical reflection might occur (for example, while they start a new job or are involved in a collaborative inquiry group) could be useful in gaining a more detailed record of actual experiences, but the quality of data is subject to people's natural inclination to keep such a log and their ability to express themselves in writing.

Repertory grids and concept maps have long been recognized as tools for promoting critical reflection (Gray, 2007; Mezirow & Associates, 1990); however, they can also serve as methods of systematic data collection. Repeated elicitations of repertory grids and concept maps could show whether people's meaning perspectives change over time or as a result of a challenging experience (for example, Farrell, 2009). Carrying out a single repertory grid interview with individuals while they are engaged in an important decision-making process might surface superordinate constructs or presuppositions that influence their decisions. Narrative analysis of people's constructed stories might reveal that they challenged presuppositions in particular contexts.

Kreber and Castleden (2009) explored whether being socialized into particular disciplinary ways of thinking is linked to university teachers' engagement in premise reflection on their teaching practice. Cranton (2000) looked at whether a psychic predisposition towards extraversion or introversion and judgment or perception plays a role in how individuals experience reflection and transformative learning. Her work might also usefully inform our understanding of why people who are very capable of objective reframing may not experience subjective reframing, and vice versa. The most interesting studies are arguably those that shed light on the distinction between the capacity to engage in critical reflection and the willingness to do so in particular situations.

I began this chapter outlining some of the frequently cited reasons why critical reflection is considered fundamental to adult life and thus is widely espoused as a principal goal of adult and higher education. These reasons included sustaining a healthy democracy, meaningful personal relationships, and well-being in the workplace. Critical reflection was shown to be considered to make learning and professional practice more profound and to nurture people's life opportunities. At the risk of sounding a touch preachy, my intent in this last section of this chapter is to explore whether as educators we can afford not to work toward critical reflection *in* and *through* our professional practice.

CRITICAL REFLECTION: AN IMPERATIVE IN OUR TIMES?

The distinction just made—between *in* and *through* professional practice—is intentional. We work towards critical reflection *in* our professional practice when we carefully consider the implications of our actions and examine whether what we say and do inadvertently sanctions or contributes to power relations that favor the interests of powerful others. At a time of increased performativity (Ball, 2008) and accountability in the education sector driven by neoliberal policies, educators often work in contexts that feel profoundly inauthentic (Kreber, 2010). Recognizing the external forces that shape both policies and the assumptions underlying our practice is part of critical reflection; so is envisioning alternatives (for example, Brookfield, 1987).

Nurturing critical reflection *in* our professional practice might lead us to acknowledge and identify ongoing problems in the provision of educational opportunities; for example, the underrepresentation of certain strata of society in adult education programs as well as the widely varying experiences of those who had a chance to join in but may feel alienated by the experience (see also Smith, 2007). The issue here is one of making our educational institutions fairer and more democratic places where all who join in have an equal opportunity to succeed.

Nurturing critical reflection *through* our professional practice as adult educators is linked to the understanding that education ultimately is aimed at making a difference to the problems faced by our societies. This implies that not only the adult education professionals or practitioners but also those who participate in adult education would seek to renew our common world after graduating from our programs (Arendt, 1958). Our world is rife with issues calling for people's capacity to reflect critically on their assumption and beliefs, and to show both courage and compassion towards those in need. One of the most pervasive human weaknesses may well be prejudice towards that with which we are unfamiliar. Such prejudice may be expressed in the attitudes displayed towards certain cultures and ways of living (as, for example, in "Islamophobia," "homophobia," or racism), but it may also be expressed, for example, in one's sentiments towards a political party whose platform one never compared with that of another (for example, "In my family we have always voted conservative"). Underlying these attitudes is an unrecognized irrationality and fear of that which is unknown or different from what one is used to, combined with a lack of capacity and willingness to engage in critical thought and, by implication, having one's assumptions challenged.

Activist groups are formed because of people who have developed both the capacity to reason and the courage as well as compassion to speak out for those in need. Although such groups are immensely important for creating a better world in which to live, being capable of critical reflection does not mean that one necessarily has to become a political activist in the sense just described. Our willingness and capacity to engage in critical reflection can also have an enormous impact in our personal relationships and the various local communities we are part of. Nonetheless, critical reflection is necessarily linked to a "political disposition" in a sense that we feel interconnected with others and care about the world (Arendt, 1958).

Arendt's (2003) call for humans "to stop and think" and to train the imagination to go "visiting" (to try to understand another person's point of view) are fundamental to critical reflection. This means that we take an interest in the happenings around us, engage in dialogue, and feel a responsibility to stand up for what we believe to be true, after careful consideration of alternative viewpoints.

What do these observations mean for the professional practice of adult and higher education? How can this willingness and capacity for critical reflection be nurtured? Nussbaum (1997) highlights the need for students to develop the Socratic capacity to reason about their beliefs; Arendt (2003) emphasized the importance of training the student's mind to go visiting. Similarly, Walker (2006), proposing Nussbaum and Sen's (1993) capabilities approach as a framework for higher education pedagogies, stresses the importance of fostering in students capabilities such as practical reason, knowledge and imagination, respect, dignity and recognition, and emotional integrity. Fostering the imagination, in particular (see also Greene, 1995), may well be fundamental for nurturing critical reflection. A potentially fruitful area for future research on critical reflection therefore might be explorations of the role of imagination in people's capacity for critical reflection as well as their willingness to apply this acquired capacity.

Infusing adult and higher education with "the spirit of the humanities" (Nussbaum, 2010) clearly is a profound challenge in some contexts; yet if it is indeed education rather than training that we intend to provide, and if our goal is that those who benefit from this education will eventually apply their developed qualities and dispositions to the complex problems of our times, is there an alternative?

References

Adorno, T. (2003). *The jargon of authenticity* (originally published by Suhrkamp Verlag in 1964). London and New York: Routledge.

Arendt, H. (1958). *The human condition*. Chicago: University of Chicago Press.

Arendt, H. (2003). *Responsibility and judgment* (edited and with an introduction by Jerome Kuhn). New York: Schocken Books.

Argyris, C., & Schön, D. (1974). *Theories in practice*. San Francisco: Jossey-Bass.

Ball, S. J. (2008). *The education debate*. Bristol, UK: The Policy Press.

Barnett, R. (1992). *Improving higher education: Total quality care*. Buckingham, UK: The Society of Research into Higher Education and Open University Press.

Barnett, R. (1997). *Higher education: A critical business*. Buckingham, UK: The Society of Research into Higher Education and Open University Press.

Basseches, M. (1984). *Dialectical thinking and adult development*. Norwood, N.J.: Ablex.

Baumgartner, L. (2001, Spring). An update on transformational learning. In S. B. Merriam (Ed.), *The new update on adult learning theory* (pp. 15–24). New Directions for Adult and Continuing Education, no. 89. San Francisco: Jossey-Bass.

Bonnett, M. (1976). Authenticity, autonomy and compulsory curriculum. *Cambridge Journal of Education*, *6*(3), 107–121.

Boud, D., Keogh, R., & Walker, D. (1985). *Reflection: Turning experience into learning*. London Kogan Page.

Bracher, M. (2006). *Radical pedagogy: Identity, generativity, and social transformation*. New York: Palgrave Macmillan.

Brookfield, S. (1987). *Developing critical thinkers*. San Francisco: Jossey-Bass.

Brookfield, S. (1994). Tales from the dark side: A phenomenography of adult critical reflection. *International Journal of Lifelong Education*, *13*(3), 203–216.

Brookfield, S. (1995). *Becoming a critically reflective teacher*. San Francisco: Jossey-Bass.

Brookfield, S. (2000). Transformative learning as ideology critique. In J. Mezirow & Associates (Eds.), *Learning as transformation: Critical perspectives on a theory in progress* (pp. 125–150). San Francisco: Jossey-Bass.

Brookfield, S. (2001). Repositioning ideology critique in a critical theory of adult learning. *Adult Education Quarterly*, *52*, 7–22.

Cranton, P. (1996). *Professional development as transformative learning*. San Francisco: Jossey-Bass.

Cranton, P. (2000). Individual differences and transformative learning. In J. Mezirow & Associates (Eds.), *Learning as transformation: Critical perspectives on a theory in progress* (pp. 181–204). San Francisco: Jossey-Bass.

Cranton, P. A., & Carusetta, E. (2004). Developing authenticity as a transformative process. *Journal of Transformative Education*, *2*(4), 276–293.

Daloz, L. A. (1986). *Effective teaching and mentoring: Realizing the transformational power of adult learning experiences*. San Francisco: Jossey Bass.

Dewey, J. (1910/1991). *How we think*. Buffalo, NY: Prometheus Books.

Dewey, J. (1916). *Democracy and education*. New York: The Free Press.

Dirkx, J. M. (1997). Nurturing the soul in adult learning. In P. Cranton (Ed.), *Transformative learning in action: Insights from practice*. New Directions for Adult and Continuing Education, no. 74. San Francisco: Jossey-Bass.

Ennis, R. H. (1991). Critical thinking: A streamlined conception. *Teaching Philosophy*, *41*(1), 5–25.

Farrell, T. S. (2009). Critical reflection in a TESL course: Mapping conceptual change. *ELT Journal, 63*(3), 221–229.

Fook, J., & Askeland, A. (2007). Challenges of critical reflection: "Nothing ventured, nothing gained." *Social Work Education*, 1–14.

Foucault, M. (1980). *Power/knowledge: Selected interviews and other writings 1972–1977* (Colin Gordon, Ed.). London: Harvester.

Freire, P. (1970). *Pedagogy of the oppressed*. New York: Herder and Herder.

Garrison, R. (1991). Critical thinking and adult education: A conceptual model for developing critical thinking in adult learners. *International Journal of Lifelong Education, 10*, 287–303.

Giroux, H. (1983). *Theory and resistance in education: A pedagogy for the opposition*. London: Heinemann Educational Books.

Giroux, H. (2010, July 12). The disappearing intellectual in the age of economic Darwinism. Truthout. Retrieved from http://www.truth-out.org/the-disappearing -intellectual-age-economic-darwinism61287

Giroux, H., & Giroux, S. (2004). *Take back higher education: Race, youth, and the crisis of democracy in the post civil rights era*. New York: Palgrave Macmillan.

Gould, R. (1978). *Transformation: Growth and change in adult life*. New York: Simon & Schuster.

Gramsci, A. (1971). *Selection from the prison notebooks*. London: Lawrence and Wishart.

Gray, D. E. (2007). Facilitating management learning: Developing critical reflection through reflective tools. *Learning Management, 38*(5). Retrieved from http://epubs.surrey.ac.uk/1190/1/fulltext.pdf

Greene, M. (1995). *Releasing the imagination: Essays on education, the arts, and social change*. San Francisco: Jossey-Bass.

Habermas, J. (1971). *Knowledge and human interests*. Boston: Beacon Press.

Habermas, J. (1983). *Theorie des kommunikativen Handelns* (vols. 1, 2). Frankfurt, Germany: Suhrkamp.

hooks, b. (1994). *Teaching to transgress: Education as the practice of freedom*. New York: Routledge.

Jacobs, G. C. (2008). The development of critical being: Reflection and reflexivity in an action learning program for health promotion practitioners in The Netherlands. *Action Learning Research and Practice, 5*(3), 221–235.

Kelly, G. A. (1955). *The psychology of personal constructs* (Vol. 1). New York: Norton and Company.

Kitchener, K. (1983). Educational goals and reflective thinking. *Educational Forum, 48*(1), 75–95.

Kreber, C. (2010). Courage and compassion in the striving for authenticity: States of complacency, compliance, and contestation. *Adult Education Quarterly, 60*, 177–198.

Kreber, C., & Castleden, H. (2009). Reflection on teaching and epistemological structure: Reflective and critically reflective processes in pure/soft and pure/hard fields. *Higher Education*, *57*, 509–531.

Kreber, C., Klampfleitner, M., McCune, V., Bayne, S., & Knottenbelt, M. (2007). What do you mean by "authentic"? A comparative review of the literature on conceptions of authenticity. *Adult Education Quarterly*, *58*(1), 22–43.

Kuhn, T. (1970). *The structure of scientific revolutions.* Chicago: University of Chicago Press.

Lauber, T. B., Knuth, B. A., & Deshler, J. D. (2002). Educating citizens about controversial issues: The case of suburban goose management. *Society and Natural Resources*, *15*, 581–597.

Lindeman, E. (1926). *The meaning of adult education.* New York: New Republic.

Loads, D. (2009). Putting ourselves in the picture: Art workshops in the professional development of university lecturers. *International Journal for Academic Development*, *14*(1), 59–67.

Loevinger, J. (1976). *Ego development.* San Francisco: Jossey-Bass.

Lyle, S., & Hendley, D. (2007). Can portfolios support critical reflection? Assessing the portfolios of schools liaison policy officers. *Journal of In Service Education*, *33*(2), 189–207.

Mackenzie, C. (2002). Critical reflection, self-knowledge, and the emotions. *Philosophical Explorations*, *5*(3), 186–206. http://www.informaworld.com/smpp/title~db=all~content=t713706422~tab=issueslist~branches=5—v5

Maher, F. A., & Tetreault, M. K. (1994). *The feminist classroom.* New York: Basic Books.

McLaren, P., & Hammer, R. (1989). Critical pedagogy and postmodern challenge: Toward a critical postmodernist pedagogy of liberation. *Educational Foundations*, *3*(3), 29–62.

Mezirow, J. (1975). *Education for perspective transformation: Women's reentry programs in community colleges.* New York: Center for Adult Education Teachers College, Columbia University.

Mezirow, J. (1981). A critical theory of adult learning and education. *Adult Education Quarterly*, *32*, 3–24.

Mezirow, J. (1991). *Transformative dimensions of adult learning.* San Francisco: Jossey-Bass.

Mezirow, J. (1998). On critical reflection. *Adult Education Quarterly*, *48*, 185–198.

Mezirow, J. (2000). Learning to think like an adult: Core concepts of transformation theory. In J. Mezirow & Associates (Ed.), *Learning as transformation: Critical perspectives on a theory in progress* (pp. 3–33). San Francisco: Jossey-Bass.

Mezirow, J., & Associates (Eds.). (1990). *Fostering critical reflection in adulthood.* San Francisco: Jossey-Bass.

Moon, J. A. (1999). *Reflection in learning and professional development*. London: Kogan Page.

Nixon, J. (2008). *Towards the virtuous university: The moral bases of academic practice*. New York: Routledge.

Nussbaum, M. (1997). *Cultivating humanity: A classical defense of reform in liberal education*. Cambridge, MA: Harvard University Press.

Nussbaum, M. (2000). *Women and human development. The capabilities approach*. Cambridge, UK: The Cambridge University Press.

Nussbaum, M. (2004). *Upheavals of thought*. Cambridge, UK: Cambridge University Press.

Nussbaum, M. (2010). *Not for profit*. Princeton, NJ: Princeton University Press.

Nussbaum, M., & Sen, A. (Eds.). (1993). *The quality of life*. Oxford: Clarendon Press.

Osmond, J., & Darlington, Y. (2005). Reflective analysis: Techniques for facilitating reflection. *Australian Social Work, 58*(1), 3–14.

Paul, R. (1992). *Critical thinking: What every person needs to survive in a rapidly changing world*. Rohnert Park, CA: Sonoma State University.

Rowland, S. (2006). *The enquiring university: Compliance and contestation in higher education*. Maidenhead, UK: Society for Research into Higher Education and Open University Press.

Rigg, C., & Trehan, K. (2008). Critical reflection in the workplace: Is it just too difficult? *Journal of European Industrial Training, 32*(5), 374–384.

Schön, D. (1983). *The reflective practitioner*. San Francisco: Jossey-Bass.

Scott, S. M. (1997). The grieving soul in the transformative process. In P. Cranton (Ed.), *Transformative learning in action: Insights from practice* (pp. 41–50). New Directions for Adult and Continuing Education, no. 74. San Francisco: Jossey-Bass.

Servage, L. (2007). Making space for critical reflection in professional learning communities. *Education Canada, 47*(1), 14–17.

Siegel, H. (1988). *Educating reason: Rationality, critical thinking, and education*. New York: Routledge.

Smith, S. R. (2007). Stop and think: Addressing social injustices though critical reflection. *Education Canada, 47*(1), 48–51.

Taylor, E. W. (2000). Analyzing research on transformative learning theory. In J. Mezirow & Associates (Eds.), *Learning as transformation: Critical perspectives on a theory in progress* (pp. 29–310). San Francisco: Jossey-Bass.

Tierney, W. G. (1993). *Building communities of difference: Higher education in the twenty-first century*. Westport, CT: Bergin and Garvey.

Tierney, W. G., & Rhoads, R. A. (1993). Postmodernism and critical theory in higher education: Implications for research and practice. In J. C. Smart (Ed.), *Higher education: Handbook of theory and research* (vol. 10) (pp. 308–344). New York: Agathon Press.

van Woerkom, M. (2010). Critical reflection as a rationalistic ideal. *Adult Education Quarterly, 60*(4), 339–356.

Walker. M. (2006). *Higher education pedagogies: A capabilities approach.* Maidenhead, Berkshire: The Society for Research into Higher Education and Open University Press.

Yorks, L., & Marsick, V. J. (2000). Organizational learning and transformation. In J. Mezirow & Associates (Eds.), *Learning as transformation: Critical perspectives on a theory in progress* (pp. 253–281). San Francisco: Jossey-Bass.

CHAPTER TWENTY-ONE

The Role of Experience in Transformative Learning

Dorothy MacKeracher

When first asked to write a chapter on the role of experience in transformative learning, I decided the only way I could approach the topic would be to write a case study. This case study focuses on my own experiences with transformative learning. I begin by defining "experience"; then I describe some of my experiences as a transformative learner, followed by an analysis of the process, and a comparison of the types of learning and the process involved with the work of various authors (Fenwick, 2000; Kolb, 1984; Mezirow, 1978; Miller, 2000; Taylor, 2011).

A DEFINITION OF EXPERIENCE

As I first started to scribble notes to myself about this chapter, I realized that I would have to provide a definition of "experience." Many writers talk about experience, but very few actually define it; most end up defining "experiential learning" or "learning from experience" rather than "experience" itself. By going back to the work of prominent writers in the field (Dewey, 1916; Kidd, 1973; Knowles, 1970; Kolb, 1984; Lewin, 1951; Piaget, 1971) and the work of newer writers (Dirkx & Lavin, 1991; Fenwick, 2000), I have cobbled together my own definition of "experience."

When considered carefully, the word "experience" is used to describe a variety of phenomena. I will consider three such definitions. In the first definition, experience is everything that happens to you between birth and death. The primal therapists would argue that this experience also includes what happens to you during the months prior to birth; and who knows, maybe during the months after death. This type of experience is always occurring in the present or the here and now. Once it slides into the past, or the there-and-then, it is retained in memory as meaning through sensations, iconic representations, or conceptual abstractions, which can be described in words. Dewey (1938) would say that one's present experience is always a function of the inter-action between the present situation and one's past experiences. In Piaget's terms (1971), past experience helps interpret and incorporate present experi-ence through assimilation, and present experience helps expand and transform past experience through accommodation.

The idea that "experience" is all derived from personal interactions is a start but isn't satisfactory. No one remembers everything that has happened since birth. So we need to distinguish life experiences that our minds have made sense of and given meaning to from those that languish unattended and senseless in our unconscious mind. I assume that even some of the experiences I have made sense of still reside in my unconscious mind waiting for my further attention.

Then I got to thinking about all the "experiences" that influenced me in my childhood but which were not events that happened to me personally. I am a child of the Depression and the Second World War. Both events became expe-riences that affected me. I gained my knowledge of them vicariously through various events that occurred around me and to me—like the air-raid drills we endured as school children or the rationing of basic foods. So the second defini-tion of experience is based on those remote experiences imposed on me by my cultural and social heritage—experiences that included a set of values, beliefs, and expectations about the roles I should aspire to and how I should behave.

So now I have two types of "experience": what was imposed on me by my social and cultural heritage and what happened to me personally and that I have made sense of. As a young child, I knew that these two "experiences" were different and that I was not supposed to discuss my personal set, especially when it differed from the imposed set. Belenky, Clinchy, Goldberger, and Tarule (1986) describe the imposed set as *received knowledge* and the personal set as *subjective knowledge*.

In the third definition, therefore, although these two sets of experience have different origins, they tend to overlap and together form a constructed whole that I refer to in this chapter as "my experience." Belenky and her associates would refer to this fused set as *constructed knowledge* and the process of developing it as *procedural knowledge*.

I think that each type of experience plays an important role in transformative learning. Perhaps transformative learning occurs when one set nudges the other (usually the subjective or personal set nudging the received or imposed set) into a new sense of awareness, with accompanying disbelief and disorientation, leading eventually to a new way to understand the world.

A CASE STUDY OF A TRANSFORMATIVE LEARNER

I will describe four instances of transformative learning selected from among many.

Learning That I Was a Teacher

I was seventeen when I first discovered I was a teacher. I was a camp counselor at a summer camp run by an altruistic organization and was working with teenaged girls from poor homes in downtown Montreal. One of my concerns was a fifteen-year-old who was afraid of the water and could not swim but wanted to learn. I told her I thought I could help; then I tried my best to imagine myself struggling in the water the way she was. The design of the swimming area forced her to swim in very shallow water infested with leeches, and I had to stand in the water with her. She and I had to keep moving to avoid the leeches. I suggested one swimming technique after another until one of my suggestions clicked and she was suddenly swimming. I don't know which of us was more surprised. The next day she jumped into the deep water and swam twenty-five feet. We all cheered! She and I had a joint transformative experience—she became a swimmer, something she thought she could never be, and I became a teacher, a role I had avoided with a passion.

Now, of course, I understand that I was facilitating her skill development. I defined myself as a "teacher" because that was the word we used in those days. I still define myself that way, even though the trend in adult education is to talk about facilitators, mentors, and guides. What did the transformation involve? I realized that I could help others learn something by doing my best to see the learning task from their point of view.

In the terms I have used in my definition of experience, my received "experience" informed me that being a teacher was not a valued role, because most were unmarried women who had no children—and heaven forbid that I would ever remain unmarried or childless. I aspired to be a medical practitioner, a much more glamorous profession. Now I am a divorced mother and a teacher with a doctoral degree.

Learning to Be a Self-Directed Learner

Since then, I have had other transformative learning experiences. In my first course as a graduate student, faced with writing my first academic paper in fifteen years, I panicked. The topic was the role of stress in learning (no more than twenty pages, typed, double-spaced). I was a young mother with three children under ten and was convinced I knew nothing worthy enough to go into an academic paper. I talked to some older, more experienced and supportive friends about my problem. One suggested that I write the paper about the stress of being a young mother. I looked at her in surprise—"Can I really do that, write about my own experience?" Her response was, "Of course—where do you think theory comes from?" So I did; I received an A+ and was transformed into a self-directed learner who could learn from her own experience, provide examples of theoretical constructs, and maybe even add new knowledge to understanding the relationship between stress and learning.

I reread the paper recently—it's the only one I saved from those heady days of being a graduate student. The first part of the paper is very academic, an informed but stilted discussion of the concept of stress. The second half is based on my own experience but is written in the third person singular; I even describe my type of learner with the pronoun "he"! My self-definition had changed, but I had not yet incorporated my newfound freedom and power into my writing. That change took much longer. Now, when I read experienced-based student papers, I recognize those who are in the middle of a similar transformation because their grammar vacillates between the first and third person singular.

In terms of my definition of experience, my received knowledge did not include much information about stress and my subjective knowledge suggested that I was inadequate to the task. When someone I respected told me I could write about my subjective experience, I was astonished and greatly relieved. I somehow managed to write about both types of knowledge with minimal connection between the two. I can still recall the relief I felt when my assumption that I was inadequate to the task was transformed into hope and excitement.

Learning to be a Professor

Then I entered the doctoral program. By this time, I was a single mother supporting the activities of three teenagers. I needed money. So I became a research assistant for a sympathetic professor who hired me to write a short monograph for the provincial Department of Education. The department had decided that, in light of declining school enrolments, some teachers might need to be retrained; and because these teachers were adults, perhaps the department should know something about adult learners and how to plan adult learning programs. I was hired to do the literature review called for in the contract. I had a great time reading my way through stacks of textbooks and journals in the library. I wrote up what I had learned as a draft of a monograph later published as *Adult Learning Principles and Their Application to Program Planning* (Brundage & MacKeracher, 1980). The short monograph ran to some 130 pages.

Then, because I needed feedback on what I had written, I made a copy for every professor in the Department of Adult Education and asked them to read it and provide me with their comments as soon as possible. Three weeks passed, then four, and still no feedback. I panicked. I imagined that my work was so dreadful that no one wanted to comment on it. I worked up the nerve to ask one professor what he thought of it. His reply was that he had never heard of most of the ideas I had written into the document and therefore wasn't able to provide me with any constructive feedback. I was stunned. I knew more than a professor! How could this be? I knew I was a good student, but not that good! This transformation was not just a change in my constructed experience of my self but a major shift in the premise I was using as a graduate student. I found myself transformed into an "expert," a doctoral student who could no longer claim to be somehow less informed or less competent that those who were helping me obtain an advanced degree. I was both terrified and exhilarated at the same time. Perhaps, in time, I could become a professor; all I had to do was complete my degree.

In my forties and fifties, I encountered some difficult life transitions. I found myself being transformed through being aware of and working through the meaning of my dreams. These dreams seemed to be another form of experience, one that came unbidden to my conscious mind, raising to awareness personal confusion about both subjective and received knowledge, and demanding attention in the here and now to make sense of the confusion and to use that sense to make changes in behavior, beliefs, and values. I described one of these transforming dreams in *Making Sense of Adult Learning* (MacKeracher, 2004), and I will not repeat that description here. Over my lifetime, I have come to know that my transformative learning involves knowledge, imagery, and sensations; body, mind, and spirit; messy and disorienting contradictions as well as clear and reorganizing choices.

Learning to Be Retired

Since then I have had other transformative learning experiences, most of them not as exhilarating or memorable as those I have described. At this time, I find myself in the middle of a learning experience that may or may not become transformative. I was forced to retire when I turned sixty-five, a requirement that I thought was unfair and unethical, not to mention ageist; unfortunately, at that time, it was not illegal. I ranted and raged to everyone who would listen to no avail. I was retired (although I still teach on contract) and found new work in the volunteer sector; and when that work was completed, I took a part-time paid position with a private, online university.

I retired from being a professor ten years ago and now am approaching my seventy-fifth birthday. I don't want to turn seventy-five; I don't know why. I have told my family and friends I plan to skip this birthday. I suspect I never completed the transformative learning associated with retirement and now I have come around to the experience again. I understand that my inner self is pushing for a resolution to the aborted transformation but my mind is not cooperating. So I am in the middle of chaos and distress again, ranting and raging at anyone who will listen. Maybe the comedians are right: Age is all a matter of verbs—we become twenty, turn thirty, push forty, reach fifty, make it to sixty, and then we gather speed so that we can hit seventy. I hope to have transformed my perspective by the time I am coasting to eighty.

ANALYSIS OF MY TRANSFORMATIVE LEARNING EVENTS

My analysis of these experiences involved examining each incident to determine any repeating patterns or themes. I have identified four steps or phases in a sequence that leads to my transformative learning.

The first phase in the sequence is that something happens that is inconsistent with "my experience," my construction of reality, and my assumptions about how the world works; that challenges my normal way of thinking; or that disconfirms at least part of my sense of self; and I am aware of this inconsistency, challenge, or disconfirmation. I assume that throughout my life I have ignored many inconsistencies, challenges, and disconfirmations because I was too busy to notice or too distracted by other experiences.

The result of this initial inconsistency is that I begin to feel distressed and start talking to myself and to any other person who will listen. I carry on a chaotic running commentary about the "problem" I am experiencing. If I am lucky, I find myself talking to someone who listens but does not judge or give advice. If the listener I have chosen has poor listening skills, I feel judged and become more distressed. I think of this as a "babbling" phase, with accompanying emotional highs and lows and an urgent need on my part to talk *ad nauseam* about my concerns. Success in this phase of change requires that I recognize that I am in a transition, that I select listeners very carefully, and that I listen to myself as I talk. This part of the sequence is very immediate: something happens, I am aware of it, I feel very emotional, I talk and I listen to myself; and when I start to listen to myself, my thinking begins to straighten itself out.

The second phase in the sequence occurs when eventually I stop talking and begin to mull things over by myself to make sense of whatever has happened. This is a reflective phase that comes easily to me. I have a "little professor" who lives in my mind somewhere above my left ear. She is a keen "observing other" who can recount my experiences in detail without judging them. She can give me a detailed description of what happened and has a talent for providing innumerable explanations about why it happened. This phase feels more conceptual, but talking to and obtaining information from my "little professor" feels like an essential experience by itself. The talking involved is slightly less messy than the babbling I do in the first phase; I feel less like I am on an emotional roller coaster, and my thinking is less chaotic. The outcome is that I experience a change either in my perspective of myself or my world or in the premises that underlie these perspectives.

The third phase in the sequence occurs when I put the change I have experienced into words that represent the change. I find it handy to have words to describe a change in order to share my experience with others, and the sharing I do is another experience by itself. I assume that some learners may carry out this part of the sequence at a subconscious level and therefore are not aware of how they have changed their perceptions. If so, then they miss the benefit of being able to share their changes with others.

The fourth phase in the sequence occurs when, once I have named it, I get on with other things and stop thinking consciously about the change I have introduced into my self-perception or my understanding of my world. My existing behavior patterns may still be consistent with the old perspective or premise, so I begin to introduce changes into my behavior that allow me to feel more congruent. This phase seems to involve many small experiences or action steps in which I try out, assess, and revise my behavior. This is an active phase that seems to take much longer than it probably should. For example, having discovered that I was competent enough to be a professor, I needed another eight years before I recognized myself in the role of "professor," and even then I was in for a surprise. I thought a professor was someone who worked alone—studying and doing research, teaching and counseling students—without having to rely on others. When I was hired as an assistant professor, I rapidly discovered I couldn't do the research component alone. Fortunately I found colleagues who asked me to work collaboratively with them, and suddenly I really was a professor in identity as well as title.

This action phase of the sequence is the hardest for me. It takes a long time to make a new perception of self an integral part of my behavior. I have talked to some learners who have more trouble with the reflective phase; but for me, the action phase is the most difficult. I think that this phase involves another type of experience in the transformative process and that the transformation is incomplete without it. Sometimes the transformation remains incomplete if the action steps do not lead to a new perception of self.

For example, my experience with retirement was distressful, and I resolved it by getting other work and continuing to teach on contract. Somehow I never integrated the concept of being a retired person into my self-perception. I cringe when someone who knows I am retired asks: "And what do you do now?" Maybe I should have stopped teaching long ago, but I enjoy working with students. Now I am beginning to think that I need to move on to other things, but I worry that this action may bring new disconfirming experiences that I will not enjoy very much—so I am resisting it just as I resisted it ten years ago.

I think that a learner can stop an experience that might lead to transformative learning by: (1) remaining unaware of or ignoring the disconfirming experience; (2) not reflecting on such experiences, even denying that they have occurred; (3) not consciously making sense of the change or force-fitting the change into an old perspective: and (4) not completing the transformation by engaging in actions based on new premises.

RELATIONSHIP OF ANALYSIS TO EXISTING THEORY

In the literature, I found little agreement about the order of the various phases and activities involved in the process of transformative learning. I also found that most articles about transformative learning were written as if the process occurred in a vacuum without emotional responses and without interaction with others. Where is the messiness, the chaos, and the emotional roller coaster that transformative learning brings to me?

The Process of Transformative Learning

My analysis of the process of my transformative learning most nearly matches the model of experiential learning proposed by David Kolb (1984). Each of the four phases I have described corresponds with Kolb's four components of experiential learning. The first phase, which begins with a disconfirming experience and then involves talking and dealing with emotional response, fits into Kolb's "concrete experience" component of experiential learning. The second phase, which involves reflection and self-reflection and my reliance on my "observing other," corresponds to Kolb's "reflective observation" component. The third phase, which involves naming my experience and construing it so that I can share it with others, seems to fit with Kolb's "abstract conceptualization" component. The fourth phase, which involves trying out new ways of behaving congruently with my new perspective, corresponds to Kolb's "active experiment" component. Consistent with my preferred learning style of assimilation (Kolb, 1984), I find the reflective part of the process much easier to manage than the active experimental part. But my experience tells me that transformative learning requires all four components of experiential learning, to ensure that a transformation has occurred and the new perspective has been fully integrated into an individual's self-identity.

Jack Mezirow's original work on transformative learning (Mezirow, 1978) outlined ten phases in the perspective transformation process; these were revised over time (Mezirow, 1991). Patricia Cranton (2002) lists these ten phases as follows:

1. Experiencing an event in society that disorients one's sense of self within a familiar role.
2. Engaging in reflection and self-reflection.
3. Critically assessing the personal assumptions and feelings that have alienated self from traditional role expectations.
4. Relating discontent to similar experiences of others; recognizing the shared problems.
5. Identifying new ways of acting within the role.
6. Building personal confidence and competence.
7. Planning a new course of action.
8. Acquiring the knowledge and skills necessary to implement this new course of action.
9. Trying out the planned action and assessing the results.
10. Reintegrating into society with the new role behaviors and with new assumptions and perspectives.

What is interesting about these ten phases is that at least five fall into the active phase of learning that I have described. Cranton (2002) revised this list into seven facets of transformative learning. In the process, she reduced Mezirow's active components to one facet—"acting on revisions, behaving, talking, and thinking in a way that is congruent with transformed assumptions or perspectives" (p. 66).

I assume that one could develop a range of activities and experiences that would fit into each of my four phases and that individual descriptions of associated activities would reflect preferred learning style. Nod Miller (2000), for example, describes her personal experience for three of Kolb's components; but for active experimentation, she describes only how she would facilitate the learning of others. In my own experience, I find I have fewer words to describe the experiences in this action phase; some of my experiences seem to occur outside of my immediate awareness, but those I am aware of are very hard to put into words. If I could only put hand gestures and facial expressions into print, I would be able to create a more complete case study.

Circumventing Transformative Learning

The idea of being able to circumvent a transformative learning process is also found in the literature. Marilyn Taylor (2011) developed the term "emergent learning" in her doctoral research (1979), which coincided with Mezirow's earliest work in 1970s. The emergent learning process is similar to the transformative learning process. It comprises four phases—disorientation, exploration, transformation, and equilibrium—and four transitions, which occur between the phases—disconfirmation of expectations, reframing, reflecting, and naming. Taylor describes two situations in which an individual learner might not be able to successfully navigate the process. The first is the possibility that a learner can become mired in the initial disorientation phase and choose to blame an outside authority for the confusion and distress while seeking others who will support this perspective. Taylor proposes that there are two ways out of this situation—withdrawing from the setting in which the disorientation occurs, or collecting critical comments about the authority to whom we attribute our duress and looking for ways to oppose the authority. The second situation that prevents us from successfully navigating the process is failing to bring together all our reflective thoughts about the change we are experiencing and to generate a synthesis that results in a conclusion. When this happens, learners may collapse back into self-doubt and recurring anxieties and find themselves back in the disorienting phase.

My experience with mandatory retirement illustrates the problem of failing to learn. I never really tried to engage in transformative learning the first time I was retired. I blamed an ageist faculty association and university for assuming that tenured individuals over sixty-five would become senile and create an insolvable problem for the university. I could not persuade them to critically reflect on this faulty assumption; no one would listen. So I changed jobs but never changed my perspective of myself as "retired." Now I am ready to move on, and I must explore my options beyond retirement to find out what seventy-five or eighty might bring. The university has finally gone through its own transformative learning process by eliminating mandatory retirement, although I suspect doubts still linger about the efficacy of this change.

Perspectives on Experiential Learning

Tara Fenwick (2000) has written about the role of experiential learning in five contemporary perspectives of cognition. These perspectives are: constructivist, psychoanalytical, situative, critical cultural, and enactivist. She states that the constructivist perspective tends to prevail in adult education. My early transformative learning experiences fall into this perspective. Fenwick (2000) describes the constructivist perspective as one that casts the individual as

> the central actor in the drama of personal meaning-making. The learner reflects on lived experience and then interprets and generalizes this experience to form mental structures. These structures are knowledge, stored in memory as concepts that can be represented, expressed, and transferred to new situations. Explanations in this perspective inquire into the ways people attend to and

perceive experience, interpret and categorize it as concepts, and then continue
adapting or transforming their conceptual structures or meaning perspectives.
(p. 248)

The descriptions I provided earlier seem to include all these activities. However, the constructivist perspective doesn't seem to encompass the messiness
and vacillating aspects of my experiences, nor the fact that some transformations seemed to occur because of pressure from my unconscious mind rather
than from reflective thought. The psychoanalytical perspective, on the other
hand, focuses on

the individual's relations between the outside world of culture and objects of
knowledge and the inside world of psychic energies and dilemmas relating to
these objects of knowledge.... These knowledge dilemmas unfold through
struggles between the unconscious and the conscious mind, which is aware of
unconscious rumblings but can neither access them fully nor understand their
language. (p. 251)

My transformative learning experiences that occurred after midlife seem to
encompass both the constructivist and psychoanalytical perspectives. I gradually became more aware of my dreams and what they were nudging me to
learn, a process Jung describes as individuation (Cranton, 2006). Some of my
dreams were frightening, some left me feeling angry, and some filled me with
wonder at the complexity of life.

As I think further about the learning experiences I have described, I conclude
that any single experience could be analyzed in terms of any of Fenwick's five
perspectives. The situative perspective "maintains that learning is rooted in
the situation in which a person participates, not in the head of that person as
intellectual concepts produced by reflection nor as inner energies produced by
psychic conflicts" (Fenwick, 2000, p. 253). My experience of learning to be a
self-directed learner seems very rooted in the situation in which I found myself
as the mother of young children trying to write an essay on stress.

The critical cultural perspective centers on power as the core issue. This
perspective encourages us to "analyze the structures of dominance that express
or govern the social relationships and competing forms of communication and
cultural practices within that system" (Fenwick, 2000, p. 256). My learning that
I had the potential to become a professor reflects the structures of dominance
that I assumed existed in graduate school.

The enactivist perspective concludes that "cognition and environment become simultaneously enacted through experiential learning. The first premise
is that the systems represented by person and context are inseparable, and
the second premise is that change occurs from emerging systems affected by
the intentional tinkering of one with the other" (Fenwick, 2000, p. 261). My description of learning that I was a teacher certainly seems to reflect the enactive

and interactive nature of my role as a camp counselor attempting to respond to the needs of a young girl.

CONCLUSION

Experience plays a crucial role in all aspects of the transformative learning process. In the initial phase of such learning, something happens—an experience in the here and now—that raises conflicts within my past experience and results in feelings of disorientation, chaotic thinking, and excessive talking about my "problem." In the second phase, I quietly reflect on and talk to myself about the source of my problem. My reflection experiences lead to a new way of understanding what has changed. In the third phase, I find words to describe the change so that I can share my experiences with others. In the fourth phase, I find ways to integrate the change into my everyday behavior. The strategies I use involve small action-oriented experiences that accumulate to a point when I can see that the change has become an integral part of my sense of self.

I believe that we need to collect more firsthand accounts of transformative learning to identify the many different ways in which experience enters into different phases of the process. This information would lead us to develop a variety of facilitating approaches to assist the learner going through a transformation. We also need to develop an integrated perspective of the process that includes the enactive nature of learning and teaching; the interactions of learners and teachers; the benefits and limitations of transformation; and the many different ways in which we can avoid transformative learning.

References

Belenky, M. F., Clinchy, B. M., Goldberger, N. R., & Tarule, J. M. (1986). *Women's ways of knowing: The development of self, voice, and mind.* New York: Basic Books.

Brundage, D. H., & MacKeracher, D. (1980). *Adult learning principles and their application to program planning.* Toronto: Ontario Ministry of Education (ERIC Reproduction Document ED 181 292).

Cranton, P. (2002). *Teaching for transformation* (pp. 63–71). New Directions for Adult and Continuing Education, no. 93. San Francisco: Jossey-Bass.

Cranton, P. (2006). *Understanding and promoting transformative learning: A guide for educators of adults* (2nd ed.). San Francisco: Jossey-Bass.

Dewey, J. (1916). *Democracy and education.* The Free Press.

Dewey, J. (1938). *Experience and education.* The Kappa Delta Pi Lecture Series. New York: Simon & Schuster.

Dirkx, J. M., & Lavin, R. (1991). Understanding and facilitating experience-based learning in adult education: The FOURthought model. Paper presented at the Midwest Research-to-Practice Conference, St. Paul, MN, October 3–4, 1991. Retrieved from https://www.msu.edu/~dirkx/EBLRVS.91.htm

Fenwick, T. (2000). Expanding conceptions of experiential learning: A review of the five contemporary perspectives on cognition. *Adult Education Quarterly*, *50*(4), 243–272.

Kidd, J. R. (1973). *How adults learn* (rev. ed.). New York: Association Press.

Knowles, M. S. (1970). *The modern practice of adult education: Andragogy versus pedagogy*. New York: Association Press.

Kolb, D. A. (1984). *Experiential learning: Experience as the source of learning and development*. Englewood Cliffs, NJ: Prentice-Hall.

Lewin, K. (1951). *Field theory in social sciences*. New York: Harper & Row.

MacKeracher, D. (2004). *Making sense of adult learning* (2nd ed.). Toronto: University of Toronto Press.

Mezirow, J. (1978). *Education for perspective transformation: Women's re-entry programs in community colleges*. New York: Columbia University, Teachers College, Center for Adult Education (ERIC Reproduction Document ED 166 367).

Mezirow, J. (1991). *Transformative dimensions of adult learning*. San Francisco: Jossey-Bass.

Miller, N. (2000). Learning from experience in adult education. In A. L. Wilson & E. R. Hayes (Eds.), *Handbook of adult and continuing education* (2000 ed.) (pp. 71–86). San Francisco: Jossey-Bass.

Piaget, J. (1971). *Psychology and epistemology: Towards a theory of knowledge*. New York: Grossman.

Taylor, M. (1979). Adult learning in an emergent learning group: Toward a theory of learning from the learner's perspective. Unpublished doctoral dissertation, University of Toronto, Toronto, ON.

Taylor, M. (2011). *Emergent learning for wisdom*. New York: Palgrave.

CHAPTER TWENTY-TWO

Group Work and Dialogue

Spaces and Processes for Transformative Learning in Relationships

Steven A. Schapiro, Ilene L. Wasserman,
and Placida V. Gallegos

A rich literature characterizes *group work* and *dialogue* as contexts and means for personal and social transformation. In the transformative learning literature, the terms "group work" and "dialogue" are usually taken as givens, but they are used in varied and often imprecise ways. In this chapter we present a framework for bringing these areas of literature together in order to explore how various kinds of groups provide a context for transformative learning, and the forms of dialogue that take place within them.

In his recent book chapter, "Fostering Transformative Learning," Taylor (2009) affirms that "engagement in dialogue with the self and others" (p. 9) is one of the core elements of a transformative approach to teaching.

> Dialogue is the essential medium through which transformation is promoted and developed.... Dialogue becomes the medium for critical reflection to be put into action, where experience is reflected on, assumptions and beliefs are questioned, and habits of mind are ultimately transformed. The dialogue is not so much analytical, point-counterpoint dialogue, but dialogue emphasizing relational and trustful communication. (p. 9)

Although this conceptualization emphasizes Mezirow's rational approach to transformative learning, it keeps open the question of how the process and content of the dialogue will vary, depending on the "educator's theoretical approach to transformative learning" (Taylor, 2009, p. 9). We explore such variations in what follows, beginning with a brief overview of the foundations of group work and dialogue as means for transformation.

The foundational literature on group work for transformation can be found in the sometimes overlapping fields of *adult education* (Lindeman, 1961; Dewey, 1916; Rose, 1996), where the emphasis has been on learning through discussion and on groups as incubators for democratic living; *psychotherapy, counseling psychology,* and *social work* (Yalom, 1986; Corey & Corey, 1977; Andrews, 2001), with a focus on the group as a context for personal growth and healing; and *social psychology* (Lewin, 1946; Lippitt, 1949), with an emphasis on intergroup and organizational relations and improving interpersonal communications.

The major threads in the literature on the transformative power of dialogue come from Carl Rogers's (1961) work on person-centered therapy and the role of deeply reflective listening and unconditional positive regard; theologian Martin Buber's (1958) work on moving from I-it to I-thou relationships through a process of what he calls *genuine dialogue*; physicist David Bohm's work (1996), later adapted by Senge (1990), Isaacs (1999), and others, on dialogue as a process through which people in groups can explore their assumptions and ways of meaning making; Paulo Freire's (1970) work on dialogue in connection with action as a means of revealing and changing our social realities; and various social constructionist perspectives (McNamee & Gergen, 1999; Anderson, Baxter, & Cissna, 2004; Wasserman & Gallegos, 2009) on transformation though the engagement of differences and the creation of dialogic moments.

Although all of these threads from both areas inform the literature on transformative learning in group settings, the connections are rarely explicit. The more aware we are of the implicit theories of change and transformation that underlie an approach to transformative learning, the more thoughtful and intentional we can be in using them.

Most of that transformative learning literature emphasizes the role of *relationships* with others as the Petri dish—the growth-supporting environment—that provides both the *container* and *space* in which such learning can occur, and the *dialogical processes* through which learning unfolds (Cranton, 2006; Taylor, 2009; Yorks & Kasl, 2006). We asked ourselves, *what is it about* groups *that can create a unique container in which transformation can occur?*

We continue our discussion with some initial answers to that question, drawing on our own practice and research as well as on the literature. We then provide a matrix that integrates and provides a framework for discussing three main kinds of transformative group work and the sorts of dialogue that support them.

GROUPS AS THE CONTAINER FOR TRANSFORMATIVE DIALOGUE

The qualities of a dialogic group provide a unique container for transformative learning, in that the norms and directional force of the relationships foster *critical self-reflection*, brought on by members' commitment to the group. Transformative dialogue groups enable profound engagements and *transformative dialogic moments* (Wasserman, 2004). *Transformative dialogic moments*, a construct that builds on Buber's (1958) concept of a dialogic moment, are facilitated by critical reflection on moments of dissonance in the context of a group. The group provides the container or holding environment to hold the complexity of seemingly incompatible personal narratives or ideas.

Qualities Vital to Transformative Dialogic Groups

> When communicating dialogically, one can listen, ask direct questions, present one's ideas, argue, debate, etc. The defining characteristic of dialogic communication is that all of these speech acts are done in ways that hold one's own position but allow others space to hold theirs, and are profoundly open to hearing others' positions without needing to oppose or assimilate them. (Pearce, 2001, p. 11)

What do we do with differences in the space of dialogue? One of the authors of this chapter (Wasserman, 2004), through her research on dialogue and the engagement of social identity group differences, identified four overlapping factors that enable and constrain transformative dialogic moments in groups, as just defined. The first two address qualities of the people involved; the third and fourth highlight the enabling of discursive processes.

○ *Continuity in members' commitment and motivation.* Participants join the group with a common motivation: to engage with others in critical reflection. The group provides a container or holding space, which is a catalyst for an encounter between and among people who might not otherwise have met. The shared commitment and motivation in a consistent space nurture a sense of expectancy to learn from mystery, and a stance of curiosity and openness to difference.

○ *Curiosity and openness.* One must suspend judgment and certainty and be prepared to discover something new about others and oneself. Inquiry, staying in the question, creates an invitation to the other's perspective. As Gurevitch (1989) warned, we must constantly challenge ourselves not to assume that our fellow human beings inhabit the same reality that we do. It is in the encounter of the strange or of not understanding that we discover meaning-making structures—the assumptions that guide us.

○ *Emotional engagement through storytelling.* Storytelling plays a key role in creating emotional engagement. Connection occurs not merely in the sharing of the story, but also in what happens once we share our story. When we feel heard and met by group members, deep emotions and a felt sense of cohesiveness often emerge.

○ *Reflection and mutual sense-making.* Reflection provides supplemental action to the stories. *Reflection in the group* provides a new episode for the group: a turn of shared social meaning. Inquiry is a catalyst for groups to think about their norms and process and to take a third-person perspective on their own experience.

Creating Group Spaces for Transformative Learning

From another perspective, one of our other coauthors (Schapiro, 2009a) drew on accounts of transformation in four varied contexts to identify key principles and practices contributing to the creation of group spaces for transformative learning. Those contexts included a class on improvisation, non-formal collaborative learning among peers, a participatory action research project in a non-profit, and mentor-guided student-centered educational programs for midlife adults (Fisher-Yoshida, Geller, & Schapiro, 2009). In describing the characteristics of these spaces, these accounts drew from a variety of theoretical perspectives that provide an overarching concept of a learning space. These include Kegan's (1982) notion of cultures of embeddedness—and the confirming, contradicting, and continuing functions of holding environments that support growth, development, and transformation (Schapiro's [2009b] model adds a fourth kind of holding environment—creating—which he argues must follow contradiction if transformation is to occur); Lewin's concept of life spaces as applied by Kolb and Kolb (2005) to learning spaces that support experiential learning, and Nonaka and Konno's (1998) articulation of the concept of "ba" as a shared space that harbors meaning. Other perspectives used focus on the nature of the learning relationships, including Buber's (1958) I-thou relationship, Belenky, Clinchy, Goldberger, and Tarule's (1986) notion of connected knowing, and Yorks and Kasl's (2006) learning within relationship.

Although there is much variation across these different perspectives and experiences, there is also much that they have in common, which Schapiro (2009a) summarized as follows:

> From this rich mix of theory and practice, we can begin to distill a set of five common themes or characteristics of transformative learning spaces: (1) learning happens in *relationships*, (2) in which there is *shared ownership* and control of the learning space, (3) room for the *whole person*—feelings as well as thoughts,

body and soul, as well as mind, (4) and *sufficient time* for collaboration, action, reflection, and integration, (5) to pursue a process of *inquiry driven by* the questions, needs, and purposes of the *learners.* (p. 112)

We can hear in these factors echoes of the discursive practices that support transformative dialogic moments described earlier—in particular, the process of inquiry, emotional engagement in the relationships, and commitment to the group demonstrated by dedicated time and space. If such elements are present, learners will have the support and the challenge—the safety, the disconfirming experiences, and the invitation to take risks—that can make transformative learning possible. Whether or not such learning happens depends on both the readiness and needs of the learner and the nature of the learning processes that unfold within the group. Thus far, we have identified overarching qualities of a group experience that can create space for transformative learning in groups of various kinds. We now turn to the variations among such groups and the dialogical processes that occur within them.

TYPES OF TRANSFORMATIVE GROUPS

Transformative learning is about both the process and content of meaning-making; the changes in our epistemologies and the assumptions, perspectives, and frames of reference that inform and underlie the meaning we make. Transformative learning is also about development: development toward more inclusive ways of understanding experience (Mezirow, 1991), higher orders of consciousness (Kegan, 1982), more critical understandings of our sociopolitical realities (Freire, 1970), greater individuation and wholeness (Dirkx, 2000), and increased capacity for empathy across cultures (Landis, Bennett, & Bennett, 2003).

We therefore find it useful to identify and discuss three main kinds of *transformative group work* (or *transformative learning in group contexts*) in terms of the developmental outcomes that they are designed to provoke:

- Personal growth and awareness
- Relational empathy across differences
- Critical systemic consciousness

These goals of group work, defined more fully in this section, are neither pure nor isolated forms. Although these forms of group work can and often do operate separately, they can sometimes be combined in the same group experience. Figure 22.1 provides a Venn diagram of the uniqueness of each type of group, of how they overlap, and of how people interact within them.

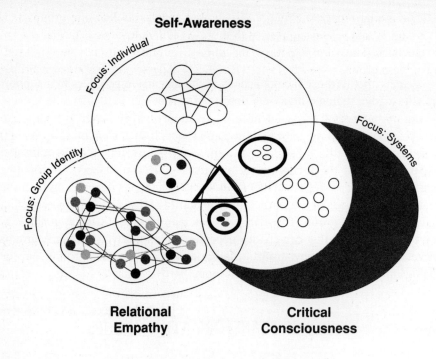

Figure 22.1 Types and Characteristics of Transformative Groups

The illustration within each circle depicts the way individuals relate to one another to accomplish their goals. In the self-awareness type of group, participants relate as distinct individuals with minimal acknowledgment of group memberships or the larger systems and structures of society. This is depicted by the small indistinct circles interacting within a group setting.

In the relational empathy across different kinds of groups, participants foreground their membership in distinct groups relative to each other, with multiple sources of identity often intersecting simultaneously. The multiple circles within the relational empathy circle and the differently shaded small circles within them are meant to represent the multiple group identities across which people interact. In the intersection between the self-awareness and relational empathy groups, the figure symbolizes the way in which these kinds of groups can be combined, with a focus on self-awareness in regard to our differences.

In the groups with critical systemic consciousness as a goal, people relate as members of social groups and systems that seek social emancipation and social change for social justice. They are illustrated as individuals within a systemic context. In the space that overlaps between the critical consciousness and relational empathy groups, the symbol represents learning groups that focus on systemic consciousness about how our multishaded differences are constructed. The symbol in the space where the critical consciousness and self-awareness groups overlap illustrates a focus on personal awareness regarding the roles we play in supporting or changing whatever systemic dynamics may be in play.

The place where all three kinds of groups overlap, indicated by the delta sign in the center of the diagram, illustrates the "sweet spot" where we have the most leverage for change through engaging simultaneously at all three levels.

Group Characteristics

These three types of transformative learning groups can be characterized in regard to five factors (see Table 22.1). The first factor concerns *the basis for group membership and relationship,* as explained above in reference to Figure 22.1. Although Daloz (2000), for one, asserted that the "presence of the other" is one of "four conditions for transformation" (p. 112), the role of the other in the transformative learning process varies according to the sort of transformation involved. (The other conditions cited by Daloz, 2000, are "reflective discourse, a mentoring community, and opportunities for committed action" [p. 112].)

A second factor in characterizing groups concerns *the experience that group members reflect on and make meaning about:* experience that is in the past, outside of the group, or both; or experience in the here and now of the group itself.

A third factor concerns the *locus of change* in the habits of mind and habits of being on which the transformative learning is focused—intrapersonal, interpersonal, intragroup, intergroup, organizational, and societal.

Fourth, we differentiate between the *form that reflection takes* in each group; and fifth, we consider the *dialogic processes* that are most often associated with each type of group, ranging from: individual sharing, listening, and feedback; to communicating differences; to collaborative inquiry in search of shared meaning and analysis. Many of these are often overlapping and combined. Table 22.1 presents a matrix for thinking about each kind of transformative group in terms of these five different factors. A fuller discussion of each of these kinds of transformative group work with implications for guiding interventions in organizations and for educational design follows.

Groups for Personal Growth and Self-Awareness

This type of group is conceptualized as a collection of individuals who are there to support each other's personal learning. In these groups, the goal is self-discovery in the context of relationship with others. The sorts of self-discovery

Table 22.1 Types and Characteristics of Transformative Groups

Group Characteristics	Group Type (in terms of the goal)		
	Personal Growth and Self-Awareness	*Relational Empathy Across Differences*	*Critical Systemic Consciousness*
Basis for group membership and relationships	Common interest in personal or intellectual growth or both	Desire to explore differences and similarities	Interest in identifying, understanding, and addressing shared social realities
Primary experience that is the object of reflection and dialogue	Individual perceptions and life experiences outside of the group and interpersonal interactions within the group	Lived experiences of social identities outside of the group, and interactions across differences within the group	Lived experiences of oppression, structural inequality, and life in systems outside of the group
Locus of change	Intrapersonal, interpersonal	Intrapersonal, interpersonal, intragroup, intergroup	Intrapersonal, organizational, societal
Form of reflection	Critical self-reflection on assumptions, images from our subconscious, the group process	Mutual meaning-making across difference	Ideology critique, collective analysis of oppressive systems, and reflection on action for social change
Dialogic process(es)	Critical dialectical discourse Dialogue with the self Listening, witnessing Feedback	Storytelling that highlights social identity group perspectives Exploring and imagining of the experiences of others	Problem-posing, storytelling, and shared inquiry and meaning-making Renaming shared social realities Reflection on action

and self-awareness involved could be primarily intellectual, emotional, soulful, or a combination of all three. In such groups, the dialogue focuses on the self: on each person's ideas, assumptions, feelings, personal qualities, dreams, and so forth.

Examples of personal growth and awareness groups include study groups, therapy groups, meditation groups, encounter groups, T-groups, councils, and various kinds of self-help groups. This type of group exemplifies the concept of *group work* as a means to achieve personal growth and change and is used most often within the fields of social work and counseling psychology.

In his construct, *circles of trust*, Palmer (2007) describes such groups as containers that support personal growth and change. These circles provide an opportunity for "being alone in community"—a concept that expresses well this idea of group support for personal change. He talks of such circles as creating "a space between us" (p. 56) that invites the soul, while recognizing that other such groups are more conducive to inviting the intellect, the emotion, the will, and the ego, all of which could involve different sorts of transformative learning.

Personal growth groups and self-awareness groups provide a context in which individuals can critically assess their assumptions and frames of reference, get in touch with and express their emotions, reflect on their own behavior, dialogue with aspects of their own subconscious, and reach new levels of personal integration and development. In such groups, the role of others is to listen and ask open and honest questions, witness and honor others' expressions of feelings, serve as a source of vicarious experience and identification, offer feedback about interpersonal behaviors, and at times challenge the validity of others' ideas and assumptions. In all such cases, others are there to help us to get in touch with, express, and clarify our own thoughts and feelings.

In these groups, the experience on which the group reflects may be either outside or inside the group, depending on the focus. For instance, in a group focused on improving skills and capacities for resolving conflict, people might reflect on their past or ongoing experience with conflict outside of the group or learn from conflict that emerges in the group itself, or both.

Two particular conceptualizations of this sort of group stand out within the transformative learning literature: Mezirow's (2003) model of perspective transformation through critical dialectical discourse, and Boyd and Myers's (1988) model of discernment and individuation through dialogue with the subconscious.

From Mezirow's perspective (2003), the transformative learning process involves a special form of dialogue, which he calls *critical reflective discourse*. "Discourse here refers to dialogue involving the assessment of beliefs, feelings, and values. Discourse involves topics referred to from the point of view of a particular frame of reference. Justification of a proposition must be assessed in relation to the particular frames of reference applied" (p. 59).

Elsewhere, following Habermas, Mezirow (1991) described the ideal conditions (never completely met) for participants to engage in this sort of discourse:

- Accurate and complete information
- Freedom from coercion and distorting self-perception
- Ability to weigh evidence and assess arguments objectively
- Openness to alternative perspectives
- Ability to reflect critically on presuppositions and their consequences
- Equal opportunity to participate
- Ability to accept an informed and objective consensus as valid (p. 78)

To the extent that these conditions are present, group members can use this rational process to critically assess and, as necessary, change their own assumptions and beliefs.

In Mezirow's model, the *locus of change* is on individual consciousness and meaning schemes. However, depending on the nature and level of the assumptions involved, those new perspectives may lead us to make changes in our interpersonal and organizational behavior, or to take action for organizational or social change.

An alternative model of groups that foster personal growth and change was described by Boyd and Myers (1988) as *transformative education*. In Boyd's (1991) view, in the broadest sense, such groups "provide a supportive structure ... [in which people can] work toward expressing their true selves in community with others" (p. 181). The goal of such transformative education is "helping individuals work towards acknowledging and understanding the dynamics between their inner and outer worlds" (Boyd & Myers, 1988, p. 261).

In the depth psychology approach to transformative learning, the dialogue does not focus solely *on* the self; it is dialogue *with* the self; that is, dialogue between the ego and other hidden parts of one's self, ultimately integrating those other parts into an expanded self-concept. In this process, the group can provide a supportive context—a container in which the person can access those previously hidden parts of the self and try on new behaviors. It is also a context that can elicit projections and other symbolic content from which we can learn, with others there to provide a mirror and be players in our own psychodrama. In such groups, the experience reflected on may be both inside and outside of the group, as well as in our own subconscious and in the external world; it is about bringing these together. The locus of change is clearly on the intrapersonal and perhaps interpersonal levels, as new learnings and personal capacities can lead to changes in our interpersonal behaviors.

Groups for Relational Empathy Across Differences

In this kind of group-level work, transformation is often understood to come about *not* primarily through an individual or intrapersonal process of critical reflection or discernment in dialogue with others and the self, but as a direct outcome of the process of our genuine dialogue with an "other" or others. From this perspective, we transform as we socially construct new meanings of self and others through hearing and being changed by each other's stories and perspectives. In this respect, dialogue does not serve as context for the individual construction of meaning, but as a process for the social construction or coordinated management of meaning (Pearce & Pearce, 2003).

Relational empathy is a process of engaging and being fully present to another in the ongoing processes of relating. Elsewhere in the literature this concept has been described as *mutual empathy*. This is a reciprocal process, as described by Jordan (1997):

> While some mutual empathy involves an acknowledgment of sameness in the other, an appreciation of the differentness of the other's experience is also vital. The movement towards the other's differentness is actually central to growth in relationship and also can provide a powerful sense of validation for both people. Growth occurs because as I stretch to match or understand your experience, something new is acknowledged or grows in me. (p. 3)

The development of empathy both is fostered by relationships and fosters relationships.

Often the engagement of differences elicits a disorienting dilemma or dissonance. This occurs when one's story of oneself in relationship to the other differs from another's own story. This dissonance or seeming contradiction among the narratives of group members is grist for this form of transformative group work (Wasserman, 2004). The group provides the learning space for members to share their stories and the time to reflect on those aspects of each other's stories that are in tension with one another. The space and time that the group work affords is consequential to enabling members to reconstruct and expand their stories to include the identity narratives of others.

To the extent that the dialogues highlight social identities, the primary loci of change can be at the intrapersonal, interpersonal, intragroup, and intergroup levels. The change process unfolds as group members come to understand more about how they have constructed their own social identities in relation to those with whom they share each identity and those who are different.

Many kinds of groups for dialogue across difference have been conceptualized and researched from a transformative learning perspective, including, for example, intergroup dialogue (Gurin, Nagda, & Zuniga, 2004), sustained dialogue (Saunders, 1999), and the Public Conversations Project (2006). Such groups focus on the here-and-now experience of communication within the group itself as the content of reflection and dialogue, as well as on sharing stories about and learning from people's lived experiences outside of the group.

Organizational practitioners often use homogenous and heterogeneous groups strategically in the process of culture change interventions (Weisbord & Janoff, 2000). Groups may initially be convened based on similarity such as gender and race to allow for connection and dialogue to occur within the group (Zane, 2002). Especially in cases where subordinated groups are ignored or not fully included, these affinity groups provide them with much-needed forums to identify their shared experiences and amplify their collective voices in the dominant cultures. Later phases of organizational interventions bring together mixed groups across social identities, with the purpose of mutual sharing and the development of relational empathy.

Groups for Critical Systemic Consciousness

Sometimes called the *social emancipatory approach to transformative learning*, the focus of this type of group is on understanding and changing shared aspects of group members' social realities, locations, and contexts. In Freire's words, education for critical *consciousness* (conscientization) is "the process through which men [*sic*] not as recipients, but as knowing subjects, achieve a deepening awareness of both the socio-cultural reality that shapes their lives and of their capacity to transform that reality" (Freire, 1976, p. 27).

Such groups work to understand the ways in which the "personal is political"; that is, the structural and systemic causes of what we may at first perceive to be our personal problems and limitations. Such a process can go on in, for example, women's consciousness raising groups, a Frierian culture circle, a community group analyzing pollution of the local environment, and an action research team in a corporate setting. It can apply to any process in which people reflect together on shared aspects of their social realities and develop a deeper understanding of the structural and systemic limitations to their full humanization and empowerment.

The transformative learning process leading to critical consciousness usually involves praxis: a continuing process of action, critical reflection, and dialogue. Transformative education from this perspective may include various forms of critical pedagogy (Darder, Baltodano, & Torres, 2003), ideology critique (Brookfield, 2005), and popular education (Horton, 1990). The dialogue process usually involves story-telling about one's experience, critical analysis of common themes and issues, problem-posing (posing the limitations people experience as problems to be solved and not as unchangeable facts of their existence), renaming of reality in ways that envision the possibility of change, and that continuing praxis cycle of action, reflection, and dialogue as people attempt to bring those changes about. Freire and others (Vella, 1994) characterize this educational meaning-making process as dialogic (that is, created through dialogue) as opposed to banking (that is, depositing meaning into students' heads).

Although such dialogue can lead to an awareness of how individuals have unconsciously internalized the rules and norms of the hegemonic status quo, the focus is not on our individual psyches alone, but on the necessarily concurrent transformation of our individual consciousness and our social contexts at various system levels—small group, organization, society, and even planetary (O'Sullivan, 1999). Such work can include the sort of critical discourse described by Mezirow, but in this case that discourse is not purely "academic" or personal, but is informed by and leads to action. This process can also involve working with and integrating images and feelings from the subconscious, as in the depth psychology approach, but again, the emphasis here is not on personality integration but rather on unpacking and transforming our internalized oppression and domination.

Such groups reflect on people's lived experiences outside of and prior to the group experience, as well as what plays out in the group's current internal dynamics as a microcosm (Slater, 1966) of the larger systems of which they are a part. Calling our attention to such dynamics and trying to change how they occur in the group can help to raise consciousness about how they are occurring elsewhere and what we do to either enable or interrupt the oppression that is all around us.

In addition to work by Freire and other critical educators in the transformative learning field, this approach can be found in what have been called the cultural-spiritual (Tisdell, 2003) and race-centric (Johnson-Bailey & Alfred, 2006) approaches to liberatory education. In addition, much of the work of what has been called *collaborative inquiry* (Yorks & Kasl, 2002) has focused on shared inquiry into issues related to oppression and liberation, including, for example, internalized anti-Semitism and the nature of whiteness and white privilege. Although collaborative inquiry can involve a group exploration of any question of shared interest and does not necessarily include critical systemic analysis, it incorporates repeated cycles of inquiry, action, reflection, and dialogue, and it can be critical if the inquiry is sociopolitical in nature. Literature involving organizational transformation (Yorks & Marsick, 2000) and group consciousness (Kasl & Elias, 2000) provides other examples of transformative group work toward critical systemic consciousness at those system levels, with the dialogue focused on the shared construction of meaning through actions for change and reflection in response.

IMPLICATIONS FOR PRACTICE

In this section we discuss the range of possibilities for drawing on the matrix (Table 22.1) and Venn diagram (Figure 22.1) of Types and Characteristics of Transformative Groups to guide interventions designed to cocreate transformative experiences for group members. As discussed in the previous sections, there is considerable overlap and complexity involved in the various types of group work focused on transformative learning. We have emphasized distinctions among them as a way of crystallizing their unique purposes and processes. As we move into the realm of praxis, distinctions become less clear and hybridization becomes predominant.

As discussed earlier, the Venn diagram in Figure 22.1 provides a graphic way of presenting both the uniqueness of each group type as well as depicting how they overlap. We turn now to the areas of overlap, with the acknowledgment that the margins between and among the different types of groups often narrow in service of the unique purpose of a particular group and the desired outcomes.

We recognize that certain combinations are more compatible, whereas others may be more difficult to integrate. For example, there is some overlap between self-awareness and relational empathy groups. Often in relational empathy groups attention must necessarily begin at the individual level, with each person coming to know more about fellow group members. This includes but is not limited to their group memberships or identities. Building connections with others at the individual level supports feelings of safety and the interest and willingness to risk being candid when exploring the difficult but often rewarding terrain of intergroup differences. Similarly, in critical consciousness groups, interpersonal and intergroup dimensions can often support the movement toward greater understanding and capacity to deal more effectively with oppressive systems.

The triangle in the middle of Figure 22.1, representing where the three kinds of group all overlap, is the place where the most integrated and powerful sorts of transformational experiences can occur. There is an ineffable element of mystery to the transformative power of group experience, and it is at that nexus—where our individual, group, and systemic levels of consciousness come together—that we have the opportunity to change in the most profound ways.

We offer the matrix as a tool for group development, facilitation, and process. The matrix can be used as a guide to more intentionally design and implement group processes that create containers that support transformative learning of various kinds. Leaders of organizations can use the matrix as a guide to forming action learning groups and action teams. Group facilitators, classroom teachers, and community-based educators can use it to support the design and facilitation of group processes. Depending on the transformative outcome or outcomes one is trying to work toward, the matrix can be used as a guide to select the most appropriate group composition as well as the focus and form of the dialogue and reflection.

CONCLUSION

We began by posing the question: What are the unique qualities of group work that foster transformative learning? We answered that question by developing a framework that delineates the different ways in which dialogue in groups is conceptualized and used as a means for transformation. Although we recognize that this typology represents just one of many ways in which these constructs could be categorized and discussed, we find this framework to be a useful tool for thinking about our own practice, and we hope that our readers will as well. We have used it to help us distinguish the different levels of systems in play in the group process and how they overlap. The model also serves as a reference for and a reminder of the full range of choices we have for where (that is, at what system level) and how to intervene to access a broader range of possibilities for transformation.

We look forward to feedback that will help us to further refine and develop our thinking. The theory and practice of transformative learning continues to develop and evolve as it is integrated with other ways of thinking about the processes of growth and transformation, and we look forward to contributing to that ongoing process.

References

Anderson, R., Baxter, L. A., & Cissna, K. N. (2004). *Dialogue: Theorizing difference in communication studies.* Thousand Oaks, CA: SAGE.

Andrews, J. C. (2001). Group work's place in social work: A historical analysis. *Journal of Sociology and Social Welfare, XXIV*(3), 211–235.

Belenky, M., Clinchy, B., Goldberger, N., & Tarule, J. (1986). *Women's ways of knowing.* New York: Basic Books.

Bohm, D. (1996). *On dialogue.* London: Routledge.

Boyd, R. D. (1991). *Personal transformation in small groups: A Jungian perspective.* London: Routledge.

Boyd, R. D., & Myers, J. G. (1988). Transformative education. *International Journal of Lifelong Education, 7*(4), 261–284.

Brookfield, S. D. (2005). *The power of critical theory: Liberating adult learning and teaching.* San Francisco: Jossey-Bass.

Buber, M. (1958). *I and thou* (R. G. Smith, Trans.). New York: T&T Clark.

Corey, M. S., & Corey, G. (1977). *Groups: Process and practice.* Belmont, CA: Wadsworth.

Cranton, P. (2006). *Understanding and promoting transformative learning* (2nd ed.). San Francisco: Jossey-Bass.

Daloz, L. (2000). Transformative learning for the common good. In J. Mezirow & Associates (Eds.), *Learning as transformation: Critical perspectives on a theory in progress.* San Francisco: Jossey-Bass.

Darder, A., Baltodano, M., & Torres, R. (2003). *The critical pedagogy reader.* New York: Routledge.

Dewey, J. (1916). *Education and democracy.* New York: Macmillan.

Dirkx, J. (2000). Transformative learning and the journey of individuation. ERIC Digest No. 223. Columbus, OH: Eric Clearinghouse on Adult, Vocational and Continuing Education.

Fisher-Yoshida, B., Geller, K. D., & Schapiro, S. (Eds.). (2009). *Innovations in transformative learning: Space, culture, and the arts.* New York: Peter Lang.

Freire, P. (1970). *Pedagogy of the oppressed.* New York: Seabury.

Freire, P. (1976). A few notes on conscientization. In R. Dale (Ed.), *Schooling and capitalism.* London: Routledge.

Gurevitch, Z. D. (1989). The power of not understanding: The meeting of conflicting identities. *Journal of Applied Behavioral Science, 25*(2), 161–173.

Gurin, P., Nagda, B.R.A., & Zuniga, X. (2004). *A multi-university evaluation of the effects of intergroup dialogue.* Ann, Arbor, MI: University of Michigan.

Horton, M. (1990). *The long haul.* Doubleday: New York.

Isaacs, W. (1999). *Dialogue: The art of thinking together.* New York: Currency Books.

Johnson-Bailey, L., & Alfred, M. (2006). Transformational teaching and the practices of Black women adult educators. In E. W. Taylor (Ed.), *Teaching for change* (pp. 49–58). New Directions in Adult and Continuing Education, no. 109. San Francisco: Jossey-Bass.

Jordan, J. (1997). Introduction. In J. Jordan (Ed.), *Women's growth in diversity* (pp. 1–8). New York City: Guilford Press.

Kasl, E., & Elias, D. (2000). Creating new habits of mind in small groups. In J. Mezirow & Associates (Eds.), *Learning as transformation: Critical perspectives on a theory in progress* (pp. 223–252). San Francisco: Jossey-Bass.

Kegan, R. (1982). *The evolving self.* New York: Harper Collins.

Kolb, A., & Kolb, D. (2005). Learning styles and learning spaces. *Academy of Management Learning and Education, 4*(2), 193–212.

Lewin, K. (1946). Action research and minority problems. *Journal of Social Issues, 2,* 34–46.

Landis, D., Bennett, J., & Bennett, M. (2003). *Handbook of intercultural training.* Thousand Oaks, CA: SAGE.

Lindeman, E. (1961). *The meaning of adult education.* Montreal: Harvest House. (Original work published 1926).

Lippitt, R. (1949). *Training in community relation: A research exploration toward new group skills.* New York: Harper.

McNamee, S., & Gergen, K. J. (1999). *Relational responsibility: Resources for sustainable dialogue.* Thousand Oaks, CA: SAGE.

Mezirow, J. (1991). *Transformative dimensions of adult learning.* San Francisco: Jossey-Bass.

Mezirow, J. (2003). Transformative learning as discourse. *Journal of Transformative Education, 1*(1), 58–63.

Nonaka, I., & Konno, N. (1998). The concept of "ba": Building for knowledge creation. *California Management Review, 40*(3), 40–54.

O'Sullivan, E. V. (1999). *Transformative learning: Educational vision for the 21st century.* London: Zed Books.

Palmer, P. (2007). *A hidden wholeness.* San Francisco: Jossey-Bass.

Pearce, W. B. (2001). *Reflections on the role of "dialogic communication" in transforming the world.* Unpublished manuscript, the Fielding Institute.

Pearce, W. B., & Pearce, K. A. (2003). Taking a communication perspective toward dialogue. In R. Anderson, L. A. Baxter, & K. N. Cissna (Eds.), *Dialogue: Theorizing difference in communication studies* (pp. 39–56). Thousand Oaks, CA: SAGE.

Public Conversations Project. (2006). Constructive conversations about challenging times: A guide to community dialogue. Retrieved from www.publicconversations.org

Rogers, C. R. (1961). *On becoming a person: A therapist's view of psychotherapy.* Boston: Houghton Mifflin.

Rose, A. D. (1996). Group learning in adult education: Its historical roots. In S. Imel (Ed.), *Learning in groups* (pp. 3–14). New Directions in Adult and Continuing Education, no. 71. San Francisco: Jossey-Bass.

Saunders, H. (1999). *A public peace process: Sustained dialogue to transform racial and ethnic conflicts.* New York: Palgrave Macmillan.

Schapiro, S. (2009a). Creating space for transformative learning. In B. Fisher-Yoshida, K. D. Geller, & S. Schapiro, (Eds.), *Innovations in transformative learning.* New York: Peter Lang.

Schapiro, S. (2009b). A crucible for transformation: The alchemy of student-centered education for adults at mid-life. In B. Fisher-Yoshida, K. D. Geller, & S. Schapiro (Eds.), *Innovations in transformative learning* (pp. 87–111). New York: Peter Lang.

Senge, P. M. (1990). *The fifth discipline.* New York: Doubleday.

Slater, P. (1966). *Microcosm.* New York: Wiley.

Taylor, E. W. (2009). Fostering transformative learning. In J. Mezirow, E. W. Taylor, & Associates (Eds.), *Transformative learning in practice* (pp. 3–17). San Francisco: Jossey-Bass.

Tisdell, E. (2003). *Exploring spirituality and culture in adult and higher education.* San Francisco: Jossey-Bass.

Vella, J. (1994). *Learning to listen, learning to teach: The power of dialogue in educating adults.* San Francisco: Jossey-Bass.

Wasserman, I. (2004). *Discursive processes that foster dialogic moments: Transformation in the engagement of social identity group differences in dialogue.* Dissertation. Santa Barbara, CA: Fielding Graduate University.

Wasserman, I., & Gallegos, P. (2009). Engaging diversity: Disorienting dilemmas that transform relationships. In B. Fisher-Yoshida, K. D. Geller, & S. Schapiro (Eds.), *Innovations in transformative learning* (pp. 177–200). New York: Peter Lang.

Weisbord, M., & Janoff, S. (2000). *Collaborating for change: Future search.* San Francisco: Berrett-Koehler.

Yalom, I. (1986). *The theory and practice of group psychotherapy.* New York: Basic Books.

Yorks, L., & Kasl, E. (Eds.). (2002). *Collaborative inquiry as a strategy for adult learning.* New Directions for Adult and Continuing Education, no. 94. San Francisco: Jossey-Bass.

Yorks, L., & Kasl, E. (2006). I know more than I can say: A taxonomy for using expressive ways of knowing to foster transformative learning. *Journal of Transformative Education, 4*(1), 43–64.

Yorks, L., & Marsick, V. (2000). Organizational learning and transformation. In J. Mezirow & Associates (Eds.), *Learning as transformation: Critical perspectives on a theory in progress* (pp. 253–284). San Francisco: Jossey-Bass.

Zane, N. C. (2002). The glass ceiling is the floor my boss walks on: Leadership challenges in managing diversity. *Journal of Applied Behavioral Science, 38,* 334–354.

CHAPTER TWENTY-THREE

Transformative Learning in the Workplace

Leading Learning for Self and Organizational Change

Karen E. Watkins, Victoria J. Marsick, and Pierre G. Faller

In this chapter, we explore the interaction of transformative learning and organization transformation theory, including organization learning, organization development, and organization transformation as they have evolved to address learning in a changing workplace context. We highlight the role that leaders (both appointed and naturally emergent) play in transformation, and the barriers and supports to transformation of the organization's culture, structure, and core practices, and we suggest a model for transformative learning in the context of organizational change.

A CHANGING WORKPLACE CONTEXT

A common organizational narrative in a rapidly changing, complex, globally linked world is that valued employees are those who can think critically, challenge assumptions, and proactively help organizations change. Global dynamics, intelligent technology, and marketplace forces have radically altered the employment contract, the nature of work, and social, collaborative dimensions of knowledge creation, work, and learning. Engeström (2004, p. 12) argues that much work today is "co-configuration" involving what Victor and Boynton (1998, cited in Engeström) call "a living, growing network . . . between customer, product, and company." Co-configuration is different from other kinds of work: craft, mass production, process enhancement, and mass customization. Engeström states that co-configuration involves "the creation of customer-intelligent products or services which adapt to the changing needs of the user," which in turn alter the frequency and nature of interaction with customers (p. 12). Co-confirmation, argues Engeström, demands new kinds of expansive learning involving ongoing negotiation and collaboration characterized in part by "transformative learning... (that emphasizes) design, modeling, textualization, objectification, conceptualization, and visibilization" along with "bridging, boundary crossing, 'knotworking,' negotiation, exchange and trading... (in) situationally constructed social spaces" (p. 16). Co-configuration is inherently social, collaborative, and collective in nature.

Heifetz (1994) argues that people today face adaptive challenges for which past solutions will not work. He advocates transformative learning in order to cope with these demands. Organizational change depends on the ability to think and act in more complex ways. Transformative learning is a natural fit to help leaders and employees engage in personal and organizational change in such circumstances.

This kind of transformative learning demands collective, critical reflection in, on, or through action to build new opportunities or to address troubling challenges, sometimes catalyzed by leaders with a mandate for organizational change. Brooks (1992), for example, studied twenty-eight managers across low, middle, and upper levels in a Fortune 500 company charged with transforming the culture of a company responding to government deregulation. She interviewed "managers identified as attempting to reestablish organizational 'fit'" with environment" to gain "insight into the relationship between individual learning and organizational transformation" (p. 325). All of these managers acted courageously to question the status quo. Additionally, they helped others transform and grow into the new culture by "providing them with varied work experiences, having them assist upper-level managers, encouraging questioning, giving direct individual feedback, involving them with both policy making and implementation, and giving open-ended assignments" (pp. 327–328). Developmentally speaking (Drago-Severson, 2010; Kegan, 1994), these opportunities could be seen as providing both challenge and support.

Other strategies are organizationally driven. Raelin (2000) catalogues a variety of these "work-based learning" approaches—action learning, action research, collaborative inquiry, and others—all of which share a process whereby:

1. It views learning as acquired in the midst of action and dedicated to the task at hand.

2. It sees knowledge creation and utilization as collective activities wherein learning becomes everyone's job.

3. Its users demonstrate a learning-to-learn aptitude, which frees them to question underlying assumptions of practice.

Work-based learning, then, differs from conventional training in that it involves conscious reflection on actual experience. Fundamental to the process is the concept of metacognition (Meisel & Fearon, 1996) which means that one constantly thinks about one's problem-solving processes.... [L]earning can be more than just the acquisition of technical skills. It also constitutes the reframing necessary to create new knowledge. (Raelin, 2000, p. 2)

Yorks and Marsick (2000) have described these work-based learning interventions as "bounded critical refection" because they create transitional space to experiment with change through which transformed individuals may engage others in the organization in transformative learning and action.

Some research supports these claims (Brooks, 2004). For example, Lamm (2000) interviewed twenty-four leaders who had participated in action learning programs over six years in a multinational car and truck company. Many individuals experienced transformative learning, but the full potential of the projects for organizational transformation was not maximized. Kuhn (2009) studied an action learning program designed to transform individuals and the organization. He documents transformative learning in individuals, but the potential for organizational transformation was limited by changes in leadership and strategy at the top. Moreover, Conger and Benjamin (1999) noted that action learning gains often remain within the group. Thus questions arise about how transformative learning in these interventions can be supported, leveraged, and sustained.

Organizations may espouse transformative learning but limit its practice because individuals who think critically and complexly challenge taken-for-granted norms and power relationships. Despite barriers like these, adaptive capacities are needed—in both the individual and the organization.

DIFFERING, DUELING FOCI OF TRANSFORMATIVE LEARNING AND ORGANIZATIONAL CHANGE

Theories of transformative learning (which are often concerned with individual growth and learning) and theories of transformative organizational change (which are typically focused on system-wide, instrumental goals) arise from different disciplines to describe, understand, and support very different purposes and processes. Henderson (2002) compared well-regarded theories in both of these categories and concluded that "these two schools of thought, although different in their approach to change, are complementary" and are more effective when taken together (p. 186). Organizational change "theorists assume that changing an organization will result in change in its individual members" but do not speak to the way that individuals can become transformed (p. 200). Essentially behaviorist in orientation, these theories assume that changing the environment (culture, structure, processes, and rewards) will push individuals to acquire new thinking and behaviors. Transformative learning theorists, in contrast, describe both how individuals transform—a process typically characterized by critical reflection—and what transformed individuals look like (p. 205). These theories are more likely to focus on intrinsic motivation, empowerment, and self-direction or autonomy. A few theorists—notably Kurt Lewin (1947) and Chris Argyris (1970, 1999)—seek to understand the change process for both individuals and the environment in the organization. Individuals who are transformed make changes in the environment that enable others to likewise transform and together act on the environment to move toward desired goals.

Lewin's and Argyris's views come from a social action perspective in which the individual acts as an agent or representative of the whole—and if individuals change how they act in the organization, other organization members will respond in new ways, creating a new social dynamic that in turn has the potential to change organizational dynamics.

UNDERSTANDING TRANSFORMATION IN ORGANIZATIONAL CHANGE AND ORGANIZATIONAL LEARNING

Organization development theorists have defined their focus as "an approach to organization change based on applied behavioral science and reliant on the action research approach" (Burke, 2008, p. 41). This definition contrasts markedly with Argyris (1970), who positioned organization development as follows: "to intervene is to enter into an ongoing system of relationship, to come between or among persons, groups, or objects for the purpose of helping them" (p. 15). The learning thrust of Argyris's definition hints of his later work with Schön on organizational learning (Argyris & Schön, 1978/1995). As Lundberg (1989) noted, organizational learning extends the distance vision of organization development. From a focus on change as an instrumental rational strategy for changing organizations, facilitated by a change agent, organizational learning moves to a focus on the learning needed by individuals and organizations in order to transform.

This social learning focus is essential, for as Schein (1996) wrote,

> The first important point to note is that systemic health can only be understood as a combination of four factors, each of which must be present to some degree:
> 1) a sense of identity, purpose, or mission; 2) a capacity on the part of the

system to adapt and maintain itself in the face of internal and external changes; 3) a capacity to perceive and test reality; and 4) some degree of internal integration or alignment of the sub-systems that make up the total system.

In a sense these four conditions are a prerequisite for learning or can be thought of as the basis of "capacity to learn." When we apply the learning concept to any complex system we note a very important distinction that has been made by most theorists, the difference between single loop and double loop learning (Argyris and Schon, 1995), or what Senge (1990) has called "the difference between adaptive and generative learning, or what others have called the difference between 1) maintenance and growth vs. 2) transformation. (p. 4)

Schein's criteria focus on generating enhanced capacity in the organization in order for it to remain healthy and viable. Argryis (1970) and Burke (2008) argue that the focus of organization development efforts is always the system as a whole. At this level, the organization changes its way of making meaning. The capacity to learn for the purpose of maintaining the status quo differs greatly from the capacity to transform. Some scholars and practitioners seek to enhance both capacities.

Meyer (1982), for example, studied organizational responses to an environmental jolt. Meyer found that environmental surprises (such as new regulations, competitors, market changes, technology) trigger organizational learning. Active scanning of the environment, both internal and external, enables the organization to proactively identify needed changes. Culture serves as a filter to focus the organization's attention. Through their separate functions, key people (separately and collectively) arrive at a strategy for responding to the trigger. The strategy's success is due in part to the organization's ability to act cohesively. This requires alignment of vision, shared meaning about intentions, and the capacity to work together across boundaries. This collaborative capacity leads to collective action. This is, as Schein observed, a culturally determined organizational capacity.

Meyer, like Argyris and others before him, found two degrees of learning that he called *resilience* (single loop) and *retention* (double loop). Resilience is the capacity to bounce back to "normal" after a jolt. Slack resources and nimble, flat structures enable this type of learning by organizations. Retention is the capacity to learn wholly new ways of responding to changes in the environment and embedding these new capacities into the ongoing operating of the organizations. Retention requires fundamental transformations of strategy and ideology (culture).

Following in this tradition, we have sought to identify cultural dimensions that support second-order learning capacity. Our model of a learning organization (Watkins & Marsick, 1993, 1996, 2003; Marsick & Watkins, 1999) maps dimensions that enhance the organization's capacity to transform itself. Learning organizations are organizations that consciously build structures, policies, and practices to support continuous renewal supported by a culture that

- Provides resources and tools for individual learning
- Ensures opportunities for dialogue and inquiry, including capturing suggestions for change
- Emphasizes team learning and collaboration to promote cross-unit learning
- Empowers people to enact a collective vision
- Creates systems to capture and share this learning
- Makes systemic connections between the organization and its environment, scanning the environment to anticipate future needs
- Provides leadership for learning through leaders who facilitate the development of employees and who themselves model learning

These learning culture dimensions open the organization to information that it must then use in some fashion in order to transform through learning.

Organization transformation theories provide additional models of how organizations can facilitate transformation. Gersick's punctuated equilibrium theory (1991) posits that organizational transformation occurs through short bursts of revolutionary activity in which core activities of the organization change fundamentally. Romanelli and Tushman (1994) confirmed this theory in a study across twenty-five microcomputer companies founded between 1967 and 1969. They coded changes across the life history of the organization as found in key documents. Interestingly, they identified twenty-three revolutionary changes, and only three evolutionary changes. Environmental conditions and CEO transitions were most often triggers of revolutionary changes, even over crises of performance. Although this theory does not provide guidance on how to initiate transformation, it does help depict the kinds of changes that constitute revolutionary change.

Burke (2008) contrasts transactional changes with transformational changes. The latter involve core organizational elements: strategy, culture, performance, context, or leadership. Yet most people can point to such changes without a profound change of perspective or transformation. *What* changes in the organization may not matter as much as the *depth* of the change; for example, the number of affected units (critical mass), the distance between present and future state, or the degree of personal change and disruption. Gephart and Marsick (forthcoming) have modified the Burke-Litwin model to include interim group organizational learning outcomes that mediate between interventions and organizational change. Using a survey-based instrument and framework, *Strategic Leverage through Learning*, they have learned that although transformational change can be linked directly to change in organizational culture, typically changes in transactional variables are easier to enact. These changes can in turn catalyze change in leadership, strategy, or culture. We next examine how leaders who themselves have changed their fundamental views through some form of transformative learning can help others engage in transformative learning to support change initiatives.

THE ROLE OF THE LEADER IN
TRANSFORMING ORGANIZATIONS

Change is critical for any organization that wants to increase performance and remain competitive. How can leaders support transformative learning to the benefit of organizational change? Although Mezirow and Associates (2000) do not focus on the organizational context, they refer to transformative learners as potential "agents of change" who can form cells of resistance and examine and challenge current norms. Meyer (2009) also notes that "many of the same capacities that allow individuals to reflect on their own experiences, question their frames of reference, and expand their ways of being are also those necessary to question organizational norms, operating assumptions, and strategic platforms" (p. 44).

Scholars have examined the role of leaders in bringing about second-order change; for example, Burns (1978) and subsequently Bass (2008) in their writing on transformational leadership. Transformational leaders are mentors—visionary, ethical, and able to stimulate creativity among followers in ways that help both individuals and organizations transform. Tichy and Cardwell (2004) see transformational leadership as interactive—a teaching and learning dynamic that enables leaders, with their team members, to learn and to transform: "In this environment, the key to winning is the leader's ability to raise the collective intelligence of his or her team and keep its members aligned, energized and working to please customers. To keep creating new value for the customers, team members must get smarter everyday" (p. 6). This view aligns well with the idea of a learning organization.

Theory U (Scharmer, 2007) brings another dimension to our understanding of transformative change leaders. According to this theory, they lead by seeing differently, from outside the normal boundaries of their own experiences and of the organization, in order to allow the future to emerge. In all of these models, harking back to Lewin's (1947) work, there is a cycling between action and reflection.

Cycles of action and reflection can build cognitive awareness of self and others in relationship to goal achievement—a constructivist view of learning from and through experience that, as Fenwick (2000, p. 248) points out, "casts the individual as a central actor in a drama of personal meaning-making." Fenwick critiques the constructivist view as individualistic, "simplistic and reductionist," and overly rational and cognitive (p. 249). We agree that learning needs to holistically engage people. This implies moving beyond Mezirow's conceptualization of transformative learning that values cognitive, rational learning even though Mezirow has also acknowledged the importance of emotions and social interaction. Organizational learning and change require alignment toward a common vision. Historically and into the present, everyone's views and vision are not equally honored in change efforts. Power, positionality, and direction from key leaders (often cascaded down through layers of management) reinforce the "bounded critical reflection" stance already noted. Change efforts encounter resistance.

Action research, action science, action learning, cooperative inquiry, and related mechanisms can support transformative learning for individuals and groups in organizations under the right conditions. Raelin (2000) describes these interventions and their dynamics, all of which involve forms of reflection on experience, experimentation in and through action, and conceptualization of what is being learned, using tacit or explicit knowledge. Although not panaceas, these strategies create a common, semi-public space for groups of people who can (but do not always) create a safe, trusting climate within which they can examine and act on circumstances in their individual or shared work lives. They are laboratories for learning, experimentation, critical reflection, and change that are often supported by a facilitator or change agent who helps people surface and examine difficult issues.

Leaders who themselves have been transformed can learn from the principles embedded in these and other strategies to create space for others to share in this process and enact transformation within the organization in various ways, such as coaching, mentoring, communities of practice or interest, and learning teams. A key principle in this dynamic is the collective identification, sharing, and examination of points of view in ways that enhance insight, understanding, and new action. Two processes enable participants to recognize limitations to their understanding and to conceive of the world in new ways: differentiation and decentration:

> *Differentiation* is the process whereby people distance themselves from their own subjectivity by experience, based on the identification of differences and diversity between their own way of understanding something from other ways, or other people's ways, of understanding the same thing.
>
> *Decentration* is a process whereby people critically validate their own assumptions to enable the perceptual reformulation of a previous point of view, shifting the given cognitive perspective.

> Differentiation and decentration are processes built on a continuously on-going cognitive movement.... The iterations of differentiation and decentration will lead to further attempts to resolve the issue or to perceptual (re) formulation. *Perceptual (re) formulation* is a transformation from one taken-for-granted cognitive perspective to another. (Bjerlöv & Docherty, 2006, p. 95)

To facilitate this transformation, then, the organization must be helped to reflect on itself—using valid single- and double-loop data about its performance, problems, and context—and align itself to take concerted action toward a possible new future.

Managing the tension between old and new ways of working can help push individuals, groups, and the organization itself into new practices and what Leonard (1998) called "creative abrasion." If leaders move too far outside the organization's tolerance level for challenge, they could commit political suicide and risk being ignored or cut off. If the culture does not support transformative learning and change, not only will learning be less than optimal, but also employees may become dispirited and experience a drop in motivation. The model that follows is designed to enable facilitators of organizational learning and transformation to lead this process.

TOWARD A MODEL OF FACILITATING TRANSFORMATIVE LEARNING FOR ORGANIZATIONAL CHANGE

One challenge of transformative learning for organizational change resides in the variety of change situations as well as the diversity of transformative learning facilitation techniques available to practitioners. We here propose a model to help change leaders who are responsible for leading and implementing change to consider choices in how they leverage transformative learning in their organizational context. Change management literature has stressed the need for effective leadership in order to conduct efficient change (Burke, 2008; Kanter, Stein, & Jick, 1992; Kotter, 1995). Laiken (2001) conducted a three-year project researching characteristics of forty-two Canadian organizations using organizational learning approaches and found that strong leadership was a characteristic of efficient learning organizations.

The Model

In our proposed facilitation model (see Figure 23.1), the distinction between a system perspective and an individual perspective offers the change leader

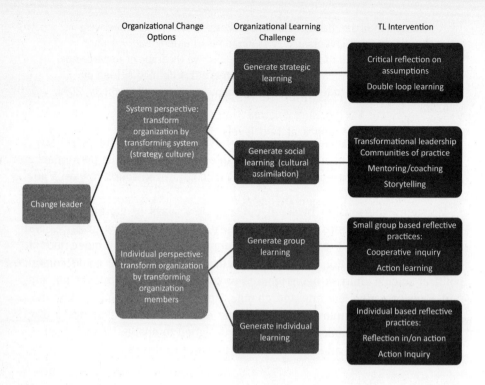

Figure 23.1 Model for Facilitating Transformative Learning in Organizational Change

different routes leading to distinctive organizational learning challenges and implying different transformative learning interventions.

The change leader can choose two routes for fostering transformational change. The first route corresponds to a vision of organizational change as a top-down process wherein goals and directions for change are first designed by the change leaders (for instance, a new vision, a new culture, a new strategy) and then spread down and implemented throughout the organization. In this option, learning focuses on the organization as a whole and assumes that individual learning will derive from the influence of the new system.

The second route is symmetrically opposite. In this route, organizational change starts with "small" change initiatives at a team or individual level, which are eventually spread throughout the organization. In this route, change leaders fully associate their teams with the definition and implementation of change and engage organization members in thinking about issues or problems. It is a more organic and collaborative conception of change, wherein change leaders promote an environment involving collaborative, group, and individual learning strategies. Yorks and Marsick (2000) have argued that this approach can produce sustained change for the organization.

We will now further detail how each route uses transformative learning to produce change.

A System Perspective

Change leaders who embark on the difficult task of defining the next vision, strategy, or structure for their organization are likely confronted with organizational learning challenges at two levels. The first challenge is to produce learning that can create sustainable winning strategies. Pietersen (2002, 2010) pioneered the concept of learning that can be converted to strategic benefits under the term "strategic learning." One of the key principles of strategic learning is to produce superior insights that can be translated into winning strategies. To do that, leaders need to question and reexamine assumptions behind the different factors that influence the organization: consumer, competition, company's own strengths and weaknesses, industry dynamics, macro environment.

For Schein, transforming the system is always changing the culture: "What then do we mean by generative learning or transformation of a system? If the organization's 'knowledge' both explicit and tacit (know-how) is embedded in the culture and in the alignment of its sub-cultures, then it follows that transformation is tantamount to a change in the culture itself—a change in the organization's sense of identity, its goals, its core values, its primary ways of working, and so on (Schein, 1985, 1992)" (as quoted in Schein, 1996, p. 5).

To help leaders reinvent their organizations and identify new business models and opportunities, different transformative learning interventions can be considered. Geller (2009), drawing on Brookfield, suggests that through the process of critical thinking, leaders become free to explore and imagine a range of alternatives, which foster innovation. Double loop learning, leading to questioning the role of the framing and learning systems that underlie actual goals and strategies (Argyris, 1992), is also a way to engage in transformative learning to generate powerful strategic insights and create enduring visions.

A second organizational learning challenge for change leaders is to create learning that contributes to building a culture aligned with the new strategy. Engaging groups and teams from the top down to adopt new ways of working or collaborating is one of the most difficult tasks that change leaders undertake (Battilana, Gilmartin, Pache, Sengul, & Alexander, 2010).

Not only is this not easy to do, but organizations are built to move toward convergence around common goals that push conformity and compliance, despite rhetoric to the contrary. Transformative leaders need to create space and opportunity within organizations for engagement in a critical cultural perspective if and when change demands wholehearted engagement of employees.

Not everyone in organizations will wish to be engaged in this way, and those who do engage may choose to diverge from the pathway urged by the organization. It is not easy or comfortable to enact these forms of learning in many organizations, but some initiatives do push in this direction. We suggest that leaders who themselves have been transformed can learn from the principles embedded in these and other strategies to create space for others to share in this process and enact transformation within the organization in various ways, such as coaching, mentoring, communities of practice or interest, and learning teams. A key principle in this dynamic is collective identification; that is, sharing and examination of points of view in ways that enhance insight, understanding, and new action.

The Individual Perspective

In this approach, change leaders create conditions for groups and individuals to become agents of change for the organization. At a group level, change leaders look at interventions such that organization members can work together to change the way the organization responds to complex challenges. This requires a specific environment and a culture in which inquiry related to change can happen and people can safely question the old ways of thinking and imagine new possibilities. To foster such transformation at a team level, change leaders can use strategies such as action research, action learning, or cooperative inquiry, which have proven effective at helping people shift perspectives and transform organizational culture.

Change leaders can also focus on helping organization members generate change at an individual level by encouraging individual-based reflective practices. The notions of reflection-in-action and reflection-on-action were central to Donald Schön's efforts in this area. It involves looking to experiences, connecting with feelings, and attending to theories in use, and it leads to building new understandings to inform our actions in the situation that is unfolding.

> The practitioner allows himself to experience surprise, puzzlement, or confusion in a situation, which he finds uncertain or unique. He reflects on the phenomenon before him, and on the prior understandings, which have been implicit in his behaviour. He carries out an experiment, which serves to generate both a new understanding of the phenomenon and a change in the situation. (Schön, 1983, p. 68)

Another potentially transformative intervention is action inquiry. Torbert and Associates (2004) describe action inquiry as "a kind of behavior that is simultaneously inquiring and productive. It is a behavior that simultaneously learns about the developing situation, accomplishes whatever task appears to have priority, and invites a redefining of the task if necessary" (p. 1). Action inquiry considers the three dimensions of human experience: subjective (first person), intersubjective (second person), and objective (third person). By interweaving subjective, intersubjective, and objective data, Torbert suggests that managers will become more aware of and less constrained by their own implicit and often untested assumptions about situations they find themselves in. He also suggests journaling as powerful techniques to generate new insights.

CONCLUSION

The workplace is so complex—with a global workforce, a harsh economic climate, and more and more dispersed, temporary, and virtual employees. Transformative learning approaches undertaken by individuals, groups, and organizations can enable the kind of learning—in the face of complexity, ambiguity, and uncertainty—that is needed for these times. Although there are many constraints, as noted in this chapter, the strategies discussed may allow a more open-ended, frank exploration of the disorienting reality of the current situation, the root causes of the problems we face, and creative alternative responses that may allow people and organizations to transform in ways that enable them to survive. In the current context, that possibility is truly significant.

References

Argyris, C. (1970). *Intervention theory and method: A behavioral science view.* Reading, MA: Addison-Wesley.

Argyris, C. (1992). *Overcoming organizational defenses: Facilitating organizational learning.* Boston: Allyn and Bacon.

Argyris, C. (1999). *On organization learning.* New York: Wiley-Blackwell.

Argyris, C., & Schön, D. (1978/1995). *Organization learning I and II: A theory of action perspective.* Reading, MA: Addison-Wesley.

Bass, B. M. (2008). *The Bass handbook of leadership: Theory, research, and managerial applications.* New York: Free Press.

Battilana, J., Gilmartin, M. J., Pache, A.-C., Sengul, M., & Alexander, J. (2010). Leadership competencies for implementing planned organizational change. *Leadership Quarterly, 21,* 422–438.

Bjerlöv, M., & Docherty, P. (2006). Collective reflection under ambiguity. In D. Boud, P. Cressey, & P. Docherty (Eds.), *Productive reflection at work* (pp. 54–66). London & New York: Routledge.

Brooks, A. K. (1992). Building learning organizations: The individual-culture interaction. *Human Resource Development Quarterly, 3*(4), 323–335.

Brooks, A. K. (2004). Transformative learning theory and implications for human resource development. *Advances in Developing Human Resources, 6*(2), 211–225.

Burke, W. W. (2008). *Organization change: Theory and practice* (2nd ed.). Thousand Oaks, CA: SAGE.

Burns, J. M. (1978). *Leadership.* New York: Harper & Row.

Conger, J., & Benjamin, B. (1999). *Building leaders: How successful companies develop the next generation.* San Francisco: Jossey-Bass.

Drago-Severson, E. (2010). *Leading adult learning.* Corwin Press and the National Council for Staff Development.

Engeström, Y. (2004). New forms of learning in co-configuration work. *Journal of Workplace Learning, 16*(1/2), 11–21.

Fenwick, T. J. (2000). Expanding conceptions of experiential learning: A review of the five contemporary perspectives on cognition. *Adult Education Quarterly, 50,* 243–272.

Geller, K. D. (2009). Transformative learning dynamics for developing relational leaders. In B. Fisher-Yoshida, K. D. Geller, & S. A. Schapiro (Eds.), *Innovations in transformative learning: Space, culture and the arts.* Counterpoints Series: Studies in the Post-Modern Theory of Education. New York: Peter Lang.

Gephart, M., & Marsick, V. U. (forthcoming). *Strategic Organizational Learning.* New York: Springer.

Gersick, C. (1991). Revolutionary change theories: A multilevel exploration of the punctuated equilibrium paradigm. *Academy of Management Review, 16,* 10–36.

Heifetz, R. (1994). *Leadership without easy answers.* Cambridge, MA: Harvard University Press.

Henderson, G. M. (2002). Transformative learning as a condition for transformational change in organizations. *Human Resource Development Review, 1*(2), 186–214.

Kanter, R. M., Stein, B., & Jick, T. (1992). *The challenge of organizational change.* New York: Free Press.

Kegan, R. (1994). *In over our heads: The mental demands of modern life.* Cambridge, MA: Harvard University Press.

Kotter, J. P. (1995). Leading change: Why transformational efforts fail. *Harvard Business Review, 72*(1), 59–64.

Kuhn, J. (2009). *Using action learning to develop the cognitive dimensions of strategic innovation: Program design, methodological and person environment considerations.* Teachers College, Columbia University. AAT 3368423. Retrieved from Proquest.

Laiken, M. (2001). Review: "Guiding change journeys: A synergistic approach to organizational transformation" by Rebecca Chan Allen. *OD Practitioner, 33*(4), 45–47.

Lamm, S. L. (2000). *The connection between Action Reflection Learning and transformative learning: An awakening of human qualities in leadership.* Unpublished doctoral dissertation, Teachers College, Columbia University.

Leonard, D. (1998). *Wellsprings of knowledge: Building and sustaining the sources of innovation.* Cambridge, MA: Harvard Business School Press.

Lewin, K. (1947). Frontiers in group dynamics. *Human Relations, 1,* 5–41.

Lundberg, G. C. (1989). On organizational learning; Implications and opportunities for expanding organization development. *Research in Organization Change and Development, 3,* 61–82.

Marsick, V. J., & Watkins, K. E. (1999). *Facilitating the learning organization.* Farnham, UK: Gower Publishers.

Meyer, A. (1982). Adapting to environmental jolts. *Administrative Science Quarterly*, *27*, 515–537.

Meyer, P. (2009). Learning space/work space: Can we make room for transformative learning in organizations? In B. Fisher-Yoshida, K. D. Geller, & S. A. Schapiro (Eds.), *Innovations in transformative learning: Space, culture and the arts* (pp. 43–64). Counterpoints Series: Studies in the Post-Modern Theory of Education. New York: Peter Lang.

Mezirow, J., & Associates (Eds.). (2000). *Learning as transformation: Critical perspectives on a theory in progress*. San Francisco: Jossey-Bass.

Pieterson, W. (2002). *Reinventing strategy: Using strategic learning to create and sustain breakthrough performance*. Hoboken, NJ: Wiley.

Pietersen, W. (2010). *Strategic learning: How to be smarter than your competition and turn key insights into competitive advantage*. Hoboken, NJ: Wiley.

Raelin, J. A. (2000). *Work-based learning: The new frontier of management development*. Englewood Cliffs, NJ: Prentice-Hall.

Romanelli, E., & Tushman, M. (1994). Organizational transformation as punctuated equilibrium: An empirical test. *Academy of Management Journal*, *37*(5), 1141–1166.

Scharmer, O. (2007). *Theory U*. San Francisco: Berrett-Koehler.

Schein, E. (1996, June 28). "Organizational learning: What is new?" Invited address to the Third Biennial International Conference on Advances in Management, Sheraton Tara Hotel, Framingham, MA.

Schön, D. (1983). *The reflective practitioner: How professionals think in action*. London: Temple Smith.

Tichy, N., & Cardwell, N. (2004). *The cycle of leadership: How great leaders teach their companies to win*. New York: Harper Collins.

Torbert, B., & Associates (2004). *Action inquiry: The secret of timely and transforming leadership*. San Francisco: Berrett-Koehler.

Watkins, K. E., & Marsick, V. J. (1993). *Sculpting the learning organization*. San Francisco: Jossey-Bass. (Translated and published in Japanese and Chinese.)

Watkins, K. E., & Marsick, V. J. (Eds.). (1996). *In action: Creating the learning organization*. Alexandria, VA: ASTD Press.

Watkins, K. E., & Marsick, V. J. (Eds.). (2003). *Making learning count! Diagnosing the learning culture in organizations. Advances in developing human resources* (vol. 5, no. 2). Thousand Oaks, CA: SAGE Publications and the Academy of Human Resource Development.

Yorks, L., & Marsick, V. J. (2000). Organizational learning and transformation. In J. Mezirow & Associates (Eds.), *Learning as transformation: Critical perspectives on a theory in progress* (pp. 253–284). San Francisco: Jossey-Bass.

CHAPTER TWENTY-FOUR

Fostering Transformative Learning in Higher Education Settings

Carol E. Kasworm and Tuere A. Bowles

ransformative learning has a historic and vibrant presence in both credit and noncredit adult and higher education. As a powerful form of learning and, for some, an intriguing perspective to define research and programmatic outcomes, transformative learning is currently imaged and understood through a diversity of descriptions and beliefs. Many current practices and research in the context of higher education represent a commitment to transformative learning through critically reflective practice, with examination of personal or societal disjunctures, of immersion in experiential as well as didactic context, and of dialogue toward new meanings of affect and cognition. For some, transformative learning is the foundation for critical pedagogy and social activism. For others, transformative learning is a helpful, albeit trendy, label to describe varied learner changes based in instructional or institutional practice. For a subset of individuals, it represents actions rigorously framed and bounded in Mezirow's theory of perspective transformation, of a focus on emancipatory learning, while others suggest conceptually related referent frames for this focus on the journey of change for individuals and groups. This chapter considers these diverse perspectives explicating key understandings and forms of research and practice. The final section presents a paradigm for transformational contexts in higher education.

TRANSFORMATIVE LEARNERS IN HIGHER EDUCATION

The authors of this chapter considered approximately 250 published reports (from 1994 to 2009) of research focused on noncredit and credit higher education learners and contexts. In these reports of research, all focused on the term "transformative learning" or perspective transformation as a grounding for their research or as an explanatory frame for their findings. However, in these varied studies there were differing understandings of the nature of the grounding theory or application of varied aspects of epistemological and philosophical understandings of transformative learning. Thus this chapter considered a range of studies, suggesting that transformative learning represented a learner or environmental process focused on learner change in perspective, worldview, and/or sense of self. This change or transformation was most often based in a self-reported shift from previously held beliefs and assumptions about self and world. For some of these studies, the predominant focus was on the learner experience of openness and engagement toward change; other studies considered the role of specific intervention through educational programs, instructors, and facilitators, or of specific instructional experiences supporting or triggering aspects of a transformative learning process.

Many of the early descriptive investigations focused on the "If it occurs?" and "How it occurs?" of transformative learning. These studies considered naturalistic examinations of diverse learner groupings, instructional strategies, and curricular or professional development programs. More recent investigations often have focused on "Can we purposefully create effective transformative learning experiences?"; they examine transformative learning outcomes-oriented programs and the impacts of related instructional strategies.

HIGHER EDUCATION AS A NATURALISTIC LANDSCAPE

Higher education, both credit and noncredit offerings, often presents cognitive, sociocultural, and emotional challenges to adult learners. Ideally, higher education offers an *invitation* to think, to be, and to act in new and enhanced ways. However, these learning environments sometimes challenge individuals to move beyond their comfort zone of the known, of self and others; thus these learners may enter higher education experiencing discrepancies in beliefs, attitudes, and understanding, and engaging in a new social environment with provocative values, ideas, and power dynamics.

As noted by the original Mezirow and Marsick study (1978), some individuals (threshold learners) entered higher education and were open to exploration and reflection, independent of intentional curricula or instructional strategies. Significant numbers of past studies have identified varied phases of this perspective transformation process through retrospective studies of learners in academic programs, professional development programs (credit and noncredit), as well as nontraditional adult degree programs. In addition, select studies documented transformative learning experiences through specific instructional strategies; through the dynamics of peer or cohort groups; through marginalized learner groups due to positionality and power structures vis-à-vis academe; through experiential clinical, internship, service learning, or study abroad field components; and through portfolio assessment. Further, a subset of studies have considered transformative learning through a cognitive developmental perspective, viewing transformative learning as correlated with self-authorship or post-formal contextual knowers (for example, Baxter Magolda, 1999; Kegan, 2000; Torosyan, 2000). In addition, a few of these studies embedded their perspectives in social justice goals, viewing the naturalistic environment as fostering transformative learning through a process of empowerment and emancipatory learning (K. M. Brown, 2005; Cox, 2009; Marmon, 2007).

In these naturalistic studies, a few caveats were reported. A number of studies (for example, Dececchi, 2006; Glisczinski, 2005; Kairson, 2009; Tsang-Chan, 2008) noted that there was no obvious starting point for the transformative learning process (with some suggesting a potential starting point prior to their academic experience). Some suggested there was no clear-cut articulation of which relationships or events were causative of transformative change; others suggested that a portion of their target research group did not experience transformative change while in the academic setting (but that it may have occurred later). These studies suggested that transformative learning seemed to be a dynamic process that takes place over time and through various interactions of people, places, opportunities, and attitudes. Thus these examinations were more often documenting adult development processes, which happened in a higher education context. Yet all of these studies suggested the catalyst was, in part, the learning environment, rather than solely the disposition of the learner. Also, in these discussions (for example, Glisczinski, 2005; Ritz, 2006) some individuals did not experience a disorienting dilemma nor did they question their current frame of reference. Thus these investigations documented students' retrospective naturalistic experiences of transformative learning (more often examined through the ten-phase perspective transformation model), as well as student-reported elements that were suggested to foster transformative learning (for example, Donahue, 2009; Erichsen, 2009; Hendershot, 2010; Kung, 2007; Warner, 2009).

INTENTIONAL INTERVENTIONS FOSTERING TRANSFORMATIVE LEARNING

Higher education learning environments can also be intentionally designed to foster select elements or a holistic process of transformative learning (TL). These intentional efforts typically focus on curriculum goals and outcomes, specific designs of courses or sets of courses and instruction, and related supports for socialization and individual development outcomes. In most of these endeavors, practitioners have viewed transformative learning embedded in the framework of experiential and active learning, using a variety of environmental, instructional, and individual engagement strategies fostering transformative learning.

Experiential and Active Learning

Intentional approaches and strategies for TL often have been framed through the principles of experiential or constructivist learning theory. The more dominant experiential programs have focused on varied forms of learning through engagement with *unfamiliar people and cultures* (including service learning), through the process of portfolio or prior learning assessment, and through unique cross-cultural and intercultural (including study abroad) engagements. These curricular approaches, as well as related strategies, have intentionally engaged the learner in examining past assumptions and disruptive experiential events; some of these studies also have individuals considering future goals and actions based on the assessment of these experiences.

Purposefully engaging with *unfamiliar others and cultures* have focused on structured engagement of learners through outreach to communities, groups of individuals, or action research projects beyond the campus. Using curricula/course activities, internships and clinical experiences, service learning projects, or applied research inquiry projects, these structures target individual experience of potentially disorienting explorations of a more diverse and complex world. From various studies, these intentional strategies have given learners opportunities for critical reflection, examination of assumptions of self and others, and a relational process stimulating new worldview understandings of more complex realities of the world (for example, Carrington & Selva, 2010; Carson & Fisher, 2006; Deeley, 2010).

Cross-cultural or intercultural experiences (study abroad programs) represent potent transformative learning environments. Reported examinations of these cross-cultural or intercultural programs provide compelling evidence of the process of transformative learning. These studies have examined culturally diverse experiences among international students in the United States, as well as culturally diverse experiences of American learners both within the United

States and in other world cultural contexts. Disorienting dilemmas were the pivotal focus of these reports in relation to experiences of cultural shock (and reverse cultural examinations), questioning of one's values and worldview, and challenges to pedagogical values (for example, Donahue, 2009; Erichsen, 2009; Hoff, 2005). The participants in these studies often suggested elements of perspective transformation, to include critical self-reflection with authentic conversations and supportive community; the development of abilities to transit through this cross-cultural experience; and an exploratory attitude toward unique and sometimes disconcerting experiences.

A third intentional approach was based in experiential learning focused on portfolio and prior learning assessment, and specifically the development of critical reflection and exploration of experiences through cognitive and emotional learning outcomes. These strategies of portfolio or prior learning assessment were often viewed through the lens of epistemic meaning-making as part of a transformational learning process (J. O. Brown, 2002; Burris, 1997; Lamoreaux, 2005).

Key Environmental, Instructional, and Individual Strategies

In these research reports, five domains of key intervention strategies supporting transformative learning have been delineated.

Domain One—Development of Self-Reflection, Emotional Capability to Openness, and Critical Disjunctures. A dominant central strategy for transformative learning focused on the intentional development of self-reflection based in a learner's openness to self-exploration through critical disjunctures. Based in a variety of strategies, reported instructional efforts have included reflective logs, critical discussions, classroom-documented reports, blogs, reflective essays, media (to include narratives), and experiential activities such as role-playing, simulated games, and cultural immersion (see, for example, Kumagai, 2008; Lee & Greene, 2004; Pasquariello, 2009). Most of these examinations recognized the power of disorienting experiences and self-reflection, thus drawing on cognitive and affective dimensions of self-awareness.

These intentional involvements were predominantly anchored in experiences of disjunctures impacting a learner's frame of reference (see, for example, Binder, 2009; Ritz, 2006; Robinson, Doberneck, Kenney, Fear, & Sterner, 2005). These catalytic strategies focused on specific types of disorienting dilemmas— often through developing self-awareness that challenged existing worldviews of self and other, as well as, for some, engaging in cultural experiences that brought attention to issues of race, gender, class, power, and privilege (Marmon, 2007). For example, some studies embedded these understandings in socialization at entry for marginalized student learners (Bowser, Danaher, & Somasundaram, 2007), reconstruction of self and related understandings of

self-reflected concerns (Dirkx & Dang, 2009), or learner openness to new experiences and new perspectives (Robinson et al., 2005). Interpersonal, collaborative groups, as well as instructor or mentor connections were significant
supportive structures for learners' engagement in these emotionally and cognitively dissonant experiences (for example, Weinski, 2006; Wing, 2000). Beyond
consideration of critical examination of a disjuncture colliding with the learner's
current sense of place and person, many of these reports also considered issues
of culture, self, and society in relation to social emancipatory perspectives (for
example, Fetherston & Kelly, 2007).

Domain Two—Strategies for Critical Reflection. Diverse strategy repertoires
were suggested for fostering critical reflection. Some studies focused on powerful narratives and discussions of role, culture, self, and other worldview
realities beyond immediate past experiences. Some identified strategies suggested in Domain One, noting the importance of journaling or reflective logs
and of having individuals reflect in private spaces, as well as dialoguing with
others to step outside of individual perspectives or experiencing a new situation beyond their comfort zone (see, for example, Carrington & Selva, 2010;
Ritz, 2006; Robinson et al., 2005). A number of intentional designs incorporated the use of action research projects, collaborative writing projects, engagements in critique, or the use of critical assessments (for example, Burns, 2009;
Glisczinski, 2005; Gravett & Petersen, 2009). Most of these reports noted structured learner processes to focus and define critical reflection as a central activity. Some of these studies considered the development of metacognitive
skills that focused on critiquing one's own metacognitive process and identified alternative assumptions and worldviews as part of the learning engagement
(for example, Pasquariello, 2009; Tsang-Chan, 2008). These activities provided
experiential-based disorienting episodes and a structured process for critical
reflection of self and others (for example, Lee & Greene, 2004).

Domain Three—Supportive Social Environment. Because individuals engaged in transformative learning are open to change and therefore emotionally
vulnerable, a significant number of the studies and reports focused on the importance of a safe, trusting, and respectful learning environment (for example,
Daly, 2007). In many intentional designs, as well as naturalistic examinations,
a supportive social environment was imperative for positive learner engagement. These environments supported and affirmed classmates and instructor,
as well as offered an active dialogue of care through which they sought new
understandings and new knowledge through one another. These environments
also fostered learning to listen more carefully, as well as consideration and
examination of other points of views and perspectives. Other strategies fostering a supportive environment included imaginal dialogue, class discussions of

educational autobiographies or life histories, or exploration of conflictual ideas (see, for example, Feller, 2009). Intentional transformative learning was based on the importance of a community of support while also providing each learner personal space to focus on issues for critical reflection. Thus many studies noted three key intentional strategies (development of self-awareness, experiencing disorienting dilemmas, and personal social supports) as the grounding for potent emotion-laden environments fostering transformative learning.

Pivotal to these strategies in a supportive environment was the importance of the leader, designer, instructor, facilitator, adviser, and/or mentor who understood and acted with purposeful expertise, guiding the process of transformative learning. Many reports noted that facilitators and instructors provided a catalyst for learner examination of knowledge, emotion, and experiences, as well as offered quiet moments and supports for reflection and redirection in the transformative learning process. Key elements structured by these expert guides included creating a democratic, respectful climate for the individual and group, as well as a positive learning environment to enhance critical discourse (see, for example, Dirkx & Dang, 2005; Elsey, 2009; Mikhael, 2009). Several studies also noted the importance of ethical and professional standards by these key designers and instructors to both challenge and protect each learner's sense of self (Sokol, 1998).

Domain Four—Use of the Arts, Literature, Film, and Drama as Tools for Transformative Learning. The fourth set of strategies focused on the purposeful use of cultural media to enhance context awareness, to engage in visual or written disjunctures from the learner's sense of life understandings and realities, and to provide experiences suggesting future options and alternatives to current worldviews and life realities. These strategies included use of literature and writing (Arnzen, 2008; Hunt, 2009; Mikhael, 2009), improvisation and theater drama (Elsey, 2009; Etmanski, 2007; Meyer, 2007), examination of video, film, and television (Goulah, 2007; Roden, 2007; Tisdell, 2008), and arts-based activities (Butterwick & Lawrence, 2009).

Domain Five—Holistic, Affective, and Spiritual Processes. Because higher education is often viewed as a rational, cognitive environment, these set of strategies focused on intentional designs based in the affective realm of emotions and other noncognitive aspects of transformative learning. In a number of investigations, transformative learning was framed as a holistic process, with multiple or expressive ways of knowing, based in emotion, spirituality, and affect in the development of critical consciousness, reflection, and altered worldview. This domain focused on empathic connections, imagery and contemplative practices, as well as forms of culturally responsive teaching strategies (Lennox, 2005; Tisdell & Tollliver, 2009; Yorks & Kasl, 2006).

HIGHER EDUCATION LEADERSHIP PROGRAMS AND PROFESSIONAL DEVELOPMENT

Today's leaders in higher education face a turbulent economy, conflicting social values, and dramatic changes in both the quantity of new knowledge expertise and the changing paradigms of valued knowledge and skills for our knowledge society. As a knowledge-generating environment, higher education requires new mind frames, both to grapple with these continuous changes and to provide a grounding to expand multicultural sensitivities, to promote effective organizational change, and to foster multiframed worldviews for decision making and action. Transformative learning has become a valued framework for engaging and fostering new mind frames through academic programs (predominantly in education for the professions), as well as through professional development of higher education faculty and administrators as leaders of institutional change. The current literature suggests two areas that draw on transformative learning for leader and organizational change. These areas include (1) academic programs fostering transformative learning for leadership, including action research and social emancipatory learning; and (2) faculty and administrator professional development to foster enhanced critical reflection and transformation in both the classroom environment and the working environment.

Academic Programs Fostering Transformative Learning

Many practitioners and researchers have explored specialized designs and outcomes in curricular programs to foster transformative learning. The dominant focus of most of these efforts has been education for the professions and the desire to enhance both the individual learner and the profession toward greater sensitivity to diverse cultures, more relevant and effective social impact by the profession, and a belief in critically reflective practice as a preferable goal in the profession. These published efforts have included intentional interventions in professional disciplines of the law (Binder, 2008), teacher education for environmental education (Burns, 2009; Caldarelli, 2004; Hashimoto, 2007), and professional preparation for teacher education (van Halen-Faber, 1997). Other key professional education curricular interventions have focused on medical and nursing education (Hanson, 2010; Morris & Faulk, 2007), theological programs (Weinski, 2006), school administration (K. M. Brown, 2006; Donaldson, 2009), and social work (Lee & Greene, 2004).

As a subset of transformative learning initiatives, a number of studies have examined changing teacher-learner perspectives through the use of action research, to include movement toward learner-centered dialogue practices (Gravett & Petersen, 2009); development of a curricular core based in action research, learner action, and societal change (Taylor & Pettit, 2007); and the use of action research for fostering learner development. The social emancipatory possibilities and challenges in transformative learning have also included faculty engaged in fostering social and professional changes in academic programs (Hanson, 2010; Jones, 2009; Pigza, 2005). A unique understanding of a transformative learning model has focused on the development of peace education representing five key sensitivities: diversity, participatory learning, globalized perspectives, indigenous knowing, and spiritual underpinnings (Turay & English, 2008).

Perhaps the most complex and comprehensive discussions of transformative learning engagement by faculty and students are from Alverno College's longitudinal studies of their four-year curriculum at this liberal arts college. These studies documented the integration of learning, development, and performance. This comprehensive presentation noted key principles, strategies, and outcomes for development of critical reflection through "three transformative cycles of learning: 1) using metacognitive strategies, 2) self-assessing role performance, and 3) engaging diverse approaches, views and activities" (Mentkowski & Associates, 2000, pp. 189–190). Beyond these programmatic designs, there have also been numerous studies on intentionally designed courses and programs reflecting aspects of transformative learning (Mezirow & Associates, 1990; Mezirow, Taylor, & Associates, 2009).

There are also significant innovative program efforts focused on transformative learning, as articulated through program websites. These select programs present clearly articulated missions and goals focused on transformative learning, to include the following:

- Challenging student perspectives and assumptions
- Promoting critical thinking and creativity
- Integrating of knowledge across the disciplines
- Engaging in community-university partnerships and collaborations
- Developing supportive and inclusive community of diverse students
- Enhancing connections between and among students and teachers.

Table 24.1 provides select examples of these innovative programs and their related goals and paraphrased mission statements from the websites.

Professional Development for Faculty and Administrators

Transformative learning theory provides an important frame for the development of innovative professional development programs. These programs incorporate strategies for faculty and administrators to experience "disorienting dilemmas" of perspective and practice; of structured critically reflective

Table 24.1 Transformative Learning Programmatic Goal and Mission Statements

Program	Mission or Goal Statement
California Institute of Integral Studies—Transformative Studies Program (Ph.D.) http://www.ciis.edu/ Academics/Graduate_ Programs/Transformative_ Studies.html	The primary focus of the doctoral program in Transformative Studies is to develop thought-leaders who are committed to exploring leading-edge issues . . . placing great value on developing the ability to participate in the scholarly discourse through publication, and on the importance of viewing academic inquiry as an opportunity for personal and social transformation, while grounding transformative processes in academic depth, rigor, and imagination. The program focuses on the development of the capacities of original transdisciplinary research; collaborative process of inquiry; engagement in inquiry as an integral, spiritual, and transformative process of personal and social transformation . . .
Clark Atlanta University http://www.cau.edu/About_ Mission_Statement.aspx	Clark Atlanta University will further extend its . . . commitment to provide a personally transformative learning environment, characterized by excellence in teaching, rigorous and innovative academic programs, dedication to the nurturing and development of its students, and the conduct of research addressing critical local, national, and global issues. . . . Clark Atlanta University graduates will demonstrate . . . inclusiveness, a disposition to serve, and a distinct appreciation for diversity in people, place, and opportunity.
Eastern University http://www.eastern.edu/ academic/ccgps/oip/PHD_ Mission.html	The mission of the Ph.D. in Organizational Leadership Program is to prepare leaders . . . through interdisciplinary studies and original research to effectively engage in the transformation of their organizations, communities, and society as practitioners and scholars. With this mission in mind, the Organizational Leadership program prepares its students to embrace the four different aspects of the transformational leader, including: The Centered Leader, The Servant Leader, The Learning Leader, and The Visionary Leader.

(continued)

Table 24.1 (*Continued*)

Program	Mission or Goal Statement
University of Toronto/OISIE http://aecp.oise.utoronto.ca/ae/areas.html	One area of emphasis for OISIE Adult Education and Community Development Graduate Program is Community, International, and Transformative Learning. Key aims include: 1) Students can challenge and support each other . . . ; . . . 3) Building mutually beneficial connections with diverse individuals, groups and communities. . . .
The Transformative Learning Centre at OISIE http://tlc.oise.utoronto.ca/wordpress/	The main goals include: 1) interdepartmental structure for community-university partnerships; 2) forum for interdisciplinary issues related to learning in community and global transformation; 3) specific networks . . . from a community-university base; and 4) interdepartmental instruction in Transformative Learning Studies . . .
The University of Central Oklahoma http://www.uco.edu/about/mission.asp	The University of Central Oklahoma (UCO) exists to help students learn by providing transformative education experiences to students so that they may become productive, creative, ethical, and engaged citizens and leaders serving our global community. UCO contributes to the intellectual, cultural, economic, and social advancement of the communities and individuals it serves.

exercises; to engage individuals in new and unique sets of knowledge and skills for teaching, research, or service; and often encouraging individuals to view themselves as emulating the transformative learning process and related strategies in their own worlds (Hussein, 2006; Riley, 2005). A few studies have raised concerns regarding ethical issues of faculty being change agents, of instructional and institutional requirements and outcomes, and of individual faculty beliefs and practices in relation to transformative learning (for example, Kumagai, 2008; Magro, 1999).

Innovative program development initiatives often have engaged faculty and administrators in analyzing their beliefs about professional or collegiate preparation and practice and of differing realities facing the profession or academy, noting disjunctures of perspectives and action in the profession or academy. A few reported projects were intentionally designed and conducted in a framework of transformative learning (Carter & Chafin, 2009; Plaza, 2006) and have also included this framework for faculty as program reviewers (Gallegos & Boverie, 2009) and in creating a supportive institutional climate of diversity (Bruning, 2006).

TOWARD AN EMERGENT TRANSFORMATIVE FRAMEWORK IN HIGHER EDUCATION

Although there are many overlapping and competing theories, concepts, and ideas focused on change processes in higher education, transformative learning offers a unifying and expansive framework for higher education. For example, in *Learning Reconsidered: A Campus-Wide Focus on the Student Experience* (Keeling, 2004), "transformative learning provides a unified theory of learning and development that transcends outmoded ideas about learning and questions the structure of most institutions of higher education" (p. 11).

Based on a meta-analysis of reports and studies reviewed for this chapter, Table 24.2 represents key elements of an emerging framework of transformative learning in higher education. The framework includes core assumptions, contextual levers of change, and exemplary strategies resulting in individual, program, and institutional outcomes.

DIRECTIONS FOR FUTURE RESEARCH AND PRACTICE

Transformative learning in higher education contexts, its practices and its related research inquiry, is a phenomenon fraught with significantly differing understandings, perspectives, and positionalities of interpretation. Key future efforts require the enhanced development of a more "disciplined," systematic body of knowledge of transformative learning. Because higher education has a key goal of generation of new knowledge, it is an ideal setting to explore and delineate alternative models, define elements for engagement, and document the impact of these strategies of transformative learning. Key future studies should consider how diverse characteristics of learners may influence or be influenced by the TL process, the relationship of specific strategies to the process, and the required environmental elements to support or deter this process.

In this process of transformative learning, there is need for enhanced reformulations of delineated stages or phase elements of the transformative experience. Most have presumed the template of the historic phases of perspective transformation, while not pursuing questions of the presence and sequence of specific elements, or of a specific progression of these elements. In addition, far too many of the previous studies have not defined the learner's cognitive

Table 24.2 Emerging Transformative Learning Framework in Higher Education

Assumptions	Contextual Levers of Change	Exemplary Strategies	Outcomes
Commitment of transformative learning in the core mission of institutions and programs	Teaching and learning settings (face-to-face and online)	– Action research – Collaborative inquiry – Critical thinking and reflection	Intellectual, emotional, social, and spiritual growth of learners
Alignment of organizational practices to support transformative learning	Programs and departments Institutions	– Cultural immersion experiences – Digital stories or videos	Enhanced reflective, analytical, and critical discourses
Supporting the whole learning and development of learners	Sociocultural external events and environmental conditions	– Experiential and active learning – Narrative, embodied, and somatic learning – Portfolio development and assessment	Development of transformative learning communities
Fostering a climate of social justice, empowerment, and intercultural awareness for all		– Transformative curriculum goals and outcomes – Developing a shared democratic and inclusive culture – Internship programs	Improved and increased retention rates Integrated system of learning
Investing resources		– Paired or clustered courses – Peer, cohort, dialogue, and/or support groups – Scholarly communities of practice – Community partnerships – Service-learning programs – Study abroad programs – Academic and social support programs – Faculty professional development opportunities	Societal change

and affective entry state prior to instructional engagement in transformative learning and have not documented either the nature of "disjuncture" as the catalyst or the blocking experience for this TL journey, or the exit state of the learner from a transformative learning experience.

As a final consideration, researchers and practitioners should consider joint development of collaborative research agendas targeted to elaborated models of TL and of longitudinal investigations of learners and programs, as well as more sophisticated instruments and protocols in support of this research and informed practice. This research needs to move beyond descriptive inquiry. Given the transformative learning experience, what difference does it make for learners, programs, and for the impact on society? These authors believe that the strength and impact of transformative learning is grounded in learners' more complex worldviews and individual or collective actions. However, there are no studies of this impact, beyond learner self-reports and program or faculty instructional goals. Thus the future strength of research and practice of transformative learning will come from more disciplined investigations focused on elaborated models, from more elaborated pre- and postassessments of learners and programs that clearly articulate the impact of transformative learning, and from research and practice that offers more complex approaches to long-term, longitudinal engagement.

References

Arnzen, M. A. (2008). The unlearning: Horror and transformative theory. *Transformative Works and Culture, 1*, 1–10. doi:10.3983/twc.2008.0037

Baxter Magolda, M. (1999). *Creating contexts for learning and self-authorship: Constructive-developmental pedagogy.* Nashville: Vanderbilt University Press.

Binder, A. (2009). *Facilitating student engagement in the legal profession's obligation to serve the public interest: Applying transformative learning and non-substantive public interest theories to Osgoode Hall Law School's curricular reform initiatives* (Master's thesis). Available from ProQuest Dissertations and Theses database. (UMI No. MR38749).

Bowser, D., Danaher, P. A., & Somasundaram, J. (2007). Indigenous, pre-undergraduate and international students at Central Queensland University, Australia: Three cases of the dynamic tension between diversity and commonality. *Teaching in Higher Education, 5*(1), 669–681. doi:10.1080/13562510701596224

Brown, J. O. (2002). Know thyself: The impact of portfolio development on adult learning *Adult Education Quarterly, 52*(3), 228–245. doi:10.1177/0741713602052003005

Brown, K. M. (2005). Transformative framework and andragogy leadership for social justice and equity: Evaluating a transformative framework and andragogy. *Educational Administration Quarterly, 42*, 5. doi:10.1177/0013161X06290650

Bruning, M. D. (2006). *Beyond access: An evaluation of attitudes and learning towards achieving equitable educational outcomes in higher education* (Doctoral dissertation). (UMI No. 3257399)

Burns, H. (2009). *Education as sustainability: An action research study of the Burns model of sustainability pedagogy* (Doctoral dissertation). Available from ProQuest Dissertations and Theses database. (UMI No. 3391670)

Burris, J. K. (1997). *The adult undergraduate's experience of portfolio development: A multiple case study* (Doctoral dissertation). Available from ProQuest Dissertations and Theses database. (UMI No. 9803091)

Butterwick, S., & Lawrence, R. L. (2009). Creating alternative realities: Arts-based approaches to transformative learning. In J. Mezirow, E. W. Taylor, & Associates (Eds.), *Transformative learning in practice: Insights from community, work, and higher education* (pp. 35–45). San Francisco: Jossey-Bass.

Caldarelli, M. K. (2004). *Targeting environmental beliefs in a community college environmental science course* (Doctoral dissertation). Available from ProQuest Dissertations and Theses database. (UMI No. 3147593)

Carrington, S., & Selva, G. (2010). Critical social theory and transformative learning: Evidence in pre-service teachers' service-learning reflection logs. *Higher Education Research and Development, 29*(1), 45–57. doi:10.1080/07294360903421384

Carson, L., & Fisher, K. (2006). Raising the bar on criticality: Students' critical reflection in an internship program. *Journal of Management Education, 30*(5), 700–723. doi:10.1177/1052562905284962

Carter, T. J., & Chafin, C. K. (2009). Transformative learning in academic medicine: Changing the way physicians think and practice as medical educators. *Proceedings of the 8th International Transformative Learning Conference*, 55–60. Retrieved from http://transformativelearning.org/index_files/TLC2009%20Proceedings.pdf

Cox, R. D. (2009). *Evolution of the soul: The transformative connection between cultural consciousness, spirituality, and self-empowerment for African American community college adult learners* (Doctoral dissertation). Available from ProQuest Dissertations and Theses database. (UMI No. 3368778)

Daly, J. (2007). *Contribution of an integrated liberal arts course to the learning identity and learning process for the adult participant* (Doctoral dissertation). Available from ProQuest Dissertations and Theses database. (UMI No. 3299624)

Dececchi, B. G. (2006). *A case study of the university training programme — Non-commissioned members of the Royal Military College of Canada* (Doctoral dissertation). Available from ProQuest Dissertations and Theses database. (UMI No. NR21806)

Deeley, S. J. (2010). Service-learning: Thinking outside the box. *Active Learning in Higher Education, 11*(1), 43–53. doi:10.1177/1469787409355870

Dirkx, J. M., & Dang, L. T. (2009). "From a dark soul to a very bright light": The role of the cohort in transformation of learner identity. *Proceedings of the 8th*

International Transformative Learning Conference, Bermuda, 90–95. Retrieved from http://transformativelearning.org/index_files/TLC2009%20Proceedings.pdf

Donahue, T. (2009). *The making of global citizens through education abroad programs: Aligning missions and visions with education abroad programs* (Doctoral dissertation). Available from ProQuest Dissertations and Theses database. (UMI No. 3355245)

Donaldson, J. (2009). Fostering transformative learning in leadership development. In J. Mezirow, E. W. Taylor, & Associates (Eds.), *Transformative learning in practice: Insights from community, workplace, and higher education* (pp. 67–77). San Francisco: Jossey-Bass.

Elsey, M. (2009). Improvisational theater art form: How an innovative adult pedagogy illuminates Mezirow's transformative learning theory. *Proceedings of the 8th International Transformative Learning Conference*, Bermuda, 101–106. Retrieved from http://transformativelearning.org/index_files/TLC2009%20Proceedings.pdf

Erichsen, E. A. (2009). *Reinventing selves: International students' conceptions of self and learning for transformation* (Doctoral dissertation). Available from ProQuest Dissertations and Theses database. (UMI No. 3387257)

Etmanski, C. (2007). *Unsettled: Embodying transformative learning and intersectionality in higher education: Popular theatre as research with international graduate students* (Doctoral dissertation). Available from ProQuest Dissertations and Theses database. (UMI No. NR37432)

Feller, A. E. (2009). Imaginal dialogue in the undergraduate classroom. *Proceedings of the 8th International Transformative Learning Conference*, Bermuda, 107–113. Retrieved from http://transformativelearning.org/index_files/TLC2009%20Proceedings.pdf

Fetherston, B., & Kelly, R. (2007). Conflict resolution and transformative pedagogy: A grounded theory research project on learning in higher education. *Journal of Transformative Education*, *5*(3), 262–285.

Gallegos, B., & Boverie, P. (2009). Transforming academic programs: Measuring the transformative change in programs and reviewers. *Proceedings of the 8th International Transformative Learning Conference*, Bermuda, 137–139. Retrieved from http://transformativelearning.org/index_files/TLC2009%20Proceedings.pdf

Glisczinski, D. J. (2005). *Transformative teacher education: A meaningful degree of understanding* (Doctoral dissertation). Available from ProQuest Dissertations and Theses database. (UMI No. 3188558)

Goulah, J. (2007). Village voices, global visions: Digital video as a transformative foreign language learning tool. *Foreign Language Annals*, *40*(1), 62–78.

Gravett, S., & Petersen, N. (2009). Promoting dialogic teaching among higher education faculty in South Africa. In J. Mezirow, E. W. Taylor, & Associates (Eds.), *Transformative learning in practice: Insights from community, workplace, and higher education* (pp. 100–110). San Francisco: Jossey-Bass.

Hanson, L. (2010). Global citizenship, global health, and the internationalization of curriculum: A study of transformative potential. *Journal of Studies in International Education, 14*(1), 70–88. doi:10.1177/1028315308323207

Hashimoto, Y. (2007). *"Becoming activated": Transformative learning and education for social change through an undergraduate course* (Doctoral dissertation). Available from ProQuest Dissertations and Theses database. (UMI No. NR39430)

Hendershot, K. (2010). *Transformative learning and global citizen identity development in undergraduates: A case study* (Doctoral dissertation). Available from ProQuest Dissertations and Theses database. (UMI No. 3389956)

Hoff, J. G. (2005). *Students' perceptions of the culture learning process during the study abroad experience* (Doctoral dissertation). Available from ProQuest Dissertations and Theses database. (UMI No. 3184937)

Hunt, C. (2009). Creative writing as a tool for transformative learning. *Proceedings of the 8th International Transformative Learning Conference*, Bermuda, 172–177. Retrieved from http://transformativelearning.org/index_files/TLC2009 %20Proceedings.pdf

Hussein, J. W. (2006). Experience-based reflections on the potential for critical practitioner inquiry to transform teacher education in Africa. *Journal of Transformative Education, 4*(4), 362–384. doi:10.1177/1541344606294463

Jones, P. (2009). Teaching for change in social work: A discipline-based argument for the use of transformative approaches to teaching and learning. *Journal of Transformative Education, 7*(1), 8–25. doi:10.1177/1541344609338053

Kairson, B. (2009). *Lives in transition: Examining transformational learning processes in ethnically diverse women* (Doctoral dissertation). Available from ProQuest Dissertations and Theses database. (UMI No. 3344519)

Keeling, R. P. (Ed.). (2004). *Learning reconsidered: A campus-wide focus on the student experience.* Washington, DC: National Association of Student Personnel Administrators.

Kegan, R. (2000). What "form" transforms? A constructive-developmental approach to transformative learning. In J. Mezirow & Associates (Eds.), *Learning as transformation: Critical perspectives on a theory in progress* (pp. 35–70). San Francisco: Jossey Bass.

Kumagai, A. K. (2008). A conceptual framework for the use of illness narratives in medical education. *Academic Medicine, 83*(7), 653–658. Retrieved from http://ovidsp.tx.ovid.com

Kung, H. C. (2007). *Dancing on the edge: International students' transformative journeys in the United States of America* (Doctoral dissertation). Available from ProQuest Dissertations and Theses database. (UMI No. 3271223)

Lamoreaux, A. J. (2005). *Adult learners' experience of change related to prior learning assessment* (Doctoral dissertation). Available from ProQuest Dissertations and Theses database. (UMI No. 3180108)

Lee, M. Y., & Greene, G. J. (2004). A teaching framework for transformative multicultural social work education. *Journal of Ethnic and Cultural Diversity in Social Work, 12*(3), 1–28. doi:10.1300/J051v12n03_01

Lennox, S. L. (2005). Contemplating the self: Holistic approaches to transformative learning in higher education. *Proceedings of the 6th International Transformative Learning Conference*, USA.

Magro, K. M. (1999). *Exploring English teachers' conceptions of teaching and learning in adult education contexts* (Doctoral dissertation). (UMI No. NQ45635)

Marmon, E. L. (2007). *Transformative learning in local, cross-cultural situations: Surprising dilemmas, reflections, and stories* (Doctoral dissertation). Available from ProQuest Dissertations and Theses database. (UMI No. 3263684)

Mentkowski, M., & Associates. (2000). *Learning that lasts: Integrating learning, development, and performance in college and beyond.* San Francisco: Jossey-Bass.

Meyer, P. (2007). Improvising learning space: Making room for difference and transformation. *Proceedings of the 7th International Transformative Learning Conference*, USA.

Mezirow, J., & Marsick, V. (1978). Education for perspective transformation. Women's re-entry programs in community colleges. New York: Center for Adult Education, Columbia University. (ERIC Reproduction Document No. ED166367)

Mezirow J., & Associates (Eds.). (1990). *Fostering critical reflection in adulthood: A guide to transformative and emancipatory learning.* San Francisco: Jossey Bass

Mezirow J., Taylor, E. W., & Associates (Eds.). (2009). *Transformative learning in practice: Insights from community, workplace, and higher education.* San Francisco: Jossey-Bass.

Mikhael, M. R. (2009). *Transformation in the Egyptian writing student: Blogs as critical reflection. Proceedings of the 8th International Transformative Learning Conference*, Bermuda. Retrieved from http://transformativelearning.org/index_files/TLC2009%20Proceedings.pdf

Morris, A. H., & Faulk, D. (2007). Perspective transformation: Enhancing the development of professionalism in RN-to-BSN students. *Journal of Nursing Education, 46*(10), 445–451.

Pasquariello, G. (2009). *The way in and the way on: A qualitative study of the catalysts and outcomes of transformative learning* (Doctoral dissertation). Available from ProQuest Dissertations and Theses database. (UMI No. 3376158)

Pigza, J. M. (2005). *Teacher seeks pupil, must be willing to change the world: A phenomenological study of professors teaching for social justice* (Doctoral dissertation). (UMI No. 3184253)

Plaza, C. M. (2006). *The application of transformative learning theory to curricular evaluation* (Doctoral dissertation). (UMI No. 3206672)

Riley, A. T. (2005). Both sides of the coin in community college faculty development: Transformative learning needs transformative leadership. *Proceedings of the 6th*

International Transformative Learning Conference, USA, 389–394. Retrieved from http://transformativelearning.org/#Conference

Ritz, A. (2006). *Transformative learning and international students in an American university.* New York City: Teachers College.

Robinson, C. F., Doberneck, D. M., Kenney, P., Fear, F., & Sterner, G. (2005). Through the looking glass: Our transformative experiences in wonderland. *6th International Transformative Learning Conference*, 395– 400. Retrieved from http://transformativelearning.org/#Conference

Roden, K. (2007). Through the lens of transformation: Considering diversity in the cinematic classroom. *Proceedings of the 7th International Transformative Learning Conference*, USA, 427–433. Retrieved from http://www.transformativelearning.org/index_files/2007_Transformative_Learning_Conference_Proceedings.pdf

Sokol, A. V. (1998). *Mezirow's transformative learning theory applied to formal adult education: A case study* (Doctoral dissertation). Available from ProQuest Dissertations and Theses database. (UMI No. 9826789)

Taylor, P., & Pettit, J. (2007). Learning and teaching participation through action research: Experiences from an innovative masters programme. *Action Research, 5*(3), 231–247. doi:10.1177/1476750307081015

Tisdell, E. J. (2008). Critical media literacy and transformative learning: Drawing on pop culture and entertainment media in teaching for diversity in adult higher education. *Journal of Transformative Education, 6*(1), 48–67. doi:10.1177/1541344608318970

Tisdell, E. J., & Tolliver, D. E. (2009). Transformative approaches to culturally responsive teaching: Engaging cultural imagination. In J. Mezirow, E. W. Taylor, & Associates (Eds.), *Transformative learning in practice: Insights from community, workplace, and higher education* (pp. 89–99). San Francisco: Jossey-Bass.

Torosyan, R. (2000). *Encouraging consciousness development in the college classroom through student-centered transformative teaching and learning* (Doctoral dissertation). Available from ProQuest Dissertations and Theses database. (UMI No. 9956409)

Tsang-Chan, G. (2008). *An exploration of the transformative learning experiences of college seniors at a Southern California Christian university* (Doctoral dissertation). Available from ProQuest Dissertations and Theses database. (UMI No. 3308530)

Turay, T. M., & English, L. M. (2008). Toward a global culture of peace: A transformative model of peace education. *Journal of Transformative Education, 6*(4), 286–301. doi:10.1177/1541344608330602

van Halen-Faber, C. (1997). Encouraging critical reflection in preservice teacher education: A narrative of a personal learning journey. In P. Cranton (Ed.), *Transformative learning in action: Insights from practice* (pp. 51–60). New Directions for Adult and Continuing Education, no. 74. San Francisco: Jossey-Bass.

Warner, C. A. (2009). *A phenomenological approach to understanding the transformative experience of adult learners in short term study abroad programs*

(Doctoral dissertation). Available from ProQuest Dissertations and Theses database. (UMI No. 3353744)

Weinski, M. C. (2006). *An inquiry into the transformative learning of evangelical theological students in Germany* (Doctoral dissertation). Available from ProQuest Dissertations and Theses database. (UMI No. 322168)

Wing, L. S. (2000). *Transforming doctoral candidates: An exploration of faculty-student relations through dissertation creation* (Doctoral dissertation). Available from ProQuest Dissertations and Theses database. (UMI No. 9956098)

Yorks, L., & Kasl, E. (2006). I know more than I can say: A taxonomy for using expressive ways of knowing to foster transformative learning. *Journal of Transformative Education, 4*(1), 43–64. doi:10.1177/1541344605283151

CHAPTER TWENTY-FIVE

Fostering Transformative Learning Online

Regina O. Smith

Both the continued growth of online learning and the use of transformative learning as a theory to help understand online learning make it important to understand how to foster this important aspect of adult learning. In this chapter "online learning" refers to courses in which at least 80 percent of the content is delivered online (Allen & Seaman, 2010). Whereas online programs were uncommon ten years ago, almost all U.S. higher education institutions now offer them (Allen & Seaman, 2010; National Center for Educational Statistics, 2009).

Juxtaposed to the growth of online learning is the interest in transformative learning in these contexts. Transformative learning, which has been around for more than twenty-five years, is one of the most researched and studied phenomena in adult education, and much of it has taken place in mainly face-to-face educational settings (Taylor, 2007). The results of this work demonstrate that transformative learning theory is useful to understand student experiences and to provide guidelines for designing and facilitating instruction that leads to this fundamental change. Nevertheless, the empirical research on ways to foster transformative learning in online contexts is more limited. The critical review of the literature in the following section both articulates the limitations of the empirical evidence and provides samples of the conceptual works that support ways to help understand how to foster transformative learning online.

A CRITICAL REVIEW OF THE LITERATURE

A review of the peer-reviewed journals revealed only one empirical study that examined the topic of fostering transformative learning online (Killeavy & Moloney, 2010). These authors conducted a small mixed methods study to explore whether maintaining a diary in an electronic format would encourage the use of the reflective journal, and whether sharing this blog would encourage peer group support among participants. They found, however, that there was little evidence of a more reflective approach attributable to the use of blogs. They suggest that perhaps the instructor should spend more time ensuring that students are familiar with reflective methods prior to implementing the use of blogs for reflection to foster transformative learning online.

A number of other empirical studies demonstrate that transformative learning is useful to understand the students' experiences in online classes, but they do not provide information about ways to foster it in these online classes. For example, Cragg, Plotnikoff, Hugo, and Casey (2001) applied transformative learning to the learning process of nursing students in a distance learning context. Benson, Guy, and Tallman (2001) attempted to document the perspective change that occurred in four students who completed two online library media courses. Reushle (2008) used transformative learning theory as the framework for an online teacher training course. These studies suggest that transformative learning theory may be a useful framework for understanding the online learning process, but they do not provide much detail in terms of how to foster transformative learning online.

There are a number of books on transformative learning online. Yuzer and Kurubacak (2010) edited a book in which authors from multiple countries examined transformative learning in a variety of settings. The book, however, focuses not on ways to foster transformative learning, but rather on ways to bring together the aesthetic dimensions of distance education and transformative learning to varying degrees. For example, one chapter of an empirical study of a multicase analysis of cross-cultural learning in a graduate-level class (Townley, Christman, Coppola, Geng, & Li, 2010) sought to understand how various course assignments helped to develop student teams into learning communities, and the type of learning activities and the level of effort that help to transform student learning. These authors relied on Mezirow's perspective transformation (2000), along with cross-cultural online learning, problem-based learning, online pedagogy, and educational technology (Garrison, Anderson, & Archer, 2000) as the conceptual frameworks for the study. The methodology included three cases representing different levels of curricular intensity based on the complexity of the assignment and varying use of technology. The curricular intensity was described as one complex assignment and an entire course, each requiring the students to engage with Chinese and United States students. According to these authors, there was evidence that an effective transformative cross-national learning community was achieved for all cases, but the type of transformative learning and links back to the theory are missing from the discussion section of the paper. The authors also failed to provide any details on how to develop complex assignments that might foster transformative learning.

Similarly, Kurubacak and Yuzer (2011) edited a book that focuses on the challenges of and barriers to using technology in ways that can bring about transformative learning for social equity. There are no empirical studies in the handbook that focus on ways to foster transformative learning. Additionally, although there are a few conceptual chapters in the handbook that help readers to understand ways to use technology to foster transformative education, many of the chapters use transformative learning tangentially, and others fail to even mention transformative learning. The focus seems to be on the use of technology (or the lack thereof) in ways that may provide transformative learning opportunities that foster social equity beyond the classroom. For example, Adeoye, Adebo, and Olakulehin (2011) discuss how poverty and fear of Internet usage among university students limit online education possibilities and thus opportunities for online transformative learning among this population. The opportunity to use transformative learning theory to promote social equity is thus unlikely to occur.

King (2009) wrote a book based on her years of experience publishing empirical work on transformative learning. Although this is useful information, the book does not discuss ways to foster transformative learning online. Finally, Rosebrough and Leverett (2011) did not mention transformative learning theory in their book written to demonstrate how to use a transformative pedagogy model, which seeks to move education to something that is transformational rather than informational. It focuses on ways to move instruction from teacher- to learner-centered on the computer. Thus it does not specifically address ways to foster transformative learning as detailed in this Handbook.

The overwhelming majority of literature on the subject of fostering transformative learning online is conceptual. A few are named in the following passages. For example, the journal *Education and Technology* produced a special issue, the March/April 2011 edition, with articles (Bolger, Rowland, Reuning-Hummel, & Coder, 2011; Harmon, 2011; Hughes, Guion, Bruce, Horton, & Prescott, 2011; King, 2011; Rogers, 2011; Veletsianos, 2011) on topics of technology and transformative learning that provide insights into the helpfulness of technologies to foster transformative learning online.

Cranton (2010) relies on her ten years of experience to help readers understand the characteristics of transformative learning in face-to-face settings that can be transferred to the online context. Dirkx and Smith (2009) use their empirical work on collaborative learning online to draw conclusions about ways to foster transformative learning through collaborative learning, including the emotional issues associated with the processes.

McCracken and Guthrie (2011) explore the capacity for transformative learning that is inherent in experientially based education such as service-learning contexts. These authors also examine the methods by which such experiences can be facilitated in web-based academic settings. They conclude that the use of technology can serve to provide for transformative learning—or can distract students from the primary learning goals, if the students do not know how to use the technology properly.

Hai-Jew (2011) discusses how to use online courses to build savvy learners who will also become responsible global citizens. These courses provide a model that promotes both liberation and transformation of students. Seo and Tindall (2011) theorize about the possibilities of fostering transformative learning through avatar role-play in online immersive virtual environments—games and social spaces in which students create roles for themselves, embodied by virtual representatives called *avatars*. The avatars interact with one another in these 3D virtual spaces to create multiple kinds of interaction like role-play and real and fantasy games. According to Seo and Tindall, these environments allow for critical reflection and opportunities to practice acting in more socially responsible ways that can foster transformational learning.

Overall, the literature suggests that it is possible to foster transformative learning with (1) deliberate attention to a strong pedagogy in the design of the online course, (2) instructors who deliberately allow for a learner-centered approach, (3) deliberate attention to the students' ability to interact with one another through sustained discussion and through the use of complex problems or issues in a safe environment, and (4) deliberate attention to students' ability to engage in self-reflection. These key considerations are discussed in the next section.

PEDAGOGICAL CONSIDERATIONS TO FOSTER TRANSFORMATIVE LEARNING ONLINE

This section begins by borrowing from information based primarily on research and conceptual papers about the use of technology in secondary school settings to demonstrate the importance of the pedagogy over the technology to foster transformative learning online. In a meta-analysis of studies on media research, Clark (1983) claims that technologies are "mere vehicles that deliver instruction but do not influence achievement any more than the truck that delivers our groceries causes changes in our nutrition" (p. 445). That is, although students gain significant learning benefits from audiovisual or computer media as opposed to conventional instruction, the same studies indicate that those benefits stem from the instructional strategies built into the learning activities rather than the particular medium for instruction. Clark (2001) reaffirmed the same conclusion. In contrast, Kozma (2001) argues that the medium does in fact influence the learning, but it is not the medium per se that makes students learn; rather, he agrees that the design of real-life models and simulations are more influential to student learning. Seo and Tindall agree with this perspective (2011).

Examples of these approaches follow. For Yuzer and Kurubacak (2010) and Kurubacak and Yuzer (2011), the approach is driven by the goals and intentions for learning and the perspective on transformative learning that is likely to help to meet those goals. According to these authors, the intended goal for the pedagogy, regardless of the discipline for the online class, is social justice. The online contexts provide opportunities for students to interact globally with students who are very different from themselves. Thus they can seriously consider worldviews extremely different from their own and create the potential for transformative learning and social equity.

Goulah (2010), in his conceptual chapter, examines the potential to foster transformative learning among second and foreign language teacher education students in an online class. He relies on O'Sullivan's (1999; 2002, as cited by Goulah, 2010) perspective on transformative learning to consider ecological issues that emphasize a "global-planetary vision combining ecological literacy, social justice, and human rights issues in interlocking structures of ableism, class ethnicity, gender, language, race and sexual orientation" (p. 304). According to Goulah, transformative learning problematizes, critiques, and resists philosophies that disrupt this ecological consciousness. Educators must help students develop an awareness and prepare them to critique such situations through critical reflection so as to create ways of seeing the interconnectedness of all lives.

Meyers (2008) wrote a conceptual article that discusses transformative pedagogy as appropriate for online teaching. Relying on Mezirow's (1991) perspective, transformative pedagogy is a way to promote critical thinking and self-examination, and to facilitate civic engagement for students. Meyers further asserts that online class discussion often appears more collegial and informal, which offers opportunities for learners to examine and question their assumptions through critical reflection as they examine materials or interact with others who have very different perspectives from than their own.

A conceptual book chapter (Sable, 2010) examined an online course that used reflective practice including mindfulness, journal writing, and contemplation as a pedagogical strategy to foster transformative learning. Sable describes contemplative practice as "an umbrella term to designate the particular set of pedagogical practices that are intended to progressively produce the conditions for transformative learning" (p. 264). He asserts that the goal of transformative learning is to produce citizens in democratic and multicultural societies where the disposition and ability to think critically and act compassionately permeate across boundaries of privilege and power. Accordingly, transformative learning should focus on the development of both insight and knowledge in the course to educate the whole person.

Dirkx and Smith (2009), in their conceptual chapter that provides advice based on their research, describe their collaborative online course intended to foster self-work and deep learning (Entwistle & McCune, 2004, as cited by Dirkx & Smith, 2009). Although social constructivism through problem-based learning and Mezirow's (1991, 2000) work informs their discussion, they focus primarily on the emotional and spiritual dimensions of students' experiences through the work of Boyd and Myers (1988). Boyd and Myers's perspective on transformative learning indicates that human lives reflect both conscious and unconscious aspects that are most influential in decision making and actions. A goal of transformative learning in their online classes is to develop a dialogical relationship with one's unconscious, so that the dynamic contents may have creative expression in our conscious lives. Dirkx and Smith assert that aspects of the online environment, such as the lack of nonverbal cues and the ambiguity of the printed word, often stimulate student presumptions regarding each other's meaning and intent, which can lead to transformative learning if the course is designed properly.

Cranton (2010) notes that one characteristic of online learning that has the potential to contribute to student engagement in transformative learning is "the stranger on the train phenomenon (speaking to people with whom you have never met nor are likely to meet in person)" (p. 4). However, one must create conditions that help students to feel safe talking to these strangers.

The issue of trust is often a challenge in creating the kinds of spaces in which students can engage in interactions that might lead to transformative learning. Empirical studies related to trust issues (unrelated specifically to transformative learning) explain that the notion of a safe learning environment, which often relies on rational approaches to promoting trust, overlooks the emotional and unconscious nature of trust and its influence on the perception of trust in the online environment (Smith, 2008, 2010). These emotional and unconscious trust issues are a by-product of intimacy (the ability to openly share with others) and epistemic challenges associated with the demands of course design, resulting in new roles for teachers and students in the online environment (Smith, 2008, 2010). Trust issues are brought into the group from students' previous personal and professional experiences; if ignored, they can hinder the students' perception of a safe space to learn regardless of the course design, facilitation, and reflection opportunities.

In summary, the most important consideration to foster transformative learning online is the pedagogical strategy embedded in the course design. Creating this kind of safe space for students—a space in which they feel free to interact with one another in ways that might foster transformative learning—remains challenging for instructors. Furthermore, Rogers (2011) in his conceptual article cautions instructors to convey, at the onset of instruction, the possibility of some moments of discomfort in the course.

The next step in fostering transformative learning online is to design learning activities and use technology to support the learning. These are discussed in the following section.

FOSTERING TRANSFORMATIVE LEARNING THROUGH DESIGN AND TECHNOLOGY

This section discusses the two main learning activities emphasized in the recommended approaches identified in the literature—discussion and reflection—and includes the technology to support these strategies. Although the interaction of discussion or dialogue among students is necessary for transformative learning in any setting, it is especially important for online environments. Both facilitators and students must establish presence. Although not directly related to transformative learning, Garrison and Anderson (2003) and Garrison, Anderson, and Archer, (2000) present two elements to establish a learning community online for online discussions: cognitive presence and social presence. Cognitive presence is defined as "the extent to which learners are able to construct and confirm meaning through sustained reflection and discourse in a critical community of learning" (Garrison & Anderson, 2003, p. 28). These authors define social presence as the "ability of participants in a community of inquiry to project themselves socially and emotionally, as 'real people' (i.e. their full personality) through the medium of communication being used" (Garrison & Archer, 2003, p. 94). If students do not participate through active engagement to establish both cognitive and social presence, it is as if they are not in the class at all (Palloff and Pratt, 1999, 2007).

The learning strategies that are used to foster discussions among students are whole class discussions, role-play, collaborative exercises such as problem-based learning, and one-on-one interactions among students. The goal of these learning activities is to allow each learner to begin to reflect upon previously held and unshared beliefs and opinions in light of the new information offered by course assignments or others in the class. These interactions can be the result of assigned or student-selected problems, cases, or projects, or reactions to videos, readings, or contemporary issues just as they arise in face-to-face settings.

A review of the conceptual literature reveals that one of the more common ways to foster transformative learning online is through collaborative group work or teams. Yuzer and Kurubacak (2010) suggest that this is especially true when students actively participate through knowledge construction, establish their own learning goals, lead discussions and share resources, and engage in collaborative decision making during project-based and problem-based learning.

During discussion, students are confronted with a different perspective, which in turn creates opportunities for reflection to examine current beliefs and behaviors (Dirkx & Smith, 2009; Sable, 2010). Collaborative learning also engenders sustained discussion and the need to coordinate different points of view, which means that the students must consider alternative perspectives.

Today there are many technologies that support interaction among students. These include technologies called *3D immersive learning environments* (Howard, Sanders, & McClannon, 2010), which are useful to foster transformative learning. These immersive learning environments include Elluminate Live!, multi-user domains (MUDs), Second Life (SL), and Skype. Elluminate Live!, a web conferencing program developed by Elluminate Inc., consists of virtual rooms called vSpaces where students, employees, and others who need to collaborate can meet via audio and video conferencing, share documents, chat, and use white boards. In addition, instructors can meet with students or student groups as well as provide lectures in this medium.

A MUD is a text-based virtual environment (Smith & Farrell, 2001). These authors postulate that MUDs provide a learning environment in which participants create imaginary worlds characterized by collaborative learning, the testing of new assumptions and perspectives in a social context, and the construction and reconstruction of the meaning of their experiences. Second Life (SL) is also a virtual world, developed by Linden Lab. Students who are called residents can engage in educational simulations in which they explore role play, meet other residents, socialize, and participate in individual and group activities. Skype is a software application that allows users to make free voice and conference calls, file transfer, file share, and instant message over the Internet. The 3D immersive technology allows students to role-play and to explore emotional and imaginative aspects of learning, which can lead to transformative learning (Howard, Sanders, & McClannon, 2010).

A second set of learning strategies useful for fostering reflection that can lead to transformative learning are what Sable (2010) refers to as "contemplative practices." These include journaling (see, for example, Dirkx & Smith, 2009; Sable, 2010) and structured contemplation (Sable, 2010). Journaling is used to ask students to write about their experiences, draw pictures, or otherwise use art to express their experiences. Students are asked to write down or draw what comes to mind without allowing the mind to edit, simply writing and drawing as the thoughts occur (see, for example, Dirkx & Smith, 2009; Sable, 2010). There are a few empirical studies that examined the use of technology such as blogs (Chandra & Chalmers, 2010; Wolf, 2010), weblog (Wopereis, Sloep, & Poortman, 2010), Twitter (Wright, 2010), mobile devices (Koole, McQuilkin, & Alley, 2010), wikis (Wen-Hoa & Nakazawa, 2010), and Web 2.0 technologies (3D immersive) (Deng & Yuen; 2011; Philip & Nicholls, 2009) to foster varying levels of self-reflection. These studies are not related to ways to foster transformative learning but are used here for illustrative purposes. These studies conclude that if used properly with direction from the instructor, each of these technologies can help to foster self-reflection on varying levels, but the technology does not foster reflection per se; rather, the ways in which the instruction is designed remain the most important component.

A blog is a type of website or a part of a website, usually maintained by an individual, with regular entries or commentaries, descriptions of events, or other materials such graphic or video files. Blogs can be private or shared with others; they allow for others to comment on the content. Something of a blog variation, Twitter is a social network that offers millions of different voices in 140-character "tweets." Basically, the member posts brief messages that can be read and responded to by other members. Wright (2010), in a study of teacher education not related to transformative learning, found that Twitter logged participants' reflective thinking during a school practicum.

Sable (2010) asserts that structured contemplation—a form of mindful meditation—is useful for online contexts. Students are asked to focus on an object—such as a drawing, a statement, or a question—and to reflect intensively on the object without trying to analyze it. Students are asked to let go of any thoughts that come to mind about the subject of their meditation. According to Sable, this first part of the process trains one's ability to remain focused on the object in the present without attachment to usual thinking patterns. Next, students are asked to pay attention to what is happening to their whole body, not just their brain. They are to notice any felt sense and stay with it, without judgment, allowing their attention to be open. By slowing down the thought processes in this way, students can discover space for fresh perspectives to emerge. Sable does not suggest any technology to help foster this kind of reflection.

Other technologies used to promote the reflective comments were discussion boards and chat rooms. Cranton (2010) suggests that although the instructor should provide suggestions for keeping reflections, students should reflect in whatever way seems comfortable to them.

There are a number of challenges to using reflective exercises in online courses. In a conceptual article, Harmon (2011) articulates the first: many adults have little to no experience or training in critical self-reflection. He further theorizes that "most adults seek to establish a rational, well-ordered world around themselves, a world with few surprises and which doesn't require them to stray outside their comfort zones. . . . Thus rather than gain experience through practice in critical-reflection, they actively seek to avoid situations that may provide transformative learning opportunities" (p. 30). In the only empirical study this author found on fostering transformative learning through blogs, Killeavy and Moloney present another challenge: they found that the students did not engage in the kinds of reflection or discussion that could lead to transformative learning; rather, they engaged in superficial discussion and reflection. These authors concluded that perhaps the teacher should spend time at the beginning of the class helping the students understand the kinds of discussion and reflection needed.

FACILITATING LEARNING TO FOSTER TRANSFORMATIVE LEARNING ONLINE

Instructors must reexamine their role in the online class. There is little information to help inform the instructors' role in fostering transformative learning online that is different from the advice offered for the face-to-face classroom. A couple of them are mentioned here. First instructors must make room for transformative learning (Palloff & Pratt, 1999, 2007). In the online environment, this means that the instructor must be knowledgeable about the technology and how to use it to foster both instructor-student and student-student interaction and reflection. The use of technology must be deliberate and not simply add bells and whistles to the course. Instructors must ask themselves, "What is it that I want to accomplish, and how can I use the technology to accomplish it?" The instructor must also make sure that the students have access to and are familiar with the technology,

Second, the instructor must create presence online. Teaching presence is defined as "the design, facilitation and direction of cognitive and social processes for the purpose of realizing personally meaningful and educationally worthwhile learning outcomes" (Anderson, Rourke, Garrison, & Archer, 2001, p. 10). Lehman and Conceição (2010) wrote a book based on an empirical study of teacher presence in online contexts that is not necessarily related to transformative learning but can provide ways for teachers to establish presence for their students. The authors explore the emotional, psychological, and social aspects from both the instructor and student perspective. Their book provides an instructional design framework and shows how a strong presence contributes to effective teaching and learning.

In summary, the instructor must rethink his or her role in the transformative process by deliberately thinking through how to take advantage of the online environment to foster transformative learning. The online environment makes it easier to keep track of student interaction and respond accordingly, but the ability to do so also presents challenges to faculty workload (Lehman & Conceição, 2010).

IMPLICATIONS AND RECOMMENDATIONS FOR FUTURE RESEARCH

The discussion in this chapter demonstrates the need to attend to the use of technology, pedagogical concerns, and course design and instructor role to foster transformative learning in online classes. Although the technology is important to help facilitate communication and reflection that can foster transformative learning, it is secondary to the pedagogical considerations, course design, and instructor role. As increasing numbers of faculty join in online teaching efforts, the ability to think through and find ways to foster transformative learning becomes critical.

This has implications for faculty development. Faculty developers will need to help faculty rethink their role as facilitators for online classes. Pedagogical considerations must include faculty beliefs about teaching and learning. Much of the literature speaks about the need for increased student-to-student interaction to foster transformative learning. When faculty hold beliefs about teaching and learning that represent a transmission model, it is necessary to help them change their beliefs to be consistent with transformative pedagogy, through more learner centered instruction (Rosebrough & Leverett, 2011). As students themselves in faculty development efforts, the faculty can be exposed to transformative pedagogy in the same ways that they will use the theory to foster transformative learning for their students.

Additional research is needed in all aspects of fostering transformative learning online. The literature review revealed only one empirical study on the topic. Thus much more empirical research is needed on the ways to use the various available technologies in the instructional design and facilitation. Second, empirical support is needed to better understand the ways that technology can either enhance or inhibit opportunities to foster transformative learning online. Third, since most of the research and conceptual papers focused narrowly on perspective transformation, more research is needed that also examines students' experiences through the other perspectives of transformative learning. Finally, further research is needed to better understand and provide empirical support for the overall helpfulness or challenges associated with the online environment and the various technologies to foster transformative learning.

References

Adeoye, B. F., Adebo, G. M., & Olakulehin, F. K. (2011). Poverty and phobia of Internet connectivity and usage among university students in southwestern Nigeria. In G. Kurubacak & T. V. Yuzer (Eds.), *Handbook of research on transformative online education and liberation: Models for social equity* (pp. 461–475). Hershey, PA: IGI Global.

Allen, I. E., & Seaman, J. (2010). *Learning on demand.* Needham, MA: The Sloan Consortium.

Anderson, T., Rourke, L., Garrison, D. R., & Archer, W. (2001). Assessing teaching presence in a computer conferencing context. *Journal of Asynchronous Learning Networks, 5*(2). Retrieved from http://communitiesofinquiry.com/files/Teaching %20Presence.pdf

Benson, A., Guy, T., & Tallman, J. (2001). Viewing online learning through the lens of perspective transformation. *Journal of Educational Telecommunications, 7*(3), 251–269.

Bolger, B. B., Rowland, G., Reuning-Hummel, C., & Codner, S. (2011). Opportunities for and barriers to powerful and transformative learning experiences in online learning environments. *Educational Technology, 52*(1), 36–40.

Boyd, R. D., & Myers, J. G. (1988). Transformative education. *International Journal of Lifelong Education, 7*(4), 261–284.

Chandra, V., & Chalmers, C. (2010). Blogs, wikis and podcasts—Collaborative knowledge building tools in a design and technology course. *Journal of Learning Design, 3*(2), 35–49.

Clark, R. E. (1983). Reconsidering research on learning from media. *Review of Educational Research, 53*(4), 445-459.

Clark, R. E. (2001). A summary of disagreements with the "mere vehicles" argument. In R. E. Clark (Ed.), *Learning from media: Arguments, analysis and evidence* (pp. 125–136). Greenwhich, CT: Information Age Publishing.

Cragg, C. E., Plotnikoff, R. C., Hugo, K., & Casey, A. (2001). Perspective transformation in RN-to-BSN distance education. *Journal of Nursing Education, 40*(7), 317–322.

Cranton, P. (2010). Transformative learning in an online environment. *International Journal of Adult Vocational Education and Technology, 1*(2), 1–9.

Deng, L., & Yuen, A.H.K. (2011). Towards a framework for educational affordances of blogs. *Computers and Education, 56*(2), 441–551.

Dirkx, J. M., & Smith, R. O. (2009). Facilitating transformative learning: Engaging emotions in an online context. In J. Mezirow, E. W. Taylor & Associates (Eds.),

Transformative learning in practice: Insights from community, workplace, and higher education (pp. 57–66). San Francisco: Jossey-Bass.

Garrison, D. R., & Anderson, T. (2003). *E-learning in the 21st century: A framework for research and practice.* New York: Routledge.

Garrison, D. R., Anderson, T., & Archer, W. (2000). Critical thinking and computer conferencing: A model and tool to assess cognitive presence. *American Journal of Distance Education, 15*(1), 7–23.

Goulah, J. (2010). Teaching transformative learning and digital/online education: From theory to practice in a second language and foreign language education context. In T. V. Yuzer and G. Kurubacak (Eds.), *Transformative learning and online education: Aesthetics, dimensions, and concepts* (pp. 301–314). Hershey, PA: IGI Global.

Hai-Jew, S. (2011). Building global citizens: Empathy, the limits of human nature, and the first steps towards social equality through e-learning assignments. In G. Kurubacak & T. V. Yuzer (Eds.), *Handbook of research on transformative online education and liberation: Models for social equity* (pp. 245–271). Hershey, PA: IGI Global.

Harmon, S. W. (2011). Virtual worlds as a trigger for transformative learning. *Educational Technology, 52*(1), 28–32.

Howard, B., Sanders, R., & McClannon, T. (2010). Constructing transformative learning communities in 3D immersive learning environments. In T. V. Yuzer and G. Kurubacak (Eds.), *Transformative learning and online education: Aesthetics, dimensions, and concepts* (pp. 34–47). Hershey, PA: IGI Global.

Hughes, J. E., Guion, J. M., Bruce, K. A., Horton, L. C., & Prescott, A. (2011). A framework for action: Intervening to increase adoption of transformative Web 2.0 learning resources. *Educational Technology, 52*(1), 53–61.

Killeavy, M., & Moloney, A. (2010). Reflection in a social space: Can blogging support reflective practice for beginning students? *Teaching and Teacher Education, 26*(4), 1070–1076.

King, K. P. (2009). *Handbook of the evolving research of transformative learning based on the learning activities survey.* Charlotte, NC: Information Age Publishing.

King, K. P. (2011). Teaching in an age of transformation: Understanding unique instructional technology choices which transformative learning affords. *Educational Technology, 52*(1), 4–10.

Koole, M., McQuilkin, J. L., & Alley, M. (2010). Mobile learning in distance education: Utility or futility? *Journal of Distance Education, 24*(2), 59–82.

Kozma, R. B. (2001). Counterpoint theory of "learning with media." In R. E. Clark (Ed.), *Learning from media: Arguments, analysis and evidence* (pp. 137–178). Greenwich, CT: Information Age Publishing.

Kurubacak, G., & Yuzer, T. V. (2011). *Handbook of research on transformative learning online education and liberation: Models for social equity.* Hershey, PA: IGI Global.

Lehman, R. M., & Conceição, S.C.O. (2010). *Creating a sense of presence in online teaching: How to "be there" for distance learners.* San Francisco: Jossey-Bass.

McCracken, H. J., & Guthrie, K. L. (2011). Using transformative pedagogy to facilitate personal growth and development in web-based service-learning courses. In G. Kurubacak & T. V. Yuzer (Eds.), *Handbook of research on transformative online education and liberation: Models for social equity* (pp. 273–291). Hershey, PA: IGI Global.

Meyers, S. A. (2008). Using transformative pedagogy when teaching online. *College Teaching, 56*(4), 219–224.

Mezirow, J. (1991). *Transformative dimensions of adult learning.* San Francisco: Jossey-Bass.

Mezirow, J., & Associates (Eds.). (2000). *Learning as transformation: Critical perspectives on a theory in progress.* San Francisco: Jossey-Bass.

National Center for Education Statistics. (2009). *The condition of education 2009.* U.S. Department of Education: Institute of Education Sciences.

O'Sullivan, E. (1999). *Transformative learning: Educational vision for the 21ˢᵗ century.* London: Zed Books.

Palloff, R. M., & Pratt, K. (1999). *Building learning communities in cyberspace: Effective strategies for the online classroom.* San Francisco: Jossey-Bass.

Palloff, R. M., & Pratt, K. (2007). *Building online learning communities: Effective strategies for the virtual classroom* (2nd ed.). San Francisco: Jossey-Bass.

Philip, R., & Nicholls, J. (2009). Group blog: Documenting collaborative drama processes. *Australasian Journal of Educational Technology, 25*(5), 883–699.

Reushle, S. E. (2008). A practitioner's journey exploring transformative approaches to the professional development of online educators. *International Journal of Pedagogies and Learning, 4*(2), 15–28.

Rogers, P. C. (2011). Shaping global citizens: Technology enhanced intercultural collaboration and transformation. *Educational Technology, 52*(1), 47–52.

Rosebrough, T. R., & Leverett, R. G. (2011). *Transformational teaching in the information age.* Alexandria, VA: ASCD.

Sable, D. (2010). Contemplative interaction: A key to transformative learning online. In T. V. Yuzer and G. Kurubacak (Eds.), *Transformative learning and online education: Aesthetics, dimensions, and concepts* (pp. 260–280). Hershey, PA: IGI Global.

Seo, K. K., & Tindall, D. A. (2011). Inspiring personal and social transformation through avatar role play in an online immersive virtual environment. In G. Kurubacak & T. V. Yuzer (Eds.), *Handbook of research on transformative online education and liberation: Models for social equity* (pp. 384–385). Hershey, PA: IGI Global.

Smith, R. O. (2008). The paradox of trust in online collaborative groups. *Distance Education, 29*(3), 325–340.

Smith, R. O. (2010). Epistemic challenges: Trust in the online collaborative group. *International Journal of Lifelong Education, 29*(1), 21–44.

Smith, R. O., & Farrell, P. (2001, June 1–3). "MUD Play": A transformative learning context. In R. O. Smith, J. M. Dirkx, P. L. Eddy, P. L. Farrell, & M. Polzin (Eds.), *Proceedings of the 42nd Annual Education Research Conference.* East Lansing, MI: Michigan State University.

Taylor, E. (2007). An update of transformative learning theory: A critical review of the empirical research (1999–2005). *International Journal of Lifelong Education, 26,* 173–191.

Townley, C., Christman, D., Coppola, B., Geng, Q., & Li, J. (2010). Cross-cultural transformative learning: Three case studies of Sino-American distance learning communities. In T. V. Yuzer & G. Kurubacak (Eds.), *Transformative learning and online education: Aesthetics, dimensions, and concepts* (pp. 14–33). Hershey, PA: IGI Global.

Veletsianos, G. (2011). Designing opportunities for transformation with emerging technologies. *Educational Technology, 52*(1), 41–46.

Wen-Hoa, D. H., & Nakazawa, K. (2010). An empirical analysis on how learners interact in wiki in a graduate level online course. *Interactive Learning Environments, 18*(3), 233–244.

Wolf, K. (2010). Bridging the distance: The use of blogs as reflective learning tools for placement students. *Higher Education Research and Development, 29*(5), 589–602.

Wopereis, I.G.G., Sloep, P. B., & Poortman, S. H. (2010). Weblogs as instruments for reflection on action in teacher education. *Interactive Learning Environments, 18*(3), 245–261.

Wright, N. (2010). Twittering in teacher education: Reflecting on practicum experiences. *Open Learning, 25*(3), 259–265.

Yuzer, T. V., & Kurubacak, G. (2010). *Transformative learning and online education: Aesthetics, dimensions, and concepts.* Hershey, PA: IGI Global.

PART FIVE

FOSTERING TRANSFORMATIVE LEARNING: PRACTICES AND ETHICS

CHAPTER TWENTY-SIX

Transformation as Embodied Narrative

M. Carolyn Clark

The moment of truth can come at strange times. For me it was in mid-May 2009—that point in the semester between receiving the piles of final papers from my graduate students and having to turn in grades. I was on campus—actually, I was *literally* on campus, because I was face down on one of the concrete sidewalks leading to my parking lot, lying spread-eagled and surprised. And cursing. Fortunately for me, I wasn't carrying anything; for years I've used a backpack purse to relieve the shoulder strain that comes with strap purses, and I was on my way to lunch, so whatever I'd brought in to work with me that day was still sitting in my office. My free hands meant that I fell unencumbered, much like Raggedy Ann, and that sprawl saved me from anything more than a few scrapes and bruises. It was the tail end of the semester, so there were few people around, but one student was nearby, and she came over.

"Are you OK? Do you need any help?"

"Thanks, I'm fine. I just tripped on these uneven sections of pavement."

She moved on, and I proceeded to get up. But as I heard myself telling her that the uneven pavement was at fault, I knew that wasn't true. If I had caught the edge of the concrete, I would've stumbled, and my body would've tensed up to catch itself as I headed to the ground. But it didn't happen that way. I was walking and then I was flat on the sidewalk, with nothing between those two moments. Even when I was still face down I knew why I was there, and that's why I was cursing. . . . My right knee had buckled under me—betrayed me, in fact—and I had given way to gravity. I was pissed. And I was scared. This knee, worn to bone by osteoarthritis and with a shredded meniscus, was no longer a part of my body I could count on, and that put the rest of my body at risk. Visions of broken bones floated in my head. I had reason to be scared.

The body has many stories, but the one I'm choosing to tell here is about physical decline. This is usually associated with aging, but, truth be told, the body can fail us at any age and leave us in a very different world and transform us into a different self. My own story is about my experience with osteoarthritis, and it has a happy ending (for now) because the wonders of medicine replaced my arthritic knee with a mechanical device that works beautifully. Her name is Daisy. We have been together for almost two years, as I write this, and she has dramatically improved my life. But she hasn't transformed me or my life, and although she plays a critical role in my story, she isn't the main character. This is a story of my body, before and after Daisy, and though my experience of a total knee replacement (TKR) is important to the plot, it is only part of the story. Illness transforms us; aging transforms us; and they are not unconnected, at least in the body story I want to tell.

This *Handbook* is about transformative learning, and this chapter is positioned in the section that examines various conceptualizations of transformative learning theory. My particular task is to explore "other ways of knowing," a phrase which typically means noncognitive knowing. There are many "other ways of knowing"; I am choosing two, which I'm interweaving: *embodied knowing* and *narrative knowing*.

Embodied knowing makes the argument that knowing is not simply a cognitive process; we also know in and through our bodies. Although our minds can and usually do reflect on knowledge that comes from our bodies, the learning that is the product of this process begins in our bodies, not in cognitive reflection on embodied experience (Michelson, 1998). In the West the mind has been privileged over the body, but more recently scholars are recognizing the value of embodied knowing (Heshusius & Ballard, 1996; Fenwick, 2003) and acknowledging that learning begins in the body. Narrative knowing has as its premise that we make sense of our experience by storying it (Bruner, 1986), which is to say, by bringing coherence to what would otherwise be chaos. We do this in a social context in several respects: there is always an audience to a story, shaping its structure and purpose; we draw from "libraries of plots" in a story-saturated world that "help us interpret our own and other people's experience" (Sarbin, 1993, p. 59); and these social narratives establish normalcy by defining reasonable causality and plausibility (Linde, 1993). Perhaps most important for my purposes here, narrative serves as a primary way of fashioning personal identity (Rosenwald & Ochberg, 1992). Given its meaning-making function, narrative is particularly important in enabling us to endure personal crises, captured best by a quote attributed to Isak Dinesen: "All sorrows can be borne if you can put them into a story" (Arendt, 1958, p. 175). The genre of illness narratives is one example of this.

My mode of exploration is autoethnography, a relatively recent type of life history research in which the researcher studies an experience of her own in order to understand it as a phenomena embedded in and interpreted through multiple cultural contexts, much as an ethnographer studies the experiences of those in specific cultures (Ellis, 2004). In my case, I am telling a story of my own body in order to understand how that embodied narrative transformed and continues to transform my sense of self. Years ago, in a chapter I wrote on transformational learning (Clark, 1993), I defined the term in a deceptively simple way: "transformational learning shapes people; they are different afterward, in ways both they and others can recognize" (p. 47). For now I'm going to stay with that simple definition and ask, How did my embodied narrative of illness and aging change me, reshaping my understanding of myself and my understanding of my life?

Any story follows an arc, and it can be helpful to know the shape of the whole in order to see how the parts fit together. In a way I'm creating an arc within an arc, telling the story of what happened in vignettes, and following those with reflections in regular text that analyze my understanding of the embodied narratives at that point. The story itself is largely chronological—you've read the low point already (my fall), and I'll flash back to give you a sense of what it was like to live with my steadily worsening arthritic knee. Then I'll move into the decision-making process, namely deciding to have TKR surgery, followed by what it was like to be within the medical narrative. The top of the arc for me follows—it is the illness narrative of the recuperation. Once through that, I'll describe what it has been like to be bionic and how this entire experience has reshaped my understanding of my self. And I'll connect that to the larger process of aging. I'll conclude with some thoughts on how we can conceptualize transformative learning in a new way, restorying it in a real sense through embodied narrative.

ONE NARRATIVE TO MAKE SENSE OF ANOTHER

My story is situated within a larger narrative; in traditional academic writing this would be called the *theoretical framework*. The body cannot speak for itself, at least not in the way that we usually understand as "speaking," so we must develop a language to enable it to speak in a way we can understand. One language we all experience any time we get sick and see a doctor is the language of Western medicine. In this language the body is understood mechanistically as a complex organism that works in a particular way when it's healthy; when the body becomes sick, the task of medicine is to find out what is going wrong and figure out how to fix it. So the goal of medicine is to cure illness and injury, and the language of medicine reflects this (the problem is diagnosed, the treatment selected, and if this process is successful, we are healed). But, except for the surgery that gave me Daisy, this language is insufficient to tell my story.

The best language, for my purposes, is that developed by people who have experienced major illness, a genre known as *illness narratives*. These stories of illness have produced ways for the body to speak, not through doctors treating the illness but through the embodied voices of those who are or have been seriously ill. From within that genre of illness narratives I have chosen the typology created by the sociologist Arthur Frank. Beginning from reflecting on his own experience of undergoing a heart attack and not long afterward being diagnosed with testicular cancer (Frank, 1991), he goes on to explore the experiences of others who have written about their illnesses, and he develops a threefold typology of illness narratives: the *restitution narrative*, the *chaos narrative*, and the *quest narrative* (Frank, 1995). The presumption he makes is that although the body itself cannot speak, we who know ourselves not in dualistic terms but holistically as mind-body can give voice to the body by telling stories *of* the body rather than *about* the body. This distinction is essential to any understanding of embodied knowing.

Frank's typology enables us to think with stories. The first of the three, the restitution narrative, is congruent with the larger medical narrative. The plot can be summarized simply: *Yesterday I was well, today I am sick, but tomorrow I'll be well again.* The agent of that restoration is medicine, and although it is a self-story, it is only marginally so, because the self is being acted on.

The chaos narrative is the opposite of the restitution narrative—life never gets better, and no one is in control—not the self, not medicine—no one. In a real sense this is an antinarrative, because it cannot be told while it is happening, it can only be lived; the suffering is beyond words. It is the most embodied narrative of the three because "chaos is told in the silences that speech cannot penetrate or illuminate" (Frank, 1995, p. 101).

The third part of the typology is the quest narrative, in which the illness is accepted and the person searches out a way to use it to benefit others. Frank uses Joseph Campbell's (1972) model of the mythic journey to describe the quest. It begins with a departure; for the ill person, that is when symptoms of the disease first manifest themselves. The second stage is initiation, and here the person crosses the threshold into suffering, the means for transformation. In that process the person is given what Campbell calls "a boon"—a significant insight that must be shared with others. The final stage of the journey is the return. The person is no longer ill, but unlike the wellness of the restitution narrative, in this return to health the person has been transformed, profoundly marked by their suffering. More important, the person is now responsible to give witness to what has been learned.

My goal is to use Frank's typology of illness narratives to both tell and listen to my own story of arthritis, my experience of knee replacement, and my ongoing story of aging. I claim no specialness for my story; in fact, it is its very lack of specialness that makes the telling of this story important. According to the Arthritis Foundation (2010), one in five adult Americans suffer from arthritis or chronic joint symptoms, and it is the leading cause of disability among those over fifteen. Likewise, TKR surgery is becoming common. Yet although there is abundant research about the medical aspects of this disease, very little research has been done on what it is like to live with this condition (Maly & Krupa, 2007). So what follows is an attempt to gain a deeper understanding of an everyday experience.

Rewinding the Tape

Although I can identify the moment of truth—when I was spread-eagled on the ground—I cannot find the beginning of all this. When was I not stiff when I got up out of a chair? When did my neck, my hands, my hips, my back, and my knee not hurt? Of course there was a time when my body didn't know it had osteoarthritis. The onset was gradual and didn't (and still doesn't) erupt in pain in all those places at once. I think the case of my knee was somewhat different, though, because that pain impacted my mobility and therefore set the circumference of my world. I simply did less of the things I loved that involved physical activity.

Not only was my world shrinking but my life was centering more and more around pain management. First came intense exercise. That worked for several years; on a good day I wouldn't start noticing the pain until the afternoon. When exercise was no longer sufficient to control the pain, I turned to drugs, then to cortisone shots. The first shot was magic—"Wow, the pain is gone!" I told my doctor as I walked around her examining room. But I knew it was temporary, and it was. Each successive shot was less magical and the pain returned sooner. Finally I couldn't sleep through the night anymore, which added sleep deprivation to my misery.

Of course I knew about total knee replacement surgery, and I knew enough to know that I wanted to avoid it as long as possible. I remember my first visit with the surgeon, standing beside him in front of a bank of lights looking at the X-rays of both my knees.

"Notice how bowed your right tibia is compared to your left? That's because the supporting cartilage is gone. You can see the femur resting directly on the tibia already. And it will only get worse."

"So how long before I'll need to have a knee replacement?"

"Till you can't stand the pain anymore."

Somehow that wasn't helpful. I wanted him to tell me there was a time certain when I'd have to have this major surgery. Instead, the message I got was that the decision about when to turn in this knee for a mechanical device was up to me. And meanwhile there would only be steadily increasing pain. Not good news.

I soldiered on. Having my world shrink meant more than limits on functionality; it also meant that I looked at my surroundings differently. I saw the world in terms of obstacles and difficulties that had to be negotiated. And I saw myself as less and less capable of doing things, more and more limited, and increasingly dependent on others. I became diminished within.

As I wrote this section, I was struck by the sound of this embodied voice of illness because it's not the voice of the person I've always considered myself to be—confident, independent, capable. Returning to the definition of transformative learning that I gave earlier, I can say that through my body, in the grip of its illness narrative, I was transformed into a different person, in ways I and others could recognize. I was a diminished self, living in a "less than" world. There are various threads of Frank's (1995) illness narratives present. I knew that restitution could come only from TKR surgery, but I resisted that, and my agency (managing the pain through exercise and drugs) was able only to postpone that step, not to change my situation. I was beginning to show elements of the chaos narrative as my body declined and my world shrank; things were only getting worse. And I began to be afraid that things would never get better. I felt like I was limping across a flat plain toward a horizon I had no power to reach. The independent and confident self I had known was fading.

Claiming Agency by Giving In

It was my trip to Chicago in June that answered the question about when I had to have the surgery. The fall in May had unnerved me, so before leaving for Chicago I decided I needed to carry a cane, just in case my knee gave out on me again. This was a major step for me—the cane constituted a public sign of disability, a sign I resisted—but I felt that I had no choice. I found one that folded up, easy to hide but available if I needed it. En route to Chicago I kept it in my carry-on bag, and once I got there, I carried it in my backpack. When I walked from my hotel to the conference the first evening, I found that my knee was hurting a lot, so I opened up the cane and used it for the first time. It felt strange, but it did make walking easier. When I got to the conference center, though, I folded it up and put it back in my bag—I didn't want anyone I knew to see me using it. That became my daily pattern; only when surrounded by strangers was I willing to use the cane. Then one evening my pride did me in. With a group of friends I went to a party across town, which meant using the subway. I climbed down and up long flights of stairs, unwilling to search out an elevator or use my cane. Surrounded by friends, I couldn't claim the mark of disability. By the time I got back to my hotel, I was in agony and fell into bed.

The next day I had a presentation in the morning, but I had planned to skip out on the conference during the afternoon and go to the Art Institute, which was across the street from the university hosting the conference. Perfect. Except not. My knee was screaming at me when I got up that morning, and it only got worse as the day progressed; the ibuprofen I took might as well have been candy. As before, I used the cane to walk to the conference site, but this time I didn't fold it up and put it back in my bag once I entered the building. Vanity had evaporated. I limped to the assigned room, catching the attention of some who knew me.

"What's wrong? Are you OK?"

"I'm fine; it's just arthritis in my knee and I'm having a flare-up."

I'm a bad liar. The pain was overwhelming. When the session was over, I knew that there was no way I could spend the rest of the day at the Art Institute. I was so frustrated—it was right across the street! I love that museum and I had longed to visit it again. But now it was absolutely impossible for me to do it—I was in far too much pain. I hobbled back to the hotel, got some ice for my knee, took more ibuprofen, and fell into a deep sleep.

The next day I flew home, this time with cane in hand. A few days later I was in my doctor's office.

"It's time," I said. "I can't do this anymore."

In choosing to have total knee replacement surgery, I was giving my body over to medicine, in search of restitution. I remembered what it was like to be well. I now knew not only that I was sick but that I could no longer endure it. I wanted to be well again.

TKR is considered elective surgery, but it's a choice that older adults are making at an increasingly high rate; according to the Centers for Disease Control (2005), between 1979 and 2002 the rate of TKR surgery in adults age sixty-five and older increased eightfold. These numbers have continued to rise in that population, from 66.8 per 10,000 in 2002 to 82.1 per 10,000 in 2007 (Centers for Disease Control, 2010). Yet to choose this major surgery is no small decision, given the risk of serious complications and the long and arduous rehabilitation that follows it.

My decision to take this step was unequivocally an embodied one; my body knew it was time, not my mind. I had, of course, been educating myself about TKR during these years; I knew a lot, but what I knew cognitively was not sufficient for me to make a decision. The body, my body, was in charge.

Becoming an Object to Be Fixed

Saying yes to TKR surgery was akin to entering a tunnel. I mark its beginning when I met with my orthopedic surgeon the second time. He was supportive, informative, direct. He agreed that it was time to do this, but before going any further he looked at me intently and said:

"You need to know that there are major risks to this surgery. A blood clot could form and you could die. The statistics on this are low, and we do everything in our power to prevent it, but the risk remains."

"I know that. But I don't think this surgery is optional anymore. I can't continue to live this way; I don't really have a choice here."

I did know the risks, and I also knew he had to tell me about them up front. I was surprisingly matter-of-fact as I talked about the possibility that I could die. It didn't seem real then; my painful, undependable knee was more real than my mortality. We scheduled the surgery, he answered my long list of questions, and I closely examined the model of the implant I would be getting. Then I began to prepare—cleaning the house, making meals and freezing them, lining up friends to drive me to physical therapy after the surgery. And I revised my will, so maybe my mortality wasn't totally out of my mind after all.

Before I arrived at the hospital, I had dealt with my situation on my terms. Once I went through those doors, I became a body that was acted on, as anyone who's been hospitalized knows. Those details aren't unique in my narrative, so I'll gloss over them here, except for one small story. As I was being prepped for surgery, the anesthesiologist came in to discuss my options for postsurgical pain control and we agreed that an epidural made the most sense for me. He told me to sit up, swing my legs off the gurney, and lean over. I felt the needle go into my back.

"I don't feel anything happening in my legs."

"Don't worry; you will soon."

But I didn't, and I don't know why I wasn't more assertive at that point. Did I trust more to his knowledge than to my own body's knowing? Clearly I did, and that was a mistake. In fact, the epidural was not inserted correctly. I paid the price in pain when I woke up, and later the epidural had to be redone.

After the surgery, hospital routine took over my life for the next three days; I was completely in the hands of others, especially physical therapists insistently pushing my body to do more than I thought reasonable.

Once home, my body continued to be regulated—by medication, by exercises, and by even more physical therapy. I found the outpatient PT program grueling. I started out at a large facility with lots of equipment, lots of patients, and a staff that was always changing. At each session I was supervised by someone different; it was August, and lots of staff were on vacation. I was a body on a conveyor belt, and that body always felt terrible—battered by drugs, lack of sleep, and pain.

On my fifth visit, it was a physical therapist named Lynn who picked me off the conveyor belt. It didn't take me long to rank her lowest on the empathy scale. We moved from machine to machine with little personal interaction. I said something about how challenging the rehab from this surgery was. She agreed that it was a slow process. I replied:

"The thing that encourages me in the midst of all this is that I'm seeing progress. For example, for the first time in years I'm able to straighten my right leg."

"Your leg isn't straight; you just think it is. It's a common misperception."

"My leg *is* straight. I can feel it. You can't see it because the dressing is still on it."

"No, it isn't."

I was furious. I knew what my body was telling me—my leg was straight. There was no point arguing further, so I did the rest of the routine in silence. That afternoon I had an appointment with my surgeon to get my stitches out. After his nurse had removed them, I was sitting on the treatment table in the examining room with my leg stretched out when the surgeon came in.

"Look at you!" he said. "Your leg is straight!"

Later that afternoon I changed physical therapy providers.

In this section I write of being within the medical narrative. This is not a category of Frank's (1995) typology, but it is in fact the larger narrative within which his typology is situated. There is a feeling of the body being given over to others (other people, other forces) and of the abdication of personal agency—which is impossible to exercise when we are in the throes of major illness. When Lynn, the obnoxious physical therapist, was telling me that she knew more about the state of my body than I did, that was what Mishler (1981/2009) calls the voice of medicine speaking. From that perspective the body is objectified and scientific or clinical knowledge provides the means for treatment. I rejected her professional knowledge in favor of my own embodied knowing. In leaving her and that clinic, I exercised agency and reclaimed responsibility for my care. My body remained an object to be fixed, but I was able to choose who would do the fixing. I chose carefully. As my story continues, though, my agency becomes more tenuous.

Being Overtaken

In the hospital I was a body being acted on; in the long weeks of physical therapy I was acted on and, in cooperation and in resistance, I was also a body that was acting; but in the timeless weeks at home, alone, I was a body that was overtaken by pain and unremitting discomfort. I was unprepared for this, and I was undone by it. The nights were the worst. I felt like my bed had turned on me, offering not rest and relief but instead greater discomfort than I experienced anywhere else in the house. Getting myself into bed, and hoisting myself out, took enormous effort. To make it worse, I could sleep for only two or three hours at a stretch, so that enormous effort had to be repeated multiple times during the night. My sleep itself was of poor quality; in addition to the interruptions, I had to deal with the discomfort of sleeping only on my back. Exhaustion was my constant state.

Then there was the pain in my leg, or more accurately, the shifting bouts of cramped muscles and bruised bones. The Vicodin took care of the pain in my knee but it did nothing for this. The trauma of the surgery—pounding the heads of the implant into the tibia and the femur, cutting two ligaments and moving others, manipulating the leg muscles to create the correct alignment and fit—was exacting its price, and it was a much greater price than I had expected. Ice packs, elevation, and exercise were my only means of treatment, but nothing took this pain away; all I could do was manage it and endure.

Then there was the price exacted by the medication I was on, Vicodin for pain and Coumadin to prevent blood clots. I felt terrible all the time. I can't find the words to describe it now, and when I was experiencing it, I could only groan, "Oh God, oh God...," as I moved through each day. I began to imagine myself living in a misery index, which I half-jokingly called my oh-God-o-meter, and it was always set high. My mind knew this was temporary; my body said this was never going to end. And it was my body that I believed.

And then there was the day I saw a front-page article in the paper about the death of a woman who was prominent in the community. I didn't know her but as I read the article a wave of cold swept over me. She had died of a blood clot several weeks after having had knee surgery. Details about the surgery weren't given, but I knew it was TKR, like mine. That could have been me. I thought of that moment in my surgeon's office when he told me of this risk and of my matter-of-fact response. I didn't have that rational composure now; I put down the paper and couldn't pick it up again. Now the risk to my mortality was not something I could dismiss so easily; now, after the fact, the possibility of dying was something my body knew in ways my mind earlier could not.

Remembering all this and writing these words makes that fear present and real again. This is the closest I come in this story to embodying the chaos narrative—that state that cannot be expressed in language but can only be lived, then later reflected on, inadequately. I've been sick before, recuperated from major surgery before, but this was my longest and most difficult experience of sustained misery. I think transformation for me in this story begins here. I have a new knee, but the rest of my body cannot be replaced in total. Decline is well under way at various sites, and their number grows; there will be no replacement parts for everything that hurts, or will hurt. More frightening is the misery that will accompany that decline and the knowledge that there will be times when I will not be able to escape or manage it. My experience this time had an endpoint that I could see, and that helped me endure it. How will I handle misery whose horizon I will be unable to see because it isn't there? I don't know. I can't know. I can only hope that I will find the strength to endure when I need it.

LIFE WITH DAISY

Being bionic is more than a little wonderful; the "I can't" world shifts toward "I can," though it never arrives there completely. I can walk without pain now, and although the distances I can cover aren't without limit, those limits are less restricting, and when I reach them it's because of fatigue, not pain. I'm again doing things that I love. I can sleep normally now, and my stamina has steadily increased. The pain of the arthritis in my knee and the misery of the recuperation are behind me. Life has come back to normal.

But it's also a new normal; if Daisy has freed me in all these ways, she has also changed me in other ways. For one thing, I find that I view the physical world and interact with it differently. I'm more deliberate in my movements, especially when I'm walking, and I'm always assessing the environment carefully to minimize my risk of falling. Outwardly I'm moving more normally, but inwardly I'm calculating, assessing, judging what is possible, what is best, as I do move through the world. Daisy has also insisted that I view my body differently. I certainly can't take her for granted; if I don't exercise regularly, her functionality will lessen. In fact, regular exercise, which used to be an option, now has become a necessity, and not just to keep my leg muscles strong. Without it my leg hurts and my stamina decreases. All of this has begun to put me in a different relationship with my body.

And that leads me to the reality of aging. Earlier in my life age was never an issue for me. I turned forty without thinking much about it; when I turned fifty, I actually threw a party (truly unusual behavior for me) because I wanted to celebrate it. But turning sixty was different; that marker was very difficult for me—I began lying about my age. I even did it on a trip to Korea, where age is valued and strangers will ask the question so that they can afford you the proper respect. Even there I lied! But in my life since Daisy that has changed. Now, when asked, I tell people I'm sixty-seven. No more lying. My age is an embodied reality now, and this embodied knowing brings a kind of inner freedom. But there is no denying the physical and cognitive decline that aging brings, and it is more difficult to embrace that willingly. I resent the limits to my energy, I am frustrated when my body creaks when I get up out of a chair, and the gradual slippage of memory frightens me more than I can say. Unlike illness, aging has no borders—there is no diagnosis here and certainly no treatment, only management and constant surprises (few of them good). I'm only in the early part of this final journey, so I don't know how it will unfold for me. But I can hope, and do hope, that what my body has taught me in the story I've told here will prepare me for the lessons yet to come.

In Frank's (1995) quest narrative, the person accepts illness, suffers, and returns to life transformed, carrying the obligation (the "boon") to witness to others what has been learned. My story falls short of the quest in the sense that Frank means it, as for me there was no return from the edge of death but rather an entry into another stage of life with a new awareness. It is an embodied awareness that I have now; my witnessing is my body speaking to my self about the naturalness of aging. As boons go, this one couldn't be more ordinary, but it is transformative—and it is welcome.

CONCEPTUALIZING TRANSFORMATION AS AN EMBODIED NARRATIVE

This story, in the end, is intended to be a story of profound change, of transformation. I return to my simple definition of transformative learning, especially the part where I noted that those who experience it "are different afterward, in ways both they and others can recognize" (Clark, 1993, p. 47). Narratively that can be made visible in many ways. I've structured this chapter around Frank's (1995) three story types to describe illness—restitution, chaos, and quest—and tried to locate my experience, as best I can, within one of those story types. But there is some slippage between Frank's categories and my experience, in large part because he is describing the experience of acute, life-threatening illness, and most of my story is about living with a chronic illness and coping with aging. It's not a perfect fit, so at this point I'm going to turn to Mattingly's (1998) more open notion of emplotment, most simply understood as people coming to realize what kind of stories they are living out at different points in their lives. I think tracking my positioning in different stories may help make the transformative learning process clearer.

Retracing my story, as it begins I am disabled, increasingly, by osteoarthritis of my right knee. In fact, I find myself more and more enmeshed in a narrative of physical disability, a narrative that I fully embody and that shapes my understanding of myself, my awareness of my world, and my engagement with and in that world. Because it is an illness narrative, it is a story of my body, and it is through my body that I both know and learn. The progression of the disease in my knee is a downward spiral, one that leads me to a place where my body knows that I cannot stay—not safely, anyway. The TKR surgery becomes the only way to claim a different narrative, one that promises restitution. I welcome Daisy, a new part of my body that is not me but that will allow me to once again be the self I've known. But the price is high: major discomfort from which I can find no relief for weeks, if not months; and sustained, painful work to strengthen and train the muscles that will make Daisy a fully functional part of my body. During that period I come close to enacting the chaos narrative, as I struggle to live with misery and not be overwhelmed by it, and as I, however briefly, know my own mortality in an embodied way. Both the experience of sustained misery and the brief gaze into the face of death shake me and make me fearful of future illness and suffering; more frightening still, they leave me uncertain about my capacity to endure what may yet come. But that is projecting myself into a future story, one I cannot fully know or grasp, and although it affects me in the present moment, what matters is what story I see myself enacting now.

Even with all the freedom that Daisy has brought me, I'm not in a restitution narrative; I am not simply well again, returning to a former, younger self. I have been changed. Although I am no longer in a disability narrative, I am abled differently now. I know through my body that life is tenuous, that age means physical decline, but also that it offers the possibility of a new kind of growth psychologically and spiritually. This is a narrative that is uncertain, and I can't yet name it for myself. But there are some elements that I can discern in the grayness. I think I have begun to grow psychologically, if recognizing that I can endure counts as a sign of growth. I think it does. I didn't give up when I was in misery—I kept on. And I reached out for support from friends who had made this journey themselves. I remember calling one friend who has had two knee replacements and asking—pitifully, I admit—"Carol, when will I start feeling better?" She responded, "I'll be right over." Her caring presence, her encouragement, and her witnessing to wellness on the other side of this particular misery made me stronger. The psychological knowledge that I am not alone, that I am connected to others in more ways than I can name, merges for me with spirituality. What I half-jokingly called my oh-God-o-meter when I physically felt the worst was a sign that I knew I wasn't alone in a deep and profound way. I reached out in faith as well. God was with me then and remains with me. As a woman of faith I have always believed this, but my knowledge of that is deeper now. How these elements of psychological and spiritual growth (and other domains I can't yet name) will play out in the future I cannot yet know, but I trust that I will continue to learn, to grow, and to become.

So welcoming Daisy has meant that I'm in a new narrative now, a narrative that is embodied in a way that I didn't know was possible when my body was well and able, qualities that for me kept my body distant, and often separate, from my understanding of myself. That distance is gone now. I don't *have* a body as I once did—I *am* my body. And my embodied self is located in a new story. We'll just have to see how it unfolds...

References

Arendt, H. (1958). *The human condition*. Chicago: University of Chicago Press.

Arthritis Foundation. (2010). Learn about arthritis. Retrieved from http://www .arthritis.org/learn-about-arthritis.php

Bruner, J. (1986). *Actual minds, possible worlds*. Cambridge, MA: Harvard University Press.

Campbell, J. (1972). *The hero with a thousand faces*. Princeton, NJ: Princeton University Press.

Centers for Disease Control and Prevention. (2005, February 25). QuickStats: Rate of total knee replacement for persons aged >65 years, by sex—United States, 1979–2002. *Morbidity and Mortality Weekly Report*. Retrieved from http://www.cdc.gov/mmwr/preview/mmwrhtml/mm5407a6.htm

Centers for Disease Control and Prevention. (2010). CDC/NCHS, National Hospital Discharge Survey. Retrieved from http://www.cdc.gov/nchs/data/hus/2010/ fig08.pdf

Clark, M. C. (1993). Transformational learning. In S. B. Merriam (Ed.), *An update on adult learning theory* (pp. 47–56). New Directions for Adult and Continuing Education, no. 57. San Francisco: Jossey-Bass.

Ellis, C. (2004). *The ethnographic I: A methodological novel about autoethnography*. Walnut Creek, CA: AltaMira Press.

Fenwick, T. J. (2003). Reclaiming and re-embodying experiential learning through complexity science. *Studies in the Education of Adults, 35*(2), 123–141.

Frank, A. W. (1991). *At the will of the body: Reflections on illness*. Boston: Houghton Mifflin.

Frank, A. W. (1995). *The wounded storyteller: Body, illness, and ethics*. Chicago: University of Chicago Press.

Heshusius, L., & Ballard, K. (1996). *From positivism to interpretivism and beyond*. New York: Teachers College Press.

Linde, C. (1993). *Life stories*. New York: Oxford University Press.

Maly, M. R., & Krupa, T. (2007). Personal experience of living with knee osteoarthritis among older adults. *Disability and Rehabilitation, 29*(18), 1423–1433.

Mattingly, C. (1998). *Healing dramas and clinical plots: The narrative structure of experience*. Cambridge, UK: Cambridge University Press.

Michelson, E. (1998). Re-membering: The return of the body to experiential learning. *Studies in Continuing Education, 20*, 217–233.

Mishler, E. G. (1981/2009). The struggle between the voice of medicine and the voice of the lifeworld. In P. Conrad (Ed.), *The sociology of health and illness: Critical perspectives* (8th ed., pp. 358–369). New York: Worth.

Rosenwald, G. C., & Ochberg, R. L. (1992). *Storied lives*. New Haven, CT: Yale University Press.

Sarbin, T. R. (1993). The narrative as the root metaphor for contextualism. In S. C. Hayes, C. J. Hayes, H. W. Reese, & T. R. Sarbin (Eds.), *Varieties of scientific contextualism* (pp. 45–65). Reno, NV: Context Press.

CHAPTER TWENTY-SEVEN

Learner-Centered Teaching and Transformative Learning

Maryellen Weimer

Learner-centered teaching—sometimes called *learning-centered teaching*, *student-centered learning*, or *student-centered teaching*—refers to efforts by faculty to use instructional approaches that develop student autonomy and responsibility for learning. College teachers from many disciplines are discovering that these approaches regularly result in experiences that permanently change how students view learning and how faculty orient to teaching. Learner-centered teaching can result in learning that transforms both the learning and the teaching experience (Blumberg, 2009; Doyle, 2008; Harris & Cullen, 2010; Weimer, 2002).

This chapter explores why and how learner-centered teaching accomplishes these changes in students and teachers. It also addresses interesting questions raised by the relationship between learner-centered teaching and transformative learning, such as these:

- Are the links between the learner-centered teaching and transformative learning strengthened when teachers use certain learner-centered approaches?

- Can learning experiences be designed so that transformative learning happens more regularly?

- What sequence of learner-centered activities, assignments, and approaches best transforms dependent learners into independent ones?

- Is learner-centered teaching a viable way to develop faculty commitment to the ideas and outcomes of transformative learning?

DEFINITIONS: HOW IS LEARNER-CENTERED
TEACHING DEFINED?

Like many ideas that become trendy in higher education, learner-centered teaching is defined loosely and variously by many who advocate its use or who want to have institutions that advocate its use. Their motivation derives from wanting to attach a popular moniker to what they do or who they are. But most faculty who incorporate these changes are not doing so to be trendy. Rather, they are looking for solutions to common classroom problems—such as passive learners who lack motivation, students not coming to class prepared, disruptive classroom behaviors, and the propensity of students who are doing poorly to place blame elsewhere. Because most faculty read pedagogical literature so sparingly and participate in technique-focused training, they are simply unaware that learner-centered strategies share common characteristics and theoretical groundings. As a result, many faculty who use learner-centered approaches would not attach that label to what they are doing or the kinds of teachers they perceive themselves to be.

Moreover, many learner-centered strategies are not new, but they have gained notoriety and become more widely used as a consequence of the Barr and Tagg article (1995) published in *Change* magazine. Since then the ideas of learner-centered teaching have been endorsed by faculty, institutions, and many professional groups. The ideas have been written about in various higher education publications, ranging from discipline-specific pedagogical periodicals to newspapers and online publications such as the *Chronicle on Higher Education* and *Inside Higher Education*.

Most faculty define learner-centered teaching operationally through activities, assignments, and approaches to teaching. Among many examples, here are some illustrations:

- Giving students a say in setting classroom policies (DiClementi & Handelsman, 2005)
- Turning over an aspect of instruction to peers, as in the model of peer-led learning developed in the field of chemistry (Lewis & Lewis, 2005)
- Letting students control how they participate in class (Litz, 2003)
- Making students responsible for coming to class prepared to discuss assigned readings (Yamane, 2006)

Examples like these and others appear regularly in the discipline-based pedagogical literature, although faculty do not always affix the learner-centered label to what they describe. A more dated cross-disciplinary collection appears in my book, *Learner-Centered Teaching* (Weimer, 2002).

Examining a collection of learner-centered techniques used by practitioners reveals characteristics and definitional attributes that tie these approaches back to the educational philosophies and tenets of constructivism, feminist pedagogy, and the radical and critical pedagogies. (For a resource that ably explains these connections, see Stage, Muller, Kinzie, & Simmons, 1998.) In a nutshell, these strategies give students choice and freedom at the same time that they hold students more responsible for learning autonomously.

Constructivism lets learners connect with content in ways that make the material meaningful to them. That does *not* involve compromising the integrity of the material to be learned by making it mean whatever the learner wishes. Rather, it is about students building bridges between what they already know and the new material. It means that students are not required to connect with the material the same way faculty do, as English professor Gregory (2005) came to realize when his students failed to see the significance of one of his favorite poems, Gray's "Elegy Written in a Country Churchyard."

> I was giving my students a reason to understand why some people—namely me or other strange persons like me—might find Gray's poem *interesting*, but I was giving them no reasons of their own for finding Gray's poem *important*. I have finally learned that unless I can make a convincing case about why the literature I love is not only interesting but important—then I seldom make much headway merely by showing why that literature interests me. And I have learned not to resent my students' skepticism on this point. (p. 95)

Feminist pedagogy attacks the assumptions of patriarchy that give faculty power over the learning process and in their relationships with students. Many learner-centered techniques change the power dynamic in the classroom. They put teachers in roles that are less authoritarian and directive, and more facilitative and supportive. Most faculty worry mightily that relinquishing power will compromise their ability to control what happens in the classroom. But most discover that students do not abuse the power they're given but instead respond maturely, taking advantage of the opportunity to facilitate their own learning and that of others. Black's (1993) observations about what happened in an organic chemistry course where he let students decide what text material they would work on in class illustrate this experience.

> Interestingly, the course does not collapse when I come in and ask what the students want to talk about, because it is always in the context of the current chapter, and the schedule for working on those chapters is in the syllabus. Going to class each day is a pleasure, and always somewhat different. I am relaxed, enjoy the time, and it shows to the students. I feel no pressure to enter a mad race to cover the material; rather, we work together on what is currently their work. (p. 144)

The radical and critical pedagogues were the first to argue that learners should be empowered to make decisions about learning processes—that doing so powerfully affects the motivation to learn—and now much research documents the regular occurrence of this outcome (Pintrich, 2003). Some learner-centered techniques give students choices about what assignments they will complete (Weimer, 2002) and occasionally how much those assignments will count, when they will be due, and what happens if a deadline is missed. Some even involve students in the assessment process (Edwards, 2007); others let students develop their own learning contracts (Hiller & Hietapelto, 2001).

Because college teachers are focused on whether or not an approach works, they often fail to see how collections of them are related and can be defined as a group. In the case of learner-centered teaching approaches, based on their theoretical underpinnings, it is fairly easy to identify approaches with these characteristics. It is much more difficult to determine when the label can justifiably be attached to a teacher. Is it a function of the number of learner-centered approaches used? Does it depend on a change in educational philosophy? Or must teachers have transformative learning experiences that enable them to see that these approaches rest on more valid assumptions about teaching and learning?

This tendency to define learner-centered teaching operationally makes the more precise defining needed for critical analysis and systematic study difficult. It also prevents learner-centered teaching from becoming an intellectually coherent teaching method. If it remains an unorganized, eclectic collection of strategies, its ability to significantly change instructional practice will be limited. This lack of definitional precision is one of the most serious impediments to ongoing development of learner-centered teaching and implicates its relationship to transformative learning.

RELATIONSHIPS: WHAT CONNECTS LEARNER-CENTERED TEACHING AND TRANSFORMATIVE LEARNING?

Transformative learning, as defined and explored by adult educators (Mezirow & Associates, 2000; Cranton, 2006), is learning that produces significant change in beliefs. It changes what people think and, often, how they act—it opens people's minds and alters how they view the world. Transformative learning can occur in any class and with any kind of content, as well as outside of class and formal educational experiences. It is a profound and lasting kind of learning and should be the goal of educators and educational institutions.

Exposure to learner-centered teaching approaches is transformative in that it regularly changes beliefs about teaching and learning. The practitioner literature is replete with accounts of how these approaches changed not only the learning experiences of students but also the teaching experiences of faculty. My book (Weimer, 2002) recounts my own instructional transformation as the effectiveness of these approaches motivated me to incorporate more and more of them until, as I often say, "I hardly recognized the teacher I'd become." At the time I was making these changes I did not think of them as being learner-centered, nor did I set out to transform my teaching. It was after the fact, when I set out to write the book, that I saw that these techniques were related and that collectively they had transformed not only how I taught but also what I believed about teaching and learning. Brookfield (1995), Tompkins (1996), and Spence (2001) offer similar detailed accounts of teacher transformation.

For students, the transformation involves beliefs about learning and perceptions of themselves as learners. For most of them, exposure to a learner-centered approach is not immediately transformative. Students (be they eighteen-year-olds or seasoned adults) come to the college classroom after having years of experience with instructional approaches based on assumptions that make them very dependent learners. Many faculty report that students begin by resisting these approaches. They want teachers to do what they're supposed to do—lecture and make decisions about learning for students (Doyle, 2008).

When change occurs, it happens more incrementally, with insights along the way leading to the larger, more profound, transformative change. For example, students discover that when they have some control over the learning process (even something as simple as being able to establish their own due dates or to select from a group of possible assignments which ones they will complete), their motivation to learn is impacted positively. When students have a role in defining the learning task, many will work harder, even on tasks that are challenging. Being in charge (even a little bit in charge) makes learning more exciting, and it brings a sense of pride and accomplishment that many students have not previously experienced. Usually the transformation comes at the culmination of a series of learner-centered experiences—say, at the end of a course. Suddenly students see themselves taking charge of their own learning. It may be that these transformative changes come more quickly for adults with more experience as self-directed learners. That has yet to be established empirically, but once learners start taking charge of their learning, they become confident, empowered, autonomous learners—perhaps not all at once, but to the point that they no longer want teachers making all the learning decisions for them (Grow, 1991).

The learner-centered transformative change in teachers and students often involves a synergistic relationship. As teachers see the positive way these approaches affect students—such as increased motivation, more of them coming to class prepared, and more time spent on assignments—this in turn motivates teachers to make more changes and to implement them with greater enthusiasm. This "better" teaching results in even "better" learning experiences. This synergistic affect does not occur automatically, nor is the progression always linear, but when the transformation of teachers and learners occurs, this synergistic relationship often magnifies the affect.

It may well be that exposure to learner-centered teaching environments increases the likelihood of transformative learning generally, especially for students. There are indications of this in many of the experiential accounts, including some already referenced (Handelsman & DiClementi, 2005; Black, 1993). However, this more general relationship between learner-centered teaching and transformative learning is not the focus of this chapter; rather, it focuses on how learner-centered approaches transform the beliefs and experiences of students and teachers with respect to learning and teaching.

Even though learner-centered approaches are frequently transformative, that outcome is not automatic. Still, it occurs frequently enough to posit a relationship between the two. But despite experiential accounts of its occurrence, I do not believe that the relationship has been explored, which makes this analysis a very initial consideration. Like many first looks, it raises a number of intriguing questions, most of which have not yet been answered.

DO SOME LEARNER-CENTERED APPROACHES PROMOTE TRANSFORMATIVE LEARNING BETTER THAN OTHERS?

Both research and practice verify that not all instructional approaches are equally effective at promoting learning. The varying effects of instructional approaches is further accentuated by the individual differences of learners and by how the content is configured within a discipline. But at this point, systematic testing of various learner-centered approaches has been almost nonexistent. Moreover, for college classroom teachers the comparison of any two instructional "treatments" presents a daunting empirical challenge. Appropriate samples are difficult to construct; the way in which students are enrolled in courses and the dynamic milieu of the classroom make it all but impossible to control enough variables to reliably attribute a set of results to any given instructional experience. Qualitative research methods are better suited for exploring the affects of learner-centered approaches.

Ascertaining the relative effectiveness of various learner-centered strategies is further complicated by the lack of definitional precision and the fact that approaches can be learner-centered to varying degrees. It would seem that before research begins, criteria need to be established to identify a strategy as learner-centered; then it may be necessary to group the various approaches so that the comparison crosses collections of approaches rather than analyzing them singly. My ongoing review of learner-centered approaches has led me to think that they might profitably be categorized according to the aspect of instruction they address. Here's a description of how that typology might work.

Learner-centered techniques could be organized into six categories. First are those approaches that *give students some decision-making power over course content.* These are not approaches that ask students what they might like to learn in an entry-level required course; rather, they are strategies that in ethically responsible ways let students make some decisions about content. They start with approaches as simple as having students decide on the topic for a paper or identifying what they would like the teacher to focus on during a review session. Sometimes teachers let students select certain readings or identify a topic of interest they would like covered in the course. Other approaches are more complex, like a carefully crafted assignment that lets students review potential course textbooks and then make recommendations to the instructor (Weimer, 2002).

Another set of strategies that deserve the learner-centered label *involve students in teaching the content to each other.* Often these approaches involve group work and use cooperative learning strategies such as jigsawing or round-robin interviewing. Three carefully designed and executed studies in chemistry document how use of this approach does not compromise content learning and actually enhances other learning outcomes (Hockings, DeAngelis, & Frey, 2008; McCreary, Golde, & Koeske, 2006; Lewis & Lewis, 2005). These approaches do significantly change the role of the teacher, as Thiel, Peterman, and Brown (2008) point out in their description of a redesigned math course in which students did most of their work and learning in lab groups, not in a classroom listening to lectures.

Other learner-centered approaches *give students some control over how they will learn course material.* Most simply, students decide whether they will write a paper or do a presentation. A bit more substantively, it may involve choice about which assignments they will complete and some control over how much each assignment is worth. For my graduate course on college teaching, I developed five assignments. Students had to complete all five, but each assignment counted for only 10 percent of their grade. I gave them the other 50 percent of the grade and let them distribute that percentage across the assignments.

Learner-centered approaches also *involve students in establishing the policies and procedures that govern how the class is run.* In some approaches they make recommendations to the teacher; in other cases they are given the opportunity to suggest revisions to what the teacher has proposed (DiClementi

& Handelsman, 2005); and in some situations, students actually develop the policy—say, for participation, classroom deportment, late submissions, and/or missed classes. Woods (1996) and I (Weimer, 2002) devised schemes that let students set the participation policy for the course. I was motivated to do so by Woods's experience. Singham (2005) and students jointly identified those areas where both felt policies and procedures were needed.

Still other approaches *let students make some determination about the pace at which they will learn course material.* Most frequently this involves setting deadlines and penalties for missing them. The online learning environment often gives students complete control over the pace at which they make their way through the material.

Finally, some learner-centered approaches *engage students in self and peer assessment activities.* These are strategies that stop far short of letting students "grade" themselves. The motivation to get grades compromises the objectivity needed to make an accurate self-assessment. Even so, there are approaches that have students look at their own work and that of their colleagues and offer feedback. Some practitioner literature offers faculty good advice on how to make this a substantive and meaningful activity (see, for example, Nilson, 2003). Some faculty use approaches and engage students in the development of the criteria that will be used to assess their work. Often this involves collectively creating a rubric.

At this point, the question of whether some learner-centered strategies are better than others at promoting transformative learning experiences is only beginning to be explored in the literature (Cranton, 2006). Much of the research scholarship and the applied practitioner scholarship are still very much focused on the use and effectiveness of individual learner-centered approaches compared with the more traditional ways of teaching (Armbruster, Patel, Johnson, & Weiss, 2009; Cheang, 2009). Moreover, the literature does not address the differentiation, made earlier in this chapter, that learner-centered teaching approaches can transform both learners and teachers. Are some approaches better at promoting transformative learning experiences for students? Are some approaches better at promoting transformative experiences for teachers? These too are interesting and important queries to which we do not have answers.

Rather than focusing on the effectiveness of individual strategies, I have proposed that it makes more sense to categorize them and look for the effectiveness of approaches across groups of techniques. With individual approaches, much depends on the context—that is, how the teacher is using the approaches. Much also depends on the nature of the content being used with the approach. Finally, much depends on the individual learner and how ready that person (student or teacher) might be for the insights offered by one set of approaches versus another. Certainly this is an area ripe for research, given that we have many accounts verifying a connection between learner-centered approaches and transformative learning experiences for both teachers and students.

CAN LEARNING EXPERIENCES BE DESIGNED TO PROMOTE TRANSFORMATIVE LEARNING?

Is it possible to incorporate design features into learner-centered classroom activities and assignments that make them more likely to result in transformative experience for students? Like the question addressed in the previous section, this query is interesting and has many ramifications for practitioners. Fortunately, the answer to this question is not quite so elusive. It has not been answered directly, but work by adult educators offers indirect answers. Cranton (2006), for example, has identified a set of activities that promote transformative learning for students. Many of those activities are consistent with learner-centered approaches. Here are two examples from her longer list.

Questioning, as it occurs in college classrooms, is not often learner-centered, as documented by several studies of classroom participation (Ellner & Barnes, 1983). "Over four-fifths of the time, instructors asked students to recall facts or ideas. This was true whether the course was at an introductory or advanced level" (p. 185). A study by Auster and MacRone (1994) documented that less participation happens in classrooms when the majority of questions are at this low cognitive level. However, questioning can be learner-centered and transformative when, as Cranton notes, the questions offer learners the chance to figure things out for themselves (p. 138). Tomasek (2009) describes a way of using prompts about assigned readings that illustrates this kind of questioning. However, even when faculty ask these more open-ended questions, that does not ensure a learner-centered focus, as cryptically pointed out by Gregory (2006). "We think we are inviting students to be active learners by asking them questions, but we can easily deceive ourselves on this point because, usually, we ask few questions to which we do not already know four different answers that we are eager to explain" (p. 313). Questioning could lead more directly to transformative learning experiences if teachers asked thoughtful questions—including those they cannot answer, at least definitively.

It also seems likely that the power of questions to promote the thinking that transforms might be enhanced if, rather than asking the questions themselves, teachers helped students generate questions. This involves creating a classroom climate where student questions are welcomed and where teachers work to help students frame questions that are relevant, substantive, and provocative. Confronted with a question of your own making adds motivation to the search for an answer. Questioning can be learner-centered, and it can be designed so that it enhances transformative learning—making it not just learning, but learning across many different knowledge domains.

Many adult educators suggest that opportunities for critical reflection play important roles in promoting transformative learning. Cranton (2006) writes about this with respect to students; Brookfield (1995), with respect to teachers. For students, these opportunities fit naturally in many learner-centered experiences. Because the approach being taken to learning is different, it is easy to ask why. Too often teachers resort to *telling* students why. They may start with a question: "Why would a teacher let students pick which assignments they will complete?" But when the first student answers, "Because the teacher wants to get good course ratings," the teacher responds by delineating in detail the educational rationale behind giving students choice. Even though students may give some wrong or inappropriate answers, the question is better used to challenge students to think about the response.

Journaling and the many other forms of reflective writing can lead both students and teachers to the insights and deeper understandings that fuel transformative learning. For students, the insights can be prompted by good questions and feedback that pushes them to discover the reasons behind the reasons. The practitioner literature contains some compelling examples of how teachers have used writing to help them understand the impact of learner-centered strategies (Noel, 2004; Albers, 2009). In both of these examples these teachers are analyzing attempts to implement learner-centered approaches that did not go as planned. They explore student resistance and how it tested their understandings of and commitments to learner-centered teaching. The practitioner literature on teaching and learning abounds with pedagogical success stories. It takes courage to publish an honest exploration of what did *not* work. I wonder if transformative learning experiences happen more often as a result of attempts to learn from mistakes—in these two cases, mistakes made implementing learner-centered approaches.

In sum, it does seem that learner-centered approaches can be designed in ways that increase the likelihood that they will be transformative learning experiences for students and teachers. Despite the cogency of this argument, I was unable to find research that has systematically tested the veracity of this claim. And there is one final interesting detail: this discussion has focused on the design of individual strategies and those changes that might enhance their transformative learning potential. What if an instructor aspires to design a learner-centered course? Are there other, larger design strategies that are relevant here? Whetten (2007) proposes three design characteristics of learner-centered courses that could be used to begin exploration of this question.

Beyond the design of courses is the assembling of a learner-centered curriculum in which experiences could build on each other.

WHAT SEQUENCE OF LEARNER-CENTERED APPROACHES BEST PROMOTES TRANSFORMATIVE LEARNING?

For both teachers and students, acceptance of learner-centered approaches seems to follow a developmental trajectory. Grow (1991) has written about this developmental progression as it relates to learners becoming self-directed—certainly a central feature of learner-centered approaches. He suggests four stages of development for both teachers and students and points out how problems occur when teachers and students find themselves at different points on the growth continuum. He also makes it clear that movement toward autonomy in learning is not always a linear process. This is useful work, although I have not been able to find that Grow's developmental theory has ever been tested. However, Grow himself makes this interesting observation: "A theory doesn't have to be right to be useful. Nearly every action we take results from a workable convergence of misconceptions" (p. 127). Thinking about becoming learner-centered as a developmental process does open the possibility that instructional approaches might be sequenced in ways that affect growth and transformation.

The question for us in this section is this: How should learner-centered approaches be sequenced if the goal is transformative learning? It's another question not yet answered. What can be done at this point is to suggest potentially relevant areas. For example, there is much evidence in the practitioner literature that learner-centered approaches initially meet with some resistance on the part of students and faculty. A variety of sources offer faculty advice on dealing with this resistance (Doyle, 2008; Felder & Brent, 1996). Most recommend not implementing too many strategies too fast. That's one of the conclusions that Noel (2004) came to in analyzing his unsuccessful attempts to implement learner-centered approaches in an organizational design course for MBA students. Others (like Doyle, 2008) suggest that this is even more of a problem when the learners are beginning students and very dependent learners.

In my own experience, I found the key was not just the number of learner-centered approaches used but how I combined innovative and conventional strategies. I could push students further with more complex and innovative approaches so long as I retained some really conventional assignments and activities in the course. For example, I used a fairly complicated group exam assignment (Weimer, 2002), but it occurred with a traditional multiple-choice test, and doing the exam in a group was an option; students could choose to take the exam individually.

From our experiences working to overcome student resistance, we have also learned that for very dependent learners, a simple-to-complex progression can be helpful—indeed, in some cases it is absolutely necessary. Early on I developed a very open-ended log assignment for my beginning students. I gave them the freedom to take the course content where they wanted, writing about its relevance in any part of their lives. But student after student asked for guidance: "I don't know what you want me to write about in my log." "This assignment is really unclear." After numerous attempts to explain, I gave up, and the following semester I wrote prompts for every log entry. But now it wasn't an assignment through which students could discover the relevance of the content. So I redesigned, attempting to make deciding what to write part of the assignment. I started by giving student prompts, I offered possible areas of relevance about which they could write, I suggested some prompts and encouraged them to write others or revise my suggestions. By the end of the log assignment I had students generating their own prompts and writing at length in response to them.

But the practitioner literature focuses on overcoming students' initial resistance to learner-centered approaches. That's a necessary first step—learner-centered approaches aren't going to result in transformative learning experiences if students don't engage with them. But advice on overcoming resistance does not directly answer how to sequence approaches so that the experiences lead more directly to transformative learning. "Sequence" implies "how many," but more directly it is about order. Moreover, this discussion has posited a connection between learner-centered approaches and transformative learning for teachers as well as students. So the question of sequence relates to both.

Does managing how many strategies are implemented in the beginning, balancing them with more conventional assignments, and moving along a simple-to-complex continuum work for teachers as it does for students? Like students, teachers are fearful of these approaches—most Ph.D.s do not admit fear, but they do willingly express reservations about what will happen when they implement learner-centered approaches. Maybe they will not be able to cover all the content. Maybe students will take advantage of what these approaches give them. Maybe students will not learn as much. And maybe the students will think the teacher is lazy or doesn't know how to teach. For teachers, like students, initial resistance must be overcome before there is any chance of these approaches leading to transformative learning.

I am proposing that what we have discovered about overcoming resistance is relevant to the question of how to sequence learner-centered approaches so that they advance transformative learning objectives. At least they offer a place to start. The literature on transformative learning also suggests that a dramatic event—a disorienting dilemma—can be instrumental in transformative learning experiences. There is some indication that interrupting a developmental sequence with an instructional event like this can effectively promote transformative thinking about teaching and learning—for both students and teachers, but especially for teachers. In fact, in my book *Inspired College Teaching* (2010), I go so far as to recommend "bone-rattling change" for midcareer faculty who may be experiencing instructional doldrums or who need to reconnect with the passion they once felt for teaching. Learner-centered approaches can provide this kind of instructional jump start. They can change instructional thinking and practice—but more often they accelerate development. Read Singham's (2005) amazement at what happened when he first abandoned his policy- and prohibition-laden syllabus. The student response was stunning and motivated Singham to make even more changes, which quite quickly led to a radical reordering of his thinking about teaching. The experience he describes is not uncommon and lends credence to the assumption that the connection between learner-centered teaching and transformative learning may also be influenced by instructional approaches very unlike what the teacher normally uses.

IS LEARNER-CENTERED TEACHING A VIABLE WAY TO DEVELOP COMMITMENT TO TRANSFORMATIVE LEARNING?

Given the significance of experiences that result from transformative learning, it ought to play a central role in the education process and be an explicit goal of college educators. Regrettably, it is neither. Transformative learning does happen in and outside of college classrooms, and teachers often play an important role, as they construct learning experiences and interact with students. But generally transformative learning is more like a side benefit of education. The failure to see its significance is ironic, because if you ask faculty to name the most important things they learned in college, most don't list items related to content acquisition. "I learned how to think." "I discovered how much I could learn and that I loved learning." "College opened my mind to a world of ideas." "I learned how to ask questions and investigate ideas." These kinds of insights are indicative of transformative learning experiences.

The question then is how to get faculty to move beyond covering content to using course material to foster these larger learning lessons—to move from a focus on the details to a sense of these larger objectives. Do learner-centered approaches connect faculty more directly to transformative learning goals? They certainly could, as the connections between transformative learning and learning-centered teaching explored in this chapter show, but that's not what they report. They describe how these approaches change their beliefs about teaching and learning, with no mention of transformative learning, by name or otherwise. Furthermore, rarely is there any acknowledgment of the role that transformative learning ought to play in their attempts to educate students.

Learner-centered approaches may make faculty more open to the idea of explicitly teaching for transformative learning, and certainly the adult education literature is rich with advice and evidence on how that can be accomplished. The problem is, until faculty become aware that what they see as an accidental side benefit of education can be an explicit and accomplishable instructional goal, learner-centered approaches alone do not seem likely to develop a commitment to transformative learning.

I see this as yet another example of important educational theory and research not having much impact on instructional practice in higher education. Transformative learning is a phenomenon known primarily to adult educators. They write about it, and other adult educators read what has been written, even though transformative learning is relevant to teachers and learners in every field. Faculty in other disciplines are not expected to read educational literature; as a consequence, the few who read anything pedagogical rarely read outside their discipline. It's one of those circular conundrums that separates research and practice, to the detriment of both.

To conclude, this chapter offers an initial exploration of the relationship between learner-centered teaching and transformative learning. Clearly there is a relationship between the two—it makes sense theoretically and has been verified experientially by both learners and teachers. These approaches to teaching can transform beliefs about learning and teaching. But many details about how the relationship works are not known—and offer intriguing areas for investigation.

References

Albers, C. (2009). Teaching: From disappointment to ecstasy. *Teaching Sociology*, *37*, 269–282.

Armbruster, P., Patel, M., Johnson, E., & Weiss, M. (2009). Active learning and student-centered pedagogy improve student attitudes and performance in introductory biology. *Cell Biology Education—Life Sciences Education*, *8*, 203–213.

Auster, C. J., & MacRone, M. (1994). The classroom as a negotiated social setting: An empirical study of the effects of faculty members' behavior on students' participation. *Teaching Sociology*, *22*, 289–300.

Barr, R. B., & Tagg, J. (1995, November-December). From teaching to learning—a new paradigm for undergraduate education. *Change*, 13–25.

Black, K. A. (1993). What to do when you stop lecturing: Become a guide and a resource. *Journal of Chemical Education*, *70*(2), 140–144.

Blumberg, P. (2009). *Developing learner-centered teaching: A practical guide for faculty*. San Francisco: Jossey-Bass.

Brookfield, S. D. (1995). *Becoming a critically reflective teacher*. San Francisco: Jossey-Bass.

Cheang, K. I. (2009). Effect of learner-centered teaching on motivation and learning strategies in a third-year pharmacotherapy course. *American Journal of Pharmaceutical Education*, *73*(3), article 42.

Cranton, P. (2006). *Understanding and promoting transformative learning* (2nd ed.). San Francisco: Jossey-Bass.

DiClementi, J. D., & Handelsman, M. M. (2005). Empowering students: Class-generated rules. *Teaching of Psychology*, *32*(1), 18–21.

Doyle, T. (2008). *Helping students learn in a learner-centered environment*. Sterling, VA: Stylus.

Edwards, N. M. (2007). Student self-grading in social statistics. *College Teaching*, *55*(2), 72–76.

Ellner, C. L., Barnes, C. P., & Associates (1983). *Studies of college teaching*. Lexington, MA: D. C. Heath.

Felder, R. M., & Brent, R. (1996). Navigating the bumpy road to student-centered instruction. *College Teaching*, *44*(2), 43–47.

Gregory, M. (2005). Turning water into wine: Giving remote texts full flavor for the audience of friends. *College Teaching*, *53*(3), 95–98.

Gregory, M. (2006). From Shakespeare on the page to Shakespeare on the stage: What I learned about teaching in acting class. *Pedagogy*, *6*(2), 309–325.

Grow, G. O. (1991). Teaching learners to be self-directed. *Adult Education Quarterly*, *41*(3), 125–149.

Harris, M., & Cullen, R. (2010). *Leading the learner-centered campus: An administrator's framework for improving student learning outcomes*. San Francisco: Jossey-Bass.

Hiller, T. H., & Hietapelto, A. B. (2001). Contract grading: Encouraging commitment to the learning process through voice in the evaluation process. *Journal of Management Education*, *25*(6), 660–684.

Hockings, S. C., DeAngelis, K. J., & Frey, R. F. (2008). Peer-led team learning in general chemistry: Implementation and evaluation. *Journal of Chemical Education*, *85*(7), 990–996.

Lewis, S. E., & Lewis, J. E. (2005). Departing from lectures: An evaluation of a peer-led guided inquiry alternative. *Journal of Chemical Education*, *82*(1), 135–139.

Litz, R. A. (2003). Red light, green light and other ideas for class participation-intensive courses: Method and implications for business ethics education. *Teaching Business Ethics*, *7*(4), 365–378.

McCreary, C. L., Golde, M. F., & Koeske, R. (2006). Peer instruction in general chemistry laboratory: Assessment of student learning. *Journal of Chemical Education*, *83*(5), 804–810.

Mezirow, J., & Associates (Eds.). (2000). *Learning as transformation: Critical perspectives on a theory in progress.* San Francisco: Jossey-Bass.

Nilson, L. B. (2003). Improving student peer feedback. *College Teaching, 51*(1), 34–38.

Noel, T. W. (2004). Lessons from the learning classroom. *Journal of Management Education, 28*(2), 188–206.

Pintrich, P. R. (2003). A motivational perspective on the role of student motivation in learning and teaching contexts. *Journal of Educational Psychology, 95*(4), 667–686.

Singham, M. (2005). Moving away from the authoritarian classroom. *Change, 37*(3), 51–57.

Spence, L. D. (2001). The case against teaching. *Change, 33*(6), 11–19.

Stage, F. K., Muller, P. A., Kinzie, J., & Simmons, A. (1998). *Creating learner-centered classrooms: What does learning theory have to say?* Washington, DC: ERIC Clearinghouse on Higher Education and the Association for the Study of Higher Education.

Thiel, T., Peterman, S., & Brown, B. (2008, July-August). Addressing the crisis in college mathematics: Designing courses for student success. *Change,* 44–49.

Tomasek, T. (2009). Critical reading: Using reading prompts to promote active engagement with text. *International Journal of Teaching and Learning in Higher Education, 21*(1), 127–132.

Tompkins, J. (1996). *A life in school: What the teacher learned.* Reading, MA: Addison-Wesley.

Weimer, M. (2002). *Learner-centered teaching: Five key changes to practice.* San Francisco: Jossey-Bass.

Weimer, M. (2010). *Inspired college teaching: A career-long resource for professional growth.* San Francisco: Jossey-Bass.

Whetten, D. A. (2007). Principles of effective course design: What I wish I had known about learner-centered teaching 30 years ago. *Journal of Management Education, 31*(3), 339–357.

Woods, D. R. (1996). Participation is more than attendance. *Journal of Engineering Education, 85*(3), 177–181.

Yamane, D. (2006, July). Course preparation assignments: A strategy for creating discussion-based courses. *Teaching Sociology,* 236–248.

CHAPTER TWENTY-EIGHT

Storytelling and Transformative Learning

Jo A. Tyler and Ann L. Swartz

T his chapter posits an integral relationship between storytelling, transformative learning, and complexity science. There are many perspectives on story, just as there are many perspectives on transformative learning. Here we are presenting ways of understanding that, in the case of both story and transformative learning, are grounded in a few decades of work inspired by complex systems thinking. This perspective is chosen because it is inherently tied to the dynamics of change, and transformative learning is about change. We are concerned with storytelling as a social process that can foster transformative learning. Our interest is in storytelling between individuals, synchronously, face-to-face (Boje, 2001; Bruner, 1986; de Certeau, 1984; Tyler, 2010) in spaces specifically created for telling, listening, and co-creating stories (Baldwin, 2005; Boje, 2001; Bruner, 1986; de Certeau, 1984; Lane, 1988; Tyler, 2010), rather than mediated by technology (including print). We use the term "storytelling" to mean the oral conveyance of personal experience, as distinct from the telling of myths, fables, or folklore. This storytelling is not a performance but a relational, emergent, and nonlinear exchange that depends on both listening and poststory conversation.

This exchange of experiences is a natural form of human communication. We can all recall a recent time when it has occurred naturally; perhaps in a bar, a parking lot, or a supermarket aisle. This storytelling in which individuals have the opportunity to freely convey their own experience of the world to engaged listeners is distinct from crafted, linearly plotted narratives with an orderly Aristotelian beginning, middle, and end (McKeon, 2001), which are often calculated as a means to persuade or mollify listeners. These practiced narratives are chosen and edited in ways that align with preconceived notions of prevailing social or organizational discourse, so that the content will be well received by listeners. The distinction we make between narrative and story here, with our focus on the latter, is that "narrative is a re-presentation (following representationalism) of a sensory remembrance, whereas living story is a matter of reflexivity upon the fragile nature of our life world" (Boje & Tyler, 2009, p. 173). Although storytelling represents a "higher order complexity than narrative" (Boje, 2006, p. 28), the distinction between them results less in a duality than in an interplay in which they reflexively define each other. The storytelling that has perhaps the most potency to foster transformative learning juxtaposes tidy, crystallized narratives with emergent, unplanned, and unfinished stories that merge with other stories. Boje (2007) simplifies our ability to notice these stories by pointing out that they tend not to be "a very coherent narrative" (p. 206).

Organic, emergent, nonlinear storytelling is connected with transformative learning's extension, especially with the threads of theory that are emerging from connections made to systems thinking and complexity science. The history of transformative learning is well known, but even earlier, when Mezirow (1962) wrote about his experience with rural farming community development in Pakistan, he was interested in fundamental change. An examination of Mezirow's 1978 and 1991 works and their references indicates that philosophy of science (Kuhn, 1962; Popper, 1962), systems thinking, and cybernetics (Bateson, 1972; Lewin, 1947) informed Mezirow from the start. His explanation of memory (Mezirow, 1991) as it supports meaning-making is grounded in neural Darwinism (Edelman, 1987) and the brain maps of neural networks.

Within all branches of science and mathematics theory, systems thinking and cybernetics evolved into chaos theory and complexity science (Aubin & Dalmedico, 2002), which have inspired new modes of thought across all major academic disciplines (Capra, 1996; Mitchell, 2009). These newer modes of thought are emerging as drivers of transformative learning theory. In their analysis of all *Proceedings of the International Transformative Learning Conferences*, 1998 through 2009, Swartz and Sprow (2010) found that consistently 30 to 40 percent of papers were grounded in systems thinking or complexity science. There are major clusters around organismic biology inspired by the developmental theory of Robert Kegan (1982), the integrative psychological theory of John Heron (1996), and the complexity informed group learning theory of Robert Boyd (1994).

Boje and Baskin (2005) point out in their own thinking about the intersection of storytelling and complexity science: "we began to suspect that this evolving hybrid field could suggest a powerful approach to the application of complexity thinking to all human systems" (p. v). This chapter expands on the concept of change generally and transformative learning specifically, by exploring the connections storytelling shares with this learning theory focused on change. It further broadens the scope of the context of change by reaching into different systems levels in and beyond the organizational; from the personal level, where change occurs within the individual, and among individuals, and between individuals and their families, their cultures, and the organizations they comprise.

A CASE STORY

To ground our exploration of these connections, it seems fitting to tell a story—really a story about a story—drawn from the transformative learning that one of us (Jo) experienced in graduate school that helped clarify the dynamic between storytelling and transformative learning.

When I was in graduate school, I took a seminar on action learning. We were in small groups called *action learning sets* and were asked to each identify a problem or opportunity that we wanted to explore. Members of the set helped each other recognize unexamined assumptions and dream up alternative assumptions. We worked through the process all semester, collaboratively and in private. The idea was to either affirm your assumptions or disconfirm them and adopt new assumptions. Around that time I had begun to question my work. I had a good job as a VP, but my boss died suddenly, the firm filed for bankruptcy, and the new CEO didn't value organizational development. The problem I chose was, "What will I do? What would a new professional persona look like?" I began to examine my relationship to work, and in one session with the group, I told this story about my grandfather:

My grandfather left school early, around grade six, to work. He worked a lot of different jobs, manual labor. Whenever he got a new job, we'd go visit. When he picked apples, he showed me how the picker worked. When he was doing landscaping, he showed me the tools he used to work on the grass and shape the bushes.

When I was twelve, I thought the best job he ever had was as the pin setter in a candle pin bowling alley, before mechanical pin setters. Bowlers would knock down the pins. My grandfather was back there, and his job was to set them back up. I thought he had a magic job, because when you were bowling you couldn't see him. The pins just suddenly were upright in place! But when we went in the back I saw that the place he worked had a really low ceiling, so my tall grandfather could never stand up straight. I said he should quit, even if it was a magic job, because it wasn't good for him to be crouched over all the time. He said, "It's not perfect, but this is a good job. You know Jo," he said, "you can't always have work that you love, so you have to find something about your work that you can love, to balance out what's not so good."

I thought to myself, So, this is how it is. Mom and Dad hate their jobs. You can't have a job you love, so there's this compromise. This is what I learned from my grandfather. Years later, I went into OD, and part of my job was talking to people about their work. I remember talking to a factory mechanic who told me, "At night, I play in a band. So during the day here, I work on my rhythm. Listen." And he started to point out "the beat" in the factory. I talked to a dancing garbage man, who had great things to say about collecting trash as a dance, and dancing up the sun every morning. I heard many stories from people who have work that I would never want to do, and maybe they don't really want to do it either, but they've found things to love about it. I saw that there was truth in what my grandfather told me.

So I tell my group that story. I explain that in my corporate job I'm being asked to compromise my values, to do things I don't want to do. I say that there is part of this job that I love, so I'm putting up with it.

The seminar ended, but this conversation with the group continued. I kept justifying why I was still in corporate. A friend said to me, "What if your grandfather story is wrong?"

I protested.

He said, "Well, we're supposed to be critiquing assumptions, but you're not critiquing that one."

I insisted my grandfather wasn't wrong.

My other friends pitched in: "Unpack that assumption. What would be the opposite of what you learned from your grandfather?"

I said right away, "That you can have work that you love."

And they said, "Yeah, OK, so how about that? What would that look like, if you actually found work that you love?"

And I resisted. I said, "But you can't."

They said, "Maybe so, but you're not playing the game. Just for a minute, assume your grandfather was wrong. What would that be like to have work you love?"

We tussled like this for several weeks. I pounded my fist on the table, and raised my voice. "Do not wreck my grandfather story! I love my grandfather story!"

I was angry. I'm not a table-pounder. I could see something was happening.

Gradually, with help, I began to assemble this imaginative, noncorporate alternative where I would teach grownups in a setting that allowed me to focus on their learning, not on reduction of errors in parts per million.

One day I made a declaration: "I want to go into academia. I want to teach." I started to move in that direction. I quit my job and transitioned to teaching at a university. It is work I love.

I no longer live by my grandfather's story, but when I introduce the concept of critical reflection to my students, I tell them this story of how what my grandfather taught me had once served me, and what happened when I saw that it no longer did.

THREE STRANDS OF THEORY

Our analysis of the case story looks at three strands of theory: storytelling, transformative learning, and complexity science. These three strands weave together a compelling transformative learning process and holistic pedagogy.

Storytelling Theory

The application of storytelling as a learning process has enjoyed increasing legitimacy as the theory of storytelling has evolved with the work of David Boje (2001, 2007), Barbara Czarniawska (1997, 2004), and Yiannis Gabriel (2000, 2004). However, we will narrow our focus here to a motif that connects storytelling to transformative learning: the notion that stories are inherently dynamic rather than static, organic rather than mechanistic, and emergent rather than linear. This animation distinguishes the stories from narrative and poises them to support the transformative learning process. Although post-transformative storytelling will foster meaning-making of the transformative outcome, our focus here is earlier in the process; specifically, on the ways in which storytelling can foster transformative learning itself.

Storytelling theory is replete with the idea that stories, unlike narratives, are connected to or possess a sort of life force. In Native American traditions of storytelling (TwoTrees, 1997; Brown, 1995), stories are alive *because* we tell them, literally inspiring them through the act of telling. With his concept of living story, Boje (2001, 2005, 2007; Boje & Tyler, 2009) extends this notion, suggesting that "living story has many authors and as a collective force has a life of its own" (2005, p. 331). He defines living story as "neither being nor non-being; it is a form of haunting. The living story is in-between dead and alive" (2007, p. 260). This revitalizing is an important link to the shifting of meaning in the process of transformative learning. Building on these ideas, Tyler's (2010) notion of story aliveness further loosens the dependence of the story on the teller, positing that stories exist whether or not we tell them.

In our case story, Jo chose a learning project that had already begun to take shape. Exploring a future direction did not prompt an immediate telling of the story. Rather, Jo remembered the story only as the inquiry unfolded with purposeful dialogue and cycles of reflection and action. There was a point where it "made sense" to tell the story. Story aliveness holds that the choice to tell a story occurs as a negotiation between the teller and the story. We see a corollary in Dirkx's (2006) notion of conversations in which the self talks with self at an unconscious level. The story is an element of the teller's self, and it also has its own aliveness, beyond the self. As Boje suggests, there is a way in which the story exists in the spaces between. These are liminal spaces shaped by ambiguity, where the normal rules of discourse relax.

Telling stories of personal experience is inherently social. Although story-telling occurs naturally, organically, it is possible to put in place structures that facilitate story emergence and attendant conversational exploration. In any case, storytelling can be a reflexive act that makes the teller vulnerable (Tyler & Rosen, 2008), but this risk is accompanied by opportunity for exploration of experience that can foster transformative learning. In our case story, Jo does not anticipate this vulnerability. She tells the story, betting that it will help her colleagues understand the importance of maintaining the status quo, so that the alternatives they explore will be confined to the context of corporate work. She feels sure of the story, but here we see the "haunting" that Boje (2007) invokes in his description of living story. Far from being crystallized narrative, Jo had never told the story before. Its potential differed greatly from narrative's insistence on a particular message. Unlike narrative, living story fragments are quite lithe, sometimes rising sharply into focus, at other times blurring into the background. Jo is surprised when, in dialogue with her listeners, the story feels turned inside-out. What she cannot see in the moment is that the story is simply morphing away from her prior understanding of her experience.

This movement of the story can be explained with Boje's theory of antenarrative (2001, 2007, 2011). He gives the term "'antenarrative' a double meaning: as being before and as a bet" (2001, p. 1). They are told while the story is still unfolding, with the teller speculating on the direction in which the story is heading. Antenarratives come prior to the story being coherent, plotted, and practiced—in essence, before it is crystallized into narrative. Antenarratives are of three types, engaged in active interplay. Linear antenarratives have a traditional beginning-middle-end structure. Cyclic antenarratives connect us with indigenous patterns of seasons and events. Unlike linear antenarratives, they do not end, but recur continuously. The third form of antenarrative is rhizomatic. Unlike cyclic antenarratives, rhizomes extend but do not repeat, moving in unpredictable directions, extending as dynamic spirals. Although most interpretations of Boje's notion of rhizomatic antenarrative are disintegrative, Boje finds Tyler's understanding of them as positive movement, imbued with potential, as a refreshing departure from more typical definitions (as Boje indicated in a personal communication to the authors on April 16, 2011).

What Jo anticipated was that her grandfather story would increase her colleagues' understanding of her previous sense-making process. Her antenarrative bet was on a linear form trending toward narrative. But in the dynamic interplay, the nature of the story shifted rhizomatically. She and her colleagues were moved by the story to prospective sense-making that eventually paved the way for a shift in her meaning perspective.

In the case story, we see rhizomatic movement beyond the restorying that took place as a result of exploratory conversations—in this case, in the context of the action learning process. The story continues to extend rhizomatically in Jo's professional experience as she now tells the larger story of conveying her grandfather story in the action learning set to the graduate classes she teaches. This "story about telling the story" is one tendril. The effect this story may have on the students, the possibility of their retelling the story in some context, represents another. Indeed, the story launches the students' own critically reflective work with stories from their own experiences, which, from time to time, results in transformative learning—a leaping, rhizomatic, co-created extension. In its aliveness, the story has an infinite capacity for these extensions. If the listeners act on the story, or co-create another story in collaboration with the first story, the teller, or other listeners, the story is living. If the listeners do not act on the story in some way, if there is no collaboration after the story, the story does not die. In this case, the story is not living with us as an actor, but it continues to retain its aliveness, waiting to be retold in different circumstances, perhaps in a different way.

Connections to Transformative Learning Theory

Fundamental to transformative learning theory is the social constructivist postulate (Berger & Luckmann, 1967) that because of the habits we have of predicting that certain things will happen, our meaning schemes and perspectives generally go unquestioned. They become our default settings for explaining all new experience, simplifying our process of moving through the world. Although we interpret things intentionally, we also incorporate culturally assimilated learning (Mezirow, 1991). This tendency toward known explanation is equivalent to antenarrative betting on an outcome that occurs before the story has fully developed. Betting on the linear antenarrative because the ending seems predictable, or relying on the cyclic antenarratives of culture that show us how things fit together, is equivalent to opting for unquestioned socially constructed assumptions when attributing meaning to new events. Overcoming the limitations of these automatic responses and moving toward a more "inclusive, differentiated, permeable...and integrated meaning perspective" (Mezirow, 1991, p. 7) makes use of reflection and rational discourse for validation as memory engages to reinterpret experience. In the same way, rhizomatic story and the dynamic interplay of all forms of antenarrative can create fertile ground for transformative learning.

Mezirow (1998) suggests that "critical reflection may be either implicit, as when we mindlessly choose between good and evil because of our assimilated values, or explicit" (p. 186). This "mindless" reliance on assimilated rules is different from the preconscious processes associated with intention, through connection with the prelinguistic process of intuition. Preconscious processes are also involved with "felt sense," an implicit awareness of how we feel about what is happening around us without the application of language (Mezirow, 1991). Presentational construal matters to both transformative learning and storytelling because the capacity for making decisions outside social convention lies in this realm (Mezirow, 1991). We reflect on felt sense, without words, to gauge the accuracy of our interpretations (Mezirow, 1991). The influences of presentational construal are brought into conscious awareness by feelings, intuition, dreams, and changes in physiologic states, all elements that are at play in story. Storytelling provides the bridge between the pre-linguistic space and the languaged space. Just as tension and communication exist between the two forms of construal, tension exists between and bridges living story with narrative. In the liminal, bridging space between established and new patterns of thought and behavior we are forming new patterns of connections. Here new understandings of authority evolve (Mezirow, 1991).

Another way of understanding this process is in terms of the core elements of transformative educational experiences. These elements include individual experience, critical reflection, dialogue, a holistic orientation, awareness of context, and authentic practice (Mezirow & Taylor, 2009). Presentational construal is clearly an individual experience. Storytelling exemplifies a holistic orientation because it calls on the whole person, using emotion, visual imagery, imagination, and metaphor to access this individual experience and allow for the possibility of integration into something unexpected. Although presentational construal reflects critically on itself to assess accuracy of interpretation, storytelling adds the reflection of the listener. The teller may also reflect on story as it is told, and make a distinction between antenarrative with a narrative trajectory and one with a rhizomatic trajectory. Jo was relying on the convincing power of narrative. She was trying to convince the listeners she was right. Even in that narrative trajectory, the story was able to influence her transformative learning process. In so doing, the story turned rhizomatic, which is how it ended up in this chapter. Awareness of context is built into the process of telling, listening, and dialogue, and authentic practice exists in learners' freedom to choose the story they will share and to define the context as they choose to define it, and in story's freedom to unwind as it chooses (Bakhtin, 1973; Benjamin, 1969; Boje, 2011; Czarniawska, 1997; Tyler, 2011).

In our case story, Jo's decisive action was the transition from the corporate world to academia. She remembers this as a process that she resisted, stretching over time. Transformation doesn't happen in a moment, but there may be a critical moment of awareness in which a feeling of being a transformed person occurs, a bridge between presentational construal and conscious awareness. For Jo, this happened when she declared, "I can do this. I'm going to quit." That was a critical point, but for a year she continued to defend and honor her grandfather's meaning perspective. In that liminal space, she had to figure out what to do with a "wrong grandfather." Ultimately, her answer was to tell this larger story.

The story's aliveness is evident in the way this story developed within Jo's relationship with her grandfather as she grew up. The basic elements of the story were always the same, but the story fit into her life in different ways. It had to transform in order to stay with her. When the corporate work world unraveled, she was confronted by a disorienting dilemma. She felt betrayed because the environment was not behaving in ways she predicted. The doctoral class was a liminal space, out of which evolved a new story of career change accompanied by some upset and uncharacteristic table pounding, grieving, and a choice to keep the story in her life within a new pattern of connections.

Connections to Complexity Science

We bring complexity science to this discussion of story because it is used in storytelling theory. Boje and Baskin (2005) organized their special edition on storytelling around this question: "Are the studies of storytelling, in its widest sense, and of complex human systems largely the same thing?" (p. v). Complexity science has the capacity to connect storytelling theory with other frameworks that contribute to our understanding of transformative learning. The ability to function as a connector among theories, creating new patterns of abstract knowing, characterizes complex systems in general. Story and storytelling, in their ability to establish new connections, and all learners, as living organisms, are also complex systems (Boje & Baskin, 2005; Capra, 1996; Karpiak, 2006).

Complexity science is an advanced form of systems thinking, a composite of theoretical concepts from multiple sciences and mathematics, a science of change (Aubin & Dalmedico, 2002; Capra, 1996; Castellani & Hafferty, 2009; Mitchell, 2009). It describes how organisms (including people) as living systems interact with their environments and adapt to stay alive: how they are impacted by forces within and outside themselves; how they have the capacity to self-organize in new ways according to their own internal principles; and how sometimes they undergo complete structural transformations to become something different (Kauffman, 1993). These processes of change are continuous, nonlinear, and unpredictable, so a living organism's properties are continually emerging, and these outcomes have sensitive dependence on the initial conditions (Lorenz, 1963). For this reason, one small influence can eventually result in a chain of major changes that are unpredictable, a concept understood in popular culture as "the butterfly effect" (Capra, 1996; Kauffman, 1993; Wilson, 1992).

Mitchell (2009) describes complex systems science as an interdisciplinary field of research that studies a phenomenon observed throughout nature and within the constructed world: large numbers of seemingly simple entities organize themselves into a collective whole capable of using information, creating patterns, and sometimes learning as they adapt. This science is a way of explaining and understanding similar concepts occurring at different scales; that is, holism, change, learning. This interdisciplinary field can help us explain the aliveness of stories weaving preconsciously within ourselves, via interpersonal connections, and within our cultural worlds.

Our immune system, economies, and the World Wide Web are examples of complex systems—large networks of individual parts following simple rules with no central controller (Mitchell, 2009). Environment, both internal and external, is the site of information creation and exchange for complex systems, so that at some scale information is always being co-created. Complex systems use evolutionary processes, or learning, to change their behavior, adapting in order to succeed.

The theoretical conception of story as dynamic, organic, emergent, multivocal, and in possession of a life force (Boje, 2001; Tyler, 2010) is consistent with our description of complex systems as they exist throughout our world. In organismic biology the *patterns of relationship* within the physical structures of living systems *are what make them whole.* The patterns are a form of *self-organization* in which systems communicate, self-replicate, and re-create themselves in new forms. Self-organization is perhaps the most central concept of systems thinking (Capra, 1996). Within the framework of systems thinking, stories are latent possibilities, a part of the networked pattern of connections. As learners self-organize, which is another way to construe learning (Karpiak, 2006), they create new networks of patterns of connections among ideas, attitudes, assumptions, feelings, behaviors, and also stories. These patterns of connection can occur within an individual and among many individuals. Stories can be elements of this networked structure and also a form of energy driving the process of connection.

Complex systems differ from simple or complicated systems in one crucial way: connections or relationships define how complex systems work. Westley, Zimmerman, and Patton (2006) explain that in our yearning for simple solutions to complex problems, we are drawn to boilerplate solutions, just as we turn first to our unquestioned assumptions when faced with new challenges. In Jo's story, she was initially tied to the simple assumptions she had carried with her grandfather's story since childhood. This is equivalent to narrative and linear antenarrative in the story world. Jo's complicated problem was the challenge presented by a forced change in employment, and the possibility of making a career change. Here the parallel is with cyclic antenarratives. With complex problems, every situation is unique. Once Jo began questioning her story and saw the uniqueness of her possibilities for major career change, the emerging complexity of the problem became evident. With complex problems, there is no formula for success. We think of rhizomatic story, with its unpredictability and nonlinear evolution, the negotiations that happen among teller and story and listener being the interactions that foster restorying, transformation. Successful social innovation combines all three types of problems (Westley et al., 2006); living story envelops all three antenarrative forms (Boje, 2011); and transformative learning, as it engages with change at multiple systems levels, encounters all three types of problems and learners using all three antenarrative forms.

In storytelling, the right context and the quality of listening create the "field" that elicits the story—an energetic negotiation between teller and story. When the system instability forces the old linear narrative to fall apart, the story can restory itself into a more complex form. A change of form may reflect a transforming of the storyteller that occurs through interpersonal interaction. By moving to this different systems level, where it is now open to interaction with other people and other stories, the story may build more complex connections and ultimately have meaning at an even greater scale.

IMPLICATIONS FOR PRACTICE IN HIGHER EDUCATION

For adult educators who wish to foster transformative learning, storytelling can play a potent role, not limited to the kind of action learning scenario included here. Storytelling effectively deepens learning, and can spark transformative learning, in a vast variety of configurations. It is often powerful to begin with students telling knee to knee, sitting in pairs, sharing their story with only one other attentive listener. As students begin to recognize both the safety of the space the educator has constructed and the potency of the storytelling and listening process, these groups can be expanded to trios, and to successively larger groups, culminating in whole-group exchanges of stories—the selection and composition of which lies entirely with the teller in the moment of telling, the timing of which is emergent and dependent in large measure on the influence of other stories present in the group. Key to this process is the ability of listeners and the teller to engage in post-telling conversations that explore the stories in ways that clarify, deepen, enlarge, expose new facets, and experiment with new meaning.

Here we touch on a few considerations for including storytelling in practice. First are the connected notions of control and time. Storytelling depends on the educator's willingness to release control of the space, to give it over not only to the collective consciousness of the group, but also to the stories themselves (Tyler, 2009). In our case story, the choice of topics lay entirely with the learner. An inquiry structure was provided, and time was available in class for unhurried conversations, giving the learners' stories such freedom that continuing the conversation beyond the boundaries of the sessions—and indeed, of the semester—felt natural. Conversations were not monitored. Outcomes were not graded.

Time limitations are problematic to storytelling, which requires decoupling efficiency from speed. Choosing to include storytelling as an element of practice means opting for a process that requires authentic engagement, and although it holds value in terms of supporting reflective work and transformative learning, it is not fast. The synthesis of telling a story and the deep engagement of listening require slowing down in the interest of eventually arriving at a destination that is more creative, integrative, sustainable, and surprising than could be achieved with acceleration. This slowing down may be foreign both to learners (who may feel that they are not being "taught") and to educators (who may need to engage differently).

Storytelling is an inclusive approach that blurs the line between educator and learner. Educators can help to create a communicative space by offering a personal story as a model. The storytelling process asks learners to engage in a form of unmasking involving choices about what story they will tell and how they will tell it. Educators who first unmask with a story that may feel risky will help learners calibrate the extent to which they can take risks with their own stories. Providing these cues can open learners to a departure from usual narratives of their experience—the ones they have been telling for years—in favor of exploring stories of experience fundamentally connected with their closely held assumptions, which may be rarely or never told. These stories deepen the possibility that their stories will spark other stories, prompt authentic dialogue, and contribute to meaning making.

Often students express concern that the storytelling process feels like therapy. Educators can alleviate this concern with an explanation at the outset that the storytelling that will occur in the classroom space will be directly connected to the content of the course. Circumscribing the world of relevant stories in this way typically assuages student ambivalence and supports their selection of appropriate stories from their repertoire of authentic experiences.

In addition to increasing their own capacity to tell stories, adult educators will be well served by increasing their capacity to listen. The listening is a form of noticing the story in a way that goes beyond the content of the story into the spaces between the lines, to listen for what is not expressed—for that which may not even be known by the teller. Distinct from what we think of as active listening—with its emphasis on eye contact, nonverbal cuing, and restatement—story listening is gentle, because it stems from an authentic curiosity and care. It is a fearless, powerful listening grounded in the profound trust that both storyteller and the story have sufficient strength to engage in exploration without strain or injury.

REFLECTIONS

As we collaborated on this chapter, we came to know our subject matter, and each other, differently. In this section we try to capture a few thoughts on a recurring theme in our conversations, and to reflect briefly on the effect of collaboration.

As we worked to unravel the theoretical threads woven into Jo's grandfather story, a motif of grief and loss developed. In Jo's case, she resisted initially, but ultimately she gently explored alternatives. The process of adopting a new alternative left her with a dilemma about where she stood, not only in relation to the story of her grandfather, but to her grandfather himself. Our conversation helped us understand that one way she managed the grief over departing from her grandfather story was to incorporate it into a new meaning perspective by telling it to her students. Understanding the way in which she figured this out is more elusive. Although the focus in the literature largely celebrates adoption of new meaning perspectives, we became curious about the fate of the old ones. Though Scott (1997) made an important contribution to this conversation with her analysis of the role of grief and loss in transformation, and Dirkx (1997) touches on it in his consideration of the soul of the adult learner, we would like to better understand what processes and rituals are associated with letting go. What can storytelling tell us about how educators can support the grief process even while they help to celebrate the integration of new meaning perspectives?

Writing this chapter, we became coauthors for the first time. Although we are colleagues in the same school at our university, are of the same generation, and share an abiding interest in transformative learning, our backgrounds only slightly overlap. Prior to writing together, we had engaged with each other's ideas as metaphors. Complexity and neuroscience became for Jo a metaphor for her working theory of story aliveness. For Ann, story aliveness worked as a useful metaphor for understanding the effects of story on the body at a cellular level. As we sat together, each typing on a laptop, a friend commented that we were engaged in parallel play. Indeed we were. As our concentration heightened, we found ourselves reimmersed in deep conversation. We came to this work with clear ideas about connections between transformative learning, storytelling, and complexity science. We leave it with more questions about the ways in which these connections occur and the roles they play in our learning as adults. And this is as it should be.

References

Aubin, D., & Dalmedico, A. D. (2002). Writing the history of dynamical systems and chaos: *Longue durée* and revolution, disciplines and cultures. *Historia Mathematica, 29*(3), 273–339.

Bakhtin, M. (1973). Problems of Dostoevsky's poetics (C. Emerson, Ed. & Trans.). Manchester, England: Manchester University Press.

Baldwin, C. (2005). *Storycatcher: Making sense of our lives through the power and practice of story.* Novato, CA: New World Library.

468 THE HANDBOOK OF TRANSFORMATIVE LEARNING

Bateson, G. (1972). *Steps to an ecology of mind.* New York: Chandler Press.

Benjamin, W. (1969). *Illuminations: Essays and reflections.* New York: Schocken Books.

Berger, P. L., & Luckmann, A. (1967). *The social construction of reality.* Harmondsworth, UK: Penguin Books.

Boje, D. M. (2001). *Narrative methods for organizational and communication research.* Thousand Oaks, CA: SAGE.

Boje, D. M. (2005). From Wilda to Disney: Living stories in family and organization research. In J. Clandinin (Ed.), *Handbook of narrative inquiry.* London: SAGE.

Boje, D. M. (2006). Breaking out of narrative's prison: Improper story in storytelling organization. *Storytelling, Self, Society: An Interdisciplinary Journal of Storytelling Studies, 2*(2), 28–49.

Boje, D. M. (2007). *Storytelling organizations.* London: SAGE.

Boje, D. M. (2011). *Storytelling and the future of organizations: An antenarrative handbook.* Routledge Press.

Boje, D. M., & Baskin, K. (2005). Guest editors' introduction: Emergence of third order cybernetics. *Emergence: Complexity & Organizations, 7*(3–4), v–viii.

Boje, D. M., & Tyler, J. A. (2009). Story and narrative noticing: Workaholism autoethnographies. *Journal of Business Ethics, 84,* 173–194. doi:10.1007/s10551–008–9702–7

Boyd, R. D. (1994). *Personal transformations in small groups: A Jungian perspective.* New York: Routledge.

Brown, A. K. (1995). Pulling Silko's thread through time: An exploration of storytelling. *American Indian Quarterly, 19*(2), 171–179.

Bruner, J. (1986). *Actual minds, possible worlds.* Cambridge, MA: Harvard University Press.

Capra, F. (1996). *The web of life: A new scientific understanding of living systems.* New York: Anchor Doubleday.

Castellani, B., & Hafferty, F. (2009). *Sociology and complexity science: A new field of inquiry.* Berlin: Springer-Verlag.

Czarniawska, B. (1997). *Narrating the organization: Dramas of institutional identity.* Chicago: University of Chicago Press.

Czarniawska, B. (2004). *Narratives in social science research.* London: SAGE.

de Certeau, M. (1988). *The practice of everyday life.* Berkeley: University of California Press.

Dirkx, J. M. (1997). Nurturing soul in adult learning. In P. Cranton (Ed.), *Transformative learning in action.* New Directions for Adult and Continuing Education, no. 74 (pp. 79–88). San Francisco: Jossey-Bass, 1997.

Dirkx, J. M. (2006). Authenticity and imagination. In P. Cranton (Ed.), *Authenticity in teaching.* New Directions for Adult and Continuing Education, no. 111 (pp. 27–39). San Francisco: Jossey-Bass.

Edelman, G. (1987). *Neural Darwinism: The theory of neuronal group selection.* New York: Basic Books.

Gabriel, Y. (2000). *Storytelling in organizations: Facts, fictions, and fantasies.* Oxford: Oxford University Press.

Gabriel, Y. (2004). *Myths, stories, and organizations: Premodern narratives for our time.* Oxford: Oxford University Press.

Heron, J. (1996). *Cooperative inquiry: Research into the human condition.* Thousand Oaks, CA: SAGE.

Karpiak, I. E. (2006). Chaos and complexity: A framework for understanding social workers at midlife. In V. A. Anfara Jr. & N. T. Mertz (Eds.), *Theoretical frameworks in qualitative research* (pp. 85–109). Thousand Oaks, CA: SAGE.

Kauffman, S. A. (1993). *Origins of order: Self-organization and selection in evolution.* New York: Oxford University Press.

Kegan, R. (1982). *The evolving self: Problem and process in human development.* Cambridge, MA: Harvard University Press.

Kuhn, T. S. (1962). *The structure of scientific revolutions.* Chicago: Chicago University Press.

Lane, B. C. (1988). *Landscapes of the sacred.* New York: Paulist Press.

Lane, B. C. (2001). *Landscapes of the sacred: Geography and narrative in American spirituality.* Baltimore: The Johns Hopkins University Press.

Lewin, K. (1947). Frontiers in group dynamics. In D. Cartwright (Ed.), *Field theory in social science* (pp. 188–237). London: Social Science Paperbacks.

Lorenz, E. N. (1963). Deterministic nonperiodic flow. *Journal of the Atmospheric Sciences, 20,* 130–141.

McKeon, R. (2001). *De Poetica* in *The basic works of Aristotle.* New York: The Modern Library.

Mezirow, J. (1962). *Dynamics of community development.* New York: Scarecrow Press.

Mezirow, J. (1978). Perspective transformation. *Adult Education, 28,* 100–110.

Mezirow, J. (1991). *Transformative dimensions of adult learning.* San Francisco: Jossey-Bass.

Mezirow, J. (1998). On critical reflection. *Adult Education Quarterly, 48*(3), 185–198.

Mezirow, J., Taylor, E. W., & Associates (Eds.). (2009). *Transformative learning in practice: Insights from community, workplace, and higher education.* San Francisco: Jossey-Bass.

Mitchell, M. (2009). *Complexity: A guided tour.* New York: Oxford University.

Popper, K. R. (1962). *Conjectures and refutations: The growth of scientific knowledge.* New York: Basic Books.

Scott, S. (1997). The grieving soul in the transformation process. In P. Cranton (Ed.), *Transformative learning in action: Insights from practice.* New Directions for Adult and Continuing Education, no. 74 (pp. 79–88). San Francisco: Jossey-Bass.

Swartz, A. L., & Sprow, K. (2010). Is complexity science embedded in transformative learning? In P. Gandy, S. Tieszen, C. Taylor-Hunt, D. Flowers, & V. Sheared (Eds.), *Proceedings of the 51st Adult Education Research Conference* (pp. 461–467). Sacramento, CA.

Twotrees, K. (1977). Presentation at the International Academy of Business Disciplines conference at Case Western Reserve. In Boje, D. (2001). *Narrative methods for organizational & communication research.* Thousand Oaks: Sage.

Tyler, J. A. (2009). Charting the course: How storytelling can foster communicative learning in the workplace. In J. Mezirow, E. W. Taylor, & Associates (Eds.), *Transformative learning in practice: Insights from community, workplace, and higher education* (pp. 136–147). San Francisco: Jossey-Bass.

Tyler, J. A. (2010). Story aliveness. In D. Boje & K. Baskin (Eds.), *Dance to the music of story: Understanding human behavior through the intersection of storytelling and complexity thinking* (pp. 62–79). Mansfield, MA: ISCE Publishing.

Tyler, J. A. (2011). Antenarrative and organizational accidents. In D. M. Boje (Ed.), *Storytelling and the future of organizations: An antenarrative handbook* (pp. 137–147). New York: Routledge.

Tyler, J. A., & Rosen, G. (2008). The story holds its heart. *Storytelling, Self, Society: An Interdisciplinary Journal of Storytelling Studies, 4*(2), 102–121.

Westley, F., Zimmerman, B., & Patton, M. Q. (2006). *Getting to maybe: How the world has changed.* Toronto: Random House Canada.

Wilson, E. O. (1992). *The diversity of life.* New York: Norton.

CHAPTER TWENTY-NINE

Transformative Learning Through Artistic Expression

Getting Out of Our Heads

Randee Lipson Lawrence

This chapter describes how the arts can be a means for transformative learning, through either the creating of art or the witnessing of art created by others. Artistic expression in the broadest sense encompasses all forms of art, including but not limited to visual arts, music, poetry, dance, drama, storytelling, and creative writing. I believe that participation in all of the arts can lead to transformative learning; in fact, the very engagement in the arts can transform assumptions of how learning occurs. Additionally, according to Maxine Greene (1995), encountering the arts can evoke the imagination, challenging conformity to taken-for-granted norms by allowing us to envision multiple alternative realities.

The artist Georgia O'Keeffe (1976) stated: "The meaning of a word to me is not as exact as the meaning of a color. Colors and shapes make a more definitive statement than words" (p. 1). The arts take us out of our heads and into our bodies, hearts, and souls in ways that allow us to connect more deeply with self and others. As Cajete (1994) notes: "The creation of art is an alchemy of process in which the artist becomes more himself through each act of true creation. He transfers his life in a dance of relationship with the life inherent in the material that he transforms into an artistic creation" (p. 149).

The arts have the capacity to transform individual worldviews and when experienced collectively can potentially transform communities. This chapter, which incorporates a blend of theory and practice of arts-based transformative learning, disrupts traditional notions of transformative learning as a rational or cognitive process of challenging distorted thought patterns or meaning schemes (Mezirow, 1991). Although critical thinking is one avenue toward transformation, the arts invite engagement that is also emotional (Dirkx, 2006) and embodied. We encounter the arts through our full *presence* (see Chapter 31 on presentational knowing). The primary focus of this chapter is on extrarational ways of knowing. The concept of extrarationality, as it relates to transformative learning through the arts, is discussed in the next section.

TRANSFORMATIVE LEARNING AS AN EXTRARATIONAL PROCESS

Mezirow (1975) is most noted for introducing the concept of transformative learning to the field of adult education. Perspective transformation was explained as a rational process of interrogating our assumptions and then correcting the distortions in our meaning schemes and perspectives. The opposite of *rational* would appear to be *irrational,* which is often expressed as a pejorative (as in "you're being irrational" or "you're not making sense"). If one were relying only on pure reasoning or cognition to make sense of a given event, then I would agree that a response that doesn't have a logical explanation might seem irrational. However, when one is confronted with a powerful emotional experience, such as the death of a loved one, there may be no rational response to one's feelings and actions. One's profound expressions of grief may not be at all rational, but neither are they irrational (Boyd & Myers, 1988; Scott, 1997).

I much prefer the term "extrarational," which does not reject rationality but is a more inclusive concept. Rather than naming something by what it is not, extrarationality goes beyond rationality. Extrarational describes a process of meaning-making expressed through symbol, image, and emotional expression. These ways of knowing—which call upon our imagination (Greene, 1995) and our intuition (Lawrence, 2009) and come to us through dreams, meditations, and other unconscious processes—are often expressed though various art forms. Boyd and Myers (1988) describe a model of transformative education that includes extrarational (symbolic, imaginative, and emotional) processes along with the rational thought process of critical reflection. They believe transformative learning occurs through a process of *discernment* or sifting through these various forms of meaning-making. Discernment, as contrasted with Mezirow's more analytical process, "leads to a contemplative insight, a personal illumination gained by putting things together and seeing them in their relational wholeness" (p. 274). The arts, which call upon our imaginal, intuitive capabilities, often lead to the types of insights just described.

Our understanding of transformative learning has expanded since first introduced by Mezirow (1975). In a recent publication (Mezirow & Taylor, 2009), Mezirow himself acknowledged the role of imagination and intuition in transformative learning (both of which are extrarational processes) and even went so far as to say that in some cases "intuition may substitute for critical reflection" (p. 28).

I previously argued (Lawrence, 2005) that creating art was a way to surface knowledge that was always present but outside of our conscious awareness. Dirkx (2006), drawing on Jung's theory of individuation, helped us to understand how transformative learning can occur through exploring the symbolic and imaginative components that arise from our unconscious. These images, which are affective in nature, can be explained only in extrarational ways. Cajete (1994) sees art making as a basic component of indigenous education, which "transforms the artist at the very core of being" (p. 154). In the remainder of this chapter I explore how the arts as an expression of extrarational knowing can promote transformative learning in adult education contexts.

ART BREAKS US OUT OF BOUNDARIES THAT CONSTRAIN

Art comes into being through our imagination. According to Greene (1995), evoking the imagination moves us from a fixed and static reality to envisioning what might be. It would seem that education would be the place most likely to nurture imaginal knowing, yet our traditional classrooms, from kindergarten through higher education, have strongly emphasized reading and writing to the exclusion of other ways of knowing and learning. Long before we reach adulthood our natural artistic tendencies have been so discouraged and repressed that many of us cease any attempts at expressing knowledge other than in traditional written discourse (London, 1989; Lawrence, 2005). Kates (2005) sees creative expression as a return to imaginal play, in which our most basic way of knowing was preverbal.

Reliance on written expression alone can limit communication. Consider a musical composition. One can read the lyrics of a song and be moved by the words; however, words alone are rather static. When words are spoken out loud, such as in a poetry reading, they come alive as the reader uses vocal expression, emphasizing certain words and offering an emotional interpretation of the passage. When the lyrics are expressed in music, such as in a song, a deeper level of communication is achieved giving a fuller and richer expression to the words. Art can be evocative (unintentional and spontaneous) or provocative (intentional and deliberate). Both have the potential for facilitating transformative learning.

The Evocative Nature of the Arts

The arts have the ability to evoke emotion and stir the imagination in unexpected ways. Most of us can recall watching a performance, viewing an art gallery showing, or listening to a musical composition and having a strong emotional reaction. The artist may not have intentionally provoked such a reaction; however, the subject matter and delivery may have triggered a response based on a person's prior experience. For example, Elton John's "The Greatest Discovery," which is about a young child being introduced to his new baby brother, always brings tears to my eyes as I recall the births of my own children.

Wilbur (1996) describes the powerful and evocative experience of witnessing works of art: "It grabs you, against your will, and then suspends your will. You are ushered into a quiet clearing, free of desire, free of grasping, free of ego, free of self contradiction. And through that opening or clearing in your own awareness may come flashes of higher truths, subtler revelations, profound connections" (p. 90).

Thomas Moore, in *The Care of the Soul* (1992), writes: "Art, broadly speaking, is that which invites us into contemplation. . . . In that moment of contemplation, art intensifies the presence of the world. We see it more vividly and more deeply" (p. 286).

Sometimes it is not a personal experience but a collective one that is evoked. It seems that in every generation music speaks to the souls of alienated youth, from Bob Dylan's "The Times They Are A-Changin'" of the 1960s to the band Anti-Flag in the 2000s.

It is not always necessary, however, to have had a relevant prior experience to be emotionally moved by a work of art. I recall reading Alice Walker's *The Color Purple* and caring deeply about the character Celie, the abuse she endured at the hands of her father and husband, and her struggle for self-acceptance. According to Eisner (2008), art provides an empathic experience for its audience, allowing one to vicariously participate in the experience. This experience calls on both emotion and imagination, which often make action possible. Patricia Cranton teaches a class on literature as transformative learning. The students read stories and relate to the characters. One can never predict where the stories will take them. "Fictional explorations allow us to penetrate more freely and intimately into the particular subject matter, to identify with the characters and situations in new ways, and to speak from the perspectives of others" (McNiff, 2008, p. 38).

Although art can evoke emotions in others, the artist can sometimes experience unexpected emotional reactions from his or her own work. According to McNiff (2008, p. 40), "In the creative process, the most meaningful insights often come by surprise, unexpectedly, and even against the will of the creator."

The Provocative Nature of the Arts

Sometimes the arts are intentionally meant to provoke, to disrupt our notions of reality, shaking us out of complacency and calling us to action. When Georgia O'Keeffe was asked why she painted flowers so much larger than they actually were, she replied: "So I said to myself—I'll paint what I see—what the flower is to me but I'll paint it big and they will be surprised into taking the time to look at it. I will make even busy New Yorkers take the time to see what I see in flowers" (1976, p. 23).

Had O'Keeffe painted the flowers their normal size, they might have been easily overlooked as something ordinary, part of our everyday experience. Mealman and Lawrence (2002) talked about the concept of *dead space.* Objects in our dead space are so familiar that we cease to see them anymore when we pass by, like the green leaves on the trees in our neighborhood. When the leaves turn colors in the fall they call our attention to them in new ways. O'Keeffe was being intentionally provocative with her large flowers, using art as a way to get us to see what Patterson (1989) refers to as the extraordinary in the ordinary.

Encouraging people to look again or re-search is what research is all about. For example, Lawrence and Cranton (2009) used photography as a metaphor for looking at the world through multiple lenses and seeing different realities. Images were presented in ways different from how we normally look at them, urging people to remove labels and reimagine taken-for-granted meanings as illustrated in the following examples: One day while riding on an airplane, I looked out of the window and was struck by the images of the clouds. Our usual way of viewing clouds is to look up at the sky, but now the clouds were below me rather than above. It gave me a whole new way to see clouds.

We normally look at flowers from the front, yet to really see an object (or a person) we need to consider it in all of its dimensions. The photo in Figure 29.1 is a sunflower taken from the back. In viewing the image, we are given the opportunity to see the flower in a different way.

Once we learn to see objects in these multiple ways, we can never go back to seeing them in our former one-dimensional ways. It is the same with people who are different from us. Once we take the time to get to know them beyond the surface, our perspectives are permanently altered.

The examples offered here illustrate how the arts can provoke us into taking the time to look at things in new ways. The arts can also provoke us to take action to work for social justice. Spehler and Slattery (1999) see the artist as "a prophet in the process of social change," particularly in educational contexts. They focus on societal injustices such as poverty, abuse, and violence along with a common self-perceived powerlessness to address such injustices.

Figure 29.1 Sunflower from a Different Perspective

They believe that "prophetic poets, visual artists, dancers, actors, lyricists, and novelists challenge us to investigate—not ignore—such despair, injustice, and paralysis" (p. 2). The arts have a unique and sometimes disturbing way of waking us up to new ways of seeing. Simply conveying a message in words sometimes is not enough to provoke action. For example, the surrealistic art of Dali and Magritte juxtaposes familiar objects that would not ordinarily be seen together such as in the famous painting *Time Transfixed*, painted by Magritte in 1938, which depicts a locomotive coming out of a fireplace. Theatre of the Absurd uses story and drama to point out the absurdity of situations. Improvisational jazz employs discordant rhythms to capture our attention. Protest music, including reggae and hip hop, uses words and cadence to call our attention to injustices.

Hayes and Yorks (2007) found that art is a way of working with conflict in constructive ways that promote learning and stimulate action and activism. These art forms can be intentionally introduced in educational settings where transformative learning is desired. Butterwick and Lawrence (2009) described how they used popular theatre in their practice to help students reflect on their life stories and create alternative realities. For example, a gay man portrayed an incident in which he was bullied as a child for being different. The class participants then acted out alternative scenarios for addressing the oppressive behavior. Butterwick and Lawrence identified three processes that promote transformative learning: (1) tapping into unconsciousness knowledge through embodying the stories, (2) making the stories public and thereby inviting others to consider alternative meanings, and (3) providing space to rehearse action to challenge injustice.

ART AS A MEANS FOR REFLECTION AND HEALING

As previously discussed, the arts cause us to slow down, to literally and metaphorically look with new eyes. Georgia O'Keeffe (1976) discussed how she deliberately painted her flowers very large so people would stop and look. Flowers, which are usually very small and low to the ground, often get overlooked because we are too preoccupied to notice them or they are so much a part of our everyday experience that we forget they are there. Similarly, the arts can offer opportunities to consider new perspectives that can get us through difficult moments and even provide entry points to open up spaces for difficult conversations to occur. We next discuss the role of the arts in transformation and healing.

Transformation and Healing Through Artistic Expression

The arts are one way that people can use to make sense of their reality, particularly in difficult or painful moments or times of despair. Moore (1992) describes how "everyday we can transform ordinary experiences into the material of the soul—in diaries, poems, drawings, music, letters, watercolors" (p. 301). He relates how, having no way to rationally deal with his strong emotions after Martin Luther King was shot, he played the music of Bach on the piano for three hours. Similarly, one might get into one's body through dance, writing poetry, or painting. Often, when the inexplicable happens, one wants to know why. However, there are usually no answers to these questions. The extrarational processes of artistic expression described earlier are all ways of tapping into the unconscious (Jung, 1964; Dirkx, 2006), providing ways of reflecting that do not involve logic or reason.

Simpson (2009) conducted research with individuals who had experienced what Mezirow (1991) referred to as a "disorienting dilemma." All of the individuals in her study had found creative outlets that helped them heal from their trauma. Examples included a man who began writing poetry to work through the emotional upheaval of losing his child in a bitter divorce, and a woman battling domestic abuse along with breast cancer who transformed her life through a series of art classes. The participants described art making as a way they made sense of and worked through their crises by bridging their inner world of the unconscious to their outer self. An unexpected outcome of Simpson's research (which included participants creating collages of their experience, along with interviews) was a theme of spirituality. Each participant, regardless of his or her religious context or lack thereof, talked about discovering a sense of spiritual renewal through his or her art, described as a "connection to purpose, or something greater than himself or herself" (p. 91).

Moore, in a later publication—*Dark Nights of the Soul* (2004)—speaks about those deep dark places where we go to in times of emotional upheaval, illness, or loss. Moore suggests that, rather than attempting to get out of those painful spaces as quickly as possible, we instead recognize that these experiences are necessary for healthy human growth and development. He further suggests that going through such experiences can deepen spirituality or give meaning to one's life. Moore shares several examples of individuals for whom creative expression was a key factor in moving from darkness into light and notes the potential for transformative learning through such expression. He states: "Whatever impulse moves us to create or to listen to a mournful song is the same impulse that begs for poetic expression of our dark feelings.... This expression of yourself is essential to the experience and whatever transformation is possible" (p. 14). We next explore how artistic expression can be a means to ease people into difficult, emotionally laden conversations.

Art as an Entry Point into Difficult Conversations

When people are dealing with emotional issues or difficult conversations, verbal communication may be very intimidating and even considered taboo in some cultures. The arts can be a way to bring people together to communicate in ways that create a sense of safety and connection. For example, Cueva (2007) was working with cancer patients in rural Alaska. The native population there was reticent to have conversations about their cancer or that of family members. Cueva created a readers' theatre script about a group of fictional characters expressing their fears and feelings of isolation. After reading through and discussing the script, the participants gradually began to talk about their own experiences. Art was a way to begin to discuss the undiscussable.

In 1989, Noris Binet, an artist and sociologist who emigrated from the Dominican Republic, was struck by the racism in her new home of Nashville, Tennessee. She brought together a multiracial group of women artists who were engaged in antiracist work. Through dance, music, poetry, and visual art, they communicated their pain and dis-ease, thus "building a bridge" toward healing racial wounds (Binet, 1994).

Scher (2007) shares similar stories in which storytelling and body movement helped immigrants from different cultures learn about community and provided space for people from different faiths to understand the oppression of Muslims after the terrorist attacks of September 11, 2001. These creative modes of expression opened doors for the difficult conversations that were so necessary in order for healing to occur. As the preceding examples illustrate, disorienting dilemmas such as diagnosis of cancer, racial tension, and fear of terrorism cannot be resolved through critical reflection alone. As part of a community process, the arts can be a dynamic way to communicate one's emotions to oneself and to others. As Hayes and Yorks (2007) discovered, the arts can be a way for individuals and communities to deconstruct and reconstruct themselves, thus transforming both individuals and the communities in which they reside.

TRANSFORMING COMMUNITIES THROUGH THE ARTS

The arts not only provide opportunities for individual transformation but also assist in transforming communities. This transformation can happen in one of two ways. As discussed earlier, witnessing art created by others can provoke community awareness and incite action to create positive change. Introducing one or more art forms into a community as an interactive project is a way for members to become more experientially involved in the process of change (Hayes & Yorks, 2007; Binet, 1994; Clover, 2006).

It has been said that art is a universal language. This means that the arts cross cultural boundaries, creating a common space in which diverse cultural perspectives can be heard (Hayes & Yorks, 2007; Lawrence, 2005). Olson (2005, p. 57) described community music as "a window into the life experience of others, which encouraged recognition, interaction, and eventually empathy among diverse groups of people." This level of empathy can lead to respect for differences, fostering collective consciousness and a desire to work together for social transformation. We now look at ways in which witnessing art can inspire community awareness and action; we then consider how participation in the arts can bring about community interaction and transformation.

Community Awareness and Action Through Witnessing Art

I've previously discussed the emotional appeal of the arts to awaken passion and move us to work for social justice (Lawrence, 2008). One recent example is Al Gore's documentary film *An Inconvenient Truth*, which prompted a generation of Americans to work for environmental sustainability. The visual imagery along with the verbal dialogue created a more powerful impact than the textual media we had been exposed to for a number of years.

Although documentary films are a deliberate attempt to deliver a message, theatrical or entertainment films can also increase our awareness about social issues and provoke action. In the 1980s, the film *Philadelphia* helped us to understand the job discrimination faced by people who were HIV positive. Likewise, the more recent film *Precious* brought our attention to issues of poverty, illiteracy, and the welfare system.

Art installation is also a provocative way to get a message across to a community. Chicago-based artist Gerda Meyer Bernstein, for example, creates room-sized scenes depicting major atrocities such as genocide, torture, and the sexual abuse of women. As one walks though the installation, one becomes a part of the space in which the action is occurring. Bernstein intentionally provokes anger, sadness, and the desire to right such wrongs.

In these examples the artist simply put his or her work out there for the pubic to experience. Adult educators are in a unique position to use these works of art deliberately to promote transformation by bringing music, poetry, fiction, film, or visual art into the classroom as catalysts for dialogue.

Arts in Community Interaction

Witnessing provocative works of art can encourage people to want to work for social change; actually participating in collective art activity can have an even more profound effect. These art activities can take many forms. Hayes and Yorks, in their book *Arts and Societal Learning* (2007), provide numerous examples of community-based activism through art, including performance with prison inmates, creating cut-paper murals as a way for low-income African Americans to learn about their heritage, and using dance to tell the stories of immigration from various cultures.

At the Highlander Folk School (currently the Highlander Research and Education Center) in Tennessee, the arts, particularly music and drama, were the cornerstone of all social change activity. Zilphia Horton staged plays with the residential students to engage them in learning about labor struggles. She also adapted an old church hymn to use as a union protest song. This song was further adapted by Pete Seeger at Highlander in the 1960s and become the well-known anthem of the civil rights movement, "We Shall Overcome" (Horton, 1990).

Olson (2005) researched the emancipatory role of music in communities, particularly among oppressed and persecuted groups, from the early settlement houses to powwows and other cultural festivals. He discovered that "music can function as a medium through which adults evaluate and critique their life experiences and consciously determine new ways to view the world" (p. 56). Music was a way to preserve cultural traditions among group members while at the same time communicating those traditions to outsiders. Furthermore, "Music created space that fostered engaged pedagogy, where hegemonic structures of power and positionality could be challenged" (p. 58).

Interactive theatre is another way in which communities can experience transformative learning and change. Theatre of the Oppressed, which is rooted in the emancipatory pedagogy of Paulo Freire, originated in Brazil by its founder, Augusto Boal, in the 1970s and has been used with communities around the world. Theatre of the Oppressed is about harnessing the power of the aesthetic space (the stage) to examine individual internalized oppressions and to place them within a larger context. The individual with the problem or issue is not a passive recipient of treatment but the director of his or her own therapeutic process. In Theatre of the Oppressed there is no distinction between actors and nonactors or audience members. They are one and the same. The audience (referred to by Boal as *spect-actors*) acts as multiple mirrors to enable new and multiple readings of past and present events. Participants in this process practice alternative responses and actions to change the oppressive situation (Boal, 2002).

Forum theatre is the process most applicable to community transformation. Forum theatre starts with a problem which has oppression at its root. Participants act out the situation, attempting to come up with a solution to challenge the oppressive situation. At any time, an audience member who thinks she or he has a better solution to the problem can call out "Stop" and then replace the protagonist in an attempt to stop the oppression. The intention of forum theatre is to "transform the spectator into the protagonist of the theatrical action and, by this transformation, try to change society rather than contenting ourselves with interpreting it" (Boal, 2002, p. 253).

Through collective art making, members of marginalized groups often find a way to communicate and take back power over their lives. Clover (2006) described a community project in British Columbia in which women explored the issue of sexual exploitation through quilt making. In doing so, the women no longer saw themselves as victims; rather, they saw themselves as people who had control over their lives. In another study, Clover (2010) found that, similar to the community music in the Olson study described earlier, women engaged in the arts, particularly the traditional crafts, found a renewed sense of cultural identity development and "cultural justice" (p. 239). The women found a way to sustain themselves economically, which instilled a sense of pride, self-respect, and personal empowerment. Most important, art was a way for the women to become active producers of knowledge as opposed to passive consumers.

This discussion has shown the various ways that art can be a catalyst for community transformation, whether one is actively engaged in creating art or is a witness or appreciator of art created by others. The transformation may not be immediate; however, the arts are a powerful way to help us see what needs to be changed and to creatively explore alternative realities. As Greene (1995, p. 22) proclaims, "Imagining things being otherwise may be a first step toward acting on the belief that they can be changed." The arts provide a medium for surfacing and exploring conflict and oppression and working through creative and productive resolution.

REFLECTION AND SYNTHESIS

This chapter provided several examples of transformative learning through the arts, using the extrarational processes of imagination, intuition, and affect. The arts were described as a way to expand the boundaries of how we learn by evoking strong emotion and provoking us to sit up and take action against injustice. Most disorienting dilemmas are fraught with pain and confusion, as our normal way of being in the world no longer makes sense (Mezirow, 1991). As the examples reveal, the arts provide holistic ways to approach painful situations in which critical reflection is not enough. Furthermore, the arts can often open the door to having difficult conversations that promote personal and community healing.

Mezirow's (1991) ten phases of the transformation process include exploring new roles and relationships, planning new courses of action, and trying out these new roles. The arts provide us ways to carry out these phases, such as using popular theatre techniques to act out alternative scenarios, or writing poems that explore and express new ways of being. Whether one is an active participant in creating art or a witness to art created by others, the arts have the potential to transform communities in positive ways.

All of the examples presented here illustrate that one does not have to be considered an "artist" to engage in artistic activities. In Native American tribal languages there is no word for artist because art is created by all (Cajete, 1994). Yet I suspect that many adult learners do not take advantage of these transformative opportunities, as they consider art to be the purview of a select group of experts. It therefore falls to the adult educator to challenge these assumptions and associations by exposing their learners to the expressive arts in a variety of ways. As Spehler and Slattery (1999, p. 10) so eloquently proclaim: "Our places of education must create spaces where we go to hear the voices of imagination calling us to justice, compassion, and ecological sustainability. If we are to survive—as educational leaders and as a human community—we must begin to hear and respond."

To create these spaces, we first need to deconstruct our notions of how knowledge is created by valuing and introducing extrarational forms of expression into our pedagogy. We can do this by bringing art, music, film, and literature into our classrooms to illustrate a particular point or provoke discussion. We can engage our students in collective art making even if it means interrogating and working through the resistance of our learners—and even our own discomfort—to engage in such activities. We can invite students to use artistic expression in completing certain assignments rather than always relying on written discourse.

Cole and Knowles (2008) have pointed out that arts-informed research makes knowledge accessible to communities in ways that written reports do not. This raises the question of whom the research is for. It would seem that artistic ways of communicating research findings can be transformative for the researcher, as she or he must think differently and creatively imagine new possibilities. Future research directly linking arts-based research with transformative learning is needed. As art taps into multiple ways of knowing, particularly the affective and spiritual domains, further research into these linkages could expand our understanding of transformative learning theory.

As adult educators, we have a responsibility to tap into the full potential of our learners and find ways to broaden our understanding of self, subject matter, and society. As we get out of our heads, we open up new avenues for transformative learning. Artistic expression offers the potential to expand our knowledge and understanding in new and exciting ways.

References

Binet, N. (1994). *Women on the inner journey.* Nashville, TN: James C. Winston.

Boal, A. (2002). *Games for actors and non-actors* (A. Jackson, Trans., 2nd ed.). London and New York: Routledge.

Boyd, R. D., & Myers, J. G. (1988). Transformative education. *International Journal of Lifelong Education, 7*(4), 261–284.

Butterwick, S., & Lawrence, R. L. (2009). Creating alternative realities: Arts-based approaches to transformative learning. In J. Mezirow, E. W. Taylor, & Associates (Eds.), *Transformative learning in practice* (pp. 35–45). San Francisco: Jossey-Bass.

Cajete, G. (1994). *Look to the mountain.* Skyland, NC: Kivaki Press.

Clover, D. E. (2006). Culture and antiracisms in adult education: An exploration of the contributions of arts-based learning. *Adult Education Quarterly, 57*(1), 46–61.

Clover, D. E. (2010). A contemporary review of feminist aesthetic practices in selective adult education journals and conference proceedings. *Adult Education Quarterly, 60*(3), 233–248.

Cole, A. L., & Knowles, J. G. (2008). Arts-informed research. In J. Knowles & A. L. Cole (Eds.), *Handbook of the arts in qualitative research* (pp. 55–70). Thousand Oaks, CA: SAGE.

Cueva, M. (2007). *Reader's theatre as cancer education.* Unpublished doctoral dissertation, National-Louis University, Chicago.

Dirkx, J. M. (2006). Engaging emotions in adult learning. In E. W. Taylor (Ed.), *Teaching for change: Fostering transformative learning in the classroom* (pp. 15–26). New Directions for Adult and Continuing Education, no. 109. San Francisco: Jossey-Bass.

Eisner, E. (2008). Art and knowledge. In J. G. Knowles & A. L. Cole (Eds.), *Handbook of the arts in qualitative research* (pp. 3–12). Thousand Oaks, CA: SAGE.

Greene, M. (1995). *Releasing the imagination.* San Francisco: Jossey-Bass.

Hayes, S., & Yorks, L. (Eds.). (2007). *Arts and societal learning: Transforming communities socially, politically, and culturally.* New Directions for Adult and Continuing Education, no. 116. San Francisco: Jossey-Bass.

Horton, M. (1990). *The long haul.* New York: Doubleday.

Jung, C. G. (1964). Approaching the unconscious. In C. G. Jung (Ed.), *Man and his symbols.* New York: Dell.

Kates, I. C. (2005). The creative journey: Personal creativity as soul work. In J. P. Miller, S. Karsten, D. Denton, D. Orr, & I. C. Kates (Eds.), *Holistic learning and spirituality in education* (pp. 193–206). New York: SUNY Press.

Lawrence, R. L. (Ed.). (2005). *Artistic ways of knowing: Expanded opportunities for teaching and learning.* New Directions for Adult and Continuing Education, no. 107. San Francisco: Jossey-Bass.

Lawrence, R. L. (2008). Powerful feelings: Exploring the affective domain of informal and arts-based learning. In J. M. Dirkx (Ed.), *Adult learning and the emotional self* (pp. 65–78). New Directions for Adult and Continuing Education, no. 120. San Francisco: Jossey-Bass.

Lawrence, R. L. (2009). The other side of the mirror: Intuitive knowing, visual imagery and transformative learning. In C. Hoggan, S. Simpson, & H. Stuckey (Eds.), *Creative expression in transformative learning* (pp. 129–144). Malabar, FL: Krieger.

Lawrence, R. L., & Cranton, P. (2009). *Looking at the world through multiple lenses: Photography as transformative learning.* Paper presented at the 8th International Transformative Learning Conference, Hamilton, Bermuda.

London, P. (1989). *No more second hand art: Awakening the artist within.* Boston: Shambala.

McNiff, S. (2008). Art-based research. In J. G. Knowles & A. L. Cole (Eds.), *Handbook of the arts in qualitative research* (pp. 29–40). Thousand Oaks, CA: SAGE.

Mealman, C. A., & Lawrence, R. L. (2002). Blue herons and black-eyed Susans: Understanding collaborative learning through natural imagery. *Thresholds in Education, XXVII*(2), 3–11.

Mezirow, J. (1975). *Education for perspective transformation: Women's reentry programs in community colleges.* New York: Center for Adult Education, Teachers College, Columbia University.

Mezirow, J. (1991). *Transformative dimensions of adult learning.* San Francisco: Jossey-Bass.

Mezirow, J., Taylor, E. W., & Associates (Eds.). (2009). *Transformative learning in practice: Insights from community, workplace, and higher education.* San Francisco: Jossey-Bass.

Moore, T. (1992). *The care of the soul.* New York: HarperCollins.

Moore, T. (2004). *Dark nights of the soul.* New York: Gotham Books.

O'Keeffe, G. (1976). *Georgia O'Keeffe.* New York: Viking.

Olson, K. (2005). Music for community education and emancipator learning. In R. L. Lawrence (Ed.), *Artistic ways of knowing* (pp. 55–64). New Directions for Adult and Continuing Education, no. 107. San Francisco: Jossey-Bass.

Patterson, F. (1989). *Photography and the art of seeing.* San Francisco: Sierra Club Books.

Scher, A. (2007). Can the arts change the world? The transformative power of community arts. In S. Hayes & L. Yorks (Eds.), *Arts and societal learning* (pp. 3–12). New Directions for Adult and Continuing Education, no. 116. San Francisco: Jossey-Bass.

Scott, S. M. (1997). The grieving soul in the transformation process. In P. Cranton (Ed.), *Transformative learning in action: Insights from practice* (pp. 41–50). New Directions for Adult and Continuing Education, no. 74. San Francisco: Jossey-Bass.

Simpson, S. (2009). Raising awareness of transformation: Collage, creative expression, and imagination. In C. Hoggan, S. Simpson, & H. Stuckey (Eds.), *Creative expression in transformative learning* (pp. 75–101). Malabar, FL: Krieger.

Spehler, R. M., & Slattery, P. (1999). Voices of imagination: The artist as prophet in the process of social change. *International Journal of Leadership in Education, 2*(1), 1–12.

Wilbur, K. (1996). Transpersonal art and literary theory. *Journal of Transpersonal Psychology, 29*(1), 63–91.

CHAPTER THIRTY

Fiction and Film and Transformative Learning

Christine Jarvis

This chapter explores the distinctive contribution of fiction and film to transformative learning. Their ability to produce intense vicarious experiences is central to this contribution. Fiction enables us to speed up the process of learning that might occur through ordinary lived experience, to imagine living other lives, including some that are rare and unusual. The use of imagery, symbolism, and sensory stimulation startles us into recognizing new patterns and connections in the world, stimulating our imaginative faculties and expanding our perceptions. In this way they can become the disorienting dilemma, the trigger for transformation that is central to the literature surrounding the constantly evolving theories of transformative learning (for example, Brookfield, 2000; Cranton, 2006; Mezirow, 1991; Mezirow & Associates, 2000; Mezirow & Taylor, 2009). Reading Marge Piercy's *Gone to Soldiers* changed my perception of a whole generation, as I felt as well as understood something of the fear, confusion, and uncertainty of success experienced by those who went through World War II; Maxine Greene describes how, in reading works of fiction like *Moby Dick* and *Heart of Darkness*, she saw for the first time her "stake in the human condition, helping me reach the ground of my being—which is also the ground of learning, of reaching beyond where one is" (2000, p. 93).

Wright and Sandlin's (2009) thorough review of the literature on adult education and popular culture makes it clear that it is not only fiction from the literary canon that has the potential to change our perspectives in this way, but also fiction from a wide range of popular cultures, such as film, television, and genre fiction.

Discussions about the transformative potential of fiction in all its forms, including film and television, are located within a range of theoretical frameworks. Sometimes these are openly acknowledged; at other times they are implicit. Such discussions are often concerned with social justice, coming from a position that can be understood in terms of critical theory more generally. They draw on concepts of hegemony and resistance, focusing on the development, through film and fiction, of a critical consciousness that will heighten awareness of power structures that maintain inequalities (Armstrong, 2005; Newman, 2006; Vandrick, 1993). Discussions also draw on postmodern theory, recognizing the shifting and constructive nature of discourses and the way that these are created through these fictional forms (Giroux, 1994; Steinnes, 2004). There is also a psychological and psychoanalytical dimension to some analyses, indicating that film and fiction tap into hidden aspects of our psyche (Dirkx, 2008; Doll, 2008). Discussions of transformative learning often operate within more than one theoretical dimension, and learning happens in ways that blur these boundaries. Therefore, rather than attempting to separate these artificially, I have focused on two aspects of film and fiction's vicarious worlds and have drawn on theoretical frameworks as appropriate. The first aspect is their power to engender empathy and identification. The second concerns their ability to enable us to stand back from our own situations; to use distancing techniques that affect our epistemologies and help us to see the constructed nature of our realities.

EMPATHY AND IDENTIFICATION

Rossiter and Clark (2007) build a powerful case for the efficacy of narrative in teaching based on its relational power; they argue that in working with narrative we develop meaning by connecting with its lifelike qualities. Such connection helps to develop empathy, a quality whose importance to transformative learning is acknowledged. Mezirow describes empathy as one of the "obvious assets for developing the ability of adults to assess alternative beliefs" (2003, p. 60). Rogers describes empathy as "entering the private perceptual world of the other . . . temporarily living the other's life" (1980, p. 142).

This process can be transformative because it shakes our preconceptions about the lives and experiences of other people. Written stories and film and television manipulate the reader's or viewer's perspectives in different ways, so that they feel they share the lives of imaginary characters.

Written fiction can use the first person, so that we appear to have a direct line to the emotions and perceptions of the subject, or they may use a narrator, whose voice has an authority that can shape the perspective we take as we view the characters' actions. Characters in written fictions may tell us directly what they feel and think, or we may have to surmise this from more oblique references. The act of reading a book is different from that of viewing a film; there is space in the process for ongoing review and reflection. We can be drawn in by narrative force and race to the end of a novel, or we can pause and step back from the central characters. We can revisit and re-experience episodes as we try to accommodate them to our frames of reference. Eagleton (1983) captures something of this when he says "We read backwards and forwards simultaneously, predicting and recollecting" (p. 77). Although this is partially true of film, viewers in the cinema cannot literally rewind the film in the same way that they can reread a section of a book before continuing to the end.

In film and television fiction, it is the camera that draws us directly into the experiences of the characters. This can create an intense and immediate experience. We literally see through characters' eyes, noticing what they notice in all its visual detail. Film also uses sound to great effect to intensify the experience (Lerner, 2010). We hear what characters hear—the anger or affection from other characters, the noise of battle, the sound of the sea. Production design also makes a major contribution to our emotional engagement with film and television (DeVries, 2010). These multisensory elements can create a degree of identification simply by virtue of the fact that viewer has a sensory experience that approximates that of the character. We can share something of a character's state of distress or confusion when the visual field becomes disjointed and the soundtrack mirrors this; we can share their wonder at a beautiful scene or person, see the welcome or pleasure in another's face as they look at "us," suffer visual impairment through illness or loss of consciousness as the visual field is clouded or spins. Sensory stimulation also works at a subliminal level to signal connections between themes and character and reinforce mood (Halfyard, 2010). For example, Fenstermacher et al. (2010) note the additional impact given to students' study of *A Lesson Before Dying* by the film adaptation's "visuals of the dark, dank death-row prison cell" (p. 4). These sensory experiences create tone and mood, and their associative qualities may directly affect our emotions. Television can use the camera and other effects in ways similar to film, and though it generally has less money for special effects, it can sometimes offer an intimacy of experience that the larger screen lacks.

Three overlapping subcategories—resonance, outsiders, and unconscious fears and desires—shape my discussion of the way that this capacity for creating empathy is integral to the transformative powers of fiction (including both written and visual fictions). "Resonance" consists of those fictional experiences that reflect aspects of the readers' own lives, enabling them to see those lives differently as they empathize with the characters. In the "Outsiders" section I consider how empathizing through film and fiction with those who might seem "other" can transform our perceptions. "Unconscious fears and desires" looks at the way films and fiction can effect deep change by enabling us to engage metaphorically with hidden aspects of ourselves.

Fiction that enables us to engage with characters who are like us and whose situations mirror ours may seem an unlikely vehicle for change; we might assume it would reinforce our world views. Gramsci, writing about the importance of hegemony—the "spontaneous consent given by great masses of the popular to the general direction imposed on social life by the dominant fundamental group" (1988, pp. 363–378)—identifies popular fiction and the media in general as conservative forces. Critical theorists have often seen popular culture this way; Adorno (1991) distinguishes between high culture and much popular culture, arguing that the latter may provoke emotion and even catharsis, but satisfies without challenging, thereby creating a contentment that diverts critique from material inequalities; Althusser (1969) includes culture and art among the institutions that contribute to the ideological state apparatus, serving to reinforce a status quo that perpetuates the interests of a dominant group.

And yet, reflection on fictional experiences that mirror our personal situations can have a profound and transformative impact. Readers are able to imagine new solutions to their problems. They may identify with the inhibitions or personality challenges of characters who overcome these and reinvent themselves. They may take inspiration from the courage and determination of a character confronting all too familiar problems. Fiction, including popular fiction, can present individuals with their own personal and social problems and help them to contextualize these and articulate resistance to injustice, rather than accept its inevitability or locate its cause in personal circumstances. For example, many of my women students have told me that they enjoy soap opera and family sagas that feature women facing poverty and family problems, precisely because they themselves have experienced similar challenges and are inspired by the strength and will of the characters to seek change in their own lives. Gramsci recognized that fiction with this capacity for resonance could contribute to the development of progressive ideologies. He described Ibsen's *A Doll's House* as a "drama of the most intellectually and morally advanced part of society" which had a "profound resonance in the popular psyche," locating its success precisely in the fact that the ideas it embodied were "represented and not expounded like a thesis or popular speech" (1988, pp. 372–373).

Giroux (2002) situates his analyses within critical theory but has synthesized this with postmodern discourse, acknowledging that popular culture produces "multiple subject positions" (p. 96). This discourse identifies complexities and multiplicities of oppression, recognizing that works are not simply conservative or progressive. He argues that film "represents a new form of pedagogical text"

(p. 8), a "powerful force for shaping public memory, hope, popular consciousness, and social agency" (p. 15). This offers, he believes, an opportunity for public dialogue. He notes the potential of films such as *Norma Rae* to create a deeper understanding of class struggle, and his analysis of the film shows that the opportunity the film affords its audience to share the detail of Norma's experience makes this possible.

Empirical work also demonstrates that individuals are significantly changed by engagement with fictional characters with whom they can identify. For instance, Wright (2007) interviewed British women who were contemporaries of *The Avengers'* character Cathy Gale and showed how, in spite of the gender restrictions they faced at that time, they identified strongly with Cathy's physical and mental strength and envisioned alternative possibilities for themselves that sometimes led to direct action. She stated: "Watching the independent, intelligent, well-educated, and athletic Gale empowered some viewers by offering them an alternative to the women their culture told them to become" (p. 67).

Popular genre fiction (such as *The Avengers*) seems to offer, through escapism, the potential for transformation through breaking out of habits of thought and related social constraints. Burr's (2010) interviews with viewers, for example, showed how identification with the core characteristics of the central character in the popular horror TV series *Buffy the Vampire Slayer* inspired women viewers and created a degree of self-belief, of confidence in their own strength.

Wright's and Burr's readers were transforming their view of themselves, making a shift in their self-concept—part of their psychological habit of mind (Mezirow & Associates, 2000, p. 17)—because they had seen what others, who were like themselves in some respects, could do. At the same time, they were challenging some beliefs about their roles as women, beliefs that they had previously taken for granted.

OUTSIDERS

Researchers have demonstrated that fiction enables us to engage with lives that are radically different from ours and with people who may be on the margins of our social world, or even seen as threats or enemies. This not only creates understanding and empathy with those who are different from us but also allows us to imagine alternatives to the way we live now. Transformative learning theory focused on social reform is particularly well served by such fiction. Brookfield (2000, 2005) argues that genuinely critical reflection must include ideology critique, an examination of "power relations and hegemonic assumptions" (2000, p. 125). He asserts that even personal reflection is ideological, because ideologies are constituent parts of our personalities. Fiction and film that connect us with outsiders often operate at an emotional, even visceral level. Sharing something intense with a character whose situation or perspective is alien to ours can shake our beliefs about ourselves. Our conviction, for example, that we could never behave in a particular way or that certain groups are wrong, or to blame for their own misfortune, starts to unravel. Changing political perspectives often begins at this level of human understanding, rather than through engagement with a theoretical perspective. Personal, sociocultural, and epistemic change are developing simultaneously, as viewers feel differently about themselves vis-à-vis an outsider group, which means they must recognize that perhaps there is no single truth or reality and thus begin a process of unraveling the constructs that they have taken for granted up to that point. This may happen simply through the stimulus of exposure to intense and powerful fictions or through repeated exposure. The political potential of the arts is summarized by Maxine Greene:

> The shocks of awareness to which the arts give rise leave us (*should* leave us) less immersed in the everyday and more impelled to wonder and to question.... They may ... move us into spaces where we can envision other ways of being and ponder what it might signify to realize them. But moving into such spaces requires a willingness to resist the forces that press people into passivity and bland acquiescence. It requires a refusal of what Foucault calls "normalization," the power which imposes homogeneity.... To resist such tendencies is to become aware of the ways in which certain dominant social practices enclose us in molds, define us in accord with extrinsic demands. (2000, p. 135)

The particular value of some form of structured, educational engagement with film and television fiction, rather than a purely unmediated encounter, lies in the capacity of educational programs to develop a framework for analysis and provide a forum for dialogue. A teacher can develop activities and promote discussion that will help the viewer to clarify and articulate the emerging new perspectives and connect the feelings and struggle for new meaning with a range of theoretical perspectives.

Film and fiction have been particularly valuable to educators engaged in transformative teaching for diversity. They use fiction to offer opportunities to students to share the experience of social and cultural groups different from their own. For example, Tisdell and Thompson's (2007) large-scale mixed methods study showed participants challenged by movies such as *Philadelphia* and *Crash* reviewing their own perspectives on sexuality and culture. Also, Tisdell's analysis of graduate students' online conversations and written papers, during a study of the movie *Crash,* demonstrated that they were living through a range of characters, and that this made them look at their own prejudices and assumptions in ways that were not always comfortable but that stimulated reflection and reevaluation (Tisdell, 2008). She stresses the importance of the group and the educator in this process. Her detailed analyses show that participants could avoid issues, and that the role of the facilitator was significant in drawing attention to these. Alexandrin (2009) also focuses on transforming understanding of cultural and ethnic diversity using television images. Her participants believed the work had "made them reflect on their perceptions of different ethnic, cultural and ability groups seen on television and how these perceptions of groups align with society's images of these groups" (p. 151). Her teaching requires participants to imagine being part of different groups and to articulate their feelings about the levels and nature of representation of those groups to other members. Similarly, Thein, Beach, and Parks (2007) focus on the way that multicultural fiction can confront students with views that clash with their own, prompting critical reflection. Again, identification is important, as students assume the subject positions of "others."

UNCONSCIOUS OR SEMICONSCIOUS FEARS AND DESIRES

Resonance and identification can create an intense emotional response that is not always immediately understandable. Fiction and film have extensive figurative properties, such as their use of symbolism, metaphor, and metonymy. They have the capacity to produce concrete manifestations of our semi- or unconscious fears and desires, stimulating powerful responses. When we engage with them, we may come to a fuller awareness of them and a better understanding of ourselves. Boyd and Myers (1988), drawing on depth psychology, have discussed the importance of symbols, images, and archetypes in fostering transformative learning, which they see as a process of personality change. Dirkx argues that transformative learning "may be fostered through the selective use of fiction, poetry and movies" (2006, p. 23). He notes that adult learning often takes place in a "powerful emotional context" and addresses unresolved conflicts that the learner may not fully recognize, which lead to "deeper insights into the self" (p. 17). He discusses the importance of recognizing the unconscious forces that shape our attitudes and behavior and examines how developing an awareness of these and their significance can lead to profound transformations, arguing that "when we take seriously the responsibility of developing a more conscious relationship with the unconscious dimensions of our being, we enter into a profoundly transformative, life-changing process" (2006, p. 19).

An example of the kind of development that can occur when fiction creates connections with hidden fears is given by Cranton, who describes how, when reading a short story, she came to an "important (and difficult) insight," as a result of reflecting on the intensity of her response, enabling her to bring "to consciousness a great fear" that she could "connect to recurring dreams and fears" about relationships (2010, p. 1). Cawelti's (1976) argument that the almost addictive power of some genre fiction lies in their revisiting of unresolvable personal and social dilemmas is relevant here, as is Bettelheim's (1976) psychoanalytical interpretation of fairy story, which locates its fascination for children in the concretization of the challenges faced at different stages of personality development.

One effect of popular fiction is its capacity to engage us intensely with characters who face conflicts of character and situation that we share but cannot resolve. This may lead to a continued revisiting of the dilemma and the gratification of a fantasy solution, in which case it acts only as a temporary respite. It may also provide us with progressive insights into those dilemmas and eventually with the courage to seek to resolve them in reality, as a result of this psychic and metaphorical rehearsal, in which case they have served a transformative function.

The monsters and ghouls of the horror genre are an excellent example of "the unconscious dimensions of our being" described by Dirkx, and the fascination we feel for these is indicative of their power. They act as concrete representations of traumas and anxieties. There has been much discussion recently about the popularity of the figure of the vampire in popular culture: *Twilight*, *Buffy the Vampire Slayer*, *True Blood*, *Vampire Diaries*, and the like. Each generation reinvents this figure in the image of its own preoccupations (Auerbach, 1995; Chandler, 2003). The extreme contemporary fascination with this character suggests that its current manifestations pick up on particularly strong desires and fears in the common psyche, and teachers have begun to use these texts with young adults, especially young women, in an attempt to work with these issues (Bloom, 2010).

CREATING CRITICAL DISTANCE

In contrast to techniques that draw the reader into the fiction, encouraging a "suspension of disbelief" (Coleridge, 1991, p. 169), there are those techniques that serve to distance readers by drawing attention to their own fictionality. Standing back and seeing the world, with its values, assumptions, and ways of being, laid bare as a piece of fiction can be a profoundly disorienting dilemma. It challenges viewers and readers to face the social construction of reality, shaking sociocultural and epistemic assumptions. Patricia Waugh (1984) defines the impact of these "metafictions" particularly succinctly: "In providing a critique of their own methods of construction, such writings not only examine the fundamental structures of narrative fiction, they also explore the possible fictionality of the world outside the literary fictional text" (p. 2).

Stimulating an awareness of the socially constructed nature of the normal world has implications for the kinds of transformative learning that can lead to an understanding of social injustice. Brecht employed techniques of *verfremdung* ("making strange") for this purpose. He made dramatic effects visible; time and place were indicated directly rather than simulated; he used narrators, and his actors addressed the audience directly, breaking the illusion of reality. He believed that the kinds of realism that led to involvement with the actors on stage meant audiences were less able to be critical observers who might take real action themselves to address social injustice. Raymond Williams (1976) calls this "a dialectical form, drawing directly on a Marxist theory of history in which, within given limits, man makes himself" (p. 318).

A range of distancing techniques are evident in film and fiction in its many forms. A common device is the use of a narrator, able to comment critically on characters and their motivations, or even to draw attention wryly to absurdities of plot or situation. The use of multiple perspectives, showing the same event through different eyes, is a particularly powerful fictional device, as is the manipulation of time and space; these strategies confront the viewer with the fragmented nature of our realities and the constructive power of memory and individual perceptions. Fiction may draw attention to its own construction by drawing on genres other than realism. *Edward Scissorhands* locates itself in an apparently twentieth-century suburb, juxtaposed with the quasi-magical gothic mansion-castle on the edge of town where the inventor-father creates the boy with scissors for hands. *Pleasantville* uses a wide range of techniques to make the viewer aware of the social construction of reality. The central protagonists, contemporary teens, are drawn into a black-and-white 1950s situation comedy. They interact with the series' characters, and as those characters challenge some of the absolute values (male dominance, family values, narrow sexual moralities) of the series, the program moves into color. The teenagers are literally inside a fiction, but this in turn reminds us that we were watching a fiction in the first place. The clash of values from one period to another foregrounds the relativity of moral perspectives and the use of color serves as a complex metaphor for the move from moral absolutism—a black-and-white view of the world—to one of moral complexity, multicolored and nuanced. The symbolism is emotionally laden; the black-and-white world seems less vibrant and pleasurable than its Technicolor alternative. In presenting us with the constructed nature of the normal in one reality, the film draws attention to the construction of reality more generally. Other fictions take questions of identity and illusion and reality as central themes; films with famous "twists," like *Fight Club* and *The Sixth Sense*, remind us that we do not always know who we are; *The Eternal Sunshine of the Spotless Mind* confronts us with the way that we are constructed by our past. The *Buffy the Vampire Slayer* episode "Normal Again" places its central character in an alternate universe, in which she lives in an institution for the mentally insane and her world, which we have watched through five and half series, is presented as nothing more than her delusions. She has to choose between the two realities.

The challenge created by these kinds of techniques can transform perspectives in all three of the dimensions originally described by Mezirow. They can profoundly shake our psychological meaning perspectives, challenging our sense of a fixed self, as we realize that we are at least partially composed of our memories, respond in ways that seem "out of character" when faced with different circumstances, and reflect on who we might have been had things been different. They challenge our sociocultural meaning perspectives by jolting us into awareness of the artificiality and performativity of aspects of social organization and interaction that we may previously have viewed as natural and inevitable. The kinds of metafictional qualities that make us stand outside our normal day-to-day realities and look on them as fictional constructs that can be made and remade, make it difficult to reify social, moral, and political imperatives. Such techniques pose special challenges to our epistemological meaning perspectives. They force us to see that the world is not singular; that reality is not fixed, but is subjective and related to individual perspectives, and can be made and remade through discourse, dialogue, and a creative reordering of the pattern of events.

Although some fiction and film can be, in effect, critical pedagogues, drawing attention to the social construction of reality, educators also have a vital role to play in using fiction to develop the critical reading skills that enable adults to do this work themselves with more general fiction. Giroux (1994, 2002) is a well-known proponent of the idea that films are forms of public pedagogy, with pleasure a significant factor in their pedagogical efficacy. He states: "They deploy power through the important role they play connecting the production of pleasure and meaning with the mechanisms and practices of powerful teaching machines" (Giroux, 2002, p. 4).

The impact created by these pleasurable experiences can reinforce social norms as well as challenge them. It may serve to normalize social practices rather than to make them strange and highlight their social construction. It is this capacity for perpetuating hegemony that has led many educationalists to focus on the importance of supporting students to develop critical media literacy, encouraging them to recognize the power of discourse, to identify alternative readings and recognize the ways meaning is constructed. McLaren and Hammer (1996) identify the importance of acquiring a critical media literacy in order to "answer the question: How do essentially arbitrarily organized cultural codes, products of historical struggle...come to represent the 'real,' the 'natural' and the 'necessary'?" (p. 112).

RECOGNIZING DISCOURSE

Educators have worked with students to help them identify powerful discourses that permeate the fictions we enjoy. Such critical pedagogies enable readers and viewers to identify the kinds of discourses that construct and reflect their realities. Guy (2007) designs his curriculum to develop critical awareness of the way fiction helps to normalize inequalities through analyses of TV series such as *Commander in Chief* or the film *Crash*. He emphasizes the importance of helping learners develop a framework for their critique that has a strong skills and cognitive base. He draws on semiotics, on the understanding of the ideological impact of representation, on the role of reader interpretation, and on learning to challenge and resist these representations.

Pervasive discourses such as heterosexual romance are normalized in our culture and can shape expectations and behavior relating to gender relations. For instance, when I worked with women returning to school who were reading popular fiction, I designed activities to draw attention to the shape and the political implications of these discourses, which led to an increased awareness of their influence on relationships and expectations (Jarvis, 1999). In this instance, and in the sessions described by Guy, critical perceptions were developed both through the design of particular activities and by the selection of fiction. *Crash* itself draws attention in an uncomfortable way to stereotypes and ideologies, and novels such as *Romance* by Joan Riley, or Carter's *Magic Toyshop*, foreground the shaping influence of romance and fairy story.

READING AGAINST THE GRAIN

This kind of critical pedagogical work with film and fictions can enable students to identify some of the contradictions and ruptures in texts that may mask hegemonic ideologies in some superficially liberal fictions. This can support the kind of ideology critique that Brookfield (2000) identifies as central to transformative learning. It also develops students' awareness of the ways these ideologies are formed, deepening their understanding of the complex construction of knowledge and discourse in a complex, media-driven society (McLaren & Hammer, 1996) and challenging epistemic meaning perspectives. For example, the film *Crazy/Beautiful*, which apparently challenges race- and class-based stereotypes, shows the impoverished Latino hero as the good student and a positive member of society with a supportive, ambitious family, and the wealthy white heroine as a wastrel whose lack of conventional family life leads to her downfall. It takes critical discussion to reveal the extent to which the movie also serves a highly assimilative function, reinforcing hegemonic assumptions about individual responsibility and failing to challenge the structural roots of poverty and oppression. The liberal values of the white family are shown to be at the root of its dysfunction, the majority of the Latino society is presented stereotypically, and the hero achieves success only through the patronage of the white girl's father, and then only by offering his services to the state through the military.

INTERTEXTUALITY AND THE ROLE OF
THE READER OR VIEWER

An important aspect of the contribution that fiction and film make to transformative learning is related to the constructive role of the reader/viewer. Meaning does not reside exclusively within the fiction itself, or with the intentions of the author, writers, or directors involved in its creation. This is what gives it so much of its power, as readers brings the force of their own creativity and emotions to the process. Greene comments: "Cathy's passion for Heathcliff in *Wuthering Heights* is our passion; Joe's murderous love for Dorcas in Toni Morrison's *Jazz* is our own epiphany—we lend it its taste and flame. Writer and reader both are responsible for the universe brought into being through the act of reading" (2000, p. 77).

The theoretical field dealing with these issues (Iser, 1980) includes views that locate meaning entirely with the reader (Holland, 1968) as well as those that acknowledge common responses within cultures that make it possible for creators to anticipate some of the likely range of meanings an audience will draw upon (Fish, 1980; McCormick, 1994). It is not necessary to come down on one side or the other to recognize the transformative potential of making viewers aware of their role in meaning-making. It is empowering almost by definition; it positions readers as active creators rather than passive recipients. Once again, it is effective in all three domains of transformative learning. Educators writing about transformative education have drawn on work on adult cognitive development. This varies in its description of stages of cognitive development and in the extent to which it sees this as a progression or something less linear. Nevertheless, models such as those developed by King and Kitchener (1994) and Belenky, Clinchy, Goldberger, and Tarule (1986) have common ground in the way they chart the movement of understanding from a position in which reality is seen to be absolute and located with authorities, to one that is capable of complex reflective judgment that acknowledges the constructed nature of reality. An individual's understanding of a work of fiction is filtered through the individual's existing meaning perspectives; discursive activities that make students aware of this help them recognize that meaning is negotiable, that knowledge is contingent on the maker, and that they themselves are a participant in this process.

CONCLUSION

When we think about the way in which the transformative power of film and fiction has been and can be theorized, it is possible to group the kinds of changes discussed into two categories. There are those changes that rely on the creation of intense and passionate emotions, empathy, and identification. Then there are those that rely, conversely, on making us stand back, stimulating awareness not only of the constructed nature of fiction itself, but also of the way we construct our daily lives and experiences.

These two aspects of film and fiction promote perspective transformation across all three of the categories originally outlined by Mezirow. The nature of transformation through film and fiction reinforces many of the claims made by those who have developed transformation theory over the last forty years, in that it draws on many aspects of our humanity, on our emotions and our unconscious fears and desires as well as on our intellectual and cognitive facilities.

In the psychic domain, film and fiction can promote greater self-awareness, enabling us to recognize and challenge some hidden aspects of ourselves that may limit our development. Sociocultural meaning perspectives are transformed as we live through the experiences of others and come to understand the validity and complexity of other subject positions. Epistemic perspectives expand as film and fiction show us the many versions of what appeared to be a shared reality; as we recognize how we construct our lives and formulate our experience into patterns and narratives; as we see the huge potential for reformulation, for telling our own stories differently.

Transformation through fiction across all dimensions integrates the emotions and the intellect. The intensity of the experience makes it an emotional and sensory as well as an intellectual process. The balance between the emotions, senses, and intellect in the transformation process will depend on the nature of the fiction itself, but also on the scope for reflection and critical dialogue available to us, either through our own resources or as a result of an educational opportunity.

There is considerable scope for more extensive work in this area. In particular, there are many theoretical areas to develop, not least the relationship between transformative learning theory and the many literary critical studies that look at the way textual meaning is created through readers' preexisting beliefs and perspectives. Important, too, would be a more systematic analysis of the implications for adult educators of the literature on readers' and viewers' empathic responses. Empirical work is needed to tease out the range of pedagogical techniques that are likely to harness the transformative potential of fictions in a way that recognizes how different students respond differently to fictional encounters. We also need a better understanding of the situations that promote unmediated transformation through fiction and film. In the current policy climate, in which the arts and humanities face exceptional challenges, it is more important than ever to strengthen the evidence base for their contribution to the capacity of human beings to transform themselves and their worlds.

References

Adorno, T. (1991). *The culture industry: Selected essays on mass culture*. London: Routledge.

Alexandrin, J. (2009). Television images; exploring how they affect people's view of self and others. *Multicultural Perspectives, 11*(3), 150–154.

Althusser, L. (1969). Ideology and ideological state apparatuses. In L. Althusser (Ed.), *Lenin and philosophy and other essays*. London: NLB.

Armstrong, P. (2005). The Simpsons and democracy: Political apathy, popular culture, and lifelong learning as satire. In R. Hill & R. Keely (Eds.), *The 46th annual adult education research conference*. Athens, GA: University of Georgia.

Auerbach, N. (1995). *Our vampires, ourselves*. Chicago: University of Chicago Press.

Belenky, M., Clinchy, B., Goldberger, N., & Tarule, J. (1986). *Women's ways of knowing*. New York: Basic Books.

Bettelheim, B. (1976). *The uses of enchantment*. Harmondsworth, UK: Peregrine.

Bloom, A. (2010, January 8). What has pale skin, drinks blood and makes a good teaching resource? *Times Educational Supplement*.

Boyd, R., & Myers, J. (1988). Transformative education. *International Journal of Lifelong Education, 7*(4), 261–284.

Brookfield, S. (2000). Transformative learning as ideology critique. In J. Mezirow & Associates (Eds.), *Learning as transformation: Critical perspectives on a theory in progress*. San Francisco: Jossey-Bass.

Brookfield, S. (2005). *The power of critical theory: Liberating adult learning and teaching*. San Francisco: Jossey-Bass.

Burr, V. (2010, June). *Buffy as role model: Her significance for female viewers*. Paper presented at the SC4 Conference on the Whedonverses, Flagler College, St. Augustine, FL.

Cawelti, J. (1976). *Adventure, mystery, romance: Formula stories as art and popular culture*. Chicago: University of Chicago Press.

Chandler, H. (2003). Slaying the patriarchy. Transfusions of the vampire metaphor in *Buffy the Vampire Slayer*. Slayageonline, 9, www.slayageonline.com.

Coleridge, S. (1991). *Biographia literaria* (G. Watson, Ed.). London: Dent.

Cranton, P. (2006). *Understanding and promoting transformative learning*. San Francisco: Jossey-Bass.

Cranton, P. (2010). *Transformative learning and social sustainability through fiction*. Paper presented at the Eighth International Transformative Learning Conference: Reframing Social Sustainability in a Multicultural World, Harrisburg, Bermuda.

DeVries, C. (2010, June). *I ate a decorator once: Production design in the Whedonverses*. Paper presented at the SC4 Conference on the Whedonverses, Flagler College, St. Augustine, FL.

Dirkx, J. (2006). Engaging emotions in adult learning: A Jungian perspective on emotion and transformative learning. In E. Taylor (Ed.), *Teaching for change: Fostering transformative learning in the classroom*. New Directions for Adult and Continuing Education, no. 109. San Francisco: Jossey-Bass.

Dirkx, J. (2008). Care of the self: Mythopoetic dimensions of professional preparation and development. In T. Leonard & P. Willis (Eds.), *Pedagogies of the imagination*. New York: Springer.

Doll, M. (2008). Capacity and Currere. In T. Leonard & P. Willis (Eds.), *Pedagogies of the imagination*. New York: Springer.

Eagleton, T. (1983). *Literary theory*. Oxford: Blackwell.

Fenstermacher, K., Moll, K., Sprow, K., Tait, B., Hayduk, D., Snyder, M., . . . Taylor, E. (2010). *A lesson before dying: Using fiction to understand transformative learning*. Paper presented at the Eighth International Transformative Learning Conference: Reframing Social Sustainability in a Multicultural World, Harrisburg, Bermuda.

Fish, S. (1980). *Is there a text in this class?* Cambridge, MA; London: Harvard University Press.

Giroux, H. (1994). *Disturbing pleasures*. New York, London: Routledge.

Giroux, H. (2002). *Breaking into the movies*. Malden, MA: Blackwell.

Gramsci, A. (1988). *An Antonio Gramsci reader, selected writings 1916–1935*. New York: Schocken Books.

Greene, M. (2000). *Releasing the imagination*. San Francisco: Jossey-Bass.

Guy, T. (2007). Learning who we (and they) are: Popular culture as pedagogy. In E. Tisdell & P. Thompson (Eds.), *Popular culture and entertainment media in adult education*. New Directions for Adult and Continuing Education, no. 115. San Francisco: Jossey-Bass.

Halfyard, J. (2010, June). *Listening to Buffy: Music, memory, meaning, and moping*. Paper presented at the SC4 Conference on the Whedonverses, Flagler College, St. Augustine, FL.

Holland, N. (1968). *The dynamics of literary response.* New York: Oxford University Press.

Iser, W. (1980). *The act of reading.* Baltimore, MD: John Hopkins.

Jarvis, C. (1999). Love changes everything. *Studies in the Education of Adults, 31*(2), 109–123.

King, P., & Kitchener, J. (1994). *Developing reflective judgment.* San Francisco: Jossey-Bass.

Lerner, N. (Ed.). (2010). *Music in the horror film.* Abingdon, NY: Taylor and Francis.

McCormick, K. (1994). *The culture of reading and the teaching of English.* Manchester: Manchester University Press.

McLaren, P., & Hammer, R. (1996). Media knowledges, warrior citizenry, and postmodern literacies. In H. Giroux, C. Lankshear, P. McLaren, & M. Peters (Eds.), *Counternarratives: Cultural studies and critical pedagogies in postmodern spaces* (pp. 81–117). New York: Routledge.

Mezirow, J. (1991). *Transformative dimensions of adult learning.* San Francisco: Jossey-Bass.

Mezirow, J. (2003). Transformative learning as discourse. *Journal of Transformative Education, 1*(1), 58–63.

Mezirow, J., & Associates (Eds.). (2000). *Learning as transformation: Critical perspectives on a theory in progress.* San Francisco: Jossey-Bass.

Mezirow, J., Taylor, E. W., & Associated (Eds.) (2009). *Transformative learning in practice: Insights from community, workplace and higher education.* San Francisco: Jossey-Bass.

Newman, M. (2006). *Teaching defiance.* San Francisco: Jossey-Bass.

Rogers, C. (1980). *A way of being.* Boston: Houghton Mifflin.

Rossiter, M., & Clark, C. (2007). *Narrative and the practice of adult education.* Malabar, FL: Krieger.

Steinnes, J. (2004). Transformative education in a poststructuralist perspective. *Journal of Transformative Education, 2,* 261–275.

Thein, A., Beach, R., & Parks, D. (2007). Perspective-taking as transformative practice in teaching multicultural literature to white students. *English Journal, 97*(2), 54–60.

Tisdell, E. (2008). Critical media literacy and transformative learning. *Journal of Transformative Education, 6*(1,) 48–67.

Tisdell, E., & Thompson, P. (2007). Seeing from a different angle: The role of pop culture in teaching for diversity and critical media literacy in adult education. *International Journal of Lifelong Education, 26*(6), 651–673.

Vandrick, S. (1993). Feminist fiction for social change. *Peace Review: A Journal of Social Justice, 14*(5), 507–510.

Waugh, P. (1984). *Metafiction.* London: Methuen.

Williams, R. (1976). *From Ibsen to Brecht*. Aylesbury, UK: Pelican.

Wright, R. (2007). *The Avengers* and the development of British women's consciousness. In E. Tisdell & P. Thompson (Eds.), *Popular culture and entertainment media in adult education*. New Directions for Adult and Continuing Education, no. 115. San Francisco: Jossey-Bass.

Wright, R., & Sandlin, J. (2009). Cult TV, hip hop, shape-shifters, and vampire slayers. *Adult Education Quarterly*, *59*(2), 118–141.

CHAPTER THIRTY-ONE

Learning to Be What We Know

The Pivotal Role of Presentational Knowing in Transformative Learning

Elizabeth Kasl and Lyle Yorks

Thinking destroys the beauty of Feeling
BUT
Without Thinking—Feeling has no meaning
Feeling and Thinking
Like
Black and White
Yin and Yang
They seem contrary
BUT
Behind the Contrast
An energy of balance flows in-between
In truth—
Feeling and Thinking
Are complementary
In
Whole-person learning.

—Michelle Wang

Note: Michelle Wang writes to Lyle Yorks about her poem: "Inspired by Franz Kline's 'Black and White' paintings, Chinese 'Yin and Yang' philosophy, and more importantly, our dialogue on presentational knowing as the connection between feeling and thinking and the art of teaching, 11/28/09."

W e describe an epistemological position known as presentational know- ing. This way of knowing fosters transformative learning in both indi- viduals and larger human systems by connecting thinking to feeling, thus providing the "flow in-between" that enriches practical action.

Presentational knowing is the name given by John Heron (1992) to a way of knowing that is intuitive and imaginal, manifested in "movement, sound, colour, shape, line" (p. 165). We gain access to presentational knowing through expressive forms such as music, dance, mime, visual or dramatic arts, story, and metaphor.

This chapter describes ways in which presentational knowing provides epistemological bridges. Within individuals or groups, presentational know- ing helps transform tacit knowledge and emotional experience into concepts and principles that become the foundation for new behavior. Between individ- uals and groups, presentational knowing creates empathic space that helps people with diverse lived experiences understand and learn from one an- other. We believe that adult educators who understand these epistemological bridges will practice a more holistic pedagogy, thus enhancing possibilities for transformation.

Over the years, we have followed the critical discourses about Jack Mezirow's transformative learning theory (1991, 2000), in particular the as- sessments of its bias toward rational ways of knowing and its failure to account for taking action (Taylor, 1998). Implicit in these critiques is a presupposition that theory about transformation should be as holistic as its lived experience. Our belief that adult educators need a learning theory that accounts holistically for feeling, thinking, and acting led us to be intrigued (Yorks & Kasl, 2002) with John Heron's ideas about epistemology, which he posits as a "theory of personhood." We believe Heron's phenomenological view of human knowing (Heron, 1992) provides a powerful explanation for how people transform their beliefs and sustain changes in behavior that reflect the transformation.

Although presentational knowing is only one among four ways of knowing in Heron's holistic epistemology, we focus on it because it is the way of knowing least likely to find a comfortable place in the pedagogical practice of North American adult educators. Before proceeding with our theoretical discussion, we provide a concrete example of one experience with presentational knowing. The example serves as an interpretive aid throughout the chapter.

Woman Emerging: An Illustrative Story of Presentational Knowing
The story is Elizabeth's and is written in the first person.

Context for Understanding the Story

To describe how presentational knowing contributed to my personal transformation, I begin with background information. I moved to San Francisco to help create a new doctoral program in transformative learning. Before the move, I had been teaching in the adult education program at Teachers College, where our view of transformative learning was limited to the work of our program's founder, Jack Mezirow. I was recruited for the new program because of my knowledge about Mezirow's theory and my strong commitment to participatory learning. This commitment predisposed me to challenge traditional assumptions about how faculty share power, authority, and responsibility with students.

Our founding faculty described the pace and generativity of our work by observing, "We are trying to run on the track while we are still laying it." We meant that although we didn't yet agree on how to actualize our program vision, we had admitted students and were already teaching a curriculum. Our espoused pedagogical philosophy for the cohort-based doctoral program was highly experiential—students would learn how to create conditions that foster transformative learning by using their cohort as a laboratory. "You will learn," we promised them, "from the text of your lived experience."

In spite of a recruitment goal for twenty students, we launched the program with nine, of whom only one was a person of color. As we began the weeklong August residency, students staged an immediate protest, challenging faculty about the gap between our curriculum promises and what we delivered. They asserted that they could not learn about transformation in human systems from the "text of student experience" when that experience was badly impoverished by the cohort's lack of racial diversity. Students petitioned the administration to reopen admissions and provide diversity scholarships. With an all-out recruitment effort from the students, eight qualified people of color were admitted into the program within a month.

I worked with a small committee of original students to plan our first experience as a newly constituted group. We extended the September weekend to four days, hoping to forge a sense of learning community in a cohort now doubled in size. The four days were both energizing and tumultuous as we explored how such a racially diverse group of people could learn from and with each other in community. At many moments I, along with the white students, felt bewildered and anxious. Still, we all seemed to experience a sense of possibility in our nascent learning venture. I asked for volunteers to help plan the October weekend.

Two students from the original group and two new students met with me several times, seeking mutual understanding about what we hoped to accomplish. It was a given that formal course work, led by school faculty, would be allocated ten to twelve hours. The remainder of our three-day, thirty-two-hour weekend was ours to design.

Our fledgling program's mission statement promised that students would be co-learners with faculty. My assumption that co-learning requires co-planning led me to create a planning committee. However, I had not reflected critically about how I would share power. I had strong pedagogical values for collaboration and participatory process, but no experience with an academic structure comparable to this one. Thus I was unprepared when students on the committee suggested an idea that I thought was a bit bizarre.

The two women of color enthusiastically proposed an activity for helping the cohort envision learning goals. We would begin with a guided meditation, followed by clay sculpting. Individuals would give themselves over to the clay and the clay would speak to them. Building on this activity, we could formulate a vision for our cohort that included each individual's hopes and goals.

I had spent years teaching adult learning theory at Teachers College, where we envisioned transformative learning as a dispassionate process of identifying assumptions and engaging in rational discourse. Nothing in my experience was remotely similar to the activities these women advocated with confident enthusiasm. I felt panic. The activity struck me as odd and potentially an object of ridicule from other students. However, I had set in motion a process that led students to believe they were empowered. Trapped in a dilemma of my own making, I felt that my credibility was on the line regarding the promise of student participation. I asked a few questions; the two white students did not seem as skeptical as I felt, and so we adopted the plan.

Elizabeth's Experience with Presentational Knowing

When our group convened on a Friday morning in October, we soon came to the planned visioning activity. We sat on the floor in a circle. Esperanza told us she had traveled to a riverbank held sacred by her people to dig the clay we would be using as part of a visioning process. She explained we would begin with guided meditation and then receive a portion of the sacred clay. Without opening our eyes we were to work the clay, to give ourselves to the wisdom in the clay. We should not make a plan about what we wanted to depict, but should let the clay reveal our wisdom.

I tried to look attentive, all the time thinking, *Good grief! What have I done?*

The meditation lasted much longer than I expected. I tried halfheartedly to follow Esperanza's instructions to visualize a path into an unknown space, but I felt agitated and preoccupied by how much time the activity was consuming. Finally, the meditation was over and I opened my eyes to see a lump of clay.

Plunging my hands into it and starting to knead, I glanced surreptitiously at what others were doing. It seemed to me they were not following the instructions to "give yourself to the clay," but were sculpting shapes with careful deliberation. Something in me wanted to be respectful of Esperanza's instructions, so I closed my eyes and tried to lose myself in the clay. After a time, I stopped sneaking peeks at the others. I was kneading and patting and feeling my clay, but not thinking about it. In contrast to my agitated state during the meditation, I felt peaceful—communing with the clay as I had been asked to do. I had somehow managed simply *to be*.

When Esperanza signaled that time was up, I opened my eyes. To my surprise, my lump of clay had taken a shape—broad at its base, tapered toward the top, with a knob at its apex. Even more surprising, I recognized the figure of a woman. When it came my turn to share, I reported, "This is a woman emerging." Inexplicably overcome with emotion, I explained through sobs, with ragged breath, that the woman was emerging from shapeless matter, not yet formed but becoming something new, becoming someone whose form was yet to be discovered. The woman was me.

For years I kept *Woman Emerging* in my living space. She signaled to me that I was living in a cauldron of growth and transformation. When I gazed on her, I felt a mystical knowing.

On the day I sculpted *Woman Emerging* I had just lived through two months of tumult—student revolt, racial challenges, and expectations for classroom practices that were completely foreign to me. *Woman Emerging* revealed my intuitive knowing that this tumult would propel me into something new. Looking back, I now know that on that Friday morning in October 1993, I was beginning a three-year experience of profound transformation—in my understanding and actions related to racism, to whiteness and systemic privilege, and to all my epistemological assumptions and pedagogical practices related to how adults learn.

Note: *Elizabeth's story originally appeared in European American Collaborative Challenging Whiteness (2003), where it is conveyed using the pseudonym "Victoria."*

THE RELATIONSHIP OF HOLISTIC EPISTEMOLOGY TO TRANSFORMATIVE LEARNING

The term "learning" can refer to changes in many different dimensions—factual knowledge, meaning perspectives brought to bear on events and encounters, skills and competencies and the ability to take action, self-awareness and emotional discernment. The term "transformative," like "learning," is also used in various ways. We perceive transformative learning as authentic, enduring change in a person's affective, cognitive, and practical being. In short, it includes, but is broader than, a change in cognitive habit of mind. Rather, it is change in *habit of being*—a holistic relationship to one's world experienced through coherence among one's multiple ways of knowing (Yorks & Kasl, 2002).

Heron's theory of personhood (Heron, 1992) provides an epistemological frame for understanding transformative change in habit of being. Based on a phenomenological empiricism of "pristine acquaintance with phenomena unadulterated by preconceptions" (Heron & Reason, 1997, p. 276), the theory grounds human knowing in deeply contemplated lived experience.

A comprehensive discussion of Heron's complex theory is beyond the scope of this chapter. We limit our discussion to a summary of core concepts that relate directly to how presentational knowing facilitates transformative learning. (In Chapter 13, Peter Willis [2011] applies Heron's theory to a different objective—understanding transformative learning as an existential process.)

MODES OF PSYCHE AND WAYS OF KNOWING

Heron distinguishes between modes of psyche and ways of knowing. "Psyche" is "a convenient generic term to use when talking about some of the basic

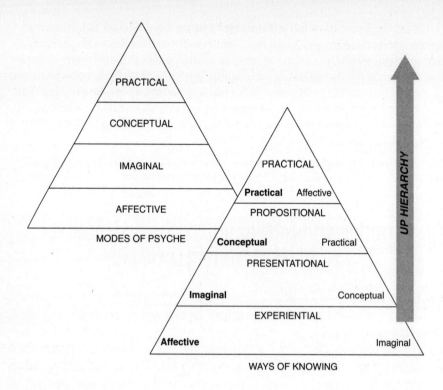

Figure 31.1 Modes of Psyche and Ways of Knowing

Note. Dominant parents are on the left in bold.
Source: Adapted from *Feeling and Personhood* (Heron, 1992), Figure 2.2 (p. 20) and Figure 8.3 (p. 174).

structures and dynamics of the human mind" (1992, p. 14). Heron posits four interdependent modes of psyche—affective, imaginal, conceptual, and practical. Figure 31.1 depicts these modes of psyche in the pyramid on the left.

The pyramid on the right in Figure 31.1 names four ways of knowing—experiential, presentational, propositional, and practical. These ways of knowing produce an *extended epistemology* (Heron & Reason, 1997, 2008); that is, "a radical epistemology . . . *extended* beyond the ways of knowing of positivist oriented academia" (2008, p. 367). The ways of knowing pyramid also shows the modes of psyche that function as "parents" to each way of knowing, with the more influential parent depicted in boldface on the left.

The base of all knowing is *experiential*, which is parented by the affective mode of the psyche, with additional support from the imaginal. Derived from direct encounters with phenomena, experiential knowing is prelinguistic, tacit, and often subconscious. It is the location of emotions, empathy, and felt resonance with presences both human and beyond human. The second way of knowing is *presentational*, an intuitive grasp of significant patterns in lived experience. This form of knowing manifests from interaction between imaginal and conceptual modes of psyche, with the imaginal being dominant. Next comes *propositional* knowing, the traditional realm for educational practice, parented by conceptual and practical modes of psyche. Propositional knowing is expressed in intellectual statements that conform to rules of logic and evidence. At the pinnacle, *practical* knowing depends on interaction between practical and affective modes of psyche and manifests as the ability to exercise some skill or behavior.

COHERENCE, CRITICAL SUBJECTIVITY, AND TRANSFORMATIVE LEARNING

Individual ways of knowing relate to each other in an "up-hierarchy," meaning that each draws from and is dependent on those beneath it. Although each way of knowing has its individual canon of validity, overall validity in a person's knowing requires coherence among the four ways of knowing (Heron, 1992; Heron & Reason, 1997). People monitor coherence by developing their capacity for critical subjectivity, which is "an awareness of the four ways of knowing, of how they are currently interacting, and of ways of changing the relations between them so that they articulate a reality that is unclouded by a restrictive and ill-disciplined subjectivity" (Heron & Reason, 1997, p. 280).

The ultimate goal of critical subjectivity is validity.

We suggest that coherence relates directly to transformative learning, which we define as *a holistic and enduring change in how a person affectively experiences and conceptually frames his or her experience of the world in order to apply new actions in life contexts that are personally developmental, socially controversial, or require personal or social healing.*

Coherence is a critical enabler for both the *holistic* and the *enduring* dimensions of transformative learning. *Holistic* knowing is governed by the up-hierarchy; that is, it is grounded authentically in felt experience that has been brought to consciousness and examined critically. The popular wry expression, "Do as I say and not as I do," points out how often people's espoused beliefs or values do not match their actions. This mismatch between propositional and practical knowing signals the need for what Heron and Reason describe as critical subjectivity; that is, an awareness of all four ways of knowing so that they can be brought into a coherent whole. Holistic knowing, in turn, becomes the guarantor of sustainability—change in one's habit of being that is *enduring*. When new thinking or behavior has not arisen authentically from emotional and tacit knowing, the new thinking and behavior typically do not endure. One falls back to old patterns of thinking and behavior because these old ways cohere with experiential knowing that has remained unexamined and unchanged.

IMPORTANCE OF PRESENTATIONAL KNOWING FOR HOLISTIC EPISTEMOLOGY

Presentational knowing is a powerful facilitator of holism because it can bring experiential knowing into conscious awareness, thus making it more accessible as a base for new ideas and actions. In presentational knowing, a person interprets felt experience by creating "a pattern of perceptual elements—in movement, sound, colour, shape, line" (Heron, 1992, p. 165). We gain access to our presentational knowing through a variety of discursive and nondiscursive expressive forms, such as poetry, metaphor, story, music, dance, and visual or dramatic arts.

When we linger in the imaginal space of presentational knowing, we stay open to multiple interpretations of our experience and protected from premature conceptualization that constrains and restricts meaning. Heron and Reason (2008) explain their practices:

> We will not rush quickly into propositions, but will hold open the presentational and imaginal space and allow it to do its sense-making magic, allowing our stories to resonate with other group members.... We can draw the stories, sculpt them in clay or psychodramatically with our bodies—thus countering our tendency to attribute one set of meanings to experience. (p. 372)

By its nature, presentational knowing slows our pace in making meaning, giving us time to resonate fully with our phenomenological world.

In assessing validity of presentational knowing, one considers the relative influence from modes of psyche that parent it. The more influential parent should be the imaginal mode. Heron (1992) warns, "While the conceptual mode bestows great freedom for the human manipulation of meaning, it is beset by its tendency to set up the subject-object split" (p. 143). This tendency will obstruct the imaginal process and, by extension, the validity of one's presentational knowledge. Returning to the expression in Michelle Wang's poem, which opened this chapter, thinking can destroy the beauty of feeling.

Positioned as it is in the up-hierarchy, presentational knowing links felt experience with conceptualizations drawn from that experience. It provides a bridging pathway that facilitates coherence between our lived experience and our thoughts and actions. It can also signal incoherence—thus the need for contemplation, critical subjectivity, and critical reflection.

Elizabeth's experience with presentational knowing demonstrates how epistemological coherence is achieved. On the October morning when she sculpts *Woman Emerging*, she is just beginning an extended experience that leads toward transformative learning. Elsewhere, her learning is described as a three-year journey in which she is bombarded constantly with disorienting challenges about race, whiteness, privilege, and pedagogical practices (European American Collaborative Challenging Whiteness, 2003). On that October morning, there is no coherence among the four ways of knowing that relate to her phenomenological world. *Emerging Woman* presents an intuitive shaping of her tumultuous experiences, but her grasp is intuitive, not yet translated into conceptual understanding. Her experiential or presentational knowing does not yet cohere with her propositional or practical knowing. As the years pass, she gradually makes conceptual sense of her experiences and mysterious intuitions. With emerging epistemological coherence, she constructs new conceptual frames that guide new actions.

HOW PRESENTATIONAL KNOWING CONTRIBUTES TO LEARNING IN HUMAN SYSTEMS

Presentational knowing influences individual meaning-making as well as the meaning space between and among individuals.

Presentational Knowing Within the Individual

In an earlier work (Yorks & Kasl, 2006), we categorized pedagogical purposes served by presentational knowing. Based on analysis of eleven case studies and seven interviews with experienced practitioners, our taxonomy identifies three ways in which presentational knowing contributes to an individual's learning.

Presentational Knowing Evokes Experience. First, presentational knowing can be used to evoke an experience in order to facilitate deeper understanding. For example, one might use presentational knowing to reexperience racial conflict—perhaps through psychodrama, a body sculpting exercise, or a collaboratively painted mural. Having deliberately evoked a direct encounter with the experience of racial conflict, learners can discern patterns revealed by their intuitive and imaginal expressions.

When Elizabeth sculpts *Woman Emerging*, her experience evokes an unfamiliar way of knowing. Elizabeth was deeply skeptical about Esperanza's assertion that the clay would speak to her, that she could find wisdom in the clay. However, she made a good-faith effort to do as Esperanza requested. By working the clay without thinking about it, Elizabeth had a direct encounter with an epistemology vastly different from her usual way of knowing. This encounter would eventually blossom into new cognitive frames and changed behavior that transformed her teaching practices.

Presentational Knowing Promotes Self-Awareness. In her analysis of six projects that use artistic ways of knowing, Randee Lipson Lawrence (2005) identifies five overarching themes. One of these is "Awareness of Self." This theme is similar to an element from our taxonomy, in which we observe that presentational knowing "Brings Feeling and Emotion into Consciousness."

This function of presentational knowing may be the most commonly understood. Individual reports abound, covering such varying topics as these:

- Becoming aware of how internalized oppression damages personal capacity for action (Johns, 2008; Rosenwasser, 2002)
- Recognizing that one's fragmented behavior in the workplace is personally debilitating (Van Stralen, 2002; McArdle, 2004)
- Learning how one's personal style can make conversations feel unsafe to others (Roberson, 2002)
- Changing self-image as a person with mental illness (Noble, 2005)
- Embracing active responsibility for personal health and well-being (Mullett, 2008)

When Elizabeth sculpts *Woman Emerging*, she is living in turmoil—buffeted by discovering how ignorant she is about white privilege and challenged by pedagogical practices that she knows nothing about. She feels very alone, without support from other faculty. Summing up her situation several years later, she observes, "Everything I thought I knew just didn't apply" (European American Collaborative Challenging Whiteness, 2003, p. 165).

Elizabeth's first look at *Woman Emerging* changes her self-awareness. She recognizes that this bit of clay suggests meaning in what she has been experiencing as chaos and confusion. When she is inexplicably overcome by wrenching sobs, she becomes consciously aware that efforts to negotiate her new experiences have left her emotionally fragile.

Presentational Knowing *Codifies Experience*. Presentational knowing is accessed through expressive form, such as music, mime, movement, visual or dramatic art, story, metaphor, poetry. The learner can relive moments of intuitive insight by engaging with the product created during the expressive activity—singing a song, reciting a poem, gazing at a drawing. Elizabeth tells us that she placed *Woman Emerging* in her living space and kept the sculpture there for years. "She signaled to me that I was living in a cauldron of growth and transformation. When I gazed on her, I felt a mystical knowing."

Presentational Knowing Between Individuals

Presentational knowing is an important catalyst for transformative learning because of its power to enhance understanding between and among individuals.
In Chapter 29 of this Handbook, for example, Lawrence (2012) describes how
the arts can serve as an entry point into difficult conversations by creating a
sense of human connection.

The possibilities for transformative learning are enhanced when people learn
from one another, but limited by what we call the *paradox of diversity* (Yorks
& Kasl, 2002). Diversity among people increases the potential for transformative learning because differences in meaning perspectives provide challenges to
taken-for-granted worldviews. However, as diversity increases, the likelihood
of transformative learning decreases. People have too much difficulty understanding the meaning perspectives generated by each other's diverse life worlds
for the potential benefit of those differences to be realized.

By communicating their lived experience through presentational knowing,
diverse persons can overcome the paradox of diversity. To learn meaningfully
with and from each other, people must be able to understand each other in
the fullness of the other's lived experience. But direct experience is a nonlin-
guistic phenomenon that is not easily shared. Presentational knowing has the
greatest potential for communicating the lived quality of experience because it
is adjacent to experiential knowing in the epistemological up-hierarchy. Thus
presentational knowing creates fertile ground in which to nurture an empathic
field that enables people to learn from one another within relationship.

When Elizabeth describes *Woman Emerging* to the students, she reveals
herself as someone deeply affected by the challenges she has been confronting
and also as someone open to new learning. Later, when pressed by a white colleague to explain why the students of color in this cohort trusted her, Elizabeth
observes, "They did, didn't they?" Reflecting on the quality of relationship she
developed with these students, she muses, "It wouldn't surprise me to learn
that they got together and caucused about it, and decided, 'This person is worth
our effort, . . . she's teachable'" (European American Collaborative Challenging
Whiteness, 2003, p. 164).

Presentational Knowing in Communities and Organizations

The dynamics that govern learning within interpersonal relationship can be
extended to larger groups, helping us understand the conditions within communities or organizations that are conducive to whole-systems learning. In their
analyses of multiple case studies that demonstrate how the arts are used to foster large-system change, Lawrence (2005) and Hayes and Yorks (2007) identify
ways in which presentational knowing leads to community building and collective action. We synthesize their discussions, along with our analysis of other

examples, into three functions of presentational knowing: signaling culture of learning, community building across diversity, and developing community will for action.

Signaling Culture of Learning. Opening the group to possibilities for new learning can be achieved with presentational knowing. In his guide for facilitators, Heron (1999) suggests leaving something unexpected and unexplained in the room, such as a stuffed toy or a puzzle box. This simple gesture sends a signal that learners should be open to the unexpected. Suzanne Van Stralen (2002) needed to help nurse managers disengage from the frenetic pace of hospital duties so they could be attentive to their thoughts and feelings. She opened each inquiry meeting with a visualization that guided participants over a bridge into a peaceful pastoral refuge. Heron and Reason (2008) describe a learning project in which doctors rearranged their offices and dressed informally to signal to patients that the doctor perceived them as whole persons, not as a set of symptoms. Adult education practitioners have long understood the symbolic power of circles, communicating their assumptions about authority and participation each time they rearrange chairs that had been set in rows facing forward.

Community Building Across Diversity. Actively engaging members of a community in presentational knowing can create a social space for conversations about the community's place within society and unify a community by bridging diversity of race, gender, and age (Armstrong, 2005; Scher, 2007).

Arnold Aprill and Richard Townsell (2007) describe a planning meeting for the Lawndale section of Chicago in which community members create mural that helps them find mutual vision. Two hundred participants self-selected into teams by areas of interest (affordable housing; arts, recreation, and culture; economic development and jobs; education; health and safety; and youth development). Participants brainstormed images to represent their hopes for their communities, developed these images by drawing and cutting out simple representations, and then arranged the cutouts into patterns to form a mural. Each team collectively reflected on the patterns and presented resulting themes to the entire group. The organizers realized that the process helped build relationships across cultural and social barriers that had traditionally fragmented the community.

Their experience parallels Lawrence's observation that, used as a participatory activity, artistic ways of knowing can be a catalyst for dialogue that builds group identity and solidarity. Kwayera Archer-Cunningham (2007) makes a similar point in describing how she uses different artistic forms to help members of the African Diaspora achieve experiential and philosophical cohesion. Cohorts in adult learning programs often (but not always) experience a similar collective awareness (Leahy & Gilly, 2009). Although Elizabeth's story focuses on her personal transformative journey, we note that it was taking place within a community that increasingly fashioned collective awareness.

Developing Community Will for Action. Beyond building group identity and solidarity, presentational knowing that manifests through community artistic engagement can be a precursor to activism (Hayes & Yorks, 2007). This is intensely experienced in the Theatre of the Oppressed, where people are encouraged to reflect on their oppression (Picher, 2007). Abby Scher (2007) describes how community organizers' stories bring to light ways they can relate more effectively to the communities they serve.

THE BRIDGING PATHWAYS PROVIDED BY PRESENTATIONAL KNOWING

Figure 31.2 provides a visual summary of our discussion about how presentational knowing contributes to transformative learning by forging two important pathways—a pathway for human connection and a pathway to epistemological coherence.

Human connection is aided by presentational knowing. By enhancing the capacity to communicate the quality of one person's lived experience to another, presentational knowing provides a pathway to an empathic field. When lived experience is very different because of ethnic, racial, gender, or other significant divisions, it is challenging to "try on" the other's point of view, as Mezirow (2000, p. 20) advocates. Presentational knowing helps people gain access to each other's phenomenological worlds. Empathic connection can extend to a large group or community, creating a sense of group identity and solidarity.

Epistemological coherence is aided by the presentational knowing pathway between experiential and propositional knowing at three levels—intrapersonal, interpersonal, and collective. The first column in Figure 31.2 describes how experiential knowing manifests as a state of being at each of these levels. At the intrapersonal level—that is, within the individual—experiential knowing provides the location of emotions, empathy, and felt resonance with presences both human and beyond human. At the interpersonal level, or between individuals, experiential knowing is a state of being we describe as an empathic field. At the collective level of groups, organizations, or communities, experiential knowing is the group's felt identity. The second column in Figure 31.2 names practices used by different levels of human systems to create frames of reference that are adopted by that system as its propositional knowing.

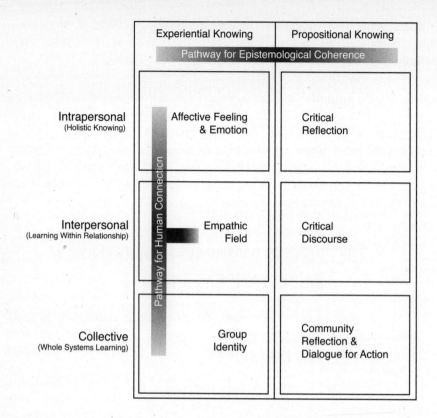

Figure 31.2 Presentational Knowing as Pathways for Connection and Coherence

Experiential knowing comes from *being in* the world; propositional knowing involves *reflecting on* the world. Presentational knowing is a pathway between these two epistemological stances; by bringing experiential knowing into conscious awareness, presentational knowing enables the system to reflect with greater clarity and forge coherence among feelings, thoughts, and actions.

COHERENCE AMONG WAYS OF KNOWING AND TRANSFORMATIVE LEARNING

The will to sustain new ways of thinking and acting resides not so much in the compelling logic of our new cognitive frames as in our emotions, felt resonances, and intuitions. Coherence among our many ways of knowing is the guardian of sustainability and transformation—especially in the face of discomfort.

Transformation as sustainable change is whimsically captured in the movie *Pleasantville*, with an exchange between George and his son Bud, who is in jail for actions flowing from his transformation:

GEORGE (EXPERIENCING HIS OWN DISORIENTING DILEMMA): One minute
> everything's fine, the next... what went wrong?

BUD: Nothing went wrong. People change.

GEORGE: People change?

BUD: Yeah, people change.

GEORGE: Can they change back?

BUD: I don't know. I think it's harder.

References

Aprill, A., & Townsell, R. (2007). The arts as an occasion for collective adult learning as authentic community development. In S. Hayes & L. Yorks (Eds.), *Arts and societal learning: Transforming communities, socially, politically, and culturally* (pp. 51–63). New Directions for Adult Education and Continuing Education, no. 116. San Francisco: Jossey-Bass.

Archer-Cunningham, K. (2007). Cultural arts education as community development: An innovative model of healing and transformation. In S. Hayes & L. Yorks (Eds.), *Arts and societal learning: Transforming communities, socially, politically, and culturally* (pp. 25–36). New Directions for Adult Education and Continuing Education, no. 116. San Francisco: Jossey-Bass.

Armstrong, K. B. (2005). Autophotography in adult education: Building creative communities for social justice and democratic education. In R. L. Lawrence (Ed.), *Artistic ways of knowing: Expanded opportunities for teaching and learning* (pp. 33–44). New Directions for Adult Education and Continuing Education, no. 107. San Francisco: Jossey-Bass.

European American Collaborative Challenging Whiteness. (2003). I'm not a social activist; I'm just a teacher. In C. A. Wiessner, S. Meyer, N. Pfhal, & P. Neaman (Eds.), *Transformative learning in action. Proceedings of the Fifth International Conference on Transformative Learning* (pp. 162–167). New York: Teachers College, Columbia University.

Hayes, S., & Yorks, L. (2007). Lessons from the lessons learned: Arts change the world when... In S. Hayes & L. Yorks (Eds.), *Arts and societal learning: Transforming communities, socially, politically, and culturally* (pp. 89–98). New Directions for Adult Education and Continuing Education, no. 116. San Francisco: Jossey-Bass.

Heron, J. (1992). *Feeling and personhood: Psychology in another key.* Thousand Oaks, CA: SAGE.

Heron, J. (1999). *The complete facilitator's handbook.* London: Kogan Page.

Heron, J., & Reason, P. (1997). A participatory inquiry paradigm. *Qualitative Inquiry, 3*(3), 274–294.

Heron, J., & Reason, P. (2008). Extending epistemology within a co-operative inquiry. In P. Reason & H. Bradbury (Eds.), *The SAGE handbook of action research* (2nd ed.) (pp. 366–380). Thousand Oaks, CA: SAGE.

Johns, T. (2008). Learning to love our black selves: Healing from internalized oppressions. In P. Reason & H. Bradbury (Eds.), *The SAGE handbook of action research* (2nd ed.) (pp. 473–486). Thousand Oaks, CA: SAGE.

Lawrence, R. L. (2005). Tying themes and threads together. In R. L. Lawrence (Ed.), *Artistic ways of knowing: Expanded opportunities for teaching and learning* (pp. 75–81). New Directions for Adult and Continuing Education, no. 107. San Francisco: Jossey-Bass.

Lawrence, R. L. (2012). Out of our heads: Transformative learning through artistic expression. In E. W. Taylor & P. Cranton (Eds.), *Handbook of transformative learning: Theory, research, and practice* (pp. 471–485). San Francisco: Jossey-Bass.

Leahy, M. J., & Gilly, M. S. (2009). Learning in the space between us. In B. Fisher-Yoshida, K. D. Geller, & S. Schapiro (Eds.), *Innovations in transformative learning: Space, culture, and the arts* (pp. 23–42). New York: Peter Lang.

McArdle, K. (2004). *In-powering spaces: A co-operative inquiry with young women in management.* Unpublished doctoral dissertation, School of Management, University of Bath, Bath, UK.

Mezirow, J. (1991). *Transformative dimensions of adult learning.* San Francisco: Jossey-Bass.

Mezirow, J. (2000). Learning to think like an adult. In J. Mezirow & Associates (Eds.), *Learning as transformation: Critical perspectives on a theory in process* (pp. 3–33). San Francisco: Jossey-Bass.

Mullett, J. (2008). Presentational knowing: Bridging experience and expression with art, poetry and song. In P. Reason & H. Bradbury (Eds.), *The SAGE handbook of action research* (2nd ed.) (pp. 450–462). Thousand Oaks, CA: SAGE.

Noble, S. E. (2005). Mental illness through popular theater: Performing (in)sanely. In R. L. Lawrence (Ed.), *Artistic ways of knowing: Expanded opportunities for teaching and learning* (pp. 45–53). New Directions for Adult Education and Continuing Education, no. 107. San Francisco: Jossey-Bass.

Picher, M. (2007). Democratic process and the theater of the oppressed. In S. Hayes & L. Yorks (Eds.), *Arts and societal learning: Transforming communities, socially, politically, and culturally* (pp. 79–88). New Directions for Adult Education and Continuing Education, no. 116. San Francisco: Jossey-Bass.

Roberson, W. (2002). Midwife to a learning community: Spirit as co-inquirer. In L. Yorks & E. Kasl (Eds.), *Collaborative inquiry as a strategy for adult learning: Creating space for generative learning* (pp. 43–52). New Directions for Adult and Continuing Education, no. 94. San Francisco: Jossey-Bass.

Rosenwasser, P. (2002). Exploring internalized oppression and healing strategies. In
L. Yorks & E. Kasl (Eds.), *Collaborative inquiry as a strategy for adult learning:
Creating space for generative learning* (pp. 53–61). New Directions for Adult and
Continuing Education, no. 94. San Francisco: Jossey-Bass.

Scher, A. (2007). Can the arts change the world? The transformative power of
community arts. In S. Hayes & L. Yorks (Eds.), *Arts and societal learning:
Transforming communities, socially, politically, and culturally* (pp. 3–11). New
Directions for Adult Education and Continuing Education, no. 116. San Francisco:
Jossey-Bass.

Taylor, E. W. (1998). *Theory and practice of transformative learning: A critical review.
Information Series No. 374.* Columbus, OH: ERIC Clearing House on Adult, Career,
and Vocational Education.

Van Stralen, S. (2002). Making sense of one's experience in the workplace. In L. Yorks
& E. Kasl (Eds.), *Collaborative inquiry as a strategy for adult learning: Creating
space for generative learning* (pp. 13–21). New Directions for Adult and Continuing
Education, no. 94. San Francisco: Jossey-Bass.

Willis, P. (2012). An existential and narrative approach to transformative learning. In
E. W. Taylor & P. Cranton (Eds.), *Handbook of transformative learning: Theory,
research, and practice.* San Francisco: Jossey-Bass.

Yorks, L., & Kasl, E. (2002). Toward a theory and practice for whole-person learning:
Reconceptualizing experience and the role of affect. *Adult Education Quarterly,
52*(3), 176–192.

Yorks, L., & Kasl, E. (2006). I know more than I can say: A taxonomy for utilizing
expressive ways of knowing to foster transformative learning. *Journal of
Transformative Education, 4*(1), 1–22.

CHAPTER THIRTY-TWO

Evaluating Transformative Learning

Patricia Cranton and Chad Hoggan

Whether in research or in teaching, how do we know when transformative learning has occurred? Are there degrees of quality of transformative learning, as we assume there to be for other kinds of learning? The researcher who describes an "increase in self-confidence" as transformative and the teacher who labels a change in a student's theoretical perspective as transformative are basing their judgments on their own notions of what transformative learning is, and herein lies a challenge. As can be seen throughout this Handbook, there are many diverse conceptualizations of transformative learning.

In this chapter, we first provide an overview of evaluation strategies based on types of knowledge. We then review the holistic approach to transformative learning that informs our discussion of evaluation strategies. We look in detail at evaluation strategies that are relevant to transformative learning, and then examine some contexts in which evaluation takes place. We conclude with a discussion of the significance to theory, practice, and research.

KINDS OF KNOWLEDGE AND EVALUATION STRATEGIES

Mezirow (1991) draws on Habermas's (1971) kinds of knowledge (communicative, instrumental, emancipatory) as a foundation for transformative learning theory. Because the kind of knowledge we are interested in evaluating determines, at least to some extent, the evaluation strategy we use, this can form a starting point for aligning theoretical perspectives on transformative learning theory and evaluation strategies.

Instrumental knowledge is that which allows us to manipulate and control the environment, predict observable physical and social events, and take appropriate actions. Instrumental knowledge is acquired through empirical, scientific research. In this paradigm, there is an objective world made up of observable phenomena (Ewert, 1991). The product or the process of the learning can be evaluated by someone who has expertise with the task at hand using objectively scored evaluation. Gillis and Griffin (2008) discuss how this kind of evaluation is used in adult education and training.

Communicative knowledge is based on our need to understand each other through language. In order for people to survive together in groups and societies, they must communicate with and understand each other. There are no scientific laws governing these communications—when we communicate with others, we interpret what they say in our own way (Ewert, 1991). This does not mean that communicative knowledge is necessarily individualistic. All societies share and transmit social knowledge; that is, a code of commonly accepted beliefs and behavior. Subjectively rated evaluation of learning comes into play here. Someone who is presumed to have the necessarily expertise judges the quality of communicative knowledge.

The third kind of knowledge, which is derived from a questioning of instrumental and communicative knowledge, Habermas calls *emancipatory*. By nature, people are interested in self-knowledge, growth, development, and freedom. Gaining emancipatory knowledge is dependent on our abilities to be self-determining and self-reflective. Self-determination can be described as the capacity both to be aware and critical of ourselves and of our social and cultural context. Self-reflection involves being aware and critical of our subjective perceptions of knowledge and of the constraints of social knowledge. Emancipatory knowledge comes from a process of critically questioning ourselves and the social systems in which we live (Ewert, 1991).

Emancipatory knowledge occurs in relation to individuals and social change. Individuals become free from the constraints of uncritically assimilated assumptions about their abilities and characteristics. On a social scale, human beings are oppressed by poverty, class, gender, race, ethnicity, and sexual orientation, and often by the intersection of several of these. People are also oppressed by government regimes, war, corporations, capitalism, and media images and messages. When people become aware of their oppression and individually and collectively challenge the social oppression, this is emancipatory learning. Evaluation of emancipatory learning must involve the learners through self-evaluation, collaboration, and dialogue. Evaluation is an appropriate strategy for emancipatory learning.

HOLISTIC APPROACH TO TRANSFORMATIVE LEARNING

Transformative learning is a deep shift in perspective during which habits of mind become more open, more permeable, and better justified (Mezirow, 2000). According to Mezirow, the process centers on critical reflection and critical self-reflection, but other theorists (for example, Dirkx, 2001, 2006) place imagination, intuition, and emotion at the heart of transformation. According to Taylor (2008), the views that focus on the individual are psychological in nature, whereas the sociocultural perspectives are about social change and take into account positionality in regards to race, gender, sexual orientation, and class. Gunnlaugson (2008) describes "first wave" and "second wave" theories of transformative learning—the first wave being those works that build on, critique, or depart from Mezirow's seminal work, and the second wave being those authors who work toward integrative, holistic, and integral perspectives. He hopes for a complex coexistence and integration of theoretical perspectives through the second wave theorists' work. It is within this inclusive, integrated view that we place our discussion of the evaluation of transformative learning.

THEORETICAL PERSPECTIVES AND EVALUATION STRATEGIES

Given the kinds of learning and evaluation strategies outlined previously and the integrative perspective just described, we next explore how transformative learning perspectives may align with evaluation strategies.

Individual transformative learning is generally psychological in nature, according to Taylor (2008), and it reflects a universal view of learning rather than a contextually or socially bound understanding. When the learning is cognitive and rational in its content (in the epistemic domain, for example), then one could assess it via one or more objectively scored methods (Gillis & Griffin, 2008). Learners could be asked to respond to a series of statements in the form of a checklist or rating scale. From the perspective of the learner, these are statements that require subjective judgment, but from the perspective of the educator, no interpretation is required.

Depending on the context, transformative learning could also be evaluated based on observations of individuals' actions and behaviors in a subjectively rated process. If someone who previously showed little tolerance of diversity, for example, now demonstrates inclusive behaviors, it could be concluded that a shift in perspective has occurred for that person. In the realm of psychodevelopmental transformative learning, Kegan's (Lahey, Souvaine, Kegan, Goodman, & Felix, 1988) system for evaluation of the phases of development through the Subject-Object Interview provides added structure.

Mezirow (1991) cautions us that transformative learning outcomes cannot be specified in advance of the educational experience, and he focuses instead on the process itself. That is, we can evaluate "changes in reflection" and the "quality of the reflection" (p. 220). He also suggests that evidence of change can focus on a growth in decontextualization and proposes that hypothetical dilemmas could be used to assess this. Focusing on the process also opens up a variety of other possible subjectively interpreted evaluation strategies, including interviews, narratives, and journals.

Learner self-evaluation is relevant for all types of individual transformation, but it is dependent on the person having not only a highly developed sense of self-awareness but also a clear understanding of what transformative learning is and what it is not. As Newman (2012) points out, it may be the case that all learning becomes viewed as transformative, and this may be exacerbated when individuals assess their experience with transformation.

In sociocultural transformative learning, people engage with the transformation of their world so that it can become a more just and equitable place to live. There is no neutrality or objectivity: teaching for sociocultural transformation is a political act. Brookfield (2005) describes four methodological approaches for this type of teaching: teaching a structuralized worldview (viewing individual experiences in terms of social and economic forces); using abstract and conceptual reasoning (considering the broad questions of how society can become equitable and fair); becoming separated or detached from cultural givens (enabling a critical view of society); and emphasizing and practicing dialogic discussion (actively promoting inclusive and critical conversation). The outcomes of this practice cannot be evaluated in a straightforward manner. We need to go back to Mezirow's (1991) suggestion that we can evaluate only the *process* of transformative learning, not the *product*. Do learners view experience in terms of social and economic forces? Do people take a critical view of society? Can participants engage in inclusive and critical conversation? It is not *what* they do or say, but *how* it is done or said that gives an indicator of transformative learning. Self-report (including journals or other forms of writing) and self-evaluation are appropriate. Also, interviews, narratives, and some arts-based techniques have the potential to assess the process of sociocultural transformative learning. In the next section, we describe in practical detail the evaluation methods relevant to assessing transformative learning.

EVALUATION METHODS RELEVANT TO TRANSFORMATIVE LEARNING

Little has been written about methods for evaluating transformative learning in educational environments. In this section, we draw on techniques used in research as well as in teaching.

Self-Evaluation

Self-evaluation is especially congruent with the philosophical foundations of emancipatory learning that have influenced the theory of transformative learning. In this method, learners evaluate themselves based on guidelines and criteria established by either the learners or the educator or both (Ross, Rolheiser, & Hogaboam-Gray, 1998). These guidelines can focus on the process of reflection, or they can offer an opportunity for learners to describe their transformative experience in innovative ways.

The basis for such an approach often stems from the educator's goal of helping "adults realize their potential for becoming more liberated, socially responsible, and autonomous learners" (Mezirow, 1990) by transferring their authority over the learning group and becoming collaborative learners. It is contradictory for an educator to hold such a goal and simultaneously to retain authority over students by assessing the extent to which they have adequately transformed their perspectives.

Interviews

Interviews are frequently used for evaluating transformative learning. Interviews can focus on the learner's story of a particular experience to gain insight into the processes or outcomes of the learning, as well as to track learners' perspective changes or developmental progression over time (Drago-Severson, 2004).

In a multisite study of adult basic education (ABE) and English for speakers of other languages (ESOL) programs, Drago-Severson and a team of researchers used semistructured, qualitative interviews as an integral part of their data collection methods. The interviews focused on the learners' experiences within the learning programs, and, among other things, were used to assess the developmental level of the learners, according to Kegan's (2000) model, as well as their progression along that model throughout their time in the program.

Narratives

Narratives are learning practices that encompass a wide variety of specific techniques, including learning journals, concept-focused autobiographical writing, and case studies (Clark & Rossiter, 2008). The common thread among these techniques is that learners articulate their stories or the ways that they organize storylines to make sense of themselves and their experiences.

Dominicé (2000), for instance, uses educational autobiographies as a form of narrative to help learners evaluate the ways in which they have come to understand their educational experiences and themselves as learners. In his approach, narratives are used to help learners become aware of the ways that they have crafted a storyline about themselves as learners, thus opening possibilities to critique their narrative habits and envision new storylines by which to understand themselves and their experiences.

Observations

Observable behavior can be used to evaluate transformative learning. This method is often more appropriate when changes in behavior, or at least the ability to document changes in behavior, is considered important. For instance, O'Neil and Marsick (2007) used observations to evaluate individual change and development in a workplace training program.

Participants in the program were observed in the course of their daily workplace routines by someone else in a position to personally see those activities. Evaluators used a critical incident form to structure the written descriptions of behavior in respect to its effectiveness for the particular activity, which related to the goals of the learning program. When used to evaluate transformative learning, O'Neil and Marsick (2007) caution that "not just any behavior occurring in the course of the activity is considered critical, only behavior where the purpose or intent of the act seems fairly clear and where its consequences are sufficiently defined to leave little doubt concerning its effect" (p. 132).

Surveys

Surveys are questionnaires designed to elicit learners' perceptions. Gatt (2009), for instance, used surveys in a three-year program designed to help teachers incorporate drama as a pedagogy in low socioeconomic schools in Malta. Surveys administered at the beginning of the program revealed insights into teachers' self-efficacy regarding the use of drama as a teaching technique. Over the course of the program, the surveys, combined with informal interviews, revealed areas in which the teachers' perceptions of themselves and their students had changed over time.

Surveys allow the evaluator to gain insights into learners' perceptions across time so as to be able to evaluate changes. Although this method is limited in the depth of information it is able to yield, it is nevertheless able to give indications of change that can be explored more thoroughly through other methods, and can accommodate large numbers of evaluations very quickly.

Checklists

Checklists comprise a written list of observable behaviors or characteristics that can be used by an educator or a learner to determine whether transformative learning has occurred. Whether the purpose is for the learner to better understand their learning experience or for the evaluator to be able to assess the learner's experience, checklists provide a tangible guideline.

King (1998, 2004) created a checklist that provides statements describing different stages of perspective transformation based on Mezirow's work. She includes free-response questions that invite respondents to choose and describe learning experiences. The evaluator then assesses the degree to which the respondent's descriptions align with the established checklist of the definition and stages of transformative learning.

Journals

Journals can take many forms, including life histories; imagined dialogues between the learner and someone else; real dialogues among multiple learners; a collection of metaphors, dreams, and images; or a life-study journal of the learner from the perspective of someone else (Progoff, 1992). Cranton (2006) cautions that educators should be sensitive to learners' privacy and to the ways in which reading their journals can be a manifestation of disciplinary power or an inducement for learners to simply write what they think the educator wants to see. She suggests some alternatives to the educator's reading journals: students could create a summary of their journal; they could work in pairs to write a dialogue back and forth; or they could use their journals as a basis of self-evaluation.

Metaphor Analysis

Metaphor theory asserts that metaphors are not simply poetic ways to express ideas; they actually represent maps that people use to understand concepts. Ubiquitous and culturally specific, metaphors use one concept to describe, relate to, and make generalizations about another concept (Lakoff, 1993). Metaphor analysis is the process of recognizing, "unpacking," and critiquing the metaphors we tacitly use to understand ourselves and our world (Deshler, 1990b).

Deshler (1990b) proposes a method for metaphor analysis by which learners select some topic and scan their memories associated with that topic in order to recognize the various metaphors that arise. They then articulate the meanings of that metaphor in relation to the topic, and reflect on and critique the embedded values, beliefs, and assumptions. Learners are encouraged to create new metaphors that express the meanings of that topic that they want to emphasize and to consider the "implications for action" of the new metaphor (p. 300). Metaphor analysis is useful in evaluating transformative learning by documenting the processes of critical reflection (Hoggan, Simpson, & Stuckey, 2009).

Conceptual Mapping

Concept maps are graphical representations of concepts, depicted as a framework of propositions (Novak & Gowin, 1984). Similar to flow charts or organizational charts in their holistic, spatial, and hierarchical representation of relationships, concept maps are used to depict essential concepts related to a topic or theme (Deshler, 1990a). Deshler (1990a) talks about conceptual mapping in transformative learning as a means to evaluate "the cognitive needs of learners" (p. 351), among other possible uses.

Deshler proposes that concept maps can be created from most any source that is "rich in concepts" (p. 351), such as essays, novels, poems, and transcripts. Through their creation, concept maps convey a synthesis of concepts, which in turn allow for evaluation. Learners can use such a graphical synthesis to evaluate their own thought structure, possibly looking for inconsistencies, concept priorities, omissions, and gaps in understanding. Similarly, educators and researchers can use concept maps to assess learners' thought structures; they can also compare multiple concept maps to assess "similarities and differences, omissions, alternative assumptions, conflicting claims, and competing paradigms" (p. 352).

Arts-Based Techniques

Arts-based techniques include a wide variety of strategies that have been applied to transformative learning, including photography and collage, creative writing, music, improvisation, body movement, and visual imagery (Hoggan, Simpson, & Stuckey, 2009). Arts-based pedagogies have long been touted for their ability to help learners gain deep insights into themselves (Greene, 1995).

Arts-based techniques, when used in evaluation of transformative learning, are designed to help learners gain personal insights, recognize ways in which they have changed, and help crystallize ways in which they may potentially change. Simpson (Hoggan et al., 2009), for instance, uses collage in her workshops with cancer survivors as a way of helping them better understand and appreciate the transformational journeys they have already undergone since their cancer experience began. Collage is helpful, she says, because it allows participants to express and understand their experiences in ways they had not been able to do through regular dialogue.

CONTEXTS IN WHICH EVALUATION OF TRANSFORMATIVE LEARNING TAKES PLACE

The literature is oddly silent on the issue of evaluation of transformative learning; to examine the contexts in which transformative learning is evaluated, we draw implications about evaluation from theoretical discussions, research studies, and descriptions of practice.

Formal Classrooms and Programs

Most of the writing on formal classrooms and programs emphasizes critical reflection, dialogue, the small group environment, and experiential learning as being integral to programs intending to foster transformative learning as a part of the curriculum. For example, Jones (2009) describes how social work education, most often a "normative profession," needs to incorporate ideology critique and facilitate learning that can lead to individual and social change in order to remain true to the basic tenets of social work practice. He emphasizes reflection, dialogue, and experience as core pedagogical concepts. Also in social work education, Rozas (2007) describes a tool called Intergroup Dialogue and identifies some of the outcomes of using such a tool: increased self-awareness and the ability to deal with ambiguity and complexity. Evaluation of transformative learning in this context relies on interviews, discussions, and reflections.

In nursing education, Lynam (2009) says that critical thinking has long been a core concept, but it tends to be confused with problem solving or reasoning rather than being viewed as ideology critique. Like Jones, she also emphasizes engagement and dialogue as ways to gain access to different points of view. Lynam's emphasis is on sociocultural transformation, and she lists several goals of nursing education in this respect: understanding how social systems operate to position people in society; appreciating our own social location and how this shapes our assumptions; gaining an understanding of social processes that create conditions of privilege or disadvantage; considering our own participation in societal practices; and appreciating the strengths and limitations of a range of individual and collective strategies for effecting transformation (p. 52).

Although these and other authors writing about formal programs do not specifically address evaluation strategies, they are describing the processes by which transformative learning is fostered (individual and social) and including some educational outcomes or consequences. These outcomes could be evaluated through interviews, narratives, case studies, journals, and self-evaluation strategies.

Workplace

Transformative learning in the workplace is sometimes addressed in relation to organizational transformation (where the organization or groups within the organization transform) and sometimes in relation to how workplaces can and do foster transformative learning among the members of the organization.

Yorks and Marsick's (2000) work on organizational transformation is based on action learning and collaborative inquiry. In action learning, individuals work in small groups on real problems and projects in the organization, and in collaborative inquiry there is an emphasis on co-inquiry, democratic process, and holistic understanding. Organizations transform on several dimensions: the nature of the environment, the vision of the organization, the management of the organization, products and services, the organizational structure, and how individual members of the organization see their roles. Each of these dimensions can be evaluated through discussions with members of the organization, the examination of documents and products, and observations of the work environment.

Choy (2009) uses Taylor's (2007) work as a framework for developing and evaluating a curriculum for "worker-learners." The curriculum was evaluated using interviews, tasks completed by the participants, facilitators' reflective notes, and a focus group discussion. The following were taken as evidence of transformative learning:

- Learners sought the meaning of what they were learning during negotiations about the content.
- Participants engaged in deliberate mindful efforts to learn, including meeting after working hours and operating as a social group.
- Learners validated and expanded their beliefs and understandings through rational discourse with their teams and interactions with the larger network of workers.
- Participants valued each other's strengths and accepted others as having justified interpretations of their experiences.
- The group validated contested beliefs through discourse.
- People became aware of the assumptions inherent in organizational policy and procedures and questioned the "truthfulness" of these assumptions.
- Learners discovered what they had previously taken for granted.
- Group members described transformed frames of reference.

Community Projects

Transformative learning is a common goal in community learning environments. Community projects do not usually offer course credit, degrees, or other benefits bestowed on the participants externally; rather, they usually arise in response to perceived social needs and result in real, lived benefits for the participants in relation to those perceived needs.

Newman (2006) places much of his work in the context of training in trade unions, teaching dialogue skills, negotiation tactics, and forms of "purposeful and political" rebelliousness. His stated goal is to help people learn feistiness, character, courage, and perspective, and to "make up their own minds and take control of their own lives" (p. 3). The benefits from such educational goals are deep changes in the learners that equip them to be more effective in pursuing their own interests in the face of powerful cultural and institutional influences that work to their detriment.

Crocco (2007) designed a curriculum based on the documentary film *When the Levees Broke: A Requiem in Four Acts* by Spike Lee. The documentary reviews the events surrounding hurricane Katrina in 2005 and the effects of the economic and racial inequities that were revealed and magnified by the disaster. Crocco's curriculum is intended to provide an organizing structure to use with the documentary to help learners reflect on the nature of government, communal, and personal responsibility; develop a sense of empathy; learn democratic dialogue skills; and "get involved in their communities to improve the common good" (p. 1). In this curriculum, Bitterman, Rimmer, and Alcantara (2007) prompt learners to articulate their own views on responsibility, heroism, and similar topics both before and after watching film segments, as well as in discussion activities. In this way, evaluation is used to help participants reflect on their learning in the program and the possible implications of that learning for future action.

Online Environments

In the literature related to online environments, learning outcomes are discussed in relation to cognitive learning (evaluated by achievement tests) and affective learning (evaluated through surveys of students' attitudes) (Tallent-Runnels et al., 2006). Morris, Xu, and Finnegan (2005) describe educators' roles in online courses based on a study of faculty's perceptions of their roles in teaching undergraduate asynchronous courses. The three main roles assumed by faculty were monitor (evaluator), facilitator, and teacher or participant.

Research and writing on fostering transformative learning online is minimal. Smith's (2005, 2008) emphasis on collaboration and group work online has the potential to encourage transformative learning, as does in-depth communication and creating a learning community (Tallent-Runnels et al., 2006), but these ideas have not been connected directly to transformative learning. The evaluation of transformative learning online is made easier by keeping the text available for the duration of the course and often beyond. The educator can carefully read the postings, looking for evidence of critical reflection, reflective discourse, questioning of assumptions, and changes in beliefs and perspectives on the part of learners (Cranton, 2010; Lin, Cranton, & Bridglall, 2005).

One-on-One and Small Group Settings

Transformative learning often takes place in one-on-one or small group contexts. One example is the use of Action Learning Conversations (ALC) (Marsick & Maltbia, 2010; O'Neil & Marsick, 2009). In this context, groups of three to seven people work as peer mentors for each other. They each identify a challenge or problem that is highly meaningful to them, and then follow a structured discussion protocol designed to help each other engage in an ongoing critical reflection related to those challenges. Evaluation can include both self-evaluation and peer-evaluation, as all participants in the ALC work to help each other "see how they can change a situation by changing the way they frame it and act on it" (O'Neil & Marsick, 2009, p. 19).

As an example of a one-on-one context, Gould proposed that psychotherapy can be approached as a developmental learning system, which he connects with transformative learning. The task of therapy is for the therapist to help the participant articulate, reflect on, and find resolution for a specific function, or the "capacities or skills necessary for work and love" (1991, p. 145). Designing a computer software program to guide the process, Gould proposed seven steps in short-term developmental therapy:

- Identifying and framing the function to be recovered
- Clarifying the action intention
- Distinguishing realistic dangers from exaggerated fears
- Isolating and exposing the fears as predictions confused with memories
- Explaining the origins of catastrophic predictions
- Demonstrating and diminishing self-fulfilling prophecies
- Consolidating new views of reality

The therapist "keeps participants on track and helps them identify errors in thinking" (p. 154). Evaluation in this context is used to guide the learning process and to measure developmental progress. For example, any of the seven developmental steps could be observed in therapy sessions or brought out in questioning and dialogue.

SIGNIFICANCE AND CONCLUDING THOUGHTS

Although the evaluation of student learning has been addressed extensively in adult education in general, this literature tends to follow a traditional outcomes-based, instructional design model, which is valuable for the evaluation of instrumental and some communicative knowledge, but largely irrelevant for transformative learning. Emancipatory knowledge cannot be predetermined, predicted, or set up as an objective for a course. Educators can create the environment and conditions that may foster transformative learning, but they cannot make it happen. Yet it can be evaluated, and it is evaluated in some way every time a researcher determines the extent to which transformative learning has occurred in a particular setting, context, or program and every time an educator realizes that some of her students have experienced a major shift in their perspectives on themselves or the world around them. But in the literature we have paid virtually no explicit and direct attention to the process of evaluating transformative learning.

The significance of this chapter to the field of transformative learning is that it brings to our attention the need to think deeply about how and when we can and should evaluate transformative learning. This thinking will make a contribution to theory, in that one of the current dilemmas in transformative learning theory is how we define and recognize transformative learning given the diverging perspectives in the field. If we think about how we can evaluate transformative learning, we need to know what it is we are evaluating. This thinking will make a contribution to practice in that educators will have some guidance and some strategies for assessing the extent to which learners engage in the *process* of transformation (discernment, dialogue, reflection, questioning). And this thinking will make a contribution to research. Currently, a standard approach to research on transformative learning is to conduct retrospective interviews with participants about their experiences and to search for themes related to the transformative process. If there were a variety of data collection techniques available for use in different contexts and for use with defined theoretical perspectives, it seems that we could make good progress in understanding the nature of the phenomenon of transformative learning.

On all three levels—theory, practice, and research—considering the evaluation of transformation helps us to think about the ethical issues involved in our work. Can we expect learners to transform as a result of what we do? Should we have transformative learning as a goal of adult education in some settings? In all settings? Is it ethical to encourage people to engage in transformative learning when this process may upset people's lives? Teaching for transformation is a political and value-laden act; it is, as Taylor (2008) says, "educating from a particular worldview, a particular educational philosophy." Theory development, educational practice, and research are never value-free, but in working toward life-altering learning, we need to take special care. Understanding the issues underlying the evaluation of transformative learning helps us to do this.

References

Bitterman, J., Rimmer, A., & Alcantara, L. (2007). Race, class, and Katrina in *When the Levees Broke*: Lessons designed for adult audiences. In M. Crocco (Ed.), *Teaching The Levees: A curriculum for democratic dialogue and civic engagement* (pp. 41–54). New York: Teachers College Press.

Brookfield, S. D. (2005). *The power of critical theory: Liberating adult learning and teaching.* San Francisco: Jossey-Bass.

Choy, S. (2009). Transformational learning in the workplace. *Journal of Transformative Education, 7*(1), 65–84.

Clark, M. C., & Rossiter, M. (2008). Narrative learning in adulthood. In S. B. Merriam (Ed.), *Third update on adult learning theory* (pp. 61–70). New Directions for Adult and Continuing Education, no. 119. San Francisco: Jossey-Bass.

Cranton, P. (2006). *Understanding and promoting transformative learning* (2nd ed.). San Francisco: Jossey-Bass.

Cranton, P. (2010). Transformative learning online. *International Journal of Adult Vocational Education and Technology, 1*(2), 1–11.

Crocco, M. (Ed.). (2007). *Teaching* The Levees: *A curriculum for democratic dialogue and civic engagement.* New York: Teachers College Press.

Deshler, D. (1990a). Conceptual mapping: Drawing charts of the mind. In J. Mezirow & Associates (Eds.), *Fostering critical reflection in adulthood: A guide to transformative and emancipatory learning* (pp. 336–353). San Francisco: Jossey-Bass.

Deshler, D. (1990b). Metaphor analysis: Exorcising social ghosts. In J. Mezirow & Associates (Eds.), *Fostering critical reflection in adulthood: A guide to transformative and emancipatory learning* (pp. 296–313). San Francisco: Jossey-Bass.

Dirkx, J. (2001). The power of feelings: Emotion, imagination, and the construction of meaning in adult learning. In S. B. Merriam (Ed.), *The new update on adult learning theory* (pp. 63–72). New Directions for Continuing and Adult Education, no. 89. San Francisco: Jossey-Bass.

Dirkx, J. (2006). Engaging emotions in adult learning: A Jungian perspective on emotion and transformative learning. In E. W. Taylor (Ed.), *Teaching for change: Fostering transformative learning in the classroom* (pp. 15–26). New Directions for Continuing and Adult Education, no. 109. San Francisco: Jossey-Bass.

Dominicé, P. (2000). *Learning from our lives: Using educational biographies with adults.* San Francisco: Jossey-Bass.

Drago-Severson, E. (2004). *Becoming adult learners: Principles and practices for effective development.* New York: Teachers College Press.

Ewert, G. D. (1991). Habermas and education: A comprehensive overview of the influence of Habermas in educational literature. *Review of Educational Research, 61*(3), 345–378.

Gatt, I. (2009). Changing perceptions, practice, and pedagogy: Challenges for and ways into teacher change. *Journal of Transformative Education, 7*(2), 164–184.

Gillis, S., & Griffin, P. (2008). Competency assessment. In J. Athanasou (Ed.), *Adult education and training* (pp. 233–256). Sydney: David Barlow Publishing.

Gould, R. (1991). The therapeutic learning program. In J. Mezirow & Associates (Eds.), *Fostering critical reflection in adulthood: A guide to transformative and emancipatory learning* (pp. 134–156). San Francisco: Jossey-Bass.

Greene, M. (1995). *Releasing the imagination: Essays on education, the arts, and social change.* San Francisco: Jossey-Bass.

Gunnlaugson, O. (2008). Metatheoretical prospects for the field of transformative learning. *Journal of Transformative Education, 6*(2), 124–135.

Habermas, J. (1971). *Knowledge and human interests.* Boston: Beacon Press.

Hoggan, C., Simpson, S., & Stuckey, H. (2009). *Creative expression in transformative learning: Tools and techniques for educators of adults.* Malabar, FL: Krieger.

Jones, P. (2009). Teaching for change in social work: A discipline-based argument for the use of transformative approaches to teaching and learning. *Journal of Transformative Education*, *7*(1), 8–25.

Kegan, R. (2000). What "form" transforms? A constructive-developmental approach to transformative learning. In J. Mezirow & Associates (Eds.), *Learning as transformation: Critical perspectives on a theory in progress* (pp. 35–70). San Francisco: Jossey-Bass.

King, K. P. (1998). *A guide to perspective transformation and learning activities: The learning activities survey*. Philadelphia, PA: Research for Better Schools.

King, K. P. (2004). Both sides now: Examining transformative learning and professional development of educators. *Innovative Higher Education*, *29*(2), 155–174.

Lahey, L., Souvaine, E., Kegan, R., Goodman, R., & Felix, S. (1988). *A guide to the subject-object interview: Its administration and interpretation.* Cambridge, MA: Harvard Graduate School of Education.

Lakoff, G. (1993). Contemporary theory of metaphor. In A. Ortony (Ed.), *Metaphor and thought* (2nd ed., pp. 202–251). Cambridge: Cambridge University Press.

Lin, L., Cranton, P., & Bridglall, B. (2005). Psychological type and asynchronous written dialogue in adult learning. *Teachers College Record*, *107*(8), 1788–1813.

Lynam, M. J. (2009). Reflecting on issues of enacting a critical pedagogy in nursing. *Journal of Transformative Education*, *7*(1), 44–64.

Marsick, V., & Maltbia, T. E. (2010). The transformative potential of action learning conversations: Developing critically reflective practice skills. In J. Mezirow & E. Taylor (Eds.), *Transformative learning in action: A handbook for practice* (pp. 160–171). San Francisco: Jossey-Bass.

Mezirow, J. (1990). How critical reflection triggers transformative learning. In J. Mezirow & Associates (Eds.), *Fostering critical reflection in adulthood: A guide to transformative and emancipatory learning* (pp 1–20). San Francisco: Jossey-Bass.

Mezirow, J. (1991). *Transformative dimensions of adult learning.* San Francisco: Jossey-Bass.

Mezirow, J. (2000). Learning to think like an adult. In J. Mezirow & Associates (Eds.), *Learning as transformation: Critical perspectives on a theory in progress* (pp. 1–34). San Francisco: Jossey-Bass.

Morris, L. V., Xu, H., & Finnegan, C. L. (2005). Roles of faculty in teaching asynchronous undergraduate courses. *Journal of Asynchronous Learning Networks*, *9*(1), 65–83.

Newman, M. (2006). *Teaching defiance: Stories and strategies for activist educators.* San Francisco: Jossey-Bass.

Newman, M. (2012). Calling transformative learning into question: Mutinous thoughts. *Adult Education Quarterly*, *62*(1), 36–55.

Novak, J. D., & Gowin, D. B. (1984). *Learning how to learn.* New York: Cambridge University Press.

O'Neil, J., & Marsick, V. (2007). *Understanding action learning.* New York: American Management Association.

O'Neil, J., & Marsick, V. (2009). Peer mentoring and action learning. *Adult Learning,* *20*(1/2), 19–24.

Progoff, I. (1992). *A journal workshop: Writing to access the power of the unconscious and evoke creative ability.* New York: Penguin Putnam.

Ross, J. A., Rolheiser, C., & Hogaboam-Gray, A. (1998). *Effects of self-evaluation and training on narrative writing.* Paper presented at the Annual Meeting of Canadian Society for Studies in Education, Ottawa.

Rozas, L. (2007). Engaging dialogue in our diverse social work student body: A multilevel theoretical process model. *Journal of Social Work Education, 43,* 5–29.

Smith, R. O. (2005). Working with differences in online collaborative groups. *Adult Education Quarterly, 53*(3), 182–199.

Smith, R. O. (2008). Adult learning and the emotional self in virtual online courses. In J. Dirkx (Ed.), *Adult learning and the emotional self* (pp. 35–44). New Directions for Adult and Continuing Education, no. 120. San Francisco: Jossey-Bass.

Tallent-Runnels, M. K., Thomas, J. A., Lan, W. Y., Cooper, S., Ahern, T. C., Shaw, S. M., & Liu, X. (2006). Teaching courses online: A review of the research. *Review of Educational Research, 76*(1), 93–135.

Taylor, E. W. (2007). An update of transformative learning theory: A critical review of the empirical research (1999–2005). *International Journal of Lifelong Education, 26*(2), 173–191.

Taylor, E. W. (2008). Transformative learning theory. In S. Merriam (Ed.), *Third update on adult learning theory* (pp. 5–16). New Directions for Adult and Continuing Education, no. 119. San Francisco: Jossey-Bass.

Yorks, L., & Marsick, V. (2000). Organizational learning and transformation. In J. Mezirow & Associates (Eds.), *Learning as transformation: Critical perspectives on a theory in progress* (pp. 253–281). San Francisco: Jossey-Bass.

CHAPTER THIRTY-THREE

Educator as Change Agent

Ethics of
Transformative Learning

Dorothy Ettling

Practitioners of transformative learning theory have a predisposition to educate for change. Even with a clear commitment to this goal, there is evidence of practitioners' discomfort in actual practice. "We can create an environment where transformative learning can occur; however, without care and attention to the power we have...we can contribute to oppression and silencing" (Butterwick & Lawrence, 2009, p. 44). Authors note that creating this kind of learning environment frequently evokes strong emotional responses from students (Dirks & Smith, 2009; Gravett & Petersen, 2009; Langan, Sheese, & Davidson, 2009). Addressing and, even more so, maneuvering the ensuing classroom tension with these emotions can be challenging. For some educators, it may even appear to cross the boundaries of appropriate pedagogical practice and evoke an ethical dilemma. This chapter presents some of the difficult positions prompted by transformative learning practice and elaborates how seasoned practitioners attend to them. Simultaneously, it addresses the importance of the educator's inner journey in the transformative learning encounter.

First, it seems important to disclose the author's personal milieu. As an adult educator committed to transformative learning theory-in-practice, I am simultaneously rooted in several contexts: a traditional world of academia, a community of practice with scholar practitioners, and a group of culturally diverse activists engaged in global NGO work. It is from these contexts, mixed and sometimes contradictory, that I reflect on the ethical implications of educating for transformation.

ETHICS OF PRACTICE

Ethics is a word much bandied about today, in every aspect of adult higher education and across business and training practices. In 1987, Paulo Freire addressed the question of the ethics of education as a transformative process. He asserted, "There is a strong, ideological dimension to this question of challenging and transforming the consciousness of students" (Shor & Freire, 1987, p. 174). Shortly thereafter, Brockett (1988) edited a compilation of essays that addressed a number of issues related to ethics in adult education. The publication was provoked, in part, by the concern of some adult educators for a stronger professional image of the field. Question was raised whether adult education should be viewed as a service profession with an agreed-upon set of guidelines to steer its professional practice. Brockett acknowledged, "As a field characterized by extreme diversity in both practice and ideology, adult education often serves as a stage for controversy and moral conflict" (Brockett, 1988, p. vii). He delineated the purpose of this 1988 edition, "to promote a greater awareness of the kinds of moral dilemmas that are inherent in the education of adults and to serve as a resource for the examination of ethical issues relative to the practice of adult education" (p. viii). The book was intended to stimulate critical reflection among practitioners, to assess their own value systems and their own ethical practice, rather than to offer an established set of guidelines for the field.

Brockett (1988) began from the perspective that it is normative ethics rather than meta-ethics that sets the stage for the ethical discussion in the context of adult education practice. "Meta-ethics focuses on an analysis of the meaning and definitions of ethical terms . . . normative ethics, on the other hand, involves the application of ethical standard and values" (Reamer, as cited in Brockett, 1988, p. 2). In other words, "ethics is a practical endeavor" (Brockett, 1988, p. 3), and as such, it relies more on the "process individuals go through in ethical decision making" (p. 9) rather than a code of ethics that will "provide prescriptive guidelines for what may be defined by some as appropriate behavior" (p. 9). Thus Brockett proposed a process model that distinguishes between three interrelated dimensions of ethical practice that he believed relevant in adult education: one's personal value system, the consideration of multiple responsibilities, and finally, the way in which values are operationalized in practice (p. 10).

Two decades later, this model still provides a useful way to approach the discussion of ethics in the practice of transformative learning and offers a partial framework for this chapter. In the TL context, the instructor's or teacher's role and self-awareness are particularly crucial. In Brockett's words, "An awareness of one's personal value system and the degree to which certain values have been internalized is an essential point of departure in understanding how one will respond in specific situations" (1988, p. 11).

His second aspect, consideration of multiple responsibilities, requires taking into account the many individuals and groups to which adult educators can be responsible. In light of this aspect, he argues that role conflict rather than role uncertainty is much more likely to confront the educator. Balancing the needs of the program, the institution, or the organization with the particular intentions of the learning process can present a dilemma. It is important to be able to set priorities with an awareness of the consequences of one's actions and then ultimately accept responsibility for those actions (Brockett, 1988).

Brockett (1988) suggests that the first two aspects, the personal value system and multiple roles, pave the way for the operationalization of values in the educational context. Acknowledging one's own worldview and standpoint, and giving serious consideration to the multiple roles played in each setting, prompts the educator to formulate a set of principles that guide interactions and steer decisions when faced with ethical dilemmas. However, he is careful to emphasize that these principles must take into account a deep respect for the context and the value system of the learner as well as the perspectives and intentions of the educator (pp. 12–13).

Ten years after Brockett, O'Sullivan (1999) stretched the ethical imperative in adult education with direct reference to transformative learning. He laid out the rationale for "education for a planetary consciousness" (p. 228). Faced with the magnitude of change and natural threats experienced in our recent history, O'Sullivan claimed, "the educational challenge is how to bring ourselves to a sustained level of consciousness concerning these problems and to hold this consciousness at the forefront of our cultural minds" (p. 19). He was calling for a deep commitment on the part of educators to include an ecological identity as part of their ethical framework in transformative learning. Other authors (Ball, 1999; Bowers, 1997; Jucker, 2002; Orr, 1992) concurred and suggested that even a radical shift in our ethical paradigm might be insufficient to address the social and ecological crises that pose the moral dilemmas of our times.

Building further, the recent impetus in the transformative learning field situates TL theory and practice within an integrally informed theory of adult development (Kegan, 2000; Cranton & Roy, 2003; Gunnlaugson, 2005, 2008). Gunnlaugson (2008) refers to this direction as "second wave frameworks" (p. 128) for transformative learning. Influenced by Wilber's (2006) extensive writing on integral human development, Gunnlaugson (2008) proposes the following:

> A first-wave theory that focused on *how* one experiences TL... within the context of a particular TL theorist's schemata could be joined by a second-wave inquiry that might involve reflexively stepping back and addressing such issues as *what form* is transforming for a student *within which* context of their lives. (p. 127)

This shift in the breadth of theoretical reflexivity on the part of the educator has implications for transformative learning practice. It presupposes another level of ethical responsibility to assess and be mindful of in the rich psychological, spiritual, social, political, and cultural contexts of the learner. In light of these multiple developments in the theory of transformative learning, a discussion of the ethics of practice is quite timely.

EDUCATING FOR CHANGE?

Experienced readers in the field of transformative learning are familiar with the two broad theoretical frameworks in transformative learning. Both of these frameworks, in varying settings, are adequately presented elsewhere in this Handbook. Jack Mezirow's approach (1990, 1991, 2000, 2003; Mezirow, Taylor, & Associates, 2009), followed by the work of a number of other authors, emphasizes personal transformation and change, with less attention to social change in the transformative experience. Critical reflection and critique of one's assumptions are paramount in this framework.

A second framework locates transformative learning in the realm of fostering social change as well as personal change and sees the two inherently linked. It is not the purpose of this chapter to differentiate among these varied nuances of transformative learning practice. Rather, it is this author's position that they all emanate from the same deep root of an educational world view that fosters creating a learning space that induces change in the adult learner: change of mind and change of behavior. Initiating educational processes that facilitate introspection into self or into one's social or work reality creates an expectation of new awareness. New awareness is, in itself, a change.

Adult development as a context for transformative change has been promoted for a number of decades. The early work of Piaget (as cited in Kasworm, 1988) in developmental psychology assumed that the journey through adulthood presupposed the reorganizing of meaning structures, which reflect transformation of the cognitive and value-related perspectives. Other authors, in developing ethical frameworks, have supported this view (Perry, Loevinger, Kohlberg, Gilligan, & Fowler, as cited in Kasworm, 1988). Kasworm claims "that adults view their world from within a cognitive and perceptual value framework, making judgments and actions based upon these perceptions" (p. 26) and that maturing through life's stages and difficulties is the natural stimulus for the change that occurs in this process. According to Kasworm, this presents the adult educator with a paradox: "What should be the role of the educator in a learner's psychosocial development and in relation to the learner's value structure" (p. 30)? Is there not a need to provide a supportive structure and a stimulus for transformation? Cunningham (1988) responds, "The ethical role of educators is to provide environments that allow people to examine critically the water in which they swim" (p. 135). Thus, Kasworm concludes, "it is possible for the adult to gain a new perspective and an alternate set of meanings for understanding one's identity and relationship to the world" (1988, p. 32). These perspectives reflect Mezirow's emphasis (1981) on critical reflexivity in the transformative learning process.

The TL educator as a change agent has a solid foundation in the literature. Teaching for change is a fundamental aspect of the transformative theoretical orientation. There is a growing recognition that the processes of transformative learning must help create reflexive conditions in both individuals and societies so that social transformation can be generated (Taylor, 1994; Mezirow & Associates, 2000; Mezirow, Taylor, & Associates, 2009). The TL practitioner is increasingly identified as a promoter of a more just world order and as a facilitator of new levels of awareness of our cosmic interdependence.

What continues to challenge practitioners is how to work responsibly, given these profound new responsibilities, making judicious use of transformative learning strategies and the balance of power and autonomy in the learning contract. The rest of this chapter will elaborate on several typical practices in the TL situation and some potential ethical issues surrounding them.

Sharing Experience

A core element in creating a transformative learning setting is the building of trust. Research indicates that establishing positive and productive relationships with others is one of the essential factors in a transformative experience (Taylor, 2009). Mezirow (2000) outlined the preconditions that allow for full participation in the reflective discourse of transformative learning (p. 13). Authors agree that it can be difficult to create those conditions in which trust can be established (Marsick & Maltbia, 2009; Taylor & Jarecke, 2009; Lange, 2009). A frequently used strategy in building the TL environment is the disclosure of one's personal story in either oral or written form. Facilitated storytelling can help set the tone for deeper dialogue. "Written narrative techniques may offer important mechanisms that can develop a level of trust and provide a safe space in which to practice the skills of self-reflexivity necessary for developing a care-full approach to deliberative engagement" (McGregor, 2004, p. 99).

These disclosures may be structured as storytelling (Tyler, 2009), journaling (Meyer, 2009; MacLeod & Egan, 2009), or critical incidents (Brookfield, 1995), or simply as personal reflections during the course of discussions or presentations. Even though individual experience is recognized as the primary medium of transformative learning (Taylor, 2009), it can still be challenging to evoke this personal sharing.

A key ethical issue in fostering disclosure is the question of voluntary participation. Langan et al. (2009) claim that "requiring students to share reflections as part of a course process can be exploitative, as it may coerce students to reveal information about themselves that they wish to keep private" (p. 53). Similarly, Butterwick and Lawrence (2009) advise that "storytelling should not be imposed or made into a requirement. We need to understand the dangers and inequalities of risk that exist in any group" (p. 43).

Implicit is a recognition of the "lens of positionality" of the educator (Taylor, 2009, p. 3) or the unequal power relations that exist among participants (Langan et al., 2009; Taylor & Jarecke, 2009). It is frequently suggested that the instructor devote time in the learning setting to directly address issues of power, marginalization, and potential areas of inequality among the learners and with the instructor. This modeling of the instructor's openness to dialogue and willingness to self-disclose can help create an ambiance of freedom in the classroom. Tisdell and Tolliver (2009) caution us, "I never ask students to do anything that I am unwilling to do myself" (p. 93). In this way, facilitators model a sense of engagement and authenticity that can dissipate resistance (Cranton, 2001). Brookfield's advice "to be as transparent as possible of one's motives, agenda, and directions" (2009, p. 134) is a useful guide.

Unveiling Conflict

An important factor in the transformative process is moving beyond one's comfort zone. When facilitating transformative learning, "educators need to create the conditions under which learners are pushed toward their learning edge, where they are challenged and encouraged toward critical reflection" (Gravett & Petersen, 2009, p. 107). Provoking the disorienting dilemma can move participants from resistance to new or expanded perspectives to acceptance of them. One suggested activity to help students push to this edge is implanting disruptions—the introduction of critical texts or lectures that challenge conventional norms and beliefs (Gravett & Petersen, 2009; Langan, Oliver, & Atkinson, as cited in Langan et al., 2009). These disruptions "typically turn classrooms into sites of contention, for they lead to complex, confrontational, and emotional responses from students and, subsequently, from us as teachers" (Langan et al., 2009, p. 52). Defending this provocation, Langan and her colleagues pose the argument that the learning space, which needs to be safe, is not guaranteed to be free from tension and even hostility. They also note that they accompany this technique with a carefully crafted analysis of the data generated by the disruption and give feedback to the students, which often leads to a deeper understanding of diverse viewpoints. But even with these supportive measures, the authors express their concern, particularly when the disruptions are offensive to some participants because of cultural or religious beliefs. This provocation can engender a dilemma for the teacher who is committed to nonviolence.

Gravett and Petersen (2009) remind us that if learners are pushed too far, they will most likely react with defensiveness and resistance—or possibly complete withdrawal from the learning process. When provocations like this are built into their praxis, an educator can model a "pedagogy of discomfort" (Boler, as cited in McGregor, 2004, p. 102) if learners are willing to recognize and acknowledge their own discomfort, resistance, and places of transformation.

Tension is not new to the learning process. There is a conflict between challenging learners and offering them a comfortable learning space in which to express questions and new ideas. Here, undoubtedly, is one place where the educator needs keen self-awareness of both intention and skill in leading the learners through this rocky terrain. Experience may be the only teacher, and willingness to risk and humility to learn are likely two of the best companions.

Evoking the Unconscious

Intense experiences in the classroom are not always initiated by design. Transformative learning often deals with material that evokes powerful feelings. Critical reflection on assumptions can lead to an eruption of old memories, unhealed areas in our lives, or deeply seated beliefs that carry enormous weight in our moral perspective. Generally speaking, strong emotions are not welcomed by students or teachers in the educational setting. For example, Dirkx and Smith (2009) claim that this lack of openness to "the presence of emotions within their learning reflects the broader tendency within our culture to regard emotions as potentially disruptive of rational and reasonable thought and action" (p. 62). They find that "helping students work through these emotional dynamics is perhaps one of the most difficult and challenging dimensions" of teaching guided by transformative learning (p. 65). Assisting students to hold the tensions arising from emotional upheavals and from addressing differences generally proves to be a complex facilitation.

Kasl and Elias (2000) stress that transformative learning educators "need to acquire competence and comfort in evoking and processing the imaginal, the archetypal, the mythic, the affective, and the somatic" (p. 249). Over the past two decades, much more emphasis has been placed on the crucial importance of the unconscious and intuition in transformative learning (Boyd, 1991; Elias, 1997; Wiessner & Mezirow, 2000; Cranton, 2000; Janik, 2005; Dirkx, 2006; Davis-Manigaulte, Yorks, & Kasl, 2006; Gozawa, 2009).

This places additional demands on the educator and holds the potential for the fear of manipulation. If the goal is to develop a "relationship with one's unconscious" (Dirkx & Smith, 2009, p. 59) and "engage learners in the process of self-work, self-change, and transformation" (p. 64), the transformative learning practitioner has an ethical obligation to be prepared and to have engaged in his or her own personal transformation process. Ultimately, "whether a learning experience is transformative rests with the learner, not us as instructors or facilitators" (p. 65). Yet as educators, we hold the process in our hands and can never take lightly the responsibility that entails. Mezirow (1991) initially reminded us that "encouraging learners to challenge and transform meaning perspectives raises serious ethical questions" (p. 201).

Expecting Collaboration

A significant impetus in adult education is a learner-centered orientation, trusting learners to share in shaping a fruitful educational experience (Taylor & Jarecke, 2009). In this framework, more discretion and direction is left in the hands of the learner. Learner-centered orientation ranges from minimal involvement to collaborative participation in creating the learning processes. Weimer (2002) described learner-centered teaching as an approach in which the teacher is seen as facilitator, as one who strives to balance power with learners through shared decision making, evaluation, and other learning responsibilities in the classroom.

There are a number of strategies in adult education that strongly focus on learner-centered practice; some of the more common are mentoring, coaching, and collaborative inquiry. All of these are presented in the literature as fertile ground for transformative learning to occur. For example, mentoring and coaching as learning practices are reflected across aspects in the literature of higher education (Mandell & Herman, 2009; Daloz, 1999) and community education (Meyer, 2009) and in the promotion of social responsibility and civic engagement (Daloz, 2000; Calderwood, 2003). Collaborative inquiry, focusing on the development of professional practice, is documented in relationship with organizational learning (Yorks & Marsick, 2000).

At first glance, the philosophy of learner-centered teaching might appear to confront transformative learning intentions. Can one expect student collaboration in designing processes to provoke a disorienting dilemma, foster uncomfortable scrutiny of buried assumptions, or activate areas of conflict? The goal of transformative learning, with its strong proclivity toward teaching for change, can seem counterintuitive to the aims of being learner-centered. But on reflection, it seems that Weimer's (2002) previous description resonates well with much of the transformative learning literature. Accounts of TL practice emphasize student inclusiveness, sharing of power, educator disclosure, and authenticity in classroom interactions. In general, there seems to be an expectation that the learner will be an active participant in creating transformative learning processes. Even so, inner conflict and ethical tension can arise for educators who carry a deep-seated orientation to education as transformative change.

A learner-centered approach has been identified as central to fostering transformative learning (Cranton, 2006; Mezirow & Associates, 2000). Yet there is minimal explanation of how this approach blends with TL's theoretical orientation and its implications in actual learning contexts. Taylor (2009) claims that more research is needed before a learner-centered orientation can be seen as an essential element of transformative learning. This author concurs. Additional research will shed more light on addressing dilemmas in the learner-centered approach.

WALKING AN ETHICAL PATH

Reflecting on the many facets of transformative learning practice presented throughout this Handbook, we may resonate with Brockett's (1988) initial premise: "Adult education is a dynamic field characterized by extreme diversity in both ideology and practice" (p. 1). Over twenty years of transformative learning theory and practice has added depth and complexity to this dynamism. To be intentional about *teaching for change* intensifies our responsibility to ourselves, to our students, and to the world community. As transformative learning educators, we are sowers of a new consciousness in adult education, a consciousness that holds promise for a human race that presently is often nonreflective. We are capable of instilling in today's learners the capacity for critical reflection on the beliefs, behaviors, and social structures we create as a human community. We no longer view education as neutral, distantly objective, or value free. We recognize that each of us, educator and student, comes to the learning context with predispositions, prejudgments, and varying degrees of openness to new knowledge. We acknowledge that transformative learning can be an inspiring yet demanding endeavor. The examples here offer concrete activities and attitudes that may be useful in dealing with issues surrounding ethical practice.

As conscientious educators committed to working for a transformed world, we are challenged to take seriously the call to personal transformation in our own lives. Rather than formulate a code of ethical guidelines to standardize our practice, we can strive to acquire what might be termed "ethical capacities" (Ettling, 2006). This refers to competencies that arise from the practice of intellectual, emotional, and spiritual rigor in our professional self-development, which can ground us and offer us guidance in our everyday practice of transformative learning. In reality, the professional journey of the transformative

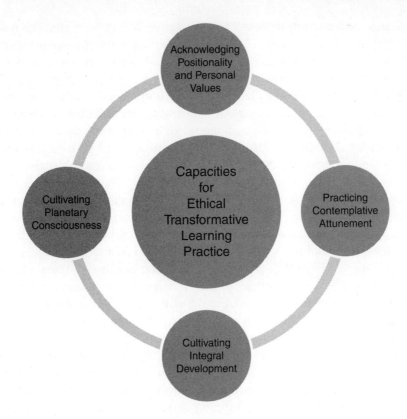

Figure 33.1 Capacities for Ethical Transformative Learning Practice

learning educator is a spiritual journey. It may draw strength from one of many different sources: humanistic, scientific, theological, or ecological. But in essence, it is the journey of the soul, and it will sometimes be shrouded in mystery and unknowing. It takes courage to pursue this path, and it is not for the fainthearted (Curry-Stevens, 2007; Fetherston & Kelly, 2007; Gozawa, 2009). Dirkx and Smith (2009) aptly term it "soul work" (p. 58). In Figure 33.1, I suggest one way of describing capacities worth striving for. I view them as spiritual competencies that prepare us for the task entrusted to us and enhance our teaching practice. They are not techniques but rather attitudes of the spirit. They reveal aspects of my journey and are drawn from many wells. They are presented not as a model but as one way to portray the path. The journey is a personal one, and each of us will explain its uniqueness in a way that reveals distinct and blessed features. With this description, I simply hope to stimulate dialogue, among us, on the process of "be-coming" transformative learning educators.

Humility and comfort with personal disclosure seem essential to the transformative learning practitioner. This requires that we work through our need to be *expert* in the learning situation, even when it is dramatically demanded of us through admiration or hostility. Acknowledging our own ideological positioning and personal values, without blame or shame, is the initial step. Closely linked is the realization that one's own position is fraught with illusions, blind spots, and prejudgments, and it can and should be readily challenged (Scharmer, 2009). Setting the stage for dialogue among learners and with us, as educators, creates the environment for change to occur, both in ourselves and in the learners.

Elaborating further on Figure 33.1, practicing *contemplative attunement* encourages us to live in a sense of awe. Wonder is practically a lost art for all us adults. The cynicism of the media and dominant cultural forces creeps into our daily interactions and hides the moments of surprise that form the hallmark of deep learning. To be able to capture the detail and beauty of a transformative change, even with its groans and grunts, renews our commitment and feeds our spirit. One learns to be attuned to detail through disciplined practice, by giving consistent time to a solitary experience of listening within. Contexts for this solitude are abundant: meditation, yoga, jogging, nature walks, to name just a few. What is crucial is a quiet activity that allows for a process of no thinking. Key is an inward turning and openness to the vulnerability that this awareness evokes. *Contemplative attunement*, on a personal level, prepares us for the essential listening in the learning context (Cannato, 2010). We begin to actually hear the learning process as it occurs, the spoken and the unspoken revelations from learners, and inspirations from within ourselves. This allows us to respond with less need to control and more readiness to facilitate pathways to transformation.

Cultivating integral development commits the TL educator to a holistic framework of human growth. Within this framework, no aspect of the human experience can be excluded from the learning situation: intellectual, emotional, physical, psychic, or spiritual. Each person is perceived as a *holon* in an interconnected field, and careful attention is given to the kind of environment that is created within that field (Wilber, 1998, 2006). This capacity, in particular, defies any desire on our part to be fully prepared or adequately ready for the transformative experience and situates transformative change in the unique context of each learner.

Developing a planetary consciousness challenges us to claim our role as educating towards a radical new consciousness, a consciousness that nurtures and affirms our place as beings of the universe, striving to create a just and peaceful planet (Bruteau, 1997, 2001; O'Sullivan, 1999; O'Sullivan, Morrell, & O'Connor, 2002). We must help learners refind their human place within community, within nature, and within the context of all life. Striving to cleanse the learning context of a pseudo-intellectual superiority, we can find our equilibrium in a balance and harmony with all life forms. This capacity is richly fed by experience outside the classroom, commitments that take us out of our comfort zone and immerse us in the transformative journeys of daily lives. There we come to understand what we try to teach, when we see, taste, and feel it in the lives of people locally and globally. In the end, we may never relieve the discomfort in our practice of TL. Perhaps we need to reframe our intention: may we simply not run from the fire.

References

Ball, G.D.S. (1999). Building a sustainable future through transformation. *Futures, 31*, 251–270.

Bowers, C. A. (1997). *The culture of denial: Why environmental movement needs a strategy for reforming universities and public schools.* Albany: State University of New York Press.

Boyd, R. D. (1991). *Personal transformations in small groups.* New York: Routledge.

Brockett, R. G. (Ed.). (1988). *Ethical issues in adult education.* New York: Teachers College, Columbia University.

Brookfield, S. D. (1995). *Becoming a critically reflective teacher.* San Francisco: Jossey-Bass.

Brookfield, S. D. (2009). Engaging critical reflection in corporate America. In J. Mezirow, E. W. Taylor, & Associates (Eds.), *Transformative learning in practice: Insights from community, workplace, and higher education* (pp. 125–135). San Francisco: Jossey-Bass.

Bruteau, B. (1997). *God's ecstasy: The creation of a self-creating world.* New York: Crossroads.

Bruteau, B. (2001). *The grand option: Personal transformation and a new creation.* Notre Dame, IN: University of Notre Dame Press.

Butterwick, S., & Lawrence, R. L. (2009). Creating alternative realities: Arts based approaches to transformative learning. In J. Mezirow, E. W. Taylor, & Associates (Eds.), *Transformative learning in practice: Insights from community, workplace, and higher education* (pp. 35–45). San Francisco: Jossey-Bass.

Calderwood, P. E. (2003). Toward a professional community for social justice. *Journal of Transformative Education, 1*(4), 301–320.

Cannato, J. (2010). *Field of compassion: How the new cosmology is transforming spiritual life.* Notre Dame, IN: Sorin Books.

Cranton, P. (2000). Individual differences and transformative learning. In J. Mezirow & Associates (Eds.), *Learning as transformation: Critical perspectives on a theory in progress* (pp. 181–204). San Francisco: Jossey-Bass.

Cranton, P. (2001). *Becoming an authentic teacher in higher education.* Malabar, FL: Krieger.

Cranton, P. (2006). *Understanding and promoting transformative learning.* San Francisco: Jossey-Bass.

Cranton, P., & Roy, M. (2003). When the bottom falls out of the bucket: Toward a holistic perspective on transformative learning. *Journal of Transformative Education, 1,* 86–98.

Cunningham, P. (1988). The adult educator and social responsibility. In R. Brockett (Ed.), *Ethical issues in adult education* (pp. 133–145). New York: Teachers College, Columbia University.

Curry-Stevens, A. (2007). New forms of transformative education: Pedagogy for the oppressed. *Journal of Transformative Education, 5*(1), 33–58.

Daloz, L. (1999). *Mentor: Guiding the journey of adult learners.* San Francisco: Jossey-Bass.

Daloz, L. (2000). Transformative learning for the common good. In J. Mezirow & Associates (Eds.), *Learning as transformation: Critical perspectives on a theory in progress* (pp. 103–123). San Francisco: Jossey-Bass.

Davis-Manigaulte, J., Yorks, L., & Kasl, E., (2006). Presentational knowing and transformative learning. In E. W. Taylor (Ed.), *Fostering transformative learning in the classroom: Challenges and innovations* (pp. 27–35). New Directions for Adult and Continuing Education, no. 109. San Francisco: Jossey-Bass.

Dirkx, J. (2006). Engaging emotions in adult learning: A Jungian perspective on emotion and transformative learning. In E. Taylor (Ed.), *Teaching for change* (pp. 15–26). New Directions in Adult and Continuing Education, no. 109. San Francisco: Jossey-Bass.

Dirkx, J. M., & Smith, R. O. (2009). Facilitating transformative learning: Engaging emotions in an online context. In J. Mezirow, E. W. Taylor, & Associates (Eds.), *Transformative learning in practice: Insights from community, workplace, and higher education* (pp. 57–66). San Francisco: Jossey-Bass.

Elias, D. (1997). It's time to change our minds: An introduction to transformative learning. *ReVision, 20*(1), 2–6.

Ettling, D. (2006). Ethical demands of transformative learning. In E. W. Taylor (Ed.), *Teaching for change* (pp. 59–68). New Directions for Adult and Continuing Education, no. 109. San Francisco: Jossey-Bass.

Fetherston, B., & Kelly, R. (2007). Conflict resolution and transformative pedagogy: A grounded theory research project on learning in higher education. *Journal of Transformative Education, 5*(3), 262–285.

Gozawa, J. (2009). The cultural complex and transformative learning environments. *Journal of Transformative Education, 7*(2), 114–133.

Gravett, S., & Petersen, N. (2009). Promoting dialogic teaching among higher education faculty in South Africa. In J. Mezirow, E. W. Taylor, & Associates (Eds.), *Transformative learning in practice: Insights from community, workplace, and higher education* (pp. 100–110). San Francisco: Jossey-Bass.

Gunnlaugson, O. (2005). Toward integrally informed theories of transformative learning. *Journal of Transformative Education, 3*(4), 331–353.

Gunnlaugson, O. (2008). Metatheoretical prospects for the field of transformative learning. *Journal of Transformative Education, 6*(2), 124–135.

Janik, D. (2005). *Unlock the genius within: Neurobiological trauma, teaching, and transformative learning.* Lanham, MD: Rowman & Littlefield.

Jucker, R. (2002). *Our common illiteracy: Education as if the Earth and people mattered.* New York: Peter Lang.

Kasl, E., & Elias, D. (2000). Creating new habits of mind in small groups. In J. Mezirow & Associates (Eds.), *Learning as transformation: Critical perspectives on a theory in progress* (pp. 229–252). San Francisco: Jossey-Bass.

Kasworm, C. (1988). Facilitating ethical development: A paradox. In R. Brockett (Ed.), *Ethical issues in adult education.* New York: Teachers College Press.

Kegan, R. (2000). What form transforms: A constructive-developmental approach to transformative learning. In J. Mezirow & Associates (Eds.), *Learning as transformation: Critical perspectives on a theory in progress* (pp. 35–69). San Francisco: Jossey-Bass.

Langan, D., Sheese, R., & Davidson, D. (2009). Constructive teaching and learning. In J. Mezirow, E. W. Taylor, & Associates (Eds.), *Transformative learning in practice: Insights from community, workplace, and higher education* (pp. 46–56). San Francisco: Jossey-Bass.

Lange, E. (2009). Fostering a learning sanctuary for transformation in sustainability education. In J. Mezirow, E. W. Taylor, & Associates (Eds.), *Transformative learning in practice: Insights from community, workplace, and higher education* (pp. 78–88). San Francisco: Jossey-Bass.

MacLeod, R., & Egan, T. (2009). Transformative palliative care education. In J. Mezirow, E. W. Taylor, & Associates (Eds.), *Transformative learning in practice: Insights from community, workplace, and higher education* (pp. 111–121). San Francisco: Jossey-Bass.

Mandell, A., & Herman, L. (2009). Mentoring: When learners make the learning. In J. Mezirow, E. W. Taylor, & Associates (Eds.), *Transformative learning in practice: Insights from community, workplace, and higher education* (pp. 78–88). San Francisco: Jossey-Bass.

Marsick, V., & Maltbia, T. (2009). The transformative potential of action learning conversations: Developing critically reflective practice skills. In J. Mezirow, E. W. Taylor, & Associates (Eds.), *Transformative learning in practice: Insights from community, workplace, and higher education* (pp. 160–171). San Francisco: Jossey-Bass.

McGregor, C. (2004). Care(full) deliberation: A pedagogy for citizenship. *Journal of Transformative Education, 2*(2), 90–106.

Meyer, S. (2009). Promoting personal empowerment with women in East Harlem through journaling and coaching. In J. Mezirow, E. W. Taylor, & Associates (Eds.),

Transformative learning in practice: Insights from community, workplace, and higher education (pp. 216–226). San Francisco: Jossey-Bass.

Mezirow, J. (1981). A critical theory of adult learning and education. *Adult Education, 32,* 3–24.

Mezirow, J. (1990). How critical reflection triggers transformative learning. In J. Mezirow & Associates (Eds.), *Fostering critical reflection in adulthood: A guide to transformative and emancipatory learning* (pp. 1–20). San Francisco: Jossey-Bass.

Mezirow, J. (1991). *Transformative dimensions of adult learning.* San Francisco: Jossey-Bass.

Mezirow, J. (2000). Learning to think like an adult: Core concepts of transformative learning. In J. Mezirow & Associates (Eds.), *Learning as transformation: Critical perspectives on a theory in progress* (pp. 3–33). San Francisco: Jossey-Bass.

Mezirow, J. (2003). Transformative learning as discourse. *Journal of Transformative Education, 1,* 58–63.

Mezirow, J., & Associates (Eds.). (2000). *Learning as transformation: Critical perspectives on a theory in progress.* San Francisco: Jossey-Bass.

Mezirow, J., Taylor, E. W., & Associates (2009). *Transformative learning in practice: Insights from community, workplace, and higher education.* San Francisco: Jossey-Bass.

Orr, D. W. (1992). *Ecological literacy—education and the transition to a postmodern world.* Albany: State University of New York Press.

O'Sullivan, E. (1999). *Transformative learning: Educational vision for the 21st century.* Toronto, Canada: University of Toronto Press.

O'Sullivan, E., Morrell, A., & O'Connor, M. (2002). *Expanding the boundaries of transformative learning.* New York: Palgrave.

Scharmer, C. O. (2009). *Theory U: Leading from the future as it emerges.* San Francisco: Berrett-Koehler.

Shor, I., & Freire, P. (1987). *A pedagogy for liberation: Dialogues on transforming education.* Westport, CT: Bergin and Garvey.

Taylor, E. W. (1994). Intercultural competency: A transformative learning process. *Adult Education Quarterly, 44,* 154–174.

Taylor, E. W. (2009). Fostering transformative learning. In J. Mezirow, E. W. Taylor, & Associates (Eds.), *Transformative learning in practice: Insights from community, workplace, and higher education* (pp. 3–17). San Francisco: Jossey-Bass.

Taylor, E. W., & Jarecke, J. (2009). Looking forward by looking back: Reflections on the practice of transformative learning. In J. Mezirow, E. W. Taylor, & Associates (Eds.), *Transformative learning in practice: Insights from community, workplace, and higher education* (pp. 275–289). San Francisco: Jossey-Bass.

Tisdell, E., & Tolliver, D. E. (2009). Transformative approaches to culturally responsive teaching. In J. Mezirow, E. W. Taylor, & Associates (Eds.),

Transformative learning in practice: Insights from community, workplace, and higher education (pp. 89–99). San Francisco: Jossey-Bass.

Tyler, J. A. (2009). Charting the course: How storytelling can foster communicative learning in the workplace. In J. Mezirow, E. W. Taylor, & Associates (Eds.), *Transformative learning in practice: Insights from community, workplace, and higher education* (pp. 136–147). San Francisco: Jossey-Bass.

Weimer, M. G. (2002). *Learner-centered teaching: Five key changes to practice.* San Francisco: Jossey-Bass.

Wiessner, C. A., & Mezirow, J. (2000). Theory building and the search for common ground. In J. Mezirow & Associates (Eds.), *Learning as transformation: Critical perspectives on a theory in progress* (pp. 329–358). San Francisco: Jossey-Bass.

Wilber, K. (1998). *The marriage of sense and soul.* New York: Random House.

Wilber, K. (2006). *Integral spirituality: An integral vision for business, politics, science, and spirituality.* Boston: Shambhala.

Yorks, L., & Marsick, V. (2000). Organizational learning and transformation. In J. Mezirow & Associates (Eds.), *Learning as transformation: Critical perspectives on a theory in progress* (pp. 253–281). San Francisco: Jossey-Bass.

PART SIX

REFLECTING ON THE FUTURE OF TRANSFORMATIVE LEARNING

CHAPTER THIRTY-FOUR

Reflecting Back and Looking Forward

Edward W. Taylor and Patricia Cranton

I n looking back over the chapters of this book, it is important to reflect on and explore what has been learned from the array of discussions about transformative learning theory. This means asking: Are we any closer to a more integrated and unified perspective of transformative learning theory? Is there greater congruency among scholars about the nature of transformative learning—its purpose, core elements, and essential practices? More fundamentally, what has been gained by bringing together all these varying views of transformative learning? And do we have a better understanding of where the study of transformative learning is headed and where it needs to head as it moves into the next decade?

In this chapter, we identify seven issues and tensions, each of which is addressed in several chapters throughout the volume. These are

- Theoretical tensions
- Imposing, coercing, and supporting
- Community-based and collaborative transformative learning
- Culture, gender, and positionality
- Emotion and rationality
- Researching transformative learning
- The transformative teacher and learner—an empathic relationship

We describe each of these areas with reference to the relevant chapters, and for each we pose some questions for future consideration, in terms of theory-building, research, and practice.

THEORETICAL TENSIONS

An objective identified in the first chapter of this Handbook was the need for a more unified theory of transformative learning. It meant recognizing that despite the range of theoretical perspectives—see, for example, Mezirow (Chapter 5), Brookfield (Chapter 8), Dirkx (Chapter 7), O'Sullivan (Chapter 10), and Taylor and Elias (Chapter 9)—and related tensions, there is much held in common by these perspectives about transformative learning theory. As we reflect back on these various chapters, we ask: Is that really the case? Is the study of transformative learning theory moving toward greater unification?

We believe readers of the Handbook will see many similarities; however, of much more significance is the greater clarity about the relationship of the different theoretical perspectives to each other and how they inform our understanding of transformative learning theory. In addition, the differences seem to lie chiefly with the theoretical discourse used by the different perspectives, the degree of emphasis on traditional conceptions of knowing (reason, logic), and the ways in which the various perspectives see the learner shaped by their social world.

We begin with a discussion of similarities: the most obvious is how transformative learning is conceptualized. Across the board, particularly in reference to what a transformation is, most conceptions of transformative learning see it associated with dramatic change. Dirkx, for example, states in Chapter 7, "Transformative learning suggests not only change in *what* we know or are able to do but also a dramatic shift in *how* we come to know and how we understand ourselves in relation to the broader world." Similarly, O'Sullivan, Morrell, and O'Connor see transformation as equally dramatic, whereby it "involves experiencing a deep, structural shift in the basic premises of thought, feelings, and actions. It is a shift of consciousness that dramatically alters our way of being in the world" (2002, p. 11).

Another way to think about this dramatic shift is metaphorically: it is a process whereby the learner—the protagonist—confronts and comes to terms with his or her nemesis in the transformative experience. For O'Sullivan, the nemesis is an undying faith in technological advancement, in concert with unabated consumerism, with little awareness of its impact on the global environment. For Dirkx, it's an overbearing ego limiting access to the inner world of the unconscious. And for Taylor and Elias, who draw on Kegan's work, it is confronting the "socialized mind" whereby learners are unknowingly constrained by the "shoulds" of their community.

The differences between these theoretical perspectives start to emerge in the discourse used to give meaning to this dramatic change. Dirkx (Chapter 7) draws on the work of depth psychology, which emphasizes exploring the inner world, the unconscious aspects of an individual's psyche, and the implications for shaping the conscious world. Developing a deeper understanding of our unconscious, of which we are often unaware, potentially leads to greater ego consciousness. The dramatic change—a paradigm shift—involves, from Dirkx's perspective, "decentering the ego and ego consciousness in the learning process and allowing our inner selves greater expression and voice, allowing for a deeper and more meaningful presence of the imagination and the spontaneous and semi-autonomous forces of the unconscious to which it is giving voice." This emphasis of discourse about the individual is also seen by Taylor and Elias (Chapter 9), who discuss a developmental perspective of transformative learning (see, for example, the works of Kegan, Daloz). They describe this transformation as individuals seeing the world in new ways and discovering "a more autonomous sense of self... [with] a new *capacity* for exploring and even embracing a broader array of ideas, feelings, and beliefs." Brookfield (Chapter 8), on the other hand, explains a transformation using the language of critical theory, wherein the change is seen as less about struggling with the self, developing ego consciousness, and more about the individual in relationship to society and developing political consciousness. This is a consciousness with a specific focus that reflects a change "from the competitive, individualist ethics and systems of capitalism to the collective, interdependent, and cooperative ethics and systems of democratic socialism."

The analysis of the different perspectives about transformative learning at this point seems quite consistent with what was previously discussed in Chapter 1, in which they are defined by their unit of analysis: the self or society. However, despite the authors' differing emphases, they all attempt to reach beyond their locus of control, in an effort to be more inclusive. For Brookfield, this involves a new discourse moving beyond the social world and discussing individual cognition; he describes transformation as a qualitative "change in the way people think, not just a change in external political and economic arrangements." Although all the while maintaining his foothold in the social world, he goes on to explore cognition through the lens of situated learning (for example, Lave, 2003). Drawing on Mezirow, Brookfield concludes that "it is within the context of these relationships [shared life world], governed by existing and changing cultural paradigms, that we become the persons we are" (Mezirow & Associates, 2000, p. 27). Furthermore, this establishes the premise of how ideology and positionality act as deterrents to fostering transformative learning.

Dirkx (Chapter 7) does something quite similar, maintaining his center with an emphasis on the self, but like Brookfield he recognizes the role of context, particularly the larger sociocultural context, in shaping learning: "Learning contexts in adult and higher education represent microcosms in which these broader psychological, social, and cultural dynamics play out. These contexts often mirror in various ways many of the processes and structures that characterize larger sociocultural contexts in which they are embedded. As such, they have the potential to evoke powerful emotions and emotion-laden images at the personal and group levels."

Like Dirkx and Brookfield, Taylor and Elias (Chapter 9) also have an appreciation of the context; however, they conceptualize it as the "social surround" within the context of an individual's community. They go on to say: "When one's community holds steadfast against challenges to its ideas—not just questions of faith, but the more pervasive and pernicious distinctions between who 'we' are and who 'they' are, and what our relationship 'should' be—the individual, already burdened by self-questioning, faces the added anxiety of potential loss of the group (family, 'tribe') that is a primary source of identity and belonging."

Despite their efforts to stretch beyond their center, the authors in Part Two still seem strongly rooted in their unit of analysis, bounded by modernist epistemological assumptions of transformative learning theory (Lange, Chapter 12). They tend to compartmentalize and reduce transformative learning to its universal essence and overlooking the related limitations associated with this approach.

A response to this limitation is made by Alhadeff-Jones (Chapter 11) through the lens of complexity theory, who views the search for "a totalizing discourse [of transformative learning theory]...tends to reduce the diversity of variables determining real-life experience in order to highlight universal characteristics." In contrast, he argues that complexity theory "privileges the reintroduction of disorder into educational practice and theory, mainly by focusing on what has been neglected, forgotten, repressed, rejected, disqualified, excluded, or silenced by traditional methodologies." This means taking into account both what is predictable about transformative learning (the importance of dialogue and reflection) and what is unplanned and unpredictable (the randomness of who experiences a transformation around a shared experience).

Both Alhadeff-Jones and Lange are informed broadly by New Science (complexity theory), whereby they use an interdisciplinary systems approach to transformative learning theory. This perspective seems to encircle both the personal and the social by engaging and fostering—not avoiding—its inherent tensions. It means embracing tensions found between a linear (such as phases) and a nonlinear (for example, recursive, spontaneity) transformative process, the singular or local and the universal, and the predictable and unpredictable. For instance, the idea of separating the self (autonomous) from the social context is incongruent, because learners are inherently linked and defined by their surroundings. Transformation for an individual potentially has no meaning until it is recognized by the community. "Individual meaning has significance only against a horizon of community meaning, a framework from which we derive, measure, and enact individual meaning" (Lange, Chapter 12). However, at the same time the uniqueness of the individual cannot be overlooked in the context of the "community." It means taking a system perspective, focusing on "multiple levels of analysis (individual, organization, institutional, societal) in order to question what characterizes their mutual relationships and how they are intertwined with each other" (Alhadeff-Jones, Chapter 11).

A way to make sense of this view is offered by Tyler and Swartz through their discussion on storytelling (Chapter 28). Storytelling, framed within complexity theory, mirrors rhizomatic stories of change, nonlinear and unpredictable, that are "dynamic, organic, emergent, multivocal, and in possession of a life force." Through stories, transformative learning seems less about change in a dramatic sense and more about continuous self-organization and ever-shifting patterns of relationships within an individual and/or collective of learners. "As learners self-organize [transform] . . . they create new networks of patterns of connections among ideas, attitudes, assumptions, feelings, behaviors" reflected in and through stories and storytelling.

By highlighting these theoretical perspectives and related tensions, greater clarity emerges about what is inherent to transformative learning regardless of perspective, identifying it as a form of learning, unique in and of itself. However, despite these commendable efforts, most research on transformative lacks a thorough theoretical analysis. For example, English and Irving (Chapter 15) find that a preponderance of writings on transformative learning— in particular, ones that refer to gender—"used the language of transformative learning in a very superficial way and did not attempt to refute or contribute to the development of theory, actions that are necessary for its ongoing conceptualization." Taylor and Snyder (Chapter 3) affirm this perspective in their review of the literature, finding that research that engages multiple theoretical perspective of transformative learning is often too deterministic and lacking critique. This concern should challenge future researchers on transformative learning to take a more analytic approach to their work. More specifically, as researchers engage in future research about transformative learning, they should reflect on the following questions: What other conceptions of transformative learning, beyond Mezirow's evolving conception, would strengthened the theoretical framework of this study? How do the findings of this study inform, confirm, and question what is theoretically known about transformative learning theory? How do these findings inform our understanding about the relationship between the various perspectives of transformative learning theory? Only by an in-depth analysis of these questions and others will new theoretical understandings emerge.

Questions for Future Consideration

1. What is the significance (if any) of having a unified theory of transformative learning? Is it feasible? Why or why not?

2. Why does Mezirow's conception of transformative learning continue to dominate the research?

3. What is needed to encourage the inclusion of other perspectives as frameworks for research?

IMPOSING, COERCING, AND SUPPORTING

A question that implicitly arises from a few of these chapters is how do educators foster change, without imposing an agenda, in the learner-center and supportive classroom. The process seems impossible or least full of contradictions. For example, in Dorothy Ettling's Chapter 33 on ethics and transformative learning, she examines the idea that educators who are facilitating transformative learning need to challenge, push, and disrupt the thinking of learners through materials and conversations that are in conflict with conventional norms and beliefs. Such practices not only raise ethical issues but also can create an environment of tension and hostility. Furthermore, how does this work, when students have a say in the process?

In a provocative paper, Baptiste (2000) is critical of the humanist foundation of adult education in general and of transformative learning more specifically. He claims not to know a world in which being nice can overcome oppressive structures, and he advocates the use of coercive restraint, defining this as "measured coercion: force appropriate in form and severity; force that matches the level of conflict" (p. 48). Recalling Baptiste's writing in this area—along with Newman's (2011) challenge of transformative learning theory and Brookfield's clear position that being an educator can never be value-neutral—led us to consider how this issue was dealt with in this volume.

In the context of the workplace, the question is addressed explicitly. In Chapter 23, Watkins, Marsick, and Faller describe two routes for transformative learning: one is top-down, "wherein goals and directions for change are first designed by the change leaders (for instance, a new vision, a new culture, a new strategy) and then spread down and implemented throughout the organization." In other words, the change is imposed on the organization and on the people working in the organization, and, as the authors say, it is assumed that "individual learning will derive from the influence of the new system." The alternative is that changes are initiated at an individual or team level and gradually spread throughout the organization through individual, group, and collaborative experiences.

In the higher education context, the issue of coercion is also present, but perhaps not directly acknowledged. For example, in Chapter 24, Kasworm and Bowles write: "Higher education, both credit and noncredit offerings, often presents cognitive, sociocultural, and emotional challenges to adult learners. Ideally, higher education offers an *invitation* to think, to be, and to act in new and enhanced ways." They go on to describe several types of "interventions" that are used to intentionally foster transformative learning. It seems that Kasworm and Bowles's vision of transformative learning in higher education is closer to Baptiste's (2000) pedagogy of coercion than it is to, for example, learner-centered or humanist perspectives.

Also writing in the context of higher education, Weimer's (Chapter 27) stance is in sharp contrast to those who impose and coerce. She describes six ways in which educators can use learner-centered strategies: giving students power over content, having students teach each other, having students control how they learn, and having students participate in determining policies for how classes are run, controlling the pace of the course, and engaging in self-assessment. Similarly, Willis (Chapter 13), in describing an existential approach to transformative learning, emphasizes freedom, choice, responsibility, and authenticity. He invites students to learn rather than coercing them into learning.

Brookfield (Chapter 8), on the other hand, applies critical theory to the practice of and research on transformative learning, and comes down on the coercion side of the debate. He writes: "critical theory ... ensures that the transformation of social and political systems is seen as necessary for any transformation of the self. If the self is understood as politically sculpted, then learning to transform the self is a political project requiring political transformation." If we take this to heart, we see immediately that the work of fostering transformative learning must involve imposition and coercion; such a task involves pushing people to the edge of their thinking and beliefs and then beyond the edge, potentially involving what Ettling (Chapter 33) refers as a "pedagogy of discomfort." Brookfield further says, "When something is transformed, its component elements undergo a profound metamorphosis so that what emerges is fundamentally different from what went before."

Despite the perspectives that offer opposing positions, there are others in the field who attempt to bridge these conflicting perspectives. For example, Jarvis (Chapter 30) takes a stance that spans these approaches, in writing about the use of film and fiction in fostering transformative learning. She notes that the discussions of film and fiction "are often concerned with social justice, coming from a position that can be understood in terms of critical theory more generally. They draw on concepts of hegemony and resistance, focusing on the development, through film and fiction, of a critical consciousness that will heighten awareness of power structures that maintain inequalities." Jarvis also emphasizes the concept of empathy and identification with the fictional characters on a personal level; she also suggests that we can engage in transformative learning through film and fiction by "standing back" and viewing the lives of the fictional characters as "other" and then working toward understanding the alternative perspectives. By operating in more than one dimension of transformative learning, working with film and fiction blurs the boundaries between the various theoretical approaches and offers a more unified approach to fostering transformative learning.

Questions For Future Consideration

1. What is the relationship between learner support, learner-centered teaching, and transformative learning?

2. How might a supportive learning environment encourage or inhibit people from choosing to engage in transformative learning?

3. What are the implications if we morally and ethically advocate for a pedagogy of coercion?

4. What are the implications for educators who ask learners to critically examine their values and beliefs? Do they have the responsibility to do so? Why?

COMMUNITY-BASED AND COLLABORATIVE TRANSFORMATIVE LEARNING

Some chapters in this volume emphasize community-based and collaborative approaches. For example, Ntseane (Chapter 17) describes adult learning in the African context to be a "webbed connection and collective process." African humanism is described as involving "sharing, compassion, respect, commitment, and sensitivity to the needs of others, patience and kindness." Further, "by being *botho* or behaving with dignity (that is, with honesty, integrity, and trustworthiness) among the collective, the individual becomes part of an empowered group of people who are honest and accommodating, sharing a commitment to a safe life at all costs and respecting the youth and the old." The process of transformative learning is spiritual and supportive; it involves dialogue and respect for all in that dialogue; and visions and dreams have a role in transformation.

In a review of the perspectives on transformative learning in Europe and especially Greece, Kokkos (Chapter 18) finds that transformative learning in relation to community development is the main interest of theorists in Europe (rather than higher education, as is the case in the United States). European writers tend to be critical of Mezirow's cognitive perspective; they prefer to focus instead on the emotional and social aspects of transformation, the collective dimension, and relational processes, among other things.

Similarly, Mejiuni's Chapter 19, on international and community-based transformation, naturally emphasizes the community-based perspectives. She defines community-based transformative learning as a "collective transformative learning of and among groups of people who share common interests and or identities and occupy a particular territory at a particular point in time." Mejiuni focuses on informal and nonformal contexts and provides five examples of community-based transformative learning from diverse settings. In examining these cases, she concludes, among other things, that community-based transformative learning begins with personal experience and moves to social and community change.

Other chapters bring in collaboration through discussing the importance of relationships to transformative learning (for example, Schapiro, Wasserman, & Gallegos, Chapter 22) or connected knowing (English & Irving, Chapter 15), or encouraging collaboration among and with learners (Weimer, Chapter 27). In contrast to the theoretical perspectives that emphasize autonomy and the development of critical-thinking skills and independent thinking, these chapters remind us of the interconnectedness of human beings in the learning process.

Questions for Future Consideration

1. How is transformative learning about breaking away from the herd, standing back, so as to examine the social norms in which we are immersed?

2. If transformation occurs through collaboration, community, relationship, and group dialogue, how does this relate to fostering independent thinking?

3. If people are interconnected in the learning process, how are they to question those things on which they agree?

CULTURE, GENDER, AND POSITIONALITY

Looking back we see that the Handbook further confirms what has long been known about transformative learning: that it does not adequately represent the voices of those who have been historically marginalized. As Ntseane (Chapter 17) reminds us, drawing on the words of Guba and Lincoln (2005), transformative learning "needs emancipation from hearing only the voices of Western Europe, emancipation from generations of silence, and emancipation from seeing the world in one color." This need to engage other voices is also discussed by English and Irving (Chapter 15) in their gendered perspective on transformative learning, in which they conclude that "the category of gender had virtually disappeared from the adult education literature as a named and separate unit of analysis, though women's issues floated beneath the surface, and women continue to make up the majority of the student body and professoriate in adult education." This lack of representation reflects an exclusion of knowledge systems, often divergent from the mainstream. Other systems include positionality (Johnson-Bailey, Chapter 16) and culture (Kokkos, Chapter 18; Netsane, Chapter 17; Mejiuni, Chapter 19) and their relationship to transformative learning theory.

Despite their marginalization, these chapters tell a story of how the margin has shaped and influenced the center. From early on in the development of transformative learning, these scholars and others have taken the theory to task concerning a number of issues. One is the theory's overemphasis on rationality and lack of attention to other ways of knowing (for example, Belenky & Stanton, 2000; Taylor, 1997; Tisdell, 2003). Through extensive research, other constructs have been found to be equally significant, such as the importance of relationships, embodied learning, and emotions. For instance, research lends "support to the teaching domain by encouraging us to give pride of place to the body in learning and to refuse to give rational, cognitive learning all the space in the teaching and learning encounter" (English & Irving, Chapter 15).

Another issue has been the lack of attention to the learner's positionality and its relationship to transformative learning. Historically, the theory has foregrounded the individual at the expense of role of context and social location, and has not appreciated the impact these have on learning. "More often than not, the mechanisms that help us to sort and categorize our world are shaped by our social positions or societal locations: race, gender, class, sexual orientation, age, physical and mental abilities. Such factors not only affect how we view the world but also influence how the world sees us" (Johnson-Bailey, Chapter 16). It is this interplay between how others see make sense of the "other" and the other sees itself that has a tremendous influence on transformative learning.

A consequence of these critiques and others reveals the inadequacy of the conceptualization of transformative learning in addressing difference and how it has contributed to a growing interest in the development of conceptions of transformative learning that more accurately reflect the learning of marginalized groups (for example, Tisdell, 2003; Taylor, 2008). A good example is the Afrocentric paradigm that places Africans and those of African descent as subjects, not objects, as the foci of the transformative experience, "as identifying African cultural values that can be incorporated in transformative learning theory to make it more culturally sensitive" (Ntseane, Chapter 17). It also reminds scholars of the context-dependent nature of the theory (shaped by cultural values), bringing to light a discourse—distinct from a Eurocentric perspective—that emphasizes unity, faith, cooperative economics, and collective work and responsibility (Duveskog, Friis-Hansen, & Taylor, 2011).

Another example of the margin addressing the inadequacy of the center is the development of the cultural-spiritual perspective of transformative learning (Tisdell, 2003). This view is "concerned with the connection between individual social structures...and notions of intersecting positionalities" (Tisdell, 2005, p. 256), in relationship to how learners construct knowledge (narratives) as a part of the transformative learning experience. It recognizes the significance of a culturally relevant and spiritually grounded approach to fostering transformative learning. Included in this approach is engaging in narrative transformation—storytelling on the personal and social level through group inquiry, engaging the learner holistically (critically, emotionally, spirituality, and somatically), contextually situated in both place and history, and with an appreciation of the moral dimensions of learning (Brooks, 2000).

By giving attention to issues of culture, positionality, and gender, the fragmentation by varying theoretical perspectives has been both enriching and bifurcating for the study of transformative learning. English and Irving, in Chapter 15, argue that we need to view change on a continuum from personal to global, which would "enable transformative learning theory to become more robust and to further strengthen its claims to both social and personal transformation." Other consequences have led to what was once considered unique to specific cultural groups but now is the norm for transformative learning. For instance, Brookfield (2010) observes that we have now come to consensus that "learning is holistic" (p. 76), an attribute that was once applied only to women's learning (English & Irving, Chapter 15).

Looking back over the preceding discussion, it is clear that the margins made a significant contribution to the dominant perspective of transformative learning. This contribution should remind future researchers of how the study of few can inform the many. By engaging margins, we can learn much about what is central and universal to transformative learning theory.

Questions for Future Consideration

1. How does the study of cultural differences work toward the goal of a unified theory of transformative learning?
2. How do educators take advantage of the positionality of learners when engaged in the practice of fostering transformative learning?

EMOTION AND RATIONALITY

In many of these chapters there emerges a tension between emotion and reason as separate entities that share significance to transformative learning. The discussion of emotion and reason or emotion and reflection has a long history in philosophical debates. Some existential philosophers see emotion and reason as bound together (Solomon, 1993); Nietzsche (as cited in Solomon, 2000) says that every emotion contains its own quantum of reason. We see these thoughts reflected in Willis's Chapter 13 on existentialism and transformative learning, in which he describes how logic, imagination, action, and sensation or feeling are interrelated and also where he distinguishes between essentialist and existentialist ways of understand human existence.

In transformative learning theory as presented in this volume, we have Mezirow's (1991) perspective, which emphasizes a rational questioning of our assumptions and revisions to our assumptions, based on that process. We also highlight the extrarational approach in which transformative learning occurs through symbols, images, and emotional expressions (for example, see Dirkx, 2001). "These ways of knowing—which call upon our imagination (Greene, 1995) and our intuition (Lawrence, 2009) and come to us through dreams, meditations, and other unconscious processes—are often expressed through various art forms" (Lawrence, Chapter 29). This is further confirmed by Kreber in Chapter 20, where she writes that critical reflection is "not only a rational activity but also calls for creative and emotive capabilities."

Historically, this tension or separation between rationality and emotions seems rooted in early critiques of Mezirow's conception of transformative learning, about which researchers concluded that too much emphasis was given to rationality in the process of change. A 1997 review of the empirical literature on transformative learning concluded that affective learning played an equally central role in transformative learning, and that "rationality, reason, and decision-making from a logical analysis constitute just one modality of the many that are central to the transformation of meaning structures" (Taylor, 1997, p. 52).

This bifurcation seems to be a by-product of a modernist conception of cognition overlooking a system's view of emotion and rationality and their inherent relationship. Literature reviews (Taylor, 1997) and other writings have contributed to this binary perspective, even though contemporary neurobiological findings substantiate that reason and emotion are biologically linked, in that reason cannot exist with feelings or emotion (Taylor, 2001). Reason without emotions is like a boat without a rudder, wandering aimlessly, unable to make decisions. "Emotion/feeling, attention, and working memory interact so intimately that they constitute the source for the energy of both external action (movement) and interaction action (thought, animation, reasoning)" (Damasio, 1994, p. 71).

The point here is that we need to cease the discussion of rationality as a separate entity, because the very existence of rationality is rooted in the presence of emotion, without which it cannot exist. It could be argued that

Brookfield's ideological critique is no less or more an example of rationality than Lawrence's arts-based ways of knowing. These other ways of knowing—an extrarational perspective—are not separate from the reason or rationality that lead to change; rather, they are (less and less overlooked) means—similar to other means that are often falsely considered to be more "rational," such as critical reflection, logic, rational discourse, and problem solving—that promote reflection and engage the unconscious. By recognizing the interrelationship of cognition and emotion, we can give greater attention to what is most necessary: ways to facilitate the transformative experience.

For future researchers and educators who recognize the significance of emotion and its inherent relationship to reason, it is important to explore ways that help learners develop emotional awareness as they engage in transformative learning. More specifically, this awareness also seems to have direct application for better understanding of why critical reflection is so central to transformative learning.

Questions for Future Consideration

1. What is needed to foster a more synergistic perspective of emotion and rationality in the study of transformative learning theory?

2. What is it about extrarational approaches to fostering transformative learning that promote reasoning and critical reflection?

RESEARCHING TRANSFORMATIVE LEARNING

The purpose of this *Handbook of Transformative Learning* is to provide a comprehensive review of more than three decades of theory development, research, and practice in transformative learning. Most chapters in this volume, whether primarily focused on theory or practice or explicitly related to research methodologies or a review of the research, are connected to the research literature in some way. This literature has grown substantially in the last two decades, to the point where it is difficult to provide a comprehensive review of the research in one place. Where have we come to? And where should we go from here?

Merriam and Kim (Chapter 4) consider the appropriateness of various methodologies for studying transformative learning based on three factors: one's philosophical perspective (positivist, constructivist, critical, postmodern), the nature of the research question, and the maturity of the phenomenon. That third factor comes into play when the area of interest has not been well-studied and exploratory qualitative research is required—a state of affairs that we have probably left behind in research on transformative learning. They further suggest that narrative inquiry, arts-based research, critical research (such as participatory action research), and action research are directions we should be considering in our choice of methodologies in the future. We can further build on these suggestions by considering methodologies from other disciplines; for example, autoethnography from anthropology (Chang, 2008) and portraiture from the fine arts (Lawrence-Lightfoot, 2005).

Most research on transformative learning has been qualitative, as the theory is built on constructivist assumptions; however, Merriam and Kim do include a positivist perspective in their discussion of how philosophical perspectives influence the choice of methodology, and in doing so they refer to some quantitative measures that have been used in mixed methods studies. Cranton and Hoggan (Chapter 32) also refer to different ways of evaluating transformative learning, including surveys and checklists. This may be a direction that can be pursued further: the development and validation of a sound quantitative survey for the assessment of the process of transformative learning, the outcome of the process, or both. For example, we could develop a theory-based list of facets of the transformative learning process, from a variety of perspectives, and a theory-based list of outcomes of transformative learning. From there a rigorous psychometric approach could be used to develop, standardize, and validate an instrument that could be used in further research.

Beyond the various ways to research transformative learning, we come to the issue of how reviews of ongoing research shape future research. For instance, there have been a number of comprehensive reviews similar to one found this Handbook (Taylor & Snyder, Chapter 3). Taylor and Snyder suggest that reliance on reviews of the literature may tend to stifle research in a field, as researchers rely on the reviews and do not approach topics outside of those reviewed. This is a courageous statement and one that we need to pay attention to. It can even be taken further. Any scholar who carries out a review of the literature has his or her own perspective, values, beliefs, and assumptions about the field. There is the possibility, then, that a whole field of study is shaped by the perspectives of those who provide the reviews that researchers rely on. It becomes difficult to challenge the perspectives of reviewers, in part because one would need to examine all of the original articles included in the review, and in part because we become accustomed to certain points of view. That is, we develop entrenched habits of mind about the theory we are working with. When we read dozens of times that Mezirow is too rational or that relationships need to be studied in research on transformative learning, we come to uncritically assimilate those statements and act on them as though they were unquestionable. Caution is called for.

Perhaps the time has come in the development of our field of study for literature reviews to be written on a smaller scale; that is, scholars could review the literature in a particular context (for example, in workplace learning, as

Watkins, Marsick, and Fuller do in Chapter 23) or the literature that follows a certain theoretical perspective (for example, as Baumgartner does in Chapter 6) or the literature concerned with a specific culture (for example, as Ntseane does in Chapter 17). This would give us a variety of reviews on different aspects of transformative learning. Each review could be more comprehensive, given its narrower focus, and perhaps this diversity in examining the literature would lead us to see some new sparks from conflict among the perspectives.

There are two issues that we need to pay attention to in future research and writing on transformative learning theory. First, we need to become conscious of expanding the methodologies we use beyond the basic interpretive approach to research, and in doing so we need to match our choice of methodologies to the theoretical perspectives we are using as a foundation for our research. Second, we need to become conscious of the extent to which reviews of the literature shape our thinking about the field, to examine original sources, and to critically question the themes and categories presented in reviews of the literature, including those presented in this volume.

Questions for Future Consideration

1. How can we introduce innovative new research methodologies into our research on transformative learning?

2. How can we use methodologies that enhance and support the theoretical perspectives in our field?

3. How much are we shaped by literature reviews of the empirical research?

4. What concrete things can we do to inject new life and energy into our research?

THE TRANSFORMATIVE TEACHER AND LEARNER: AN EMPATHIC RELATIONSHIP

One area into which we had hoped to provide more insight as a result of this Handbook is that of teachers and learners who engage in the practice of fostering transformative learning. This is a teaching approach that is often fraught with challenges, conflict, and blind alleys and dead ends, and it can potentially lead to highly emotional reactions from learners and teachers. As Dorothy Ettling reminds us in Chapter 33, this approach to teaching "may even appear to cross the boundaries of appropriate pedagogical practice and evoke an ethical dilemma." Recognizing the challenges and risk, what do teachers and learners need to bring to the transformative classroom?

This question is asked of both teachers and learners because of their interdependent relationship in the classroom. This perspective is particularly relevant when considering that some authors in this Handbook strongly advocate for a learner-centered approach to fostering transformative learning, which blurs the boundaries between the teacher and learner and further confounds their roles and responsibilities in the transformative classroom. Many of the suppositions about teachers could easily be applied to the learner as well.

Returning to the previous question of what teachers and learners need to bring the transformative classroom, probably the most significant is self-awareness. "An awareness of one's personal value system and the degree to which certain values have been internalized is an essential point of departure in understanding how one will respond in specific situations" (Brockett, 1988, p. 11).

Another way to think about the importance of awareness for both the teacher and learner is through the lens of empathy, an essential construct of transformative learning that deserves much greater attention than it receives. Several authors (such as Jarvis, Chapter 30; Willis, Chapter 13) start to foreground empathy as important, though most of the discussion is in reference to teachers and ways that they can engender empathy among learners. Mezirow (2003) found empathy to be one of "the obvious assets for developing the ability of adults to assess alternative beliefs" (p. 60).

Empathy seems to have particular relevancy in the context of close personal relationships. Willis sees empathy as a by-product of the dialectic between the self and other. Interpreting this in the context of teaching, this dialectic, this social tension, is found in the relationships among teacher and learners, potentially generating empathy and compassion. Existentially, it is the shared experience of teaching and learning, wherein both learners and teacher, in concert with each other, learn to develop greater awareness of and understanding about themselves and others.

Developing awareness, both of self and others, involves interacting in a world that is often risky and fraught with mishaps. Willis alludes to this risk that a teacher faces in transformative education in a poem titled "Invitation," metaphorically inviting learners "to engage in similar learning and to allow room in their heart for a similar experience." Taking this metaphor of invitation even further—looking at it as a mutual process involving both the teacher and learners, in which each is inviting the other to engage in transformative learning—reframes risk as a shared experience. And self-awareness and empathy lead to a greater appreciation of the risk for both parties.

Ways to manage this risk, however, are limited, or at least not discussed much—although a few authors offer us some strategies that indirectly lead to greater empathy toward others, awareness about ourselves, and potentially lessoning risk. Jarvis (Chapter 30), for example, refers to the practice of "creating critical distance," a technique that distances "readers by drawing attention to their own fictionality. . . . It challenges . . . readers to face the social construction of reality, shaking sociocultural and epistemic assumptions." Even though Jarvis discusses this approach in the context of a literary text, it also has application in a variety of areas, all of which can foster greater empathy—an appreciation of how others view or feel about the world. For example, encouraging the sharing of multiple perspectives, discussing value-laden experiences—whether fiction, real, or otherwise—confronts teachers and learners with "the fragmented nature of [their] realities, the constructive power of memory, and individual perceptions" (Jarvis).

One other strategy, for both teachers and learners, that fosters self-awareness and empathy and addresses risk—to a degree—in the practice of transformative learning, is listening. Tyler and Swartz (Chapter 28) talk about listening in the context of storytelling, in which listening is seen as "a form of noticing the story in a way that goes beyond the content of the story, into the spaces between the lines, to listen for what is not expressed—for that which may not even be known by the teller." It is through acute attention to listening that empathy comes forth, as described by a participant in the Charaniya and West Walsh (2001) study: "if you are really listening, you can't help but be moved by whatever it is that moved them. So you have to say, 'Wow, that's a pretty powerful force that has made this person's . . . ,' you know it resonates with you" (p. 191). Listening rooted in a deep authentic and intellectual curiosity allows both teachers and learners to "read" between the lines, engendering empathy among themselves and others in the transformative classroom.

Questions for Future Consideration

1. What challenges do educators face when taking an empathic stance with learners when fostering transformative learning?
2. How do educators manage empathy when coercing, encouraging, or inviting students to engage in transformative learning?
3. What is the relationship between empathy and critical reflection?

CONCLUSION

As this Handbook comes to fruition, it is particularly exciting to see the vitality that exists around the study and practice of transformative learning. It is clear that as scholars and practitioners we have only scratched the surface of what is presently known about this exciting form of adult learning. One area of research that needs particular attention is that of giving much greater thought to theoretical analysis in relationship to research findings. This in-depth theoretical analysis will help us to, for example, move beyond the old emotion-and-reason debates to other related areas that need greater attention, such as empathy and joy and their relationship to transformative learning.

From a practice perspective, practitioners and scholars need to grapple with what is often unspoken—the value-laden nature of fostering transformative learning, which is often counter to its learner-centered image. Even educators who attempt to be learner-centered in their teaching approach are imposing a way of teaching on learners. It seems relevant not only to identify effective practices to foster transformative learning but also, and more important, to identify ways that foster a transparency of practice—a view of practice that is understood and shared by both the learner and the educator.

Finally, this Handbook should challenge scholars to pay particular attention to voices on the margins—voices of transformative experiences that often are overlooked and inadequately understood. The study of transformative learning in non-Western countries, positionality, and cultural difference holds great promise of offering new understanding of this way of adult learning.

References

Baptiste, I. (2000). Beyond reason and personal integrity: Toward a pedagogy of coercive restraint. *Canadian Journal for the Study of Adult Education, 14*(11), 27–50.

Belenky, M. F., & Stanton, A. V. (2000). Inequality, development, and connected knowing. In J. Mezirow & Associates (Eds.), *Learning as transformation: Critical perspectives on a theory in progress* (pp. 3–34). San Francisco: Jossey-Bass.

Brockett, R. G. (Ed.). (1988). *Ethical issues in adult education.* New York: Teachers College Press.

Brookfield, S. D. (2010). Theoretical frameworks for understanding the field. In C. E. Kasworm, A. D. Rose, & J. M. Ross-Gordon (Eds.), *Handbook of adult and continuing education* (pp. 71–81). Thousand Oaks, CA: SAGE.

Brooks, A. (2000). Cultures of transformation. In A. L. Wilson & E. R. Hayes (Eds.), *Handbook of adult and continuing education* (pp. 161–170). San Francisco: Jossey-Bass.

Chang, H. (2008). *Autoethnography as method.* Walnut Creek, CA: Left Coast Press.

Charaniya, N., & West Walsh, J. (2001). *Adult learning in the context of interreligious dialogue: A collaborative research study involving Christians, Jews, and Muslims* (Doctoral dissertation, National-Louis University).

Damasio, A. R. (1994). *Descartes' error: Emotion, reason, and the human brain.* New York: Putnam.

Dirkx, J. (2001). Images, transformative learning, and the work of soul. *Adult Learning, 12*(3), 15–16.

Duveskog, D., Fris-Hasen, E., & Taylor, E. W. (2011). Farmer field school in rural Kenya: A transformative learning experience. *Journal of Development Studies*, *47*(10), 1–16.

Lawrence-Lightfoot, S. (2005, February). Reflections on portraiture: A dialogue between art and science. *Qualitative Inquiry*, *11*(1), 3–15.

Lave, J. (2003). Producing the future: Getting to be British. *Antipode*, *35*(3), 492–511.

Mezirow, J. (1991). *Transformative dimensions of adult learning*. San Francisco: Jossey-Bass.

Mezirow, J. (2003). Epistemology of transformative learning. Proceedings from the Fifth International Conference on Transformative Learning: *Transformative Learning in Action: Building Bridges Across Contexts and Disciplines*, Teachers College, Columbia University.

Mezirow, J., & Associates (Eds.). (2000). *Learning as transformation: Critical perspectives on a theory in progress*. San Francisco: Jossey-Bass.

Newman, M. (2011). Calling transformative learning into question: Some mutinous thought. *Adult Education Quarterly*. doi:10.1177/0741713610392768

O'Sullivan, E. V., Morrell, A., & O'Connor, M. A. (2002). *Expanding the boundaries of transformative learning: Essays on theory and praxis*. New York: Palgrave.

Solomon, R. C. (1993). *The passions: Emotions and the meaning of life*. Indianapolis, IN: Hackett Publishing.

Solomon, R. C. (2000). *What Nietzsche really said*. New York: Random House.

Taylor, E. W. (1997). Building upon the theoretical debate: A critical review of the empirical studies of Mezirow's transformative learning theory. *Adult Education Quarterly*, *48*, 34–59.

Taylor, E. W. (2001). Transformative learning theory: A neurobiological perspective of the role of emotions and unconscious ways of knowing. *International Journal of Lifelong Education*, *20*(3), 218–236.

Taylor, E. W. (2008). Teaching and emotions in a nonformal educational setting. In J. Dirkx (Ed.), *Adult learning and the emotional self* (pp. 79–87). New Directions for Adult and Continuing Education, no. 120. San Francisco: Jossey-Bass.

Tisdell, E. J. (2003). *Exploring spirituality and culture in adult and higher education*. San Francisco: Jossey-Bass.

Tisdell, E. J. (2005). Feminism. In L. M. English (Ed.), *International encyclopedia of adult education* (pp. 254–257). London: Palgrave.

NAME INDEX

A

Abalos, D., 27
Abrams, D., 206
Adebo, G. M., 410
Adeoye, B. F., 410
Adeyinka, A. A., 76
Adkins, N. R., 139
Adorno, T., 297, 332, 489
Aga Khan, K., 233
Agyekum, S. K., 100
Ahern, T. C., 530
Albareda, R., 126
Albers, C., 448
Alcantara, L., 530
Alexander, J., 383
Alexandrin, J., 493
Alfred, M. V., 11, 24, 48, 249, 260, 265, 367
Alhadeff, M., 293, 294
Alhadeff-Jones, M., 178–180, 184–186, 188–190, 558, 559
Alheit, P., 182
Allen, I. E., 408
Alley, M., 416
Althusser, L., 297, 489
Amorok, T., 22, 30
Anderson, A. S., 182
Anderson, R., 356

Anderson, T., 409, 414, 417
Andrews, J. C., 356
Anfara, V. A., Jr., 41
Applebee, A. N., 156–157
Apps, J. W., 240, 297
Aprill, A., 513
Archer, W., 409, 414, 417
Archer-Cunningham, K., 514
Archimides, 218
Ardoino, J., 178–180, 185, 187
Arendt, H., 327, 335, 336, 426
Argyris, C., 87, 326, 376, 377, 383
Aristotle, 456
Armacost, L. K., 247, 251, 253, 254
Armbruster, P., 446
Armot, M., 275
Armstrong, J. L., 237–238
Armstrong, K., 66
Armstrong, K. B., 514
Armstrong, P., 487
Arnot, M., 247
Arnzen, M. A., 394
Asante, M. K., 280
Askeland, A., 330
Asùn, J. M., 184, 185
Aubin, D., 456, 463
Auerbach, N., 493
Auster, C. J., 447

B

Bache, C., 180, 205
Bachelard, G., 180
Bagnall, R. G., 181
Baillie, C., 25–26
Bakhtin, M., 297, 462
Balan, B. N., 247, 254
Baldwin, C., 455
Ball, G.D.S., 538
Ball, S. J., 335
Ballard, K., 190, 426
Baltodano, M., 366
Banathy, B. H., 178–179
Bandura, A., 110–111
Bangxiang, L., 39, 43
Banks, J. A., 25
Baptiste, I., 560, 561
Barnacle, R., 251
Barnes, C. P., 447
Barnett, R., 330
Barr, R. B., 440
Baskin, K., 457, 463
Bass, B. M., 359
Basseches, M., 92, 188, 325
Bateson, G., 456
Bateson, M. C., 239
Battilana, J., 383
Baumgartner, L., 10, 60, 62, 99, 232, 238, 264–267, 291, 329, 569
Baxter, L. A., 356
Baxter Magolda, M., 390
Bayne, S., 331
Beach, R., 492
Belenky, M., 8, 41, 81, 188, 205, 246–248, 254, 291, 295, 343, 358, 497, 564
Bellah, R., 81
Benjamin, B., 375
Benjamin, W., 462
Bennett, J., 359
Bennett, M., 359
Bennis, W., 79
Benson, A., 409
Berger, J. G., 49
Berger, P. L., 461
Bernstein, G. M., 479–480
Berry, T., 24, 165, 169, 175, 201, 207
Bettelheim, B., 493
Bey, G. J., 39, 41, 43, 44
Biesta, G., 178–179
Binder, A., 392, 395
Binet, N., 478, 479
Biro, S. C., 265, 267–270
Bitterman, J. E., 186, 189, 530
Bjerlöv, M., 381

Black, K. A., 441, 444
Bloom, A., 493
Bloom, L. R., 60, 66, 249
Blumberg, P., 439
Blumer, H., 100
Blunt, K., 254
Boal, A., 480, 481
Bohm, D., 356
Bohr, N., 199
Boje, D. M., 455–457, 459, 460, 462–464
Bokou, P., 297
Bolger, B. B., 410
Bonazzi, R., 219
Bond, D. S., 116, 123
Bonetti, M., 184
Bonnett, M., 332
Boud, D., 311, 330–331
Bourdieu, P., 268, 297
Boverie, P., 260, 398–399
Bowers, C. A., 538
Bowles, T. A., 388, 561
Bowser, D., 392
Boyd, D., 39, 41, 42
Boyd, R. D., 11, 13, 38, 41, 42, 47, 83, 87, 110, 116–118, 120, 122, 212, 260, 265–266, 269, 291, 295, 296, 363, 364, 413, 456, 472, 492, 542
Boyer, N., 39, 40, 46
Boynton, A. C., 373
Bracher, M., 330
Bradshaw, E. I., 110
Brecht, B., 494
Brent, C. P., 449
Bridglall, B., 530
Briggs, J., 200, 203
Brigham, S. M., 41, 43
Briscoe, D. B., 260
Brock, S., 39–41
Brockett, R. G., 537, 538, 544, 570
Brookfield, S. D., 4, 8–9, 41–42, 85, 93, 110, 131, 142, 185, 249, 250, 255, 265–266, 290, 291, 295, 297, 298, 323, 324, 326, 329–331, 335, 366, 383, 443, 448, 486, 490, 496, 523, 541, 557, 558, 560, 561, 565–567
Brooks, A. K., 249, 250, 254, 374, 375, 565
Brown, A. K., 459
Brown, B., 445
Brown, J. O., 392
Brown, K. M., 39, 41–42, 58, 390, 395
Brown, M. Y., 165, 166
Brown-Haywood, F., 238
Bruce, K. A., 410
Brundage, D., 4, 345

Bruner, J., 74, 80, 426, 455
Bruning, M. D., 399
Bruteau, B., 546
Bryant, I., 181, 186
Buber, M., 356, 358
Buck, M. A., 247, 248, 250, 251, 254
Burke, W. W., 376–378, 381
Burns, H., 393, 395
Burns, J. M., 379
Burr, V., 490
Burris, J. K., 392
Butterwick, S., 65, 394, 476, 536, 541

C

Caffarella, R. S., 10, 60, 260, 291,
    311–312
Cajete, G., 207, 471, 473, 482
Caldarelli, M. K., 395
Calderwood, P. E., 543
Campbell, J., 428
Candy, P., 91
Cannato, J., 546
Capra, F., 32, 197, 199, 456, 463, 464
Carawan, L., 39–40, 250, 253
Cardwell, N., 379
Carmody, J., 31–32
Carr, W., 57
Carrington, S., 39–41, 59, 66, 391, 393
Carson, L., 40, 391
Carter, A., 496
Carter, T. J., 254, 398–399
Carusetta, E., 331
Casey, A., 409
Castellani, B., 463
Castledon, H., 334
Cawelti, J., 493
Ceballos, R. M., 137
Cervero, R. M., 59, 260, 265, 267
Chafin, C. K., 398–399
Chalmers, C., 416
Chandler, H., 493
Chandra, V., 416
Chang, H., 568
Charaniya, N. K., 231, 234–238, 571
Chasidou, M., 297
Cheang, K. I., 446
Chesser-Smyth, P., 293, 294
Chilisa, B., 274, 277, 278, 285
Chin, S. S., 39–41, 44, 45, 48, 49
Chistman, D., 409
Chomsky, N., 133
Choy, S., 39–40, 46, 529
Cissna, K. N., 356
Clandinin, D. J., 64

Clare, R., 39–42, 46, 47
Clark, C., 13, 87, 204, 232–235, 245, 251, 252,
    487
Clark, M. C., 22, 91, 107, 116, 205, 260, 264,
    265, 425, 427, 435, 524
Clark, R. E., 411, 412
Clarkson, A., 118
Clements, A., 163, 164
Clénet, J., 178–179
Clinchy, B. M., 81, 188, 205, 246, 247, 254,
    343, 358, 497
Clover, D., 65, 208, 247, 253, 254
Clover, D. E., 479, 481
Coady, M., 4
Codner, S., 410
Cohen, L., 86
Cole, A. L., 64, 482
Coleridge, S., 493
Colin, S.A.J., III, 260
Collard, S., 7, 13, 104, 185, 265
Collins, M., 132
Collins, P., 268
Conceição, S.C.O., 417, 418
Conger, J., 375
Congleton, C., 31–32
Congram, S., 118
Conrad, J., 486
Cook, B. J., 58
Cooley, L., 39–40, 46, 247, 250, 254
Cooper, S., 530
Coppola, B., 409
Corbin, H., 124, 217
Corey, G., 356
Corey, M. S., 356
Courtenay, B. C., 59, 265, 267
Cox, R. D., 390
Cragg, C. E., 409
Cranton, P., 3, 11, 23, 38, 39, 41, 44, 45, 116,
    126, 142, 157, 212, 246–248, 250, 251, 254,
    260, 264–266, 291, 295, 297, 298, 304, 316,
    317, 329–331, 333, 334, 350, 356, 410, 413,
    416, 442, 446–448, 474, 475, 486, 493, 520,
    526, 530, 538, 541, 542, 544, 555, 568
Cresswell, J. W., 56, 58, 60
Crocco, M., 529, 530
Cross, J., 214–215
Cross, W. E., 267
Crotty, M., 59
Cueva, M., 478
Cullen, R., 439
Cunningham, P. M., 41, 107, 279, 540
Curry, R., 279
Curry-Stevens, A., 46, 545
Czarniawska, B., 459, 462

D

Dall'Alba, G., 216
Dalmedico, A. D., 456, 463
Daloz, L. A., 110, 148, 149, 155, 157, 159, 232, 239, 241, 265–266, 269, 291, 332, 361, 543, 557
Daly, J., 393
Damasio, A. R., 566
Danaher, P. A., 92
Dang, N.L.T., 124, 392–394
Darder, A., 366
Darlington, Y., 330
Datan, N., 111
Davidson, D., 536, 541
Davis, A., 249
Davis, B., 204, 205
Davis, D., 231
Davis, F., 100
Davis, R. H., 116, 117
Davis, W., 207
Davis-Manigaulte, J., 183–184, 542
Dawson, T., 116, 117
de Certeau, M., 455
de Gaulejac, V., 184
DeAngelis, K. J., 445
Dececchi, B. G., 390
Deeley, S. J., 391
Deng, L., 416
Descartes, R., 278
Descendre, D., 184
Deshler, D., 526–527
Deshler, J. D., 333
Devereux, G., 187, 188
DeVries, C., 488
Dewey, J., 41, 213–214, 222, 323, 324, 328, 342, 343, 356
Dickinson, G., 100
DiClementi, J. D., 440, 444–446
Dinesen, I., 426
Dirkx, J., 8, 11, 23, 24, 27, 41, 42, 75, 116, 117, 120–124, 154, 185, 212, 213, 231, 235, 236, 245, 252, 260, 265–267, 291, 295, 297, 298, 331, 333, 342, 359, 392–394, 410–411, 413, 415, 416, 459, 467, 472, 473, 477, 486, 492, 522, 536, 542, 543, 545, 556–558, 566
Dixson, A., 247, 251, 252
Doberneck, D. M., 392, 393
Döbert, R., 89
Dobson, D., 120
Docherty, P., 381
Doll, M., 487
Dominicé, P., 182, 186, 291, 293, 295, 524
Donahue, T., 390, 392
Donaldson, J. F., 15, 395

Douglass, Fredrick, 139
Doyle, T., 439, 443, 449
Drago-Severson, E., 374, 524
DuBois, W.E.B., 260
Dubouloz, C.-J., 293, 295
Durand, G., 124
Duveskog, D., 39, 41, 43, 291, 293, 294, 296, 305, 306, 311, 313–315, 564–565

E

Eagleton, T., 488
Easton, P., 15
Edelman, G., 456
Edwards, A., 196, 197
Edwards, N. M., 442
Egan, T., 15, 541
Einstein, A., 147, 199
Eisner, E., 474
Elias, D., 147, 159, 291, 295, 367, 542, 556–558
Elias, J. L., 6, 102, 106
Ellis, C., 427
Ellner, C. L., 447
Ellsworth, E., 186
Elsey, M., 394
Elvy, J. C., 247, 250, 253
Engels, F., 141
Engeström, Y., 297, 373, 374
English, L. M., 231, 233, 245, 246, 250, 396, 559, 563–565
Ennis, R. H., 324
Entwistle, N., 413
Epley, D., 100
Erichsen, E. A., 390, 392
Esteva, G., 208
Estrela, A., 216
Ethier, K. A., 111
Etmanski, C., 394
Ettling, D., 247, 248, 536, 544, 560, 561, 569
Ewert, G. D., 521

F

Faller, P. G., 373, 560, 568–569
Farrell, P., 415
Farrell, T. S., 334
Faulk, D., 39, 40, 395
Faundez, A., 266
Fear, F., 392, 393
Fearon, D., 375
Felder, R. M., 449
Felix, S., 522
Feller, A. E., 393–394
Fennell, S., 275
Fenson, S., 293, 294
Fenstermacher, K., 488

Fenwick, T., 201, 342, 351–353, 379–380, 426
Ferrer, J., 122
Fetherston, B., 39, 40, 46, 47, 293–296, 393, 545
Fiddler, M., 157
Fingarette, H., 102
Finger, M., 184, 185
Finnegan, C. L., 530
Fish, S., 497
Fisher, K., 40, 391
Fisher-Yoshida, B., 24, 173, 358
Flannery, D., 246, 251
Fleming, T., 293, 295, 296
Fook, J., 330
Forest, C., 247, 248, 251, 252, 254
Forrester, G., 39, 43
Foucault, M., 9, 132, 133, 268, 297, 330, 491
Fowler, J. W., 235, 539
Fowler, R., 316
Frank, A. W., 428, 430, 432, 435, 436
Freire, P., 4, 13, 22, 24, 38, 41, 42, 59, 66, 87, 102, 126, 212, 252, 254, 266–269, 291, 295, 298, 311, 324, 325, 356, 359, 366, 367, 480, 537
Freud, S., 83
Frey, R. F., 445
Friis-Hanson, E., 39, 41, 43, 291, 293, 294, 296, 305, 306, 311, 313–315, 564–565
Fromm, E., 135, 208, 297
Frosty, S., 87
Fulghum, R., 82

G
Gabriel, Y., 459
Gajanayake, J., 247, 248
Gallegos, B., 398–399
Gallegos, P. V., 355, 356, 563
Gandhi, M., 159, 205
Gard, T., 31–32
Gardner, M., 24, 173
Gare, A., 168
Garman, N., 217
Garrison, D. R., 409, 414, 417
Garrison, R., 330–331
Gatt, I., 525
Gee, J. P., 316
Geller, K. D., 24, 157, 173, 358, 383
Geng, Q., 409
Gephart, M., 378
Gerber, D., 39
Gergen, K. J., 356
Gershman, K., 213
Gersick, C., 378
Gillen, M. A., 231, 232–233

Gilligan, C., 205, 539
Gillis, S., 521, 522
Gilly, M. S., 514–515
Gilmartin, M. J., 383
Giroux, H., 268, 297, 323, 487, 489, 495
Giroux, S., 323
Glaser, B. G., 100
Gleick, J., 200, 203
Glisczinski, D., 39, 40, 390, 393
Goduka, I. N., 278
Goldberger, N. R., 81, 188, 246, 247, 254, 343, 358, 497
Golde, M. F., 445
Goleman, D., 79
Goodman, R., 522
Gore, A., 479
Goulah, J., 39–41, 43, 173, 394, 412
Gould, R., 83, 291, 325, 326, 531
Govender, P., 306, 307, 311–313
Gowin, D. B., 526
Gozawa, J., 120, 542, 545
Gramsci, A., 131, 297, 324, 489
Grant, L. D., 250
Gravett, S., 67, 393, 395–396, 536, 541, 542
Gray, D., 293–296, 334
Gray, T., 441
Greene, G. J., 392, 393, 395
Greene, M., 89, 213–214, 216, 222, 295, 330, 336, 471–473, 481, 486, 491, 497, 527
Gregory, M., 441, 447
Griffin, J. H., 219–221, 224, 225
Griffin, P., 521, 522
Griffin-Bonazzi, E., 219
Groome, T., 29
Grow, G. O., 443, 449
Guba, E. G., 275, 563
Guilian, L., 247, 248
Guion, J. M., 410
Gunnlaugson, O., 5, 12, 30, 38, 522, 538
Gurevich, Z. D., 377
Gurin, P., 366
Guthrie, K. L., 411
Guy, T. C., 260, 409, 496
Guy-Sheftall, B., 269

H
Habermas, J., 59, 77, 78, 89, 99, 102, 103, 110, 111, 135, 136, 144, 297, 315–316, 324–328, 364, 520, 521
Hafferty, F., 463
Hai-Jew, S., 411
Halfyard, J., 488
Hall, S., 260
Hammer, R., 330, 495, 496

Hamp, J., 247–249
Hamza, A., 43
Handelsman, M. M., 440, 444–446
Hanley, M. S., 187
Hanlin-Rowney, A., 39–41, 46
Hansman, C. A., 247, 253, 254, 309, 311, 313–315
Hanson, L., 39–42, 395, 396
Harding, M. E., 121–122, 274
Harding, S., 274
Harmon, S. W., 410, 417
Harris, M., 439
Hart, M., 7, 13, 77, 92
Hart, M. U., 311
Hart, T., 30, 32
Harvey, B., 293, 294, 296
Hashimoto, Y., 395
Havel, V., 203
Hawken, P., 186
Hawkensworth, M., 107, 111
Hayduk, D., 488
Hayes, E., 246
Hayes, S., 476, 478–480, 513, 515
Heidegger, M., 216
Heifitz, R., 374
Heisenberg, W., 199
Helms, J. E., 267
Hendershot, K., 390
Henderson, G. M., 375
Hendley, D., 333–334
Hendra, R., 39
Herman, E., 133
Herman, L., 543
Hernandez-Serrano, J., 63
Hernendez, A., 312
Heron, J., 15, 41, 46, 75, 216–218, 221, 224, 297, 456, 504, 507–510, 513
Heshusius, L., 190, 426
Hiebert, P., 30
Hietapelto, A. B., 442
Hill, P. C., 233
Hill Collins, P., 252
Hiller, T. H., 442
Hillman, J., 116, 217
Hockings, S. C., 445
Hodge, S., 39
Hoff, J. G., 392
Hogaboam-Gray, A., 524
Hoggan, C., 520, 526, 527, 568
Holland, N, 497
Holland, P., 217
Hollis, J., 120
Holst, J. D., 131, 140
Hölzel, B., 31–32

Homer, 223
Hood, R. W., 233
hooks, b., 252, 268, 297, 330
Hoppers, C.A.O., 286
Horell, H., 29
Horkheimer, M., 7, 131, 297
Horton, L. C., 410
Horton, M., 4, 22, 24, 366, 480
Horton, Z., 480
Houle, C. O., 60
Howard, B., 415
Hughes, J. E., 410
Hugo, K., 409
Hundleby, C., 274
Hunt, C., 293, 294, 296, 394
Hussein, J. W., 398
Hutchison, A., 43

I
Ibsen, H., 489
Ickovics, J. R., 111
Illeris, K., 293, 295, 297
Illich, I., 187
Irving, C. J., 245, 246, 559, 563–565
Irwin, R., 29
Isaacs, W., 87, 356
Iser, W., 497
Isopahkala-Bouret, U., 39–40

J
Jackson, M. G., 29–30
Jackson, S., 253
Jacobs, G. C., 333
James, M., 410
Janik, D., 542
Janoff, S., 366
Jansen, T., 90
Jarecke, J., 14–15, 66, 540, 541, 543
Jaruszewicz, C., 39, 40, 67
Jarvis, C., 486, 496, 561, 570, 571
Jarvis, P., 290, 297
Jaspers, K., 215
Jeanetta, S., 247, 248, 252, 254
Jenlink, P. M., 178–179
Jeris, L., 247, 248
Jick, T., 381
Johns, T., 512
Johnson, E., 446
Johnson-Bailey, J., 11, 24, 48, 187, 249, 252, 254, 260, 265, 267–270, 367, 564
Johnston, R., 181, 186
Jokikokko, K., 39, 40, 43–45
Jonassen, D. H., 63
Jones, P., 396, 528

Jones, R. A., 118
Jordan, J., 365
Jucker, R., 538
Jung, C. G., 83, 116–127, 158, 217, 477

K

Kagiavi, M., 297
Kairson, B., 390
Kalogridi, S., 297
Kanter, R. M., 381
Karalis, T., 293, 295, 296, 298, 299
Karpiak, I., 200, 463, 464
Kasl, E., 15, 39, 41, 46, 183–184, 216, 291, 295, 356, 358, 367, 394, 503, 504, 507, 511, 513, 542, 543
Kasworm, C. E., 388, 539, 540, 561
Kates, I. C., 473
Kauffman, S. A., 463
Keeling, R. P., 399
Kegan, R., 2, 11, 25, 29, 30, 38, 41, 48, 78, 89, 92, 126, 147, 150–158, 239, 249, 275, 291, 295, 359, 374, 390, 456, 522, 524, 538, 556, 557
Kelly, G. A., 326
Kelly, R., 39, 40, 46, 47, 293–296, 393, 545
Kelly, U., 24, 173
Kemmis, S., 57
Kennedy, P., 162, 163, 195
Kennedy, R., 159
Kenney, P., 392, 393
Keogh, R., 330–331
Kerton, S., 39
Khan, H. I., 28
Kidd, J. R., 342
Kilgore, D., 60, 66, 249
Killeavy, M., 409, 417
Kim, S., 56, 567, 568
Kimbles, S. L., 122
Kincheloe, J. L., 59
King, A. P., 58
King, K., 39–41, 46, 47, 58, 291, 295
King, K. P., 6, 265, 267–270, 410, 525
King, M. L., Jr., 159
King, P., 89, 105, 497
Kinzie, J., 441
Kirkman, S., 39–40, 46
Kitchener, J., 105, 291, 295, 497
Kitchener, K., 74, 89, 325, 326
Kitchenham, A., 102, 260, 266
Klampfleitner, M., 331
Kluge, M. A., 247, 249–251
Knight, S., 39–40, 250, 253
Knottenbelt, M., 331
Knowles, J. G., 64, 482

Knowles, M., 4, 6
Knowles, M. S., 100, 342
Knuth, B. A., 333
Koeske, R., 445
Kokkos, A., 289, 293, 294, 296–298, 562, 564
Kolb, A., 358
Kolb, D. A., 156, 342, 349, 350, 358
Konate, M., 280
Konno, N., 358
Koole, M., 416
Korten, D. C., 168, 196
Kossak, M., 31
Kotter, J. P., 381
Koulaouzides, G., 297
Kozma,R. B., 412
Krauss, S. E., 60, 61
Kreber, C., 323, 331, 334, 335
Kriesberg, J., 126
Kroth, M., 260
Krupa, T., 429
Kucukaydin, I., 251
Kuhn, J. S., 311, 375
Kuhn, T. S., 102, 107, 111, 326, 456
Kumagai, A. K., 392, 398
Kundera, M., 73
Kung, H. C., 390
Kuntzelman, K., 39–40
Kurubacak, G., 409, 410, 412, 415
Kyi, Aung San Suu, 159

L

Laenui, P., 277
Lahey, L. L., 126, 522
Laiken, M., 381
Lakoff, G., 207, 526
Lamm, S. L., 375
Lamoreaux, A. J., 392
Lan, W. Y., 530
Land, R., 25–26
Landis, D., 359
Lane, B. S., 455
Langan, D., 536, 541
Langdom, J., 293, 294, 296
Lange, E. A, 48, 195, 204, 208, 213, 540, 558, 559
Langer, E., 76
Langer, J. A., 156–157
Lani-Bayle, M., 182, 184
Lara, M., 39–40
Larson, D. B., 233
Laszlo, E., 197, 199, 200, 204, 205, 209
Lather, P., 57
Lauber, T. B., 333

Lave, J., 143, 557
Lavin, R., 342
Law, M., 7, 13, 104, 185, 265
Lawrence, R. L., 65, 291, 394, 471–473, 475, 476, 479, 512, 513, 536, 541, 566–567
Lawrence-Lightfoot, S., 568
Lazar, S., 31–32
Lazaridou, T., 297
Le Grand, J.-L., 184
Leahy, M. J., 514–515
Lear, G., 213
Lee, E., 247, 251
Lee, G.C.M., 236–237
Lee, M. Y., 392, 393, 395
Lee, S., 529
Lehman, R. M., 417, 418
Lennox, S. L., 394
Leonard, D., 381
Leonard, T., 124
Lerner, N, 488
Lesourd, F., 184
Leverett, R. G., 410, 418
Lewin, K., 342, 356, 376, 379, 456
Lewis, J. E., 440, 445
Lewis, S. E., 440, 445
Li, J., 409
Lin, L., 530
Lincoln, E. Y., 275, 563
Linde, C., 426
Lindeman, E., 4, 147, 323, 356
Lintzeris, P., 297, 299
Lippitt, R., 356
Litwin, G. H., 378
Litz, R. A., 440
Liu, J., 315
Liu, X., 530
Loads, D., 330
Loder, J., 29
Loevinger, J., 325, 539
London, P., 473
Long, H. B., 100
Lorenz, E. N., 463
Loue, S., 29
Lourau, R., 187, 188
Louv, R., 208
Luckmann, A., 461
Lundberg, G. C., 376
Lyle, S., 333–334
Lynam, M. J., 528

M
Macdonald, J., 217
Macedo, D. P., 267
Mackenzie, C., 331

MacKeracher, D., 4, 342, 345, 346
MacLoed, R., 15, 541
MacRone, M., 447
Macy, J., 165, 166, 200
Madsen, S., 43, 58
Magro, K., 41–43, 398
Maher, F. A., 260, 330
Maher, P., 39–40, 46
Makgoba, M. W., 276
Mallett, M. A., 182, 184
Mallory, J. L., 58
Maltbia, T. E., 530, 540
Maly, M. R., 429
Mandela, N., 158–159
Mandell, A., 543
Maney, J. S., 110
Manicom, L., 24, 254
Marcuse, H., 9, 140
Marienau, C., 157
Markos, L., 10
Marmon, E. L., 392
Marschke, M., 39
Marshall, G., 314
Marsick, V. J., 291, 295, 311, 323, 367, 373, 375, 377, 378, 382, 390, 525, 528, 530–531, 540, 560, 568–569
Martin, L. G., 260
Marx, K., 83, 132, 142, 297
Maslow, A. H., 6
Mathison, J., 294, 296
Matthieson, J., 110
Mattingly, C., 436
Maturana, H., 199
Mayes, C., 118
Mayo, P., 297, 308–312
Mayuzumi, K., 247, 249, 251, 252
Mazama, A., 279
McAdams, D. P., 116, 123
McArdle, K., 512
McBrien, J., 39, 40
McCaffery, J., 254
McClannon, T., 415
McCormick, K., 497
McCracken, H. J., 411
McCreary, C. L., 445
McCullough, M. E., 233
McCune, V., 331, 413
McDonald, B., 59, 265, 267
McGregor, C., 540, 542
McIntosh, P., 260
McKeon, R., 456
McLaren, P., 59, 142, 297, 330, 495, 496
McLuhan, M., 167
McNamee, S., 356

McNiff, S., 474

McQuilkin, J. L., 416

McRae, M. B., 119

McTaggert, L., 205

McWhinney, W., 10

Mead, M., 41

Mealman, C. A., 475

Meisel, S., 375

Mejiuni, O., 247, 250–252, 304, 307, 308, 313–315, 563, 564

Melville, H., 486

Mentkowski, M., 396

Merriam, S. B., 4–6, 10, 13, 41–43, 60, 91, 102, 106, 107, 110, 112, 116, 232, 260, 267, 280, 291, 311–312, 315, 567, 568

Merrill, B., 182

Mertz, N. T., 41

Metzger, D., 167

Meyer, A., 377

Meyer, J., 25–26

Meyer, P., 379, 394

Meyer, S., 248, 251, 541, 543

Meyers, S. A., 299, 412

Mezirow, J., 3–16, 22–26, 30, 31, 37, 38, 41–43, 45, 48, 56, 58, 59, 61, 64, 66, 68, 69, 93, 99–112, 117, 126, 132, 135, 142, 143, 153, 157, 158, 178, 181, 182, 188, 203, 212, 233, 235, 236, 239, 240, 246, 254, 260, 261, 265, 266, 268, 275, 280, 291, 304, 314–317, 323, 325, 328, 329, 331, 333, 334, 342, 349–351, 359, 363, 364, 367, 390, 396, 412, 442, 456, 461, 472, 473, 477, 482, 486, 487, 490, 495, 503, 513, 515, 520, 522, 523, 539, 540, 542–544, 566, 570

Michelli, D., 293, 294, 296

Michelson, E., 251, 426

Mikhael, M. R., 394

Miles, R., 15

Miller, E., 164

Miller, J., 231, 236

Miller, N., 342, 350

Mills, S., 316, 317

Ming-Dao, D., 206

Mishler, E. G., 64, 433

Mitchell, M., 456, 463, 464

Moll, K., 488

Moloney, A., 409, 417

Monkman, K., 15

Montuori, A., 180, 186, 187, 189, 190

Moon, J. A., 330

Moon, P., 60

Moore, T., 474, 477, 478

Morin, E., 178–180, 182–184, 186, 187, 189, 190, 297

Morrell, A., 24, 116, 126, 164–166, 171, 172, 175–176, 183–184, 546, 556

Morris, A., 39, 40

Morris, A. H., 395

Morris, L. V., 530

Morris, V. C., 214

Morrison, A., 223

Morrison, T., 497

Moser, S., 260

Mott, V. W., 39–40, 43, 45, 46

Motteram, G., 39, 43

Muhammad, C. G., 247, 251, 252

Muller, P. A., 441

Mullett, J., 512

Mwebi, B. M., 41, 43

Myers, J. G., 11, 13, 42, 116, 117, 120, 212, 264–266, 291, 295, 296, 363, 364, 413, 472, 492

Myers, K. D., 156

Myers, P. B., 156

N

Na, S., 247, 251

Nagda, B.R.A., 366

Nakazawa, K., 416

Nash, S. T., 247, 248, 252

Neugarten, B. L., 111

Neville, B., 118

Newberg, A., 32

Newman, M., 10, 13, 14, 107, 224, 487, 523, 529, 560

Nicholls, J., 416

Nichols, T., 39–40

Nietsche, F., 565

Nieuwenhuis, L., 293–295

Nilson, L. B., 446

Nixon, J., 332

Noble, S. E., 512

Noel, T. W., 448, 449

Nohl, A. M., 39, 41, 42, 44, 48, 49

Nonaka, I., 358

Novak, J. D., 526

Ntiri, D., 39, 40, 46, 47

Ntseane, G., 41–43, 110, 232, 274, 276, 280, 281, 315, 562–564

Nunner-Winkler, G., 89

Nussbaum, M., 323–325, 332, 336

O

Obilade, O. O., 307, 308, 313–315

Ochberg, R. L., 426

Ocitti, J. P., 276

O'Connor, M., 24, 116, 126, 164–166, 171, 172, 175–176, 183–184, 546, 556

O'Keefe, G., 471, 475, 477
Olakulehin, F. K., 410
Oliver, D., 213, 541
Olson, K., 479, 481
O'Neil, J., 525, 530–531
O'Neill, E., 172, 173
Orr, D., 195, 197, 199, 201, 208, 538
Osberg, D., 179
Osmond, J., 330
O'Sullivan, E., 13, 23–24, 27, 29–31, 38, 41, 42, 116, 126, 162–166, 171, 172, 175–176, 183–184, 207, 367, 412, 538, 546, 556
Ozanne, J. L., 139

P
Pache, A.-C., 383
Pagès, M., 184–186
Palloff, R. M., 414, 417
Palmer, P., 363
Palmer, P. J., 120, 285
Paprock, K., 88
Pargament, K. I., 233
Parks, D., 492
Parks, S., 22
Pasquariello, G., 392, 393
Patel, M., 446
Patterson, F., 475
Patton, M. Q., 56, 59, 464
Paul, P., 178–180, 190
Paul, R., 324, 330–331
Pearce, K. A., 365
Pearce, W. B., 357, 363
Peat, D., 200, 203
Perry, W. G., 156, 539
Peterman, S., 445
Peters, J. M., 237–238
Peters, N., 250
Petersen, N., 393, 395–396, 536, 541, 542
Pettit, J., 294–296, 395–396
Philip, R., 416
Piaget, J., 342, 343, 539
Picher, M., 515
Piercy, M., 486
Pietersen, W., 383
Pietrykowski, B., 107, 181
Pigza, J. M., 396
Pineau, G., 178–180, 190
Pintrich, P. R., 442
Plaza, C. M., 398–399
Plotnikoff, R. C., 409
Poisson, D., 178–179
Pokorny, M., 39–40, 250, 253
Polyzoi, E., 41–43

Poortman, S. H., 416
Pope, S. J., 267
Popper, K. R., 456
Prah, K. K., 280
Prakash, M., 208
Prasad, P., 57
Pratt, K., 414, 417
Preciphs, T. K., 260
Preece, J., 277, 290, 293–296
Prescott, A., 410
Progoff, I., 526

Q
Quinn, R. E., 282

R
Rachal, J. R., 16
Raelin, J. A., 374, 375, 380
Randall, W. L., 63
Rasheed, S., 214, 216
Rea, T., 43
Reamer, F. G., 537
Reason, P., 507–510, 513
Reuning-Hummel, S., 410
Reushle, S. E., 409
Revans, R., 87
Rhoads, R. A., 324
Riessman, C. K., 64
Rigg, C., 323, 333
Riley, A. T., 398
Riley, J., 496
Rimmer, A., 530
Ritz, A., 390, 392, 393
Roberson, W., 512
Roberts, N. A., 110
Robinson, C. F., 392, 393
Roden, K., 394
Roffman, K., 39–40
Rogers, C., 6, 487
Rogers, C. R., 356
Rogers, P. C., 410, 414
Rolheiser, C., 524
Rollings, G., 159
Romanelli, E., 378
Romero, M., 126
Roosevelt, Eleanor, 159
Roquet, P., 184
Rose, A. D., 356
Rosebrough, T. R., 410, 418
Rosen, G., 460
Rosenau, P. M., 181
Rosenfield, I., 74–75
Rosenwald, G. C., 426

Rosenwasser, P., 512
Ross, J. A., 524
Ross-Gordon, J. M., 260
Rossiter, M., 487, 524
Rourke, L., 417
Rowland, G., 410
Rowland, S., 330
Roy, M., 538
Rozas, L., 528
Rubenson, K., 90
Rush, B., 39, 40
Rusnell, D., 100

S
Sable, D., 412, 413, 415, 416
Sanders, R., 28, 415
Sandlin, J. A., 39, 41, 43, 44, 139, 486
Sands, D., 39–42, 44, 49, 63
Santopolo, F. A., 100
Sarbin, T. R., 426
Sardello, R., 122
Sartre, J., 213–214, 222
Saul, J. R., 167
Saunders, H., 366
Schapiro, S. A., 24, 58, 155–156, 173, 355, 358, 563
Scharmer, C. O., 546
Scharmer, O., 379
Schein, E., 376–377, 383
Scher, A., 478, 513, 515
Schlitz, M., 22, 30, 164
Schön, D., 323, 324, 326, 330–331, 376, 384
Schugurensky, D., 186
Scott, S., 49, 200, 467
Scott, S. M., 331, 472
Seaman, J., 408
Seeger, P., 480
Sek Kim, Yi, 5
Selva, G., 39–41, 59, 66, 391, 393
Sen, A., 336
Senge, P. M., 356
Sengul, M., 383
Seo, K. K., 411, 412
Servage, L., 333
Shaw, S. M., 530
Sheared, V., 48
Sheese, R., 536, 541
Shiva, V., 208
Shor, I., 537
Short, E. L., 119
Siegal, H., 90
Siegel, D., 32

Siegel, H., 324, 325
Sifakis, N., 297
Simmons, A., 441
Simpson, S., 477, 526, 527
Sims, L., 39, 43
Sinclair, A. J., 39, 43
Singer, T., 122
Singham, M., 451
Sinha, S., 216, 222
Sinnott, J. D., 178–179, 182, 183
Slater, P., 367
Slattery, P., 475, 482
Sloep, P. B., 416
Smith, L., 277, 278
Smith, R. O., 124, 408, 410–413, 415, 416, 530, 536, 542, 543, 545
Smith, S. R., 335
Snyder, C., 110
Snyder, M. J., 37, 488, 559, 568
Sobel, D., 208
Socrates, 151, 336
Sokol, A. V., 394
Solomon, R. C., 566
Somasundaram, J., 392
Sonik, M., 117
Souvaine, E., 522
Spehler, R. M., 475, 482
Spence, L. D., 443
Spretnak, C., 199
Sprow, K., 456, 488
Stackpool-Moore, L., 293, 295
Stage, F. K., 441
Stanton, A., 8, 41, 564
Stanton, A. V., 247–248, 254
Stapley, L. F., 119
Stein, B., 381
Stein, M., 116–122
Steinmetz, D., 26
Steinnes, J., 487
Sterner, G., 392
Stevens, A., 116, 123
Stevens, K., 39
Stewart, M., 39, 40, 46, 47
Stratton, N., 118
Strauss, A. L., 100
Strenger, C., 215
Stromquist, N. P., 247, 254
Stuckey, H., 526, 527
Sumara, D., 204, 205
Sumner, J., 208
Sussman, A., 31
Swartz, A. L., 455, 456, 559, 571
Swimme, B., 168, 175, 201, 207

Swyers, J. P., 233
Sztompka, P., 202

T

Tagg, J., 440
Tait, B., 488
Takacs, D., 264
Takaki, R., 260
Tallent-Runnels, M. K., 530
Tallis, Thomas, 21, 28, 33
Tallman, J., 409
Tannen, D., 79
Tarnas, R., 201
Tarnoczi, T., 39
Tarule, J. M., 188, 246, 247, 254, 343, 358, 497
Taylor, C., 205
Taylor, E. T., 250, 251, 253
Taylor, E. W., 9, 12–16, 23, 24, 37, 39, 41, 43,
    44, 48, 56, 59, 60, 64–67, 69, 100, 108, 111,
    112, 178, 181, 183, 184, 187, 236, 245, 246,
    265, 284, 291, 293–295, 297, 298, 316, 331,
    355, 356, 396, 408, 462, 473, 486, 488, 504,
    522, 529, 532, 539, 540, 543, 544, 555, 559,
    564, 566, 568
Taylor, K., 147, 153, 156, 157, 291, 556–558
Taylor, M., 163, 166, 172, 342, 350
Taylor, P., 293–296, 395–396
Tennant, M., 39–42, 44, 49, 63, 88, 91, 108,
    150
Tetreault, M. K., 260, 330
Thayaparan, B., 111
Thein, A., 492
Thiel, T., 445
Thomas, J. A., 530
Thompson, J., 252, 297
Thompson, P., 491
Thurman, R., 31
Tichy, N., 379
Tierney, W. G., 324
Tindall, D. A., 411, 412
Tisdell, E. J., 11, 21, 24–25, 38, 39, 41, 46,
    187, 231–233, 238–240, 260, 283, 291, 367,
    394, 491–492, 541, 564, 565
Tolliver, D. E., 231, 232, 239, 240, 283, 394,
    541
Tolliver, E., 11, 24–25
Tomasek, T., 447
Tompkins, J., 443
Torbert, B., 384–385
Torosyan, R., 390
Torres, R., 366
Tosey, P., 110, 293, 294, 296
Tough, A., 60, 100
Toulmin, S., 167

Tournas, S. A., 279
Townley, C., 409
Townsell, R., 513
Trehan, K., 323, 333
Trule, J., 81
Tsabouri, U., 297
Tsang-Chan, G., 393
Turay, T. M., 396
Tushman, M., 378
TwoTrees, K., 459
Tyler, J. A., 63, 455, 456, 459, 460, 462, 464,
    465, 541, 559, 571

U

Usher, R., 181, 186

V

van Halen-Faber, C., 395
Van Stralen, S., 512, 513
van Woerkom, M., 293–295, 331
Vandrick, S., 487
Vangel, M., 31–32
Varela, F., 199
Velde, B. P., 39, 40, 43, 45, 250, 253
Veletsianos, G., 410
Vella, J., 367
Vergidis, D., 298, 299
Victor, B., 373
Vieten, C., 22, 30
Vygotsky, L., 41

W

Waldman, M., 32
Walker, A., 474
Walker, D., 330–331
Walker, M., 336
Walters, S., 24, 254
Walton, J., 39, 40, 46, 47
Wang, M., 503, 510
Wang, V.C.X., 6
Wangoola, P., 269
Warner, C. A., 390
Warren, M., 91, 160
Warren, M. A., 159
Wasserman, I. L., 355–357, 365, 563
Watkins, K. E., 373, 377, 560, 568–569
Watkins, M., 116, 124, 125
Waugh, P., 493–494
Weaver, W., 179
Weber, M., 201
Weimer, M., 439, 440, 442, 443, 445, 446,
    449–450, 543, 561, 563
Weimer, M. G., 439, 440, 442, 443, 445, 446,
    449

Weinski, M. C., 393, 395
Weisbord, M., 366
Weiss, J., 75
Weiss, M., 446
Welsh, L., 39–40
Welton, M. R., 132, 185
Wenger, E., 143
Wen-Hoa, D. H., 416
West, C., 135
West, L., 182
West Walsh, J., 234–238, 571
Westley, F., 464–465
Wheatley, M., 205–206
Whetten, D. A., 448
Whitmont, E. C., 116, 117
Wiessner, C. A., 109, 253, 542
Wilber, K., 30, 538–539, 546
Wilbur, K., 474
Wildemeersch, D., 90
Wilhelmson, L., 39–40, 44, 293–296
Williams, I. D., 247, 249–250
Williams, R., 494
Williams, S. H., 48
Willis, P., 124, 212, 222, 223, 507, 561, 566, 570
Wilner, A., 293, 295
Wilson, A., 13, 107, 260, 265
Wilson, E. O., 463
Wing, L. S., 393
Wittman, P. P., 39, 40, 43, 45, 46, 253
Wolf, K., 416
Wolf, S., 126

Woods, D. R., 446
Wopereis, I.G.G., 416
Wright, B., 39, 41, 44–46, 247, 248, 251, 254
Wright, J. K., 247, 253, 254, 309, 310, 313–315
Wright, N., 416
Wright, R., 486, 490

X
Xu, H., 530

Y
Yalom, I., 356
Yamane, D., 440
Yerramsetti, S., 31–32
Yorks, L., 15, 39, 41, 46, 183–184, 216, 291, 323, 356, 358, 367, 375, 382, 394, 476, 478–480, 503, 504, 507, 511, 513, 515, 528, 542, 543
Young Brown, M., 200
Young-Eisendrath, P., 17, 116
Youngman, F., 269
Yuen, A.H.K., 416
Yuzer, T. V., 409, 410, 412, 415

Z
Zane, N. C., 366
Zarifis, G., 297
Zimmerman, B., 464
Zinnbauer, B. J., 243
Zuniga, X., 366
Zweig, C., 126

SUBJECT INDEX

A

Action Learning Conversations (ALC), 530–531

Action research, 67–68

Action Research (SAGE), 292

Active learning, 391–394

Adult Basic Education (ABE) programs, 40, 66, 524

Adult Basic Education programs, 66

Adult education: and learning to think like adult, 73–93; overlaps and integration in, and beyond, 24–25; toward a philosophy of, 89–93; and transformational and emancipatory learning, 23–27

Adult Education (journal; Greece), 299

Adult Education Quarterly (SAGE), 100, 292

Adult learning: as context for transformative learning, 4–5; nurturing soul in, 122–125; working with emotions and emotion-laden images in, 124–125

Adult Learning Principles and Their Application to Program Planning (Brundage and MacKeracher), 345

Adulthood, 88–89

African Diaspora, 514

African National Conference (ANC), 159, 306–307

African perspective: and African worldviews informing transformative learning, 276–280, 562; and Afrocentric paradigm, 279–280, 564; and colonization and imperialism, 277–278; and Dingaka (Diviners) practices: communal practices to transformative learning (case 3), 282–283; and role of community support (case 2), 282–283; and traditional African education, 276–277; and transformative learning in Botswana, 280–285; and *Ubuntu*, 278–279; and visionary transformative learning: interview with sixty-year-old divorcee (case 1), 281–282

African tradition, 268

ALC. *See* Action Learning Conversations (ALC)

Alienation, overcoming, 9

American Association of Community and Junior colleges, 101

ANC. *See* African National Conference (ANC)

Andragogy, 16

Antenarrative, 460

Anti-Flag (band), 474

Archetypes, 217

Argument culture, 79

Artistic expression: and breaking out of constraining boundaries, 473–477; and evocative nature of arts, 474; and provocative nature of arts, 475–476; reflection and synthesis on, 481–483;

transformation and healing through, 477; and transformative learning as extrarational process, 472–473; transformative learning through, 471–483

Art, 253; community awareness through witnessing, 479–480; in community interaction, 480–481; as entry point into difficult conversations, 478–479; as means for reflection and healing, 477–479; transforming communities through, 479–481

Arthritis Foundation, 428–429

Arts and Societal Learning (Hayes and Yorks), 480

Assumptions, 77, 151–152

Autonomy, 89–92; and autonomous thinking, 91; and dependence, 186–187

Avengers (genre fiction), 490

Aymara language (South America), 310

B

Bach, J. S., 477

Batswana, 43

Belief, 151–152

Bifurcation point, 202–203

Birbeck College, University of London, 253

Black Like Me (Griffin), 219–222, 224

Bolivia, 309–312

Book of Laughter and Forgetting (Kundera), 73

Botho, 278–279, 562

Botswana, 278–279; transformative learning in, 280–285

Boundary situations, 214, 218; choice and, 215

Brazil, 266

British Columbia, 481

Buffy the Vampire Slayer (television series), 490, 493, 495

Bush administration, 140

C

California Institute of Integral Studies-Transformative Studies Program, 397

Care of the Soul (Moore), 474

Center for Studies and Self-Directed Learning (Greece), 298, 299

Centers for Disease Control, 431

Change magazine, 440

Chaos narrative, 428

Choice, and boundaries, 215

Christian belief, 83

Chronicle of Higher Education, 440

Circles of trust (Palmer), 363

Civil Rights movement, 269

Clark Atlanta University, 397

Client-centered therapy (Rogers), 6

Clinton, Hillary, 264

Cochabamba, Bolivia, 309–310

Coercing, 560–562

Cognitive processing, three levels of, 74

Coherence, 509–510; among ways of knowing and transformative knowing, 516–517

Collaborative inquiry, 367

Colonialism, 277–280, 285

Color Purple (Walker), 474

Columbia University, 31

Commander in Chief (television series), 496

Communicative learning, 77

Community will for action, 515

Complexity: challenges of, as sources of transformative learning, 188–189; and conceiving emerging nature of transformation through levels of organization, 183–184; introducing paradigm of, 179–180; and negotiating tensions between generality and singularity, 181–182; as object of study and dimension of research, 189–190; and recognizing heterogeneity and multireferentiality, 184–186; and reconsidering linearity and nonlinearity, 182–183; and reconsidering relationship between autonomy and dependence, 186–187; and reintroducing knower in any knowledge, 187–188; revisiting transformative learning through paradigm of, 181–188; transformational learning and challenges of, 178–190

Complicity: An International Journal of Complexity and Education, 178–179

Conscientization, 59, 87, 102, 247, 254, 264, 266, 299, 366

Consciousness studies, 30–32

Consensus building, 79–80

Constructed knowledge, 343

Constructive-developmental theory (Kegan), 151

Constructivist assumptions, 5–6

Constructivist philosophical orientation, 58–59

Contemplative attunement, 546

Contextualized Model of Adult Learning (CMAL), 41

Convergence and Adults Learning Journal (NIACE), 292

Counter-discourse, case for, 316–317

CRA. *See* Critical reflection on assumptions (CRA)

Crash (film), 491, 492, 496

Crazy/Beautiful (film), 496–497

Creative abrasion, 381

Creativity, 253

Critical and emancipatory approaches, 65–66
Critical and emancipatory self-assumptions (CRSA), 105
Critical philosophical orientation, 59–60
Critical race theory, 59
Critical reflection, 88; and emotions, 331–332; fostering, 329–336; as imperative in our times, 334–336; influence of Habermas and Dewey on Mezirow's concept of, 328–329; researching, 332–334; strategies for, 393; theoretical influences, 325–327; theory of communicative action and, 327–329; and transformative learning, 323–336; two levels of, 327–328; what is critical about, 324–325
Critical reflection on assumptions (CRA), 105, 329, 333
Critical research, 59
Critical self-reflection, 357
Critical self-reflections on assumptions (CSRA), 105, 329, 331–333
Critical Social Theory, 7
Critical subjectivity, 509–510
Critical theory, 59; adult learning project embedded in, 138–142; defining, 134–136; and definition of learning, 136–138; and definition of transformative, 142–144; seven learning tasks associated with (Brookfield), 8–9; tradition, 324; and transformative learning, 132–144
"Critical Theory of Adult Learning and Education" (Mezirow), 291
Critical thinking, 324
CSRA. See Critical self-reflections on assumptions (CSRA)
Cuban Literacy Campaign, 250
Cultural and Educational Issues Survey (Version B), 58
Cultural paradigms, 82–83
"Cultural Transformative Learning and Planetary Literacy in the Foreign Classroom" (Goulah), 173
Cultural-spiritual perspective: and conditions for transformation, 235–238; implications of, for adult educator, 239–242; overview of, 232–235; and question of what trans-forms, 238–239; of transformational learning, 231–242
Culture, issues with, 563–565
Cumulative Index to Nursing and Allied Health Literature (CINAHL), 38

D

Dark Nights of the Soul (Moore), 478
Darwinism, 456

Decentration, 380
Decolonization, 277–278
Deep transformation: and critical resistance education (critique mode), 167–168; and dynamism of transformation at personal level, 170–171; and holism, 173–174; integral modes of, 166–170; and integral transformative learning, 173–176; planetary context of, 169–170; and spirituality, 175–176; and survival education (survive mode), 166–167; timeline for, 165; and transformative learning at level of emergent practices, 171–173; and visionary transformative education (create mode), 168–169; and wisdom of indigenous peoples, 174–175; and wisdom of women, 174
Democracy, practicing, 9
Democratic theory, reciprocity of, with Transformative Theory, 91
Depth psychology, 118, 364
Developmental intentions, 157
"Dialogic thinkers," 92
Dialogue, 316–317; versus discourse, 266; genuine (Buber), 356; group work and, 355–369
Differentiation, 380
Discernment, 472
Discomfort, pedagogy of, 541
Discourse, 78, 88, 316; critical reflective, 363–364; dialogue versus, 266; recognizing, 496; reflective, 316–317
Disorienting dilemma, 150, 212, 265, 477
Diversity: community building across, 514–515; paradox of, 513
Doll's House (Ibsen), 486–499
Dominant ideology, 7
Double loop learning (retention), 377
Dylan, Bob, 474

E

Eastern University, 397
Education and Technology, 410
Education and Training (Emerald), 292
Edward Scissorhands (film), 494
Effective Teaching and Mentoring: Realizing the Transformational Power of Adult Learning Experiences (Daloz), 269
Ego consciousness, idea of, 118–119
8th International Transformative Learning Conference, 197
"Elegy Written in a Country Churchyard" (Gray), 441
ElluminateLive!, 415
Emancipation, 78, 91–92

Emancipatory education, 24

Emancipatory learning, 22. *See also* Transformational and emancipatory learning

Embodied narrative: and Becoming an Object to Be Fixed, 431–432; and Being Overtaken, 433–434; and Claiming Agency by Giving In, 430–431; conceptualizing transformation as, 435–437; and Life with Daisy, 434–435; and one narrative to make sense of another, 427–434; and Rewinding the Tape, 429; transformation as, 425–437

Emerald Group, 292

Emergent learning (M. Taylor), 350–351

Emotion, and rationality, 565–569; working with, and emotion-laden images in adult education, 124–125

Emotional intelligence, 79

Empathy, 80, 487–490; cultivating, 157

English as a Second Language programs, 40

Enlightenment, 200–201

Epistemological adulthood, 152

Epistemological coherence, 515

Epochal transformations, 25, 31

Epoche, 80

ERIC database, 38

Eternal Sunshine of the Spotless Mind (film), 494–495

Ethics, of transformative learning: and educating for change, 539–544; and educator as change agent, 536–547; and ethical capacities, 544–545; and ethics of practice, 537–539; and evoking unconscious, 542–543; and expecting collaboration, 543–544; and sharing experience, 540–541; and unveiling conflict, 541–542; and walking ethical path, 544–547

Europe: and defining theoretical framework of transformative learning, 291–292; findings on transformative learning activities in countries of, 293–297; literature review methodology for transformative learning in, 292–293; transformative learning in, 289–300, 562–563; and transformative learning in Greece (case study), 297–300

European American Collaborative Challenging Whiteness, 507, 511–513

European Union, 290

Evaluation strategies: and art-based techniques, 527; and checklists, 525–526; and conceptual mapping, 526–527; and contexts for evaluation, 527–531; and evaluation methods relevant to transformative learning, 523–531; and interviews, 524; and journals, 526; kinds of knowledge and, 520–521; and metaphor analysis, 526; and narratives, 524–525; and observations, 525; and self-evaluation, 524; and surveys, 525; theoretical perspectives, 522–523

Evocative pedagogy, 221

Existential perspective, 213–216; choice and boundary situations in, 215; and existence and transcendence, 214–215; and existential pedagogy and transformative learning, 222–224; and narrative dimensions of existential transformation, 218–219; self and other in, 215–216; and transformative learning as existential process, 216–218

Exodus 3 (Hebrew Bible), 26

Expanding the Boundaries of Transformative Learning (O'Sullivan, Morrell, and O'Connor), 164–165, 171–172

Experience, defining, 22–23

Experience, role of, in transformative learning, 342–353; and case study of transformative leader, 344–349; and circumnavigating transformative learning, 350–351; and definition of experience, 342–344; and perspectives on experiential learning, 351–353; and process of transformative learning, 349–350; and relationship of analysis to existing theory, 349–353

Experiential learning, 392–394

Extended epistemology, 508

F

Facilitating environments (Schapiro), 155

Farmer Field Schools (FFS), 305, 311, 313–315

Feeling and Parenthood (Heron), 508

Feminist theory, 59

FFS. *See* Farmer Field Schools (FFS)

Fiction, 486–499; and creating critical distance, 493–496; and intertextuality and role of reader and viewer, 497–498; outsiders in, 490–492; and reading against grain, 496–497; and recognizing discourse, 496; and unconscious or semiconscious fears and desires, 492–493

Fielding Institute and Associates, 173

Fight Club (film), 494–495

Film, 486–499

Fort Worth, Texas, 219

Fostering Critical Reflection in Adulthood (Mezirow and Associates), 5

"Fostering Transformative Learning" (Taylor), 355

Fourth order (self-authorizing) consciousness, 153

Frame of reference, 82–84, 109, 152–153

Frankfurt School of Critical Social Theory, 7, 297–298, 325

Freudian orientation, 83

Frommelt Attitude Toward Care of the Dying (FATCOD), 58

G

Gale, Cathy (*Avengers'* character), 490

Gandhi, M., 159

Garment and Allied Workers' Union (GAWU; South Africa), 306

Garment Workers' Industrial Union (GWIU; South Africa), 306

GAWU. *See* Garment and Allied Workers' Union (GAWU; South Africa)

Gender, 563–565. *See also* Women, and transformative learning

Generative images, 217

Globalization, language of, 169

Gone to Soldiers (Piercy), 486

Great Turning, 165

"Greatest Discovery" (John), 474

Greece, 293, 562

Greek Skeptics, 80

Griffin, John Howard, 219–222, 224

Group work: and creating group spaces for transformational learning, 358–359; and dialogue, 355–369; and group as container for transformative dialogue, 357–359; and qualities vital to transformative dialogic groups, 357–358; and types of transformative groups, 359–368

GWIU. *See* Garment Workers' Industrial Union (GWIU; South Africa)

H

Habit of mind, 83, 109, 325

Handbook of Adult and Continuing Education, 142

Heart of Darkness (Conrad), 486

Hegemonic assumptions (Gramsci), 324

Hegemony, 9; contesting, 9

Hellenic Adult Education Association, 299

Heteronomy, 89

Higher education: and academic programs fostering transformative learning, 395–396; directions for future research and practice in, 399–401; emergent transformative framework in, 399; fostering transformative learning in, 388–401; leadership programs and professional development in, 395–399; as naturalistic landscape, 389–390; and

professional development for faculty and administrators, 396–399; transformative learners in, 389; and transformative learning programmatic goal and mission statements, 397–398

Highlander Folk School (Tennessee), 24, 480

Holding environment, 150

"Holding Flames: Women Illuminating Knowledge of s/Self Transformation" (O'Neill), 172

Holism, 173–174

Holistic epistemology, 507, 509; importance of presentational knowing for, 510–511

Human Condition (Arendt), 327

Human connection, 515

Human Resource Development Review (SAGE), 292

Humanism, 6

Hurricane Katrina, 529–530

I

Identification, 487–490

Ideology, 9; challenging, 9; critique, 11, 12, 324, 326, 329, 362, 366, 490, 496, 528; dominant, 7, 131–134, 139, 141, 143

"If Ye Love Me" (Tallis), 21, 28, 33

Iliad (Homer), 223

Illness narratives, 428

Imperialism, 277–278

Imposing, 560–562

Impressionistic learning, 78

Improvisational jazz, 476

In Defense of the Lifeworld (Welton), 132

Inconvenient Truth, An (Gore), 479

India, 29–30

Innovations in Transformative Learning (Fielding Institute and Associates), 173

Inside Higher Education, 440

Instinct for Freedom (Clements), 163

Institute of Noetic Sciences, 27, 30

Instituto Costarricense de Electricidad (ICE; Costa Rica), 43

Instrumental learning, 77, 103

Integral development, cultivating, 546

Integral transformative learning, 173–176

International Conference on Transformative Learning, 11, 289, 293, 300

International Encyclopedia of Adult Education, 142

International Journal of Lifelong Education (Taylor and Francis-Routledge), 292

Intertextuality, 497–498

Intervention strategies: and experiential and active learning, 391–394; and key

environmental, instructional, and individual strategies, 392–394
Invictus (film), 159
"Invitation" (Willis), 223
Iraq, war in, 140
I-thou relationship (Buber), 356, 358

J

Jazz (Morrison), 497
Jewish women, 250
John, Elton, 474
John Wiley & Sons, Inc., 292
Journal of Transformative Education (SAGE), 10, 247, 249, 292, 293
Journal of Workplace Learning (Emerald), 292
Jungian approach, 83; to transformative learning, 116–127

K

Kennedy, Robert, 159
Kenya, 305–306, 311, 313
King, M. L., Jr., 159, 477
Knowledge: kinds of, and evaluation strategies, 520–521; received, 343

L

La Pensée Complexe en Recheches et en Pratique, 178–179, 190
Landscape and Human Health Lab (University of Illinois), 208
Learner-centered teaching: defining, 440–442; and possibility of designing learning experiences to promote transformative learning, 447–449; and promoting transformative learning, 444–447; and relationships, 442–444; and transformative learning, 439–452; *versus* transformative learning intentions, 543–544; as viable way to develop commitment to transformative learning, 451–452; what sequence of, best promotes transformative learning, 449–451
Learner-Centered Teaching (Weimer), 440
Learning: definition of, 136–138; domains of, 77–78
Learning Activities Survey Questionnaire, 39, 58
Learning as Transformation: Critical Perspectives on a Theory in Progress (Mezirow), 291
Learning Toward an Ecologicals Consciousness-Selected Transformative Practices (O'Sullivan and Taylor), 172
Learning-Style Inventory (Kolb), 156

Lee, Spike, 529–530
Lesson Before Dying (film), 488
LGBT sexual identity development, 268
Liberation, learning, 9
LindenLab, 415
Logos (Ancient Greece), 83

M

Maat (African), 280
Magic Toyshop (Carter), 496
Magritte, R., 476
Making Sense of Adult Learning (MacKeracher), 346
Malta, 308–309, 311
Management Learning (SAGE), 292
Mandela, Nelson, 158–159
MaraMediterra, 309
Marxism, 184
Marxist orientation, 83, 132
Maturity of phenomenon, 60–62___
Meaning making, 151; four modes of, 74; as learning process, 73–82; and meaning perspective, 82; and phases of meaning, 86; and structures of meaning, 82–84
Meaning of Adult Education, The (Lindemann), 4
Meaning perspective, 109
Medline database, 38
Mentor (Greek mythical character), 223
Mephato, 276
Middle Ages, 83
Mindlessness, 76
Mindsight, 32
Minneapolis, 140
Moby Dick (Melville), 486
Modeling, 75
Moses, 26, 28
Mothers of the Plaza de Mayo (Argentina), 141
MUDs. *See* Multi-user domains (MUDs)
Multi-user domains (MUDs), 415
Mutual empathy, 365
Myers-Briggs Type Indicator, 156

N

Narrating Transformative Learning in Education (Gardner and Kelly), 173
Narrative analysis, 63–64
Nashville, Tennessee, 478
National Institute of Adult Continuing Education (NIACE), 292
Native American storytelling tradition, 459
Neuroscience, 32
New Directions for Adult and Continuing Education (Wiley), 292

New science, 202, 209; and living systems theories, 200–201

NIACE. *See* National Institute of Adult Continuing Education (NIACE)

Nigeria, 251, 307–308, 311, 312, 314

Nommo (African; Nile Valley civilization), 280

Normative ethics, *versus* meta-ethics, 537

Normative learning, 78

Nurturing soul work: in adult learning, 122–125; and attending to expressions of soul in teaching and learning, 123–124; and idea of ego consciousness, 118–119; implications of, for transformative education, 125–127; as Jungian approach to transformative learning, 116–127; and map of soul, 117–122; and structures and dynamics of unconscious, 120–122

O

Oakwood College (Alabama), 159

Obama, Barack, 264

Objective reframing, 87

Occupy movement, 206

Officina Juridica Para la Mujer (Women's Legal Office; OJM), 309–314

OJM. *See* Officina Juridica Para la Mujer (Women's Legal Office; OJM)

One America in the 21st Century: Forging a New Future. (President's Institute on Race: The Advisory Board's Report to the President; 1998), 262

One-Dimensional Man (Marcuse), 9

Oracle at Delphi, 151

Organizational change: differing, dueling foci of transformative learning and, 375–376; and individual perspective, 384–385; model of facilitating transformative learning for, 381–385; system perspective for, 383–384; understanding transformation in, 376–379

Organizational learning, 376–379

Outsiders, 490–492

P

Pakistan, 456

Palin, Sarah, 264

Parks, Rosa, 205

Participatory action research (PAR), 65–66

Pedagogy of Freedom (Freire), 311

Pedagogy of the Oppressed (Freire), 266

Personal transformation, 66

Personal Transformation in Small Groups: A Jungian Perspective (Boyd), 269

Personhood, theory of (Heron), 504, 507

Perspective transformation, 472

Philadelphia (film), 479, 491

Philosophical perspective, 57–60

Planetary consciousness, developing, 546–547

Pleasantville (film), 494

Point of view, 83–84

Positionality, and transformational learning, 260–270, 563–565; coexistence of transformational learning and positionality, 267–270; complexity of, 262–264; example of, 261–262; lens of, 541; and two perspectives of transformational learning and social locations, 264–267

Positive perspective, 57–58

Postcolonial theory, 59

Postmodernist philosophical perspective, 60

Power, unmasking, 9

Praxis, 66, 218, 219, 325

Precious (film), 479

Preparing for the Twenty-First Century (Kennedy), 162–163

Presentational knowing: bridging pathways provided by, 515–516; and codifying experience, 512; in communities and organizations, 513–515; contribution of, to learning in human systems, 511–515; Elizabeth's experience with, 506–507; and evoking experience, 511–512; within individual, 511–513; between individuals, 513; and promoting self-awareness, 512; role of, in transformative learning, 503–517; "Woman Emerging": illustrative story of, 504–506, 511–513

President's Commission on Race (1998), 262

Procedural knowledge, 343

Proceedings of the International Transformative Learning Conferences, 456

Professional Development as Transformative Learning (Cranton), 269

Proquest data base, 38, 247

Psyche, modes of, 507–509; and ways of knowing, 508

Psychoanalysis, 184

Psychosociology, 184

Public Conversations Project, 366

Q

Quechaua language (South America), 310

Queer theory, 59

Quest narrative, 428

R

Rationality, emotion and, 565–569

Reason, reclaiming, 9

Received knowledge, 343

Reflective action, 88, 218
Reflective discourse, 78–82, 316–317
Reflective practice, 324
Reflective thinking, 324
Reflectivity, 103
Reformation, 83
Reframing Social Sustainability in a Multicultural World (8th International Transformative Learning Conference), 197
Relationships, 356; and learner-centered teaching, 442–444
Repressive tolerance, 140
Research in Post-Complimentary Education (Taylor and Francis-Routledge), 292
Research methodology, for studying transformative learning: and action research, 67; and arts-based research, 64–65; and challenges in studying transformative learning, 68–69; and critical and emancipatory approaches, 65–66; factors in selection of, 57–62; for future study, 62–68; and narrative analysis, 63–64; and philosophical perspectives, 57–60; selection of, 56–62
Restitution narrative, 428
Restorative transformation (Lange), 213
Return to Cosmology (Toulmin), 167
Rhodes, Cecil, 277
Rhodesia, 277
Romance (Riley), 496
Roosevelt, Eleanor, 159

S

SAGE Publications, 38, 247, 292
Scientific Committee on the 9th International Transformative Learning Center, 293
Scottish Clydeside shipbuilding plants, 141
SCUTREA (Standing Conference on University Teaching and Research in the Education of Adults), 292
Second Life (SL), 415
Seeger, P., 480
Self-actualization, concept of (Maslow), 6
Self-authorizing, 153
Self-directed learning (Knowles), 6
Self-transforming way of knowing, 158
September 11, 2001, terrorist attacks of, 478
Signaling culture of learning, 514
Single loop learning (resilience), 377
Sixth Sense (film), 494–495
Skype, 415
Social environment, supportive, 393–394
Social locations, 264–267
Socialism (Engels), 141–142

Socialization, beyond, 153
Socrates, 151
South Africa, 306–307, 311, 312
Spirit Matters Gathering, 173
Spirituality, 175–176; what is meant by, 232
Springboks (South African rugby team), 159
Sri Lanka, 248
Storytelling: case story, 457–458; connection of, to complexity science, 463–465; connection of, to transformative learning theory, 461–463; and implications for practice in higher education, 465–466; reflections on, 466–467; theory, 459–461; and transformative learning, 439–452
Strategic Leverage through Learning framework, 378–379
Studies in Continuing Education (Taylor and Francis-Routledge), 292
Studies in the Education of Adults (NIACE), 292
Subjective knowledge, 343
Subjective reframing, 87
Subject-object: interview, 522; relationship, 151; shifts, 152
Supporting, 560–562
Sustainability: contested visions of, 197–199; and sustainable development and sustainability, 198; transforming transformative learning through, 195–209

T

Taylor and Francis-Routledge Group, 292
Technology, 414–417
Telemachus (Greek mythical character), 223
Templeton Foundation, 27, 30
Text, 64
Theatre of the Absurd, 476
Theatre of the Oppressed, 480–481, 515
Theoretical tensions, 556–560
Theory of Communicative Action (Habermas), 327
Theory U, 379
Third order consciousness, 152
Third World scholars, 278
3D immersive learning environments, 415, 416
Threshold concepts, 25–26
Time Transfixed (Magritte), 476
"Times They Are A-Changin' " (Dylan), 474
Towards a Transformative Political Economy of Adult Education: Theoretical and Practical Challenges (Wangoola and Youngman), 269
Transcending process, 222
Transference, 75
Transformation, 10, 22–23

Transformation process, ten phases in (Cranton), 349–350

Transformation theory: core concepts of, 73–93

Transformational and emancipatory learning, 23–27; adult education and, 23–27; consciousness studies and, 30–32; and consideration of forms that change and transform, 25–27; and expanding vision: love, death, and big questions, 27; neuroscience and complexity in, 32; new directions for, and research on, 33; new variations on, and influences from other disciplines, 29–33; and overlaps and integration in adult education and beyond, 24–25; overview, 21–23; themes and variations of, 21–34; three primary discourses of, 23–24

Transformations, 84–88

Transformations of consciousness, 147; analysis of, 149–154; application, 154–157; caveat and challenge for, 159–160; and cultivating empathy, 157; and forging mutuality and welcoming difference, 156; illustration of, 148–149; and invocation, 158–160; and shifting authority, 156–157; support and challenge for, 155–156; two stories in illustration of, 147–149

Transformative, 22, 25, 26

Transformative dialogue, 357–359; and transformative dialogic moments, 357

Transformative Dimensions of Adult Learning (Mezirow), 5, 108, 266

Transformative education (Boyd and Myers), 364

Transformative groups: and group characteristics, 361; and groups for critical systemic consciousness, 366–367; and groups for personal growth and self-awareness, 361–365; and groups for relational empathy across differences, 365–366; implications for practice in, 368–369; types and characteristics of, 360, 362; types of, 359–368

Transformative learning: coherence, critical subjectivity and, 509–510; conceptualization of (Mezirow), 6; and critical reflection, 323–336; critical theory and, 131–144; cultural-spiritual perspective of, 231–242; as developmental perspective, 147–160; ethics of, 536–547; in Europe, 289–300; evaluating, 520–532; existential approach to, 212–225; fiction, film and, 486–499; holistic approach to, 522; intentional interventions fostering, 391–394; international and community-based, 304–318; Jungian approach to, 116–127; learner-centered teaching and, 439–452; as "new andragogy," 16; and object of study and dimension of research, 189–190; online, 408–419; positionality and, 260–270; relationship of holistic epistemology to, 507; role of experience in, 342–353; role of presentational knowing in, 503–517; role of transpersonal in, 122; storytelling and, 455–467; through artistic expression, 471–483; women and, 245–255

Transformative learning, international and community-based: in Bolivia (South America), 309–310; and bonding and unity forged during educational interactions, 313; common themes in, 310–313; and community-based transformative learning projects and activities, 304–310; and dialogue, reflective discourse, and case for counter-discourse, 316–317; and experience and frame of reference, 311; implications for practice and future research in, 317–318; and issues as yet unresolved, 313–316; and issues with community-based and transformative learning, 562–563; in Kenya and Uganda (East Africa), 305–306; in Malta (Europe), 308–309; in Nigeria (West Africa), 307–308; from particular to general and personal to social in, 312–313; and role of facilitators, 312; in South Africa, 306–307; and triggers for transformative learning, 311–312

Transformative learning, Mezirow's theory of (1975–present), 99–112; beginning of, 100–102; Collard and Law critique of, 104; critique of (1990s), 106–108; expansion and refinement of (1980s), 102–104; and meaning perspectives, reflection, phase revision (1990s), 104–106; Mezirow publications prior to formulation of, 99–100; and reflections on past and predictions for future, 110–112; as theory-in-progress (2000s), 108–110

Transformative learning, online: critical review of literature on, 409–411; facilitating learning to foster, 417–418; fostering, 408–419; implications and recommendations for future research on, 418–419; pedagogical considerations to foster, 411–414; use of design and technology to foster, 414–417

Transformative learning, transforming, through sustainability and new science, 195–209; and contested visions of sustainability, 197–199; and rethinking ethics of transformative learning, 206–208; and rethinking outcomes of transformative learning, 205–206; and rethinking pedagogy of transformational learning, 204–205; and rethinking process of transformation, 202–204; and rethinking scope of transformative learning, 208–209; and shedding modernist clothing, 199–201; and transforming transformative learning, 201–209

"Transformative Learning as Discourse" (Mezirow), 316

Transformative Learning Center, 171, 173, 398

Transformative Learning Conference, 247, 292, 299

Transformative Learning: Educational Vision for the 21st Century (O'Sullivan), 207

Transformative Learning in Practice (Taylor and Janecke), 66

"Transformative Learning Perspective of Continuing Sexual Identity Development in the Workplace" (King and Biro), 268

Transformative learning theory: African perspective on, 274–286; boundaries of field of, 10–11; cognitive rational approach to, 8; constructivist assumptions underlying, 5–6; in context of adult learning, 4–5; critical social theory assumptions underlying, 7; dominant perspectives on, 7–10; fragmentation and integration in, 11–12; humanist assumptions underlying, 6; issues in practice of, 14–15; overview of, 3–4; philosophical underpinnings of, 5–10; social-individual tensions in, 12; stagnation in, 12–14; tensions and issues in field of, 10–16

Transformative learning theory, research on: critical review of, 37–50; cross cultural, 42–44; discussion and implications of, 47–50; and fostering transformative learning, 45–47; growing significance of relationships in, 44–45; issues with, 567–569; methodologies and general trends used in, 39–41; multiple theoretical frameworks in, 41–42

Transformative teacher and learner, empathic relationship between, 569–571

Transformed epistemology, 151

"Transpose," 22

"Triple loop learning" (Isaacs), 87

True Blood (television series), 493

Truth and Reconciliation hearings (South Africa), 141

Twilight (film), 493

Twitter, 416

U

Übuntu, 278–279, 285

Uganda, 305–306

Unconscious, structure and dynamics of, 120–122

Unconscious civilization, 167–168

Understanding and Facilitating Adult Learning (Brookfield), 4

Understanding and Promoting Transformative Learning: A Guide for Educators of Adults (Cranton), 269

UNESCO, 299

United Kingdom, 253, 254, 290

Universal Sufism, 28

Universe Story (Swimme and Berry), 175, 207

University of Central Oklahoma, 398

University of Lesotho, 290

University of Pennsylvania, 32

University of Sussex, Institute for Development Studies, 254

University of Toronto, Ontario Institute for Studies in Education (OISE), 254, 398

V

Vampire Diaries, 493

Verfremdung (Brecht), 494

vSpaces, 415

W

WARSHE. *See* Women Against Rape, Sexual Harassment, and Sexual Exploitation (WARSHE)

Watershed Management Agricultural Programme (WMAP; Costa Rica), 43

Web 2.0 technologies, 416

When the Levees Broke: A Requiem in Four Acts (Lee; documentary film), 529

Wikis, 416

Women, and transformative learning, 245–255; background and rationale for category of, 245–255; and connection to race, class, and oppression, 248–249; and directions for future research and practice, 253–255; and engagement of women's learning with theory, 247; and facilitating women's transformation, 250–253; and importance of body, 251–252; and importance of creativity and arts, 253; and importance of emotion, 252; and importance of race and class, 252–253; importance of relationship in, 250–251; observations on literature on, 247; and silence on transformative learning theory, 249–250

Women against Rape, Sexual Harassment, and Sexual Exploitation (WARSHE), 307, 308, 311–315

Women's Ways of Knowing (Belenky et al.), 247–248

Workplace, transformative learning in, 373–385; and changing workplace context, 373–375; and differing foci of transformative learning and organizational change, 375–376; and role of leader in transforming organizations, 378–381; and understanding transformation in organizational change and organizational learning, 376–379

World Café process, 205

Wuthering Heights (Brontë), 497

Y

Yoruba language (Nigeria), 308

Z

Zimbabwe, 277